MORAL
REASONING
Ethical Theory and Some
Contemporary Moral Problems

VICTOR GRASSIAN

Harbor College
Wilmington, California

PRENTICE-HALL, INC., Englewood Cliffs, New Jersey   07632

Library of Congress Cataloging in Publication Data

GRASSIAN, VICTOR.
   Moral Reasoning.

   Includes bibliographies and index.
   1. Ethics. 2. Social ethics. I. Title.
BJ1012.G68   270   80-14893
ISBN 0-13-600759-7

© 1981 by Prentice-Hall, Inc., Englewood Cliffs, N.J. 07632

Printed in the United States of America

10 9 8 7

Editorial/production supervision and interior design: Robert Hunter
Cover design: Infield/D'Astolofo Associates
Manufacturing buyer: Harry P. Baisley

PRENTICE-HALL INTERNATIONAL, INC., *London*
PRENTICE-HALL OF AUSTRALIA PTY. LIMITED, *Sydney*
PRENTICE-HALL OF CANADA, LTD., *Toronto*
PRENTICE-HALL OF INDIA PRIVATE LIMITED, *New Delhi*
PRENTICE-HALL OF JAPAN, INC., *Tokyo*
PRENTICE-HALL OF SOUTHEAST ASIA PTE. LTD., *Singapore*
WHITEHALL BOOKS LIMITED, *Wellington, New Zealand*

To my parents
David and Ann Grassian
who toiled so their sons would have
the opportunities they never did

Contents

2
Theories of Normative Ethics   43

5
Abortion   236

6
Euthanasia   259

7
Racial and Sexual Discrimination and the Problem of "Reverse Discrimination" 293

8
Punishment and Rehabilitation 338

9
The Death Penalty   386

10
The Morality of War   407

Preface

I have attempted to provide an ethics text which is readable and enlighteningly relevant to the unsophisticated philosophical novice without being superficial to the more sophisticated. Although there is an abundant supply of introductory ethics texts currently available, I have found none of them satisfying. The anthologies of excerpts from the ethical classics are much too difficult for most beginning students of philosophy who find themselves adrift in the intricacies of reasoning, often couched in a technical and pedantic language style. On the other hand, the several quite readable general introductions to the problems of traditional normative ethics and metaethical theory by contemporary philosophers are too abstract and of dubious value in elucidating the complicated moral issues of our day. One can imagine the disappointment of bright and inquisitive students who, seeking to scrutinize, clarify, and unify their own ethical beliefs about practical moral issues, come away from their introductory ethics course with a knowledge of abstract philosophical terminology and theories whose application to the solution of concrete moral problems is never made clear. Although considerations of concrete moral problems may lack the abstractness and antiseptic generality of which philosophers are so fond, what use is the study of ethics, the student may wonder, if such a study does not serve to sharpen one's ability to think clearly, intelligently, and logically about the pressing moral problems which generate passionate argument among ordinary people.

On the other hand, those texts which are devoted to philosophical discussions of the contemporary moral and social issues of our day are usually not preceded by any general discussion of the issues of traditional ethical theory. The student is exposed to arguments on contemporary moral issues without any general consideration of the nature of moral reasoning and the possibility of formulating general moral principles which can be applied to a resolution of these issues; therefore, the student will often find himself without the principles and theoretical perspectives that can serve to organize his thinking about a concrete moral problem. Furthermore, the numerous texts on contemporary moral problems tend to be either too abstract or too superficial. Most are anthologies of philosophical articles extracted from philosophical journals. These articles are generally directed to the philosophically sophisticated reader who can be assumed to understand the terminology and methodology they presuppose and to appreciate their dry professional analytic style. Although the main purpose of an introductory ethics course should always be to foster a critical and analytic spirit in a student, one cannot expect the philosophical novice to grasp the intricacies of reasoning and analytic "concept chopping" that is often found in contemporary philosophical journals. Those texts, however, which are written with the beginning student in mind, are disappointing in their oversimplification of moral issues and arguments whose meaning, presuppositions, and implications are not adequately explored. While it is one thing to say that the most important objective of an introductory ethics course is to encourage students to think intelligently about concrete contemporary moral problems, it is something else to exclude considerations of abstract issues of ethical theory that attempt to provide moral reasoning with a structure and coherence that has been an essential part of traditional ethics. No doubt, this abstractness will not appeal to all, but an ethics course that dispenses with it entirely is apt to purchase relevance at the cost of *philosophic* substance.

In addition, discussions of contemporary moral issues by philosophers, regardless of their level of philosophical sophistication, are very rarely ever related to contemporary scientific findings and theories of the nature of man and society or to the complexities and practical workings of the law which can infuse these problems with greater meaning. Although one can, for example, talk in generalities about the concept of justice and the issue of "reverse discrimination," philosophical discussions of this concept and this issue can be made much more significant to an introductory student if they are related to specific legal cases, and the conflicting judicial decisions that such cases have generated. Similarly, a discussion of the morality of homosexuality should be anchored in some broad understanding of the various scientific theories about the nature and causes of homosexuality. Indeed, it is not only contemporary moral problems that are made more meaningful and engaging to an introductory philosophy student by being related to the findings and theories of science; the same is certainly true of the traditional ethical questions relating to human motivation and moral responsibility. Consequently, in the discussions in this text of psychological egoism and the free will controversy the student is made aware of how scientific findings and theories bear upon the resolution of these traditional philosophical concerns.

This text attempts to provide a reasonable balance between considerations of some controversial contemporary moral issues and of the more general and abstract questions of ethical theory which underlie these issues. A study of the contemporary moral issues is best attempted after the student has at least briefly been exposed to some of the fundamental questions of metaethics (such as "the objectivity of moral knowledge") and some of the general theories of normative ethics. A general understanding of the issues of ethical theory can provide the student with a theoretical and conceptual framework which can be drawn upon to elucidate and organize the later discussions of the contemporary moral issues. The section entitled "Some Reflections on Theories of Normative Ethics" is devoted primarily to a discussion of the relevance of theories of normative ethics to the solution of concrete moral problems, providing a necessary bridge from the abstract issues in the first part of the text to the concrete issues of the second part. In addition, hopefully, the discussions of the issues of normative ethics will serve to foster a recognition of the need for a judicious balancing of conflicting moral principles in the resolution of concrete moral issues.

The aim of the text throughout is to encourage the student to think more clearly and critically about the answers that have been provided to both practical and abstract moral questions. The student will be exposed constantly to the two-fold task of analytic philosophy—conceptual clarity and principled justification (that is, "What does this mean and how, if at all, can it be justified?") Although a text can never substitute for the skillful use of the Socratic method of inquiry in class, it is my hope that this text will act as a stimulant to the student's latent analytic spirit. I hope that it will, by its own example, encourage him to clarify his beliefs (such as, "What do we mean by a 'heroic' life-support measure in the context of the euthanasia debate?"), to think through their implications and mutual consistency (such as, "What implications does one's position on the abortion issue have on the euthanasia issue?") and finally to weigh their relative strengths and weaknesses. In this spirit, the success of this text should be measured by the degree to which it leads the student toward the Socratic ideal of critical thinking which strives always to dig beneath the surface of the often passionate though logically hollow rhetoric of popular moral reasoning.

I am grateful for the helpful comments of Herbert Morris, William J. Winslade, Richard Wasserstrom, Murray Schwartz, my brother Stuart Grassian, and an anonymous reviewer. Special thanks are due my wife, Esther, who shared with me the joys and frustrations of seeing this manuscript to completion and the cheerless task of many hours of painstaking proofreading. Her concern meant much. The interdisciplinary breadth of this text as well as my strong desire to make it philosophically stimulating and insightful, as well as analytically clear and logical, owes much to the example and encouragement of Herbert Morris. Thomas E. Hill, Jr. deserves special thanks for his many specific criticisms and generous sacrifice of time.

VICTOR GRASSIAN

ETHICAL THEORY

Reason is, and ought only to be the slave of the passions . . .

DAVID HUME

. . . the will is a faculty of choosing only that which reason, independently of inclination, recognizes . . . as good.

IMMANUEL KANT

The foundations of morality are like all other foundations: if you dig too much about them the superstructure will come tumbling down.

SAMUEL BUTLER

A philosophy is characterized more by the formulation of its problems than by the solution of them.

SUSANNE LANGER

1

The Nature
of
Moral Reasoning

1. INTRODUCTION

What Is Ethics?

Ethics may be defined as the philosophical study of morality—that is, of right conduct, moral obligation, moral character, moral responsibility, social justice, and the nature of the good life. The philosophical study of morality should be distinguished from the descriptive or scientific study of the same subject matter. It is not the philosopher's task, as it is that of the anthropologist, sociologist, or psychologist, to describe the various positions individuals and societies take on the various questions of morality (such as, What is right? What is the good life? Who is responsible? How should the goods of society be distributed?) nor to devise explanations as to why individuals and societies have the moral views that they do. Although philosophers often make use of the results of descriptive and scientific studies of morality, their tasks are different. First, philosophers attempt to provide some view or theory of the "right" answers to these questions. Yet this characterization alone does not uniquely identify the philosophical study of morality, for such great literary figures as Shakespeare and Dostoyevsky have also enriched our lives with great insight into the answers to moral questions, as have psychologists and psychiatrists who can grasp the psychological consequences of the adoption of various moral positions. What distinguishes the specifically philosophical account of morality is its generality, systematic nature, and above all its attempt to prove its claims through arguments which purportedly can demonstrate that the ideal morality a philosopher proposes is indeed ideal.

3

The attempt to provide coherent, systematic, and justifiable answers to moral questions has been called *normative ethics* and has been distinguished from the second task of the philosophical study of morality, *metaethics,* which consists of an inquiry into the meaning and logic of moral language. First, metaethics is an attempt to supply some enlightening account of the nature of morality and the meanings and interrelationships of the fundamental concepts of moral language. Answers to such questions as the following are sought: "How does a moral principle differ from a nonmoral one—such as a principle of etiquette?" "What do we mean when we say that an act is right?" "Can the notion of 'right conduct' be defined in terms of the notion of what is 'good' (that is, worth seeking) and can this notion in turn be defined in terms of some nonmoral quality such as 'pleasure'?" "What does one mean by saying that an individual has 'free will' or is 'morally responsible' for his actions?" Second, metaethics is an attempt to supply an account of the nature of moral reasoning. In this area of metaethics, questions such as the following are considered: "How does moral reasoning differ from scientific reasoning?" "In what sense, if at all, can a moral claim be said to be 'true' or 'false'?" "Is there such a thing as moral knowledge or is morality, in the last analysis, simply a 'matter of taste'?"

Why Study Ethics?

Although a study of ethics will not in itself make one into a good person, it can certainly provide us with more than the knowledge of abstract philosophical theories and terminologies that seem incapable of aiding us in the solution of our own practical moral problems. A study of ethics can serve to help us better understand and classify our own moral principles; most of all, it can help refine, develop, and sometimes change these principles. The beginning student of ethics comes to this study laden with beliefs on many moral issues, but rarely has he adequately thought out the implications of these beliefs and whether or not they "hang together" as a unit without leading into unforeseen contradictions (that is, whether or not his moral beliefs form a "consistent set").

The study of ethics can lead one from the blind and irrational acceptance of moral dogmas gleaned from parental and cultural influences, which were never subjected to logical scrutiny, into the development of a critical reflective morality of one's own. Certainly, all reflective people at one time or another in their lives have been struck by the intolerable vagueness and apparent inconsistencies of conventional morality, where general moral principles are called upon in certain contexts only to be conveniently forgotten in others. Similarly, who has not at one time or another suspected that some cherished moral belief was simply a deeply felt "prejudice"? Aware of the many apparently divergent moralities that seem to coexist in the world around us, many of us wonder whether our moral beliefs are capable of rational justification or are nothing more than a reflection of the prevailing, although ever changing mores of our culture—no more right or wrong than those of the innumerable cultures that have existed through the ages. Some of us may shudder to think that sometime in the future a student of anthropology may laugh as he reads about some of the strange moral beliefs and practices that we now hold, just as many of us now laugh at the moral beliefs and practices of some ancient cultures. It is in the face of such intellectual uneasiness or perplexity that the philosophical spirit of questioning and inquiry often begins. By studying the arguments that philosophers give for their ethical positions and the objections they pose to the views of others, a person's ability to defend his own positions and recognize their shortcomings will itself be sharpened. This is by far the most important thing that the study of ethics has to offer.

Socratic Method and the Ideal of Consistency

As the ancient Greek philosopher, Socrates, noticed long ago, most of us have strong opinions on moral matters, but are, nevertheless, neither capable of adequately justifying these opinions nor indeed of defining their key concepts. Philosophical reflection begins, as it began with Socrates, with the questioning of one's own beliefs. Socrates is remembered today not for his philosophical positions (he claimed he had none), but for a method of doing philosophy that bears his name—Socratic Method. As he walked the streets of Athens, conversing with his contemporaries on philosophical topics, Socrates did not play the role of an advocate, attempting to convince others of the correctness of his views, but instead simply questioned them as to the meanings of their opinions, their presuppositions and implications; and in the process, he uncovered their logical weaknesses.

As you subject your moral beliefs to critical Socratic scrutiny, you may be embarrassed to discover that many of the moral principles you claim to hold and act upon are unclear in meaning, are difficult to justify, and appear to have contradictory implications. As we shall later discuss, although there may be no way to prove that a given set of moral principles is "true" to the exclusion of all others, nevertheless, rationality demands that one strive to make one's moral principles clear and mutually consistent.

Each of us comes to the study of ethics with a multitude of judgments on concrete moral questions (such as, Should X lie in situation Y? Should homosexuality be illegal? Are abortions ever morally justified?). The task of philosophical reflection is to unify these particular moral judgments into some systematic and consistent whole. As you attempt to discern *general* underlying moral principles that can account for your particular moral judgments, you may find that a principle accepted in one type of concrete moral situation appears unacceptable in another situation. Unless you can point to some morally relevant difference in the two situations, the ideal of consistency demands that you either modify your initial commitment to the general moral principle or revise your moral judgment of the concrete moral situation. The difficulty of developing some unified and consistent system of underlying moral principles which can guide you in the resolution of concrete moral problems can be clearly seen when you are faced with a serious moral dilemma in which conflicting moral principles to which you feel some allegiance seem to demand different answers. We shall turn to a sample of such moral dilemmas in the next section.

DISCUSSION QUESTIONS

1. If you were an anthropologist studying a strange culture, what criteria (standards) would you use to distinguish the principles of "morality" of that culture from its principles of "etiquette"? What difference(s) in meaning do you attach to these two concepts?

2. Consider the following dialogue:

   A: I admit that conventional morality requires that I keep my promise in this situation and I accept that demand of conventional morality as a correct one. Nevertheless, I do not intend to keep my promise and furthermore do not think that I ought to. Other considerations override the moral ones for me in this situation. Although breaking my promise in this situation is wrong according to the morality I accept, it is not wrong for me, all things considered.

   B: I do not think that what you say makes sense. If, as you say, you accept as proper conventional morality's demand that one ought to keep one's promises in situations such as yours, then you must, as a matter of logic, admit that you will be acting wrongly when you break your promise— not wrongly according to conventional morality alone, but wrongly from your own point of view as well. If you do not think that you are acting wrongly in your particular situation, then you must really be rejecting as incorrect conventional morality's demand that one ought to keep one's promises in situations such as yours. You cannot have it both ways.

   Whose side would you take in this debate? Why? Do you think that *A* and *B* are attributing the same meaning to the concept of "morality"? Explain.

3. Consider the following dialogue:

   A: The only way to really find out what a person's moral beliefs are is by having him honestly tell you. One can never discover the moral principles a person accepts by simply observing his behavior, for some people consistently act contrary to their moral principles.

   B: It seems to me that if a person consistently acts contrary to the moral beliefs he professes, he really cannot meaningfully be said to "accept" those moral principles. People, after all, sometimes lie to themselves about what they really believe.

What do you think of *B*'s reply? Is there some essential connection between a person's actual behavior and the moral beliefs he accepts? How do you see the nature of this connection?

2. SOME MORAL DILEMMAS

In each of the following cases try to extract the underlying moral principle that justifies the moral position you take. Be on guard for a moral principle that you are inclined to use in one example but not in another. When this happens, ask yourself what differences there are in the two cases that incline you to treat them differently.

As you proceed through these moral dilemmas, see if there is some set of general moral principles on which you consistently rely. Is it possible for your moral principles to be arranged in some type of hierarchical order where certain *basic* general moral principles are used as a means of justifying derivative ones but are themselves incapable of justification in terms of some higher level moral principle? Do you accept more than one basic moral principle? If so, can they not conflict, and how would you choose among them in such a case? Can you *justify* your choice of basic moral principles? Ponder these questions as you consider the moral dilemmas. After we have critically studied some general theories of normative ethics provided by famous philosophers, we may inquire as to how these philosophers would resolve our moral dilemmas. Most important, after having subjected your own moral views to reasoned criticism, you may find that your initial reactions to these moral dilemmas have themselves undergone some degree of change or development.

1. The Overcrowded Lifeboat

In 1842, a ship struck an iceberg and more than 30 survivors were crowded into a lifeboat intended to hold only 7. As a storm threatened, it became obvious that the lifeboat would have to be lightened of its human load if anyone were to survive. The captain reasoned that the right thing to do in this situation was to force some individuals to go over the side and drown. Such an action, he reasoned, was not unjust to those thrown overboard, for they would have drowned anyway. If he did nothing, however, he would be responsible for the deaths of those whom he could have saved. Some people opposed the captain's decision. They claimed that if nothing were done and everyone died as a result, no one would be responsible for these deaths. On the other hand, if the captain attempted to save some, he would be able to do so only by killing others and their deaths would be his responsibility. It was claimed that this would be worse than doing nothing and letting all die. The captain rejected this reasoning and decided that he must throw some people overboard. Since the only possibility for rescue required great efforts of rowing by the survivors, the captain decided that the weakest would have to be sacrificed. In this situation, it would be absurd, he thought, to decide by drawing lots who should be thrown overboard.

As it turned out, after days of hard rowing, the survivors were rescued and the captain was tried for his action. If you were on the jury, how would you have decided? Why?

2. A Father's Agonizing Choice

You are an inmate in a concentration camp. A sadistic guard is about to hang your son who tried to escape and wants you to pull the chair from underneath him. He says that if you don't he will not only kill your son but some other innocent inmate as well. You don't have any doubt that he means what he says. What should you do?

3. The Fat Man and the Impending Doom

A fat man leading a group of people out of a cave on a coast is stuck in the mouth of that cave. In a very short time high tide will be upon them, and unless he is promptly unstuck, they will all be drowned except the fat man, whose head is out of the cave. But, fortunately, or unfortunately, someone has with him a stick of dynamite. There seems no way to get the fat man loose from the opening without using that dynamite which will inevitably kill him; but if they do not use it everyone will drown. What should they do?

4. Jean Valjean's Conscience

In Victor Hugo's *Les Miserables,* the hero, Jean Valjean, is an ex-convict, living illegally under an assumed name and wanted for a robbery he committed many years ago. Although he will be returned to the galleys, probably for life, if he is caught, he is a good man who does not deserve to be punished. He has established himself in a town, becoming mayor and a public benefactor. One day, Jean learns that another man, a vagabond, has been arrested for a minor crime and identified as Jean Valjean. Jean is first tempted to remain quiet, reasoning to himself that since he had nothing to do with the false identification of the hapless vagabond, he has no obligation to save him. Perhaps this man's false identification, Jean reflects, is "an act of Providence meant to save me." Upon reflection, however, Jean judges such reasoning "monstrous and hypocritical." He now feels certain that it is his duty to reveal his identity, regardless of the disastrous personal consequences. His resolve is disturbed, however, as he reflects on the shattering and irreparable harm his return to the galleys will mean to so many people who depend upon him for their livelihood—especially troubling is a helpless woman and her small child to whom he feels a special obligation. He now reproaches himself for being too selfish, for thinking only of his own conscience and not of others. The right thing to do, he now claims to himself, is to remain quiet, to continue making money, while using it to help others. The vagabond, he now comforts himself, is not a worthy person, anyway. Still unconvinced and tormented by the decision he must make, Jean goes to the trial and confesses. Did he do the right thing?

5. A Callous Passerby

Roger Smith, a quite competent swimmer, is out for a leisurely stroll. During the course of his walk he passes by a deserted pier from which a teenage boy who apparently cannot swim has fallen into the water. The boy is screaming for help. Smith recognizes that there is absolutely no danger to himself if he jumps in to save the boy. He could easily succeed if he tried. Nevertheless, he chooses to ignore the boy's cries. The water is cold, Smith thinks to himself, and he is afraid of catching a cold and doesn't want to get his good clothes wet either. "Why should I inconvenience myself for this kid," Smith says to himself, and passes on. Does Smith have a moral obligation to save the boy? If so, should he have a legal obligation as well? Why?

6. A Poisonous Cup of Coffee

Tom, hating his wife and wanting her dead, puts poison in her coffee, thereby killing her. Joe also hates his wife and would like her dead. One day, Joe's wife accidentally puts poison in her coffee, thinking it's cream. Joe, who happens to be a chemist, has the antidote, but he does not give it to her. Knowing that he is the only one who can save her, he lets her die. Is Joe's failure to act as bad as Tom's action? Why or why not?

7. The Torture of the Mad Bomber

A madman who has already killed many people by planting bombs in crowded areas has finally been apprehended. It is known, however, that this fiend has already planted several bombs which are scheduled to go off in a very short time. It is possible that hundreds of people may die. The authorities seem unable to make him divulge the location of the bombs by conventional methods. He refuses to say anything and his lawyer is there to protect his fifth amendment right against self-incrimination. Finally, in exasperation, some high-level official suggests that some type of truth serum or, if necessary, torture, be used to prevent the looming tragedy. This would, of course, be illegal, but the official thinks that it is nevertheless the right thing to do in this desperate situation. Do you agree? If you do, would it also be morally justifiable to torture the mad bomber's innocent wife if that is the only way to make him talk? Why? If you believe that this would be wrong, how do you square this with your view concerning the morality of war?

8. Political Assassination

You are the director of the C.I.A. A mentally unstable tyrant is in control of a small nation and is ruthlessly killing his real and imagined opposition. He has, however, assumed control legally. You are presented with a plan to have him assassinated which you think has a good chance of succeeding. Should you go ahead? If it depends, on what does it depend?

9. Involuntary Euthanasia and the Common Good

Most of us would feel great moral repugnance at the Nazi program of involuntary euthanasia of the chronically and hopelessly ill, the insane, the senile, and congenital idiots. The rationale given for this program by the Nazis was that the immense amount of money it would cost to care for such people could be better spent on social programs for those with greater capacities for meaningful lives. Indeed, with current technology, the bodies of the victims of involuntary euthanasia would provide "spare parts" to save the lives or greatly increase the quality of life of many people with much greater potential for meaningful life. "This is wrong," most of us will say. "It is wrong to sacrifice people for the common good like this." Yet if this is so, how can we justify having, let us say, 60 mile per hour speed limits, when we know that a 55 mile per hour speed limit would save a considerable number of lives? Are we not in this case sacrificing innocent lives for the common good? Furthermore, many people feel justified in sacrificing innocent lives for the greater good in a war. What, if anything, are the relevant moral differences in these cases?

10. The Cog in an Unjust System

You have just been offered a high position in your corrupt city government. If you attempt to buck the system, you will be thrown out at once and a person with fewer scruples will take your place. Since this is so, would it be right for you to accept the position, going along with the corrupt system when you must but trying to do as much good as you can?

11. The Principle of Psychiatric Confidentiality

You are a psychiatrist and your patient has just confided to you that he intends to kill a woman. You're inclined to dismiss the threat as idle, but you aren't sure. Should you report the threat to the police and the woman or should you remain silent as the principle of confidentiality between psychiatrist and patient demands? Should there be a law that compels you to report such threats?

12. Two Drowning Men

There are two men on the verge of drowning who desperately need your help. You can probably save one of them; the other will surely drown. One of the men is your father, a person you deeply love but realize is of no particular importance to anyone but his own immediate family. The other man, however, is a world renowned scientist who is on the verge of finding a cure for cancer. No one else, you realize, is likely to take his place for some time. Your initial impulse is to swim towards your struggling father, but seeing the other man and thinking of his importance, you hesitate. What should you do?

13. A Father's Right in a Pregnancy

Joan, an unmarried 18-year-old finds herself pregnant. Does she have a moral obligation to inform the baby's father and allow him to participate in the decision about whether she should have an abortion? What if Joan were married and wanted an abortion but knew that her husband would disapprove?

14. The Deathbed Promise

You and a friend have been shipwrecked on a deserted island. There is only a limited amount of food available and it is extremely doubtful that you can both survive on it until you are rescued. Your friend has been injured and is more likely to succumb than you. He tells you that you can have all the food, as long as you promise to see to it that his son gets his share of the treasure the two of you have uncovered. You promise. Your friend dies and you are rescued. Intending to keep your promise, you find your dead friend's son, his only living relative. You are dismayed when you discover the life he is leading and are convinced that he would certainly waste his father's share of the treasure on the extravagances of which he is so fond. If your friend did not know the life his son was leading, you would feel absolutely no guilt in breaking your promise, but you are convinced that he did know. You hesitate and then decide that since your friend is dead, you can't hurt him by breaking your promise. (You don't believe in an afterlife.) You decide that the right thing to do in this situation is to break that promise. Feeling guilty about your decision and even though you believe that guilt to be irrational, you decide that you should give your friend's share of the treasure to charity in his name. This is what you do. You continue, however, to feel guilty about your action, and sometimes wonder whether you really did right. But you keep telling yourself that you're being irrational and that your action was morally justified. Right?

15. The Promise or the Innocent Man

A friend of yours has confided to you that he has committed a particular crime and you have promised never to tell. Discovering that an innocent man has been accused of your friend's crime, you plead with him to give himself up to the authorities. He refuses and reminds you of your promise. What should you do?

16. The Reluctant Voter

You are on your way home from work on a Presidential election day. You were planning to vote, but you're rather tired and would like very much to get home quickly, relax, and have a couple of drinks before supper. You really don't want to spend the extra half hour or more that it would take you to get to the polling place, vote, and get home. You think about it and convince yourself that you might as well go home. After all, your vote certainly will not make a difference in this national election. Since others may criticize you, you decide not to tell anyone you didn't vote. The more you think about it, the more convinced you become that it really is foolish for people to vote when they know their refusal to vote will not make a difference towards the outcome or to the voting behavior of others. What, if anything, is wrong with this sort of moral reasoning?

17. The Soft-Hearted Professor

You are a professor of philosophy. A student who is doing D work comes to you just before the final and explains to you that he needs a C in your class to be admitted next semester to the business school to which he hopes to transfer. He claims that he's been working hard in your class but just doesn't seem to understand what is going on. You offer to help him, but soon discover that there isn't much you can do short of giving him the questions and answers to the final. He seems quite sincere, however, and you would hate to have his admission rejected on the basis of your grade. You're very tempted to give him the C and attempt to justify this to yourself by reflecting that "a good business administration major doesn't have to have any aptitude for philosophy." But then again, you think, "It would be unfair to the other students." What should you do?

3. SOME PITFALLS OF MORAL REASONING

Since philosophers attempt to justify their moral positions, they provide *arguments* in support of them. As we shall see, lack of agreement as to what counts as a "good" moral argument, seems to be a distinctive characteristic of the questions we shall be discussing. As such, there is no list of fallacies (that is, types of incorrect reasoning) that we can hope to learn and then mechanically apply to test the correctness of a person's moral reasoning. Nevertheless, there are certain very distinctive pitfalls of moral reasoning to which the uninitiated can easily fall victim. Consequently, it is important that these potential stumbling blocks to sound moral reasoning be pointed out at the very outset of our inquiry into the problems of ethics. Let us turn then to a discussion of the following pitfalls of moral reasoning:

1. The failure to recognize that the concepts we use in making moral distinctions often have no precise definition—that is, they are vague
2. The tendency to mistakenly assume that certain concepts are value-free ones which simply report "the facts," when they actually are moral ones which make some value judgment about these facts
3. The tendency to utilize a statement which appears on the surface to be an informative one that tells us something about the world in a way which makes it trivially *true by definition*—that is, turns it into a *tautology*
4. The tendency to accept general moral principles on the basis of an insufficient sample of concrete cases
5. The tendency towards rationalization
6. The tendency to dismiss moral positions on the basis of their causes, without considering the reasons that are given in their support—that is, the *genetic* or *argumentum ad hominem* fallacy
7. The confusion between what one would be inclined to do and what one morally ought to do

The Problem of Vagueness

It is common to find people defending moral principles without any clear understanding of their meanings. Consider, for example, the moral principle "never lie." What is a lie? "A false statement that is made with the intention of deceiving," one might answer. But is this really an adequate definition, for is it not possible for one to lie without making any statement at all? For example, suppose I am asked if I agree with a statement and refuse to answer, knowing that my silence will be taken as a tacit affirmation of that statement. Assuming that I know that statement to be false but want to mislead others into believing it's true, have I lied? Similarly, have I lied when someone asks me to lend him a $10 bill and I say, "Sorry, I don't have it," and although it is true that I

13

don't have a $10 bill, I do have a couple of $20 bills and know that I can easily get change? If both of these examples should count as instances of lying, perhaps we should revise our definition to cover "all that one does or refrains from doing with the intent of misleading." But, is this definition too broad? Do we really want to say, for example, that a person who intentionally misleads a friend into thinking that he is far more successful than he really is, through a lavish show of generosity that he can ill-afford, has lied to his friend, even though he never said anything that was false? As you can see, the concept of a lie is a vague one which does not sharply limit the range of things that fall within its definition. Consequently, the claim that "lies are always wrong" does not clearly specify which things are wrong.

The same can be said for the concept of killing. What is it to kill someone? That seems very easy. "You have killed someone," you might say, "when he dies as a result of what you have done to him." This definition can be applied with no problem in many cases. For example, if you shoot someone directly in the heart and he dies immediately as a result, you have obviously killed him. But, imagine that, intending to merely scare him, you point a gun at him and pretend you are going to shoot him, and as a result he dies of a heart attack. Have you killed him? Similarly, in which of the following cases do you think that the accused person can be said to have killed (that is, *caused* the death of someone)?

1. Accused gravely injures his victim. The victim is taken to a hospital where he dies as a result of negligent medical treatment. Given proper medical treatment, he would most likely have survived.

2. Accused gravely injures his victim who is hospitalized with almost no chance of survival. While lying in his hospital bed, the victim is stabbed by a maniac.

3. Accused brutally rapes X who, distracted by intense pain and grief, jumps into a creek and drowns.

4. Accused throws a live grenade into X's room, intending to kill him. X seizes it and throws it out of his window where it falls to the crowded street below, exploding and killing several persons.

5. Accused engages in an armed robbery, not intending to kill anyone. However, in the course of his apprehension by the police, a policeman accidently kills an innocent bystander.

6. Accused negligently strikes X with his automobile, throwing him about 20 feet and breaking his thighbone. Soon afterward, X dies from delirium tremens which was precipitated by his injury. The injury would not have led to delirium tremens, however, if X were not an alcoholic.

In addition to facing the problem of how far back we should go in a single causal chain of events (this problem is reflected in the legal distinction between *proximate* and *remote* causation), we must also face the problem of when one can be said to have *caused* the death of another through some omission. Practically everyone will agree that if a parent lets a newborn baby die by refusing to feed it, that person has *caused* the death of the baby (that is, has killed it) by his omission. But if failure to do something can be called killing, aren't we in the affluent part of the world guilty of killing starving people in other parts of the world whose lives could be saved if we were more willing to share our wealth with them? Again, we can see that the concept of killing is not the sharply defined one that many people seem to think it is.

The Conflation of Factual and Value Judgments

It is tempting to think that the question of whether an omission *is really a cause* of a given event or whether a given event in a causal chain is *the true cause* of a resulting event is a purely "factual" one. This is not so. The decision as to whether a given event should be picked out as *a cause* or *the cause* of a given event is often based on some moral judgment. Consider, for example, a two car automobile accident that would not have occurred but for the convergence of several independent factors (that is, these factors were all necessary conditions for the accident). Let us say that the accident would have been avoided had:

1. there been better street lighting;
2. the brakes on one of the cars had been in better condition;
3. the driver of the other car had reacted with quicker reflexes.

Since all three features were equally necessary ingredients in causing the accident, the question of which of these factors should be singled out as *the cause* of the accident is not at all a factual question but rather a question concerning where we choose to place the responsibility for this accident. It is for this reason that the question "What caused X?" is often equivalent to the question "What ought we to consider responsible for X?" The answer to this question might in turn reflect some general social policy decision as to how we ought best to attempt to control the occurrence of X.

There are many concepts that misleadingly appear to be value-free which turn out under closer inspection to presuppose a particular moral standpoint. For example, many philosophers have claimed that "a voluntary act" should be defined as "an act which is not a result of coercion." But the trouble with this definition is that the notion of coercion is itself in need of clarification. Indeed, after seeing the differing uses philosophers make of this concept, one may come to the justifiable conclusion that the question of what is or is not to count as *coercion* is not at all a purely factual one, but reflects a commitment to particular moral standards as to the distinction between *proper* and *improper* causal influence. If this is true, then it is a mistake to think that the judgment of whether something is truly voluntary is a purely factual matter that justifies the moral stands we take (Since his action is involuntary, he ought not to be held responsible) rather than a reflection of our moral judgment (Since

I do not believe that it would be morally proper to hold him responsible for his action, I judge his action to be an involuntary one).

The concepts of mental health and mental illness are also good examples of concepts that can often be used to present particular moral commitments under the guise of value-free diagnoses. Consider, for example, the following definition of mental health given by the noted psychiatrist Karl Menninger:

> Mental health is the adjustment of human beings to the world and to each other with a maximum of effectiveness and happiness. Not just efficiency or just contentment—or the grace of obeying the rules of the game cheerfully. It is all of these together. It is the ability to maintain an even temper, an alert intelligence, socially considerate behavior, and a happy disposition. This, I think, is a healthy mind.[1]

Though Menninger offers this definition in his capacity as a psychiatric expert, such a definition does not rely upon any psychiatric insight but reflects value judgments that Menninger is no more qualified to make than any of us. In effect, Menninger, by conceiving of mental health in terms of "adjustment," prescribes that we come to terms with our culture and its institutions, making a claim which reflects a conservative political bias. It is a question open to moral debate, after all, whether one *ought to* adjust to a given society or accept life in that society with a happy disposition.

As many sociologists have pointed out, when some psychiatrists classify behavior as a manifestation of mental health or mental illness, they are at the same time labelling that behavior as, at least to some extent, morally desirable or morally undesirable. Two psychiatrists, fully agreeing on the nature and causes of a given pattern of thought, feeling, and behavior, might disagree as to whether this pattern should be described as a mental illness (Is homosexuality a mental illness?), precisely because of their differing moral judgments as to the moral desirability of that pattern of thought, feeling, and behavior. In calling someone mentally ill, one is often not merely describing the facts but taking a moral position on these facts. People, unfortunately, are often not aware of this, camouflaging their moral positions behind the facade of terms that give the mistaken impression of being value-neutral.[2]

---

[1] Karl Menninger, *The Human Mind*, 3rd ed. (New York: 1946), p. 2.

[2] Freud, himself, was quite aware of this problem. The concept of "mental health," he once wrote, is "a purely conventional practical concept and has no real scientific meaning. It simply means that a person gets on well; it doesn't mean that the person is particularly worthy." Freud's disavowal of the scientific nature of the distinction between "health" and "illness" anticipated the contemporary sociological view that a diagnosis of "mental illness" is best conceived as a negative cultural judgment of a person's social performance (for a person may get on well in one culture, but not in another). From such a perspective, though the question of whether a pattern of behavior should be classified as a "mental illness" is not a scientific question, once a person is so classified, one must turn to science to discover the causes and methods of altering that person's maladaptive behavior.

Moral Principles Can Be Reduced to Tautologies

In the course of defending a moral principle, this principle may be diluted into a tautology—that is, a statement which might appear to be informative but is really not and is true merely by definition. For example, a person, after initially claiming that "lying is always wrong," may be forced to admit that it is sometimes right to say things that are false with the intention of deceiving. For example, he may admit that it would be all right to lie to a maniac who asks you where someone is with the intention of killing that person. It is all right, too, he admits, to untruthfully tell a gracious hostess that you enjoyed the meal she prepared. But he is still unwilling to abandon his principle that lying is always wrong. Instead, he claims that such lies are merely "white lies," and he did not mean to include them in his principle. But when we press him to be specific as to what should count as a white lie, he seems unable to give us any specific definition and finally simply says that a white lie is a morally justifiable lie. But if he accepts this definition of a white lie, his principle that "all lies, except white lies, are always wrong," reduces to the empty tautology that "all lies which are not morally justifiable are wrong." This statement is no more informative than Calvin Coolidge's famous remark that "when large numbers of people are out of work, unemployment results," for it, too, is simply true by definition.

Similarly, a person who bases his morality on the Ten Commandments might initially claim that "it is always wrong to kill." But upon being pressed to consider various possible counter-examples to his principle, he admits that it is not wrong to kill animals or kill human beings in self-defense or as a just punishment for their criminal deeds. It may be right, he now says, to kill, but it is never right to *murder* human beings. When asked to define what he means by "murder," he initially says that murder is the intentional taking of a human life neither in self-defense nor as a just punishment.[3] But under questioning, he is willing to grant that it is also morally permissible to kill a person if this is essential to prevent him from killing innocent people and that it may be morally permissible as well for a spy to kill himself rather than to divulge vital information to the enemy. As other cases are thrust before him (such as hastening the death of someone who is bound to die in a short time, in order to ease his excrutiating pain), he admits that there are many types of justifiable intentional homicides which should not count as murder. But he now finds himself hesitant to attempt to specify the categories that should incorporate the exceptional cases he now has in mind, for he realizes that there is no guarantee that other unanticipated cases of what he would consider justifiable homicide probably exist that would necessitate new revisions in his categories of exceptions. So rather than attempt to specify the exceptions to his principle, he simply asserts in

---

[3] Notice that one could pursue the question of why the death penalty is a "just" punishment, as well as the question of what exactly should count as an act of "self-defense."

the end that murder should be defined as "the unjustifiable taking of human life." But if this definition is accepted, the principle that "murder is always wrong" turns into a tautology.

As we shall see in our various discussions of moral issues, assertions that may appear to be telling us something about the world or making some substantial moral point may turn out to be disguised tautologies that reflect a particular stipulation as to how a concept is to be used. For example, as we shall see, many philosophers have claimed that the plausibility of the view that "all voluntary human actions are selfishly motivated" comes from the tendency of its adherents to use the concept of selfishness with such an expanded meaning as to make it synonymous with the notion of a voluntary action, rendering their view into a tautology.

The Fallacy of the Hasty Moral Generalization

The process of extracting moral principles from concrete cases, such as those on our list of moral dilemmas, requires great care. As you reflect upon a concrete moral problem which your moral "intuitions" lead you to evaluate in a particular way and search for some underlying general principle which can justify your particular evaluation, you may find yourself embracing some generalization which you would be inclined to reject upon consideration of a wider spectrum of cases. Since all concrete moral problems possess many features, it is quite possible that you may have focused on a given feature as the solely morally relevant one (say F_1) when other features (F_2 . . . F_n) may be having an unconscious effect upon your moral appraisal. Consequently, given another situation which possesses F_1, but not F_2 . . . F_n, you may find your moral reaction to be quite different. If this happens, you must reconsider your generalization as to the importance of F_1 when taken in isolation. Perhaps, F_1 is morally relevant to you only when it is combined with some other feature or combination of features, or perhaps you may even find that F_1 is a morally irrelevant feature, focusing your attention now on the moral relevance of other features, previously neglected.

Let us consider, for example, the case of the poisonous cup of coffee. It is my experience that practically everyone will claim that Joe's action is as morally wrong as that of Tom. Yet Tom's action must be described as one of *killing* his wife, whereas many will claim that it is improper to so describe Joe's action which should be seen as one of *letting* his wife *die*. Some will disagree, however, claiming that in this case Joe's letting his wife die is a way of killing her. The description of an act of letting die as equivalent not only morally but conceptually, as well, to that of killing reflects the fact, previously discussed, that the description of an action as one of killing may reflect a decision as to how the facts are to be morally evaluated. Regardless of how one chooses to describe Joe's action, most people will perceive Joe's action as morally equivalent to that of Tom's. Consequently, one may hastily conclude that there is no morally relevant distinction between the notion of killing and that of letting die, dismissing the contention of some that this distinction has great moral weight. (As we shall see in our discussion of the euthanasia issue, it has been claimed that although we have no justification *to kill* the hopelessly dying, we do have a right to *let them die.*) We may feel confirmed in this appraisal when we compare allowing an infant to die by the refusal to feed it with that of directly killing it by a lethal injection. Although cases such as these may indicate that letting someone die in some situations is morally equivalent to killing that person, one would be rash to jump to the conclusion that this distinction has no moral relevance whatsoever.

For example, practically everybody would agree that there is a tremendous moral difference between killing a child with a gun so that one may be freed of the burden of its support and the situation of letting many children die in the poverty stricken parts of this world by our refusal to donate the funds necessary to feed them. Certainly, in this case, most of us would claim that killing is worse than letting die. We would also accept this appraisal in considering the case of a great surgeon who is contemplating killing a skid row bum, who is useless to himself and others, in order to obtain a kidney and heart which are required to keep two highly productive and well-loved human beings alive—one of whom is dying of heart failure, the other of kidney failure. Even if we were convinced that these two human beings would certainly die unless the surgeon obtained the needed "spare parts" in such a manner, most of us would condemn such action. The surgeon, we will say, must not *kill* the bum, but must *let* the others *die.* Considering such cases, we may now reconsider our claim that these two notions are morally equivalent, claiming instead that killing is generally, though not always, worse than letting die.

Maybe so, but one can also point to cases where killing seems to be preferable to letting die. Consider, for example, our case of the fat man. If the dynamite is not used, one will certainly be letting many people die, yet if one uses it, one will be killing the fat man. Yet many people who would consider it morally reprehensible for the surgeon to kill the bum will claim that the dynamite should be used in this situation. Consider, as well, the situation of a President who is told that a missile carrying an atomic bomb has been launched and is aimed towards New York City. The only way this bomb can be prevented from striking New York City and killing millions, the President is told, is by deflecting it toward the Atlantic Ocean; but unfortunately the bomb will still have a devastating effect on the tip of Long Island, killing thousands. Considering the savings of life and the importance of New York City to the economic well-being of the nation, the President decides to deflect the bomb. Most of us will agree with his action. Yet his action can be described as one of choosing to kill rather than letting die. The conclusion that must be drawn from a consideration of these various cases of choosing between *killing* and *letting die* is that this distinction will not form the foundations of some general and simple moral principle which can mechanically yield conclusions about specific moral problems, as some think it can. One must delve deeper than this distinction in order to obtain some insight into the factors that motivate us to make the moral distinctions that we do.

Why, for example, do so many of us believe that Joe's action is equally as wrong as that of Tom's in the case of the poisonous cup of coffee? There seem to be several factors here that determine our judgment. First, Joe's motive is certainly morally relevant, for we are assuming that he hates his wife and wants her dead, and this is a black mark against him. But the most important factor, it would seem to me, is the great ease with which Joe could save his wife, coupled with the fact that he alone can help her. Similar remarks can be made of the refusal to feed a newborn infant. Certainly, our judgment that such an omission is the moral equivalent of directly killing the infant stems both from the fact that feeding an infant requires so little effort and from the special responsibility that we place upon parents and doctors for the care of the newborn. Clearly, we feel that there is a marked difference in the degree of responsibility parents and doctors have for the children in their care than we consider ourselves to have for starving children who bear no special relationship toward us. Why is this so? I think the best way to answer this question is to consider what would happen if all human beings were considered to have an equal claim to our aid? Would this not so diffuse our responsibilities that we would become incapable of ever fully discharging them, for it is impossible to aid everyone who might profit from our aid. Furthermore, we may ask, why should we assume the burden of helping individuals to whom we have no special responsibilities when others, who could equally as well assume this obligation, refuse? Does not this fact to some extent explain why we often consider the distinction between taking life and saving it to be a very important one?

Do we not also draw this distinction because of an underlying belief that individuals have *rights* to noninterference which should not be violated out of a belief that by so doing greater general happiness or welfare will be created? Is it not for this reason that practically all of us recoil with horror at the contemplation of the surgeon killing individuals in order to save others whose potential for happiness or social productivity is greater? Perhaps, our reaction here stems from our fear of living in a society where individuals do not have rights to noninterference that can override the demands of the common good. We fear that human beings would prove incapable of wisely and impartially judging both the demands of the common good and the necessity for sacrificing innocent individuals to meet its demands.

How can those many individuals who believe that it would be morally permissible to use the dynamite on the fat man distinguish this case from other cases of sacrificing innocent individuals for the common good, such as that of the surgeon, which they would strongly condemn? It would appear that the *causal responsibility* of the fat man for the plight of the others has a strong effect upon our moral judgment. Even though the fat man might have absolutely no moral responsibility for the sad predicament of his companions, he is no doubt causally responsible for it, whereas the surgeon's contemplated victim, we may assume, has no connection to those who would profit by his sacrifice.

In the case of the President deflecting the bomb from New York City to the tip of Long Island, this distinction does not play a role. It has been suggested that the relevant consideration here is that the President is not *creating a threat* but *deflecting an already existing threat*. In addition, the more momentous nature of the consequences for the general good and a President's special responsibility to consider these consequences, and even to decide to sacrifice innocent human lives if necessary in an act of war, leads us to allow the President to act on a principle which we would preclude from the surgeon.

As you can see, the factors that motivate us to make moral distinctions are complex. After studying various theories of normative ethics which attempt to unify and criticize the various factors that form our collective moral "intuitions," you might feel, as I do, that philosophers should give more attention than they often do to understanding the interrelationships of diverse and conflicting moral considerations instead of pursuing the task of providing a specious sense of unity to diverse and independent moral factors. This is a central criticism you shall find threaded through my critical evaluation of various theories of normative ethics.

The Tendency Toward Rationalization

While people often quite knowingly act in ways they believe to be wrong, it is perhaps even more common for people to convince themselves that what they want to do is what they ought to do. Since it is very important to most of us to have a moral self-image of ourselves, there is a marked human tendency to engage in a process of self-deception in which one devises superficially rational justifications for actions which are motivated by other factors. Psychiatrists call this process rationalization. Since rationalizations are merely rational cover-ups of one's true and often unflattering motives which are devised after one has already arrived at some decision, one is apt to conveniently forget these same reasons when it is in one's interest to so forget. For example, when Jones cheats on an important test, he will say that "everyone does it sometimes" or that "the test was unfair anyway"; but if Smith should cheat when Jones doesn't, Jones will be morally indignant and accuse Smith of "not having any personal integrity" or of "being unfair to those who are honest." Similarly, if Brown is reprimanded by his boss for being late, he might very well think ill of him for his "stern and inhumane attitude" and for his refusal "to give a guy a break once in a while," but if his wife is late with the supper, he will quickly and sternly reproach her for her "lack of consideration" or "laziness." The human capacity for inconsistency and self-deception is certainly, at times, staggering. Indeed, one of the greatest virtues of subjecting one's own moral beliefs to philosophical scrutiny is that under the light of such scrutiny, such self-deception and inconsistency can be brought to consciousness and there dealt with rationally.

The Genetic or Argumentum ad Hominem Fallacy

As the common tendency toward rationalization demonstrates, the *reasons* people give for their beliefs are often quite different from the factors that actually motivate or *cause* them to have these beliefs; or, as it is often put, they are not their *real reasons*. It is, however, misleading to equate the notions of *a cause* and *a reason*, as this common figure of speech does. The causes of a person's beliefs may not at all be reasons in the precise logical sense of rational considerations or arguments that are taken as supporting or justifying these beliefs. For example, although Jack may be capable of giving arguments for believing in the Judaic-Christian God, his belief in God may not have been influenced by these arguments at all. Instead, this belief may have been motivated purely by his needs and fears.

Since people often arrive at their moral beliefs as a result of non-rational factors of which they are not aware, it is tempting for us not to pay any heed to the reasons they give for their nonrationally motivated moral beliefs—assuming, quite mistakenly, that these reasons cannot be good reasons. Clearly, however wrong people may be in their self-knowledge of why they hold the moral beliefs they do, they can, nevertheless, be quite capable of rationally defending them. For example, although Mary may believe that abortion is wrong as a result of nonrational factors, she may still be capable of giving good arguments in defense of her belief. If Mary's position on the abortion issue is not a result of her consideration of these reasons, we have grounds for challenging the rational self-image she may have of herself, but we have no justifiable basis for dismissing her belief about abortion as unwarranted unless we can counter the arguments she presents. Consequently, when one assumes that a belief is false or unjustifiable because of its causal origin (that is, its genesis) one has committed a fallacy—*the genetic fallacy* or, as it is often called, *the fallacy of argumentum ad hominem* (literally: an argument directed to the man; that is, to the *source* of the argument rather than to the argument itself).

It is important that we realize that the reasons people offer in support of their beliefs must always be evaluated on their own merits, even if these reasons did not motivate (cause) the acceptance of these beliefs. We must not lose sight of the fact that although people will often search for good reasons to justify their nonrationally preconceived beliefs, they may very well find that justification.

Although a person may have plausible reasons for a belief that he arrived at on self-interested or purely emotional grounds, if these reasons are sufficient to justify acceptance of his belief and if he is a truly rational person who is motivated to act by the reasons he gives, he should continue to find these reasons sufficient to motivate his acceptance of the belief they support even without the further impetus of the nonrational factors that motivated him previously. This is, unfortunately, often not the case, and, consequently, we are right in being suspicious of the motivating power of the reasons people often give in defense of their moral positions. As psychiatrists stress, human beings are often much less rational in their behavior than their rational self-images of themselves would have them believe.

The Confusion Between What One Ought to Do and What One Would Be Inclined to Do

Although the distinction between what one morally ought to do and what one would be inclined to do is an obvious one, in a debate over the resolution of specific moral dilemmas, such as those on our list, it is quite common for a person to challenge the worth of this enterprise, claiming that most of us simply do not know how we would react in the situations described. No doubt, this is very often true. Our quest, however, is not the psychological one of what an individual would as a matter of fact be inclined to do in a given situation but, rather, the normative one of what he morally ought to do. The mere fact that an individual might be inclined to act in a particular way does not show that that is the way he should act. Once pointed out, this is obvious, and most will be satisfied with such an answer, especially when it is suggested that we are more apt to make rational moral judgments about what is right when we are not personally involved in a situation. For example, one would not expect most people to do their best moral deliberation when their very lives are at stake and their deliberation must be done very quickly. Nevertheless, such an answer is, perhaps, not fully adequate. If moral judgments were "objective" in the sense that they could be said to be true or false, independently of the way human beings happen to *feel* about things, then, it would appear, one would be more apt to arrive at "correct" moral judgments when one detaches oneself from the corrupting influence of emotional factors which cloud one's moral reason. On the other hand, if one takes the "subjective" view that moral judgments are ultimately dependent on human feelings, the value of "armchair moral speculation," as opposed to moral reflection made in "the heat of action," becomes a more difficult question. A person who takes the subjective view of moral judgments, in response to a request to give his view of what he thinks is right in a complex moral situation might reply as follows:

I really don't know what I think is right here, and I don't think I would know until I were in such a situation myself and discovered how much certain things meant to me or how vividly I would empathize with certain individuals if I were involved in their situation. Without this knowledge of what my own subjective feelings would be in the situation described, I really don't know what *I think* is right in this situation. Indeed, if I were in this situation, forced to choose between different options, I would probably discover something about my own true moral values and their relative importance that I am simply ignorant about now.

One's reaction to this claim will depend on one's view of the objectivity or subjectivity of moral judgments, and it is to this problem that we now turn.

DISCUSSION QUESTIONS

1. Which of the following moral rules do you think turn out to be tautologies? Why?
    a. A person should always do what is best.
    b. A person should always do as he thinks best.
    c. Cowardice is always wrong.
    d. Selfishness is not a desirable moral trait.
    e. It is always unjust to punish the innocent.
    f. It is always wrong to punish the innocent.
    g. When a person makes a promise, she has an obligation to keep it.
    h. When a person makes a promise, she ought to keep it.
    i. One ought always to like those whom one loves.

2. Consider the following case:

   > Jones is driving a tram in a crowded amusement park. Seeing two little children darting in front of the moving tram, Jones quickly slams his foot on the brake, but there is no response. Frantic, he looks quickly to his left and right, noticing to his left a lone pedestrian and to his right a crowd of them. Jones realizes that the tram is bound to hit, and most likely kill, someone regardless of what he does. Attempting to minimize the number of people who will be hit, Jones steers the tram in the direction of the lone pedestrian who is critically injured as the tram finally comes to a halt.

    a. Did Jones do the right thing?
    b. In what morally relevant ways, if any, does Jones' decision to sacrifice one to save two differ from the surgeon who also decides to sacrifice one to save two? (See p. 19.)

4. THE OBJECTIVITY OR SUBJECTIVITY OF VALUES

As any discussion of moral dilemmas, such as those on our list, would amply illustrate, moral opinions often differ. Is there some way to resolve these differences, some way to distinguish *true* moral opinions from *false* ones, or is this a hopeless task? Are these opinions merely a matter of taste, and whatever agreement exists, merely a matter of social convention? It has often been suggested that if there is to be an objective standard for distinguishing correct from incorrect moral beliefs, this standard must be a religious one. A right act, on this view, consists of obedience to God's will. This, it has been claimed, is the only genuine basis for morality. An atheist may live according to the moral point of view, but if his life is to have any objective justification, apart from his own personal preference, it must come from its correspondence to the independent will of God. As Dostoyevsky's Ivan Karamazov puts it, "If there is no God, then anything is permissible." Let us briefly consider this view.

Religious Absolutism

Assuming that we were created by some type of supernatural God, there are two different claims that can be made about the connection between God and morality. First, one may claim that, even though we can understand what morality demands of us without relating it to the will of God, the existence of God gives the only adequate reason for being moral at all times. Second, one may claim that morality must *be defined* in terms of God's will. The first view is usually understood in terms of a belief in an afterlife and an eventual day of moral reckoning in which the virtuous will be rewarded and the wicked punished. This view, which we shall not pursue here, appeals to one's self-interest as a reason for being moral. It is the second view which is relevant to our concern, for we are interested at this point not in why one ought to be moral, but in the logically more basic question of what ought to count as moral behavior.

The question of the legitimacy of defining morality in terms of God's will is the subject of an early Platonic dialogue called the *Euthyphro*. In this dialogue, which is representative of the Socratic method of doing philosophy, Socrates attempts to make Euthyphro distinguish between the claim that "an act is right because God wills it" and "God wills an act because it is right." According to the former claim, right action must be defined in terms of God's will, while according to the latter, there is some logically independent standard of right action to which God's will adheres. It is the former claim that Socrates finds objectionable. Why should the fiat of any being, even God, in itself make an act right? Is it because God is our creator and as such has the right to demand our total obedience? Bishop Robert C. Mortimer advocates this view, writing,

> God made us and all the world. Because of that he has an absolute claim on our obedience. We do not exist in our own right, but only as His creatures, who ought therefore to do and be what He desires.[1]

This, however, seems clearly inadequate, for is it not conceivable that we were created by an evil deity for some malevolent purpose. If we are to do what such a being wants, it would not be out of respect, but simply out of fear for the consequences of his power, should we disobey. "This is absurd!" a critic is bound to retort. "We were not created by such a God, but a morally perfect one—to suggest otherwise is to blasphemize the Judaic-Christian God." This is indeed the case, but it also brings out the circularity in attempting to define morality in terms of God's will. It is precisely because the Judaic-Christian God is defined partially in terms of moral perfection that a denial of God's goodness is itself a rejection of the Judaic-Christian God. The traditional Judaic-Christian answer to the question "Why ought we to worship and obey God?" is that "God *deserves* our worship and obedience *since* he is morally perfect." Such a claim, however, can only make sense if we understand the notion of moral perfection before we relate it to God. The very fact that we refuse out of hand to consider the possibility of a fiendish and sadistic creator reflects the fact that we are employing some logically independent standard in morally judging the appropriateness of respecting the God in whom we were taught to believe. Granted, we may have faith in the morality of an act which we believe to be willed by God, in spite of the fact that it appears immoral to our finite human intellect; yet, this is not a result of a *total* willingness to abandon our own independent moral appraisal.

Consider, for example, the biblical story of Abraham and his willingness to sacrifice to God his innocent and only son, Isaac. Although it would have appeared to Abraham that God was asking him to do an act which would in normal circumstances certainly be immoral, Abraham had faith that God had his reasons, reasons which, if made known to Abraham, would have been accepted as morally proper. In no sense should it have been morally acceptable to Abraham, had he sacrificed his son Isaac, to find that the God, who was the subject of his worship, simply enjoyed the anguish of his fatherly heart and especially gloated at it precisely because Abraham had so much innocent faith in him. We may have faith that God has his reasons and that, due to our ignorance of his purposes or perhaps even due to our muddled thinking, we cannot appreciate them now, but we certainly should believe that God has reasons which are worthy of respect. Consequently, it is not the fiat of a God that

---

[1] Robert C. Mortimer, *Christian Ethics* (1950) in Raziel Abelson and Marie-Louise Friquegnon, eds., *Ethics for Modern Life* (New York: St. Martin's Press, 1975), pp. 127–28.

makes an act right, but the reasons that a God who we believe or define to be good would give for his actions. These reasons would have their logical force (if not practical efficacy) even if there were no God, and can be studied in their own right.

The considerations which have led us to reject the view that there is no logically independent standard for distinguishing right from wrong apart from the blind acceptance of the will of God should lead us equally as well to dismiss the view that *conscience* is the correct standard. Even if we are to assume, what secular psychologists and psychiatrists would strongly contest, that the urgings of one's conscience reflect the inborn knowledge of "moral law" instilled in us by God, there is no sure mark by which the notoriously divergent promptings of conscience can be distinguished as correct or incorrect. The conscience of a religious pacifist, for example, tells him that war is contrary to the moral law, whereas the consciences of his nonpacifistic brethren speak with a different voice.

If we are to distinguish *enlightened consciences* from *misled* ones or from the disguised promptings of some other source, we must have some standard for making this distinction. If, as is often suggested, the mark of an enlightened conscience consists in its correspondence with the revealed word of God as found in the Bible, we must have some standard for choosing the *right* bible and its *proper* interpretation. The widespread disagreement of theologians is ample testimony to the fact that the words of a given book of holy writings are open to differing interpretations and disagreements as to proper translation. More fundamentally, there is no agreement as to the standard that should be used in deciding which book of allegedly divinely inspired writings should be accepted. Should we turn to the Christian Bible? If so, which version? Should we, perhaps, restrict our attention to the Old Testament as Judaism does, or should we turn to the Koran or the holy writings found in eastern religion? The lessons to be learned will differ depending on where we turn. Again, there is no way to escape using our own independent moral standards as at least a partial standard for the acceptance or rejection of the divinely inspired nature of some religious writing. If we picked up an alleged bible only to find that it seemed to have been written by the Marquis de Sade, we would dismiss it as uninspired by the good Judaic-Christian God, either believing that it was not the result of any supernatural influence or attributing it to some malicious supernatural force.

Ethical Relativism

If we cannot establish what is right or wrong by turning to a God and if, as we shall soon see, there are incompatible *ethical theories* as to the standard to be used in resolving moral disputes, perhaps these disputes are, in the last analysis, of a nonrational nature and can only be decided on the basis of one's personal emotional preferences or commitments. Perhaps, ethical choice should be assimilated more to the model of choosing the flavor of ice cream than to discerning the objective color or size of a physical object, for there are no *correct* answers as to which flavor of ice cream is *right* or *best*. This is the position of *ethical relativism* which claims that there is no way to justify a single morality as the *correct* one and others as *mistaken*. The belief in ethical relativism is often based on the observation that, as a matter of fact, different societies or cultures have fundamentally different moral beliefs. This doctrine is called *sociological* or *cultural relativism* and has been held by many students of anthropology to be obviously true. Not all cultural relativists, however, have been ethical relativists. One may accept the alleged *fact* of cultural relativism, while taking the *metaethical* position that only one morality can be justified as *correct*.

According to the cultural relativists, the fact of cultural moral variability has been conclusively established. None but the most insulated of people can remain unaware of the abundant differences in the mores of different cultures, the changing mores of a given culture through time or of a pluralistic society like ours where varieties of life-styles coexist at a given time. Furthermore, the cultural relativist will often point out that moral beliefs are neither inborn nor the result of logical reasoning but are rather the *internalized* reflection of the views of our culture, transmitted to us by our parents and other environmental influences. The process of acquiring moral beliefs is based on an unconscious psychological process which plays not upon our capacity for logical reasoning but on our emotional natures. Consequently, this learning process results in an essentially emotional nonreasoning acceptance of the norms of one's culture. These norms, which are explained and reinforced by a society's religious beliefs and practices, function as instruments for maintaining social stability and coherence. It is precisely man's desire to cling to a group and to reject external groups as in some way inferior which explains the tendency to believe that the moral norms of one's culture are the only true ones, and those of other cultures, mistaken. This ethnocentric (group centered) feeling, based as it is primarily on nonreasoning emotion, often causes people to be narrow-minded in their ethical outlook and afraid to subject their moral beliefs to logical scrutiny. This, in brief, is the case often presented for sociological relativism, and by inference, ethical relativism, by their adherents.

The case for sociological relativism is, however, open to challenge. Although there can be no doubt that different societies often seem to be guided by very different attitudes concerning the morality of homicide, suicide, euthanasia, sexual conduct, etc., and seem to place different degrees of emphasis upon such possibly conflicting principles as individual freedom and social welfare, it is open to question whether these different attitudes on specific moral issues reflect deeper differences in ultimate moral perspectives or are instead reflections of differing circumstances or factual or religious beliefs. Perhaps if agreement could be obtained upon these nonmoral factors, agreement would be unanimous on moral issues as well.

It is quite conceivable that all societies share the same *basic* moral

principles (that is, moral principles which are used to justify other derivative moral principles but are themselves incapable of justification in
terms of more fundamental moral principles). Consider, for example, the
issue of sexual morality. Let us imagine that in society A premarital sex
and polygamy may be encouraged, whereas they are condemned in society B. Clearly, we have moral disagreements here, but they need not be
ultimate. Perhaps both societies are committed to the same basic moral
principle that "one should always do what is conducive to the general
happiness." The differences in the two societies' positions on sexual morality may stem from differences in their circumstances and factual beliefs.
Perhaps women in society A greatly outnumber men and most people in
that society believe that sexual experience in general and with one's
prospective spouse in particular, is a necessary condition for the maximization of human happiness, whereas most members of society B disagree. Similarly, a given society may approve of cannibalism, while we
condemn it, only because it accepts what is, to us, the erroneous belief
that eating the flesh of one's enemy is necessary for the survival of one's
group. Similarly, we may morally condemn the practice in Western
civilization during the religious Inquisition of burning people at the
stake, but this does not at all imply that our disagreement is ultimately
of a moral nature. Perhaps, in this case, the disagreement stems from a
fundamental divergence of religious conceptions. During the period of
the Inquisition, when there was greater fear of eternal damnation than
there is today, it was generally fervently believed that burning people at
the stake was the only way to save them from the far worse fate of eternal
damnation. If we shared the same religious belief, would we not also
approve of this distasteful and desperate action?

Granted then that a mere difference in moral position need not
reflect a disagreement in ultimate or basic ethical principle, is there any
reason to think that all cultures actually do share the same basic moral
principles? Some people, perhaps in overreaction to the quick and
thoughtless defenses of sociological relativism, have pointed to the underlying similarities of human beings the world over and of the conditions
necessary for survival and mutual cooperation as sufficient to disprove
this doctrine. For example, the psychologist S.E. Asch writes, "We do not
know of societies in which bravery is despised and cowardice held up to
honor, in which generosity is considered a vice and ingratitude a virtue."[2]
Even if this were true,[3] Asch neglects the fact that different cultures have
different conceptions of bravery and generosity. Similarly, one may accept
the observation that no society tolerates the indiscriminate killing of
members of its group but distinguishes between justifiable and unjustifiable homicide. Yet the nature of this distinction may be quite different
in different societies.

[2] Solomon Asch, *Social Psychology* (Englewood Cliffs, N.J.: Prentice-Hall, Inc.,
1952), p. 378.

[3] For a refutation of Asch's claim that all societies consider generosity a virtue,
see Colin Turnbull, *The Mountain People* (New York: Simon & Schuster, 1972).

If all societies consider bravery a virtue as Asch says they do, why is this so? No doubt, as Asch recognizes, this explanation would have to be sought in some universal similarity in human nature. Given the human tendency toward selfishness and the struggle for survival and happiness that the nature of the world we inhabit imposes upon us, societies of human beings are invariably governed by principles which function to restrain individual selfishness for the common good. Again, given the realities of human nature, all societies will recognize that there will be times when abiding by the moral and legal principles of the group will prove very difficult and there will also be times when the common good requires individual sacrifices that go beyond the normal obligations imposed upon members by these principles. Consequently, societies may inevitably have some concept of bravery—that is, some concept of behavior in the common good that is beyond the call of duty. Societies, *by the very definition* of "bravery" will naturally support and encourage such behavior. Yet societies may have very different conceptions of the common good and of the specific behavior or degree of sacrifice that counts as an act of bravery. Although Asch does not make this distinction himself, it is important to recognize that all social moralities may share a common *structure* (that is, a way of conceptualizing morality) while they differ in *content* (that is, the specific meanings they attribute to their basic moral principles). This similarity in structure might in turn be a reflection of the basic psychological characteristics and needs that all human beings share—such as, the fact that they are at least partially selfish and need the cooperation of others—while the differences in content will be a reflection of differences in human desires and values.

Certainly, it is important to see the vast similarities of the human condition the world over—environmental, emotional, and motivational —but one should not neglect the differences that exist as well. It is one thing to say that all societies will encourage cooperation and have some notion of property, some rules prohibiting theft and distinguishing permissible from impermissible homicide, and certain procedures for recognizing sexual unions as having legal consequences;[4] it is, however, something quite different to say that this similarity in itself negates the thesis of sociological relativism. The mere fact that human beings share similar emotions, such as love, hate, happiness, sadness, pride, and shame, can in no way establish that they share the same basic moral outlook. Clearly, it would make a difference, for example, whether one takes pride in the number of people one helps or in the number of people one kills.

As we will see later in our discussion of specific ethical theories, key moral principles, such as "always act to maximize human happiness" and "always act to preserve the value of human freedom," can take on quite different meanings corresponding to the different meanings that are attributed to such key notions as "happiness" and "freedom." Consequently,

---

4 Indeed, such notions are built into the very *definition* of a "society." Consequently, a claim such as "All societies encourage cooperation and prohibit indiscriminate deception, violence, and theft" is tautological.

two societies committed to a moral principle, such as that of the "maximization of human happiness," may turn out to be committed to quite different moral ideals. Indeed, a cultural relativist might suggest that it is possible for two different cultures to inhabit such differing moral universes that it is impossible to translate one culture's moral categories into that of the other. Different cultures, we may want to say, simply *see the world differently*. But are ways of *seeing the world* differences in *factual* or *moral* belief? These differences may not be clearly distinguishable in some cases. For example, it is not at all easy to separate the factual from the moral beliefs found in the Buddhist religious worldview. Some may claim that the essence of the Buddhist religion is a commitment to a particular moral stance which makes Buddhists organize the facts of the world in a particular way. On the other hand, others can claim that the essence of the Buddhist religion is a way of looking at the facts of the world which makes Buddhists assume a particular moral stance.

Furthermore, even if it could be shown that two societies, whose external ways of life appear so different, actually share the same basic moral principles, their disagreement could still be of a moral nature, if they did not agree on the *ranking of these moral principles* in cases of conflict. For example, two societies might both share a basic commitment to the ideals of individual liberty and the general happiness, but disagree on when society has the right to make people happy *in spite of themselves*. Similarly, a society may accept some basic moral principle which confers a certain right of concern to animals, but this principle may be much lower in the hierarchy of this society's values than it is in the hierarchy of another society's values. In addition, it is quite possible for two societies to agree on the same basic moral principle but to disagree on its range of application (Does the moral principle of "the greatest happiness for the greatest number" include the happiness of animals as well as persons? If it is only to apply to persons, which ones? Everybody in the world? Everyone in our nation? Everyone in our subculture? Everyone in our immediate family?).

Although the grave difficulties involved in isolating a society's basic moral principles and determining their exact meanings and ranking make the truth of sociological relativism open to debate, I would suggest that societies, as well as individuals, most certainly appear to rank their basic moral principles differently and accept different ranges of application for them. I would also suggest more tentatively that they seem to differ in the basic principles they accept.

The truth of sociological relativism does not, of course, in itself establish the truth of ethical relativism. It is quite possible that there is a single correct morality even though few, and perhaps even no given society accepts it. But again, is there any good reason for believing that this is so? Many philosophers have thought so. As we have seen, for some this single correct morality has been identified with the will of God. Not all philosophers who believe that there is only one correct morality have, however, taken this view. For example, W.T. Stace (1886–1967) in a widely reprinted section of his book *The Concept of Morals* argues against ethical relativism and for the existence of a single correct morality that is not based on the will of God. Although one would naturally expect a person who takes such a view to present us with a moral code and then to present some argument which supports his contention that this morality is the solely *correct* one, this is not Stace's procedure. Instead, he indirectly argues for his position by pointing out what he sees as the highly undesirable consequences that must follow from the acceptance of ethical relativism. Counting on us also to see these consequerces as undesirable and inevitable implications of the doctrine of ethical relativism, Stace assumes that we will, in our desire to avoid these consequences, reject the doctrine of ethical relativism that must lead to them. As Stace puts it:

> Ethical relativity can only end in destroying . . . morality altogether, in undermining its practical efficacy . . . in robbing human beings of any incentive to strive for a better world, in taking the life-blood out of every ideal and every aspiration which has ennobled the life of man.[5]

This criticism is quite inadequate. First, one should notice that even if Stace were right that ethical relativism does indeed lead to such consequences, this does not show that ethical relativism is false. The truth, after all, need not be pleasant. Stace's argument here is reminiscent of the argument often utilized in the nineteenth century for belief in God. The idea was not that one should believe in God because such a belief was true or at least probably true, but rather that one should believe in God because the consequences would be better if one did so. In particular, it was argued that one would be happier or more inclined to accept conventional moral standards if one thought that God existed. The attitude that we ought to believe things simply because they make us feel better or have better social consequences—regardless of their truth—will be strongly opposed by those moralists who believe that knowing the truth is a value in and of itself. At any rate, it is clearly not the attitude a philosopher should take who is seeking the truth. Second, Stace seems quite unjustified in claiming that individuals would cease to strive for the realization of their moral principles and for a better world, as they see it, unless they thought that their moral principles and their conception of a good world was the only reasonable one. I see no reason why this should be so. It is certainly possible for a person to *feel* strongly enough about *his* ideals and to strive to get others to accept them, even if he admits that people equally as reasonable as he can accept conflicting ideals and that there is no way for him to prove them "wrong." Nevertheless, he may be able to convince them to accept his ideals if he can succeed in getting them *to care* about the things that he cares about, and he might try very hard to do precisely that. Does not the "life-blood of

5 W.T. Stace, *The Concept of Morals* (New York: Macmillan, 1937), p. 45.

our ideals" come from the strength of our *feelings* about them rather than from the possibility of their "objective" justification?

As Stace sees it, if there were no single correct morality, then moral ideals would be purely arbitrary and incapable of any rational justification. These are not, however, the only two possibilities. As we have defined it, ethical relativism is the view that there is no *single* correct morality, but this does not imply that all moralities, or alleged moralities, are equally good. Perhaps, although there is no way to pick one morality as the solely correct one, there are principles which allow us to dismiss certain moral or alleged moral views as inadequate—that is, there may be necessary factors that any adequate morality must possess, even though different moralities may possess them all. Exactly what these factors are is a controversial philosophical issue, but let me suggest here that logical consistency definitely would be one of these factors: consistency among the basic ethical principles that form one's ultimate ethical outlook; consistency between these basic moral principles and those particular moral judgments which are alleged to follow from them; and consistency between one's emotional attitudes and actions, on one hand, and the moral principles and judgments one claims to accept, on the other. In addition, ethical beliefs should certainly be informed ones—that is, an ethical belief can be criticized as based on a misapprehension of circumstances, facts, scientific theories, or ideological or religious doctrine. Perhaps, in addition, all justified ethical beliefs must pass some test of generalizability and impartiality similar to "the golden rule" or Kant's "categorical imperative," which we shall later discuss. If this is true, there is much that can be said in criticism of a person's alleged moral stand, even if individuals might in the end hold fundamentally different moral outlooks which can never be reconciled by reason alone. Yet, this might happen much less often than Stace suggests.

When we have reached this fundamental impasse, existentialists, such as Sartre, are correct when they emphasize the fact that one's ultimate moral values must be based on a *choice* of a particular way of life for which no full agreement is possible and no single choice "objectively" right. We may be guided to some extent by our knowledge of the sort of persons we are and the sort of life we can best live with; but there will be, at times, the choice between conflicting, though equally personally compelling, values which help to define the sort of person we are to become.

Whether ethical relativism is true or false depends on the exact meaning one assigns to this concept. As is often the case with philosophical concepts, philosophers have attributed different meanings to the concept of ethical relativism. Consequently, philosophers, in debating the merits of ethical relativism, can become engaged in a *merely verbal dispute,* hinged on the fact that they have defined the key concept of ethical relativism differently, rather than on any substantial factual or philosophical disagreement. Indeed, a philosopher may use apparently different definitions of ethical relativism in his discussion of this topic, without resolving the question of whether these definitions are equivalent in meaning or relevant implication. As you shall see, when philosophers inquire into the justification of certain basic beliefs underlying our understanding of things, it becomes necessary to clarify (analyze) the meaning of these beliefs. As we progress through our study of ethics, we shall see that the meaning that should be attributed to key moral concepts is often at issue when philosophers discuss such questions as *the subjectivity of values* or the truth of the doctrine of *ethical relativism* or whether everyone is or ought to be *selfish* or whether anyone has *free will* or is *morally responsible* for his actions.

The definition I have attributed to ethical relativism is the most defendable, and it is for this reason that I have used it. In addition, if we use this definition, ethical relativism can be contrasted with its denial, the view often called ethical absolutism, which asserts that there is a single correct morality which can be used to determine which acts are (really) right, regardless of prevalent moral standards. Very often, however, ethical relativism is defined as the view that "whatever a given society's (culture's) moral beliefs are, these moral beliefs are correct for them and are logically immune from rational criticism"—that is, whatever a society *believes* is right *is actually* right for them. Behind such a view is often the metaethical assumption that the logic of proper moral reasoning varies from society to society and that there are no universal principles of moral reasoning which must be assumed by anyone, in any culture, who thinks reasonably about moral matters.

The definition of ethical relativism as the view that whatever a society believes is right actually is right for them breaks down as inadequate under analysis. First, according to this definition, all moral reformers who revolt against the established morality of their society must be taken as "mistaken" when they are rebels, although if they succeed in converting the members of their culture to their beliefs, their beliefs will then become "correct." Consequently, the "correctness" of a moral view is to be understood in terms of its shifting acceptability, regardless of the *grounds* for that acceptability. For example, if some "mad scientist" were capable of involuntarily manipulating the minds of members of a society so that they would all come to share the most preposterous of ungrounded moral beliefs (such as, "One can kill whomever one chooses on Sundays but not on any other day of the week"), these moral beliefs would be "correct" for the members of such a society and nonmembers of that society would have no basis for criticizing the "correctness" of such a morality. Any doctrine that leads to such a conclusion should certainly be rejected.

Furthermore, this definition does not tell us what is to count as a "society" or "culture" and does not stipulate how this definition is to be applied when, as is often the case, we find a group of people who, though certainly united into what we would reasonably want to call a "culture" or "society," tolerate great divergence in moral beliefs. This is, after all, the case here in the United States where many different "subcultures" coexist, with importantly different standards of morality. Since there clearly does not seem to be anything that can be described as "the morality of the United States," are we to speak instead of the moralities of a rural community, of an inner city ghetto minority, of religious fundamentalists, or of liberal Protestants? However morally homogeneous and small we make the groups we are to consider, we will still find some divergence in moral opinion. Are we then to take the view of the majority of some group, assuming that the will of the majority is always "correct" while the minority always "mistaken"? It would appear that the definition of ethical relativism under discussion would best be amended to refer to individuals rather than to societies or cultures, and consequently be taken to state that "whatever an individual believes is right is right for that individual." But according to such a view, an individual would be speaking in a logically incoherent manner were he to say "I thought about the issue of abortion more deeply and have come to the opinion that my previous beliefs on this issue were *mistaken*." According to our amended definition of ethical relativism, when an individual changes his moral opinions, he cannot reasonably make judgments about their relative justifiability. This is a mistake.

The Roles of Reason and Feeling in Moral Judgment

Underlying Stace's rejection of ethical relativism is undoubtedly his belief that if there were no single objective rational standard for appraising moral judgments, they would become totally capricious and subjective—a reflection of feelings formed on the shifting sands of constitutional predisposition and social conditioning rather than based on the invariable and durable dictates of reason. There can be no doubt that both reason and feeling play a part in our moral judgments—morality is something most of us deeply *care* about and *argue* about. In this respect, moral judgments are quite unlike purely subjective preferences, such as one's choice of ice cream flavors. Preferences for ice cream flavors, we would all agree, are appropriately described as subjective for they cannot meaningfully be said to be either "true" or "false," as observational and scientific judgments can, but are instead merely reflections of one's own feelings.

A perennial question of ethical philosophy concerns the proper classification of ethical judgments as either objective or subjective. For some philosophers, such as Plato, just as there are "scientific facts" waiting in the world to be discovered by ordinary sense perception or by the discerning scientist, there is also a "moral order" in the world waiting to be discovered either by the average person's ordinary "moral sense" or by that of a penetrating moralist. As we have discussed, some philosophers who hold this objective view of morality identify this moral order with the revealed commands of a God; others, like Plato, seem to believe that there is some faculty of reason which can reveal immutable "moral facts" which allow us to discover what is good and what is right and to regulate our desires and emotions accordingly.

Many contemporary philosophers have claimed that this view is fundamentally mistaken and have pointed with approval to the moral writings of the famous Scottish philosopher David Hume (1711–1776). According to Hume's classical statement on the bearing of reason and feeling to moral judgment, although reason is necessary to guide and direct our sentiments (feelings) in such a way that we may best achieve our objectives, it is ultimately sentiment itself and not reason which moves us to judge things as good, bad, right, or wrong. It is our feelings of approval or disapproval toward things, Hume contends, that determine our moral judgments and not the other way around. On this perspective, since morality is a function of temperament, it becomes logically possible that individuals of fundamentally different temperaments may reach a point of *ultimate moral disagreement*—that is, a disagreement which would persist even with total agreement on all possibly relevant nonmoral "facts."

For example, there would appear to be an ultimate moral disagreement, irreconcilable by reason alone, between the ethical philosophies of the English philosopher Jeremy Bentham (1748–1832) and the German philosopher Friedrich Nietzsche (1844–1900) which reflects the irreconcilable differences in the feelings of these two men. Focusing upon the similarities in the abilities of all human beings to experience happiness and pain, and feeling a certain universal benevolence toward all mankind, Bentham afforded all human beings an equal moral importance. Nietzsche, on the other hand, did not share Bentham's basic benevolent feelings toward all humanity, and a different ethical perspective was the result. Nietzsche, and some of his less acute followers who interpreted his subtle writings in ways that he did not intend, were struck by the vast differences in the capabilities of human beings. Some human beings, they believed, the so-called *ubermensch* (supermen), were far more worthy of moral consideration than others, many of whom were seen as no better than animals. As such, they could be sacrificed for the betterment of the supermen in precisely the same manner that we who eat meat are willing to sacrifice animals for our own good, with little or no regard for their interests. Persons sharing the sentiments of Bentham may shake their heads in moral disagreement, but, nevertheless, rational means alone can never generate the feeling for the happiness of the average human being that is required to cause a Nietzschian to change his views. Rational argument in a case of such fundamental divergence of attitude is a "mere beating of wings in the void," for which even perfect agreement on the nonmoral facts can be of no avail.

On a personal note, I remember myself, as a student at the height of the Vietnam war, listening to a defense of the war by the then Secretary of State, Dean Rusk. I remember being struck by the realization that the disagreement between Rusk and the antiwar movement reached a fundamental impasse which went deeper than their obvious disagreements over beliefs as to the likely effects and bearing of our actions in Vietnam upon our own national interests. At that moment, it appeared to me that the Secretary of State simply did not *feel* sufficient sympathy for the vast suffering of human beings who were being sacrificed for unclear ideals of American security. As I listened to Rusk, my predominant reaction was not to argue with him rationally, but in some sense to shake him into an emotional realization of the enormity of human suffering we as a nation were creating in Vietnam. An emotional conversion was required here, not simply cold rational arguments, for there are no rational arguments or calculations that can tell us how much human suffering should be sacrificed for the achievement of certain desired ends.

Hume's insight that ultimate moral disagreements are possible is, I believe, a sound one. One must admit that human needs are various, widely adaptable, and often conflicting and that this plurality of needs can generate a plurality of human ideals. Where there is no background of mutually accepted ideals, rational argument reaches an impasse and the various techniques of emotional arousal are our only recourse. Yet, it is equally a mistake to overplay the importance of emotion in ethical assertions as did the twentieth century ethical disciples of Hume, the emotivists.[6] One must realize, to begin with, that it is quite unlikely that two ethical disputants will not share certain moral feelings or attitudes which can provide some basis for rational argument. Furthermore, even though there is an irreducible element of feeling in moral judgment, a moral judgment is more than the mere reflection of strong and transitory feelings. One must use reason to organize one's desires into some coherent whole (one's *reasoned preferences*) which can withstand rational scrutiny and embody those feelings one chooses to be guided by when momentary feelings are at less than their best. Although Hume was right that the ultimate source of our moral principles resides in our feelings, one should not assume that we must be slaves to our feelings. One cannot only change one's principles when they conflict intolerably with one's natural feelings,[7] one can also attempt to adjust one's feelings when they

6 According to emotivists, ethical assertions are "nonfactual" ones which cannot meaningfully be said to be either true or false. Emotivists do not, however, agree on the proper analysis of ethical assertions. They have been analyzed as (a) expressions of feelings or attitudes (b) linguistical devices for arousing feelings of approval or disapproval (c) commands (d) universal prescriptions (that is, recommendations that *everyone* ought to behave in a given way in a given situation).

7 The Humean insight that our morality should not be seen as something external to our feelings, but rather as an attempt to organize feelings into some coherent whole, is lost on Twain's Huck Finn when he helps his slave friend Jim escape. Although Huck's natural sympathies are clearly with Jim, his socially conditioned conscience tells him that he is acting wrongly. Incapable of realizing that he can and should reconsider the promptings of his socially conditioned conscience in the light of his natural sympathies and criticize the morality of his day as a bad one, Huck sees himself as a person of weak moral will who is sacrificing an "objective" morality for the promptings of his own personal feelings. Consider, for example, the following passage:

> Jim was saying how the first thing he would do when he got to a free state he would go to saving up money . . . and when he got enough he would buy his wife. . . . and then they would both work to buy the two children, and if their master wouldn't sell them, they'd get an Ab'litionist to go and steal them.

conflict with one's reasoned preferences. The moral life is a constant interplay between reason and feeling.

Since reason and feeling are both essential to the moral life, it is a fundamental mistake to make it appear, as some philosophers do, that one must choose between a view which claims that morality is "objective" in the sense that moral judgments are true or false, depending upon the "objective nature of things," independent of considerations of human psychology, and the view that morality is "subjective" in the sense that moral claims are nothing more than "nonrational emotional responses" or mere expressions of "capricious and arbitrary taste." Although these two views may be presented as mutually exhaustive (that is, if one rejects one view, one must accept the other), this is simply not so. One can say, as I would, that both views are inadequate, that moral claims are neither "objective" nor "subjective" in the above senses. In choosing between competing ethical views, an essential part of one's task is to *clarify and refine the philosophical choices that are possible.* In addition, as we have mentioned before, one should always be on the alert to the possibility that philosophers may be attributing different meanings to the key concepts they employ. For example, even though philosophers X and Y may call themselves "moral objectivists," while philosopher Z calls himself a "moral subjectivist," it may still be possible that X's view is more like Z's than Y's, and that these philosophers simply define these concepts quite differently. As such, philosophical labels can at times cause more confusion than understanding. This is the case with the familiar distinction often presented between "moral objectivism" and "moral subjectivism." It is a fundamental mistake to assume that these, as well as other basic philosophical concepts, have a single clear meaning and that learning philosophy consists of placing philosophers and philosophical theories in the right conceptual "pigeon hole." No, quite often sophisticated philosophical views straddle the simple "pigeon holes" that are presented to us and, indeed, at times, the very objective of philosophical reflection involves molding new and more enlightening ways of classifying things.

It most froze me to hear such talk. . . . Thinks I, this is what comes of my not thinking. Here was this nigger, which I had as good as helped to run away, coming right out flat-footed and saying he would steal his children —children that belonged to a man I didn't even know; a man that hadn't ever done me no harm. I was sorry to hear Jim say that, it was such a lowering of him. My conscience got to stirring me up hotter than ever. . . .

. . . I go aboard the raft, feeling bad and low, because I knowed very well I had done wrong. . . . Then I thought a minute, and says to myself, hold on; s'pose you'd 'a' done right and give Jim up, would you felt better than what you do now? No, says I, I'd feel bad. . . .

(Samuel L. Clemens, *The Adventures of Huckleberry Finn*, New York: Dodd, Mead, 1953 edition, pp. 97, 100)

DISCUSSION QUESTIONS

1. Practically all of us would consider it morally reprehensible to kill our aged parents when their care creates hardship for us as well as for others. Yet Eskimos used to consider it quite proper to kill aged parents who would endanger their tribe in their nomadic journey from winter to summer quarters. Do you think this fact provides a good example of a cultural disagreement in basic moral principles? Explain.

2. Do you see the disagreement between principled vegetarians who believe that animals have a right not to be killed by humans for food and those who do not believe that animals have such a right as one that would be resolved if the disputants agreed on all their nonmoral facts? Explain.

3. After claiming that there is no inconsistency in believing that ethical judgments are ultimately based on human feeling, while at the same time expressing emphatic opinions on ethical questions, Bertrand Russell, the famous twentieth century philosopher, goes on to admit,

   > Certainly there seems to be something more. Suppose, for example, that someone were to advocate the introduction of bull-fighting in this country. In opposing the proposal, I should *feel*, not only that I was expressing my desires, but that my desires in the matter are *right,* whatever that may mean. As a matter of argument, I can, I think, show that I am not guilty of any logical inconsistency in holding to . . . [a subjective] interpretation of ethics and at the same time expressing strong ethical preferences. But in feeling I am not satisfied.[8]

   What conclusion do you draw from this?

4. Argue for or against the view that we have a "moral sense" that enables us to immediately "see" whether or not certain actions are right or wrong.

5. Are there some moral rules which every reasonable person would accept? If so, what are they and how would you account for their universal acceptability?

6. Some philosophers have suggested the following definition of what it *means* to say that an act is right:

   > "X is right" means that an ideal observer would approve of it. An "ideal observer" is defined to be impartial, fully informed and vividly aware of the relevant facts, and in a calm frame of mind.

[8] Paul Schilpp, ed., *The Philosophy of Bertrand Russell* (New York: Tudor Publishing Company, 1954), p. 724.

Supporters of this definition have suggested that its acceptance makes moral judgments capable of being confirmed or disconfirmed by scientific observation. What do you think of this claim and the preceding analysis of what it means to say that "an act is right"?

7. Solomon Asch writes,

> If . . . we are to speak of relativism with reference to infanticide we must assume that the *same* action which is tolerated under one set of conditions is outlawed under other conditions. This assumption is . . . dubious. . . . In the first few days of life, an infant may be regarded as not yet human. . . . Therefore, the act of killing will not have the same meaning. . . .[9]

Asch suggests that even though individuals may disagree as to the morality of infanticide, this may not indicate a difference in basic moral value if there is disagreement as to the "humanity" of an infant. For example, a society that prohibits infanticide may see an infant as a "human being," while a society that tolerates it may see the same infant as less than a "human being." Is Asch right in his apparent assumption that one's perception of the nature of an infant is a nonmoral perception that determines one's moral attitude toward infanticide or is this perception itself a moral one? If so, is it simply tautologically true that "Whenever individuals disagree as to the morality of an action, there is a difference in *the meaning* they attribute to this action," as Asch suggests? Carefully explain.

8. How do rational "moral judgments" differ from mere "prejudices"? Give some examples.

9. What does the following disagreement indicate about the concept of a "moral judgment"?

A: The moral judgment that homosexuality is wrong is a mere prejudice.
B: Since it is a mere prejudice it cannot, by definition, be a moral judgment.

10. How would you resolve the following issue?

Principled Vegetarian: How can you eat meat with a clear conscience? Don't you realize that a conscious, feeling creature had to be killed so that you could gratify your carnivorous appetite?

Meat Eater: There you go again with your obsessive concern about the killing of animals for food. It might be wrong for you to eat meat, but it's not wrong for me. Let's leave it at that.

Principled Vegetarian: You can call my concern "obsessive," but I think your lack of concern is improper and your belief that it's all right to eat meat a prejudice that allows you to do as you like with a clear conscience.

[9] Solomon Asch, *Social Psychology* (Englewood Cliffs, N.J.: Prentice-Hall, 1952), pp. 376–77.

Meat Eater: Look, you and I have an ultimate moral disagreement in this matter that reflects differences in our attitudes toward animals. Since such differences are not over facts, you have no right to call my attitude toward animals a prejudice. I know you don't like my attitude, but there's no way you can prove it to be mistaken, just as I can't prove your opposed attitude mistaken. That's the way it is when you come to basic moral commitments.

Principled Vegetarian: That's not so. If I told you that people with brown eyes should be afforded less respect than people with blue eyes and that this was a basic moral principle with me, you'd think me crazy. Basic moral principles must themselves be rational.

11. Consider the following quotation from the anthropologist Ruth Benedict:

> From all that we know of contrasting cultures it seems clear that . . . there is an ascertainable range of human behavior that is found [in every society]. . . . But the proportion in which behavior types stand to one another in different societies is not universal. The vast majority of the individuals in any group are shaped to the fashion of that culture. In other words, most individuals are plastic to the moulding force of the society into which they are born. . . . The deviants, whatever the type of behavior the culture has institutionalized, will remain few in number. . . . The small proportion of the number of the deviants in any culture is not a function of the sure instinct with which that society has built itself upon the fundamental sanities, but of the universal fact that, happily, the majority of mankind quite readily take any shape that is presented to them . . .[10]

Do you agree with Benedict? Do you think that the divergent behavior patterns of different cultures reflect divergent moral outlooks, as Benedict does? If so, is it unreasonable, as Benedict claims, to distinguish correct from incorrect moral outlooks? Argue carefully for your position.

FURTHER READINGS

Asch, Solomon, *Social Psychology,* chapter 13. Englewood Cliffs, N.J.: Prentice-Hall, Inc., 1952. Criticizes ethical relativism on the basis of Gestalt theory.

Brandt, Richard, *Ethical Theory,* chapters 2–5 and 7–11. Englewood Cliffs, N.J.: Prentice-Hall, Inc., 1959. I recommend this book very highly for the student who would like a more detailed discussion of the issues of this chapter. Brandt's discussions effectively combine the virtues of clarity and philosophical rigor. Brandt enriches his discussion of ethical relativism with a knowledge of anthropology and especially with his own first-hand experiences of the Hopi Indian culture.

[10] Ruth Benedict, "Anthropology and the Abnormal" in the *Journal of General Psychology,* 1934, 10, 59–82.

The Encyclopedia of Philosophy. New York: Macmillan, 1967. This is an excellent reference source which contains well-written articles by professional philosophers on topics in traditional ethics as well as on the ethical views of famous philosophers. Articles especially relevant to this chapter are: "Ethical Relativism," "Ethical Objectivism," "Ethical Subjectivism," "Ultimate Moral Principles: Their Justification," and "Emotive Theory of Ethics."

HUME, DAVID, *A Treatise of Human Nature.* Oxford: Clarendon Press, 1964, first published in 1739. Also, *An Enquiry Concerning the Principles of Morals.* Oxford: Clarendon Press, 1975, first published in this final revised form in 1777 (from the original 1751 publication). Hume's most provocative presentation of his thesis that moral questions are decided by "sentiment" and not "reason" is found in the *Treatise,* Book II, Part III, Section III. It is in this section that Hume makes his famous remark that "reason is . . . the slave of the passions." It is here too that Hume provocatively claims that as long as a "passion is neither founded on false suppositions, nor . . . [chooses] means insufficient for the end. . . . [reason] can neither justify nor condemn it. 'Tis not contrary to reason to prefer the destruction of the whole world to the scratching of my finger." Disappointed by the poor literary reception of the *Treatise,* Hume reformulated his ideas on ethics into the more popular form of his *Enquiries Concerning the Principles of Morals.* Hume's treatment of the relationship between reason and feeling is found in Appendix I of this work. While Hume is one of the most readable of classical philosophers, he does employ technical philosophical terms in this work which would make it hard going for students not familiar with Hume's general philosophy.

LADD, JOHN, ed., *Ethical Relativism.* Belmont, Calif.: Wadsworth, 1973. An anthology of articles arguing for and against ethical relativism.

MINTON, ARTHUR, ed., *Philosophy: Paradox and Discovery.* New York: McGraw-Hill, 1976. The section "Sources of Morality" serves as an excellent anthology of material relevant to our discussion in this chapter. It contains excerpts from Plato's "Euthyphro" (against religious absolutism), Sartre's "Existentialism" (against objectivism), a defense of ethical relativism by the anthropologist Ruth Benedict, and excerpts from the psychologist Asch (see above) and from the philosophers Russell and Blanshard (for and against subjectivism).

SELLARS, WILFRED, and JOHN HOSPERS, eds., *Readings in Ethical Theory* (2nd ed.), sections IID, E, and F. Englewood Cliffs, N.J.: Prentice-Hall, Inc., 1970. This anthology contains an extensive collection of essays on the topics of this chapter by contemporary analytic philosophers for the more philosophically sophisticated reader.

STACE, W.T., *The Concept of Morals.* New York: Macmillan, 1937. Stace believes that there is a single correct morality for human beings based on a *universal* human nature which is not a function of cultural factors. Stace calls this position "ethical universalism," and not "ethical absolutism" which he defines to be the view that moral judgments are "valid independently of all conditions." Since Stace believes that morality depends on human nature and would be different *if* human nature were different, he rejects "ethical absolutism."

2

Theories
of
Normative Ethics

5. THE TERMINOLOGY OF NORMATIVE ETHICS

It would be helpful to begin our study of normative ethics with a general discussion of some of the key concepts philosophers tend to employ in this area of study. A preliminary acquaintance with these concepts will help us to perceive in broad outline the issues and conflicting positions we will be discussing in the next several sections.

The question that has preoccupied moralists most is, as one would expect, the question of what actions are morally right or obligatory. General answers to this question are provided in what philosophers call *theories of moral obligation*. Moral judgments can also be made about the intentions, motives, and character of moral agents, such as whether they are good, bad, praiseworthy, blameworthy, or morally responsible. The standards philosophers provide for answering such questions are called *theories of moral value*. Moral questions also arise as to what things in life are worthwhile or desirable. In discussing this issue, philosophers often make a distinction between those things that are merely *instrumentally good* (that is, good because of their consequences) and those things which are *intrinsically good* (that is, good in and of themselves). For example, unless a person has masochistic desires, having a dentist drill one's teeth to fill a cavity is merely instrumentally good, not intrinsically good; the drilling is not good in and of itself, but rather for its consequences. Similarly, if we ask a person why he works, he might reply that he works for the money he can earn. If we go on to ask why he wants money, he might say that it is necessary in order to buy the things that he wants, and if we pursue the questioning further and ask him why he wants to buy things, he might reply that it gives him pleasure. If we then ask him why he desires pleasure, there would seem to be no

43

answer he could give, for he does not seek pleasure in order to gain something else—that is, pleasure is intrinsically good. Philosophers have had different views concerning what is intrinsically good. The most famous view is *hedonism* which asserts that pleasure is *the only* intrinsic good. For example, according to the hedonist, knowledge has value, not as an end in itself, but only as a means for obtaining pleasure—that is, knowledge is only instrumentally good.[1]

Theories of moral obligation can be distinguished on the basis of whether or not they hold that the rightness of an act or rule of conduct depends solely on its consequences. The *teleologist* believes that it does, while the *deontologist* does not.[2]

As the teleologist sees it, the right act or rule of conduct in a given situation is that act or rule which will produce the greatest balance of good over evil of any available alternative. Consequently, a teleological theory of moral obligation is dependent upon some theory of intrinsic good; in order to determine whether something is right, we must first determine which things are worth seeking, without regard to their consequences.[3] Although teleologists have often been hedonists, this has not always been the case. Some teleologists have been nonhedonists, identifying intrinsic good with such things as power, knowledge, self-realization, or several distinct qualities. Teleologists have differed not only on the question of what is intrinsically good, but also on the question of whose intrinsic good should be sought. *Ethical egoism* holds that one should always do what will promote one's own greatest good, while *utilitarianism*

---

[1] Since many philosophers have identified the intrinsic good with those things that are *worthwhile apart from any moral consideration,* theories of intrinsic value are sometimes called theories of *nonmoral value.* Not all philosophers, however, have identified intrinsic good with nonmoral qualities. Some, for example, have claimed that certain qualities of moral character—such as honesty, integrity, and conscientiousness—are intrinsic goods. In addition, considerations of justice (such as, that the good should prosper and the wicked suffer) have been taken by some philosophers to be intrinsic goods.

[2] The word "teleological" derives from the Greek word *telos* which means end or purpose; the word "deontological" derives from the Greek word *deon* which means duty or that which is binding. Some philosophers use the term "deontological" to refer only to those theories of moral obligation which justify acts in terms of general rules, seen as justified by some factor other than their consequences. If we were to accept this usage, then some theories of moral obligation would be neither "teleological" nor "deontological." The way we will be employing the term, however, "deontological" means no more than "nonteleological."

[3] Again, the assumption often made here is that those things that are "intrinsically good" are those things that are worthwhile apart from any moral consideration. If this assumption is made, one can define a "teleologist" to be a person who believes that what is morally right is that which maximizes nonmoral value. Since not all philosophers have made this assumption, however, it is best not to accept this definition which is sometimes given. If it were to be accepted, a philosopher such as G.E. Moore, whose ethical theory we shall briefly discuss, could not be classified as a "teleologist" (since he accepted the value of justice as an "intrinsic good"); yet, he usually is so classified (since he believed that what is morally right is that which maximizes intrinsic good).

holds that one should always do what will promote the greatest good for everyone. Since the most famous utilitarians, Jeremy Bentham and John Stuart Mill, were also hedonists, the principle of utilitarianism is often given as the principle of "the greatest happiness (or pleasure) for the greatest number."

Deontologists deny what teleologists affirm—that is, that the rightness of an action or rule depends only on its consequences. Some deontologists have claimed that the rightness of an action has nothing to do with its consequences. Other more moderate deontologists see the consequences of an act as one among several factors to be considered. For example, in deciding whether to keep a promise, one should consider the consequences, either good or bad, of keeping the promise; nevertheless, it is sometimes right to keep a promise even though the consequences in balance would be worse if one does so. Deontologists also disagree as to the role that general rules should play in determining what is right. At one extreme, there are those who believe that since each situation of moral choice is unique, we must somehow "intuit" or decide separately in each particular situation the right thing to do without any appeal to general rules or to the consequences of our actions. At the other extreme, there are those deontologists who claim that the standard of right and wrong consists of total allegiance to one or more rules. These rules may be either very concrete ones such as "Always keep promises," "Never lie," and "Never kill innocent people," or abstract ones such as Kant's categorical imperative which asserts (in one of its formulations) that one should "act only on that maxim which you can at the same time will be a universal law." By reducing all of morality to this single basic moral rule, Kant attempts to avoid the difficulty that besets those deontologists (*ethical pluralists*) who accept more than one basic rule and have no rule for resolving possible conflicts among them.

The disagreement between the teleologist and deontologist is the most basic one in normative ethics. The teleologist will look ahead to the consequences of his actions, whereas the deontologist will look back upon the nature of the act itself, seeing it within the context of the duties and obligations one has either simply by virtue of being a human being (such as the duty to be just, honest, or benevolent) or by virtue of the specific personal and social relationships that one assumes (such as the duty of being a parent, of citizenship, or of one's profession). The moral life for most of us is a mixture of deontological and teleological considerations, and that indeed, as I shall later argue, is the way it should be.

6. THE UTILITARIAN THEORY

The utilitarian view that the rightness or wrongness of actions and moral rules should be evaluated solely in terms of their consequences for all concerned—that is, in terms of their ability "to maximize the good"—

like so many other philosophical ideas, can be traced back to ancient Greek philosophy. Nevertheless, the term "utilitarianism" is used today primarily to refer to the specific systematic ethical theory of the British philosopher Jeremy Bentham (1748–1832) who was the first to coin this term and to the various later refinements of Bentham's theory at the hands of his many disciples, in particular, John Stuart Mill (1806–1873). Although Bentham was primarily a moral reformer bent on criticizing and changing the existing legal and social institutions of the England of his day, he also believed, as did many of his disciples, that his utilitarian ethical theory was implicit in the generally accepted moral "common sense" or "intuitions" of the average person *insofar as* this common sense or intuition was justifiable. Seeing his utilitarian theory *as the only* defensible moral theory, it was Bentham's belief that those who accepted moral beliefs inconsistent with his utilitarian theory would under more careful analysis renounce these beliefs as either unintelligible or unjustified and come to accept the utilitarian theory as the ultimate theoretical underpinning of their own moral reasoning.

Bentham's Criticism of Intuitionism in Ethics

Trained as a lawyer at Oxford under the tutelage of the famous legal theorist and constitutional scholar Sir William Blackstone, Bentham found himself quite dissatisfied with both the practical operations of the law of his day and its theoretical justification by Blackstone and others, a justification which Bentham saw as no more than elaborate and ultimately indefensible rationalizations for the status quo. The prevalent legal theory of his day was that the ultimate standards for moral appraisal to be utilized in evaluating the soundness of law were certain clearly recognizable "natural laws" engrained upon the consciences of mankind by God. In order to discover whether a given act was right or wrong, a person was not supposed to inquire as to its effects, but rather to consult the "inner moral light" of conscience whose pronouncements were seen as "self-evident." It was this aspect of the ethical philosophy of his predecessor John Locke (1632–1704), the philosophical force behind the American Declaration of Independence, that Bentham totally rejected. Locke's notion of certain "self-evident natural rights," Bentham dismissed as nothing but "nonsense on stilts." When Locke and other moral and legal philosophers turned to "intuited" moral rules and principles, they inevitably, Bentham believed, turned to their own learned, and often irrational, moral feelings.

Similarly, when legislators felt greatly revolted by certain actions, they would punish them heavily, even when these actions caused little or no suffering to anyone (such as certain sexual offenses). On the other hand, if legislators did not have strong feelings of repugnance toward certain actions, they were either left unpunished or punished lightly, regardless of their capacity to cause human suffering (such as certain business practices). But the legislator, faithful to the obscurist philosophy of his day, would not admit that the ultimate source of his moral sentiments were certain visceral feelings and would instead describe these feelings in a way which made them quite unjustifiably appear to have some objective basis (for instance, it was not said that homosexuality should be condemned because most people felt revolted by the practice, but that it should be condemned since "the clear light of moral conscience reveals the self-evident unnaturalness of homosexuality"). The moral intuitionism of philosophers such as Locke seemed to be nothing more than an appeal to sentiment—or as Bentham called it, to "the principle of sympathy and antipathy"—which by some verbal magic exalted prejudices into seeming eternal and immutable principles. Bentham wanted to do away with such rationalization. It must be recognized, he argued, that the sole aim of morality and law is to maximize human happiness, not to intuit certain unchangeable moral laws that stigmatize actions as bad in themselves, without regard to their consequences.

It was not only the criminal law that Bentham saw inflicted with this error in moral theory; the civil law was equally a victim, for the generally accepted pronouncement of conscience was that one's moral obligations, such as the obligation to keep one's promises, were absolutely binding. For example, since a contract is a legally enforceable promise, the view was that contracts, once made, should always be kept. Occasionally, however, those who enforced the law were unwilling to enforce a contract that clearly seemed to go against the public interest, but instead of admitting that contracts were not absolutely binding but subordinate to the general public interest, it would be said that the contract was null and void—that there never was a valid contract. In other words, the facts would be distorted to save a mistaken moral theory.

The Universalistic Element of Bentham's Utilitarianism

As well as criticizing the legal theorists of his day for unjustifiably elevating the status quo into immutable dictates of reason, Bentham criticized them for blinding themselves to the widespread exploitation of the new and burgeoning class of city workers that resulted from the "Industrial Revolution." Torn from the security of the English countryside and herded into factories, this new class found itself exposed to inhumanly long and grueling working conditions for a pay scarcely adequate to maintain a bare subsistence. Sheltered from the cruelty of this sort of life, legal theorists spoke complacently of the "natural" and "inalienable rights" of property of the privileged class, blinding themselves to the legalized inequalities and exploitation that the exercise of these rights entailed. As Bentham saw it, some kind of universal principle of moral criticism was needed that could cut through the partiality of the status quo and the abstract talk of "natural rights" that supplied its moral rationale. This principle Bentham saw as that of "the greatest happiness for the greatest number"—or, as he also called it, "the principle of utility." This principle had, he thought, two great virtues. First, it was a universalistic one that referred equally to all human beings and not just to some. As such, it could be utilized as a principle for criticism of the partiality of the status quo. As he passionately wrote,

> Government has, under every form comprehending laws and institutions, had for its object the greatest happiness not of those over whom, but of those by whom, it has been exercised; the interest not of the many, but of the few, or even of the one, has been the prevalent interest; and to that interest all others have been at all times sacrificed. To these few, or to this one, depredation has everywhere been the grand object.[1]

Second, by equating morality with the "maximization of happiness" which he saw as a determinable "real entity" capable of scientific measure, it afforded morality the "objective" status that the purely "subjective" intuitionistic view lacked.

The Attack on Fictitious Entities

Armed with the principle of utility, Bentham attempted to cut through the obscure ethical and legal theory of his day and the undefined abstract terms in which it was formulated. Although the legal theorists of his day spoke abstractly of the existence of "obligations" and "rights" as if these words referred to specific abstract "things" that people had or did not have, Bentham rejected such an idea which he dismissed as a belief in "fictitious entities." If abstract moral terms are to be accepted as meaningful, they must, he believed, be translated into concrete terms that have some real reference. As Bentham saw it, the abstract notion of an individual's obligations to behave in particular ways must, in order to be made meaningful, be translated into talk about the concrete feelings of pleasure and pain. As Bentham put it "An obligation . . . is incumbent on a man . . . insofar as, in the event of his failing to conduct himself in that manner, pain, or loss of pleasure, is considered as about to be experienced by him." Consequently, for Bentham, the notion of an obligation was to be defined in terms of the notion of a sanction—that is, on the pain or loss of pleasure that normally resulted from its neglect. Legal and moral obligations, as he saw it, differed only in the types of sanctions they involved. If the sanction was a physical or political or economic one which officials of government are able and disposed to inflict, the obligation was a legal one. If, on the other hand, the pain was merely the loss of others' or one's own esteem, the obligation was a moral one. (Such a view of legal obligation was later to be developed by John Austin, the famous legal theorist and disciple of Bentham.)

[1] Jeremy Bentham, *The Theory of Legislation* (London: Harcourt Brace Jovanovich, Inc., 1931), p. xxviii.

Similarly, as Bentham saw it, when we say that an individual has a political or moral "right," we are speaking of "a general disposition, on the part of those by whom the powers of government are exercised, to cause him to possess . . . the benefit to which he has a right." Since no such disposition to confer benefits exists in the case of alleged "natural rights," this notion has no definite sense, Bentham declared. (Notice that a religious moralist can claim that such a disposition exists in God. Indeed, Locke, himself, believed that natural rights were derived from God.) The most that one can be taken to mean by asserting that someone has a "natural right" to something, Bentham wrote, is that "I am of the opinion that he ought to have a political right to it; that . . . he ought to be protected and secured in the use of it"; in other words, that "the idea of his being so is pleasing to me, and the idea of the opposite result displeasing."

Bentham's Utilitarian Perspective

With this criticism as a backdrop, Bentham developed his hedonistic utilitarian theory. The goal of life, as Bentham saw it, was quite simply to create as much human happiness as possible. Those religious moralists who condemned the gratification of certain desires as inherently evil were mistaken. A human desire should only be condemned when it comes into conflict with other desires which promise to create greater human happiness in the long run. Morality should not be perceived as a conflict between inclination and an abstract duty having nothing to do with human happiness, but rather as an attempt to arbitrate between these conflicting inclinations in such a way as to maximize the amount of happiness in this world. Either in a situation of individual moral choice or in the legislative task of deciding between conflicting laws, the right act or law to choose was that act or law which among all the alternatives produced "the greatest happiness for the greatest number." Perhaps in overreaction to the "unscientific" method of his intuitionistic opponents, Bentham assumed that the concepts of happiness or pleasure and unhappiness or pain could be measured and compared in quantitative terms. For each alternative, one would add up the sum of pleasure that would likely be experienced and subtract from it the amount of likely pain, choosing that alternative with the greatest net sum. From such a perspective, Bentham envisioned moral reasoning as a type of "moral arithmetic" or "moral accounting." In this type of moral arithmetic, all individuals would be treated equally, no individual's pleasure or pain counting more heavily than another's. In addition, since for Bentham the rightness of an act depends on its never fully foreseeable consequences, moral judgment was always subject to correction as new and unforeseeable consequences come into focus. Given the possibility of unforeseeable consequences and the difficulty of estimating the probability of foreseeable ones, even the most wisely made moral judgments are subject to error. This is the inevitable price one must pay for the finiteness of human foresight.

Since in the utilitarian view the rightness of an action depends solely on its consequences, it followed, Bentham believed, that there could be no absolute exceptionless moral rules other than the principle of utility. It seemed clear to Bentham that in certain circumstances the consequences of lying, breaking promises, stealing, and even killing the innocent, might be more desirable than refraining from these actions. Consequently, conventional moral rules, such as "never lie," "never break promises," "never steal," and "never kill the innocent," were not to be taken as the absolute moral rules that they are often presented as. Bentham did not, however, totally reject these rules of conventional morality. Many of them, he argued, were useful rules of thumb which served in most cases to maximize human happiness. Given the difficulty of foreseeing possible consequences, one has need for moral guides other than the principle of utility. The rules of conventional morality often provide these guides. Furthermore, they provide a background of stability and predictability of human behavior which enables individuals to better anticipate the actions of others and to plan their own actions accordingly. Nevertheless, Bentham believed, these rules should never be used blindly. Given important choices or a conflict in the conventional rules themselves, one should always resort to the principle of utility itself in deciding what to do.

In deciding whether a conventional moral rule should be violated, it was essential, Bentham claimed, to consider *the long-range consequences* of such a violation. Quite often, even though the short-range consequences of breaking a rule may be advantageous, its long-range consequences may be quite undesirable. For example, even though in the short run my refusal to keep my promise to repay a debt of money to a wealthy friend may be justified from a utilitarian perspective if I use this money instead to help a more needy person, such an action may not be so justified in the long run. Among the long-range consequences, I must always consider the effect of my action on people's confidence in my reliability or on the general practice of promise-keeping which serves the general interest. Whatever short-range beneficial consequences I might have gained in this particular instance of breaking my promise might be more than offset by its undesirable long-range effect on my ability to have my promises accepted in the future. Furthermore, if most people broke promises whenever they thought the beneficial consequences to specific individuals would be maximized—however slightly—public confidence in the practice of promise-keeping, which has great utility, would soon be shattered.

Criticisms and Modifications of Bentham's Utilitarianism

Bentham's utilitarian theory has been subjected to much criticism both by those fundamentally opposed to it as well as by those sympathetic to its main tenets who sought to strengthen, refine, or modify it. Let us briefly consider some of these criticisms.

The "Truth" of the Principle of Utility

Although Bentham saw the principle of utility as a "true" principle which was more than simply a statement of his own personal commitment, the sense in which this principle is "true" is quite questionable. According to Bentham, our ultimate and sole basic moral obligation is to maximize human happiness. Nowhere, however, does he explicitly present an argument to convince those who are not motivated by a feeling of universal benevolence and believe that they have no moral obligation to be so motivated that they nevertheless do have this moral obligation. Similarly, nowhere does he explicitly present an argument to establish that the principle of utility is the only basic moral principle that is "rational" or "correct." In one of his writings, Bentham is willing to concede that he cannot prove the principle of utility to be correct since "it is used to prove everything else and a chain of proofs must have their commencement somewhere." At this point, it is open to a utilitarian to say, as the early twentieth century utilitarian Henry Sidgwick said, that this principle is known by "intuition" or is "self-evident." This view, however, was not open to Bentham who saw such notions as rationalizations for one's own "prejudices."

Bentham and his disciple John Stuart Mill attempted in some of their writings to anchor the principle of utility to the doctrine of psychological egoism which asserts that the pursuit of individual pleasure is, as a matter of fact, the *sole* human motive. (We shall discuss the adequacy of this theory in section 13.) According to this theory of motivation, however, each person seeks only to maximize his or her own pleasure. As the psychological egoist sees it, one is concerned about the pleasures of others only insofar as they are seen *as means* to the satisfaction of one's own pleasure. Clearly, however, individuals do not always, as a matter of fact, feel concern or sympathy for others or see the pleasure of others as means to their own pleasure. Indeed, both Bentham and Mill stress the need to *induce* people (especially children) through sanctions to develop such feelings and to associate the pleasure of others with their own pleasure. Consequently, they both seem to admit that there is no guarantee that self-interest would naturally lead one inevitably to a concern for the interests of others or more specifically to consider all human beings equally, whether they be oneself, one's family, or total strangers. Indeed, even if one could be conditioned to feel this way, it is certainly open for some to claim, as the philosopher and novelist Ayn Rand would, that it is not in one's ultimate interest to feel this way. Consequently, there is a fundamental logical gap between the doctrine of psychological egoism and the principle of utility. This gap is never explicitly bridged by Bentham who never explains the source of our ultimate moral obligation to maximize human happiness, especially when this obligation seems to conflict with our own interests. While Bentham does not make this claim himself, perhaps implicit in his thinking is the assumption made by his contemporary, the philosopher and economist

Adam Smith, that somehow in the nature of things, the purely self-seeking pursuit of pleasure will tend in the long run to coincide with the general interest. For example, according to Adam Smith's classical "laissez-faire" theory of economics, a situation of unfettered economic competition, where each producer attempts to sell his own products and maximize his own profit, leads in the long run *without any conscious intention* to the most efficient economic system for all concerned. Adam Smith's faith in the ultimate convergence of self and community interest would, however, be widely rejected today as overly optimistic.

Utilitarianism and the Need for Specific Moral Rules

Some philosophers sympathetic to the utilitarian point of view have been reluctant to accept Bentham's claim that all moral principles, other than the principle of utility itself, are subject to exceptions or that one can at times justify the utilization of means that promise to have bad consequences in order to achieve ends which one believes will produce enough good to outweigh this evil. For example, G.E. Moore, a very influential British philosopher of the early twentieth century argued in his *Principia Ethica* (1903) that there are certain moral rules whose violation so regularly leads to bad consequences that one would be mistaken in violating them in any given situation. (Consider, for example, the rule "Never torture.") As Moore saw it, even though from a purely utilitarian perspective there are justified exceptions to all conventional moral rules, a person will never have sufficient information in a concrete situation of moral choice to know that *in this situation* breaking such a rule will have the best consequences. Experience has often shown that the expected good consequences that are utilized as a justification for breaking moral rules often turn out to be unattainable or much less good in the long run than the evil means employed in false anticipation of greater good. Furthermore, when one assumes that moral rules can always be broken as long as it appears that human happiness will be maximized by so doing, one often becomes a victim of selfishly motivated rationalization. We may find ourselves breaking rules for selfish reasons and then conveniently (though often unconsciously) weighing the consequences in such a way as to justify the actions we desire. In addition, even if we were correct in a given situation that the violation of a conventional moral rule were justified on utilitarian grounds, breaking the rule might be a dangerous example to ourselves in future, less clear, cases and to other individuals, less scrupulous and impartial in weighing the consequences.

Moore's fear of individuals taking upon themselves the task of weighing the consequences of the observance of even the most deeply cherished of conventional moral rules is quite justified. It is certainly arguable that a constant reliance upon the principle of utility in deciding what one ought to do is likely in practice to produce a greater threat to the ultimate utilitarian ideal than that of individuals blindly following moral rules which generally serve the common good. Nevertheless, if the stakes are high enough, I do not see how a person truly committed to the utilitarian point of view can consider any moral rule, other than the principle of utility itself, totally inviolate. For example, consider the sad situation facing the President of the United States in the novel *Fail Safe*. One of his nuclear bombers is mistakenly on its way to bomb Moscow. Certainly as we read the novel (or watch the movie), we tend to agree with the President's decision to attempt to shoot down his own plane. (He fails.) Yet this would seem to be a violation of the moral rule forbidding us to kill the innocent. It certainly is a colossal violation of this principle when the President, in desperation, decides to drop a nuclear bomb on New York City as a price the Soviets will accept for the now unavoidable bombing of Moscow. This is a horrible choice, but it seems the only way to avert a total nuclear confrontation. Most of us will accept the President's decision as justified on utilitarian grounds. Even though the President cannot be absolutely sure that the consequences of his decision will be as he anticipates, he has very good reason to believe this and good reason to believe that any other choice will have the most tragic of consequences. He must, most of us believe, attempt to avoid these tragic consequences in a way that minimizes human misery, regardless of the moral or legal rules he breaks in the process.

Similarly, if it seemed quite clear that the tragedy of a nuclear war could be averted only by torturing one or several innocent people, such an action would also seem to be justifiable from a utilitarian perspective. Granted that one should never do such things in doubtful or insignificant cases, nevertheless, sometimes the situation does appear clear or the consequences so momentous that such a painful choice seems required from a utilitarian perspective. If actions are to be evaluated solely by their consequences, it seems inescapable that, given the complexities and tragedies of this world, all conventional moral rules will, as Bentham saw, be subject to exceptions. If one does not want to accept this conclusion, one must either reject the principle of utility as the sole ultimate ethical standard, or claim, as some contemporary philosophers have, that although the principle of utility should be used to justify moral rules which should then be used to justify particular acts, it is somehow wrong to justify particular acts directly by an appeal to the principle of utility. (We shall discuss this modern view called "rule utilitarianism" in section 9.)

Utilitarianism and Special Responsibilities

As critics of utilitarianism have often pointed out, a commitment to the utilitarian point of view would seem to lead us in some situations to justify actions that would go contrary to many, if not most, people's intuitive moral reactions. For example, in the case of the two drowning men in our list of moral dilemmas, a utilitarian would seem to be committed to the view that if a choice must be made, one ought to save the scientist over one's own father. Yet many of us would disagree, claiming that one has a *special moral responsibility* toward one's father that one does not have toward strangers, however illustrious. Traditional utilitarianism is, however, silent about the notion of special responsibilities. On the face of it, our common belief that we have special moral obligations to particular individuals seems quite foreign to utilitarianism, which claims that in attempting to maximize the total good in the world we should consider everyone equally. Although it is open for a utilitarian to claim that human happiness can only be maximized in the long run if individuals assume special moral responsibilities to each other, the specific nature and force of such special responsibilities has never been worked out by any utilitarian. The utilitarian neglect of special moral obligations has been considered by many to be a serious failure of utilitarianism as a comprehensive ethical theory.

Utilitarianism and the Principles of Distributive Justice

Even if we are to accept the utilitarian view of the secondary place of moral rules in the moral life, as Bentham did, Bentham's utilitarian theory suffers from an inherent ambiguity in its formulation. According to Bentham's formula, the right act or rule in a given situation is that act or rule which produces "the greatest happiness for the greatest number," counting each person's happiness equally. There are, however, two notions conflated into this formula, the maximization of both the *total happiness* for all individuals and the *total number of individuals* who share in that happiness. Bentham and Mill never did distinguish these two factors, nor realize the possibility of conflict when one must choose between a greater total amount of happiness for those involved or a wider distribution of it. Since Bentham often spoke of "the greatest happiness" principle, deleting the reference to "the greatest number," it would appear that the meaning he intended for his formula was that one should always attempt to maximize the amount of happiness, regardless of its method of distribution. This is, however, clearly inadequate. The same quantity of happiness can be distributed in many different ways. One arrangement might give all, or most, of that happiness to a relatively small number of people who do not especially "deserve it" while other arrangements might spread it more evenly or in accord with desert. In morality, one cannot do without principles of distributive justice, which Bentham and Mill never did supply. Certainly it is possible that an act which maximizes the sum of human happiness is nevertheless wrong if that happiness is unjustly distributed.

For example, today most of us will readily condemn the institution of slavery as unjust, even if its existence can in some situations maximize human happiness, as some historians have suggested. To use a more frivolous example, most of us would certainly condemn a group of sadists for inflicting pain on some unwilling innocent victims even if we were convinced that the sum of happiness the sadists were experiencing outweighed the sum of the pain of their victims. Consider, as well, the Russian Communist practice, under Stalin, of repressing civil liberties and unjustly imprisoning or executing individuals who were seen as a threat to the social order. All this was justified as a necessary means to the maximization of the general happiness for this and future generations. Yet even if this were true, it would not guarantee that such practices were right. Granted that justice should at times be sacrificed for the common good (such as, killing innocent people in war), the point is that there are different, and possibly conflicting, principles involved here— general utility versus individual justice. Bentham and Mill never did recognize this. Although Mill attempted to reconcile the utilitarian desire to maximize the general happiness with the principle of individual liberty in his essay *On Liberty,* there is no guarantee that these values will always coincide. Given today's more pessimistic view of human rationality, one may reject Mill's essential assumption that each individual is the best judge of his own happiness. If this is so, a possible implication of utilitarian thinking is that we ought to force people to be happy "in spite of themselves." The conflict between governmental paternalism and individual freedom is for most of us a conflict over differing principles and not a question of the proper application of the single utilitarian principle, as Mill suggested. Similarly, although Bentham and Mill were strong proponents of greater equality, particularly of plans for the more even distribution of wealth, their theoretical justification for this aim was that a more equal distribution of goods was the most likely *means* toward a greater total happiness for society as a whole. There is again no good reason to believe that these two values will necessarily coincide. When they do not, some of us will choose to sacrifice some degree of equality to achieve a greater total of happiness, whereas others will choose to accept a smaller sum of happiness for a more equal distribution of it. Such situations of moral choice seem to involve a conflict of independent basic moral principles that cannot be resolved by an appeal to a higher moral principle.

DISCUSSION QUESTIONS

1. Consider the following criticism of utilitarianism by the American philosopher William James:

> If the hypothesis were offered us of a world in which Messrs. Fourier's and Bellamy's and Morris's utopias should be all outdone, and millions kept permanently happy on the one simple condition that a certain lost soul on the far-off edge of things should lead a life of lonely torture, . . . [would we not] immediately feel, even though an impulse arose within us to clutch at the happiness so offered, how hideous a thing would be its enjoyment when deliberately accepted as the fruit of such a bargain.[2]

2 William James, *The Will to Believe and Other Essays in Popular Philosophy* (New York: Longman, 1896), p. 188.

Do you agree with James? If you do, what is your reaction to the following claim by the American philosopher Morris R. Cohen:

> Moral feelings are very strong, but this does not prevent them from appearing as irrational taboos to those who do not share our conventions. This should warn us against the tendency to make ethical philosophy an apology or justification of the conventional customs that happen to be established. Suppose that someone were to offer our country a wonderfully convenient mechanism, but demand in return the privilege of killing thousands of our people every year. How many of those who would indignantly refuse such a request will condemn the use of the automobile now that it is already with us?[3]

Can you see any relevant moral differences between the cases James and Cohen mention?

2. No doubt, most of us feel strongly that our obligation not *to harm* people is much more stringent than our obligation *to help* people. Can a utilitarian give any justification for this moral distinction? Similarly, do you think a utilitarian could give a plausible defense of our tendency to distinguish such claims as "It would be *morally ideal* for Jones to do X" from "Jones is *morally obligated* to do X"? If so, how do you think a utilitarian would analyze the different meanings of these two claims?

3. There is an unresolved problem that utilitarians must face of the scope of the principle of utility. Should it apply only to human beings and not to animals? Only to presently existing human beings or to future generations as well? If we are to consider future generations, how are we to weigh the interests of an indefinite posterity against the interests of the existing generation?

   How do you think we should weigh the rights of animals against those of human beings? If, let us fancifully imagine, beating animals before killing them resulted in making the animals' meat far more tender and succulent, would we be morally justified in this sort of action? If not, what justifies us in eating them at all? If you think we are justified in using animals for our benefit as we do, would it be morally correct for beings from some other part of our universe whose abilities are vastly superior to ours to use us in a similar manner? If not, why not?

4. According to the (hedonistic) utilitarian formula, our concern should always be with the maximization of *the sum* of happiness in this world. Assuming then that a world filled with ten billion marginally happy people yields more happiness in sum than a world filled with three billion individuals who are individually far happier, does this mean that a utilitarian should claim that the more populated world

---

[3] Morris R. Cohen, *Studies in Philosophy and Science* (New York: Ungar, 1949), pp. 24–25.

even with its more thinly distributed happiness is a better world? If not, how do you think a utilitarian should handle this situation?

5. According to the (hedonistic) utilitarian formula, in choosing between alternative courses of action, the right choice is that alternative which maximizes the general happiness. Does this mean, then, that you can break promises or refuse to pay debts in *all* situations where, by so doing, the general happiness would be made greater by this course of action? Can you accept as proper an ethic that is *always* willing to renounce our special obligations to particular individuals in behalf of the general happiness? In addition, if you were committed to the view that the right thing to do is always to act so as to maximize the general happiness, would you be acting immorally whenever you spent money on some personal luxury for yourself when this same money would create greater happiness if given to the poor and starving of this world? If so, is the principle of utility a principle that the average person can reasonably be expected to follow or is it one only for saints?

6. Consider the following quotation from Ayn Rand's *Atlas Shrugged:*

> "the good of others" is a magic formula that transforms anything into gold. . . . your code hands out, as its version of the absolute, the following rule of moral conduct: if *you* wish it, it's evil; if others wish it, it's good; if the motive of your action is *your* welfare, don't do it; if the motive is the welfare of others, then anything goes. . . . For those of you who might ask questions, your code provides a consolation prize and booby-trap: it is your own happiness, it says, that you serve the happiness of others, the only way to achieve your joy is to give it up to others . . . and if you find no joy in this procedure, it is your own fault and the proof of your evil. . . . a morality that teaches you to scorn a whore who gives her body indiscriminately to all men—this same morality demands that you surrender your soul to promiscuous love for all comers.[4]

To what extent does Rand misinterpret the utilitarian point of view? To what extent do you agree with her?

7. In upholding the involuntary sterilization of a retarded 16-year-old girl, a 1925 Michigan court (*Smith v. Command*) claimed in justification that "No citizen has any right superior to the common welfare." First argue for or against this general principle and then consider its application to the particular question of the involuntary sterilization of the mentally retarded.

8. Evaluate our list of moral dilemmas from the utilitarian point of view. In which cases, if any, do you find this point of view inadequate? Why? In particular, focus on the utilitarian relevance of the

[4] Ayn Rand, *Atlas Shrugged* (New York: Random House, 1957), pp. 1030, 1031, 1033.

secrecy of one's act in the cases of "the Deathbed Promise," "The Reluctant Voter," and the "Soft-Hearted Professor."

9. A popular objection to utilitarianism is that it can lead to the punishment of the innocent. If we are to assume, as Bentham did, that the main aim of punishment is deterrence (that is, frightening people into obeying the law through the fear of punishment), law enforcement officials, it has been claimed, would be justified in particular situations in framing innocent individuals as a deterrent to future crimes when the guilty parties cannot be found and the framing can be kept secret. Yet such a practice is clearly wrong, it is claimed. What is the most plausible reply a utilitarian could make to this criticism? Does it convince you?

10. It seems clear that a utilitarian must admit that some widely held moral intuitions are unjustified. Can he, however, offer a plausible explanation of their source which can serve to weaken their force?

FURTHER READINGS

BAYLES, MICHAEL D., ed., *Contemporary Utilitarianism*, Garden City, N.Y.: Doubleday, 1968. A good collection of essays pro and con by contemporary philosophers.

BENTHAM, JEREMY, *An Introduction to the Principles of Morals and Legislation*. New York: Hafner Press, 1948, first published in 1789. A rather long and involved book, not suited for beginning students. The detailed table of contents in the work, however, makes it a good reference source for the serious student of utilitarianism.

MILL, JOHN STUART, *Utilitarianism*. Indianapolis: Bobbs-Merrill, 1957, first published in 1863. A very readable and short account of utilitarianism by Bentham's foremost disciple.

MONRO, D.H., "Bentham," *The Encyclopedia of Philosophy* (1967), 1, 280–85. An excellent short summary of Bentham's ethical philosophy.

MONRO, D.H., "Utilitarianism," *The Dictionary of the History of Ideas*, 4, 444–49. New York: Scribner's, 1973. An excellent short survey of the utilitarian philosophy (*The Dictionary of the History of Ideas* is another excellent reference source for broad general surveys of philosophical ideas. Unlike *The Encyclopedia of Philosophy*, however, there are no articles on particular individuals.)

SIDGWICK, HENRY, *The Methods of Ethics* (7th ed.). New York: Macmillan, 1907. The most thorough attempt at developing a hedonistic utilitarian ethical theory. While Sidgwick writes clearly, this long book (528 pgs.) is for the more philosophically sophisticated.

SMART, J.J.C., "Utilitarianism," *The Encyclopedia of Philosophy*, 8, 206–12. An excellent short survey of the utilitarian philosophy.

SMART, J.J.C., and BERNARD WILLIAMS, *Utilitarianism: For and Against*. Cambridge: Cambridge University Press, 1973. Consists of an essay by Smart defining and defending a utilitarian point of view and one by Williams in criticism.

7. HEDONISM

Introduction

Let us turn our attention now to the hedonistic underpinnings of Bentham and Mill's utilitarianism. According to the hedonist, you may recall, only pleasure is worthwhile in and of itself (that is, is intrinsically good). The hedonistic point of view has been embraced by many philosophers. Its roots can be traced back to Aristippus (435–350 B.C.) who was an older contemporary of Plato and, like him, a student of Socrates. The most famous supporter of hedonism, however, was Epicurus (342–270 B.C.), the founder of the school of philosophy known as epicureanism. Ironically, this word has now come to describe a view of the good life against which Epicurus would strongly protest. As it is currently used, an "epicurean" is a gourmet whose main delights consist in the enjoyment of exquisite food and drink. Epicurus was anything but an epicurean in this sense. He is said to have suffered from stomach trouble and to have subsisted on the blandest of food and drink.

While embracing the hedonistic view that pleasure alone is good, Epicurus viewed pleasure more as the absence of painful wants or longings than as the positive gratification of longings. From this perspective, he made a central distinction in his philosophy between those pleasures which have painful consequences and those which do not. A life devoted to the gratification of bodily sensations was bound to prove unsatisfying in the long run, he believed, since the price of such pleasures is often greater pain in the long run. For example, sexual love, he warned, often proves unsatisfying since it is usually "accompanied by fatigue, remorse, and depression." Similarly, gluttony and indulgence in alcoholic beverages are unsatisfying in the long run since they lead to indigestion and hangovers. Since the good life, as Epicurus saw it, was essentially a life containing as few painful experiences as possible, such a life, he believed, could not be achieved if one turned to the physical pleasures for gratification. One should turn instead, he preached, to the more tranquil modes of enjoyment which are not accompanied with the unpleasant side effects of the bodily pleasures. These modes of enjoyment embraced the joys of friendship, good conversation, and philosophical and artistic contemplation.

Epicurus' advocacy of the sort of tranquil pleasure or happiness that comes to one who is free of strong passions and pains has not been shared by all hedonists. For example, Aristippus claimed that the aim of life should not be tranquility but the maximization of as many particular pleasures as our intelligence can procure and assimilate. Very intense pleasures, Aristippus claimed, are to be sought even when they are the occasion of considerable pain, for a life without excitement would be dull and uninteresting.

Since the word "pleasure" often suggests bodily or physical enjoyment which many hedonists such as Epicurus did not at all advocate, some have preferred substituting the term "happiness" for that of "pleasure" in expressing their hedonistic commitment. They have preferred this concept since it suggests longer lasting enjoyment which need not refer to specific bodily pleasures. Not all philosophers, however, have been willing to identify pleasure with happiness. According to Aristotle, for example, the good should be identified with happiness, but not with pleasure. As he perceived it, happiness refers to "activity in accordance with the moral and intellectual virtues," and not to a particular sensation such as that of pleasure. Although pleasure accompanies such activities, Aristotle believed, it is not the proper end of our desires but simply a by-product of that end.

There have been many other philosophers who have refused to accept the hedonistic thesis that pleasure alone is intrinsically good. The good has been equated by nonhedonistic philosophers with such things as knowledge, moral virtue, beauty, self-realization, power, friendship, communion with God, and the just apportionment of happiness to desert. Many philosophers have also accepted a pluralistic view of intrinsic good, taking the position, shared by Plato, that the good life is "a mixed life" consisting of various different intrinsically good things. The hedonist, one should realize, will not deny that there are many different things —such as knowledge and moral virtue—which are desirable; what he will deny is that anything other than pleasure is intrinsically good. The things in life that are good other than pleasure are merely instrumentally good as a means for obtaining pleasure, he will say. For example, knowledge, the hedonist would say, is generally valuable because it enables us to understand and satisfy the needs of individuals and, consequently, is a source of pleasure. In addition, the very pursuit of knowledge is for many a very pleasurable activity in itself. In those situations, however, where knowledge does not lead to human pleasure, the hedonist would claim that it has no value. The same is true, he would say, of the various moral virtues, such as benevolence and courage, for the only justifiable moral virtues are those which promote human pleasure. Similarly, the hedonist would contend, it is not the existence of "beauty," "friendship" or "self-realization" in some impersonal and inexperienced (and, perhaps, meaningless) sense that is of value, but rather the satisfactory or pleasurable experience that human beings obtain from such things as aesthetic experience, having friends, and realizing their potentialities.

If the hedonist is also a utilitarian who (unlike the ethical egoist) places equal value on the pleasures of others, he will stress that a person's pursuit of a given pleasure can be bad not only when it leads in the long run to greater dissatisfaction for himself, but also when it causes greater dissatisfaction for others. It is for this reason, the hedonistic utilitarian would say, that many pleasures are to be condemned. The cruel man, for example, may obtain pleasure from his cruelty, but his cruelty is to be condemned for it is likely to cause greater pain to others and indeed possibly to himself in the long run. Any pleasure, however revolting we may find it (such as the pleasures of sado-masochists) is never to be condemned in and of itself, but only for its consequences (that is, on the grounds that it leads to greater human dissatisfaction than satisfaction in the long run), the hedonist contends.

Bentham's Quantitative Hedonism

As we have seen, it was Bentham's ideal that ethics should be made into a science whose subject matter would be capable of quantitative measure. Born into an age that had witnessed rapid development in the mathematical sciences, it was Bentham's hope that, just as scientists could measure the quantities of such things as heat and sound, it should also be possible for psychologists to measure the quantities of pleasure and pain. In arriving at a judgment of a pleasure's worth, it would be necessary, Bentham believed, to measure the following seven features of pleasure:

1. intensity (how strong or weak it is)
2. duration (how long it lasts)
3. certainty (the degree of probability that it will occur)
4. propinquity (how soon it will be fulfilled)
5. fecundity (its ability to lead to other pleasures)
6. purity (the likelihood that it will not be mixed with or followed by pain)
7. extent (the number of people who will experience it) (note that a hedonistic ethical egoist would accept the relevance of Bentham's first six features, but not the seventh, which reflects Bentham's utilitarian commitment)

If these features could prove mathematically quantifiable and capable of being incorporated into a mathematical formula for determining what one ought to do, moral reasoning could become a type of "hedonistic calculus" capable of giving exact guidance to action and legislation. Although Bentham clearly assumed that it was at least theoretically possible that pleasure could be "quantified," he never did give a method for computing the "quantity" of a given pleasure. As Bentham's critics have pointed out, while it may be possible to roughly rank certain pleasures according to their relative strength, exact mathematical measurement seems out of the question. Indeed, different sorts of pleasures often appear incommensurate. How can we, for example, compare the relative "amount" of pleasure that one obtains from a good meal as opposed to pleasure obtained from an invigorating and relaxing swim or from a good book? Indeed, does it really make sense to attempt to compare in any exact manner the "relative amount" of even similar sorts of pleasures? (Did the hamburger I had for lunch give me 1/10, 1/4, or perhaps 1/2 of the pleasure of yesterday's steak?) Furthermore, pleasures, unlike calories, change their amounts when they are combined with other pleasures. For example, the pleasure one obtains from a good dinner, wine, and the company of some loved one in romantic surroundings could be considerably greater when these pleasurable elements are taken together than they would be if they were experienced separately and then added together. Finally, as we shall discuss later, Bentham's attempt to quantify pleasures might be based on the fundamental error of assuming that the concept of pleasure refers to specific identifiable sensations or feelings. Perhaps, as behavioristic psychologists have suggested, the concept of pleasure should be taken to refer instead to dispositions (tendencies) to behave, think, and feel in certain general ways which render inappropriate any type of exact quantitative measure.

In addition to assuming that pleasures were capable of quantitative measure, Bentham also firmly held the view that pleasures should be ranked only on the basis of the seven features previously mentioned. Bentham fully rejected the view that some pleasures, apart from their quantity or consequences, were simply of a "higher level" or "quality" than others. If pleasures were to be said to differ in "quality" as well as "quantity," Bentham feared, the result would be unresolvable debates as to the "true worth" or "level" of a given pleasure, where conflicting statements of personal preference would falsely be made to appear to be dictated by impersonally justifiable standards of value. Such, of course, would make a shambles of his attempt to reduce ethics to "moral arithmetic." Bentham's view that pleasures should not be said to differ in "quality" as well as "quantity" was summed up in his famous remark that "quantity of pleasure being equal, pushpin [an old English table game] is as good as poetry."

Bentham's refusal to rank pleasures according to their "quality" as well as "quantity" led many of his critics to describe his hedonistic utilitarianism as "a philosophy fit only for pigs." Such critics shared Plato's disdain for the "lower" bodily pleasures that human beings share with other animals and his view that there are distinctively "human" sorts of pleasures that are more worthwhile apart from their amount or consequences. Bentham's reply was that even though a life limited to the bodily pleasures would be as good as one devoted to intellectual sorts of pleasures *if* their quantities were the same, as a matter of fact, the latter sort of life allows for a more varied and complex level of enjoyment which generally results in a far greater amount of pleasurable experience in the long run.

Mill's Qualitative Hedonism

This sort of reply did not seem sufficient to John Stuart Mill, Bentham's foremost disciple. Much taken by the characterization of Bentham's ethical philosophy as a "doctrine worthy of swine," Mill introduced a qualitative element into Bentham's quantitative hedonism. "It is better to be a human being dissatisfied than a pig satisfied, better to be Socrates dissatisfied than a fool satisfied," he asserted. According to Mill, "there is but one possible answer" to the question of the relative ranking of different pleasures, and he gives it as follows:

> . . . of two pleasures, if there be one to which all or almost all who have experience of both give a decided preference, irrespective of any feeling of moral obligation to prefer it, that is the more desirable pleasure. If one of the two is, by those who are competently acquainted with both, placed so far above the other that they prefer it, even though knowing it to be attended with a greater amount of discontent, and would not resign it for any quantity of the other pleasure which their nature is capable of, we are justified in ascribing to the preferred enjoyment a superiority of quality, so far outweighing quantity as to render it, in comparison, of small account.
>
> Now it is an unquestionable fact that those who are equally acquainted with, and equally capable of appreciating and enjoying both, do give a most marked preference to the manner of existence which employs their higher faculties. Few human creatures would consent to be changed into any of the lower animals, for a promise of the fullest allowance of a beast's pleasures; no intelligent human being would consent to be a fool, no instructed person would be an ignoramus, no person of feeling and conscience would be selfish and base, even though they should be persuaded that the fool, the dunce, or the rascal is better satisfied with his lot than they are with theirs.[1]

According to Mill, then, the relative qualities of two different pleasures are to be determined by asking those who have experienced both to rank them. Mill's account is quite inadequate. First, individuals who are familiar with different sorts of pleasures will rarely come close to a unanimous agreement on their ranking. In addition, it is no more adequate to claim that the pleasure preferences of "most" people is the ultimate standard of the "quality" of a pleasure than it is to say that the standard for determining what is right is what most people think is right. Clearly, the vast majority of people can sometimes be very wrong. For example, as many a frustrated teacher of literature or art will confirm, a great many, and perhaps even most, individuals who are exposed to "great literature or art" do not prefer it to simpler and less demanding forms of literary or artistic enjoyment. It is not the preferences of all those who have been exposed to literature and art which should be used as the standard of literary or artistic value, but the preferences of those who are competent to judge. The same is true of the relative qualities of different sorts of pleasures. Yet, as Bentham rightly saw, there are no clear agreed-upon standards for determining who is and is not "competent" to make such judgments.

One should also consider that if we were to employ Mill's test of "quality," then most of us would apparently have no right to judge the

---

[1] John Stuart Mill, *Utilitarianism* (Indianapolis: Bobbs-Merrill, 1957), p. 12.

quality of pleasure experienced by such individuals as the guilt-free psychopathic killer whose mode of enjoyment we have not experienced. In addition, it is possible that the sort of "higher level" intellectual pleasures that Mill advocates act to dull one's former appreciation of the simpler less cerebral type of pleasure. If this were true, one may, like Tolstoy, express a preference for these simpler pleasures even at the price of the more intellectual ones. Furthermore, it is one thing to say that a human being capable of reason, aesthetic satisfaction, and complicated feeling would not want to be turned into a "lower animal" who is incapable of these experiences; it is something else to say that the pleasures we share with animals are less valuable than those we uniquely enjoy. It could be claimed, for example, by those hedonists who emphasize the pursuit of the bodily pleasures that although intellectual and aesthetic experiences help to "enhance" the bodily ones, it is, nevertheless, the bodily ones that are more valuable in and of themselves.

Such a view cannot be "refuted" simply by pointing out that it is a minority opinion. Those of us who find the life of those primarily devoted to the titillation of the bodily senses inadequate, it would seem, would have to base our objection either on the claim that such a life does not usually produce as much pleasure in the long run as other forms of life or be forthright and renounce the hedonistic point of view that pleasure alone is intrinsically good, as Mill should have done. Does it really make any difference, after all, to say that "two pleasures can be equal in amount and consequences and yet one can be 'better' than the other" instead of saying that "pleasure is not the only intrinsic good"? I think not.

The Marxist Challenge: Which Pleasures Are Really Satisfying?

Even if one accepts the hedonistic thesis that pleasure alone is intrinsically good, it is clear that the various objects of human desire vary greatly in their capacity to generate lasting pleasure or happiness. If a person seeking advice as to the proper end or ends of "the good life," were told nothing more than "seek pleasure," this advice would not in itself inform him as to which of the multitude of possibly pleasurable activities he could seek would most likely prove satisfying in the long run. Indeed, according to the "hedonistic paradox," those who aim directly at pleasure rarely achieve it, while those who direct their attention to other pursuits more often do. We may, like Bentham, be committed to the maximization of human pleasure or happiness, but without specific goals and some insight into "human nature" we will have no specific view of "the good life." As we have seen, philosophers committed to a hedonistic view of intrinsic good often arrive at different views of the manner in which pleasure should be obtained. Each specific view is built upon assumptions as to the nature of man and his place in the universe he inhabits, as well as upon value judgments based on those assumptions. For example, a value judgment must be made as to whether it is better "to live dangerously," risking great pain as a price for great happiness, or "to play it safe," seeking the tranquility of the perhaps less intense but more pain-free pleasures.

Often these assumptions and value judgments, while exerting their strong influence on a given ideal of "the good life," are not fully brought to consciousness and subjected to scrutiny. This is precisely the criticism Karl Marx (1818–1883) directed towards Bentham's hedonistic utilitarianism. Given Marx's view that ethical philosophies are often "ideologies" in which naked power clothes itself in the robes of legitimate authority, Marx looked with suspicion at the pronouncements of Bentham and his followers. Referring to Bentham's hedonistic utilitarian principle of "the greatest happiness for the greatest number," Marx contemptuously wrote, "at no time and in no country has the most trivial commonplace ever before strutted about with such appalling self-satisfaction." In a similar vein, Marx went on to remark that this principle is quite useless apart from a definite conception of the nature of man.

> To know what is useful for a dog, we must study dog nature. This nature cannot be excogitated from the "principle of utility." If man is in question, human nature and its historical transformations must be studied. But Bentham makes short work of it. In his arid and simple way, he assumes the modern petty bourgeois, and above all the modern English petty bourgeois, to be the normal man. Whatever seems useful to this queer sort of normal man and to his world is regarded as useful in and by itself.[2]

Marx, we should note, is not criticizing Bentham as many others did, for identifying the good with pleasure, but is rather willing to take this as a "trivial commonplace." The real question to answer, Marx tells us, is which pleasures are truly satisfying to human beings. This cannot be discovered by an appeal to the principle of utility, but requires understanding of the psychological nature and social conditions of mankind. Bentham, however, Marx says, neglects any such explicit considerations and when one "reads between the lines" to discover which sorts of activities he focuses upon as pleasurable, one finds him taking it for granted that the good life is a life which satisfies the desires of the English middle class. But the real unanswered question here, as Marx perceived it, was whether these desires are truly satisfying in the long run or are merely "false" needs created by a capitalistic society. According to Marx, it is a fundamental mistake to take an individual's desires as given and unchallengeable, as Bentham so readily did, for these desires can be the reflection of social conditioning that does not reflect the true psychological nature of man. To understand the nature of the good life,

2 Karl Marx, *Capital*, volume III, trans. F. Engels (Chicago: Charles H. Kerr, 1909), p. 671.

one must understand human psychology, and for Marx this in turn meant that one must understand sociology. An individual's psyche, Marx fervently believed, is molded by social forces. Accepting Montesquieu's insight that "institutions form men," Marx, in his many writings, presented a theory of how social institutions are themselves rooted in economic conditions. The capitalistic economic system, he believed, produces as a chief motivating factor the desire for money and property, while other economic systems can produce quite different desires. Some of these desires, such as those generated by capitalism, Marx claimed, create "false needs" that are not psychologically satisfying in the long run. On the other hand, the communist society he envisioned would cater only to man's "true needs."[3] Regardless of the inadequacies in Marx' conception of the nature of man and society, his criticism is certainly sound that philosophical inquiry as to the nature of the good life is useless apart from a commitment to some general conception of "human nature."

Theories of Self Realization

Once a hedonist accepts the necessity for formulating a specific conception of human nature, his theory can become indistinguishable from the various, historically competing, philosophical theories which have identified intrinsic good with human self-realization. Such theories, which can be traced back to the ancient Greek philosophers, notably Aristotle, are united in their view that the good life for an individual is one in which one strives to realize one's potentialities. Such an unrefined view is open to the obvious objection that human beings have many, often conflicting, potentialities which we neither could nor would want fully realized. If one asserts that each of us should develop his own special talents, we must certainly face the sad fact that some predominant potentialities (such as brutality, greed, and dishonesty) should never be fully realized. Philosophers and psychologists have often camouflaged their own personal preferences as to the ideals that we should strive to realize by speaking of "true" self-realization or of what is to be "genuinely" human—conveniently using these terms to describe those human potentialities of which they approve. Of course, however, those human tendencies which supporters of a particular view of self-realization would disapprove are just as "real" and "human" as those they admire. Even though many philosophical theories of self-realization are nothing more than statements of personal preference, others, especially those of such psychologists as Erich Fromm, Carl Rogers, and A.H. Maslow, do provide us with great insight into human nature and those things that are necessary for long-range human satisfaction.

[3] Although Marx makes it appear that his conception of man's "true needs" is purely "scientific," and does not reflect his own basic value preferences, this is open to serious question. Marx, unfortunately, never clearly distinguished the moral judgments he made from the "scientific facts" that he used to back them up.

The Linguistic Challenge: What Is "Pleasure"?

Marx' criticism that hedonism is not so much a mistaken doctrine as it is an empty one has been further strengthened by contemporary analyses of the concept of pleasure by psychologists and philosophers. Like many other philosophers of his day who were under the influence of the philosopher Descartes, Bentham believed that the most certain knowledge possible is that which results from the introspection of the workings of one's mind. From this perspective, Bentham assumed that "pleasure" was the name of a single distinctly introspected sort of feeling or sensation that every human being could easily identify. Is this, however, true? Is there some common element present in the various activities that we describe as pleasurable or enjoyable? As I focus on some of the things that give me pleasure, I cannot find a common felt quality that they all share. Indeed, although some pleasurable activities are accompanied with discernable sensations or feelings, this does not always seem to be the case. If "pleasure" is not the name of a sensation, what then is it? Contemporary philosophers are not universally agreed, but many would accept the view that to say that "X is pleasurable" simply means that "X is an experience that one would rather have than not have, apart from any considerations as to its morality or possible consequences." Similarly, to say that "X is more pleasurable than Y" does not mean that "the sensations of pleasure accompanying X are greater than those accompanying Y," but rather that "one would prefer X over Y if one were asked to choose between them without regard to consequences or moral considerations." If we accept this general conception of the meaning of "pleasure," we can easily understand why a person who says "I find X pleasurable but see no reason to do it," seems to be talking nonsense, and we can see, too, why we often discover what things really give us pleasure only when we compare our preferences for different things. Consider, for example, the following analysis of the concept of pleasure that is found in Gilbert Ryle's (1900–76) *The Concept of Mind:*

> The words "pleasure" and "desire" play a large role in the terminology of moral philosophers and of some schools of psychology. It is important briefly to indicate some of the differences between the supposed logic of their use and its actual logic.
>
> First, it seems to be generally supposed that "pleasure" and "desire" are always used to signify feelings. And there certainly are feelings which can be described as feelings of pleasure and desire. . . .
>
> . . . But there is another sense in which we say that a person who is so absorbed in some activity, such as golf or argument, that he is reluctant to stop, or even to think of anything else, is "taking pleasure in" or "enjoying" doing what he is doing, though he is in no degree convulsed or beside himself, and though he is not, therefore, experiencing any particular feelings.
>
> Doubtless the absorbed golfer experiences numerous flutters and glows of rapture, excitement, and self-approbation in the course of his game. But when asked whether or not he had enjoyed the periods of

the game between the occurrences of such feelings, he would obviously reply that he had, for he had enjoyed the whole game. He would at no moment of it have welcomed an interruption: he was never inclined to turn his thoughts or conversation from the circumstances of the game to other matters. . . .

In this sense, to enjoy doing something, to want to do it and not to want to do anything else are different ways of phrasing the same thing.[4]

The essential point Ryle is making here is that when we say that we are getting pleasure from something, we usually mean not that we are doing that thing and experiencing something else, but merely that we are doing it "wanting to do it and not wanting to stop." Since we may want to do things as a means to other things or on the basis of some sense of moral obligation, and since we may be willing to stop engaging in some pleasurable activity out of a sense of moral obligation or because an even more pleasurable activity can be pursued, the initial definition of "pleasure" provided is a better one. So let us assume now that "X is pleasurable to Y" means that "X is an experience that Y would rather have than not have, apart from any considerations as to its morality or possible consequences," which would seem to be just another way of saying that "X is an experience that Y would desire to prolong for its own sake." But if this definition is accepted, the hedonistic view that "pleasure alone is intrinsically good" would reduce to the view that "something is intrinsically desirable to a person only if it is an experience that that person would want to prolong for its own sake." Such a definition, however, invites the Marxist challenge that hedonism is a "trivial commonplace." Indeed, if one takes for granted that the only things desirable are states of consciousness, then hedonism would be rendered an uninformative tautology. Since not all philosophers have identified intrinsic good with states of consciousness, hedonism is to some extent informative, even though many of us would consider it beyond question that the only things human beings ought to seek are states of consciousness that can be experienced as satisfactory.

The actual desires and preferences of human beings is, of course, the province of the science of psychology. The scientific study of psychological phenomena can also provide insight into the causal connections among our desires, providing us with knowledge of the coherence of our desires and their capability of providing long-range satisfaction. This is very important, for as the philosopher Morris R. Cohen (1880–1947) rightly observed:

One of the obvious facts of human nature is that our unhappiness comes not only from the fact that we cannot have what we want, but very often we are most miserable because we succeed in getting what we thought we wanted. Wisdom, therefore, consists in surveying our various

---

[4] Gilbert Ryle, *The Concept of Mind* (New York: Harper & Row Pubs., 1949), pp. 107–8.

conflicting desires with a view to the attainment of a harmony, or a maximum of happiness. A man may prefer a short but a merry life. Another may prefer suicide. But, if we regard our life as a continuing one, that is, if we have some regard for our own personality, we must integrate all of our desires into one coherent system, so that we can attain self-respect. Just as all of our judgments of perception of nature can be integrated by physical science into a view of the world, so may our judgments of preference be integrated with them into a view of the most desirable mode of life.[5]

While psychologists and psychiatrists today differ in their conceptions of the exact interrelationships of our desires, there is general acceptance of the Platonic view that the only satisfactory type of life is "a mixed one" devoted to the pursuit of a plurality of things which are deemed intrinsically valuable. Furthermore, there is general consensus that the realization of one value is often achieved only at the price of another. Psychologists and psychiatrists can help us to realize the price we must pay for "a way of life," but ultimately each of us must choose for ourselves whether the price is one we are willing to pay. There is no way of life that has no cost and no single "right" price to pay. There is no reason to believe that rationality demands that all people choose the same way; what it does demand is that we know what we are choosing. When we attempt, as hedonists do, to reduce all desires to the common denominator of "pleasure" we run the risk of deceiving ourselves, through a linguistic trick, into believing that human desires are more unified than they really are.

DISCUSSION QUESTIONS

1. According to G.E. Moore, an undesirable consequence of Bentham's hedonism is that:

   > . . . the state of mind of a drunkard, when he is intensely pleased with breaking crockery, is just as valuable in itself—just as well worth having, as that of a man who is fully realizing all that is exquisite in the tragedy of *King Lear*, provided only the mere quantity of pleasure in both cases is the same.[6]

   How would a defender of Bentham reply? What do you think of this reply?

2. Bertrand Russell, a famous twentieth century philosopher, was once asked whether criminals sentenced to life imprisonment (without

5 Morris R. Cohen, *A Preface to Logic* (New York: Holt, Rinehart & Winston, 1944), p. 170.

6 G.E. Moore, *Principia Ethica* (Cambridge: Cambridge University Press, 1959), first published in 1903, p. 147.

chance of parole) should be sent to the South Sea Islands instead, if they could be equally as well removed from society that way. Russell claimed that this would be fine as long as the South Sea Islanders' security was not endangered and it was kept secret. (If it weren't kept secret, such treatment would not serve as a deterrent to would-be criminals.) Do you agree with Russell that convicted criminals should be allowed to experience as much pleasure as possible as long as no hedonistic utilitarian purpose can be served by making them suffer pain? Do you accept the hedonistic view that the experience of pleasure is always in itself good?

3. In Mark Twain's *The Mysterious Stranger,* an angel promises an unhappy old man that he will make him happy. He accomplishes this by making the old man insane. Deluded into thinking that he is very rich, the old man takes great joy in giving away things that he doesn't possess to his friends and relatives. Wouldn't a hedonist have to claim that this old man is better off insane than sane? Do you agree? Why, or why not? If you disagree, do you think a person can ever be said to be better off if, after taking a drug, he finds himself much happier than he was before, although not as intellectually capable?

4. Assuming that a community of sado-masochists would maximize their pleasure (in the long run) by indulging their sado-masochistic desires, without this having any adverse effect upon individuals outside of their community, a hedonist would be committed to the view that "the good life" for them is one in which they satisfy their sado-masochistic desires. Do you agree? If not, why not? (Do not claim that they could not "really" be happy or that they would be happier if they did not possess their sado-masochistic desires, for we are to accept as a premise of this case that this is simply not so. If you refuse to make this assumption about human beings, imagine it to be true of creatures from some strange world.)

5. Aldous Huxley depicts a society committed to the hedonistic ideal in his novel *Brave New World.* In this society, people are immunized from all diseases and are genetically engineered and behaviorally conditioned so that they quite naturally do as they ought to do. The euphoric drug *soma* is used to combat any depression in life and to create the most pleasurable of sensations. The merits of Huxley's imagined society are debated within the novel by the "Controller," Mustapha Mond, who directs the society and a "Savage" who has not yet been "civilized." Consider the following excerpt from this dialogue:

> The Savage nodded . . . "Yes, that's just like you. Getting rid of everything unpleasant instead of learning to put up with it. Whether 'tis better in the mind to suffer the slings and arrows of outrageous fortune, or to take arms against a sea of troubles and by opposing end them. . . . But you don't do either. Neither suffer nor oppose. You just

abolish the slings and arrows. It's too easy. . . . Isn't there something in living dangerously?"

"There's a great deal in it," the Controller replied, "Men and women must have their adrenals stimulated from time to time. . . . It's one of the conditions of perfect health. That's why we've made the V.P.S. treatments compulsory."

"V.P.S.?"

"Violent Passion Surrogate. Regularly once a month. We flood the whole system with adrenin. It's the complete physiological equivalent of fear and rage . . . without any of the inconveniences."

"But I like the inconveniences." . . .

"In fact," said Mustapha Mond, "you're claiming the right to be unhappy. . . . Not to mention the right to grow old and ugly and impotent; the right to have syphilis and cancer; the right to have too little to eat . . . the right to live in constant apprehension of what may happen tomorrow . . . the right to be tortured by unspeakable pains of every kind."

There was a long silence.

"I claim them all," said the Savage at last.

Mustapha Mond shrugged his shoulders. "You're welcome," he said.[7]

Do you agree with the Savage that there is something seriously lacking in Huxley's imagined society? If so, what is it?

6. It is now possible to implant electrodes in a region of the brain (the septal region) which can be electrically stimulated to cause very pleasurable sensations. One can consequently imagine a "Brave New World" of the future where individuals spend their leisure time "stimulating their implanted electrodes," and thoroughly enjoying themselves. Let us take this a step further and imagine a "dream machine" to which people can connect themselves to create the most vivid and coherent of dreams. While one is connected to this "dream machine," one's experiences appear as real as they do when one is awake. There is no sensory, physical, or psychological experience that the dream machine is incapable of reproducing. Furthermore, it is possible to individually program the dream machine to cater to the differing psychological needs of different people. Now, let us imagine someone who is quite dissatisfied with his experience of the "real world" and decides to opt out by having himself connected to "the dream machine" for the remainder of his life. (Let us assume that he can be kept physically healthy this way—that is, he will be fed intravenously, his body wastes removed, etc.—and that the efficient society of the future has no need for his labor.) What do you think of the desirability of such a life? What, if anything, is missing from it?

7 From *Brave New World* by Aldous Huxley. Copyright 1932, 1960 by Aldous Huxley. By permission of Harper & Row, Publishers, Inc., pp. 286–88.

FURTHER READINGS

ALSTON, WILLIAM P., "Pleasure," *The Encyclopedia of Philosophy* (1967), 6, 341–47. A critical discussion of different analyses of the concept of pleasure.

BENTHAM, JEREMY, *An Introduction to the Principles of Morals and Legislation,* chapters 4 and 5. New York: Hafner Press, 1948, first published in 1789.

HOSPERS, JOHN, *Human Conduct,* chapter 3. New York: Harcourt Brace Jovanovich, Inc., 1972. A very readable and engaging discussion of hedonism.

HUXLEY, ALDOUS, *Brave New World.* New York: Harper & Row Pub., 1946. Huxley's classic unsympathetic portrait of a futuristic society dedicated to the hedonistic ideal.

MILL, JOHN STUART, *Utilitarianism,* chapters 2 and 4. Indianapolis: Bobbs-Merrill, 1957, first published in 1863.

MOORE, G.E., *Principia Ethica,* chapter VII. Cambridge: Cambridge University Press, 1959, first published in 1903. An influential early twentieth century utilitarian's arguments for rejecting hedonism and with it the view that there is only one intrinsic good.

RYLE, GILBERT, *The Concept of Mind.* New York: Harper & Row, Pub., 1949. Ryle's behaviorist analysis of the concept of "pleasure" is in chapter IV, section 6: "Enjoying and Wanting." It would be worthwhile also to read the first chapter for background. In this chapter, Ryle expresses his central thesis that most mental terms do not refer to "mental events" that occur in "immaterial things" called "minds." In later chapters, Ryle defends his view that most mental terms including those relating to knowledge and emotion refer, instead, to dispositions (that is, tendencies) to behave in particular ways in particular situations.

SMART, J.J.C., "An Outline of a System of Utilitarian Ethics," section 3, in *Utilitarianism: For and Against.* Cambridge: Cambridge University Press, 1973.

8. KANTIAN ETHICS

Introduction

The ethical theory of the very influential philosopher Immanuel Kant (1724–1804) stands in marked contrast to that of the utilitarians. Unlike the utilitarians, Kant did not think that the ordinary person needed guidance in arriving at more enlightened moral judgments. The central question of morality for Kant was not, "What would be the right thing for a person to do in this specific situation?" The answer to such a question, he assumed, would usually be perfectly clear to every decent human being. Perhaps due to his deeply religious background, discerning the right was not a major problem for Kant; the problem was maintaining the self-control to do what is right. As a result, Kant does not seriously consider the type of moral perplexity, emphasized by the existentialist Sartre, that arises from confusion as to what is right when one feels oneself torn between conflicting obligations.

From such a perspective, the task Kant set for himself was not one of demonstrating that the ordinary person's moral intuitions made sense; this he simply assumed. The task, instead, as he saw it, was to formulate some comprehensive theory of the nature of morality, human beings, the physical world, the after-life, and God, which could *explain how* morality, as the common person understood it, was possible and rational. In particular, Kant was struck by the apparent incompatibility of human "free will" and the assumption of the developing deterministic sciences of his day that every event, including human behavior, could in principle be predicted from a knowledge of scientific causal laws. It seemed clear to Kant that if human choices ("acts of will") were entirely governed by causes, as the deterministic view seemed to entail, then "free will" would be an illusion. Since, as Kant saw it, it makes sense to tell people what they morally *ought* to do only when we believe that they *can* do it, morality presupposes the existence of free will, which determinism seems to deny. In order to remove the apparent inconsistency between freedom and determinism, Kant made a radical distinction between that part of man—his sensual or animal nature—that was fully determined by causes capable of scientific understanding and prediction, and that distinctive part of him—his nature as a rational, moral being—which stood outside of the stream of these causes. Consequently, for Kant, man's uniqueness among the animals resided in the fact that he alone among them was a creature capable of rational moral choice; it was in this that man found his special dignity.

Kant's ethical theory can be best understood as a reaction to what Kant saw as the two fundamental inadequacies of the hedonistic utilitarianism of Jeremy Bentham: its reliance upon the notion of "happiness" as the ultimate ground of morality and its potential for injustice. First, Kant rejected the utilitarian assumption that morality should be based on the actual desires of human beings—that morality is nothing more than the maximization of human desires, such as the desire for happiness. From this point of view, human reason must be subservient to the direction of one's desires or passions. As the philosopher David Hume, who accepted this view, put it, "reason is the slave of the passions." Kant fully rejected this view. As Kant saw it, morality should be grounded in a value which gives human beings their distinctive worth. Such a value cannot be a desire such as the desire for happiness which, as a matter of psychological fact, human beings simply happen to desire. People may desire happiness, but they do not derive their dignity or worth as persons from desiring it. (Consider the traditional dismissal of hedonism as a "pigs'" philosophy.) According to Kant, they derive this dignity from their freedom and ability to reason, the characteristics which distinguish human beings from other animals. People alone can act from reasons, as opposed to being acted upon by external causes; people alone can act freely. Morality, then, as Kant saw it, must be based on the values of rationality and freedom. Only by acting as a free and fully rational human being would act, Kant believed, does man reveal his dignity—asserts that autonomy of action that distinguishes him from the brutes. Believing, as Hume before him believed, that there was an unbridgeable gap between reason and desire—that desires could never in themselves be said to be "reasonable"—the way Kant saw it, one cannot be acting morally when one justifies one's actions by an appeal to one's desires.

Second, Kant feared that a complete commitment to the principle of utility could lead to grave injustices. As we have seen, a glaring in-adequacy of the traditional utilitarian theory developed by Bentham was its neglect of the notion of distributive justice. In his preoccupation with the maximization of happiness, Bentham never inquired into the principles that should be utilized to assure that the distribution of that happiness be fair. While the utilitarians neglected the concept of justice in the development of their moral theory, Kant makes it the focal point of his. For Kant, the rightness of an action must be determined indepen-dently of a consideration of a person's actual desires which could be quite unjust. It is the fear that utilitarian ethics could lead one to justify un-just actions in certain situations that led Kant to speak warningly of "the serpent windings of utilitarianism." Kant believed that Bentham and his followers, in their desire to maximize human happiness, failed to realize that (in this world) happiness can sometimes be maximized only by sacrificing justice. According to Kant, such a sacrifice could never be morally justified. As Kant saw it, legal systems exist in order to secure the value of justice. Justice, in turn, demands that each person enjoy the fullest possible liberty compatible with a like liberty for all. The law can legitimately interfere with a person's freedom only when that person illegitimately interferes with the liberty of some other person. It is improper for the law to interfere with a person's liberty to enforce such nebulous goals as the "maximization of human happiness" or "the common good." Such goals, Kant saw, are subject to conflicting interpre-tations and have the potential for gravely interfering with individual liberty—the very value that gives human beings their dignity.

Although the utilitarian Mill argued in his famous essay *On Liberty* that the principle of utility implies a commitment to the value of free-dom which allows individuals to make their own decisions as to what is best for themselves, there is no guarantee that these two values will al-ways coincide. It is not at all hard to imagine, as Aldous Huxley did in his novel *Brave New World,* a society of happy, though minimally free, individuals. The widely felt revulsion towards Huxley's envisioned totali-tarian society stems not from the belief that the people in such a society "cannot really be happy" but from the fact that they are not allowed the freedom to make their own decisions as to how to find their happiness. Clearly perceiving the potential conflict between freedom and utility and seeing the dignity of man in his freedom, Kant attempts to solidly anchor the value of freedom to a basic and absolute principle of justice.

Unlike the utilitarians who did not have much to say about the principles to be utilized in the evaluation of moral character,[1] Kant provides us not only with a theory of moral obligation (that is, a theory of how we should determine when an act is right), but also with a theory of moral value (that is, a theory of how we should determine when a person is morally good). Let us turn to a consideration of the main elements of these two very influential theories.

Kant's Theory of Moral Value

How do we determine if a person is a morally good person? Clearly, it is insufficient to look at the person's actions and their consequences without considering the person's motives and intentions. Indeed, a person's actions may give no indication at all about his moral character. Certainly, a "bad" person may do right things for the wrong reasons, and a "good" person, having only good intentions, may nevertheless do bad things. Accepting the familiar distinction we all make between the goodness of a person's character and the rightness of his actions, Kant asserts that the only motive that should be taken as a sign of good character is the motive of conscientiousness (that is, acting from duty). According to Kant, a morally good person (or as he prefers to put it, a person with "good will") is a person "who intends to do his duty because it is his duty and summons all the means in his power to do that duty." It is this, and this alone, which determines "a good will," Kant declares. A person who does his duty for any other reason does not have a good will and is consequently unworthy of moral praise. As an example, Kant mentions a shopkeeper who is honest, not because he believes that it is his moral duty to be so, but because he believes that honesty pays off by giving him a good reputation which in turn brings him more customers and more profit. Such a person, who is fortunate to find himself motivated by self-interest to do as duty demands, does not have a good will and is unworthy of moral praise, Kant would say. In addition, Kant asserts, the "naturally good person" who does what is right simply because that is what he is naturally inclined to do without any consideration of his duty also does not have a good will and is unworthy of moral praise. For example, if Jones helps others, not out of a sense of moral duty, but simply out of his kindly nature, Kant would not consider him worthy of moral praise.

Is it reasonable to ignore inclination in determining a person's moral goodness? Critics of Kant have contended that the sign of moral

[1] Like many philosophers of his age, Jeremy Bentham was committed to the doctrine of psychological egoism which asserts that all (voluntary) human motives are ultimately "selfish." Given this assumption, Bentham understandably felt little impetus to delve into the subtleties of human motives. Instead his concern with human motivation centered on the problem of how to motivate rational self-interested people to obey moral and legal rules which aim at the general interest.

maturity is when one does what is right without being tempted to do otherwise, and consequently without having to think about duty. For example, imagine that at first you want very much to steal, but, recognizing your duty to refrain, you don't. After awhile, however, you find yourself no longer even tempted to steal. Many philosophers have claimed that it is quite unreasonable to say as Kant does, that your action is now no longer a morally praiseworthy one.

Kant, however, would have a reply. First, he would agree that it is best for people not to always have to think about their duty and to train themselves into developing habits of restraint. The important thing, as he saw it, was that one have *a disposition to act from duty* (that is, that one would do what is right out of a sense of duty *even if* one had no natural inclination to do so). A "morally good" person is not necessarily a person who always acts from duty, he is rather a person who *would* choose duty over inclination *if* he had to make such a choice. As Kant saw it, a person should not get credit for his natural inclinations, since they are largely determined by his heredity and environment over which he has no control. People who do the right thing out of natural inclination, Kant would say, are simply lucky to have their natural inclinations coincide with their duty.

An adequate criticism of Kant's position here would involve coming to grips with the traditional philosophical problem of determinism and free will which we shall tackle in section 14. For our purposes at this point, it will suffice to say that critics of Kant would say that he is fundamentally mistaken in claiming that people act more freely and are consequently more worthy of praise when they act from duty than when they act from any other motive. The disposition to do one's duty, the critics would say, is as much determined by hereditary and environmental factors as are other inclinations. If a person does not have free choice in determining whether he should have a kindly or courageous character, for example, why should he be said to have free choice when it comes to his disposition to act from duty? If an individual who is kindly by nature is simply lucky, as Kant believed, why isn't the same true of the person who has a strong sense of duty? After all, a person's sense of duty might be as much a result of childhood training as another person's kindness. If, on the other hand, one is properly subject to moral praise or blame for the choices he makes between the demands of duty and conflicting natural inclinations, why can't one equally as well be subject to moral praise or blame for choosing between these inclinations themselves and, consequently, be held morally accountable for one's very temperament?

Regardless of the inadequacies of Kant's view of moral character, this view does bring out the important point that some people find it much easier than others to do their duty as a result of hereditary and environmental factors that they had no hand in choosing. If, for example, Jones has a much less violent and imperturbable nature than Smith, it will be much easier for Jones than for Smith to control himself from reacting with unjustified violence to some very strong provocation. If we can ultimately trace the difference between Jones' and Smith's nature to hereditary or early environmental factors over which neither had control, is it to Jones' moral credit that he is a more self-controlled individual than Smith? I would think not. Indeed, is it not the case that if Smith and Jones both restrain themselves equally well, Smith's behavior would be more to his moral credit and consequently more worthy of praise than Jones' since it involved more moral effort? I would think so. It is the virtue of Kant that he makes us think about such issues.

Another problem with Kant's view of moral character relates to the fact that he rivets his attention upon people who not only act from duty but are also correct in their appraisal of what duty demands. Consequently, he does not tell us whether people who act from a *mistaken* conception of duty are worthy of moral praise. In judging moral character, must we not consider what a conscientious person is conscientious about? As we have mentioned, Kant did not focus on this problem, for he, like so many others of his age, tended to think that every "right-minded" person would have the same conception of his duty. But it is clear, nevertheless, that people often profoundly disagree as to the demands of duty. Consider, for example the following two cases:

Mr. and Mrs. Jones are Christian Scientists who believe that it is their moral duty to refuse any medical interference with the functioning of their bodies. Their little son, whom they love dearly, is involved in a serious accident. The doctors who examine him say that without a blood transfusion he will surely die. Even though it strongly goes against their natural inclination, Mr. and Mrs. Jones say no. It would be wrong, they believe, to allow the blood transfusion; it would be contrary to the will of God.

Mr. Smith is a person who acts in complete ignorance and superstition but with utter devotion to duty; he whips his children every day, telling them that it hurts him more than it hurts them, but sparing the rod spoils the child. He persecutes minority groups in this country because he is convinced that this country is too small to hold people like himself and all those second-rate and disruptive minority groups that make life in this country more difficult for others. In fact, he wouldn't mind liquidating these minority groups in order to cleanse the country of them once and for all. We try to convince Mr. Smith that he is wrong, but he staunchly adheres to what he believes to be his duty and calls us wicked instruments of the devil because we are trying to undermine his moral convictions.[2]

Assuming, as most of us would, that the Jones' are mistaken about what their duty demands, what should our judgment be of their moral character? If we are to consider them praiseworthy for their conscientiousness, it is doubtful that we would feel the same way about Mr. Smith. What is the morally relevant difference in these two cases? Does the dif-

[2] This example is taken, with minor changes, from John Hosper, *Human Conduct* (New York: Harcourt Brace Jovanovich, Inc., 1972), p. 273, exercise 1.

ference, perhaps, reside in the fact that we are willing to accept the Jones' conflict between duty and inclination as a real one, but are not at all apt to do the same with Mr. Smith? We may sympathize with the Jones', seeing their choice as a genuine case of self-sacrifice. We may shake our heads in sadness over their "ignorance," but may feel that they cannot reasonably be blamed for it. When we turn to Smith, however, we are apt to distrust his claim that "it hurts him more than it hurts them." We suspect that he is lying to himself, that he is simply rationalizing. We suspect that deep down he wants to hurt others and then conveniently convinces himself that his duty demands that he do what he is inclined to do anyway. Consider, for example, the following imaginary dialogue:

> **X:** A person who always acts on principle is much more to be trusted than a person who acts on the basis of his desires or inclinations. Such a person can be counted on, regardless of how he might happen to feel at a given moment. We all know how fickle one's feelings can be.
>
> **Y:** No doubt people's feelings are often fickle, but it seems to me that people's senses of duty can be equally fickle. How common, indeed, it is for the "person of principle" to trim and interpret his principles in such a manner that he can justify doing exactly what he wants to do, with a good conscience.

Does not *Y* have a good point here? Certainly, one can never neglect the possibility that one's sense of duty is a convenient rationalization for doing as one would want to do apart from any moral consideration. Holden Caulfield, the hero of J.D. Salinger's *The Catcher in the Rye* reflects on this possibility when he says:

> Even if you did go around saving guys' lives and all, how would you know if you did it because you really wanted to save guys' lives, or whether you did it because what you really wanted to do was be a terrific lawyer, with everybody slapping you on the back and congratulating you in court when the goddam trial was over, the reporters and everybody . . . How would you know you weren't being a phony?[3]

Is one, however, "being a phony" if one helps others only when one gets something out of helping them, or is one being a phony when one does something out of a sense of duty that does not really reflect one's own desires? Ayn Rand, for example, the foremost contemporary advocate of "the virtue of selfishness," would claim that it is the second, and not the first, person who is the true phony. As she puts it in her novel *Atlas Shrugged*:

> If you wish to save the last of your dignity, do not call your best actions a 'sacrifice': that term brands you as immoral. If a mother buys food for

---

[3] J.D. Salinger, *The Catcher in the Rye* (New York: Bantam, 1964), p. 172.

her hungry child rather than a hat for herself, it is not a sacrifice if she values the child higher than the hat; but it is a sacrifice to the kind of mother whose higher value is the hat, who would prefer her child to starve and feeds him only from a sense of duty.[4]

Kant's Theory of Moral Obligation

Fundamental to most people's conception of morality is a commitment to the value of justice. Although, like the utilitarians, we are all concerned with maximizing the good in society, most of us would not consider such value as a typically "moral" one. It is an "efficient" society, we are apt to say, that is most capable of maximizing the good of its citizens, but such a society is not a "moral" one unless its goods are justly distributed. Clearly, for most of us, any adequate moral theory must find a central place for the notion of justice. It is this notion that forms the cornerstone of Kant's theory of moral obligation. In this theory, the notion of justice is inseparably tied to the notions of freedom and rationality. As Kant saw it, justice in its most basic respect involves treating individuals fairly, and this in turn involves considering them as rational moral agents who have the right to make their own choices unless these choices interfere with the freedom of others. From such a perspective, it is fundamentally wrong to "use" individuals, as the utilitarian scheme would invite us to do, as mere instruments or means to be manipulated in our quest for the maximization of human happiness. To treat individuals in such a way, Kant would claim, is to treat them as less than "persons"—that is, as less than free rational moral agents.

Just like the utilitarians who attempted to reduce all of morality to the single basic principle of utility, Kant attempts to reduce all of morality to a single basic principle which he calls the "categorical imperative." By calling this principle a "categorical" one, Kant means to assert that our obligation to abide by it depends in no way upon our actual desires. In this respect, the categorical imperative, Kant asserts, differs from mere "hypothetical imperatives" which prescribe the necessary means for achieving our desires. For example, if one wants to lose weight, then it is rational for one to eat less. The imperative (command) to eat less, Kant would say is hypothetical in that it will bind us only insofar as we accept the end of losing weight. If we reject this end, the command "to eat less" will have no force for us. A demand of morality, on the other hand, Kant asserts, is "categorical" in the sense that it presents "an action as of itself objectively necessary, without regard to any other end" (that is, it constitutes a rational principle of action even in the absence of any desire in that direction). For example, according to Kant, our moral obligation to keep our promises in no way depends upon whether or not we desire to keep them.

According to Kant, there are three equivalent ways of expressing the meaning of the categorical imperative. They are

---

[4] Ayn Rand, *Atlas Shrugged* (New York: Random House, 1957), p. 1029.

1. Act only according to that maxim by which you can at the same time will that it should become a universal law of nature.

2. Act in such a way that you always treat humanity, whether in your own person, or in the person of any other, never simply as a means, but always at the same time as an end.

3. All maxims which spring from your own making of laws ought to accord with a possible kingdom of ends as of kingdom of nature. (*Foundations of the Metaphysics of Morals*)

Kant's second and third formulations of the categorical imperative express his central concern with the notion of "treating individuals with respect as persons." The second formulation expresses this idea best by commanding us never to treat people "simply as a means, but always at the same time as an end." An individual is treated "simply as a means" when our response to him is motivated not by his choices but by ours in disregard of his. This same notion is central to Kant's concept of a "kingdom of ends" which is used in the third formulation—that is, a society of free moral agents, all of whom govern their actions by reason and all of whom are considered as ends-in-themselves and never simply as means. As Kant saw it, since the very dignity of human beings resides in their freedom and rationality, human beings are not treated with respect whenever they are not treated as rational moral agents who are given the freedom to set their own goals. To be "treated as a person" is simply to be afforded this respect. This is illustrated by the teenager yelling at his parents who insist on making his decisions for him, "You aren't treating me as a person; I'm rational enough to make my own decisions. I'm not a child anymore." It is inconsistent with treating an individual as a person, Kant believed, to ever use him as a mere means to the satisfaction of any goal—even that of his own ultimate happiness—for to treat a human being in this respect is to lower him to the level of an animal, whom we may love but do not respect.[5]

It is Kant's first formulation of the categorical imperative, however, which is usually considered to be the most informative and important of the three formulations and it is certainly the most well known. When Kant asserts that you "should act only according to that maxim [that is, rule] by which you can at the same time will that it would become a universal law of nature [that is, that everyone should follow that maxim]," he is expressing the idea, so deeply a part of practically everyone's moral sense, that morality demands impartiality and empathy. As a parent might tell a child, "You were wrong to take Billy's toy away from him. If it's right for you to do it, then it would be right for him to do it to you. How would you like that?" It is this idea of impartiality and concern for those who might be affected by one's action that is at the heart of the Golden Rule of Judaic-Christian ethics which commands that you "Do unto others as you would have others do unto you" and it is this

---

[5] Notice that if we do respect an animal, that animal ceases to be seen as a "mere animal," but is seen more as a "person."

same idea, stated in a less demanding and more passive way, that is expressed in the Confucian rule to "Do not do unto others as you would not have them do unto you." For most of us, impartiality is essential to the "moral point of view." When a person acts on a "moral principle" we tend to believe he must be willing to accept the right of everyone else to act on that same principle—that is, he must be willing to accept the "universalization" of the rule under which he acts.

The categorical imperative was Kant's attempt to formulate in a more precise manner the spirit behind the Golden Rule. Taken literally, unfortunately, this rule seems to lead to absurd consequences. For example, if Jones is a sado-masochist who enjoys being hurt and hurting others, we would certainly think that Jones is violating "the spirit behind" the Golden Rule, if not its "letter," when he hurts Smith and justifies it by saying that he is merely "doing unto Smith as he would have Smith do unto him." As George Bernard Shaw, the English literary figure, once remarked, the Golden Rule seems to neglect the fact that people's tastes may be different. Given this observation, one can either reject the Golden Rule as a useless guide to moral conduct (some have) or try to dig more deeply into the ideas that underlie it. This is what Kant attempted. It is, however, far from clear if Kant's first formulation of the categorical imperative is any clearer than the Golden Rule it so much resembles.

When Kant tells us that we should do only what we *can* will that everyone else do, what exactly is the force of the "can" here? Does it mean what we *can logically will* (that is, what it is possible to conceive), or what is *scientifically possible for us to will* (that is, what is consistent with "the laws of nature"), or what we can *rationally will*, or merely what *we would desire as a matter of psychological fact*. Kant himself does not clearly say and what he does say points in different directions. Consequently, Kantian scholars disagree as to the precise meaning that should be attributed to the categorical imperative.

Whatever else Kant might have meant when he tells us that we should only act according to maxims that *we can universalize,* he certainly and most fundamentally meant to exclude actions that it would be *logically impossible* for everyone to follow. For example, it would be logically impossible for everyone to act in accordance with the maxim "Never offer to contribute to projects in the common good, instead let your neighbors make the necessary sacrifices, while you share in the benefits these sacrifices make possible." Obviously, a person who acts under such a maxim assumes that not everyone will, for it is logically impossible for everyone to follow it. A person who reaps the benefits of a community without assuming the burdens that make them possible is a parasite who counts on others not acting the way he acts.

An example Kant himself gives of a maxim that it would be logically impossible to universalize is the following one: "When I think myself in need of money, I shall borrow and promise to repay, although I know that I can never do so." Although Kant says this is the maxim he is considering, it would appear that the maxim he actually is focusing upon is the broader one, "Whenever necessary to obtain the things that I desire, I shall make promises that I know I cannot keep." So let us consider this maxim. The way Kant seems to see it, it is "logically impossible" to universalize this maxim in the sense that if everyone were to follow it, promises would cease to have any force and the institution of promise-keeping would be destroyed. As Kant put it, "There would be no promises at all. . . . Thus my maxim would necessarily destroy itself as soon as it was made a universal law." Notice that, unlike the preceding example, the universalization of the maxim in question does not "destroy itself" in the straight-forward logical sense that the preceding maxim did. Certainly, like Kant, we tend to assume that if everyone were always willing to make promises they knew they could not keep in order to obtain things they desired, the institution of promise-keeping would soon be destroyed. But it would be destroyed only if we make the *factual assumption* that people often find themselves in situations where they desire things that can be obtained only by making promises that cannot be kept and that the frequency of dishonest promise-making would lead people to refuse to accept promises. This is, no doubt, true; it is not, however, "logically true" but involves some basic assumptions about the nature of people and the world they inhabit.

While one can see the categorical imperative in the preceding two examples as a demand that the universalization of one's maxims of action be neither logically impossible nor self-defeating of one's purposes in acting, it is not at all clear what the force of the categorical imperative is in examples Kant himself gives of its use. He tells us that it would be contrary to the categorical imperative for us

1. not to help individuals who are in need of help, whenever we find it inconvenient.
2. not to develop our special talents.
3. to commit suicide if life's prospects include more pain than pleasure.

What are we to say to such examples?

According to a common interpretation, the categorical imperative should be taken to prohibit not only those maxims which it is logically impossible to universalize, but also those which one *would not choose* to have universalized after one had *impartially* thought through what such a universalization would involve. According to this view, even though there is no inconsistency involved in everyone acting under the maxim "Don't help others who need help when you find it inconvenient," it would be wrong for us to act under this maxim if we would be unwilling to live in a world where this maxim was universally followed. What Kant is claiming, these interpreters suggest, is that since we all realize that we may one day desire help from others, none of us would want to live in such a world. Consequently, Kant concludes that it would be wrong for us not to help those in need. But, one may protest, it is possible that a person sure of his own material and psychological resources may have no fear at all of ever needing help from anyone else. It has been suggested that Kant would insist at this point that an individual must be willing to accept a situation where everyone follows the same principles of behavior even if he did not know what he would stand to gain or lose in such a situation. He must be willing to empathize with all who stand to be affected by the universalization of his act and be willing to accept the desirability of that universalization without taking advantage of his own specific psychological attributes and specific social role. Would a person, for example, be willing to live in a society where no one helped those in need, even if, by some magic, a cosmic roulette wheel were to randomly spin and he were to find himself occupying someone else's body and someone else's social role?

Even on this fanciful assumption, however, it seems that some people might very well be willing to live in a world where everyone follows the principle "Look out for yourself, give no help to others and expect none in return." A rugged and selfish individualist might very well be willing to take his chance on the spin of the wheel, hoping that he would fare well but willing to accept the consequences if he should not. Similarly, a successful thief, desiring to live in a more adventurous type of world, might be quite willing to accept the universalization of self-seeking theft even if he were not at all assured that he would possess the requisite abilities to fare well in such a world. It would seem that if Kant meant to assert that an act is right as long as one is merely psychologically capable of willing the universalization of one's act, Kant's standard would become a subjective one which would make the rightness of an action a function of one's desires. Yet this is clearly what Kant did not want to do. As Kant most likely saw it, the selfish individualist, the self-seeking thief, the person who refuses to cultivate his special talents, and a person contemplating suicide could not will that everyone else act as they are acting *if they were fully rational.* But it is not at all clear how Kant can justify the "irrationality" of those whose views of "the good life" are quite different from his own.

Although Kant claimed that utilitarian considerations should have no bearing on the determination of one's moral obligations, it has been suggested by some philosophers that, in deciding which maxims a "rational" person would be willing to see universalized, the standard Kant appears to use in some of his examples concerns itself with the *desirability of the consequences of the universalization of that maxim.* This, as we shall see in the next section, is the position of "rule-utilitarians" who assert that an act is right if and only if it falls under a moral rule whose general observance has the best consequences—that is, the question is not "What will the consequences be if I do this?" but rather "What would the consequences be if everyone were to do it?" Most Kantian scholars, however, would dismiss this interpretation of Kant as quite inconsistent with his intention. One may, however, grant this and nevertheless suggest that some of Kant's own examples of maxims that cannot ("rationally") be universalized can be made intelligible only by the assumption of a rule-utilitarian point of view. Such a contention would generate heated debate among philosophers and need not concern us here.

Aside from the unresolved question of the force of the word "can" in Kant's first formulation of the categorical imperative, there are other very serious problems involved in interpreting the meaning of the categorical imperative. Kant, at least in some of his writings, made it quite clear that he believed that the categorical imperative would lead one to embrace all sorts or exceptionless moral rules—such as, "never break promises and never lie, regardless of the circumstances." For example, in an article entitled "On the Supposed Right To Lie from Benevolent Motives," Kant claims that it would always be wrong for an individual to lie since, if everyone did so, the very purpose of communication would be defeated. With all due respect to Kant, his argument here seems absurd. Certainly, common sense would reply that there are all sorts of lies. Although one can reject with Kant the universalization of the maxim "Lie whenever it suits your purpose," why cannot one accept more specific maxims such as "Lie whenever it is necessary to save an innocent human life"? The same can be said for promises. Although one would not will the universalization of the maxim "Break your promises whenever it suits your purpose," there seems to be no problem in willing the universalization of more specific maxims which allow the breaking of promises in particular circumstances. Kant ignored the fact that acts do not come with ready labels. The very same act can, for example, be described as a lie which suits one's purpose, an unselfish lie, or a lie which is necessary to save an innocent human life. Each of these different descriptions generates a different maxim. Following Kant, one will not want to universalize the first maxim, but practically all of us will want to universalize the last. Although Kant categorizes his actions very broadly, he fails to give any justification for rejecting a narrower categorization. A principle for deciding upon the proper categorization of an act is lacking in Kantian ethics.

As critics of Kant have pointed out, without such a principle a person can always categorize his action so narrowly that his maxim covers only his own specific case. For example, even if we assume that no rational person would want to live in a world where everyone lied whenever they wanted to, it might very well be quite rational for Jones to want to live in a world where "all five-foot-eleven inch Los Angeles stockbrokers with two-inch scars over their right temples lie whenever they want to," knowing he is most likely to be the only one that would fit such a description. No doubt, such a flagrantly narrow maxim would be dismissed as morally absurd.[6] But without some principle for determin-

---

[6] Certainly, we would not believe that our stockbroker actually had such a maxim in mind when he acted. It is important to realize that the Kantian view that the rightness of an action is to be judged by the maxim under which one acts makes it impossible to judge the rightness of an act apart from an agent's

ing how to properly categorize one's act, an individual can always build enough specific details into his maxim of action that he has no compunction at all in willing its universalization. Certainly, we are all aware of the common human tendency to qualify and interpret rules in such a way that they seem to be capable of justifying almost anything.

Although, no doubt, rules can at times be qualified and interpreted in such a manner as to render them virtually useless as guides to action, there is no way to escape the need for qualifying and interpreting such rules as "never lie," "never break promises," and "never steal" that Kant takes to be absolute. Without a principle for qualifying such rules, for example, there will be no way to resolve possible conflicts in these duties. For example, what is one to do when one must lie in order to keep a promise? Kant gives us no clue at all as to how conflicts of duty such as this are to be resolved. Similarly, Kant is much too uncritical in his acceptance of such concepts as "lying," "promising," and "stealing."

As we have seen in our discussion of the problem of vagueness in the section on "The Pitfalls of Moral Reasoning," concepts which we employ so readily in everyday life are often quite vague. For example, we saw some of the difficulties involved in pinning down the meaning of the concept of lying. Consider, as well, the concept of stealing. Although this concept might have been unproblematic to Kant, people can disagree as to what should and should not count as an act of stealing. For example, to many socialists, the inheritance of wealth is a type of stealing. Consequently, for such socialists, strict adherence to the command "never steal" should rule out the inheritance of wealth. Kant, no doubt, had no such radical proposal in mind, assuming quite uncritically that stealing is what the common person sees as stealing. Yet, as a Marxist would be quick to point out, the common person often sees things through an ideological structure of beliefs that serves as a rationalization for the self-interest of a particular class of people.

Kant, unfortunately, never came to grips with the legitimacy of the underlying institutions that are unquestioningly assumed by our familiar moral intuitions. Instead, the way Kant tended to see it, a person who acted to destroy these institutions was always acting immorally.

---

perception of what he is doing. In this respect, Kant's first formulation of the categorical imperative is quite unlike the principle of utility which judges the rightness of actions in terms of what actually will (or is likely to) contribute to the greatest good and not in terms of what an agent believes will do so. While a person's mistaken beliefs about the rightness of his actions will not affect the "objective rightness" of his actions for the utilitarian, it will affect the moral judgments we make about his character and the legal judgments we make in deciding whether to punish him for acting on those mistaken beliefs. Consequently, for a utilitarian, there will be an important difference between what actually *is* right ("objective rightness") and what *is thought to be* right ("subjective rightness"). Kant's first formulation of the categorical imperative, however, does not enable us to draw this important distinction. In addition, it neglects the fact that people often act impulsively under no maxim at all. Yet, such actions are ordinarily subject to moral judgment as "right" or "wrong."

For example, Kant would most likely accuse a poor person who steals from the rich as acting immorally since, if everyone were to steal from those who had more than they, the entire institution of private property would be destroyed. Yet this might be exactly what the poor man wants. Just as classical utilitarianism must be rejected as fundamentally incomplete as a moral theory, so too must we reject the categorical imperative as a sufficient standard for determining what one ought to do. There is more to the moral point of view than Kant's theory is willing to grant.

Reflections on Kantian Ethics

Kant's ethical theory has an importance which transcends the difficulties of his formulations of specific ethical principles. It provides us with a conceptual framework for the solution of moral problems, deeply reflected in ordinary moral thinking and especially in the Judaic-Christian religious tradition. For Kant, the central moral concept was not, as it was for Bentham, Mill, and the socialistic thinkers who followed them, the maximization of "human happiness" or "the common good," but rather the "maximization of human freedom."[7] The language of Kantian morality is the deontological one of rights and obligations. Within the Kantian moral framework, our obligation to respect *the rights* of others to be left alone always overrides our obligation to provide positive assistance to those to whom we have no specific obligation. As Kant saw it, while we ought to attempt to contribute to the general happiness, no one can demand *by right* that we do so. On the other hand, people can demand *by right* that they be given the freedom to work out their lives as they see fit. Indeed, as Kant saw it, since man's noblest feature was his capacity to govern himself by principles of reason that he has himself chosen, man's very humanity required that he have a right to noninterference. As Kant saw it, a person's right to noninterference by others can only be forfeited when that individual has himself interfered with the legitimate rights of others. In particular, we cannot violate his right to be left alone on the grounds that we believe that we can make him happier or provide for a greater "common good."

As our discussion of the rehabilitative philosophy that threatens to drastically change or eliminate our present system of criminal punishment will make clear, the twentieth century tendency to see criminals as "sick" and "nonrational" individuals poses a great contemporary threat to the notion of justice. As Kant clearly saw, of all tyrannies, a tyranny exercised for "the good" of its victims may be the most oppressive, for those who have power over us can strip us of our freedom and dignity

---

[7] Actually, the "maximization of freedom" is Kant's central concept under his theory of "justice" (*The Metaphysical Elements of Justice*) but not under his theory of "virtue" (*The Metaphysical Principles of Virtue*). Here the ends of "happiness of others" and "one's own perfection" are the central concepts. See my brief remarks in the annotated bibliography at the end of this section.

as persons with a clear conscience that they are helping us when, in reality, they are doing nothing of the kind. The development of more and more effective and sophisticated techniques of behavioral control testifies to the potential tyranny of a utilitarian commitment to "the common good" which is unlimited by a Kantian concern for *the rights* of individuals and their dignity as persons. As we shall see, as well, in our discussions of the moral issues of abortion, euthanasia, and war, the Kantian way of thinking permeates very influential (especially religious) views of these problems. According to these views, central distinctions must be made between our duties of noninterference and benevolent aid and between the direct intentions of our acts and their likely consequences. As our discussions of these moral issues, as well as the issue of punishment, will indicate, for most of us the moral life is an uneasy balance between the utilitarian and Kantian moral perspectives.

Two Contemporary Theories of Justice in the Kantian Tradition: Rawls and Nozick

The Kantian moral vision has also been quite influential upon professional contemporary philosophers. Two competing theories of justice, the liberal-welfare-state theory of John Rawls[8] and the libertarian theory of Robert Nozick[9] are deeply Kantian in outlook. Fundamental to both theories is an acceptance of the Kantian view of human beings as autonomous rational moral agents and a rejection of the utilitarian view of them as mere pleasure-seekers. Following Kant, both Rawls and Nozick see justice and not utility as the primary moral value. Like Kant, they see justice as the cornerstone of human dignity and self-respect. Yet their theories of justice are very much different.

The central notion in Nozick's theory of justice is that of "entitlement." Like Kant before him, Nozick equates justice with the respecting of people's rights. As he sees it, people's rights are respected only when they are allowed to keep and control that to which they are "entitled." An individual is entitled to those things which he has acquired without resort to force, theft, and fraud, Nozick believes. This is all one can demand *by right*. Although individuals can demand by right that they be left alone to make their own decisions as to how they are to live their

8 Rawl's theory is elaborately developed in this *Theory of Justice* (Cambridge, Mass.: Harvard University Press, 1971), a book which is the product of many years of development in Rawl's thinking about the concept of justice. The first version of Rawl's theory appeared in his essay "Justice as Fairness," published in 1958 in *The Philosophical Review* and reprinted in many anthologies. An altered version of the theory was presented by Rawls in his 1967 essay "Distributive Justice" which appeared for the first time in P. Laslett and W.G. Runciman, eds., *Philosophy, Politics and Society* (third series).

9 Robert Nozick, *Anarchy, State and Utopia* (New York: Basic Books, 1974).

lives, they cannot demand by right that the state provide them with assistance in the pursuits of their ends, Nozick declares, echoing Kant. Such positive interferences by the state are illegitimate impositions upon personal autonomy since the state can help some only by violating the entitlements of others. Given this extreme anti-utilitarian view and concern for human freedom, Nozick argues for a "minimum state" which is limited to the narrow passive functions of protection against force, theft, and fraud, and the enforcement of contracts. Nozick argues first that a minimum state would naturally arise out of an association of human beings "even though no one intended this or tried to bring it about, by a process which need not violate anyone's rights." He then goes on to argue that a more extensive state cannot be justified. In particular, he argues that a state is not justified in redistributing the wealth of its citizens or in paternalistic legislation (which aims at protecting people from themselves). Consequently, such things as the progressive income tax, publicly supported education and welfare, and mandatory seat-belts in automobiles are all unjustified infringements of human liberty for Nozick. If people want such things as education and health or unemployment insurance, they will be free in Nozick's minimal state to voluntarily contract for it themselves. Nozick's extreme libertarianism is shared today by members of the Libertarian Party who are united in their commitment to individual freedom and opposition to the welfare state.

Unlike Nozick, Rawls is quite concerned with human welfare in his theory of justice. Nevertheless, like Nozick, he accepts the basic Kantian view that individual liberty takes precedence over the utilitarian concern with "the common good." As Rawls puts it,

> Each person possesses an inviolability founded on justice that even the welfare of society as a whole cannot override. For this reason justice denies that the loss of freedom for some is made right by a greater good shared by others . . . the rights secured by justice are not subject to political bargaining or to the calculus of social interests.[10]

Like Kant, Rawls attempts to show that the value of justice can be derived from the idea of rationality. As the "social contract" theorists before him, Rawls tries to derive principles of morality from a hypothetical consideration of the moral principles that purely self-interested rational people would unanimously choose to regulate the practices of their society. Realizing that self-interested people, seeking to maximize their own vested interests, would never unanimously agree on any specific principles, Rawls hypothesizes that they are ignorant of their individual mental and physical attributes, tastes, and values, and of the particular place they will occupy in their society. In other words, Rawls imagines rational self-seeking individuals committing themselves to abide by the unanimous decisions arrived at behind such a "veil of ignorance."

[10] Rawls, *A Theory of Justice*, pp. 3–4.

Subject to certain other constraints,[11] Rawls argues that given this veil of ignorance, rational and purely self-interested persons would choose certain principles of justice to rule their lives over utilitarian principles. According to Rawls, the participants would agree that

1. each person is to have an equal right to the most extensive basic liberty compatible with a similar liberty for others.
2. social and economic inequalities are to be arranged so that they are both (*a*) reasonably expected to be to everyone's advantage, and (*b*) attached to positions and offices open to all.[12]

The most widely discussed part of these two principles is 2*a*, according to which inequalities in power, wealth and other resources must not exist except insofar as they work to everyone's advantage. For example, imagine a base-level society where everyone shares equally. Such a society is, however, not too efficient. We can make it more efficient only by rewarding people unequally. Such unequal rewards would be justified according to principle 2*a* only if *every* person fares better in this new unequal society. Similarly, we can justify making this unequal society even more unequal if this works out to everyone's advantage. In his later formulations of his theory, Rawls modifies this principle so that it is not necessary that everyone fare better as long as the worst-off members of the society do. No greater disadvantage, however small, for the worst-off members of society, can justify a greater advantage, however large, for those better off. From this perspective, Rawls views rational people as very cautious people who plan their lives on the basis of the least favorable possibility about how things will turn out.[13]

Rawls's and Nozick's theories of justice, like Kant's before them, are works of intellectual brilliance. But perhaps like Kant, too, they overplay the role of reason in moral judgment and underplay the role of feeling.

---

[11] As Rawls sets it up, a contracting party has no idea as to the probabilities that attach to the various psychological characteristics he may possess and social positions that he may occupy. Second, each party has "a conception of the good such that he cares very little, if anything, for what he might gain above the minimum stipend." Third, he accepts certain outcomes as simply "intolerable." Fourth, he is not so envious of the positions of others that he would be willing to accept a lesser reward to prevent someone else from receiving a greater reward.

[12] Rawls, *A Theory of Justice*, p. 60.

[13] Critics of Rawls have contended that a rational person need not be as aversive to risk as Rawls claims he will be. Perhaps under a "veil of ignorance" a rational person would agree on some minimum floor under which no one can fall—that is, he would insure himself against the worst calamities, but once he is protected against this he might very well be willing to take his chances. While Rawls would admit that his theory of justice will appeal only to people who have particular values and preferences, he tends to write as if he believes that all rational people would share these same values and preferences. This is, however, not the case.

Neither Rawls nor Nozick, nor their predecessor Kant, seems willing to accept the existence of conflicts of basic moral principle, irreconcilable by reason alone. As such, they construct elaborate moral systems that do justice to some of our moral intuitions only at the expense of conflicting ones that most of us are unwilling to abandon. For example, Nozick in his preoccupation with individual freedom and entitlement finds no place for benevolence in his moral system, while Rawls in his preoccupation with freedom and equality finds no place for merit or entitlement in his system. Both systems are inadequate to the complexity of the moral life and for that reason do not provide a pattern for living to which most of us would be willing to fully commit ourselves. Indeed, perhaps the truth for most of us is that the principles we choose to live by cannot be reconciled into a single coherent moral system.

DISCUSSION QUESTIONS

1. Consider the following:

Kantian: Man's greatest moral virture is his capacity to be rational and to be self-governing. It is this capacity which enables him to adopt moral principles and to live by them, regardless of the contingencies of his feelings.

Utilitarian: The most important moral virtue is the capacity to feel sympathy for one's fellow creatures. Conscientiousness itself is unimportant. What is important is that one be conscientious about the right things and this requires that one be motivated by feelings of benevolence.

What do you think?

2. What do you think is the most plausible meaning that can be attributed to the Golden Rule?

3. Defend either *A's* or *B's* position.

A: I know it would be right for me to lie in these circumstances, but I don't know if it would be right for anyone else in the same circumstances.

B: What you say makes no sense. If you really thought that *all* the relevant circumstances were the same, you would have to make the same moral judgments; otherwise, you're simply misusing moral language. What is right for one person cannot be wrong for someone else unless there is some relevant difference in their circumstances. The very meaning of moral language requires this.

4. Kant tells us that we should never treat individuals as "mere means." Are soldiers who are drafted into the army treated as "mere means"? Are criminals who are punished? Explain.

5. Critically consider the following claim:

Kant's picture of human beings as autonomous rational moral agents unfortunately does not fit most human beings who tend to be quite irrational. Although Kant says that human beings should be "respected as persons," most human beings should be treated as children.

6. Argue as forcefully as you can either for or against the claim "Let justice be done though the heavens fall" (in less poetic language: "When justice and utility conflict, as they may, always choose justice over utility").

7. Consider the following criticism of Kantian morality: The central idea of Kantian morality is the importance of treating people as persons worthy of respect, as "free beings" rather than as "things" to be manipulated for some end they do not voluntarily choose, even if that end be their own happiness. As Kant saw it, moral rights can only be rightfully conferred upon those who are worthy of respect—that is, only upon rational creatures. I fully disagree. Influenced by Christian philosophy, Kant places too much emphasis on the rationality that supposedly separates human beings from animals, while he wrongfully neglects their similar capacity *to feel* pleasure and pain. Compare, for example, the following quotations from Bentham and Kant:

> The day *may* come when the rest of the animal creation may acquire those rights which never could have been withholden from them but by the hand of tyranny. The French have already discovered that the blackness of the skin is no reason why a human being should be abandoned without redress to the caprice of a tormentor. It may come one day to be recognized that the number of the legs, the villosity of the skin, or the termination of the *os sacrum*, are reasons equally insufficient for abandoning a sensitive being to the same fate. What else is it that should trace the insuperable line? Is it the faculty of reason, or perhaps the faculty of discourse? But a full-grown horse or dog is beyond comparison a more rational, as well as a more conversable animal, than an infant of a day, or a week, or even a month old. But suppose the case were otherwise, what would it avail? The question is not, Can they *reason*? nor, Can they talk? but, Can they *suffer*?[14]

> But so far as animals are concerned, we have no direct duties. Animals . . . are there merely as a means to an end. That end is man. . . . Our duties towards animals are merely indirect duties towards humanity. Animal nature has analogies to human nature, and by doing our duties to animals, . . . we indirectly do our duty towards humanity. Thus, if a dog has served his master long and faithfully, his service, on the analogy of human service, deserves reward, and when the dog has grown too old to serve, his master ought to keep him until he dies. Such action helps to support us in our duties toward human beings. . . . If a man shoots his dog because the animal is no longer capable of service, he does not

---

14 Jeremy Bentham, *The Principles of Morals and Legislation* (New York, Hafner Press, 1948), p. 311, footnote 1.

fail in his duty to the dog, for the dog cannot judge, but his act is inhuman and damages in himself that humanity which it is his duty to show toward mankind. If he is not to stifle his human feelings, he must practice kindness toward animals, for he who is cruel to animals becomes hard also in his dealings with men.[15]

I must say that my sympathies lie with Bentham and not with Kant. Can we really say as Kant does, that we do not have a duty to a dog and that decent behavior to a dog is merely practice for decent behavior toward human beings? Dogs may not be able to "judge," but neither are many human beings (consider children and the mentally retarded), but certainly we have duties to them. No, Bentham was right. The important moral question is not "Is that creature rational?" but rather, "Can it feel?" What do you think?

8. Consider the following claim:

> When Rawls speaks of "our intuitive conviction of the primacy of justice," he is speaking for himself and not for the majority of human beings. For them, I am sure, it is security and not justice which is the most important virtue of social systems.

What do you think?

FURTHER READINGS

Kant's philosophical writings are exceedingly difficult and obscure. Given the conflicting strands in Kant's ethical writings, any attempt to provide a single clear and coherent account of "Kantian morality" is bound to be incomplete. This is certainly the case with all elementary expositions of Kantian ethics, including my own. The more comprehensive expositions of Kant, on the other hand, are usually written for the philosophical scholar, and beginning students of philosophy will have a difficult time with them. In reading Kant's own works (translated from the German), it is very helpful to read the introductions by the editors.

Kant's Main Writings on Ethics

Kant's most abstract, comprehensive, and difficult ethical writing is the *Foundations* (or *Groundwork* or *Fundamental Principles,* depending on the translation) *of the Metaphysics of Morals* (1785). There are several translations of this classic work. The one I recommend is by the Kantian scholar H.J. Paton which is preceded by Paton's own section-by-section short summary and analysis of the work—Paton, H.J., trans.,

---

15 Immanuel Kant, "Duties Toward Animals and Spirits," in *Lectures on Ethics* (New York: Harper & Row, Pub., 1963), pp. 239–40.

Groundwork of the Metaphysics of Morals. New York: Harper & Row Pubs., Inc., 1964. Another widely used translation is by the Kantian scholar Lewis White Beck—*Foundations of the Metaphysics of Morals.* Indianapolis, Bobbs-Merrill, 1959. This same translation is also included in Robert Paul Wolff's *Foundations of the Metaphysics of Morals: Text and Critical Essays.* Indianapolis: Bobbs-Merrill, 1969. The nine critical essays included with Kant's work, with the exception of the article, "The Categorical Imperative," by Jonathan Harrison, are, in my opinion, too difficult for beginning students.

In *The Metaphysics of Morals,* Kant applies the categorical imperative to derive more specific moral directives. Its two parts have been translated and printed separately, the first as *The Metaphysical Elements of Justice,* and the second as *The Metaphysical Principles of Virtue.* In *The Metaphysical Elements of Justice,* Kant is concerned with the notions of legality and rights and the general question of the state's moral right to use coercion to limit the freedom of individuals. The picture I paint in the preceding chapter of "Kantian morality" comes from this work. (John Ladd, trans., *The Metaphysical Elements of Justice.* Indianapolis, Bobbs-Merrill, 1965.) While Kant is concerned with the question of external legal compulsion in *The Metaphysical Elements of Justice,* in *The Metaphysical Principles of Virtue* he turns his attention to those moral virtues and vices that he claims should be enforced from within by one's sense of duty. Kant considers various "duties to oneself" as well as "duties to others." (James Ellington, trans., *The Metaphysical Principles of Virtue.* Indianapolis: Bobbs-Merrill, 1964. The same work is translated by Mary Gregor as *The Doctrine of Virtue.* New York: Harper & Row Pubs., 1964.) Kant's application of his general ethical theory is also found in his *Lectures on Ethics* which consists of the lecture notes of three of his students. This work, along with *The Metaphysics of Morals,* helps put flesh on the bare bones of Kant's theoretical discussion of ethics in the *Foundations of the Metaphysics of Morals.* (Infield, Louis, trans., *Lectures on Ethics.* New York: Harper & Row Pubs., 1963.)

Commentaries on Kant

MURPHY, JEFFRIE, *Kant: The Philosophy of Right.* London: Macmillan, 1970. A good short account of Kant's underlying ethical theory in the *Foundations of the Metaphysics of Morals* and its application to *The Metaphysical Elements of Justice* which would prove quite helpful to beginning students.

PATON, H.J., *The Categorical Imperative.* New York: Harper & Row Pubs., 1967. This detailed analysis and commentary on the *Foundations of the Metaphysics of Morals* is for the philosophically sophisticated.

WOLFF, ROBERT PAUL, *The Autonomy of Reason.* Harper & Row Pubs., 1973. A detailed analysis and commentary on the *Foundations of the Metaphysics of Morals* for the more philosophically sophisticated.

Works by Contemporary Philosophers
Especially Relevant to Kant

BAIER, KURT, *The Moral Point of View*, chapter 8. Ithaca, N.Y.: Cornell University Press, 1958. Following Kant, Baier sees the moral point of view as one of acting from rational principles. As Baier sees it, "universalization" is a *logical* requirement of "the moral point of view." Baier specifies certain conditions which he sees as implicit requirements of "universalization." For example, he says that moral rules must be "universally teachable" and cannot be "self-frustrating" or "self-defeating."

GLICKMAN, JACK, ed., *Moral Philosophy: An Introduction*. New York: St. Martin's Press, 1976. Contains a good selection of critical articles by influential contemporary philosophers on different aspects of Kantian ethics as well as Kant's own *Fundamental Principles of the Metaphysics of Morals*.

HARE, R.M., "Universalizability," *Proceedings of the Aristotelian Society*, 55 (1954), pp. 295–313. A defense of the thesis that moral judgments must *by definition* be "universalizable." Hare incorporates his view that universalizability is a necessary condition of the moral point of view with the subjectivistic view that one must choose one's moral principles and not discover them, in his influential book *The Language of Morals*, London: Oxford University Press, 1952. In this respect, Hare's point of view is quite different from that of Baier.

NOZICK, ROBERT, *Anarchy, State and Utopia*. New York: Basic Books, 1974.

RAWLS, JOHN, *A Theory of Justice*. Cambridge, Mass.: Harvard University Press, 1970.

9. RULE UTILITARIANISM

"Rule Utilitarianism" is not the name of any single theory of moral obligation but refers to a cluster of different theories developed and supported by many twentieth century philosophers who have found themselves dissatisfied with both the potential injustice of traditional utilitarianism and the Kantian attempt to detach morality from a consideration of consequences and the actual desires of human beings. Although utilitarian in its ultimate concern with beneficial consequences, rule utilitarianism incorporates this concern with a Kantian requirement either that one's actions should be capable of universalization or that they should be guided by specific moral rules and not by a direct appeal to the principle of utility. The simplest version of this general cluster of theories employs the Kantian notion of universalization. As this theory sees it, in determining how one is to act, the relevant moral question is not "what would the likely consequences of *this act* be," but rather "what would the likely consequences be if *everyone* were to do the same"— that is, according to this view, the morality of an individual act is to be judged by the utility of the general performance of acts relevantly similar to the given act. For convenience, let us label this view of moral obligation "general-rule-utilitarianism."

While general-rule-utilitarianism makes the rightness of a given action depend on the consequences of its universalization (philosophers call this "utilitarian generalization") and not on its correspondence to independently specifiable and binding moral rules, this is not the case with other rule-utilitarian theories. These theories draw a fundamental distinction between the proper procedures to be employed in justifying specific actions on the one hand and moral rules on the other. As these theories see it, when determining how one ought to act, one should not appeal directly to the principle of utility, focusing on whether a specific action is likely to have the best consequences. Instead, one should determine what one ought to do on the basis of specific moral rules which are themselves justified in terms of their utility. Some of these theories claim that actions should be justified in terms of the actual and recognized rules of a given society, while others claim that actions should be justified in terms of moral rules which would be ideal for a given society, from a utilitarian point of view. For convenience, let us call the former class of theories of moral obligation "actual-rule-utilitarianism"[1] and the latter class "ideal-rule-utilitarianism," and let us call the traditional utilitarian theory, which claims that the rightness or wrongness of an action should be judged by the consequences of the act itself, "act-utilitarianism."[2]

The merits of the various theories of rule-utilitarianism over act-utilitarianism have been a subject of controversy among contemporary philosophers. While some of the most influential of contemporary philosophers have, at one time or another, defended some rule-utilitarian theory, such theories have also been subjected to sharp criticism. Indeed, some philosophers have argued that some versions of rule-utiliarianism reduce to act-utilitarianism (that is, their moral implications are the same),

---

[1] There are different forms of "actual-rule-utilitarianism." According to some forms, a person has an obligation to abide by the moral code of his society only if it is, in some loose sense, "reasonable" from a utilitarian point of view—even if it is less than "ideal" from that point of view. More commonly, however, "actual-rule-utilitarianism" is used to refer to that theory of moral obligation that asserts that a person has no moral obligations apart from the obligations imposed on him by the moral code of his society. Consequently, this theory is quite anti-utilitarian in its conception of an individual's moral obligations. It is utilitarian, however, in asserting that it is utility that justifies decisions as to whether a moral code is itself justifiable or ought to be changed. In this section, "actual-rule-utilitarianism" shall be used to refer to the second and not the first theory.

[2] The distinction between act and rule utilitarianism is a purely twentieth century one which was never explicitly made by Bentham and Mill. Given Bentham and Mill's concern with amending the laws of England into greater conformity with the principle of utility, they naturally often focused on justifying rules of conduct rather than specific acts and therefore could be seen as anticipating the rule utilitarian point of view. Indeed, some philosophers have suggested that Mill's utilitarianism, unlike that of his predecessor, Bentham, is more attuned to the rule than act utilitarian point of view.

and that those theories that are different from act-utilitarianism involve a type of valueless "rule-worship." Furthermore, if, as actual- and ideal-rule-utilitarians claim, the principle of utility is the sole standard to be used in justifying moral rules, then these rules can allow unjust social practices that most of us would consider clearly wrong. As these critics see it, utilitarianism, in any of its forms, must be supplemented by independent and possibly conflicting principles of justice. It is my belief that these criticisms of rule-utilitarianism are justified. Let us briefly see why, turning our attention first to general-rule-utilitarianism and then to actual- and ideal-rule-utilitarianism.

The difficulty in distinguishing general-rule-utilitarianism from act-utilitarianism resides in the problem, mentioned in our discussion of Kantian ethics, of deciding upon the proper categorization of an act. To illustrate this problem, let us turn to the case of "the mad bomber" in our list of moral dilemmas. If we were to reason as act-utilitarians in deciding whether the mad bomber should be tortured, we would focus upon the likely consequences of this course of action as opposed to that of the various alternatives open to us which, in this case, appears to be simply to do nothing. Certainly, immediate utility would be maximized by torturing the mad bomber as a necessary means for saving the lives of many innocent people. Of course, the perceptive act-utilitarian will also have to focus upon the more remote consequences of this act—in particular, the effect torturing the bomber will have upon general respect for law and upon those law enforcement officials who would have clearly broken the law by torturing the bomber. Nevertheless, the monumental undesirable consequences of doing nothing and allowing the bombs to explode would seem to justify the act of torturing the mad bomber from a purely act-utilitarian point of view. Indeed, the act-utilitarian justification for this course of action would be greatly strengthened if it could be done in secret (perhaps by killing the bomber and falsely claiming that he died in an escape attempt after voluntarily divulging the information).

Now, a general-rule-utilitarian will most likely claim that his standard does not lead to the same conclusion, morally repugnant to many of us. According to our general-rule-utilitarian, we must weigh the consequences, not of the specific act of torture against the refusal to so act in this case, but rather against the consequences of everyone taking the law into their own hands as a way of averting violence. Certainly, our general-rule-utilitarian will claim, the consequences of this becoming a general practice would be disastrous. Consequently, it is wrong for us to so act, even if in this particular situation such an act would have the best consequences. Since it would be wrong for everyone to act in such a manner, it is wrong for anyone to do so.

The reasoning here is, however, unclear. According to our general-rule-utilitarian we must focus upon the consequences of *everyone* doing the *same*. But who is to count as "everyone"? All those who find themselves in a situation where breaking the law might have desirable consequences? All law enforcement officials who are inclined to break the law for altruistic reasons and risk undesirable consequences to themselves when this seems the only way to avoid great violence? Similarly, what is to count as a situation which is relevantly similar to the given situation? One where *violence* is threatened and *can be averted* by the use of *torture?* One where *mass murder* is threatened and *can be averted only* by *torturing the responsible party?* One where *mass murder* is threatened and *can be averted only by torturing the responsible party* in a situation where one can be reasonably assured that this action can be kept *secret?* It would appear that if we incorporate every relevant utilitarian consideration into our description of the act in question it would make no difference if we ask "What would happen if everyone did the same?" instead of "What would happen if this act were performed?" In our example, if one could be reasonably assured that the torture of the bomber could be kept secret and consequently not act as a precedent to be followed in less clear cases or lead to a more diffuse lessening of general respect for law, it would appear that a general-rule-utilitarian should incorporate this relevant utilitarian characteristic into his description of the act in question and conclude that the consequences of the general performance of *such* acts would have the best consequences.

Similarly, it would be absurd for a general-rule-utilitarian to abide by a "keep off the grass" sign that is posted to preserve a lawn *already* ruined by trampling and to justify his action by claiming that the consequences of general disregard for such signs would be undesirable. Certainly, a general-rule-utilitarian should narrow his focus to include all relevant utilitarian circumstances surrounding his situation and as such should focus upon the consequences of everyone disregarding "keep off the grass" signs that *do not serve the purpose for which they were intended.* But once all relevant utilitarian factors are incorporated into one's description of one's act, general-rule-utilitarianism will justify whatever traditional act-utilitarianism can justify and consequently is equally subject to the charge of being potentially unjust.

For example, consider a group of people engaged in some cooperative enterprise—let us say, preparing a cooperative vegetable garden, requiring the participation of most, but not all, of those who will benefit from this enterprise. Practically everyone is willing to do his share *out of a sense of justice,* but one general-rule-utilitarian is not. Realizing that his effort is not especially needed and that no one will even realize that he did not participate in the work, he decides to spend his time in a more personally enjoyable manner. Although he is acting *unfairly,* accepting the benefits of the vegetable garden without assuming the burden that others have assumed, he need not care if *everyone* who shares his reasoning does likewise if he knows that most people do not think that way and that the necessary work will be done. Supporters of the general-rule-utilitarian point of view will object that our reluctant gardener should

not focus on the consequences of everyone who thinks like him not working on the garden, but rather on the consequences of absolutely everyone connected with the garden not working; but no utilitarian reason
can be given for a rejection of the narrower categorization. It is our
sense of justice, and not utility, that so strongly inclines us to reject it.

Let us turn our attention now to actual-rule-utilitarianism. Underlying this view is the assumption that it is for the greatest good for individuals to act always on the basis of specific moral rules, less general
in scope than the principle of utility itself. If individuals always felt
justified in abandoning specific moral rules whenever it was believed that
the consequences would be maximized by so doing, confusion, it is
claimed, would be the natural result. The predictability and guidance
that specific rules of conduct provide would be lost if the principle of
utility itself could be directly applied to the justification of specific actions. The moral life requires individuals to subject themselves to certain
established ways of doing things—that is, to practices—that are defined
by rules and require abdication of full liberty to act on utilitarian
grounds. To accept a practice is to commit oneself to follow the rules that
define it. For example, to accept the practice of promising, one must
abdicate the right to decide on particular occasions whether it would be
best on the whole to keep the promise. To refuse to do so is to refuse to
participate in the practice of promise-keeping. Similarly, to accept the
practice of punishment that exists in this country is to accept a system
for making and applying criminal laws defined by certain rules. Under
these rules, legislators in deciding upon the justification of criminal laws
are permitted to appeal to general utilitarian considerations which are
precluded from the judge who is bound to abide by general rules of law
which serve to guide and limit his discretion to act as he thinks best
in a given situation (such as, by punishing a defendant more than the
law allows by appeal to its deterrent utility in a specific situation).

Once one distinguishes between practices and acts falling within a
practice, the actual-rule-utilitarian claims, it can be seen that utilitarian
justifications should be reserved for decisions relating to the moral desirability of certain practices but, once a practice is instituted, they do
not properly belong to questions of what one should do within that
practice. Such questions are answered by reference to the rules defining
the practice and not to the principle of utility itself. This view of the
logically indispensable place of rules within the moral life stands in contrast to traditional act-utilitarianism. As you may recall, for traditional
utilitarians such as Bentham, specific moral rules of conduct were not
logically indispensable to the moral life, but rather were needed as practical guides for conduct, necessitated only by the brute facts of man's
finite knowledge of the consequences of his actions and of his tendency
toward partiality and rationalization. If man were a god, endowed by
perfect omniscience and concern for others, such rules could be discarded
in favor of the principle of utility. Given man's limitations, however,
specific moral rules are necessary as "rules of thumb" that experience

has shown us usually maximize utility. Nevertheless, one ought to break any such rule in a given situation whenever it is clear that to do so will have greater utility in the long run than will abiding by it. As the foremost act-utilitarian of our day, J.J.C. Smart puts it,

> Suppose that there is a rule R and that in 99 percent of cases the best possible results are obtained by acting in accordance with R. Then clearly R is a useful rule of thumb; if we have not time or are not impartial enough to assess the consequences of an action it is an extremely good bet that the thing to do is to act in accordance with R. But is it not monstrous to suppose that if we have worked out the consequences and if we have perfect faith in the impartiality of our calculations, and if we know that in this instance to break R will produce better results than to keep it, we should nevertheless obey the rule? Is it not to erect R into a sort of idol if we keep it when breaking it will prevent, say, some avoidable misery? Is not this a form of superstitious rule-worship (easily explicable psychologically) and not the rational thought of a philosopher.[3]

Certainly, the actual-rule-utilitarian who would deny the justification of breaking moral rules in the cases Smart describes seems to be in a very unstable position. If specific moral rules are, as he claims, means to the end of utility, why should they not be put aside when they fail that end? If utility can justify a rule, why not an act? As Smart suggests, the rule utilitarian seems committed to a type of rule-worship that the principle of utility should disallow. It is one thing to point out the need for the stability and guidance provided by moral rules and the practices they define; it is something else to say that the rules defining a practice, however good they may be in general, should never be violated regardless of the consequences.

For example, if the law enforcement officials in our mad bomber case decide to torture the bomber, they will be violating the rules defining the practice of punishment in this country. And, even if we assume that this practice can be justified on a purely utilitarian basis, it certainly does not appear unreasonable for these law enforcement officials to consider their moral obligation to humanity as a whole to be of such overriding moment in this situation as to outweigh their obligations as defined by a practice to which they may have a deep commitment. Although breaking these obligations often would be logically incompatible with such a commitment, breaking them once or very infrequently would not. The commitment to any practice and to the roles defined by it should never be absolute and blind us to our foremost obligation to humanity as a whole, an act-utilitarian would contend, and I must agree.

Indeed, actual-rule-ultilitarianism neglects the fact that our responsibilities, as defined by the different roles we occupy under different practices, can often conflict and that the rules that are supposed to ab-

---

[3] J.J.C. Smart, "Extreme and Restricted Utilitarianism," *The Philosophical Quarterly,* 6 (1956), p. 348.

solutely guide the moral life will inevitably be incomplete and lead to conflicts. In such cases, the actual-rule-utilitarian would have to appeal directly to the principle of utility to determine what one ought to do. This may happen much more than he foresees.

Actual-rule-utilitarianism, like so many theories of normative ethics, captures something important about the moral life, but then goes on to overemphasize its importance. What this theory captures is our feeling that we usually have a moral obligation to abide by the rules and practices that actually exist in our society, even if they are less than ideal. Although irrational social conditioning no doubt plays a part, many of us recognize that it is usually *unfair* for one to accept the benefits that the rule-governed behavior of others makes possible while refusing, oneself, to submit to these same rules. As Kant before us, we are sensitive to the special *injustice* that such behavior usually involves. Nevertheless, while it is reasonable to claim that we have some obligation to abide by the moral code of our society, it is quite unreasonable to claim, as actual-rule-utilitarians do, that one cannot speak of one's moral obligations apart from the moral code of one's society. Clearly, most of us believe, as indeed we should, that acts can be judged right or wrong apart from the prevalent moral standards of our society. If this were not the case, we would have had no moral right to try Nazis in Nuremberg for "crimes against humanity," for they, after all, just went along with the moral code of their society. Clearly, we believe that the Nazis who "went along" acted "wrongly," while those who refused to do so, acted "rightly," regardless of what their society said. There is more to the moral life than actual-rule-utilitarianism is willing to allow. Recognizing this, many philosophers have turned to the ideal-rule-utilitarian point of view.

While there are different types of rule-utilitarian theories which relate the rightness of actions to "possible" as opposed to "actual" moral rules, the term ideal-rule-utilitarianism is usually reserved for the view that "an act is right in a given society if and only if it conforms to a moral code whose general acceptance in that society would maximize utility." The great virtue of this theory is that it allows us to judge the rightness or wrongness of actions independently of the moral standards that actually exist in a given society. On the other hand, it achieves this objective, I would charge, at the cost of providing an alleged standard for judging the rightness of actions that is totally impractical and serves to distort the true nature of moral choice. According to this theory, a morally perplexed person is not supposed to ask "will my act have the best consequences" or "does the moral code of my society allow me to do this," but rather "what would the moral code of my society allow me to do in this situation if it were that code, among all possible moral codes, which would maximize utility in this society." It is difficult enough to know in many cases what the first two standards prescribe; the third, however, seems designed only for an omniscient god.

As those familiar with the law well know, legal theorists often disagree over which legal rules would exist in ideal utilitarian legal codes.

Certainly, at any rate, such questions, if they are to be at all useful, must take place within the context of proposals for specific changes within an on-going complex legal system. According to the ideal-rule-utilitarian, however, moral questions are not to be related to a specific functioning legal system or to an existent moral code but to an "ideal moral code" that has never existed. In addition, underlying the ideal-rule-utilitarian view is the myth that in principle, if not in practice, there is an objective way to determine which moral code would be ideal for a given society. Utilitarians may speak as if all the various elements of "the good life" can somehow be reduced to a single scale and weighed objectively against each other, but, as I have suggested before, this may be an illusion. If this is so, the utilitarian quest, in whatever form, for the "maximization of the good" is a quest that can lead us in different directions.[4] Given the apparent impossibility of objectively measuring the "utility" of things, one should be suspicious of the ideal-rule-utilitarian's claim that "an ideal moral code would allow (prohibit) . . ." While such claims are easy to make, it is quite another matter to justify them. It is my belief that such claims often serve as convenient rationalizations for moral beliefs whose sources lie elsewhere. The true motives for defending a moral position of even the most rational of philosophers can often be hidden behind a self-deceiving and ultimately indefensible facade of rationality; it is just that the rational facades of philosophers are more abstractly and intricately woven.

Assuming, however, that I am wrong and that we can attach some definite meaning to the notion of "ideal moral code" and can agree on what such a code would prescribe in concrete situations, why ought we to follow this ideal moral code when we know that others will not and consequently that the good that general compliance would bring cannot be achieved? Using our "keep off the grass" sign as an example, and assuming that it would be best if everyone (or most people) refrained from walking on the grass, is it wrong for one not to abide by the sign when practically no one else does and one's action will have absolutely no effect upon the grass? Similarly, and of more moment, one would certainly assume that it would be best for nations to accept a rule which foreswears the use of nuclear weapons. But ought a nation to do so when it knows, or is reasonably assured, that if it does so other nations will not follow suit? The ideal-rule-utilitarian principle to always act in accord with those rules, general conformity to which would maximize utility, would seem to have a place only in a world where one could rely upon others to do similarly; yet this is a description of an ideal world

---

4 Notice that even if there were an objective way to measure and compare the utility of different moral codes, it is still possible that two or more different moral codes might have the same maximum utility for a given society and consequently that there would be more than one ideal moral code for that society.

sadly different from the world in which we find ourselves and in which we must make our moral decisions.

Some critics of ideal-rule-utilitarianism have suggested that it, no less than general-rule-utilitarianism, reduces to act-utilitarianism. As they see it, one of the rules of an ideal moral code would be always to do what will maximize utility, and another rule would be to appeal directly to the principle of utility when the rules of the ideal moral code conflict. Clearly, if both these rules are accepted, the ideal moral code collapses into the act-utilitarian principle. Defenders of ideal-rule-utilitarianism have replied that no ideal moral code would have a rule allowing people to appeal directly to the principle of utility in deciding what act is right. Life, they have claimed, would be chaotic if such a rule were generally accepted and acted on by members of a given society. Such a claim deserves careful attention. First of all, it is interesting to note that the influential American Law Institute does indeed accept the principle of utility itself as a rule which supersedes all other rules in its (1958) Model Penal Code. According to the A.L.I.,

> Conduct which the actor believes to be necessary to avoid an evil to himself or to another is justifiable, provided that the evil sought to be avoided by such conduct is greater than that sought to be prevented by the law defining the offense charged. . . .[5]

Although the A.L.I. considered this rule to provide "a general justification for conduct that otherwise would constitute an offense," it obviously did not think that such a rule would lead to chaos. In the real world, the mere existence of a generally accepted moral or legal rule does not mean that people will always or usually act on such a rule whenever they think that they are justified in doing so. In the case at issue, the A.L.I. expected that in unclear cases those who violate established rules on the grounds that utility demands such action would have the burden of defending their moral judgment in court. This itself is a powerful deterrent to acting lightly in such cases.

It is very important, it seems to me, that we draw a distinction between those moral rules that are incorporated in legal systems which function as constraints on human behavior and those rules that a person should appeal to in deciding how he morally ought to act in a given situation. Any rational person, of whatever ethical persuasion, would want the law to encourage people to follow specific rules and not to directly appeal to the principle of utility in most situations of moral choice. Similarly, any rational person would want a law that is effective in motivating people to comply with its directives. In addition, any rational person would want people to be morally trained to have respect for

---

[5] Sanford H. Kadish and Monrad G. Paulsen, eds., *Criminal Law and Its Processes: Cases and Materials*, 3rd ed. (Boston: Little, Brown, 1975), p. 547. There are some minor qualifications the A.L.I. places on this rule, but they do not affect the point I am making.

specific moral rules (such as, "keep your promises") and to feel guilty when these rules are broken. In the moral education of children, it must be specific rules and not their exceptions or abstract ones like the principle of utility that must be first impressed upon the developing moral conscience. If moral education succeeds, people will be naturally hesitant to appeal directly to the principle of utility instead of to the specific moral prohibitions which were so deeply engrained into them by their early moral training. It is because of this early moral training that people naturally feel guilty when they lie or break promises, but not when they violate the principle of utility.

But the question still arises: Is it right for a person to break a moral or legal rule when he is reasonably assured that this would have the best consequences? Let us take the example of "the deathbed promise" on our list of moral dilemmas. One may safely assume that no ideal moral code would allow for this.[6] Should the survivor break the promise? The act-utilitarian will say that he should and his reasoning is clear. Since my friend is dead, his son would waste the money, and no one knows about the promise, etc., it follows that more good would come from my giving the money to charity. Since in this case the rule about keeping promises does not serve the utilitarian purpose which provides its justification, the rule should be broken, he will say. The ideal-rule-utilitarian will advocate abiding by the rule. But what justification can he give for his position. To say simply "the rules don't allow it" subjects him to Smart's charge that he is a "rule worshiper," who follows rules as an end in itself. He can't say "it would be unfair (or dishonest)," for as a utilitarian, questions of justice (or honesty) that are not based on utilitarian considerations are not supposed to have any affect upon his rational moral decisions. So what can he say?

The most fundamental charge that can be made against ideal-rule-utilitarianism is that it fails in its underlying objective to avoid the charge leveled against traditional act-utilitarianism—that it is an incomplete moral theory which neglects necessary and *independent* moral considerations, such as that of distributive justice. There is absolutely no guarantee that a single-minded pursuit of utility will not lead an ideal-rule-utilitarian to embrace moral rules which go against one's sense of justice. For example, our criminal justice system might very well be made more efficient, from a solely utilitarian standpoint, if harsher punishments, now considered inhumane, were instituted, if less "due process of law" were afforded criminals, if collective punishments were allowed (punishment of a group for the acts of one of its members), and if strict liability (liability without fault) were used much more than it is now. It is the *injustice* of these measures that makes us so apt to reject them

---

6 If the ideal-rule-utilitarian claims that there would be a rule that allows individuals to break promises in situations such as this, his "ideal" moral code is likely to be an ad hoc one which he creates as he goes along on the basis of his moral "intuitions" (or better "feelings"). There is, of course, no guarantee that such a system will be a coherent and consistent one.

and not their ultimate disutility. Indeed, incorporated, in uneasy balance, within our criminal law are two basically conflicting models—the utilitarian one of maximizing the *efficiency* of our crime control procedures and the Kantian one of respecting *the rights* of individuals caught up within the criminal *justice* system. The proper balance that should exist in a functioning legal system between these two conflicting models is a perennial topic for debate, but practically all of us would shudder at the thought of a criminal law ruthlessly devoted toward the general welfare and eradication of crime and unwilling to ever sacrifice that objective to even a small degree by a desire to protect the rights of individuals caught up in the criminal process.

Most of us in the United States today, for example, would loudly morally condemn the Russian experience under Stalin, where many people were unjustly imprisoned and executed. Nevertheless, such measures were often defended by supporters of the Stalinist regime as being necessary to create a more stable and economically and militarily viable nation. Although it was unfortunate that the Soviet Union had to treat some individuals unjustly and repress civil liberties, a Stalinist apologist would argue, such actions were necessary to enable the economically underdeveloped and militarily second-rate Soviet Union to catch up with the western democracies. The Soviet Union could not achieve these ends without ruthlessly repressing internal dissension. The Soviet Union simply could not afford the "luxury" of civil liberties at this critical stage in its development. This critical stage, admittedly, was a frightening and unjust one for many people; nevertheless, it was justified on the utilitarian ground that it was necessary for the happiness of Soviet citizens in this and future generations. Now, doubtlessly, many will attack such an argument as mistaken, on utilitarian grounds alone, suggesting that the greatest happiness of the Russian people did not at all require such drastic action; but this is not obviously so. Most important philosophically, however, is that even if such measures were justifiable on purely utilitarian grounds, most of us here in the United States would still morally object on the ground that such practices offend our sense of justice. The same could be said of the institution of slavery in the ancient world, which some historians have said was necessary to enable a minority of people to have the leisure essential for the cultivation of art, human learning, and the development of such momentous achievements as a written alphabet. If this were true, the institution of slavery would appear justified from a purely utilitarian standpoint; yet even if many of us today would accept slavery under such circumstances, we would do so only with the sad sense that we have sacrificed principles of justice to obtain our ends.

It has been suggested by some utilitarians that although it is theoretically possible for justice to conflict with utility, this is impossible in practice, given a realistic knowledge of human nature. Injustice, it is claimed, will never lead to the maximization of human happiness in the long run. For example, Paul Taylor relates such an argument in his

Principles of Ethics. He tells us to imagine a society which unfairly distributes its benefits and burdens. In such a society, the argument goes, an individual unfairly treated will not accept the rules of this society as fair and will conform to the rules only because he is forced to. Taylor continues the argument, writing,

> ... To make sure that social conflict will not get out of hand, let those who accept the rules establish a power structure which will ensure their domination over those who reject them. . . . To this the utilitarian replies, history has shown us that no such power structure can last for long; even while it does last, the effort spent by the "ins" on maintaining domination over the "outs" makes it impossible for the "ins" to obtain much happiness in life. A social system of this kind is constantly liable to break down. The need to preserve their position of power drives the "ins" to even greater measures of surveillance and repression. The society as a whole becomes a closed system in which the freedom of all individuals is diminished. . . . Inevitably, there develops an intolerance of diversity in thought, in speech, in styles of life. A narrow conformity of taste, ideas, and outward behavior becomes the main concern of everyone. What kind of "happiness" is this?
>
> The upshot of the argument is now apparent: Given a clear-headed view of the world as it is and a realistic understanding of man's nature, it becomes more and more evident that injustice will never have, in the long run, greater utility than justice. Even if the two principles of justice and utility can logically be separated in the abstract and even if they can be shown to yield contradictory results in hypothetical cases, it does not follow that the fundamental idea of utilitarianism must be given up. For it remains the case that, when we are dealing with the actual practices of people in their social and historical settings, to maximize happiness . . . requires an open, freely given commitment on the part of *everyone* to comply with the rules for settling conflicts among them. Anyone who is coerced into following the rules when he, in good conscience, cannot accept them as being fair . . . will not consider himself morally obligated to abide by them. . . . From his point of view, he will have good reason to do what he can to change or abolish the rules. He will join with anyone else who rejects them as unfair, in an effort to overcome his powerlessness. Thus injustice becomes, in actual practice, a source of great social disutility.[7]

Taylor does not give any indication of his view of the cogency of this argument, leaving its consideration simply "for the reader's own reflection."

Although such an argument can, at best (and this is highly questionable) support the contention that social injustice *generally* will not maximize utility in the long run, it cannot support the contention that it will *never* do so. First, the minority unjustly treated could be so few in number or so powerless or fearful as to prove no threat to those who

---

[7] From *Principles of Ethics: An Introduction* by Paul W. Taylor. © 1975 by Dickenson Publishing Company, Inc., Belmont, California 94002. Reprinted by permission of Wadsworth Publishing Company, Inc.

exploit them. Secondly, and most menacingly of all, the exploited could be brainwashed into accepting their plight on the basis of some ideology or religion. As Marx clearly saw, those in power often do not need physical power to exploit others, but can more effectively achieve this end through the vast power of ideological or religious persuasion where they may cloak their vested interests in the garments of morality. This is precisely why Marx called religion "the opium of the people," for those in power can use religion as an instrument for perpetuating the injustice of the status quo. (Consider, for example, the American experience under slavery, where the Southern plantation owner often encouraged religion among his slaves as a vehicle for teaching them to accept their plight or, at least, not to revolt against it.)

History does not seem to support the contention that unjust power structures are inherently unstable and consequently do not last as long as just power structures or that societies which tolerate more individual freedom tend to be happier. In addition, there seems to be no invariable connection between social and economic injustice on one hand and lack of individual freedom on the other, as the argument Taylor presents suggests. A society can be quite devoted to political and economic justice for all its citizens and yet be quite intolerant, by popular opinion if not criminal law, to divergent lifestyles. Conversely, a society can be quite politically and economically unjust but allow its minorities great cultural freedom and diversity of lifestyles as long as this diversity does not threaten the political and economic order. It would be nice if this world were so constituted that injustice would always be unprofitable in the long run, even to those who initially profit from it, but this is simply not the way it is in this world. As Henry Fielding, the author of *Tom Jones* put it in a slightly different context:

> There are a set of . . . moral writers who teach that virtue is the certain road to happiness and vice to misery, in this world. A very wholesome and comfortable doctrine, and to which we have but one objection, namely, that it is not true.[8]

The fact that philosophers so often use arguments such as the one presented by Taylor is an indication of the tendency of some philosophers to distort the facts in order to save a moral theory which would otherwise run counter to strong moral sensibilities.

The ultimate failure of rule-utilitarianism in any of its forms is that it, no less than traditional act-utilitarianism, when unlimited by other moral principles, can simply justify more than most people's moral sensibilities are willing to allow. Rule-utilitarianism, with its emphasis on utilitarian generalization or the general following of moral rules, may give the appearance of preventing this from happening, but it does not. Certainly, as rule-utilitarians point out, many of us would feel that

[8] Henry Fielding, *The History of Tom Jones, a Foundling* (New York: Modern Library, 1931), p. 672.

it is wrong not to vote for the candidate of our choice when we are assured that he will win without our vote. We feel this way, however, not because of some abstract commitment to general moral rules or to a nebulous principle of utilitarian generalization, but simply as a result of our realization that if others vote when we refrain, we are acting *unfairly* since we have no special claim to so act, and consequently our happiness is parasitic upon the efforts of others. Such notions are part of the general concept of justice and cannot be assimilated to that of utility. The moral life cannot be reduced to a purely teleological model and remain faithful to our deepest moral sensibilities. This is, indeed, the claim of David Ross, a twentieth century philosopher to whom we now turn.

DISCUSSION QUESTIONS

1. You are driving in a deserted area and have stopped at a red light. You are already late for a social engagement and are impatiently waiting for the light to change. You are absolutely positive that there are no vehicles coming, nor any pedestrians or policemen. (The visibility is excellent and unobstructed in every direction.) You want very much to run the redlight, but you feel that it's "wrong." Is it?

2. Evaluate our moral dilemmas as you think the different sorts of rule-utilitarians would, comparing their evaluation of these cases to those of an act-utilitarian.

FURTHER READINGS

BAYLES, MICHAEL D., ed., *Contemporary Utilitarianism*. Garden City, N.Y.: Doubleday, 1968. This anthology has an excellent collection of articles on the act- versus rule-utilitarianism controversy by contemporary philosophers. In particular, the articles mentioned in this bibliography by Smart, Rawls, McCloskey, and Urmson are reprinted in this anthology.

BRANDT, RICHARD, "Some Merits of One Form of Rule-Utilitarianism," *University of Colorado Series in Philosophy*, 3 (1967), 39–65. Brandt defends ideal-rule-utilitarianism, and discusses and criticizes other forms of rule-utilitarianism. This article is reprinted in the Feinberg and West anthology.

CUPPLES, BRIAN, "A Defense of the Received Interpretation of J.S. Mill," *Australasian Journal of Philosophy*, 50 (1972), 131–37. Cupples argues against Urmson's claim that Mill was a rule-utilitarian.

FEINBERG, JOEL, and HENRY WEST, eds., *Moral Philosophy: Classic Texts and Contemporary Problems*. Encino, Calif.: Dickenson, 1977. This anthology contains the articles by Brandt and Rawls listed in this bibliography, along with Smart's discussion of "The Place of Rules in Act-Utilitarianism," a section of his article "An Outline of a System of Utilitarian Ethics."

LYONS, DAVID, *Forms and Limits of Utilitarianism*. Oxford: Clarendon Press, 1964. In this intricate and difficult book, Lyons argues that general-rule-utilitarianism reduces to act-utilitarianism and criticizes ideal-rule-utilitarianism.

McCLOSKEY, H.J., "An Examination of Restricted Utilitarianism," *Philosophical Review*, 66 (1957), 466–85. A very clear nontechnical criticism of act- and rule-utilitarianism by one of its forceful critics. Reprinted in the Bayles anthology.

RAWLS, JOHN, "Two Concepts of Rules," *Philosophical Review*, 64 (1955), 3–32. Rawls argues for the merits of a type of limited actual-rule-utilitarianism over act-utilitarianism. As he sees it, some of our actions (but not all of them) can only be morally evaluated in terms of certain rules or practices (which are justified in terms of their utility) that *define* these actions as the sorts of actions they are taken to be. This article is reprinted in the Bayles and Feinberg-West anthologies.

SELLARS, WILFRED, and JOHN HOSPERS, eds., *Readings in Ethical Theory* (2nd ed.), section IIB. Englewood Cliffs, N.J.: Prentice Hall, Inc., 1970. This anthology contains excerpts from Lyons's and Singer's books mentioned in this bibliography, as well as articles by Don Locke and J. Howard Sobel on universalizability and utilitarian generalization. With the exception of the Locke article, this collection of readings is quite technical and directed to the philosophically sophisticated.

SINGER, MARCUS G., *Generalization in Ethics*. New York: Knopf, 1961. In this very technical discussion of utilitarian generalization, Singer attempts to specify which "generalization arguments" are successful. (That is, arguments of the form: "If everyone were to do that, the consequences would be disastrous (undesirable), therefore, no one ought to do that.") For example, in rejecting the argument: "Since if everyone were to produce food, the consequences would be disastrous, then no one should produce food" as an illegitimate generalization argument, Singer claims that all valid generalization arguments must be "invertable,"—that is, it cannot be the case that the consequences would be disastrous if no one did the thing in question, as well as if everyone did.

SMART, J.J.C., "Extreme and Restricted Utilitarianism," *Philosophical Quarterly*, 6 (1956), 344–54. A criticism of rule-utilitarianism by the foremost defender of act-utilitarianism. This original article which Smart claims "contains some serious errors" has been revised and the revised article is included in the Bayles anthology.

URMSON, J.O., "The Interpretation of the Moral Philosophy of J.S. Mill," *The Philosophical Quarterly*, 3 (1953), 33–39. Urmson claims that Mill was a rule- and not an act-utilitarian.

10. THE ETHICS OF W.D. ROSS

As we have seen, a full commitment to the utilitarian principle as the single basic moral principle would seem to have logical consequences which go contrary to most people's moral convictions. Clearly, for example, most people believe themselves to have special obligations to particular individuals which should be put before their general obligation (if one accepts such an obligation) to aid mankind in general. Our moral obligations, it would appear, are often *past-looking* as well as *future-looking*—that is, some of our duties rest on our previous actions and not on the possible future good that their fulfillment will create. For example, in the case of the deathbed promise in our list of moral dilemmas, most of us would perceive this situation as a dilemma precisely because we feel torn between our desire to see that some future good is done and our desire to keep our promises, even when to do so is not likely to have the best consequences. Some of us, in this situation, will weigh our obligation to keep our promise more heavily than the obligation of "maximize the good," and will consequently believe that the deathbed promise should have been kept. However, if keeping the promise would most likely lead to disastrous consequences (such as if the son is a terrorist, planning to manufacture bombs to kill innocent people), few will hold that a promise once made must always be kept. This position, for practically all of us, seems clearly inadequate, for we feel that a moral person should not be blind to the consequences of his actions.

Perhaps any adequate morality will have to incorporate elements of both utilitarianism and Kantian ethics. It would have to accept the Kantian view that the demands of justice are essential aspects of the moral life which are independent of the utilitarian commitment to the common good. Yet it would reject the Kantian view that considerations of justice can never be sacrificed for the common good. Similarly, it would accept the utilitarian view that the various specific duties that form the core of conventional morality—such as our duty to keep our promises and to be truthful—are not absolute. Nevertheless, it would reject the utilitarian view that one ought to consider only the consequences of one's action in deciding when a conventional duty should be kept. It may be wrong to assume, as both utilitarians and Kantians do, that moral reasoning must come to rest on a single basic moral principle. It would certainly do more justice to the moral life if we were to assume, instead, that there are several independent and possibly conflicting moral principles. This is the essential position of the English philosopher W.D. Ross (1877–1971) in his influential book *The Right and the Good*, published in 1930.

According to Ross, utilitarianism in all its forms is an inadequate moral theory because it is inconsistent with the moral convictions of the ordinary man. The essential defect of utilitarianism, Ross writes,

> . . . is that it ignores, or at least does not do full justice to, the highly personal character of duty. If the only duty is to produce the maximum of good, the question of who is to have the good—whether it is myself, or my benefactor, or a person to whom I have made a promise to confer that good on him, or a mere fellow man to whom I stand in no such special relation—should make no difference to my having a duty to produce that good. But we are all in fact sure that it makes a vast difference.[1]

[1] W.D. Ross, *The Right and the Good* (Oxford: Oxford University Press, 1930), p. 22.

Kant was also wrong, Ross claims, because he failed to distinguish absolute and unconditional duties—those things we must always do, no matter what—from *prima facie* duties—those nonabsolute duties which we must do, if no other conflicting *prima facie* duties interfere. (The Latin term *prima facie* means "at first sight.") As Ross used the term, a *prima facie* duty was simply a duty that could in certain circumstances be overridden by a more compelling conflicting duty. One's actual duty in a given situation, Ross claimed, is determined by consulting one's *prima facie* duties. For example, according to Ross, we do indeed have a duty to produce the most good possible, as the utilitarians claimed, and, when this duty does not interfere with any of our other *prima facie duties*, it should be followed. Nevertheless, such a duty can conflict with our other *prima facie* duties—such as the duty to keep one's promises. If this were to occur, we would have to choose between these *prima facie* duties. If breaking a promise will create only a slightly greater amount of good, the promise should be kept, but if the amount of good that can be created is very great, it should be broken. In describing our *prima facie* duties, Ross writes,

(1) Some duties rest on previous acts of my own. These duties seem to include two kinds, (a) those resting on a promise or what may fairly be called an implicit promise, such as the implicit undertaking not to tell lies. . . . These may be called the duties of fidelity; (b) those resting on a previous wrongful act. These may be called the duties of reparation. (2) Some rest on previous acts of other men, i.e., services done by them to me. These may be loosely described as the duties of gratitude. (3) Some rest on the fact or possibility of a distribution of pleasure or happiness (or of the means thereto) which is not in accordance with the merit of the persons concerned; in such cases there arises a duty to upset or prevent such a distribution. These are the duties of justice. (4) Some rest on the mere fact that there are other beings in the world whose condition we can make better in respect of virtue, or of intelligence, or of pleasure. These are the duties of beneficence. (5) Some rest on the fact that we can improve our own conditions in respect of virtue or of intelligence. These are the duties of self-improvement. (6) I think that we should distinguish from (4) the duties that may be summed up under the title of "not injuring others." No doubt to injure others is incidentally to fail to do them good; but it seems to me clear that nonmaleficence is apprehended as a duty distinct from that of beneficence, and as a duty of a more stringent character.[2]

Ross admits that his list of *prima facie* duties may be incomplete and that other duties could perhaps be listed. In compiling his list, Ross accepts the viewpoint that clear-thinking people can simply "intuit" or "see" what their *prima facie* duties are. He writes, for example, that

[2] Ibid., p. 21.

I should make it plain at this stage that I am *assuming* the correctness of some of our main convictions as to *prima facie* duties, or, more strictly, am claiming that we *know* them to be true. To me it seems as self-evident as anything could be, that to make a promise, for instance, is to create a moral claim on us in someone else. Many readers will perhaps say that they do *not* know this to be true. If so, I certainly cannot prove it to them; I can only ask them to reflect again, in the hope that they will ultimately agree that they also know it to be true. The main moral convictions of the plain man seem to me to be, not opinions which it is for philosophy to prove or disprove, but knowledge from the start; and in my own case I seem to find little difficulty in distinguishing these essential convictions from other moral convictions which I also have, which are merely fallible opinions based on an imperfect study of the working for good or evil of certain institutions or types of action.[3]

As this quotation indicates, Ross does not conceive his task to be that of guiding individuals into developing a more justifiable moral code, but rather perceives it to be that of properly describing the nature of a "thoughtful and well-educated" person's moral reasoning. In taking this stand, Ross neglects the incontestable fact that "thoughtful and well-educated people" often disagree on the question of what our moral duties should be and especially disagree on the question of how moral duties should be weighed in cases where they happen to conflict.

It is indeed the case, as Ross claims, that making a promise "is to create a demand on us in someone else." This can be known to be true, however, not by some special insight into a realm of "moral truths" that can be used to guide us in making moral choices. On the contrary, it is simply a definitional truth that promising "creates a demand on us in someone else." Ross' *prima facie* duties, however, are moral and not merely conceptual demands, and as such can, and have been, rejected as *proper moral* demands by other less conventional moralists. It is open to debate, for example, that self-improvement should be considered a *moral* demand. And even if this is granted, the differing meanings that can be attributed to this obligation—as indeed to all Ross' *prima facie* obligations—is sufficient to generate very different sorts of moralities. In addition, there are some possible moral duties that other moralists would consider legitimate that are absent from Ross' list of *prima facie* duties. For instance, under the first category of *prima facie* duties, duties based on our own previous actions, Ross lists two subdivisions, those based on past promises and those based on past wrongful acts—the first subdivision leads to duties of fidelity, the second to duties of reparation. Why, one may well ask, are there not two subdivisions also in the second category of *prima facie* duties, those based on previous acts of others? One might very well have expected this duty to be subdivided into the duties of gratitude for favors done us and that of retribution for wrongs done us, but the second of these subdivisions does not appear on

[3] Ibid., p. 22.

Ross' list. Since there have been quite a few very "thoughtful and well-educated" retributivists who, like Kant, believed that justice demands that a wrongdoer be punished for his wicked deeds, regardless of the consequences, Ross gives no reason why the duty of retribution should not be included in his list of *prima facie* duties.[4] If he intuits that such a duty does not exist, he gives no reason to reject the conflicting moral intuitions of retributivists such as Kant. Similarly, Ross nowhere mentions as a possible candidate for a *prima facie* duty the duty not to participate in injustice even if less injustice will be done if one does participate. (Consider the ethical dilemma of "The Cog in an Unjust System.") Again, Ross may intuit that such a duty does not exist, but others will disagree.

Even if most of us would accept Ross' list of *prima facie* duties, perhaps with minor revisions and additions, we would, I am convinced, disagree to a very substantial extent when it comes to interpreting these *prima facie* duties and weighing them in cases of conflict. Apart from telling us that the duties of noninterference (nonmaleficence) and promise-keeping *normally* override the duty of benevolence, Ross does not place his *prima facie* duties in hierarchical order from the most to the least stringent. He does not supply us with any standard to aid us in determining what we ought to do when our *prima facie* duties conflict. Although he tells us, for example, that promises should sometimes be kept and sometimes be broken, depending on the magnitude of the consequences, he does not give us any guidance as to how much good must be produced before we are justified in breaking a promise for its sake. If the man who made the deathbed promise was not justified in breaking that promise in the situation described on our list of moral dilemmas, but would have been, had this been necessary to save civilization, where exactly is the line to be drawn? Ross is very insensitive to this sort of problem, assuming that in some mysterious way we can recognize how to weigh our *prima facie* duties through some type of direct moral intuition. But, as we have said before, moral intuitions notoriously differ. It is a fundamental mistake to assume, as Ross does, that even though no precise rules can be given as to how to weigh conflicting obligations, there nevertheless exist uniquely correct answers to specific moral problems which can be recognized as such through a mysterious capacity of direct moral insight into a realm of values that exists apart from the shifting sentiments of human beings and the social forces that help mold them.

Nevertheless, one would expect a moralist to provide us with some

---

[4] While Ross does reject that type of "retributive" theory of punishment which asserts that criminals ought to be punished simply because they "deserve it" and that the degree of punishment inflicted on a criminal should be proportionate to his "moral guilt," he does not, on the other hand, accept the utilitarian view that punishment can be justified simply by its beneficial consequences. As Ross sees it, society derives its right to punish from the *prima facie* duties of beneficence (that is, promoting the general interest), of justice (punishment should be proportional to the offense committed), and of fidelity to promises (the promise to the law-abiding that criminals will be punished and the law-abiding will not). See pp. 56–64 of *The Right and the Good.*

pattern of rational moral choice that can *guide* us in making moral decisions. This Ross does not do. However, his theory is not without value, for it makes us focus on a plurality of independent moral obligations and although this complicates the moral life it also does it greater justice.

Ideal Utilitarianism versus Rossian Ethics:
How Rival Philosophical Theories Can Be Made to Converge

A central theme of Ross' *The Right and the Good* was that the utilitarian point of view in vogue during the early part of the twientieth century among English philosophers was inadequate. In particular, Ross meant to criticize the "ideal utilitarianism" presented by his contemporary, the philosopher G.E. Moore, in his very influential *Principia Ethica*. While accepting the utilitarian position that the right action to perform in a given situation is that act which maximizes intrinsic good, Moore was unwilling to embrace the hedonistic viewpoint of Bentham and Mill. While he accepted pleasure as an intrinsic good, he accepted other intrinsic goods as well. For example, he claimed that it is good in and of itself that the wicked be punished, writing:

> . . . the infliction of pain on a person whose state of mind is bad may, if the pain be not too intense, create a state of things that is better on the whole than if the evil state of mind had existed unpunished.[5]

Once one recognizes a plurality of intrinsic goods, as Moore did, an ideal utilitarian point of view can become indistinguishable from the Rossian point of view. All the ideal utilitarian has to do is to claim that all of Ross' *prima facie* duties are intrinsic goods—such as, that it is intrinsically good that one keep one's promises, that one make reparation for injuries done, etc. Since the list of intrinsic goods supplied by an ideal utilitarian can be identical to Ross' list of *prima facie* duties, such rival theories of normative ethics can be made to converge into the same theory, one formulated in a language of "goods" while the other is formulated in a language of "duties." If this were to happen, the choice between a Rossian type of ethics and an ideal utilitarian one would become one of choosing a more preferable mode of expressing one's moral commitments and would not express differing moral commitments.

DISCUSSION QUESTIONS

In his book *Thinking About Ethics*, Richard Purtill suggests that "other things being equal" (such as, the needs of individuals), Ross' *prima facie* duties can be ranked in terms of their relative stringency as follows:

5 G.E. Moore, *Principia Ethica* (Cambridge: Cambridge University Press, 1959), p. 214. First published in 1903.

1. Not to harm others
2. To make reparations for harm done by us
3. To keep our commitments
4. To repay our benefactors
5. To treat people as well as they deserve to be treated
6. To do some good to some people, deserving or not
7. To improve ourselves in some ways

Do you agree with this ranking? If not, how would you change it? Would you want to make any changes, deletions, or additions to this list of our basic moral obligations? How useful do you think a list like this is in providing guidance to the solution of moral problems?

FURTHER READINGS

PURTILL, RICHARD, *Thinking About Ethics.* Englewood Cliffs, N.J.: Prentice-Hall, Inc., 1976. Purtill embraces the Rossian point of view in this very readable introductory ethics text. It would be profitable to compare Purtill's treatment of Ross (chapter 4) with my own. It would also be worthwhile to consider Purtill's application of the Rossian point of view in his chapter on situation ethics. While reading these two chapters, focus on the points of disagreement between Purtill and myself. Does Purtill tend to overemphasize the practical usefulness of the Rossian rules or do I tend to underemphasize it?

ROSS, DAVID, *The Right and the Good.* Oxford: Oxford University Press, 1930.

11. SITUATION ETHICS

If traditional religious ethics tends to overemphasize the guidance that moral rules can provide, Joseph Fletcher, the foremost spokesman for "situation ethics" tends to underemphasize it. As the philosopher Hegel noted, and as Marx later echoed, philosophical reflection often takes the form of a "dialectic," where the inadequacies of one view give rise to a competing one which, in its attempt to eliminate these deficiencies, tends to overcompensate. The result is a view that suffers from inadequacies of an opposite nature. Such is the case with the ideas Joseph Fletcher, a contemporary spokesman for liberal Protestant moral thinking, expounds in his widely influential book *Situation Ethics.* Published in 1966, Fletcher's book immediately generated controversy among preachers and religious scholars. Some acclaimed it in such glowing terms as "a watershed in the history of moral theology," or as an "idea whose hour has come," while others denounced it as "frightening" or "shocking" in its implications. Unlike most expositions on normative ethics, however, Fletcher's book attracted a very wide lay audience, who, perhaps frustrated by the rigidity and mechanical legalism of more traditional religious ethics, were quite receptive to the more liberal and permissive tone of *Situation Ethics* and the "new morality" which it exemplified. The great attraction they found in *Situation Ethics* was its central precept that the most important aspect of the moral life was not a blind adherence to "the letter of the law," but rather to the spirit of "loving concern" which should always underlie it.

Fletcher begins his book with a description of three different approaches to the nature of moral decision making—legalism, antinomianism, and situationism. According to Fletcher,

> . . . [The legalist] enters into every decision-making situation encumbered with a whole apparatus of prefabricated rules . . . Not just the spirit but the letter of the law reigns. Its principles, codified in rules, are not merely guidelines or maxims to illuminate the situation; they are *directives* to be followed. . . .
>
> . . . all major Western religious traditions have been legalistic. . . .
>
> Statutory and code law inevitably piles up, ruling upon ruling, because the complications of life and the claims of mercy and compassion combine—even with code legalists—to accumulate an elaborate system of exceptions and compromise. . . . It leads to that tricky and tortuous . . . business of interpretation that the rabbis called pilpul. . . .
>
> . . . With Catholics it has taken the form of a fairly ingenious moral theology that, as its twists and involutions have increased, . . . appears . . . to evade the very "laws" of right and wrong laid down in its textbooks and manuals. Love, even with the most stiff-necked of system builders, continues to plead mercy's cause and to win at least partial release from law's cold abstractions. . . .
>
> Protestantism has rarely constructed such intricate codes and systems of law, but what it has gained by its simplicity it has lost through its rigidity, its puritanical insistence on moral rules.
>
> . . . This is really unavoidable whenever law instead of love is put first. The "puritan" type is a well-known example of it. But even if the legalist is truly *sorry* that the law requires unloving or disastrous decisions, he still cries, *"Fiat justitia, ruat caelum!"* (Do the "right" even if the sky falls down). He is the man Mark Twain called "a good man in the worst sense of the word." . . . [He is the sort of person who accepts Cardinal Newman's view that] "The Church holds that it were better for sun and moon to drop from heaven, for the earth to fail, and for all the millions who are upon it to die of starvation in extremest agony . . . than that one soul, I will not say should be lost, but should commit one single venial sin."[1]

Antinomianism, on the other hand,

> . . . is the approach with which one enters into the decision-making situation armed with no principles or maxims whatsoever, to say nothing of *rules*. In every "existential moment" or "unique" situation, it declares,

[1] From *Situation Ethics: The New Morality,* by Joseph Fletcher. Copyright © MCMLXVI, W.L. Jenkins. Used by permission of The Westminster Press.

one must rely upon the situation of itself, *there and then,* to provide its ethical solution.

> While legalists are preoccupied with law . . . [the antinomians] are so flatly opposed to law—even in principle—that their moral decisions are random, unpredictable. . . .[2]

The Situationist, however,

> . . . enters into every decision-making situation fully armed with . . . ethical maxims . . . and he treats them with respect as illuminators of his problems. Just the same he is prepared in any situation to compromise them or set them aside *in the situation* if love seems better served by doing so.[3]

Although at the outset of his book Fletcher attempts to distinguish the "situational" from the "antinomian" approach, his subsequent discussion of the situational approach to specific moral problems makes this approach appear indistinguishable from the unprincipled antinomian one. In spite of Fletcher's claim that the situationist is "fully armed with ethical maxims," there is very little mention in his book of the use the situationist makes of these maxims and much talk about apprehending, in some apparently immediate and intuitive way, the dictates of love. For example, in describing the famous Sheri Fishbein abortion case of the early 1960s, Fletcher writes,

> When a lady in Arizona learned, a few years ago, she *might* bear a defective baby because she had taken Thalidomide, how was she to decide? She asked the court to back her doctor and his hospital in terminating the pregnancy, and it refused, to the judge's chagrin, since the law prohibits nonmedically indicated abortions without exception. Her husband took her to Sweden, where love has more control of law, and there she was aborted, God be thanked, since the embryo was hideously deformed. But nobody could know for sure. It was a brave and responsible and right decision, even if the embryo had been all right.[4]

Nowhere, however, does Fletcher give us any idea of which principles are relevant in deciding what the dictates of "love" are in this situation. Clearly, given his "liberal" sensibilities in the abortion issue, Fletcher focuses his "loving concern" upon Sheri Fishbein, the pregnant woman, but those who would strongly oppose her abortion will also perceive their opposition as stemming from "loving concern," but, in their case, it will be for the unborn fetus. In a troublesome case such as this, one's moral choice should be illuminated and guided by moral principles. It is one thing to stress that moral principles are incapable of purely mechanical, computer-like application to complicated situations of moral

[2] Ibid., pp. 22–23.

[3] Ibid., p. 26.

[4] Ibid., pp. 135–36.

choice, but it is something else to dispense entirely with their guidance, as Fletcher seems to do in the examples he uses. Given Fletcher's initial characterization of situation ethics, one would expect that the image of the situationist that will emerge from his discussion is one of a wise judge who uses his intuitive sense of justice (or loving concern) within the framework of existing rules and principles. Yet, this expectation is never satisfied.

As Fletcher himself initially perceived, such decisions, although not mechanically predictable, are not arbitrary either. A wise judge must always *justify* his decisions. His decisions about particular cases are not "mechanically predictable," in the sense that more than one decision is often capable of justification. Yet, there are constraints, such as that of consistency, within which a wise judge must work. The present case must be examined within the backdrop of one's existing moral principles and rules and on the basis of similar precedents. This is exactly the legalistic model that Fletcher holds in such little regard. The problem with religious legalism is not its legalistic procedure but its underlying otherworldly concerns and assumptions as to the source and unchallengeable status of precedents (such as revelation). Unless we are to accept the existence of a "moral sense" that enables us to "see" what is right in particular situations, without an appeal to moral principles, there is no recourse but to the legalistic method of principled justification that Fletcher so scorns. However strongly we may feel that a given action is right, if these feelings are to be more than "prejudices," they must be justified in terms of general moral principles that one is willing to embrace in other situations. Since our moral principles, however complex, will never prove complex enough to solve all unforeseeable moral problems, the rational moral agent—like the legal judge—will find himself occasionally faced with "special" cases that require him to interpret, qualify, refine, and even at times abandon a moral principle. Such legalistic procedure may indeed be "tricky and tortuous" as Fletcher describes it, but it is essential if our moral decisions are to have a rational pattern and predictability.

Instead of the picture of a person constantly on the alert to interpret, modify, and enlarge his repertoire of moral principles, Fletcher, in his various examples, depicts the situationist as a person who, in some mysterious way, intuits the loving thing to do, without recourse to principles. The concept of love, as Fletcher's treatment of the abortion issue demonstrates, is not as unproblematic as he makes it appear and can only be made less problematic by being anchored to more specific moral principles and rules. For example, in the context of the question of the morality of the Vietnam war (which was being waged as the book was written), Fletcher, disagreeing with both "doves" and "hawks," counsels us that the situationist's motto should be "Be not a dove, nor a hawk, but an owl." Who, however, will find any fault with such an uninformative claim. The problem, of course, untouched by Fletcher, resides in specifying the conditions that must be satisfied before one can qualify as an "owl"—and, one would hope, a moral one to boot! This is the problem. The rest is empty rhetoric. To tell us to let "love" decide as Fletcher seems to is to tell us nothing.

The question of the demands of distributive justice is cast aside by Fletcher who tells us that *"Love and justice are the same, for justice is love* distributed, nothing else."[5] The principles of procedures by which love is to be distributed in a just way are, however, never hinted at by Fletcher. Are we, perhaps, simply to intuit how to weigh the conflicting needs of individuals so that love may be equitably distributed? Fletcher is characteristically silent, simply thrusting the anchorless concept of love toward us in a sea of rhetoric and leaving us to navigate for ourselves. Although Fletcher tells us that love should be "thoughtful" and "is a matter of intelligence, not sentiment," one is justified in claiming that it is sentiment more than intelligence that emerges in Fletcher's much too facile treatment of difficult moral issues. The Marxist criticism of utilitarianism as an incomplete amorphous system that can be bent into various different shapes to suit the differing sensibilities of its adherents seems quite apropros as a criticism of Fletcher. Concern for others does not stipulate the direction this concern should take until we ask what in general is *the good for human beings;* this ultimate question is, however, never tackled in *Situation Ethics.* As Fletcher divulges his specific moral stands in the various examples he uses, his beliefs appear no different from those of many educated moral "liberals" of our day. He does not, however, attempt to justify his liberal stands, and therein lies the ultimate failure of his ethical outlook.

In addition to this basic failure of *Situation Ethics,* Fletcher is quite ambivalent in the statement of his thesis, at times claiming that it is the *motive* of loving concern, and at other times, the *maximization of beneficial consequences* to everyone concerned that makes an act right. For example, in discussing sexual ethics, Fletcher writes,

> . . . if people do not believe it is wrong to have sex relations outside marriage, it isn't, unless they hurt themselves, their partners, or others. This is, of course, a very big "unless" and gives reason to many to abstain altogether except within the full mutual commitment of marriage.[6]

Here Fletcher, as would a utilitarian, focuses his attention upon the consequences of our actions and not the motives behind them. Fletcher never resolves the basic tension in his position between its traditional utilitarian element and its reliance upon the motive of loving concern; it is, however, the latter view which is emphasized throughout Fletcher's book. Yet is it not much easier to deceive ourselves of the "purity" of our motives than it is to deceive ourselves of the probable consequences of our actions? At least when we focus upon the consequences of our actions we realize that our moral decisions require knowledge and fore-

5 Ibid., p. 99.

6 Ibid., p. 140.

sight which may be sadly lacking when we rivet our attention upon the immediate motive behind our actions. As history so amply demonstrates, opposing armies can easily convince themselves that it is on the basis of the motive of "Christian love" that they kill each other and innocent noncombatants. In a truly astounding claim, Fletcher tells us that President Truman's decision to drop atomic bombs on Hiroshima and Nagasaki were acts of love.[7] This claim cries out for justification, yet Fletcher says not a word in its defense. One wonders how Fletcher arrived at this decision. Was it on the basis of Truman's professed motive in dropping the bombs—the saving of American lives? If so, we may ask Fletcher, if it was morally right for President Truman to focus all his "loving concern" upon Americans, to the exclusion of the Japanese, when the outcome of the war was not at stake. Furthermore, most certainly in a case such as this, Truman's motive is not nearly as important for us to consider today as a consideration of the alternatives of action open to him and their probable consequences. Yet Fletcher does not mention that the utilitarian justification of Truman's action has been seriously questioned. Certainly, in those many situations, such as those found in the context of war, when we face a moral dilemma of hurting some to help others, we need facts and vision more than love or purity of heart.

Fletcher is much too sanguine about such sad moral choices as those faced in the context of a war. He makes it a point to tell us that we should not wallow in guilt for having chosen in accordance with the dictates of love. Yet it seems to me that when one feels forced to violate a moral principle which conflicts in a given situation with a more stringent one, one ought often to make one's choice only with a deep sense of regret and tension and even, at times, guilt, if for no other reason than that no better way can be found. This sense of moral tension seems to be totally lacking in Fletcher. Yet, I fear, without it, people are apt to become too callous and less inclined to care about others. In addition, since we must sometimes act in accordance with much less than complete knowledge, momentous moral choices can sometimes only be made hesitantly "in fear and trembling" that the facts as they become known will prove us wrong. There is, however, no sense of tragic loss and uncertainty in the many examples Fletcher cites. For example, there is none in the case, heartrending to any loving parent, of a mother in the old American West who, convinced that the cries of her baby will alert the Indians as to the whereabouts of a wagon train of settlers, suffocates her child to save the rest of the wagon train. One may see the actions of such a woman, as Fletcher evidently does, as one of heroic and loving sacrifice, but would we not drastically change our view of the moral character of this woman were we to discover that she could live her life after making such a decision without guilt and the deepest of regrets?

Another important inadequacy of Fletcher's moral thinking is his tendency, frequently found in philosophers, to dwell upon the exceptional case rather than the more commonplace one. It is one thing to

---

[7] Ibid., p. 98.

use special cases as a wedge to bring out the inadequacies of conventional moral principles and rules or as a vehicle for generating critical thought. This is the role of the traditional philosophical "gadfly," such as Socrates, who is not attempting to offer his own comprehensive moral theory —the role of the philosophical "sage." Yet it is something quite different when one assumes the role of a sage who is presenting some comprehensive moral view which is meant to be a guide to the average person in his everyday life. Here an overreliance upon the exceptional is bound to cause a distortion in one's own view. This is the case, I am convinced, with Fletcher.

For example, Fletcher relates to us the case of a German mother in a Russian prisoner of war camp who could gain release and rejoin her family only by being impregnated by one of the prison guards.[8] Many will agree with Fletcher that her decision was morally right in the circumstances, but what guidance does this rare case give to young Americans seeking a rational sexual morality? None at all. A more conservative sexual moralist than Fletcher can claim that the moral rule prohibiting extramarital sexual relations, which may have a justifiable exception in the case of the German woman, does not have any exceptions when applied to an average American contemplating an extramarital affair.

Fletcher, in his preoccupation with the exceptional case, blinds himself to how disruptive of his own conception of proper human relationships, his exceptional cases, would be if they were to become the general rule. It would be very dangerous for a child to learn morality from Fletcher's book. How is a child, for example, to understand that it may be morally right to cheat in certain situations out of love for some classmate and not feel that it is equally right for him to cheat when he is simply not adequately prepared? Again the child, as indeed all of us, needs moral rules and principles as a necessary source of restraint, let alone as a guide in making the "loving choice."

DISCUSSION QUESTIONS

Do you think that the "legalistic," "situational," and "antinomian" points of view can be clearly distinguished? Is there, perhaps, some truth in all three views? Explain.

FURTHER READINGS

Cox, Harvey (ed.), *The Situation Ethics Debate*. Philadelphia: Westminster Press, 1968. A collection of essays and short comments by Protestant clergymen in support of and in opposition to Fletcher.

Fletcher, Joseph, *Situation Ethics: The New Morality*. Philadelphia: Westminster Press, 1966.

8 Ibid., pp. 164–65.

12. SOME REFLECTIONS ON THEORIES
OF NORMATIVE ETHICS

The various theories of normative ethics that we have critically discussed all seem incomplete and inadequate to the task of providing specific directives toward the solution of moral problems. Given the vague nature of such principles as the categorical imperative and the greatest happiness for the greatest number, different philosophers committed to the same basic moral principle can arrive at very different specific moral conclusions. For example, the principle of utility has been used by some as the ultimate justification for pacifism, while for others it has been used as the ultimate justification for the morality of war. There can be no doubt that the vague nature of these principles allows them to be used as rationalizations for particular moral judgments that are based on other considerations. (Recall the Marxist criticism of utilitarianism.) For example, given the indefinite consequences of one's actions and their uncertain bearing upon the creation of human happiness or pleasure, a hedonistic utilitarian can often be quite adept at meeting the challenges of his critics by bending the principle of ultility in the direction that he would like it to lead. When his critics reply that a commitment to his theory, unsupplemented by other independent basic moral principles, is inadequate since it does not provide individuals with *rights* against having their individual liberty restricted in the name of social welfare or paternalistic benevolence, he will often counter by claiming that the provision of rights of noninterference in human liberty is an essential condition for the maximization of human happiness. Behind such claims are often dubious psychological and sociological assumptions, such as the assumption that a human being is the best judge of how to maximize his own happiness (Mill's assumption) or that an unjust society will eventually prove to be an unstable one (the argument Taylor presents).

Realizing the slender threads by which human liberty is tied to the principle of utility, given the uncertainties of actual human desires and the world around us, the Kantian unsuccessfully attempts to totally detach morality from these psychological and worldly uncertainties. The result is an abstract principle, such as the categorical imperative, which lacks any definite content. It is fine and well to claim, as Kantians do, that "similar cases must be treated similarly" or that "individuals should be treated as persons and not as things," but lacking any definite conception of what is to count as a morally revelant similarity or what it is to treat someone "as a person," such principles do not guide. Indeed, some utilitarians would claim that the notion of "respect for persons" implies nothing more than a relationship of involvement with others, such that our choices are governed by their aims and aspirations as well as our own. As such, these utilitarians will say, rather than being opposed to this notion, utilitarianism is built upon its very foundations and indeed helps to clarify its meaning.

Clearly, a Kantian would rightfully protest that one can be "concerned" about those whom one does not "respect" (such as animals). As the Kantian sees it, "respect" implies an acknowledgment of a person's *rational* status and *right* to *self-determination*. Nevertheless, the Kantian, like any reasonable person, would have to admit that human choices are not always "rational" or "voluntary." One does not necessarily show "disrespect for a person" when one ignores his momentary "nonrational" or "nonvoluntary" wishes. For example, one is not necessarily showing "disrespect for a person" when one forcefully prevents him from committing suicide in the belief that *he himself will later repudiate this wish upon more rational consideration*. But given the ambivalence and flux of human desires, the notion of "what one would choose if one thought about it rationally" is quite indeterminate itself. As such, there will be a strong temptation for utilitarian notions of a person's "best interests" to be smuggled surreptitiously into one's notion of that person's rational or voluntary choices. For example, those who see suicide as clearly being against a person's "best interests" will be apt to refuse to see suicidal wishes as rational or voluntary wishes which reflect one's "true self." (*"You don't really want* to commit suicide; *you're just temporarily overpowered* by depression.")

The traditional utilitarian theory is, however, no less unclear and indefinite in application than the Kantian theory. Its apparent simplicity and unity are seen to be an illusion as the many unanswered questions it poses are brought to light. What, for example, does "pleasure" denote? How are we to measure and compare different degrees of it? Is it not the case that some individuals may have the capacity for experiencing stronger pleasures (or have stronger desires) than others? If so, how is this to be taken into consideration in a utilitarian calculation of the "maximization of human happiness"? Similarly, how are we to take into consideration the fact that some people are unhappier than others, not because they experience less pleasure, but because their *expectation* of the pleasures they would like to be experiencing is greater? Are we to rank pleasures according to their quality as well as their quantity? If so, how do we determine the quality of a given pleasure and its importance relative to its quantity? Are we to be concerned with the distribution of pleasure as well as its aggregate maximization? Are we to be concerned about the pleasures of animals as well as of human beings, of future generations as well as the present generation? Is it right for us to create more and more people to inhabit this world as long as the total amount of pleasure experienced keeps increasing, or should we be concerned with maximizing the average pleasure experienced? As such questions crowd upon us, the clarity of the utilitarian vision grows dimmer. It is clear that the "utilitarian calculus," which Bentham believed would reduce morality to a type of "moral arithmetic," is a myth.

Given the inadequacies of traditional utilitarian and Kantian conceptions of morality which attempt to reduce our moral obligations to a single basic moral principle, other philosophers have turned to the ideal utilitarian or pluralistic deontological theories of such individuals as G.E. Moore and David Ross, which stress the existence of independent and possibly conflicting intrinsic goods or *prima facie* duties. Such theories, although more adequate to the realities and perplexities of moral choice, can no longer disguise the fact that they are incapable of generating determinate answers to specific moral questions. A morally perplexed person, faced with some moral dilemma, will be no more capable of resolving his difficulty after being exposed to such theories than he was before. He will have only learned how to formulate the nature of his moral perplexity in the more academic language of "conflicts between *prima facie* duties" or between "intrinsic goods." The perplexity will remain unless one assumes that there exists some inner moral voice which can allow one to intuit the demands of morality in a given situation. How we are to distinguish this inner voice of moral truth from the promptings of nonmoral factors and of social conditioning is never made clear.

One must always be wary of abstract principles which are made to appear to provide more guidance than they really do. For example, in discussing sexual morality in his book *Thinking about Ethics,* Richard Purtill advocates the utilization of the golden rule—"treating others as you would like to be treated in their place"—as a "guide for personal relationships." As we have mentioned before, this is a very indefinite guide. The function of such a principle, it seems to me, is to point out that a necessary condition of *any* adequate morality is that equal consideration be given each member of one's moral community. Indeed, such a principle is so fundamental to most conceptions of morality, that for many it is true by definition that a moral way of life must involve an equal consideration for others. The exact form this equal consideration should take differs, however, from one specific conception of morality to another. The golden rule that Purtill so approvingly quotes is a very poor guide to sexual morality since it does not in any way tell us what we are to do when the desires of different people conflict. I might very well know how I would like to be treated, were I Susan, and how I would want to be treated, were I Joan. But what if I cannot treat Susan the way she would like to be treated without treating Joan in a way that she would not like to be treated? Alas, most problems of sexual morality are of this nature. Indeed, the concept of "empathy" is a philosophically puzzling one, for in the course of empathy one is supposed to remain oneself and yet become someone else. It may be logically impossible for an individual of a given temperament to empathize with an individual of a fundamentally different temperament. Finally, even if one succeeds in vividly imagining what it would be like to "see" and "feel" the world with the emotions and thought structure of someone else, why should one feel a moral obligation to treat all individuals the way they would like to be treated? Is it not obviously the case that some individuals simply *ought* not to be treated the way they would like to be treated? There is a difference, after all, between understanding someone and giving him his way. Purtill does not, however, point out these difficulties, creating the false impression that the golden rule provides guidance to the resolution of specific moral problems, which it does not.

While the theories of normative ethics we have discussed are incapable of providing determinate answers to specific moral problems, they can provide a conceptual framework for the resolution of these problems and by so doing function to organize one's moral thinking. Such conceptual frameworks can have the effect of pointing a person's thought in a particular direction and can consequently serve to some extent to narrow the field of morally relevant factors. For example, there is no guarantee how a person committed to the hedonistic utilitarian standpoint will resolve specific moral problems, such as those concerning the morality of adultery, euthanasia, and capital punishment. We do know, however, that such an individual will focus upon the consequences that one's actions are likely to have on the ultimate well-being or happiness of individuals in this world, and this does at least serve to narrow the scope of moral relevance. We know the direction of the hedonistic utilitarian's thought, if not the ultimate outcome. This is often the case with other theories as well. Although one cannot predict how a Kantian will resolve a particular moral issue, one knows how he will organize his thoughts about this issue. For example, in the question of the justification of punishment, a Kantian will direct this justification *to the criminal himself,* attempting to show him why he *deserves* to be punished, while the utilitarian will direct this justification to *society as a whole,* attempting to show how punishment can act to *prevent* crime. While there is no unique utilitarian or unique Kantian way to resolve *specific* moral questions relating to punishment, one does have some idea of how utilitarians and Kantians will conceptualize and approach their moral questions in this area. As different moral theories become more complex and pluralistic, the differences in approach may reside in no more than a difference in the relative emphasis that is placed on different morally relevant factors.

As we proceed from the abstract conceptualizing, characteristic of theories of normative ethics, to a consideration of concrete cases of moral choice, such very general and abstract principles as the categorical imperative and the greatest happiness for the greatest number must give way to more specific moral principles. Each of us, in arriving at these specific moral principles and in determining how to balance them in cases of conflict, must refer to our deeply felt (and doubtlessly, at least to some extent, socially conditioned) judgments about the morality of particular actions. This is the given frame of reference from which moral reasoning begins. From these particular moral judgments we can then attempt to extract general principles that render these particular judgments into a consistent and unified whole. These general principles can then be called upon as a guide to the solution of different moral problems. If some general moral principle to which we have up until now been committed leads us to a conclusion that goes counter to deeply felt moral sentiments in a new and unforeseen moral problem, one can either abandon this principle, or, more likely, attempt to modify it in some way. On the other hand, when a certain general moral principle has proven itself to be a very worthwhile guide to many different sorts of moral problems, one may tend to cling to that principle when it seems to go counter to some nonreflective but deeply felt particular moral judgment and reject that judgment in favor of the reflective moral principle. For example, a person's initial judgment that homosexuality is wrong, might eventually give way to a growing commitment to a general principle of respect for human autonomy. As one's commitment toward this principle grows, one's immediate feelings of tolerance to divergent life-styles is likely to grow as well.

This process of on-going mutual adjustment between general moral principles and particular nonreflective moral judgments is very much like the sort of reasoning that can be found in judicial decisions in courts of law. Legal precedents play the same logical role for the legal judge as particular nonreflective moral judgments ("moral feelings" or "moral intuitions"[1]) do for the rational moral agent. Recognizing the inconsistencies of precedents or particular nonreflective moral judgments, the legal judge and rational moral agent accept the obligation *to act on principle,* even when their principles go counter to a deeply felt moral feeling that a particular case should be resolved in a particular way. They will attempt to modify their principles to accommodate these feelings or, if this is not possible, to abandon these feelings, but there is no guarantee that they will always be able to do this.

As we shall see in our discussions of some contemporary moral issues, the complexities of life often present us with unavoidable and painful choices between conflicting values and moral principles that cannot be resolved by an appeal to a higher value or moral principle. Faced with such dilemmas, we must choose, realizing that whatever we choose will exact a price and become a precedent for the future. It is no doubt psychologically easier to believe that there is some supreme moral authority that we can always turn to in times of moral doubt, be it God or some basic moral principle, which can generate uniquely correct moral answers, but this is an illusion. Ultimately, we must choose for ourselves how we want to live as individuals and as a society, but at least we can endeavor to choose rationally.

> 1 While many philosophers use the notion of a "moral intuition" to mean a "nonreflective specific moral judgment," I prefer not using this concept myself, since it still carries along for some the implication that "moral intuitions" are intellectual perceptions of a realm of "objective" moral truths which are not dependent upon the differing preferences of human beings. Just as the notion of a "moral intuition" can prove misleading, so too can the notion of a "moral feeling" about the rightness of an action. Consider, for example, a person who, when asked, "Why do you think that wars are wrong?" simply answers, "I *feel* it." If such a person's "feelings" about war are indeed *"moral* feelings," we expect that person to be able to tell us *what it is about war that makes him feel that way* (such as that it results in the deaths of innocent people). In general, it is a logical requirement of moral language that "moral feelings" about the rightness or wrongness of an action be anchored in nonmoral features of that action.

3

Morality, Self-Interest, Free-Will, and Moral Responsibility

Since we cannot reasonably make moral evaluations of peoples' behavior and character without understanding the limits of possible human behavior, moral philosophers have always been concerned with psychological questions relating to "human nature." This is especially true when philosophers supply standards for the appraisal of moral character and moral responsibility. Clearly, the factual information gathered and theoretical perspectives assumed by the psychological sciences have an important bearing on such standards. Consequently, ethical reflection in this area becomes intertwined with philosophical reflections upon human psychology. In addition, unlike many abstract philosophical questions that seem to interest few people other than professional philosophers, philosophical questions relating to human character, motivation, and moral responsibility interest many people. Although one would expect only the philosophically trained to argue over the relative virtues of different abstract theories of normative ethics, practically all of us, at times, argue over questions like "Is everyone really selfish?" "Why should I sacrifice my interests for others, if there's nothing in it for me?" "Is our behavior totally caused by environment and heredity and, as such, in principle fully predictable by science?" "If this is so, can we be said to have free will?", and "Is anyone ever really morally responsible?" Philosophers and laypersons alike often question the quite familiar distinctions that people make in characterizing individuals as selfish or unselfish, as free or unfree, and as morally responsible or morally nonresponsible. "We are all selfish," some say. "We are never free or morally responsible," others assert.

It is to these widely intriguing questions and issues that we shall

turn in the next two sections. As we shall see, these questions are partially *about words*—that is, what we mean or should mean by such concepts as "selfish behavior," "free choice" or "free action," and "moral
responsibility," and partially *about the underlying facts* that these concepts are meant to describe—that is, the facts of human psychology and
the nature of the world we inhabit that lead us to distinguish people as
selfish or unselfish, as free or unfree, and as morally responsible or morally nonresponsible.

13. MORALITY AND SELF-INTEREST

Psychological Egoism

Psychological egoism is a theory of human motivation, not an ethical theory. It is held today, as always, by many ordinary people, and was
once almost universally held to be true by philosophers. Today philosophers tend equally strongly to reject it. Whether they have good reasons
for rejecting it is another matter, depending in part on the meaning we
attribute to it. The following are some typical formulations of this
theory.

1. All voluntary human acts are ultimately selfishly motivated.
2. Every person always acts so as to promote his own self-interest.
3. People do things for others only because they expect something in
   return.

As is the case with most philosophical controversies, it is exceedingly important that we attempt to extract the most plausible formulation of this doctrine before we pursue the question of its truth or falsity.
The question at issue is not, as many have posed it, "Is psychological
egoism true?" assuming that this doctrine has a single clear meaning;
it is rather the more murky one, "Is there some fundamental insight
about human nature that the above statements are getting at, and if so,
what is the most enlightening and scientifically defendable way to
formulate that insight?" Contemporary philosophers have often been
much too quick in dismissing some clearly imprecise and inadequate
formulations of the doctrine of psychological egoism without attempting
to delve deeper into the ideas underlying it. The tenacity of the hold
that psychological egoism has had on the minds of many may reflect
some view of human motivation which goes beyond the imprecise formulations of this doctrine and the conceptually confused arguments that
are often used in its defense. While there are many contemporary scientific views of human motivation which would reject any attempt to reduce all human motivation to a single "self-interested" or "selfish" base,
there are other theories that would seem to be much more sympathetic

to such an attempt and would indeed serve to clarify the exact meaning that should be attributed to the doctrine of psychological egoism. The issue of psychological egoism, like many philosophical issues that touch upon scientific concerns, requires scientific understanding as well as conceptual clarity and clear logical reasoning.

Reasons for the Initial Plausibility of the Doctrine of Psychological Egoism

The widespread acceptance of the belief that everyone is, in some sense, motivated only by "self-interested" or "selfish" considerations in acting as they do can clearly be given some degree of plausibility when one considers the prevalence of self-deception and the process by which we are taught to be moral or to be concerned about the interests of others. Let us briefly consider these factors.

Self-Deception   It is a sad fact of human nature that to some extent we all deceive others, as well as ourselves, as to the true nature of our motives. Who has not had occasion to realize that the apparently kindly, concerned, and unselfish attitude of others can be nothing more than a facade behind which lurks exclusively selfish desires? Although this deception may take the form of consciously intended duplicity, there are many occasions when people conceal their true motives from themselves. It is a short step for some from the realization that one's true motives can appear to be unselfish, while being in reality quite selfish, to the cynical view that this may always be the case. Behind every seemingly unselfish action the cynic will seek some underlying selfish concern. Politicians who loudly profess their love for the people will be seen as self-seeking power-hungry individuals, while the love of parents for their children will be seen as nothing more than "ego-fulfillment" or a source of vicarious selfish pleasure. Similarly, friendship will be seen as nothing more than the conscious or unconscious use of others to satisfy one's own desires. Nothing will be sacred from the piercing eyes of the truly convinced cynic. Religion, with its belief in heaven and hell, will be seen as a prime example of man's ultimate selfishness, for although we are told that we should worship and obey God because he deserves this response from us, we are motivated to so act by the security such action provides and by our fear of the undesirable personal consequences of doing otherwise. Conventional morality will be seen by the cynic to be, as Marx suggested, nothing more than "a racket" by which those in power attempt to maintain their position at the expense of the gullible. Charitable deeds will be seen as a source of self-congratulation on one's own good fortune or as a means of alleviating deep-seated guilt feelings which have been conditioned into us by the use of rewards and punishments. This claim brings us to the next important factor which has led people to the doctrine of psychological egoism.

Moral Education and Depth Psychology   According to almost all schools of psychology, moral education draws upon associations with rewards and punishments. For example, the way behaviorists would see it, since a child is dependent upon his parents for the satisfaction of his inborn (primary) self-centered needs, such as food and security, he comes to associate the satisfaction of these needs with the moral injunctions his parents utilize in rewarding and punishing him for his behavior. By such a process, a child learns to consider the interests of others and to feel guilty when he does not. Such a view can be supplemented by psychoanalytic theory. As the psychoanalyst sees it, a child learns to be moral by a process of "identification" with his parents. By so doing, the child is made to feel safer. Instead of being terrified by a cold impersonal world upon which he is fully dependent for the sustenance of life, the child develops a sense of self-reliance. Normally, as the child's sense of self-reliance develops, he also stops seeing his parents as the powerful and awe-inspiring figures he once perceived them to be. They begin to be perceived as similar to him, having similar sorts of needs and feelings. The child is now able "to identify" with the feelings of his parents. Eventually the process generalizes and the child develops "empathy" or "fellow-feeling" with people in general. Nevertheless, psychiatrists tell us that such other-regarding feelings and concerns are always integrally hooked-up with the maintenance of a sense of self-worth, which provides in subtle unconscious ways for a sense of security. As we delve into the unconscious depths and interrelations of human motives, a psychological egoist may contend, we will discover that behavior which is conventionally classified as "unselfish" in nature is really no different in underlying motivational structure from behavior which we would classify as "selfish" in nature. Since all voluntary human action will turn out to be capable of being traced back to some purely self-regarding motivational component, such actions are ultimately selfish in nature, our psychological egoist will contend.

The Linguistic Ploy: Reducing the Doctrine of Psychological Egoism to a Tautology

Given the multitude of possibly selfish motives, a cynic can contend that underlying all apparently unselfish actions lurks some selfish motive, which may or may not be consciously perceived as such. For example, if a person sacrifices his life for someone else or for some cause, the cynical psychological egoist can claim that such an action was motivated by such selfish desires as the following:

a. to be rewarded in heaven for one's deed
b. to avoid guilt feelings
c. to be thought of highly by others
d. to escape from a meaningless life

In some cases, however, no concrete selfish desires, such as the preceding, seem to underlie an apparently unselfish action. There are certainly, for example, individuals who sacrifice their lives with no conscious desire to be rewarded in heaven (the agent might be an atheist) or to avoid guilt feelings (not everyone is troubled by strong guilt feelings and such feelings would have to be immense to outweigh all the satisfactions life might have to offer). As concrete selfish motives are suggested and dismissed as clearly unsupported in a given case, one begins to wonder what a psychological egoist is claiming when he says that all actions are "really selfish." Consider, for example, the following:

> **A:** Cats are selfish. They want you only for the meal-ticket which you supply. But dogs will really sacrifice for you—they will starve at your feet rather than leave you, and they will travel a thousand miles, undergoing great hardship, just to be with you again.
>
> **B:** I disagree with you. Even dogs are selfish. They won't do anything for you unless there's something in it for *them*. They want your love and affection more than they want food, and they fear insecurity more than hunger.
>
> **A:** In the Arctic some time ago an explorer was found who had been dead for three weeks. His dog lay starving at his feet, while his cat was eating his eyes out. Don't you consider that evidence for my position?
>
> **B:** No. Both the dog and cat were selfish, but in different ways. And the same for human beings. They are always selfish too, but their selfishness more often includes a concern (selfish concern, of course) for the welfare of others.
>
> **A:** I disagree once again. Dogs are less selfish than cats, and human beings *can* be more unselfish than either. Neither dogs nor cats act contrary to their own interests from principles of duty, but people do. Perhaps the dog finds it easier or less unpleasant to be with his master even if he himself is starving, but people often do the more difficult thing and the thing that they *don't* want. You have commanded the dog not to go outside; although he wants to go out, perhaps he stays indoors because he fears punishment or loss of affection. But people sometimes do things for others without expecting anything in return—not even the satisfaction or security which the dog expects.
>
> **B:** I think all three species are equally selfish, always. I grant that a person may act from a sense of duty, unlike the dog, but I don't believe he would do so if he didn't think he would derive more satisfaction (or avoid dissatisfaction) by so doing.[1]

This example is illustrative of two common faults of debates as to the truth of psychological egoism. First, it demonstrates the tendency of individuals to debate this issue without agreeing upon the definition that ought to be attributed to the key concept of "selfishness." Clearly, *A* and *B* do not share the same understanding of the meaning of this concept, and, as such, their disagreement is, at least to some extent, a verbal or conceptual one. This is often the case in philosophical debates. Second, this example demonstrates the tendency that the doctrine

---

[1] John Hospers, *Human Conduct* (New York: Harcourt Brace Jovanovich, Inc., 1972), pp. 156–57. By permission.

of psychological egoism has of degenerating into a mere tautology. Let us see why this is so.

While it is quite unclear what definition *A* is attributing to the notion of "selfishness," it is clear from *B's* last remark that he rests his conviction that all voluntary human actions are selfish on the ground that such actions are always performed in order to "gain satisfaction or avoid dissatisfaction." Let us consider this claim more fully. On the surface, it seems clearly false. For example, what possible "satisfaction" is gained or "dissatisfaction" avoided by those who "screw up" their courage to do what they believe is their moral duty in spite of their conviction that they would be much happier if they did not do so? Although, no doubt, some such individuals would experience some degree of guilt feelings if they did not do their duty, this is not universally true, and at any rate the "dissatisfaction" one will experience from doing one's duty may seem to far outweigh the "dissatisfaction" that guilt feelings might bring. How then can the psychological egoist be so convinced that individuals who perform voluntary acts "must get satisfaction out of their actions?" What is the force of the "must" here? Certainly, there is no unique feeling of "satisfaction" (or "dissatisfaction") that accompanies all voluntary action. What then does the psychological egoist mean by "satisfaction"? One ploy open to the psychological egoist is to claim that "satisfaction" simply means "satisfying one's desire." But if this definition of "satisfaction" is accepted, the psychological egoistic thesis that "All voluntary actions are selfish" reduces to a tautology. This is so since the psychological egoist's reason for claiming that all voluntary actions are "selfish" is that such actions give one "satisfaction" and by "satisfaction" all he means is "satisfying one's own desire"—that is, "doing as one wants"—but this would appear to be precisely the definition of a voluntary act. Consequently, when such a psychological egoist says that all voluntary actions are selfish, he is only saying that whenever an individual does as he wants, he does as he wants—a tautology.

The initial appearance that psychological egoism was a profound observation of human nature—that things could have been otherwise, but alas are not—is a misinterpretation when this doctrine is turned into a tautology. Given the linguistic assumption that merely "doing as one wants" is to count as a "selfish" action, the notion of a voluntary unselfish action—that is, an action where one does as one wants, but not as one wants—becomes a logical impossibility, just as a four-sided triangle would be. Consequently, under such an interpretation the doctrine of psychological egoism is not at all based on *an observation of the facts* of human nature but simply reflects a *linguistic decision* to use the notion of "selfishness" in a very inflated and uncommon way. But if this inflated definition of "selfishness" is employed, no longer is it possible to contrast the notion of selfishness with that of unselfishness. Yet the notions of selfishness and unselfishness gain whatever meaning they possess in ordinary language precisely by virtue of the fact that they are used to describe contrasting actions within the class of voluntary actions.

To assert that all voluntary actions are selfish would be informative only if we could contrast such actions with actions which could at least conceivably be unselfish. Yet this can no longer be done when the doctrine of psychological egoism is reduced to a tautology.

The First Step in Resolving Philosophical Issues: Conceptual Clarification

As the preceding discussion indicates, if the doctrine of psychological egoism is not to be reduced to a tautology, it must be stated in terms which make its truth depend on the facts of human psychology and not simply on definitional fiat. It must be possible for us to imagine a state of affairs that would make it true as well as a state of affairs that would show it to be false. With this objective in mind, what exactly should we take the doctrine of psychological egoism to be asserting. Let us turn back to the preliminary formulations of the doctrine of psychological egoism previously given.

1. All voluntary human acts are ultimately selfishly motivated.
2. Every person always acts so as to promote his own self-interest.
3. People do things for others only because they expect something in return.

Now, if the concepts in these definitions are taken according to their ordinary usage, these definitions are not at all equivalent in meaning. Let us consider the first definition. According to two dictionaries, "selfish" is defined as follows:

> Concerned excessively or exclusively with oneself: seeking or concentrating on one's own advantage, pleasure, or well-being without regard for others.[2]

> Having such regard for one's own interests and advantage that the happiness and welfare of others becomes of less concern than is considered right or just; too much concerned with one's own welfare.[3]

As these two definitions indicate (especially the second one), the word "selfish" functions in ordinary language as a moral term which implies an *undue* disregard for the interests of others. Indeed, the notions of selfishness and unselfishness are used in ordinary language only in those contexts where an individual's interests conflict with the interests of others. A selfish person is one who unduly disregards the interests of others for the sake of his own interests, while an unselfish person is one who tends to act on the interests of others in disregard of his own interests. In those contexts where the interests of others are not involved, it is inappropriate in ordinary language to speak of actions as being either selfish or unselfish. For example, if, upon dressing in the morning, I

[2] *Webster's Unabridged Dictionary*, 3rd ed., 1971.

[3] *Webster's New World Dictionary, College Edition*, 1966.

choose a blue shirt over a white one, one would be at a loss to understand what could be meant by calling such an action a selfish one. Similarly, although it is certainly to my self-interest to have a well-balanced diet, it would seem inappropriate to call such a concern a selfish one. Consequently, if the notion of selfishness is given its ordinary meaning, the first formulation of psychological egoism would be trivially false, since there are many actions which can neither be said to be selfish nor unselfish. The second definition of psychological egoism fares no better when taken literally. Clearly, there are many people who habitually act contrary to their self-interest. This includes not only those individuals who fail to see what their self-interest demands, but also those of "weak-will" who quite knowingly act contrary to their own self-interest for some momentary satisfaction (such as smoking) or simply on impulse. Indeed, there are countless individuals whose actions reveal a self-destructive tendency, quite opposed to any of their rational self-interests.

The third definition of psychological egoism is the most promising. Unlike the other two, it does not attempt to specify a single motive that underlies all voluntary human actions, but instead attempts to rule out a particular type of motive—"acting on the interests of others, without expecting something in return"—that is, one never voluntarily acts to promote the interests of others as an end in itself. Let us call this motive the motive of "pure altruism." According to the third definition of psychological egoism, then, "pure altruistic actions do not exist." According to this thesis, one acts to promote the interests of others only as a means to the promotion of one's own interests. This definition, though better than the preceding ones, is also open to grave difficulties. Certainly there is no plausibility in the claim that individuals will never voluntarily do anything for someone else unless they consciously expect something in return. Clearly, people sometimes act impulsively to aid others without any thought of some "reward."

At this point, the defender of the third definition of psychological egoism is likely to begin speaking of "unconscious expectations." Yet one will find no support in any of the various psychological theories of human motivation for the claim that one is always "rewarded" in some unconscious, if not conscious, way whenever one voluntarily acts on the interests of others—let alone that some type of reward is the *aim* of one's other-regarding actions. Consider, for example, the following: Walking home, Jones sees an old woman carrying a heavy package. Jones notices that it is clearly to the woman's interest to have someone carry that package for her. The woman is walking in the same direction as Jones and it is absolutely no trouble for him to aid her, and this he does impulsively, without giving it any thought. Is it not implausible to claim that Jones must be expecting some "reward" for such an easy and non-self-sacrificing action? Upon consideration of examples such as this, the psychological egoist should, at the very least, grant that one need not expect to be rewarded for every single other-regarding action. More plausibly, he could contend that although individuals do at times act on altruistic motives—not expecting or receiving anything in return for some acts of benevolence to others—such a motive would not exist unless it were *associated with and generally reinforced* by some purely self-regarding interest.

Psychological Egoism and Behavioral Psychology

One can find support for this formulation of the doctrine of psychological egoism in the psychological theories of such behavioral psychologists as B.F. Skinner. According to this controversial view, all human motives are either unlearned self-regarding ones, such as the desire for security, food, and sex, or "higher order" ones which derive from (by the "laws of reinforcement") and are always dependent upon these primary self-regarding ones. These higher order motives, which would include any consideration for the interests of others, are dependent upon the primary self-regarding motives in that individuals would not indefinitely continue acting from them if they were no longer *in general* associated with the satisfaction of the primary self-regarding motives. In the more technical language of behavioral psychology, without reinforcement from the primary motives, the higher order ones would eventually become "extinguished"—that is, they are not "functionally autonomous." Skinner's belief that higher order motives are not functionally autonomous has been rejected, however, by other psychologists (such as Gordon Allport). As they see it, although the higher order motives derive from the primary ones by a learning process of association and reinforcement, once learned, they no longer are dependent upon further reinforcement from the primary ones. There are other more complex possibilities. For example, even if altruistic acts always satisfy primary self-regarding motives, it is still possible that some altruistic acts are acts of self-sacrifice in which one "gives more than one receives." One can also assume that people act from altruistic motives only if certain primary self-regarding needs like security and food are to some extent satisfied.[4] But once these

---

4 Such a view is supported by Colin Turnbull's description in his *The Mountain People* of an obscure tribe of African hunter-gatherers in Northern Uganda, the Ik. Given the constant struggle the Ik must maintain for bare survival, they live a life fully devoid of consideration for others. Love and generosity and all the various other ramifications of other-regarding concerns which we see as essential aspects of "humanity" and "morality" are nonexistent in the Ik's culture. As a result of his study of the Ik, Turnbull emphasizes the precarious and ultimately unstable nature of other-regarding motives. Turnbull's pessimistic picture of the human capacity under unfavorable circumstances to revert to primitive "inhumane" lack of concern for others is, however, not fully supported by our knowledge of how human beings responded to the chronic terror of life in Nazi concentration camps. Although many inmates lost any concern for the welfare of others, not all did so. Many could not kill to stay alive; they could not wish the other dead rather than themselves. Understandably, such people died more frequently than those who regressed into a more primitive and selfish way of seeing themselves and others, but while they lived they were perhaps able to maintain a "higher" self-image than those who succumbed to their more primitive needs.

needs are satisfied to some minimal extent, altruistic motives can flourish even if they are not in any way reinforced by the satisfaction of any primary self-regarding motives.

Psychological Egoism and Depth Psychology

Even if it is true, as Skinner and other behavioral psychologists have suggested, that people usually "get something in return" for their other-regarding actions and would not perform these actions unless they generally did so, it might still be quite misleading to say that people are never "really unselfish." Would this not depend on exactly what people "get out" of their actions? Perhaps if one delved more deeply into the cognitive and emotional structures of the human psyche, one would still want to distinguish some of the things one "gets out" of other-regarding actions as selfish and others as unselfish. It seems to me that behavioral psychology is not rich enough to help us in our dilemma here, for behaviorists find no utility in delving into the underlying nature of human motives. Psychoanalytic theory, on the other hand, does and thereby provides us with insight into the "murky depths" of human motives which can enable us to develop a more coherent and scientifically enlightening way of talking about the relative selfishness of people. Without this insight, statements that all people are or are not "really selfish" tend to be simplistic and misleading.

This is the case with most discussions of the doctrine of psychological egoism by professional philosophers who tend to dismiss it as either "trivially false" or "logically confused." Even if they are right about this, given the ordinary language meaning of the concept of selfishness, perhaps the fault is not with psychological egoism but with the scientifically imprecise and vague meaning attributed to the concept of selfishness in ordinary language. At times the indefinite and vague concepts of ordinary language must give way to the sort of refinement that scientific understanding can provide. Without this understanding, quick dismissals of the doctrine of psychological egoism by philosophers leave the more psychologically sophisticated person uneasy that not enough has been said.

For example, many philosophers today, in dismissing psychological egoism as stemming from linguistic confusion, claim that one must make a distinction between *the object* of one's desire and *the results* of satisfying one's desires. Even if it turned out that everyone did receive some satisfaction or pleasure from their altruistic actions (in a sense that does not trivialize this into a tautology), this would not necessarily imply, such philosophers rightfully point out, that one's (conscious) intention in acting altruistically must be the attainment of that satisfaction or pleasure. We do not begin by desiring some type of satisfaction or pleasure and then attempt to figure out how to achieve it, but rather desire all sorts of other things—friendship, health, money, power, etc.—and *because* we desire these things find ourselves deriving pleasure or satisfaction when we obtain them. No doubt this is true and it is an important distinction for a philosopher to make, for we tend to see a moral difference between what a person directly intends and what he indirectly achieves. (As we shall see, the Roman Catholic doctrine of "the double effect" is based on this distinction.) Philosophers have quite mistakenly, however, often assumed that people can be said to be selfish only when they do something with the (conscious) intention of obtaining pleasure or satisfaction for themselves. Typical of such claims are the following:

> . . . it is the *object* of a want that determines whether it is selfish or not. The mere fact that I am acting on *my* wants does not mean that I am acting selfishly; that depends on *what it is* that I want. If I want only my own good, and care nothing for others, then I am selfish; but if I also want other people to be well-off and happy, and if I act on that desire, then my action is not selfish.[5]

> Now take the case of a person who does an action with the *conscious aim* of helping someone who is in trouble. If the person who performs such an act gets pleasure as a result of achieving his aim, are we to say that he is therefore really behaving from self-interest, since he obtains the pleasure of satisfying a desire (namely, fulfilling his aim) by doing the action? The answer is no because the motive of an action is determined by the goal being sought . . . not by the effects of achieving that goal. In fact, a person who gets pleasure or satisfaction as a result of his achieving the goal of helping someone in trouble is *by definition* an unselfish person. The pleasure he gets is the *sign* that what he desired was to assist the other person, since he would feel frustrated and unhappy if he were unable by his action to fulfill his goal. In other words, one who acts to alleviate the suffering of another and *experiences satisfaction just because and insofar as he successfully accomplishes that purpose* is precisely the person who would be described as having acted unselfishly![6]

Such claims tacitly assume that the falsity of psychological egoism can be demonstrated without delving beneath the surface to the unconscious causes of our conscious intentions. According to the above statements, if a person's conscious intention or desire is to aid someone else and is not to receive some satisfaction or pleasure from his action, such a person should, if one is to speak correctly, be said to be an unselfish person. Since such people clearly exist, psychological egoism becomes a trivially false doctrine. But a psychologically perceptive person would want to go beneath the surface of one's conscious intentions and desires, realizing that even if one consciously aims at the welfare of someone else, it is quite possible on an unconscious level that one's concern for others is never an end in itself. Although it is obvious that people often act on the interests of others, without consciously expecting or wanting any-

---

[5] James Rachels, "Egoism and Moral Skepticism," in Arthur J. Minton, *Philosophy: Paradox and Discovery* (New York: McGraw-Hill, 1976), p. 275.

[6] Paul Taylor, *Principles of Ethics* (Encino, Calif.: Dickenson, 1975), pp. 43–44.

thing in return, it is not at all obvious that once we plumb the unconscious depths of human motives we will still want to say that such persons ought to be described as acting unselfishly. Perhaps, once we learn more about the hidden sources of human motives, a sceptic might claim, it will be discovered that in a much more enlightening sense "all motives are really ultimately the same" or that "truly unselfish actions do not exist." Such claims cannot be dismissed in the easy way that philosophers often dismiss them.

If we are to dig deeper into human motives, it is necessary for us to utilize the concepts of psychoanalytically oriented psychiatry. Let us turn our attention briefly then to some common personality types and look at their motives as a psychiatrist would.

The Psychopath: Pure Selfishness   Acting on the basis of the most primitive of human motives, the psychopath[7] is exploitative and parasitic in his relationships with others. He is concerned about other people's feelings only insofar as the recipient of his concern can give him something concrete in return for that concern; if he perceives that this is not the case, he loses interest. Since he has no genuine concern for the feelings of others, he often commits acts injurious to others, and thus often finds himself in trouble with the law. Clinically, psychiatrists have observed that such individuals tend to be very insecure people who feel dependent upon others for their own security. When someone does not fill their needs, they feel panic and rage.

The psychopath's relationship with his psychiatrist tells us much about his personality. Such an individual will voluntarily seek the services of a psychiatrist only when there is something concrete to be gained —often the psychiatrist's help in avoiding a jail sentence. The psychopath is usually clever enough not to mention what his "hidden agenda" really is, but instead, with appropriate tears, relates the misery of his childhood, etc., comes faithfully to his appointments, and expresses his unending appreciation to his psychiatrist. This goes on precisely until the psychopath's day in court; after that, the psychopath loses all interest in his psychotherapy and turns elsewhere for the support he needs.

The Oversolicitous Mother: Selfishness Masked as Unselfishness
The oversolicitous mother who sacrifices continually for her children while making sure that they know this is an example of an individual

---

[7] For a study of case histories of "psychopathic" or "sociopathic" personalities, see H. Cleckley, *The Mask of Sanity*, 4th ed. (St. Louis, Mo.: C.V. Mosby, 1964). According to Cleckley, psychopaths are incapable of empathizing with others and caring about anyone other than themselves. Yet they tend to have a higher than average shrewdness when it comes to knowing the motives of others and how to manipulate these motives to their own advantage. Projecting a facade of superficial charm, the psychopath hides his unreliability, insincerity and untruthfulness. While free of delusions and other signs of irrational thinking, as well as of nervous or neurotic symptoms, the psychopath is characteristically incapable of adjusting to society, learning by experience and following a life plan.

whose apparently unselfish actions are tainted with an underlying self-regarding motive. By giving so much of herself, she is capable of inducing guilt and feelings of obligation in her children. As a result, she is often much more efficient in satisfying her desire for security than she would be were she to utilize the concrete and simple quid pro quo of the psychopath. In addition, by acting as she does, she feels self-righteous and this boost to her often fragile self-esteem can act as a powerful unconscious motive. Psychiatrists call her "the moral masochist," but whatever the name, the syndrome is quite familiar to them. On the surface, she is quite the opposite of the psychopath. When she comes to see a psychiatrist, she is suffering. Yet, she is reluctant to incur the expense of psychiatric treatment; perhaps her boy Joey needs a car and she says that despite her terrible depression she doesn't want to deprive him of it by indulging herself. Her whole life, it soon appears, she has been sacrificing herself for others—even now she doesn't want to sit in her psychiatrist's comfortable chair. ("Save the furniture for your other patients.") She seems, in fact, determined to sacrifice and suffer. How unlike the psychopath! How unselfish!

Yet, is she really responding to other people's needs or to her own? For example, during treatment, her psychiatrist becomes aware of how determined she is to suffer, and he begins to notice how, despite how intensely she complains, she rejects all his attempts to help. Finally, he brings Joey in for a visit and discovers that Joey, who has been given so much by mother, is an unhappy boy—one of his chief feelings being a feeling of inadequacy. It soon becomes apparent that mother doesn't know what Joey really wants from her. Joey needs to feel competent and capable, and does not enjoy mother's excessive concern. Yet he feels too guilty and inadequate to confront mother or to leave home.

Ultimately, the oversolicitous mother's motives do seem selfish—although in a different way from the psychopath's. Unlike the psychopath, she wants long-standing relationships with people, but she gets them by trapping people in an unconscious cycle of feelings of inadequacy and guilt. Not only does she trap people, but she constantly boosts her self-esteem at the expense of others. On the surface, she seems the model of the unselfish person, but on a deeper level, she too can be seen as a manipulator who *uses others* as a means for satisfying her own needs. She can be said to be selfish because her needs so often motivate her actions instead of the needs of those whom she cares about and thinks she is helping. Unlike the psychopath, she cares deeply about others, but her concern is so wrapped up in her own self-regarding concerns that she is incapable of perceiving the true needs of those upon whom she showers her concern and upon whom she is so unknowingly dependent. Essential to her lifestyle is a mode of behavior toward her children that is oblivious to their need for growth, autonomy, and freedom from guilt. On the surface, she sacrifices for them; but on a deeper level, they are being sacrificed for her.

The Empathic Person: The Psychological Roots of Unselfishness

If the notion of unselfishness is to be a viable concept, it must be one which finds its proper application in the sort of person who is capable of empathically comprehending and caring about the feelings of others. Such an individual does not respond to others as objects to be manipulated, but rather as persons whose feelings have worth in and of themselves. Although such a person may feel gratified by doing things for others, she does not expect some concrete reward for her altruistic acts. Simply seeing the recipient of her benevolence better off is reward enough. Nevertheless, a psychiatrist could claim that the unconscious motive reinforcing such actions is the same as that in the preceding examples—security and self-esteem. Indeed, consciously requiring and expecting less from others, the empathic and caring person usually gets much more in return. Others, perceiving her empathic concern, tend to trust her and respond to her in a similar way. Consequently, over the long haul, empathic concern is strongly reinforced and is most successful in satisfying one's "basic" self-regarding motives. Although one may call the capacity for empathic concern a "secondary motive," such motives are very firm and difficult to disrupt in some people. Even the fear of death may not shake such motives, and a person may die to help others without expecting anything in return. Are these motives, however, never fully autonomous, that is, would they eventually be extinguished if all (unconscious as well as conscious) rewards were to cease? Given the differences in psychological theories of human nature and the complexity of human motives, this question has no clear answer.

Concluding Comments:
The Plausibility of Psychological Egoism

As we have seen, taken in the stronger forms in which it is often presented, psychological egoism is a trivially false doctrine if the concepts in its definitions are used with their ordinary language meanings. On the other hand, these concepts can be so expanded in meaning as to render the doctrine into a tautology. Yet, there was a weaker version of the doctrine of psychological egoism which has some plausibility—a view which makes us focus upon the connection between other-regarding interests and self-regarding ones; this connection is one which both behavioral psychologists and psychiatrists would claim to be an important one. According to our weaker formulation of psychological egoism, people who consistently act on the interests of others would eventually cease to behave in such a manner if their own self-regarding interests were not generally satisfied by so acting. Yet, even if such a view were true, this is certainly a far cry from the view that "everyone is selfish." To say that all people are selfish may enlighten in that it forces us to focus on the rewards that people get for their other-regarding actions, but it makes us neglect the vast differences in the nature of the rewards people receive. What it neglects is of much more moment than what it emphasizes.

Only the psychopath in aiding others expects to get something very specific from the recipient of his other-regarding actions. What the empathic person may get—even though she may not be consciously seeking it—is a reinforcement of her sense of self and the love and concern of others. Ironically, if the psychopath could respond similarly, he would most likely be much more efficient in receiving the sorts of things he consciously strives to receive. The psychopath is clearly the model of the truly selfish person—the person who does not care about others but manipulates them as if they were unfeeling objects. If the oversolicitous mother is to be said to be selfish, her selfishness is quite different from that of the psychopath. Unlike him, she certainly does care about other people, but like him, her needs motivate her actions and therefore she is often very incapable of perceiving the desires of those whom she helps. To go further and call the empathic person selfish is to so expand the notion of selfishness as to make it a useless one for theoretical as well as ordinary purposes. Intuitively, most of us know that there are people totally wrapped up in their own concerns who don't seem to perceive the feelings of others and who never go out of their way for anyone. On the other hand, there are caring people who seem to feel the joy and pain of others. Among these are some who give us an uneasy feeling. They are going to want something specific back in return or they are going to exact a good measure of guilt (by making us feel guilty, they can feel self-righteous). But others seem to give quite easily and with no strings attached. Clearly then, different people feel differently in a selfish-unselfish dimension. Since psychological theories of human behavior do not explain away this intuition, but rather serve to explicate it, it would serve no good purpose and can gravely mislead to dissolve this distinction by calling all human beings selfish. If we were to accept such a broadening of the concept of selfishness, we would very likely find the old distinction between selfishness and unselfishness creeping back into our language now in the guise of different sorts of selfish motives; such is often the case in philosophical attempts to dissolve conceptual distinctions that play an important role in ordinary discourse.

Morality and Self-Interest:
Can Self-Interest Alone Always Motivate
A Person To Do the Right Thing?

The thesis that everyone is motivated only by self-interest has had a profound grip on many influential philosophers. Such a view was held, for example, by Plato, Thomas Hobbes, and Jeremy Bentham. Nevertheless, morality certainly at times seems to demand that we sacrifice our own interests for the interests of others. Although we are often taught as children that following the dictates of morality always pays off in the end—that "honesty is the best policy" and that "crime does not pay"—we come to learn that there is no invariable connection between moral virtue and material happiness or prosperity, at least in this world. Immorality clearly seems to pay off handsomely for some people, while following the dictates of morality often does not. If this is so, how can we reconcile the harsh realities of life in this world with the belief that following the dictates of morality will always be consistent with one's enlightened self-interest? The most famous attempt at such a reconciliation is to be found in Plato's longest and most famous philosophical dialogue, *The Republic,* which is devoted primarily to the solution of this problem. Although Plato is willing to grant that material prosperity need not accompany the pursuit of morality, he argues that immoral people suffer from a type of psychic imbalance which always precludes the possibility of happiness. An immoral person may be possessed of all sorts of materialistic goods, but he will always lack the most important good of all—a "good soul" or "healthy psyche." The identification of virtue with psychic health was a central element in Plato's moral teaching. Let us consider this view.

Plato's Conception of Morality as Mental Health

Plato begins his detailed discussion of morality and self-interest in *The Republic* by observing that it often pays to live a moral life since immoral individuals are not apt to obtain the cooperation and respect of others that is required for faring well in this world. Nevertheless, Plato realizes the inadequacy of such a view, for if the only reason that can be given for being moral is the effect that such behavior has upon others, then it is not essential that one really be moral but merely that one appear to be so. If one could create the false impression that one were moral while secretly giving not one whit of consideration for the interests of others and acting accordingly whenever one could with impunity do so, one could apparently reap the beneficial consequences both of being thought moral as well as of actually being immoral. Plato puts such an argument in the mouth of one of the participants of the dialogue in *The Republic,* Glaucon. The dictates of morality and law, Glaucon claims, are a compromise between one's basic immoral instincts and one's desire for security. (This view will be echoed later in the political philosophy of Thomas Hobbes.) The best sort of world for each of us would be one in which we could with impunity act immorally while those around us act morally toward us. But since such a world does not exist, we are willing to compromise, binding ourselves to moral and legal restraints on condition that others do likewise. No rational person, however, who was capable of acting immorally with impunity would live up to such an agreement. In order to vividly illustrate his point, Glaucon relates the mythological story of Gyges who found a magic ring which enabled him to become invisible. Possessed of this ring, Gyges took what he wanted from others, untroubled by the demands of morality. All rational people in Gyges' place would have been moved by self-interest to act similarly, Glaucon asserts. If a person refused to employ Gyges' ring to wrong his neighbors with impunity when it was in his self-interest to do so, people would think him "a miserable fool" however much they might praise him in public. In order to show how injustice often seems to pay off so much more handsomely in this world than justice, Glaucon asks us to imagine two men—one a perfect model of justice, the other of injustice. The unjust man, he tells us,

> . . . must be like any consummate master of a craft . . . who, knowing just what his art can do, never tries to do more, and can always retrieve a false step. The unjust man, if he is to reach perfection, must be equally discreet in his criminal attempts, and he must not be found out . . . for the highest pitch of injustice is to seem just when you are not. . . . we must allow him to have secured a spotless reputation for virtue while committing the blackest crimes; he must be able to retrieve any mistake, to defend himself with convincing eloquence if his misdeeds are denounced, and, when force is required, to bear down all opposition by his courage and strength and by his command of friends and money.[8]

The just man, on the other hand,

> . . . must be stripped of everything but justice, and denied every advantage the other enjoyed. Doing no wrong, he must have the worst reputation for wrong-doing . . . and under this lifelong imputation of wickedness, let him hold on his course of justice unwavering to the point of death.[9]

Plato, through Glaucon's challenge, has placed before himself an extremely difficult task. He will cast aside all of the external rewards that morality often brings to those who accept its dictates and imagine a just man who is universally thought to be unjust, who is vilified by others and receives no material reward for his goodness. On the other hand, we are also to imagine a thoroughly immoral, but clever and rich, man who is the recipient of the lavish praise of others. Even in such a situation, Plato intends to show us, the moral man is far happier than the immoral one, for he alone possesses the inner peace and harmony of a healthy psyche or "good soul." Plato argues for this point on the basis of his psychological theory of the tripartite nature of the human psyche ("mind" or "soul"). In a mentally healthy person, Plato claims, the appetitive (bodily desires) and spirited (will or emotion) elements of the psyche are under the control of the third rational element. A mentally unhealthy person, on the other hand, is a person whose appetitive or spirited element is out of the control of reason. Such a person, lacking the inner harmony of an orderly psyche, is bound to be unhappy regardless of how great his external rewards may be. According to Plato's characterization of the immoral person, such a person is victimized by insatiable desires which his reason cannot control. To try to gratify such a person's desires, Plato claims, is like trying to pour water into a leaky vessel: the more water one pours, the greater the leak becomes because of the weight of

---

[8] Francis M. Cornford, trans., *The Republic of Plato* (New York: Oxford University Press, 1945), pp. 45–46.

[9] Ibid., p. 46.

the water; and the larger the leak becomes, the more rapidly one continues pouring, in the self-defeating attempt to compensate. A person who is victimized by insatiable desires, Plato claims, is incapable of happiness.

Although one may agree with Plato's assessment of such a person, there is certainly no reason to believe that *all* immoral persons are of the type Plato describes. The person who threatens the prestige of justice is not the unreasoning sensualist or unchecked tyrant that Plato depicts, but rather the immoral person of moderation, the person whose reason restrains his vice today in the interests, not of virtue, but of vice, tomorrow. This is the person who praises virtue for what he can get out of it in the way of wealth, power, and reputation, and this is the person whose picture Glaucon so aptly paints. Such a person is not at all like the sick individual who passes on heedlessly from one action to the next without foresight. Nowhere in *The Republic* does Plato ever show that those who follow the demands of conventional justice (such as, telling the truth and not stealing) are always happier than those who do not follow these demands, since the just alone have "harmonious psyches." Indeed, contemporary psychiatrists would attest to the fact that psychic imbalance befalls the "good" as well as the "bad" and that some "bad" people are among the psychologically healthiest of human beings. While psychiatrists would defend the view that a person totally devoid of a moral sense —that is, the psychopath—is a sick person who can never really find long-lasting happiness, such individuals form only a small percentage of the immoral people in this world. At any rate, even if we accept the view that the acceptance of *some* moral obligations to others is a necessary condition of happiness, such a view in no way specifies the exact nature of the moral obligations one must assume to others and the stringency of these obligations when they seem to conflict with one's own self-regarding concerns. Perhaps total dishonesty or untrustworthiness is always inconsistent with psychic health and happiness, but *moderate* dishonesty or untrustworthiness may not be at all.

Concluding Comments

If Plato's attempt to draw an invariable connection in this world between the demands of conventional morality and self-interest is doomed to failure, one can always appeal to the belief in an after-life where virtue will always be rewarded and wickedness punished. To nonbelievers, however, this is merely a psychologically comforting myth that cannot be rationally justified. If this is so, what reasons can we give individuals for sacrificing their interests for the interests of others in those situations where morality seems to require this? Clearly, if a person is motivated only by reasons of self-interest, there is no reason we can give such a person that will cause him to behave morally. But, as we have discussed, most of us are motivated by more than pure self-interest. A person genuinely concerned about others will often need no reason to behave morally other than the simple reason "because it will hurt someone else" or "because it is right."

Granted then that one can at times sacrifice one's own self-interest for the interests of others, the question still arises as to whether or not *one ought* to do so. It is to this question that we now turn.

Ethical Egoism

Even if individuals *do as a matter of fact* sometimes act on purely other-regarding motives without expecting or receiving anything in return, one could argue that individuals *ought* never to so act. This is the position known as "ethical egoism." According to the ethical egoist, self-interest is the only *rational* or *justifiable* motive an individual could ever have for acting.

Surprisingly, philosophers, who are quite aware of the need for clarifying the meaning of the doctrine of psychological egoism, seem to assume that the doctrine of ethical egoism has some transparently clear and unambiguous meaning. This is not so. The result, it seems to me, is that philosophers tend to attribute a meaning or implication to this doctrine that no one can be found to defend. For example, Richard Purtill in his *Thinking about Ethics* tells us that "the pure egoist considers no one's feelings but his own. To value others' respect or friendship is not to be a pure egoist."[10] Similarly, James Rachels, in his article "Egoism and Moral Skepticism," assumes that an ethical egoist "doesn't care about other people" and that he does not accept "it would harm another person" as a reason not to do something. Therefore, the ethical egoist is a person who "has no affection for friends or family," who "never feels pity or compassion, who is the sort of person who can look on scenes of human misery with complete indifference, so long as he is not the one suffering." After depicting the ethical egoist in this way Rachels admits that "Genuine egoists, people who really don't care at all about anyone other than themselves, are rare."[11] Doubtlessly! But, more important for our purposes, there is no philosopher who has advocated such a view. Indeed, I am sure that any psychiatrist or psychologist would contend that such a person could never be a happy or contented human being. Certainly, the picture Rachels paints of an ethical egoist who is willing to set fire to a department store "just for the fascination of watching the spectacular blaze," while not caring a whit for the people who might be burned to death as a result of his act, would be classified immediately as "sick." It is very difficult to believe that by acting in such a way such a person is acting in his own ultimate "self-interest."

Instead of attacking a position that no one advocates, it would be much more valuable to discuss the ethical beliefs of the popular philoso-

[10] Richard Purtill, *Thinking About Ethics* (Englewood Cliffs, N.J.: Prentice-Hall, Inc., 1976), p. 50.

[11] Rachels, "Egoism and Moral Skepticism," p. 281 of Minton anthology.

pher and novelist Ayn Rand who is noted for her advocacy of "selfishness."[12] Certainly, Rand and the followers of her so called "objectivistic" moral philosophy, while advocating "selfishness," do not advocate that we should not care about anyone other than ourselves. Although there is much ambiguity, and even inconsistency, in Rand's many expressions of her view, its essential theme is best seen in the quotation from her novel *Atlas Shrugged* that was utilized in our discussion of Kantian ethics (see pp. 78–9). The underlying sentiment behind so much of Rand's writings is not that one should not care about others, but rather that one should not accept a moral obligation to sacrifice one's interests for those about whom one happens not to care. This is clearly a different (and more plausible) view of ethical egoism than that attributed to it by Purtill and Rachels.

According to Rand, one ought to act on the interests of others only insofar as these interests are one's own. For example, if one genuinely loves someone else, one will have a desire for (an interest in) the welfare of that person. If one were a person (or God) with the sentiment of universal benevolence that utilitarians advocate—a person for whom the interests of all other human beings are an integral part of one's own interests—then ethical egoism would coincide with universal benevolence. Rand would claim, however, that given human nature, universal benevolence is both unnatural and undesirable. Human beings who attempt to follow the utilitarian point of view, she would claim, must of necessity restrict their desires out of an artificially created sense of moral duty which is incapable of rational justification. As Rand sees it, while utilitarians and Kantians enjoin us "to love our neighbors as ourselves," love is "a profoundly personal and selfish value" that people "should have to earn by means of their virtues and which one cannot grant to mere acquaintances or strangers." As an example, Rand tells us to imagine a man who spends a fortune to cure a woman whom he passionately loves. It is absurd, she argues, to claim that this is a *sacrifice in her behalf,* for her welfare *is* his welfare. On the other hand, suppose that he lets her die in order to spend his money on saving the lives of ten other women, none of whom mean anything personally to him, as utilitarianism would advocate. This would be a *sacrifice.* But this is a sacrifice that we have no moral right to request of human beings, and that human beings cannot make without forfeiting their very individuality—that is, their integrity—as human beings, Rand passionately argues.

Philosophical Criticism of Ethical Egoism

Many philosophers, in attacking the ethical egoist's contention that one ought not to act on the interests of others unless by so doing one satisfies one's own interests, have not been content with merely expressing their strong disagreement with such a view, but have attempted instead to show that in some fundamental respect this view is incoherent *as a moral point of view.* Without inquiring too deeply into the metaethical thickets of this issue, let us briefly consider certain typical philosophical refutations of ethical egoism and the manner in which such a doctrine might be defended.

First, a critic could attempt to convince an ethical egoist to abandon his position by pointing out to him that it is to his advantage to respect the rights and interests of those for whom he has no special feelings, since it is to his advantage to live in a society in which people's rights and interests are respected. Life in a society of ethical egoists, each pursuing his own uncurbed self-interest would be, in Thomas Hobbes's famous words, "solitary, poor, nasty, brutish, and short." Consequently, rational egoists, faced with the prospect of insecurity and death that general uncurbed egoism would bring, would agree to curb their egoism through a convenant (agreement) to abide by general laws which provide for mutual noninterference and cooperation and punishment for those who disobey. Nevertheless, if an egoist could with impunity act contrary to this covenant he would, for he is bound to it not by respect but by fear. For an egoist, the best sort of world would be one where he can break the law with impunity but those around him cannot. On the basis of this apparent consequence of ethical egoism, philosophers have argued that it cannot be conceived as a moral point of view. By definition, they have claimed, a moral point of view must be a *disinterested* one which requires that one be willing to universalize one's desires. Since the ethical egoist is unwilling to accept a disinterested point of view and would not want everyone to act as he wants to act, his position must be taken as a rejection of the moral point of view, it is claimed.

There are several replies an ethical egoist can make to this sort of criticism. First, he could reject the metaethical contention that all legitimate moral principles must be disinterested ones, for such a view of morality assumes that a moral person must be willing to submit himself to a good other than his own, and this is simply not so, our ethical egoist may contend. As we can see, the point of disagreement between our imagined ethical egoist and his critic is to some extent a *verbal* (conceptual) one concerning the proper use of the term "moral." However, unlike a *merely verbal disagreement,* this disagreement cannot be resolved simply by recognizing the fact that different meanings are being attributed to a concept. As in most philosophical debates that hinge on the meaning that should be attributed to a key concept, underlying the verbal disagreement is a deeper and more substantial one—in this case, a disagreement over *the sorts of reasons that should be most binding on human beings.*

Doubtlessly, in ordinary language, we speak primarily of moral demands in the context of conflicts of interest with others and, as such, moral demands are social demands that involve a consideration of the interests of others. Nevertheless, we sometimes do speak of individuals as having moral obligations to themselves—for just as it is often very difficult for people to put aside their own self-interest for the interests of others, it is sometimes very difficult for people to accept the self-denial of momentary impulses that is often necessary if one is to provide for one's good in the long run. There would appear to be a personal dimension to the moral point of view as well as the obvious social dimension. The critics of ethical egoism, by claiming that a moral principle must be disinterested, are focusing exclusively upon the social dimension, whereas the ethical egoist is focusing exclusively upon the personal dimension. If the critics' view is to be accepted, purely personal commitments to a way of life, however seriously binding they are considered to be, are not to count as *moral* commitments. Such a contention is not merely a description of what the concept of "morality" means in ordinary language, for this concept has no single clear meaning, but is rather a prescription of how it ought to be used. It is precisely this prescription that the ethical egoist might very well refuse to accept, arguing that any rational commitment to act in a particular way, in spite of external obstacles and internal temptations which move one to act otherwise, should count as *moral* commitments.

Indeed, even if our ethical egoist would be willing to grant, for the sake of argument, that ethical egoism is not *a moral point of view,* it is still, he would argue, *a reasonable* (or *the only reasonable*) point of view. Even if one's seriously binding personal commitments should not be called moral ones, this does not settle the issue of whether they should always, or at least sometimes, take precedence over one's moral commitments. One may be willing to accept that only other-regarding reasons should count as moral reasons but strongly disagree on the substantive nonlinguistic issue of what reasons ought to be seriously binding on human beings. The real issue separating the egoist and the nonegoist is not the meaning of the term "moral," but *what is to count as a rational reason for action.* As the egoist sees it, such reasons should always be reasons of self-interest. Insofar as conventional morality counsels us to sacrifice our own self-interest to the interests of others, conventional morality is unreasonable and ought to be disregarded, the egoist claims.

It is precisely because the notion of a moral reason carries for many the tacit implication of being the most binding of reasons for action that egoist and nonegoist alike will attempt to cling to this concept although offering different definitions of its content. Any attempt to find the "real" definition of a very key concept which is intertwined with other concepts whose meanings and exact interrelationships have shifted through the ages is bound to result in a stipulation as to how that concept ought to be used and therefore must reflect some substantial philosophical commitment which goes beyond ordinary usage. As we shall see, for example, in our discussion of the issue of punishment, the traditional philosophical question of defining the concept of punishment has often camouflaged substantial moral questions concerning how we ought to respond to criminal offenders.

Second, although admitting that universalization, though not disinterestedness, is a necessary requirement of the moral point of view, an ethical egoist could claim that he does not at all reject this notion, for he is claiming that everyone, and not only he himself, should act exclusively in terms of self-interest. Although from his own selfish point of view, he may very well not *want* others to do so, he will, however, admit that others, from their own point of view, ought to so act. If the "universalizability principle" simply means that whatever principles one believes are right for oneself to follow one must be ready to accept as right for everyone else to follow, he will be quite willing to accept the "universalizability principle" as a necessary requirement of the moral point of view. If, however, a commitment to this principle is to be taken to imply that one must *want* others to accept the same principles as one accepts, then he might very well reject this principle as a necessary condition of the moral point of view.

Finally, an ethical egoist will reject the claim made by some philosophers that "ethical egoism is an inconsistent doctrine since it leads to inconsistent directives." According to this argument, if one is committed to the view that everyone ought to act exclusively in his own interest, then if doing X is in A's interest, A ought to do X. However, if doing X is contrary to B's interest, then B would correctly judge that X ought not to be done by A. Thus, we have two contradictory judgments—"A ought to do X" and "A ought not to do X"—which follow from the doctrine of ethical egoism. Consequently, it has been claimed, ethical egoism must be rejected as an internally inconsistent doctrine.

This argument is, however, a confused one for the ethical egoist, for it will not make sense to him to speak of what "morally ought" to be done in a strictly impersonal sense. As he will see it, judgments of what ought to be done *presuppose* and are *relative to* a given person's interests. Consequently, the alleged contradictory judgments are not, according to him, really contradictory if they are written in their complete form as "A ought to do X, from A's point of view" and "A ought not to do X, from B's point of view." Now, granted that such statements do not stipulate how such a conflict of interest should be resolved, an ethical egoist might very well not presume that morality can resolve conflicts of interest among individuals. He may simply claim that each individual ought to attempt from his own point of view to emerge victorious from a conflict of interests with others and give this advice to others when asked. Of course, if his own interests are involved, he may very well choose to remain silent or even to "propagandize" others to accept an impersonal viewpoint. We might very well find such a view distasteful, but it is not at all an inconsistent view, as some philosophers have claimed.

Ethical egoism may not be an inconsistent or illogical view, but is it a reasonable one? Is it reasonable to say that we ought never to act contrary to our own self-interest? Even if one defines "self-interest" broadly, as Rand does, to incorporate a natural (as opposed to morally induced) concern for others, given human nature, will it not be to one's self-interest at times to injure others in order to obtain what one desires? In reply to this question, an ethical egoist could concede the need for a *social morality* which acts to curb individual desires, but would maintain, nevertheless, that this *social morality* should be distinguished from one's *private morality*. As an egoist making this distinction would see it, it is to everyone's interest that social morality should act to curb the natural inclinations of individuals by giving individuals certain rights of noninterference. Such an egoist might well agree that individuals should be conditioned to internalize such obligations. Yet, he would recognize the possibility that one's private morality—that is, a general all-inclusive theory of conduct based on self-interest—could quite conceivably conflict with this social morality. When this happens, it would be his belief that individuals would always be justified in sacrificing the demands of social morality for the demands of private morality. It will, of course, be to all our interests to have a strong criminal law that acts, through the fear of punishment, to make the demands of social morality coincide with the demands of private morality. Nevertheless, these demands will not always coincide and, no doubt, there will be occasions when a person can be reasonably assured that he will not be punished if he violates the rights of others. According to our ethical egoist, when this is the case, a wise person would violate the law.

Most of us would not, however, be willing to accept such a position. How many of us would be willing to accept the ethical egoist's apparent belief that one is justified in killing and stealing from others whenever one can be reasonably assured that this will be in one's ultimate self-interest? It would appear that even Ayn Rand doesn't hold such a view, since she places some curb on human selfishness by requiring that an individual's actions be consistent with *rational* self-interest. Although, as far as I am aware, Rand never carefully spells out the force of the word "rational" here, it would appear that this word serves to provide individuals with rights of noninterference from others. As she perceives it, the *rational* interests of human beings do not clash, since *rational* human beings (by definition) do not "desire the unearned," and treat other human beings as *traders,* "giving value for value." The principle of trade, she claims, is "the only rational ethical principle for all human relationships. . . . It is the principle of justice."[13]

As we see, according to Rand, a *rational* desire is a *just* desire. While Rand's notion of justice is never spelled out, it would appear that she advocates her egoistic philosophy within the background of a (Kantian) framework of rules which respect persons and property and which aim at maximizing human liberty (and minimizing governmental interference). As such, Rand seems to be committed to the moral position that individuals have an obligation not to violate the rights of others to their life and property, apart from the effect that such forbearance will have on their ultimate self-interest. Although Rand exhorts us not to

---

[13] Ibid., p. 28.

accept a moral obligation to *aid* those whom we do not care about, she accepts obligations of *forbearance* (not harming). Consequently, Rand's ethical egoistic commitment to one's *supreme* moral obligation to oneself is limited by other moral principles. Her ethical philosophy, in the last analysis, would seem to reduce itself to the more carefully spelled out libertarian philosophy of Robert Nozick that we briefly discussed in the chapter on Kantian ethics.

As we have seen, even Ayn Rand, who is considered the foremost contemporary advocate of ethical egoism, does not seem to accept the doctrine that individuals have no moral obligations whatsoever to people other than themselves and should always act in their own self-interest regardless of the effect that such action will have on others. Understandably, Rand and her followers do not claim that an individual would be justified in doing anything he pleases to others—including robbing and killing them—as long as such action serves his long-range interests. If, as many philosophical critics of ethical egoism assume, this is what the doctrine of ethical egoism asserts, then Rand is not an ethical egoist and indeed there is no contemporary advocate of this pure version of ethical egoism, of which I am aware. Although one can quibble over whether or not Rand should be called an ethical egoist, there can be no doubt that she accepts a moral point of view very much opposed to the utilitarian point of view. In essence, Rand is telling us that *our primary moral obligation is to ourselves* and that, although we have obligations of forbearance toward others, we do not have any (utilitarian) obligation to help total strangers for whom we have no special feeling. We ought not, Rand tells us over and over again in her many writings, sacrifice ourselves or those we care about on the altar of universal benevolence.

Certainly the point of view that Rand expresses has some plausibility and cannot be dismissed as confused or irrational. Is she not right, for example, that we ought sometimes to reproach a person for being *too* altruistic? I think so. Nevertheless, I cannot accept Rand's view that we have no obligation whatsoever to help mere acquaintances or strangers. If Rand is right that an individual whose moral choices were always motivated by the utilitarian principle of universal benevolence would lack a very essential attribute of humanity, so, it seems to me, would a person who feels absolutely no empathy and inclination to help mere acquaintances or strangers whom he knows he can help. It would seem to me that a morally wise person should accept the existence of independent, purely self-regarding moral obligations as well as the more typical other-regarding moral obligations. The ancient Greeks, for example, certainly believed this, emphasizing the purely personal moral virtues of prudence, self-courage, and temperance. Exactly how we are to weigh the moral demands of others against our own moral demands must, as we have said before, ultimately reflect the actual preferences we find within ourselves or those preferences by which we choose to be guided. We may shun, lock up, or even kill, those who do not care for others as much as we think they should or who are willing to disregard the interests of others in ways we consider morally unjustified, but we cannot always hope to have a rational basis for proving that such individuals are wrong or irrational for not caring or not considering.

DISCUSSION QUESTIONS

1. Consider the following argument:

> The doctrine of psychological egoism is incompatible with true friendship. True friendship, by definition, involves a concern for the welfare of someone else as an end in itself. A concern for the welfare of someone else that is purely self-regarding is not true friendship. Yet the psychological egoist claims that all motives for action are self-regarding. Consequently, the psychological egoist rules out the possibility of true friendship.

How do you think a psychological egoist would reply? How would Ayn Rand?

2. Consider the following often-quoted incident attributed to Abraham Lincoln:

> Mr. Lincoln once remarked to a fellow-passenger on an old-time mud coach that all men were prompted by selfishness in doing good. His fellow-passenger was antagonizing this position when they were passing over a corduroy bridge that spanned a slough. As they crossed this bridge they espied an old razor-backed sow on the bank making a terrible noise because her pigs had got into the slough and were in danger of drowning. As the old coach began to climb the hill, Mr. Lincoln called out, "Driver, can't you stop just a moment?" Then Mr. Lincoln jumped out, ran back and lifted the little pigs out of the mud and water, and placed them on the bank. When he returned, his companion remarked: "Now, Abe, where does selfishness come in on this little episode?" "Why, bless your soul, Ed, that was the very essence of selfishness. I should have had no peace of mind all day had I gone on and left that suffering old sow worrying over those pigs. I did it to get peace of mind, don't you see?"[14]

Do you agree with Lincoln that his action was a selfish one or would you say, as some philosophers have, that his action was definitely an unselfish one or do you think that it depends? If so, on what does it depend? Can you think of some test that would decide the issue?

3. In depicting a person who successfully feigns an unselfish concern for the feelings and interests of others, Glaucon imagines a thoroughly unjust person who cunningly deceives others into believing him just. Is it at all likely in the real world for a person to successfully practice

[14] Quoted from the *Springfield* (Ill.) *Monitor* in the *Outlook*, 56, p. 1059.

such duplicity over the long haul? Are such dishonest people likely to be as happy as those who are motivated by a genuine unselfish concern for others? Explain.

FURTHER READINGS

FEINBERG, JOEL, ed., *Reason and Responsibility* (3rd ed.), Part G. Encino, Calif.: Dickenson, 1975. This anthology contains a good selection of material on the topics of this chapter, including Glaucon's challenge from Plato's *The Republic* that was referred to in this chapter. Feinberg's own essay "Psychological Egoism" and his introduction to Part G are especially written for beginning students.

PLATO, *The Republic of Plato,* trans. Francis Cornford. New York: Oxford University Press, 1945. Glaucon's challenge is found in Chapter 5.

RACHELS, JAMES, "Egoism and Moral Skepticism," in *Philosophy: Paradox and Discovery*, 272–81, ed. Arthur J. Minton. New York: McGraw-Hill, 1976.

RAND, AYN, *The Virtue of Selfishness: A New Concept of Egoism.* New York: New American Library, 1964.

14. DETERMINISM, FREE WILL, AND MORAL RESPONSIBILITY

As the philosopher Kant emphasized, deeply a part of our conception of morality is a picture of human beings as free and morally responsible persons whose moral choices are justly the subject of judgments of moral praise or censure. Yet the picture science presents of human beings is quite different. As science tends to see it, human beings are complex machines whose actions are fully determined (caused) by environmental and genetic factors that make people behave as they do. Are these two pictures incompatible, as they appear to be? From the very first stirrings of the scientific spirit, people have pondered this question in perplexity. This is no less true of philosophers. "Are human beings *really* morally responsible?" philosophers have asked. "Is it *really* right that human beings should be punished and blamed for their wrongdoing?" they have wondered. Traditionally, these questions have centered on the compatibility of the notions of free will and moral responsibility, with the doctrine of *determinism*.

Determinism is the philosophical theory that everything in the universe, including human actions and choices, is entirely governed by causal laws of the sort that science attempts to discover. To put this thesis another way, determinism is the belief that for any event, *E*, in this universe, there is some *cause, C. C*, in turn, is called a *cause* of *E*, because there is a "law of nature" which asserts that "whenever *C* occurs, *E* will occur." According to determinism, then, nothing happens purely by chance, if "by chance" one means "without any cause." Although we do, of course, often say that events happen "without any cause," if we accept the deterministic thesis such assertions cannot be taken literally.

When we say, for example, that "Jones quit his job without any cause," the determinist will take such a statement to mean not that Jones' action was an uncaused one, but rather that the cause is either unknown to the speaker or that Jones' reasons for leaving his job appear unjustified to the speaker. If determinism is true, every event that happens in this universe is in principle predictable if one knows the relevant laws of nature and the events leading up to that event. If, for example, there were some type of superscientist who knew absolutely everything that was happening in the universe at a given moment and every causal law, then he could predict the entire future of the universe from that moment on. This would be so, for any event E that will occur from this moment on will be related to some cause C through a law of nature that asserts that "whenever C occurs, E will occur"; and our superscientist will, according to our assumption, know of this law and of the existence of the event C which this law says will cause E.

Now, although it is impossible to prove that determinism is true, for there are clearly many things that happen whose causes are at present unknown to us, this doctrine is, nevertheless, a fundamental presupposition of scientific method as well as the reasoning of the ordinary person. For example, whenever we plug in a machine or plant seeds or mix certain chemicals, we act in accordance with the belief that events will occur in accordance with laws of nature. Indeed, without the knowledge of such laws, we would be powerless to control the future. Although there are many things whose causes we do not know, we rarely, if ever, consider the possibility that these events are uncaused, and consequently seek to discover a cause which we believe exists but is simply unknown to us. For example, doctors at present will admit that they do not know what the cause or causes of cancer are, but we would be at a loss if some doctor asserted that cancer, or some type of cancer, had no cause at all. We are ready to admit that there are diseases whose causes are unknown to us, but are not at all ready to admit that there are diseases without causes. Similarly, we all tend to readily accept the claim that human physical characteristics, such as the color of one's eyes, one's height, and general health and susceptibility to diseases, are fully determined by heredity and environment.

Is it not equally true that human temperament, intelligence, emotion, and behavior are determined by causal laws? After all, isn't the science of psychology slowly discovering the causal laws governing human behavior? If the science of psychology were as developed as the science of physics, could we not predict the behavior of human beings just as we can now predict the motion of physical objects according to the laws of mechanics? Many philosophers and scientists have thought so, believing that a human being is a complex conscious machine whose feelings, thoughts, choices, and behavior are subject to scientific explanation no less than other parts of nature. Given the complexity of the human organism and the innumerable forces that act upon it in complex and ever-changing combinations, there will always, most likely, be some element of uncertainty in the predictions scientists make about the expected choices and behavior of human beings. Nevertheless, in principle, what a human being chooses or does is subject to scientific laws no less than is a pebble which, once thrown up in the air with a particular force and particular air resistance, eventually begins to fall at a velocity and rate of acceleration predictable by the science of mechanics. As the sciences of psychology, sociology, and anthropology advance, we learn more and more about how a human being's choices and behavior are part of an order of causes and effects and are not the scientifically impenetrable acts of some mysterious "self" or "soul" whose choices are themselves undetermined, as some thinkers would have us believe.

While we appear to assume the doctrine of determinism in our everyday judgments about so many different things, we also assume that individuals perform actions "of their own free will" in situations where they were quite capable of doing something other than what they in fact did, and therefore, are proper subjects of judgments of moral responsibility and blame. Yet many philosophers have found it impossible to reconcile the common-sense assumption that people act freely with the doctrine of determinism which seems to imply that every event that occurs is *the only one that could have occurred* in the circumstances. For example, assuming that determinism is true, if Jones kills Smith at time *T*, given the forces both internal and external acting on Jones just prior to *T*, his killing of Smith had to happen. Given the causal factors at work in this situation, as in all situations of human choice, nothing can happen except what does happen. Thus, it seems to follow that if determinism is true, human beings can never act differently from the way they do act—that what occurs must occur, given the causal factors involved—and that, consequently, people are not really morally responsible or morally praiseworthy or blameworthy for their acts. Given the causal antecedents of their actions, they really have no choice but to act as they do. If determinism is true, the argument continues, then the feeling a person has that there are a number of alternative courses of action open to him is an illusion. Actually, only one of the imagined alternatives is possible—and indeed inevitable—given the causal law or laws involved.

Many philosophers as well as well-known thinkers outside of the fold of professional philosophy have accepted the soundness of the preceding argument and have, as a consequence, argued that one must choose between the belief in universal determinism and that of the existence of human free will.[1] Others have disagreed and have held that any

---

[1] There is no general agreement by philosophers over what can "properly" be said to be "free" (such as "will," "choice," or "action"). Although many philosophers use these concepts interchangeably (as we will), there are some philosophers who would consider them importantly different. For example, a philosopher might believe that our actions are free when determined by our choices but that our choices are never free or are free when not determined or determined in a particular way. As in many philosophical controversies, an essential part of the philosophical issue at hand is to decide upon its very formulation.

apparent conflict between determinism and human freedom is itself an illusion. Some who take this point of view merely assert that determinism is compatible with human free will and judgments of moral responsibility, while some go further, asserting that free will and judgments of moral responsibility presuppose the belief in determinism. Human freedom and moral responsibility, instead of being incompatible with determinism, they assert, is incomprehensible without it. There are, thus, three possible positions one can take on the determinism-free will issue and one can find influential supporters of all three.

First, there are those who, agreeing that determinism is incompatible with human freedom and moral responsibility, accept freedom and moral responsibility and reject determinism. Utilizing the generally accepted philosophical terminology, we shall call this the "libertarian" position. Most who take this position assert that the existence of free choice is a given fact of immediate experience. As the philosopher Henry Sidgwick put it, "It is impossible for me to think (at a moment of choice) that my volition is completely determined by my formed character and the motives acting upon it. The opposite conviction is so strong as to be absolutely unshaken by the evidence brought against it; I cannot believe it to be illusory." Since free choice seems to be so intuitively certain and is incompatible with determinism—a doctrine that is unproven and believed on scientific faith—one should reject determinism. Many who take this point of view emphasize the feeling of freedom that we have when engaged in a moral choice. Our belief that we are moral agents, they say, presupposes that we have free choice. As Kant put it, "ought implies can" (that is, to tell a person that he ought to do something makes sense only when that person has the freedom to do that act or to refrain from doing it). If an abstract and unproven theory such as determinism conflicts with our consciousness of being moral beings, the scientific theory must be discarded, and not the immediate and strong testimony of our consciousness. Such a view has been defended by the American philosopher William James and the famous English physicist Sir Arthur Eddington, who believed that the ideas of contemporary quantum physics are incompatible with determinism. While James and Eddington were willing to identify freedom with chance, this is not true of all libertarians. For example, Kant and his twentieth century disciple, C.A. Campbell, insist that acts of will are neither capable of a full causal scientific explanation nor are they mere chance occurrences. According to this point of view, true freedom of choice implies the existence of an autonomous (moral) self (soul) that can transcend the biological, psychological, and social conditions of one's being. The essence of this version of libertarianism is not that a free act is uncaused, but rather that the decisions of this autonomous (moral) self are not themselves fully determined by biological, psychological, and social conditions that are studied by science and related to each other through causal laws. Those who take this position distinguish a person's *moral self* from his *empirical self,* which is subject to determination by such factors.

Second, there are those who, agreeing that determinism is incompatible with freedom and moral responsibility, accept determinism and reject freedom and moral responsibility. Following William James's terminology, such individuals are often called "hard determinists."[2] According to this point of view, the constant advances in scientific explanation of phenomena, including human behavior, strongly favors belief in determinism. Any feeling we may have of freedom of choice and action that transcends causal determination by physical, psychological, and social conditions is a reflection of our ignorance of the causes that act through us. Human choices and actions are simply the determined responses of complex machines subject to scientific understanding and control. Since we do not choose the hereditary and environmental factors that fully determine our psychological makeup, which in turn determines our choices and actions, we are not ultimately morally responsible for what we do. We do what we do because we are what we are; but what we are is what our genes and environment make us. In holding people morally responsible for their actions and in praising them for their "good" actions and blaming them for their "bad" ones, we like to think that people are "morally praiseworthy" or "morally blameworthy" for their actions; in doing this, we forget that those who do well are simply those who have been *lucky* enough to inherit desirable characteristics or to be exposed to environmental circumstances which cause them to develop the wherewithal to do well. This hard-deterministic perspective was held by the famous philosophers Hobbes, Spinoza, and Schopenhauer and also by the scientists Freud and Einstein, as well as by the novelists Thomas Hardy and Mark Twain. The famous twentieth century lawyer, Clarence Darrow, often expressed such a view, both in his writings and in his successful court pleas—in particular, in his defense of the kidnap-murderers Leopold and Loeb.

Third, there are those who maintain that determinism is compatible with freedom and moral responsibility and that any appearance of conflict is a result of various philosophical confusions. Following the widely used terminology, we will call those who hold such a view "soft determinists." According to this point of view, once we clearly consider what we mean—or at least ought to mean, if we are thinking clearly—when we call an act or choice "free," we shall see that we in no way imply that free choices or actions are uncaused choices or actions. It is *specific types of causes* that make acts or choices unfree, not the mere fact that they are caused. Yet soft determinists disagree as to what these

---

2 James called those determinists who believe that determinism and free will are compatible "soft determinists." Although the terms James coined are currently used with no evaluative connotations, they were not intended as such. As a libertarian, James rejected the attempt to reconcile determinism with free will and, in calling those who attempted to do this soft determinists, James meant to imply that they were "soft-headed" thinkers who refused to accept the unpleasant, but inevitable, consequences of the belief in determinism. On the other hand, James believed, hard determinists were "hard-headed" enough to accept these unpleasant consequences.

causes are and therefore disagree as to the proper analysis of the notion of free choice or free action. According to a soft deterministic viewpoint held by the famous philosophers David Hume and John Stuart Mill, a free action is one that is not due to external compulsion or constraint. Even though all human actions are caused, those many human actions which are not a result of compulsion or constraint are free. Other soft determinists choose different analyses of "free action." For example, a free action has been defined as

1. one in which the agent could (or would) have decided otherwise *if* he had chosen otherwise or tried to do otherwise. For instance, X's knee reflex was not a free action. If he had tried (chosen) not to move his leg when the doctor hit his knee, he would have failed. (Freedom as hypothetical behavior)

2. one in which the agent had the power to decide and act otherwise. For instance, X's raising his hand when told to was not a free action. He was under hypnotic suggestion and even though he would not have raised his hand if he had chosen not to, he simply did not have the power to make this choice. (Freedom as power to do otherwise)

3. one in which the agent could have been persuaded to choose or act otherwise in light of rational considerations which would make it reasonable to act otherwise. For instance, the neurotic's continual washing of his hands is not a free action. (Freedom as capacity for rational action)

Let us now turn to a critical discussion of some representative statements and defenses of the various positions on the free will-determinism issue that we have briefly outlined. As we shall see, every position has its weaknesses. After presenting the various positions and mentioning the criticisms that can be raised against them, I will briefly share with you my own philosophical reflections about an adequate resolution of this classic philosophical problem.

Hard Determinism: Darrow, Twain, and Hospers

The most sensational American crime of 1924 was the brutal kidnapping and murder of fourteen-year-old Bobby Franks by two brilliant students, eighteen-year-old Nathan Leopold, Jr. and seventeen-year-old Richard Loeb. The killers, both from wealthy Chicago families, had the distinction of being the youngest graduates of the University of Chicago and the University of Michigan. In order to demonstrate their contempt for conventional morality, the two planned to commit "the perfect crime." Their attempt, however, proved flawed; and captured, they confessed. The state demanded the death penalty, while the attorney for the defense, Clarence Darrow, already famous for his defense of unpopular causes, pleaded that the killers' lives be spared. For over twelve hours in his summation to the jury, Darrow passionately pleaded for mercy for the defendants. This plea proved successful and the defendants were sentenced to life imprisonment. Over and over again in his summation, Darrow implored that Leopold and Loeb were helpless victims of hereditary and environmental forces which they did not choose, but which, nevertheless, molded them into the murderers that they had eventually become.

> Nature is strong and she is pitiless. She works in her own mysterious way, and we are victims. We have not much to do with it ourselves. Nature takes this job in hand, and we play our parts. . . .
> What had this boy to do with it? He was not his own father; he was not his own mother; he was not his own grandparents. All of this was handed to him. He did not surround himself with governesses and wealth. He did not make himself. And yet he is to be compelled to pay. . . .
> To believe that any boy is responsible for himself or his early training is an absurdity. . . . If his failing came from his heredity, I do not know where or how. None of us are bred perfect and pure; and the color of our hair, the color of our eyes, our stature, the weight and fineness of our brain, and everything about us could, with full knowledge, be traced with absolute certainty to somewhere. If we had the pedigree it could be traced just the same in a boy as it could in a dog. . . .
> If it did not come that way, then . . . if he had been understood, if he had been trained as he should have been it would not have happened.
> If there is responsibility anywhere, it is back of him; somewhere in the infinite number of his ancestors, or in his surroundings, or in both. And I submit, Your Honor, that under every principle of . . . right, and of law, he should not be made responsible for the acts of someone else.[3]

Similar sentiments were expressed by Mark Twain, when he wrote,

> Man is not to blame for what he is. He didn't make himself. He has no control over himself. All the control is vested in his temperament—which he did not create—and in the circumstances which hedge him round from the cradle to the grave and which he did not devise. . . . He is as purely a piece of automatic mechanism as is a watch, and can no more dictate or influence his actions than can the watch. He is a subject for pity, not blame. . . .[4]

At the heart of the hard deterministic perspective shared by Darrow and Twain is the contention that we are never justified in holding a person morally responsible or blameworthy for his actions since "he

[3] Clarence Darrow, *Attorney for the Damned*, in *Philosophy: Paradox and Discovery*, Arthur J. Minton, ed., (New York: McGraw-Hill, 1976), pp. 302–4.

[4] Mark Twain, "Reflections on Religion" quoted in Paul Edwards and Arthur Pap, eds., *A Modern Introduction to Philosophy*, 3rd ed., (New York: Free Press, 1973), p. 5.

didn't make himself." (Notice that Darrow and Twain use this very same expression.) A person may be free to act in accordance with his own desires, but since a person's very desires and capacity to find the will power and motivation to combat these desires are reflections of his character—a character which has itself been molded by hereditary and environmental forces that he did not choose—he does not really have free will and is not really morally responsible or morally blameworthy. The notion that individuals are not morally responsible in a determined world since in such a world individuals do not "choose their own characters" is a central idea that one finds in expressions of the hard deterministic point of view. Yet the notion of "choosing one's character" is a quite puzzling one which seems to be self-contradictory, for in order to choose something, one would seem to need to already possess some type of character. Consequently, when we speak of choosing one's character, are we not assuming that one already has some type of character? Although we can attach meaning to the notion of an individual who has a particular type of character choosing to change or develop certain personality traits, the idea of a type of characterless blob (which cannot be identified as a person) choosing its entire character from scratch seems to be nonsensical. It would seem to be as self-contradictory to talk about choosing one's (entire) character as it is to talk of a foursided triangle. Yet it seems to be this notion that hard determinists have in mind. Hard determinists, such as Darrow and Twain, bemoan the fact that since determinism is true, no one can choose his character; but even if determinism were false, it would appear that people would be equally incapable of choosing their character, for this notion appears self-contradictory. Consequently, it is misleading for a hard determinist to make it appear that the truth or falsity of determinism has any bearing on a person's free will or moral responsibility. The real problem here is to understand what possible sense can be attributed to this puzzling notion of choosing one's character.

Darrow and Twain, as well as other hard determinists, can also be criticized for their tendency to move imperceptibly from the idea that individuals do not make themselves to the idea that individuals are not morally responsible since they have no control over themselves. One can, however, admit that even though people do not make themselves (assuming we can attach some meaning to this expression), they often, nevertheless, have the power to control themselves and can therefore be held morally responsible and blameworthy for not exercising such control. For example, even though Jones may not have chosen to have the violent temper that he does, if he is not the victim of some type of "irresistible impulse," we expect him to have some degree of control over that temper. Assuming this to be true, even if Jones experiences himself as victimized by his violent temper which interferes with his "normal" personality and which inclines him to act against his value system, would we accept this fact alone to be sufficient to excuse him from accepting any responsibility for controlling that temper? Certainly not. Indeed, it is a fundamental psychoanalytic premise that the first step in controlling an "alien" desire is to accept responsibility for it—to recognize that we have the power to help direct and determine *the future course of our lives.* Without such an assumption, psychotherapy would be impossible. Is it not the case that once people are treated as and look upon themselves as being *helpless* or as *not having control* or as being *acted upon by forces outside of themselves* they tend not to exert the effort they have the power to command which would enable them to change themselves. As Sidney Hook, a contemporary American philosopher puts it,

> Far from diminishing the amount of needless cruelty and suffering in the world, I am firmly convinced that the belief that nobody is ever morally responsible, in addition to being false, is quite certain to have a mischievous effect and to increase the amount of needless cruelty and suffering. For it justifies Smerdyakov's formula in *The Brothers Karamazov:* "All things are permissible." One of the commonest experiences is to meet someone whose belief that he can't help doing what he is doing (or failing to do) is often an excuse for not doing as well as he can or at least better than he is at present doing. . . . We are responsible . . . for what it is in our power to do . . . In spite of the alleged inevitabilities in personal life and history, human effort can redetermine the direction of events. . . . It is not true that everything that happens to us is like "being struck down by a dread disease." The treatment and cure of disease—to use an illustration that can serve as a moral paradigm for the whole human situation—would never have begun unless we believed that some things that were did not have to be, that they could be different, and that *we* could make them different. And what we can make different we are responsible for.[5]

Furthermore, is it not the case that our very dignity as human beings consists in our conception of ourselves as responsible beings? To consider oneself as a passive object or machine that is simply acted upon by forces that one cannot control is to rob oneself of one's dignity as a responsible and rational human being. One can well understand a person's plea that he *is* responsible and ought to be treated as such and not as a passive object of forces beyond his control.

With these criticisms in mind, let us turn to a defense of the hard deterministic point of view by the contemporary American philosopher John Hospers, which is much more sophisticated than the defenses presented by Darrow and Twain. In his widely reprinted article, "What Means This Freedom," Hospers is quite willing to admit that for practical purposes we must hold people morally responsible for their actions and treat them as if they had free will. Nevertheless, when we reflect more deeply about the determinants of a person's behavior, we realize that in a deeper sense no one is ever morally responsible for his actions. Although we like to look down upon wrongdoers from a position of

---

5 Sidney Hook, "Necessity, Indeterminism and Sentimentalism," in *Philosophy,* ed. Minton, p. 356.

moral superiority believing them to be proper recipients of our moral feelings of righteous indignation and resentment, such feelings, Hospers believes, are out of place on deeper-level reflection. Since determinism is true, there is a causal chain stretching from conditions that existed before our birth to our present characters and present choices. This means that if we go back far enough we will find our characters to be causally determined by conditions over which we had no control. Thoughtful persons, Hospers believes, once recognizing this fact, will find feelings of moral superiority out of place.

> . . . the more *thoroughly* and *in detail* we know the causal factors leading a person to behave as he does, the more we tend to exempt him from responsibility. When we know nothing of the man except what we see him do, we say he is an ungrateful cad who expects much of other people and does nothing in return, and we are usually indignant. When we learn that his parents were the same way and, having no guilt feelings about this mode of behavior themselves, brought him up to be greedy and avaricious, we see that we could hardly expect him to have developed moral feelings in this direction. When we learn, in addition, that he is not aware of being ungrateful or selfish, but unconsciously represses the memory of events unfavorable to himself, we feel that the situation is unfortunate but "not really his fault." When we know that this behavior of his, which makes others angry, occurs more constantly when he feels tense or insecure, and that he now feels tense and insecure, and that relief from pressure will diminish it, then we tend to "feel sorry for the poor guy" and say he's more to be pitied than censured. We no longer want to say that he is personally responsible.[6]

As a famous French saying puts it, "To understand all is to forgive all" ("tout comprendre, tout pardonner"). But a critic is bound to reply, "this is certainly not always the case. Sometimes, the more I learn about a person, the more inclined I am to blame him for not making an effort to change himself. An individual is not simply passively acted upon by forces, but can exert the effort to change himself. Some individuals, alas, do not exert that effort and for that very reason should be blamed. Individuals who succeed often do so precisely because of *their* effort and are not simply the lucky and passive recipients of forces acting upon them." Hospers has a reply to such a critic:

> But, one persists, it isn't a matter simply of luck; it is a matter of effort. Very well then, it's a matter of effort; without exerting the effort you may not overcome the deficiency. But whether or not you are the kind of person who has it in him to exert the effort is a matter of luck. . . .
>   The position, then, is this: if we can overcome the effects of early environment, the ability to do so is itself a product of the early environ-

6 John Hospers, "What Means This Freedom," in *Philosophy*, ed. Minton, pp. 332–33. Reprinted by permission of New York University Press, the publisher of the original hardcover edition.

ment. We did not give ourselves this ability; and if we lack it we cannot be blamed for not having it. Sometimes, to be sure, moral exhortation brings out an ability that is there but not being used, and in this lies its *occasional utility;* but very often its use is pointless, because the ability is not there. The only thing that can overcome a desire . . . is a stronger contrary desire; and many times there simply is no wherewithal for producing a stronger contrary desire. Those of us who have the wherewithal are lucky.[7]

What are we to make of such sentiments? Is Hospers not right that there is a basic ambivalence in our attitude toward wrongdoers? On one hand, we feel inclined to blame and hold them morally responsible for the choices that stem from their own defective characters. Yet, on the other hand, when we understand the causal factors that produced that defective character, we often find ourselves inclined to "feel sorry for the poor guy" and fortunate in having avoided the same causal influences. If we are good at empathy, we might be able to imagine ourselves turning out no different from the person we originally judged with feelings of moral superiority, saying, "there but for the grace of God, go I," or perhaps, more appropriately, "there, but for the grace of my causal antecedents, go I." When we see things this way, as so many of us can at times, the righteous indignation and resentment that we initially feel toward a wrongdoer undergoes a metamorphosis into a sort of cosmic sadness that the forces of the world created such a person. It is not the individual as a locus of responsibility to whom we direct our scorn but to those causes that molded him. "If only his physiology were different, or his early environment, or his parents, . . . he would not have turned out as he did," we muse. And if there is anything at all that we find redeeming about this person, as we often will, we can imagine *him* existing without his "bad" qualities and direct our sorrow for the loss of what could have been at that "good" part of him we see before us.

Like Darrow and Twain, however, Hospers tends to confuse the notion that we are not morally responsible for our actions because they stem from qualities of character that can ultimately be traced back to causal antecedents over which we had no control, with the quite different thesis that we have no power to control our actions. For example, Hospers writes,

Let us suppose it were established that a man commits murder only if, sometime during the previous week, he has eaten a certain combination of foods—say tuna fish salad at a meal also including peas, mushroom soup, and blueberry pie. What if we were to track down the factors common to all murders committed in this country during the last twenty years and found this factor present in all of them, and only in them? The example is, of course, empirically absurd; but may it not be that there is *some* combination of factors that regularly leads to homocide? . . . When such

7 Ibid., pp. 334–35.

specific factors are discovered, won't they make it clear that it is foolish and pointless, as well as immoral, to hold human beings responsible for crimes? Or, if one prefers biological to psychological factors, suppose a neurologist is called in to testify at a murder trial and produces X-ray pictures of the brain of the criminal; anyone can see, he argues, that the *cella turcica* was already calcified at the age of nineteen; it should be a flexible bone, enabling the gland to grow. All the defendant's disorders might have resulted from this early calcification. Now, this particular explanation may be empirically false; but who can say that no such factors, far more complex, to be sure, exist?[8]

This passage is worthy of careful scrutiny. First, one should realize that even if a person would not commit a given crime if he had not eaten a certain combination of foods or if he did not have a "calcified *cella turcica*," it still need not be "pointless, as well as immoral" to hold such an individual responsible for his crime, as Hospers suggests, *if the individual had some control over the effects of these factors.* For example, if Jones would not have committed a crime had he not been in an agitated condition, and he would not have been in an agitated condition had he not eaten that particular combination of food, there is certainly a point in holding him responsible if he were conscious of his agitated condition and had the power to combat the desires that sprang from it. After all, we often find ourselves victimized by unexpected changes of mood—stemming from we know not where—which incline us to do things we normally would not; but clearly, this is precisely the time that it is important for us to accept responsibility for controlling the desires that we find imposing themselves upon us. Even though Hospers does not explicitly say this, he would appear to be assuming in the examples that he gives that the forces that *cause* a person to commit a crime do so in ways that bypass any conscious deliberation. Clearly, if certain combinations of food or a "calcified *cella turcica*" are in themselves *sufficient* to cause a crime, as Hospers seems to assume, then individuals are powerless victims of these forces. But is there any reason to believe that human behavior is *fully* determined by such uncontrollable forces. I think not. As psychoanalysts and Hospers point out, many actions which appear to be determined through conscious and rational deliberation are actually fully caused by unconscious factors over which we have no knowledge or control. Nevertheless, there is no good reason to believe that this is always or usually the case. The psychoanalytic insights Hospers so readily relies upon suggest not that actions are *never free,* but that they are perhaps *less free* than we originally thought. Indeed, the cornerstone of psychoanalytic thought is the belief that unconscious causes can be brought to consciousness and there be subject to control. From the psychoanalytic perspective it is in this that our freedom lies.

Doubtlessly, a newborn baby or a very young child is a fully passive recipient of environmental influences, but as the child grows older, he

[8] Ibid., p. 332.

helps mold and direct that environment. If it could be shown that all or most conscious human deliberation over momentous personal choices is nothing but a rationalization for acting in ways that are fully determined by the unconscious effects of early childhood experiences, there would be justification for looking at individuals as mere pawns of fate, but there is no reason to believe that this is generally true. Indeed, agreed upon scientific laws relating early childhood experience to an adult's later capacity for conscious and rational choice are nonexistent.

Libertarianism

James: Freedom as Chance

William James (1842–1910), an influential philosopher and psychologist of the turn of the century and one of the key figures in the development of the school of American philosophy known as "pragmatism," argues passionately for an acceptance of the libertarian point of view in his famous article "The Dilemma of Determinism." James begins his article by sketching the essential difference, as he sees it, between determinism and indeterminism. He writes,

> . . . [Determinism] professes that those parts of the universe already laid down absolutely appoint and decree what the other parts shall be. The future has no ambiguous possibilities hidden in its womb. . . .
>
> > With earth's first clay they did the last man knead,
> > And there of the last harvest sowed the seed,
> > And the first morning of creation wrote
> > What the last dawn of reckoning shall read.
>
> Indeterminism, on the contrary, says that the parts have a certain amount of loose play on one another, so that the laying down of one of them does not necessarily determine what the others shall be. It admits that possibilities may be in excess of actualities. . . . Of two alternative futures which we conceive, both may now be possible; and the one become impossible only at the very moment when the other excludes it by becoming real itself. Indeterminism thus denies the world to be one unbending unit of fact It says there is a certain ultimate pluralism in it; . . .[9]

According to James, determinism is inconsistent with our unsophisticated view that "what has happened need not have happened." If determinism is true then our common intuitive experience that there are possibilities of action open to us must be an illusion. On the other hand, if this experience is not an illusion, then there must be some chance factor in the universe which makes complete scientific predictions of events impossible. James unhesitantly identifies "freedom of action" with

[9] William James, "The Dilemma of Determinism" in *Philosophy*, ed. Minton, p. 307.

acts due to "chance." Nevertheless, James admits that we cannot be sure of the veracity of our intuitive feeling that there really are alternatives of action open to us; all we know is that this experience appears quite real to us.

As well as going against our immediate experience of freedom, the doctrine of determinism, James argues, is inconsistent with our deep moral feelings of regret that some things that happen need not have happened. He writes,

> I wish first of all to show you just what the notion that this is a deterministic world implies. The implications I call your attention to are all bound up with the fact that this is a world in which we constantly have to make what I shall, with your permission, call judgments of regret. Hardly an hour passes in which we do not wish that something might be otherwise; and happy indeed are those of us whose hearts have never echoed the wish of Omar Khayam—
>
> . . .
>
> Ah! Love, could you and I with fate conspire
> To mend this sorry scheme of things entire,
> Would we not shatter it to bits, and then
> Remould it nearer to the heart's desire?[10]

Thinking now of the story he had just recently read in the newspaper of a brutal murder in Brockton, Massachusetts, James reflects that in a determined world our feeling of regret that such a crime happened becomes irrational, for given the causes acting in the universe, such a crime was inevitable.

> But for the deterministic philosophy the murder, the sentence, and the prisoner's optimism were all necessary from eternity; and nothing else for a moment had a ghost of a chance of being put into their place. . . .
> If this Brockton murder was called for by the rest of the universe, if it had to come at its preappointed hour, and if nothing else would have been consistent with the sense of the whole, what are we to think of the universe? Are we stubbornly to stick to our judgment of regret, and say, though it *couldn't* be, yet it *would* have been a better universe with something different from this Brockton murder in it? . . . the judgment of regret calls the murder bad. Calling a thing bad means, if it means anything at all, that the thing ought not to be, that something else ought to be in its stead. Determinism, in denying that anything else can be in its stead, virtually defines the universe as a place in which what ought to be is impossible . . .[11]

The acceptance of determinism, James claims, must lead to the very depressing conclusion that what is, however bad it might be, must be—

10 Ibid., p. 309.

11 Ibid., p. 310.

that regret over particular events is irrational. (If regret makes any sense at all in a determined world, James goes on, such regret must be directed not to particular events, but to the "whole sorry scheme of things.")

There are many serious difficulties with James's view. First, it is doubtful that the introspective "feeling of freedom" that James relies upon in any way supports his belief that our actions are not caused. According to the determinist, this feeling is nothing more than the feeling that one can do as one chooses. Although it is conceptually impossible for a person who is in the course of deliberating to know what the outcome of that deliberation will be, this does not mean that his act of deliberation is uncaused and could not be known beforehand by some superscientist who was aware of all the conscious and unconscious factors influencing his decision. The fact that one is not aware of the causes of one's action in no way shows that there is no cause for that action. For example, it was Freud's contention that many apparently uncaused or random slips of the tongue were quite significant revelations of unconscious mental processes that are capable of causal explanation.

Second, it would certainly seem unreasonable to identify free actions with those that are due to chance. If, for example, Jones's decision to murder Smith was due to chance—to, let us say, some random firing of certain neurons in his brain—how can we call such an action a free one for which Jones is morally responsible? As one soft determinist put it, "in proportion as an act of volition starts of itself without cause it is exactly, so far as freedom of the individual is concerned, as if it had been thrown into his mind from without—'suggested to him by a freakish demon!'" If, as James contends, our feelings of regret that a murder occurred would be inappropriate in a determined world, would they be appropriate in a world governed by chance? Certainly not. If undesirable events are due to chance, we would have no control over the future. On the other hand, if they are caused, we can learn how to prevent similar events from occurring *again*. Is it not the case that the intelligibility of feelings of regret resides precisely in the fact that the future is open to our control through a knowledge of causes?

Although an omniscient God would know beforehand of all the murders that ever will occur, the important thing for us as human beings who live at a particular point in time is that our actions can have some causal influence on the future. As soft determinists often point out, it is essential that one carefully distinguish—as James does not—the doctrine of determinism from that of fatalism. In a fatalistic world, human choices and actions are powerless to affect the future. Determinism, however, need not entail such a bleak view. The determinist is committed to the view that all events are caused, not that they will occur *in spite of* human actions to avoid them. Quite often, the nonfatalistic determinist would assert, human choices and actions can act as causes. While we cannot erase what has already happened, we can study the causes that made it happen and utilize this knowledge to create the causal conditions that will assure, or at least make less probable, its occurrence in the future. From such a perspective, human freedom resides in human control, which in turn presupposes a deterministic universe and not one ruled by chance.

Campbell: Freedom as Causation by a Nondetermined Moral Self

Given the implausibility of equating freedom with chance, most libertarians will grant that free acts are caused, but will insist that they are caused by a "self" whose actions are themselves not caused and, as such, are incapable of scientific prediction.

The most influential contemporary proponent of this point of view is C.A. Campbell (1897–   ). According to Campbell, the distinctive characteristic of human beings is that they are moral agents whose actions can transcend the promptings of *character* as formed by heredity and environment. Although the various states of consciousness and dispositions to behave in particular ways that comprise a person's character at a given moment are capable of scientific explanation and prediction, a person is more than just his character; he is also an autonomous *moral agent (self)* whose choices are *influenced* but not determined by the promptings of his character. The metaphysical picture Campbell presents of the nature of a moral self is quite in accord with the traditional Judaic-Christian conception of a "soul" as an "immaterial substance" whose distinctive characteristics are its free will and knowledge of right and wrong. According to this conception, scientific knowledge of a person's character and the external forces acting upon it will give us some idea of the degree of moral effort that the moral self will have to exert to make a certain choice. In addition, given our general knowledge of how human beings tend to respond, it is possible to develop scientific laws which can tell us that a certain percentage of human beings with a given type of character will act in a particular way in given circumstances. Consequently, it is possible to know beforehand what the *probability* is that a given person will so behave, but it is impossible for us to scientifically know with *absolute certainty* how a person will act since it is possible for the moral self to transcend the desires and tendencies toward action that comprise the promptings of character.

According to Campbell, most of our choices are fully determined and, as such, are not free. It is only in a situation of moral conflict, where our characters prompt us to do one thing and our sense of moral duty prompts us to do something else, that the moral self is capable of making a causally undetermined choice for which it is the sole author.[12]

---

12 Campbell's view of free will is clearly influenced by, but not identical to, Kant's view. While it was the existence of conflicts between duty and inclination which led Kant to postulate the existence of free will, he did not believe that freedom existed only in such situations of conflict, as Campbell does. Furthermore, unlike Campbell, Kant believed that all human (externally observable) behavior was fully determined; what he thought was not fully determined was the human "will," which in some mysterious way stood outside of the flux of events in the empirical world.

As Campbell puts it,

> Here, and here alone, so far as I can see, in the act of deciding whether to put forth or withhold the moral effort required to resist temptation and rise to duty, is to be found an act which is free in the sense required for moral responsibility; an act of which the self is sole author, and of which it is true to say that "it could be" (or, after the event, "could have been") "otherwise." . . .
>
> There is *X*, the course which we believe we ought to follow, and *Y*, the course towards which we feel our desire is strongest. The freedom which we ascribe to the agent is the freedom to put forth or refrain from putting forth the moral effort required to resist the pressure of desire and to do what he thinks he ought to do.
>
> But then there is surely an immense range of practical situations—covering by far the greater part of life—in which there is no question of a conflict within the self between what he most desires to do and what he thinks he ought to do. . . . over that whole vast range there is nothing whatever in our version of Libertarianism to prevent our agreeing that character determines conduct. In the absence, real or supposed, of any "moral" issue, what a man chooses will be simply that course which, after such reflection as seems called for, he deems most likely to bring him what he most strongly desires; and that is the same as to say the course to which his present character inclines him. . . .
>
> . . . the very function of moral effort, as it appears to the agent engaged in the act, is to enable the self to act against the line of least resistance, against the line to which his character as so far formed strongly inclines him. But if the self is thus conscious here of *combatting* his formed character, he surely cannot possibly suppose that the act, although his own act, *issues from* his formed character? I submit, therefore, that the self knows very well indeed—from the inner standpoint—what is meant by an act which is the *self's* act and which nevertheless does not follow from the self's *character*. . . . the "nature" of the self and what we commonly call the "character" of the self are by no means the same thing. The "nature" of the self comprehends, but is not without remainder reducible to, its "character"; it must, if we are to be true to the testimony of our experience of it, be taken as including *also* the authentic creative power of fashioning and refashioning "character."[13]

There are many difficulties with Campbell's view. Without getting into the thickets of metaphysical reflection, which any complete treatment of Campbell's position would require, let me briefly sketch what I see as the main problems. First, it is difficult to understand what to make of Campbell's notion of a "self" as some type of a "substantial entity" that can be understood as being distinct from the various states of consciousness and dispositions to behave that comprise one's "character." Indeed, many philosophers, following the philosopher David Hume, have

[13] C.A. Campbell, *On Selfhood and Godhood*, in *Philosophy*, ed. Arthur J. Minton, pp. 342–43, 345–46. By permission of George Allen & Unwin, Ltd., publishers.

found this notion unintelligible. Although Campbell says that he can intuit the existence of this self, other philosophers would strongly disagree. Second, it is quite contrary to current scientific teachings to believe, as Campbell does, that the choice between duty and desire is any less under the sway of causal determination than other choices between desires that Campbell is willing to grant are fully determined. Is Campbell not under the influence of an old religious metaphysics that has been discredited by modern science? Third, is it not implausible to maintain, as Campbell does, that although a person is free to choose between duty and desire, he is, nevertheless, not free in any other of the choices that he makes? Fourth, Campbell asserts that a person who struggles to overcome desires that lead contrary to the promptings of duty has free will, but if he gets to the point where doing his duty is the natural thing to do, he is no longer free. Does this make sense? Fifth, since Campbell claims that a person is only free when he consciously faces a choice between desire and duty, a very strange consequence of Campbell's view would be that a person is not free or morally responsible when he does not think about his duty. This, however, runs clearly counter to our common practice of holding people morally responsible for not thinking of their duty when we think that they had the power to do so.

Sixth, Campbell seems to imply that any choice between duty and desire is a free choice and, as such, one for which we can always hold people responsible; this does not always seem to be the case. For example, let us assume that Jones deliberates about whether to kill Smith with his gun (that which he desires) or by poison (that which he believes to be his duty), and, having the power to choose either way, he chooses one rather than the other. If, however, Jones did not have the power to refrain from killing Smith in some manner, we would certainly not want to say that Jones's action was a free one for which he is morally responsible, as Campbell's view would seem to imply. This would, in particular, be the case if Jones's conception of his duty appears to us to be irrational (or "insane").

Finally, Campbell admits that the self is *influenced* by the promptings of character as determined by heredity and environment which can make it more or less difficult for the self to "rise to duty." But, why isn't it possible that these promptings are so strong that the self is *powerless* to overcome them? Certainly, some people clearly see what they think they ought to do, try very hard to overcome desires that lead them to do otherwise, and fail. Are they free? Imagine, too, a person who is involuntarily hypnotized or "programmed" to consider his duty and to struggle fiercely to do it, and then to decide not to. Is he free? It would certainly seem that whatever problems we initially had in explaining when a human being is free Campbell will have in explaining when a self is free. Campbell has not really solved our problem, he has simply side-stepped it. Before, we had the problem of when a human being is free; now we have the problem of when a self is free; as far as I can see, we have gained nothing. In addition, since Campbell speaks of the self exerting more or less moral effort, ought he not to speak of *degrees of human freedom* and focus on the problem of how we are to compare and measure differences in the amount of moral effort individuals exert? Would it not be more reasonable to use this notion as the basis for assessing an individual's moral responsibility, and not rely upon the mysterious notion of a self that transcends scientific understanding?

Soft Determinism

The Belief that Determinism Is Incompatible with Free Will Is a Result of Conceptual Confusion

Although soft determinists do not agree upon what is, or ought to be, meant by calling human acts "free" in the sense required for justifiably holding individuals morally responsible, all soft determinists agree that the mere fact that acts are determined does not make them "unfree." As they see it, acts are unfree only when they are caused *in particular ways*. Indeed, for many soft determinists, the notion of a free but causally undetermined act is logically incoherent. As one philosopher put it,

> An action which is not causally determined by the character of the agent (together with the situation in which he is acting) cannot be said to have stemmed from *him,* from the particular person that he is, and hence is not anything for which *he* can be held responsible. If it is causally determined by something independent of his character, it is not *his* act; while if it is not causally determined at all, it is a chance happening and, again, something for which he cannot be held responsible.[14]

For most soft determinists, the widespread belief that determinism is incompatible with free will is merely a result of certain conceptual confusions and can easily be dispelled once those conceptual confusions are uncovered. Primary among those confusions, according to the soft determinist, is the tendency to confuse determinism with fatalism, which we have briefly touched upon. While freedom is incompatible with fatalism, it is not incompatible with determinism if the chain of causes that determine our actions operates through our desires and decisions.

As many soft determinists have seen it, the widespread tendency to equate the doctrine of determinism with the fatalistic belief that human actions are fully determined by forces that impose themselves unwillingly upon us stems from a confusion between *descriptive* laws of nature which merely describe how people *actually* behave and *prescriptive* man-made laws which prescribe how people *ought* to behave. While human beings often experience themselves as being under the *constraint* of prescriptive laws which *make* them behave in ways they would not *naturally* or *freely*

---

[14] R.B. Hobart, "Free Will as Involving Determination and Inconceivable Without It," *Mind,* 43 (1934), p. 7.

choose without the existence of such laws, human choices and actions are not *subject* to descriptive laws of nature in the same sense. The laws of human behavior that behavioral scientists attempt to discover do not *constrain* us or *make* us behave in any particular way, these laws simply explain how we *choose to behave*. Behavioral scientists attempt to uncover the patterns of connection that exist between our choices and the various physical and psychological factors upon which they depend. These physical and psychological factors, however, in free actions are not constraints which go contrary to our free will. They simply are the causal antecedents of that free will. If our free choices are determined, someone could, in principle, predict what we will choose, but this does not, in itself, take away our freedom to choose. Indeed, do we not all, at times, find ourselves fully confident of our ability to predict the actions of those whose characters we know well? Yet this confidence in our ability to predict a person's actions in particular circumstances in no way affects our belief that such a person is acting freely and is morally responsible for his actions.

Soft Deterministic Analyses of "Free Action"

United in their belief that human acts can be said to be free even though they are fully determined and, as such, capable of scientific prediction, soft determinists diverge when it comes to the analysis they give of the sense of freedom they consider to be required for judgments of moral responsibility. There are four basic analyses that soft determinists have offered for the concept of free action:

1. *Freedom as the Absence of Compulsion:* According to this view, a person's actions are free when they are not a result of *compulsion* or *constraint* or, to put it in a positive way, when they result from the agent's own *unimpeded desire*.

2. *Freedom as Hypothetical Behavior:* According to this view, a human action is a free one as long as the agent *could (or would) have been able to do otherwise if he had chosen (or tried) to do otherwise*.

3. *Freedom as the Power to Choose and Do Otherwise:* This analysis of free action differs from the preceding one in that proponents of this view admit that it is possible that a person who could or would have done otherwise, if he had chosen otherwise or tried, might nevertheless still not be free if he did not have the power to choose otherwise or to try.

4. *Freedom as Capacity for Rational Action:* According to this view, only creatures capable of modifying their actions as a result of rational deliberation can be said to be free and morally responsible creatures. An individual is responsible for his actions when our responses to him—such as holding him morally responsible, blaming or praising him, punishing him—can in some rational way influence him to make different decisions in the future.

Let us consider these different views. (As is often the case in philosophy, views which appear different on the surface might under deeper-level analysis turn out to be the same view, expressed differently. How different these views are depends on the precise meaning that one chooses to attribute to them.)

Freedom as the Absence of Compulsion   The view that freedom of action or choice should be defined in terms of the lack of external compulsion or constraint can be traced back to the ancient Greek philosopher Aristotle who, in drawing a distinction between "voluntary" and "involuntary" behavior, declared, "Those things, then, are thought involuntary, which take place under compulsion or owing to ignorance; and that is compulsory of which the moving principle is outside, being a principle in which nothing is contributed by the person who is acting . . . for example, if he were carried somewhere by a wind or by men who had him in their power." In more modern times, such famous philosophers as Hobbes (1588–1679), Hume (1711–1776), Mill (1806–1873), Schlick (1882–1936), and Russell (1872–1970) have defined freedom in terms of the lack of compulsion. For example, according to Schlick, "Freedom means the opposite of compulsion; a man is free if he does not act under compulsion, and he is compelled or unfree when he is hindered from without in the realization of his natural desires."[15] According to this commonly accepted view, free acts are by definition those acts caused by the unimpeded desires of the agent, while unfree acts are defined as those which are caused by forces or conditions outside the agent.

The main difficulty with this influential soft deterministic analysis of a free act resides in the conceptual obscurity that surrounds the notions of compulsion or constraint. There are, no doubt, clear cases of human behavior that we would all agree are due to compulsion or constraint and, for that reason, are clearly unfree. For example, we would all agree that an epileptic is behaving under the influence of a constraint or compulsion and, consequently, is acting unfreely when he finds himself helplessly in the midst of a seizure. Similarly, if someone, by virtue of overpowering physical force, flings me across a room, I am certainly under the physical constraint of the laws of physics as I fly through the room against my own free will. In these two clear-cut cases of unfree behavior, due to external physical compulsion or constraint, one should note that there is really no element of choice at all. Indeed, since this is so, many philosophers would refuse to describe such behavior as "actions," for according to their usage of this term, a human action must, by definition, involve some element of choice or intention. If one accepts this usage, since the examples we have given are not examples of "actions," neither are they examples of "unfree actions."

However one resolves this conceptual question, when we turn away from these clear-cut cases of involuntary behavior and turn to those

---

15 Moritz Schlick, "Problems in Ethics," in *A Modern Introduction to Philosophy,* 3rd ed., eds., Paul Edwards and Arthur Pap, p. 62.

actions which do involve some element of choice, it becomes very difficult to understand exactly what we mean or ought to mean when we say that an action is due to external compulsion or constraint. An example often given of such an action is that of a person doing something under the threat of death—such as when someone holds a gun over you and asks you to divulge some information. When a person acts as a result of such compulsion, it is said, such an act is an unfree one for which the actor is not morally responsible. This is, however, quite problematic. A person who chooses to divulge information rather than to face the clear and immediate prospect of his death could have chosen death rather than divulge the information if he had wanted to. Indeed, if the actor were a captured soldier or spy, we would consider it his obligation to choose death rather than to divulge any information that was vital to the interests of his country and as a result would consider him free to choose death and morally responsible if he did not.

The very important conclusion that we must draw from such considerations is that our notion of what is to count as a compulsion or a constraint is a reflection of what we are willing to excuse. Since in most circumstances we are quite willing to excuse, if not justify, an individual's choice to act in a particular way under the threat of death, we call such an act unfree. But is a person acting unfreely when he succumbs to the threat of a severe beating or the loss of his job or the loss of his reputation? Indeed, should a person be said to be acting under compulsion or constraint and for that reason unfreely if he does something in order to obtain a reward? For example, if some rich person promises to give me $100 if I slap Ms. Jones in the face and say something unpleasant to her, have I acted unfreely if I do this? If you say, as most of you will, that I am certainly under no compulsion here, would you change your mind if you found that I was a poor person who desperately could use that $100 to obtain an operation that my child needs? Does not our inclination to call an action unfree vary directly with our belief about whether an individual *ought to succumb* to a particular temptation? It is precisely because people will disagree as to what we ought to accept as a good excuse or justification for a particular type of behavior that no clear answers exist for the questions we have posed. This fact is, unfortunately, often lost on those many philosophers who present the notion of compulsion or constraint as if it were a purely *factual* notion that could be used to justify particular judgments about the freedom of action or moral responsibility of an individual. Since we are often faced with unpleasant choices that we perceive as being at least to some extent "imposed on us from without," a decision must be made as to what type or degree of external constraint upon our behavior renders that behavior unfree and this decision is a *moral* one that cannot be resolved simply by "looking at the facts."

For example, F. Lee Bailey argued in defense of Patty Hearst that she was "brainwashed" into robbing a bank with members of the S.L.A. According to Bailey, the pressures under which Ms. Hearst was forced to choose whether or not to accept the wishes of her captors were so compulsive as to render her action an unfree one. No doubt, Ms. Hearst was in a very unpleasant situation when she allowed herself to be influenced by her S.L.A. captors to become the seemingly self-assured and proud S.L.A. member that she became, but was she not also in a very unpleasant situation when she was influenced by her parents and her attorney to appear in court as a humble, timid girl who repentently became again the dutiful daughter she once was? If a choice made under the possible threat of death at the hands of the S.L.A. can justify calling Ms. Hearst's choice a compulsive one, why shouldn't a choice made under the threat of a long imprisonment equally as well qualify as a compulsive one?

It is precisely because the answer to such a question requires a moral decision as to which factors ought to render one's action "unduly" caused that psychiatric experts on brainwashing find themselves in the unflattering position of seemingly never to agree on their diagnoses. "Yes, she was brainwashed," "Yes, she did act under compulsion," some say. "No, she was not brainwashed," "No, she did not act under compulsion," others say. And though such a debate is often presented in courts of law as being over a purely "factual issue" for which psychiatrists are especially qualified to offer testimony, this is simply not the case. The fact is that psychiatrists, like the rest of us, simply do not agree on what *ought* to count as rendering an action so "unduly" caused as to justify calling it one due to compulsion or constraint and for that reason unfree. Two psychiatrists might very well agree on the nature of the pressures that a person faced and disagree over whether or not these pressures had compulsive force for they, like the rest of us, *do not clearly know what we mean by a compulsive force.* If we are to say, for example, that a person who makes a particular choice acts under compulsion only when he is under the influence of an *irresistible impulse,* we must have some way of distinguishing between impulses which are so strong that they *cannot be resisted* and those impulses that *can be resisted if sufficient effort is exerted.* This, as the law courts have discovered, is no simple task. (See p. 359 for a discussion of "The irresistible impulse" test for insanity.)

As we grapple with what it means to say that an act is due to compulsion or constraint, our heads may swim in a swirl of conceptual confusion. If acting under compulsion is to be identified with acting under an irresistible impulse, am I acting under compulsion when I run to help my small child who has severely hurt himself? Clearly, we do not want to say this, for we tend to call actions compulsive only when an individual's choices are determined by internal states with which he does not identify himself or with which he does not approve. Consequently, the notion of a compulsive action carries along the suggestion of fighting against alien and strong desires which incline one to do something that does not fit in with one's normal personality or which goes against one's value system. Yet, one may wonder, why should a person's failure to identify himself with his desires be considered an excusing factor, for is not the decisive factor in the determination of moral responsibility whether an individual can control his desires and not that he consider them as parts of his normal self? After all, we all, at one time or another find within ourselves very strong desires which seem alien to our nature, which seem as if they were "imposed upon us from without." Yet as long as we have some degree of control over them, should we not be responsible for them? But as our minds continue swimming in philosophical confusion, we wonder how we can determine "the degree of control" individuals have over their desires. This becomes especially puzzling when we realize that a person can appear to us and himself as being blatantly free of any external constraint or compulsion but nevertheless be a victim of some type of *internal* constraint or compulsion over which he is not even aware. For instance, he might be acting under the influence of a hypnotic suggestion. But if acting under a hypnotic suggestion renders one's action as due to internal compulsion and for that reason unfree, what if someone acts in a particular way because of some childhood experience or purely biochemical condition over which he is equally unaware; are these not unfree actions as well? If Freud and other psychiatrists are right, is it not the case that the sphere of compulsive actions is much wider than we thought? How wide is it? Are any of our actions ever totally free of internal unconscious influences that can be said to function as compulsive forces? Even if they sometimes are free of such forces, how can we ever know when this is so?

In addition, even if we could clearly agree upon a definition of that sort of internal or external compulsion or constraint that negates human freedom and could specify a range of human actions which is exempt from it, it still would seem to be wrong to claim that all acts which are performed free of compulsion or constraint may for that reason alone be said to be free actions which justify the ascription of moral responsibility. If we accept this point of view, it follows that nonrational creatures, such as ants, dogs and very young human children, act freely and are morally responsible, for they often act without internal or external compulsion or constraint. Clearly, however, such a conclusion would be rejected. But why? Part of the answer seems clear. We can justify our rejection of the claim that ants act freely by claiming that only conscious creatures can be said to act freely and be morally responsible for their actions. But what are we to say about dogs and very young children? Do they act freely? Even if you are inclined to say yes, I doubt that you would want to say that they are morally responsible for their actions. Why is this so? Is it not because dogs and very young children are not *rational* creatures that have a capacity for reasoned choice and moral reflection? If animals and very young children are not ordinarily considered free and morally responsible agents because they are incapable (or not sufficiently capable) of altering their behavior in accordance with rational considerations, cannot the same sometimes be said of human beings? Would we call a person free who acts as he chooses without any internal or external constraint but is incapable of perceiving and rationally weighing alternative courses of action? I would think not. Consequently, it would appear that individuals should not be said to act freely unless they are capable of rationally considering the nature and consequences of possible courses of action.

Freedom as Modifiability or Capacity for Rational Choice The identification of free action with the capacity for rational choice also has a long philosophical history. According to the Greek philosopher, Plato, acting freely implies being rational and virtuous. A free man, for Plato, is a man who is ruled by reason, not by passions, and under the guidance of reason decides as he ought to decide. Furthermore, Plato conceived the rational and virtuous part of man's nature, and not his passionate nature, to be his true nature. Consequently, for Plato, the notions of freedom, rationality, virtue, and self-expression were interrelated. This classical Greek conception of freedom is well expressed by the philosopher Plotinus:

> When the Soul has been modified by outer forces and acts under that pressure so that what it does is no more than an unreflecting acceptance of stimulus, neither the act nor the state can be described as voluntary; so, too, when even from within itself, it falls at times below its best. . . . But when our Soul holds to its Reason-Principle . . . only then can we speak of [a] voluntary act. Things so done may truly be described as our doing.[16]

Saint Thomas Aquinas (1225–1274), the most influential of Christian philosophers, also closely associated the notion of freedom with that of rationality, as did the famous philosophers Descartes (1596–1650), Spinoza (1632–1677), Leibniz (1646–1716), and Kant (1724–1804). In contemporary times, the identification of rationality with free action was one of the central themes of the American philosopher John Dewey (1859–1952). The free man, for Dewey, is the man who, possessed of scientific knowledge of himself and the world about him, utilizes that knowledge to mold himself and his environment in ways that are more conducive to human fulfillment.

Contemporary soft deterministic philosophers who analyze the notion of free action in terms of the capacity for rational choice tend to assume a utilitarian moral perspective and, in particular, a utilitarian view of the nature and justification of punishment and reward. According to this perspective, we ask whether or not a person acted freely because we want to know whether or not to hold that person responsible and as a fit subject for judgments of moral praise or blame. In order to determine the answer to this question, supporters of this viewpoint would contend, the concept of moral responsibility should be seen as a forward-looking one. The question of whether an individual deserves reward or punishment should be taken as equivalent to the question of whether or not he should be rewarded or punished and that question should be

---

[16] Plotinus, "Enneads," III, *First Tractate*, 9.

answered on the basis of the probable consequences of rewarding or punishing him. A free and responsible individual, according to this perspective, is a person who is rational enough to be influenced by rewards and punishment which can affect the strength of his motives to behave in particular ways. In holding such an individual morally accountable for his behavior, we should not focus on the causal antecedents of his behavior, but rather on the best way to control his *future behavior*. While the free and responsible person is the person who is capable of modifying his behavior as a result of rational considerations, the unfree and nonresponsible person is the person who cannot so respond.

Such a view of responsibility is reflected in traditional utilitarian justifications of the insanity defense in the criminal law. Following Bentham, most utilitarians who have attempted to justify the existence of such a defense have claimed that the "insane" are those adult human beings who, because of "mental disorder" are "incapable of being deterred" through the threat or infliction of punishment. Furthermore, utilitarians have claimed, it is precisely because such individuals are nondeterrable that they are not morally blameworthy.

The notion of deterrability is, however, no less exasperating to analyze than the notion of compulsion. In particular, one must face the difficulty of distinguishing those who are *incapable* of being affected by the threat or infliction of punishment from those who are merely *indisposed* to be so affected. For example, would we not want to say that some *free* individuals are so courageous that no threat or infliction of any punishment that the law presently allows could ever intimidate them or cause them to modify their behavior in the future? For example, an "incorrigible" civil disobedient, such as Gandhi, would seem to be a model of nondeterrability, but we would clearly not consider him a model of the unfree and nonresponsible individual who does not deserve praise for his actions. It is not clear, however, how we are to distinguish Gandhi, whom we may want to say was simply *indisposed* to conform to the law from those individuals whom we would want to say were *incapable* of so conforming.

Freedom as Hypothetical Behavior   According to another commonly held soft deterministic analysis of "free action," to say that an individual (X) acted freely in doing something (A) in situation (S) means that X would have been *capable* of acting otherwise *if* he had tried (or chosen) to. This statement has often been taken by soft determinists to be equivalent to "X would have done other than A in S if he had tried (chosen) to."

As many philosophers have pointed out, however, such an analysis of "free action" seems to have very serious shortcomings. First, since a person often may try to do something and fail, and yet still be thought to have been *capable* of doing otherwise, it seems clearly mistaken to assert that the notion of what an individual is *capable* of achieving can be analyzed in terms of what he *would* achieve *on any given occasion*. As the influential twentieth century philosopher, J. L. Austin (1911–1960) observed,

> Consider the case where I miss a very short putt and kick myself because I could have holed it. It is not that I should have holed it if I had tried; I did try, and missed. . . . Nor does "I can hole it this time" mean that I shall hole it this time if I try . . . for I may try and miss and yet not be convinced that I couldn't have done it; indeed, further experiments may confirm my belief that I could have done it that time although I didn't.[17]

In addition, we can well imagine cases where X would have refrained from A in S *if* he had tried (chosen) to, where we would not want to say that X had the power or ability to refrain from A in S. We might feel this way, for example, because we believe that X did not have the power to try to refrain from A in S. (This is especially the case if we take the concept of trying to involve the making of some strong effort.) For example, if we deliberate over whether some criminal could have avoided his crime, our deliberation will rarely hinge on the question of whether that criminal could (or would) have done otherwise *if* he had tried (chosen) to, but rather over whether he had the power within himself to try (choose) not to commit that crime. Similarly, a person, who under hypnotic suggestion takes a sip of a drink whenever a particular word is said could, of course, have refrained from taking those sips if he had chosen to, but the hypnotic suggestion may have rendered him incapable of so choosing.

Freedom as Involving the Power To Choose or Try   If we reject the view that "a person's act is free" means no more than that he could have done otherwise if he chose (tried) to, we may modify this view and now claim that "a person's act is free" means that he "could have done otherwise if he chose (tried) to and *he had the power to so choose (try)*." (Let us call this "The Power To Do Otherwise.") If we take this line, as some philosophers have, we will again be faced with the difficult problem of spelling out exactly what is involved in having the "power to do otherwise." No doubt one of the most important factors that we tend to focus on in determining a person's "power to do otherwise" is the strength of his desires and the amount of effort that he would have to exert in order to refrain from these desires. There are, however, other important factors which ought to be considered relevant in determining a person's "power to do otherwise." For example, one's knowledge of the alternatives of action open to him certainly affects this power. A person who has little ability to think about the alternatives of action open to him or their consequences may have very little "power to do otherwise"; yet such a person does not yield to overpowering forces, nor does he try to

---

[17] J. L. Austin, "Ifs and Cans," in *Free Will and Determinism,* ed., Bernard Berofsky (New York: Harper & Row, Pubs., 1966), p. 308 (footnote).

overcome them and fail. Similarly, a person's "power to do otherwise" may be severely limited by his moral convictions or lack of them. A person who has a very strong moral sense may have very little power to do other than what he believes to be right, and a person who has no moral sense might have very little power to attend to the considerations that would lead him to do what we think is right. An individual whose character or moral convictions make it impossible for him to believe that behavior of a different kind would be desirable has no real choice between competing options of behavior. Such a person may clearly perceive the alternatives of action open to him and their probable consequences, but they will make no appeal to his emotional or moral nature. It may be psychologically soothing for us to believe that great evildoers, such as Hitler, had the "full power to do otherwise" and as such were maximally morally guilty for their actions, but I think we will find that such individuals are often very limited in their power to do otherwise by their very limited knowledge or moral understanding.

Since many concepts are packed into the notion of "power to do otherwise," a person may be said to have a high degree of power to do otherwise from one perspective, but a low degree of power from another perspective. For example, a person may have great power to do something if he tries, but little power to attend to considerations which would lead him to realize why he ought to try. This makes comparisons of degrees of power to do otherwise conceptually uncertain. Nevertheless, I think we can make sense of the notion of "full power to do otherwise" which human beings seldom possess. To say that "X had full power to do $A2$ (a morally right action) rather than $A1$ (a morally wrong action) in S" can be analyzed as follows:

1. X fully recognized and appreciated the nature and relevant consequences of $A1$ and why it would be morally wrong for him to do $A1$ in S.
2. X fully recognized and appreciated the nature and relevant consequences of $A2$ and why it would be morally right for him to do $A2$ in S.
3. X did not try to do $A2$ instead of $A1$ in S although he realized that no effort or only a minimal degree of effort was necessary to have refrained from $A1$ and done $A2$.

Once we depart from this concept of "full power to do otherwise" and attempt to distinguish different "degrees of power to do otherwise," we may very well find the different factors that go into this notion pulling us in different directions. At any rate, the many factors which go into the determination of a person's "power to do otherwise" are incapable of precise scientific definition and measurement. If such power can be determined at all at the present time, it is only on the basis of very imprecise generalizations about how roughly similar persons in roughly similar situations have been observed to behave.

The Hard Deterministic Rejoinder
to the Soft Determinist

Even if we could clearly define what we mean by "degrees of power to do otherwise" and had some scientific means for measuring and comparing such power, a hard determinist will argue that any distinction that a soft determinist makes between "free" and "unfree" actions is overly narrow in focusing its attention only on the present capacities or incapacities of an individual without focusing on the causal antecedents of those capacities or incapacities. Clearly, our hard determinist will contend, we are often willing to lessen our harsh moral judgment of an individual when we find that he suffered from certain environmental or hereditary disadvantages from which most of us have been spared. Indeed, our hard determinist will contend, if we attempt to trace back the causes of why any individual chooses to act in one way rather than another we will find that a person's character is ultimately the product of factors over which he had no control, namely, heredity and early childhood experiences. Since a person is not responsible for these factors, how can he be justifiably held responsible for his later actions which stem from a character that was molded by these forces, the hard determinist will protest. As the philosopher Schopenhauer (1780–1860) put it, "A man can surely do what he wills to do, but he cannot determine what he wills." As we have pointed out, however, it is difficult to know what conceivable circumstances a hard determinist would count as justifying the ascription of moral responsibility, for the notion of an individual fully forming his own character from scratch seems to be unintelligible. Consequently, it would appear that our hard determinist should not be taken as asserting that free will is incompatible with determinism—tacitly seeming to imply that freedom would be possible if determinism were not true—but should rather be taken to be asserting that the notion of moral responsibility is actually a meaningless one.

Once we realize that a person's act can be traced back to hereditary and environmental causes belonging to a world that he had no part in making, we will realize, our hard determinist will say, that there is no distinction that can be made between free and unfree actions that can sustain the moral weight it is made to bear when we hold individuals morally responsible or nonresponsible for their actions. No doubt, our hard determinist will say, there can be a utilitarian justification for holding some individuals morally accountable for their actions as a way of affecting their future behavior, but, if we put aside any practical concerns about the future and simply try to rank individuals in terms of their moral responsibility for their actions as the traditional Judaic-Christian tradition assumes God ultimately will, we will find that the distinction between free and unfree acts must be meaningless to an all-knowing God who can grasp the full network of causes that serve to explain why individuals behave as they do. For such a God, the feelings of righteous indignation and resentment that we as human beings so naturally feel toward those whom we perceive to have freely acted wrongly must be replaced by an understanding that transcends such feelings and makes it impossible to rank people in terms of moral worth. At the highest level of moral development, the notion of a type of divine justice where individuals are rewarded or punished in accordance with their "deserts" must be seen as unintelligible, our hard determinist will argue.

Some Reflections on the Free Will Problem

As is often the case in philosophical problems, the free will problem is a quite tangled one that must be untangled before it can be solved. Each of the traditional solutions of this problem oversimplifies a multi-dimensional problem that involves the resolution of conceptual, scientific, and moral questions. For example, we must first decide upon the moral principles we are to use in making judgments of moral responsibility. With these principles in mind, we must then agree on the meanings to be attributed to key concepts in this controversy, such as "compulsion," "deterrability," and "trying." Once we settle on definitions of these concepts, we must attempt to answer such scientific questions as "How wide is the area of compulsive behavior?" "How deterrable, if at all, was this individual in this instance?" and "How much, if at all, did this individual in this instance have it in his power to try to do otherwise?"

While a complete solution of the free will problem is impossible without the resolution of issues such as these, there are certain, often neglected, observations that can be made about this problem that can serve to put it in a much clearer perspective. Let me share with you these observations, along with my own views about the direction a proper resolution of this problem must take. First, it seems to me that the soft determinists are right that although many things may interfere with a person's power to do otherwise, the principle that "everything in this world is subject to scientific explanation and prediction" is not one of them. If the distinction between free and unfree actions is to have any meaning at all, it must be understood in terms of the differences in the nature of the causes behind one's acts. Furthermore, we cannot obtain any solution to this problem by claiming that some causes are subject to scientific understanding and prediction and that others, in some mysterious way, are in principle beyond the reaches of such understanding and prediction as libertarians like Campbell claim. The problem with soft determinists, however, is that they tend to provide oversimplified analyses of "free action" that neglect the *many different and vague meanings* we attribute to these notions in ordinary usage. In particular, hard determinists are quite right that when we deeply reflect about a person's responsibility—free of the immediate concern of trying to influence his behavior—we do not find ourselves focusing simply on his current capacities or incapacities, but consider it quite relevant to inquire into their causal antecedents. Such considerations are, however, fully neglected by soft determinists.

The first step in resolving the free will problem comes with the realization that the real problem we are facing is not one of explaining whether or not "free will" is compatible with determinism, but rather of explaining what the concept of "free will" should be taken to mean. It is a fundamental mistake to begin this inquiry, as many philosophers do, with the tacit assumption that the notion of a free act has a single meaning in ordinary usage. There are many different things we mean when we say that a person acted freely or unfreely. Judgments about whether or not a person acted freely or was morally responsible or blameworthy for his action are made from varying moral perspectives, reflecting different human concerns and attitudes. Who among us has not had occasion, when considering whether a person is morally blameworthy for his action, to feel torn between different perspectives, pulling us first this way, then that. "He should be blamed," we say, "after all, . . ." but then again we reflect "Maybe he really shouldn't be blamed, after all, we have to consider . . . ," coming at the end to no resolution. Consider, for example, the following imaginary dialogue:

A: I don't think that Bill was really responsible for his crime.

B: Come now! Bill knew what he was doing. He could have done otherwise if he had wanted to; he wasn't at all under any constraint to act the way he did.

A: I admit that and I guess I would agree with you that Bill should be held legally responsible. After all, there is some chance (though I don't think it's too great) that punishment might teach him a lesson. More important, his punishment will serve as a warning to others of the possible consequences of a similar act. Yes, Bill should be held legally accountable, but what bothers me is that I don't really think that he is *morally* responsible.

B: What in the world do you mean?

A: Well, considering Bill's early environment—his drunken father and uncaring mother—one couldn't reasonably expect him to turn out any better.

B: Others have in similar circumstances.

A: Circumstances are never fully the same. If some other fellow turned out better than Bill, he must have been lucky enough to have had some advantage Bill did not have.

B: That's nonsense. The logical implication of a view such as yours would be that no one is ever responsible and I don't think you really want to say that. Furthermore, I think you are wrong to say it's only a matter of luck whether or not we turn out well. You make it appear that people are always the passive recipients of lucky or unlucky breaks. Doubtless, this is sometimes the case, but quite often things come or don't come to people only as a result of the effort they choose or choose not to exert and for which they deserve praise or blame. It's often a question of whether or not people have enough motivation and not simply a question of whether or not they have lucky breaks.

A: I'm really confused about this. I see what you're saying about my view leading logically to the conclusion that no one is ever really morally responsible, and I suppose that deep down that is really what I believe. Remember I did say that Bill should be held legally responsible; it's just that I don't see how we can really blame him, thinking in the process that we're better than he. No, we're just lucky. According to you, it isn't just luck, it's also a matter of effort, but don't you see that whether or not a person has it within him to make that effort is itself ultimately determined by his heredity and early childhood environment which is not chosen in any way.

B: Boy, you really are confused over this whole matter.

A: I know I am, but I think your seeming clarity on this issue stems from your narrow-minded refusal to see the whole picture. By the way, as we were talking, something else occurred to me. I'm not so sure any more that I want to say as I did before that Bill knew what he was doing or that he wasn't acting under some type of a constraint.

B: What do you have in mind now?

A: Well, I'd grant that Bill knew that his act was wrong in the sense that he knew that society would condemn it and I suppose that his act was contrary to his own professed moral code, but I don't know how deep Bill's adherence to traditional morality goes. Sometimes, I think it's all just words with him—he simply doesn't *feel* deeply enough about the things that he should, and for this reason, I hesitate to say that Bill really knew what he was doing.

B: What about Bill acting under some type of constraint?

A: Well, you know sometimes people aren't aware of the constraints under which they act. Perhaps this was true of Bill. After all, he's got so many hangups that work their way through him without his being aware of them. Furthermore, by calling something a constraint, it seems to me all we mean is that it is something that limits one's options of choice, and Bill's options of choice are certainly limited by his environment and even by his very way of thinking. Sure Bill isn't stupid. He can reason and judge consequences as well as you and I. He has the intelligence, no doubt, to make it in this world, if only he wants to. But it seems to me, his childhood experiences have provided him with an unrealistic picture of people and the world that makes it impossible for him to realize what possibilities of action are open to him and to care about the things you and I think are important. Isn't this a type of constraint?

B: You should change your major to philosophy and spend your time attempting to solve problems that arise out of your own conceptual confusion. Once you start playing this game of Bill didn't *really* know what he was doing or *really* acted under some type of constraint, I think you'll find yourself saying that every criminal either didn't really know what he was doing or really was acting under some type of constraint. Again, you'd be left with the absurd result that no one is ever responsible for wrongdoing. It seems to me that you are so inflating the meanings of the concepts of knowledge and constraint as to make them meaningless. You shouldn't misuse concepts that way.

A: I'm not so sure I'm misusing these concepts. Sometimes we use these concepts very broadly, the way I am. Anyway, I doubt that they have any clear meaning, and if you could settle on some simple definition of them, I think you'd want to say that some people are not morally responsible for their actions even though they knew what they were doing and weren't acting under any constraint. You'll just simply have to find other words to describe what I am describing under the heading of "lack of real knowledge" or the "presence of some constraining factor."

Perhaps neither *A* nor *B* has the full monopoly on truth here. *A* is right that his sentiments are indeed reflections of common ways of thinking about who is or is not morally responsible, and *B* is right that some of the common ways of thinking about this question will, if taken to their full logical conclusion, lead to conclusions most of us would be unwilling to accept. Perhaps the truth of the matter is that most of us work with all sorts of different ideas about who should or should not be considered morally responsible—ideas which are not clearly spelled out in our minds and can, at times, pull us in different directions, and even generate outright inconsistencies.

Although philosophers have often made it appear that the question of whether or not an individual is free is a factual one that can justify ascriptions of moral responsibility, the fact is that a judgment of whether or not an individual is free *presupposes* some view of the conditions under which it is proper to hold individuals morally responsible. The resolution of the question of when an individual should properly be held morally responsible, however, involves taking a moral position and not simply uncovering the relevant facts, for it is our moral decision that will specify which of the facts are to be considered relevant. Consider, for example, a typical case of an individual acting under external compulsion. Smith is informed that if he does not assist in a particular crime his wife will be raped. Smith, acting under compulsion, commits the crime. Did he act freely? Did he have a choice? The answer we give to this question will depend *on what we are willing to excuse.* Those who want to excuse Smith may say, "he really didn't have a choice," or claim that his choice was forced and hence unfree. Those who do not want to excuse him will not call his choice a forced one, attributing it to a very unpleasant but nevertheless free choice. If the crime Smith was pressured to commit involved some horrid act like killing several people, most of us would say that he acted freely, but if the crime were a minor one, that he acted unfreely.

Similarly, consider a prisoner of war who is tortured into giving the enemy some intelligence. Did he have a choice? Did he act freely? "He was free to remain silent and suffer; he had a choice," some of us will say, while others will say, "he was not free; he had no choice." It is very important to realize that what we say will depend on what we think a reasonable person ought to do in such circumstances. (If the prisoner were a spy, we would expect much more of him and consequently be much less inclined to excuse him by saying he acted unfreely.) Consider, too, the possible excuses of accident and mistake. It might seem that in such cases a person clearly has no choice—for one does not choose to be careless or to make mistakes. Assuming this to be the case (psychiatrists would say that it is not always the case), this is still not the whole story. Even though accidents and mistakes are not (consciously) chosen, we can still make a distinction between avoidable and unavoidable accidents and mistakes, as the law does. For example, if an intoxicated person gets himself involved in an automobile accident, which would not have occurred but for his intoxication, the law will claim that his accident was avoidable, for he did not have to drink (that is, the law takes the view that even though an accident is not in itself chosen, one can choose the events leading to it). Such an action is considered avoidable because we demand that reasonable people should refrain from driving when they are intoxicated or, at the very least, be prepared to accept the responsibility of any accident they might cause as a result of that intoxication. In general, whether or not a given accident or mistake is said to be unavoidable in the law is decided on the basis of our judgment of whether or not it was a reasonable one, and what one considers reasonable depends upon what one is willing to excuse. Consider, too, the excuse of insanity. A person might say, "Jones was not morally responsible; he did not act freely as a result of his insanity." For such a person, the judgment that an individual is insane will often be seen as a factual psychiatric one that justifies the claim that an individual is not morally responsible. But the fact is that "insanity" is not a psychiatric term at all, but is a legal one which is defined on the basis of an insanity rule. There is, however, much legal disagreement as to which insanity rule best picks out those who *morally ought* to be considered insane.

Since the decision as to whether or not an individual acted freely presupposes a moral standard under which the proper conditions for moral responsibility are defined, the question of whether or not a person acted freely reduces to the question of whether or not there is some single uniquely justifiable moral perspective from which judgments of moral responsibility should be made. It is my opinion that there is not— that any single perspective will prove inadequate to achieve all reasonable human purposes and to express all reasonable human attitudes; as a consequence, we move from perspective to perspective as our shifting purposes and attitudes lead us. Indeed, philosophers have a tendency of overly intellectualizing the factors that motivate us to classify individuals as morally responsible or morally nonresponsible, neglecting the often unconscious factors that motivate us to make such discriminations and often reveal more about us than they do about those whom we judge.

For example, most of us will be inclined to excuse a kleptomaniac who steals valueless objects on the grounds that he is acting under the force of a compulsion. But what this exactly means, we rarely ask. Certainly we cannot say that the kleptomaniac's desires are overpowering in the same sense that the epileptic's seizure is overpowering, for the kleptomaniac, unlike the epileptic, can refrain if he tries hard enough and often does refrain either because he is ashamed of his desires or fears apprehension. Can we claim, perhaps, that his desires, though not totally

overpowering, are, nevertheless, sufficiently strong so as to make it unreasonable for us to hold him responsible for succumbing to them? Yet
what does this claim really mean? It surely would not be unreasonable
for us to hold him responsible if our sole concern were to maximize
compliance with the law, for then we should say, as one jurist did, that
"if an influence is so powerful as to be termed irresistible, so much the
more reason why we should not withdraw any of the safeguards tending
to counteract it." Do we, perhaps, mean that if an ordinary person were
a victim of the desires of the kleptomaniac, he too would prove unable
to control them? If so, how do we know this is true? And even if it is,
there are surely some criminals whom we have no inclination to excuse
who succumb to desires which the average person would also succumb to
if he possessed them.

Why, for example, would many of us be willing to excuse the kleptomaniac, but not nearly as willing to excuse a thief who steals as a result
of poverty or a ghetto youth who steals as an act of rebellion against a
social system he finds unbearable? We surely have no reason for believing
that the kleptomaniac's desires are invariably stronger (whatever this
should be taken to mean) than those of the poor man or the ghetto
youth. Indeed, why is it that when we find a rich man stealing valueless
items, we are quite willing to assume, on the basis of no evidence at all,
that he is the victim of a compulsion, but are, on the other hand, inclined to reject evidence which points to the great strength of the desires of others? We may no doubt assume that the kleptomaniac struggles against impulses which he rejects as alien and which generate much
internal anxiety for him, and this may make his moral position seem
more favorable than that of the thief who fully accepts his desires and
feels no anxiety over them. Yet, we can just as easily assume that the
poor man and the ghetto youth fight against their impulses and suffer
much anxiety over them—impulses which they perhaps realize are not in
their ultimate self-interest.

The best explanation for our tendency to hold the poor thief or the
ghetto youth morally responsible, but not the kleptomaniac, is, I think,
the classical psychoanalytical one. According to this view, we consider
the poor man and the ghetto youth to be "ordinary" criminals and consequently feel justified in holding them morally and legally responsible
for their actions because they act out of quite ordinary and understandable motives which we all find within ourselves at one time or another
and have to repress or control. For example, we often want things we
cannot afford (the poor man), or feel inclined to react unlawfully to
what appear to us to be social injustices (the ghetto youth). Consequently, we naturally feel disposed to blame the poor man and the
ghetto youth who have not assumed the burden of control that we have;
by punishing such individuals, *we attempt to prove to ourselves* that
"crime does not pay." Similarly, we tend to exonerate the kleptomaniac
because his motive for stealing appears to us to be so different from *the
motives that we find within ourselves*. Although I would certainly not be

so rash as to suggest that this is always true, I strongly suspect that it is true much more often than most of us would like to believe. Indeed, given the general vagueness of the concept of power to do otherwise and our present inability to scientifically measure the various factors upon which it depends, it is inevitable that even those of us who sincerely attempt to dispassionately assess a person's power to do otherwise will be swayed by those factors which psychologically determine for us whether that person arouses our sympathy and understanding or our indignation and resentment.

DISCUSSION QUESTIONS

1. According to the Judaic-Christian tradition, God is conceived to be an all-powerful (omnipotent), all-knowing (omniscient), and all-good creator of all else that exists. Essential to the traditional conception is a view of human beings as free and morally responsible beings who will ultimately be judged by God for their actions in this world.

    a. Which of the following attempts to reconcile the belief in God's omniscience with the conception of God as moral judge and of human beings as free and morally responsible before God do you find the most plausible?

    1. God does not have foreknowledge of our actions. This is not, however, a limitation on his omniscience, for it is logically impossible to have foreknowledge of the actions of free beings. Since human actions are free, they cannot be fully determined.
    2. God has foreknowledge of our actions and, since we are free beings, our actions cannot be fully determined.
    3. God has foreknowledge of our actions and, since we are free beings, our actions must be determined.
    4. God has foreknowledge of our actions and we are free. It is irrelevant whether our actions are fully determined or not.

    b. Are any of these positions acceptable to you? Assuming that God does have foreknowledge of our actions, can this fact be reconciled with the belief that God sees us as morally responsible individuals who deserve punishment or reward for our actions? If this reconciliation can be made as far as God's foreknowledge goes, can it still be made once one adds the fact that God is conceived as an all-powerful creator of all else that exists?

2. a. From Darrow's perspective, can anyone reasonably be held responsible for Leopold and Loebs's crime?

    b. How would Hook criticize this point of view?

    c. Can Darrow's position be defended against this criticism?

3. a. Is the "feeling of freedom" that libertarians emphasize inconsistent with the belief in determinism? Why, or why not?

b. According to Campbell, free acts are acts in which "the self is sole author." What do you think this means? Is this condition ever satisfied.

4. Consider the following imaginary dialogue:

> **A:** I wish I could take a pill which would make me always want to do what I morally should.
>
> **B:** The cost of such a pill would be the loss of your freedom as a human being.
>
> **A:** On the contrary, it would provide me with the freedom I've always sought.

What do *A* and *B* mean by freedom? Can a person ever be "forced to be free"? Explain.

5. In B.F. Skinner's utopian novel *Walden II*, children are conditioned by the methods of behavioral engineering to become happy and adjusted citizens of their community. The psychologist director of this program is a hard determinist (as is Skinner) who claims, "I deny that freedom exists at all. I must deny it—or my program would be absurd. You cannot have a science about a subject matter which hops capriciously about." How would a soft determinist reply? A libertarian?

6. How plausible is the psychoanalytic explanation Grassian gives for our tendency to excuse the kleptomaniac who steals valueless objects? Is there some other plausible explanation for this tendency? Under what conditions, if any, ought we to morally or legally excuse such an individual?

FURTHER READINGS

BEROFSKY, BERNARD, ed., *Free Will and Determinism*. New York: Harper & Row, Pub., 1966. The best and most comprehensive anthology of material on the free will-determinism issue. The articles by Campbell ("Is 'Free Will' a Pseudo-Problem"), Hobart and Hospers ("What Means This Freedom"); and excerpts from Melden and Schlick, listed separately in this bibliography, are included in this anthology. /

CAMPBELL, C.A., *On Selfhood and Godhood,* lecture IX, 1957, reprinted (with minor deletions) in the Minton anthology, pp. 338–46. Campbell defends his version of libertarianism and criticizes soft-deterministic analyses of free action as hypothetical behavior (that is, "could have . . . if"). Campbell also defends his libertarian position and attacks soft determinism in general, and Schlick's position in particular in his earlier (1951) article "Is 'Free Will' a Pseudo-Problem" which is reprinted in the Edwards and Pap anthology (pp. 67–82) and in the Berofsky anthology.

DARROW, CLARENCE, "The Crime of Compulsion," in *Attorney for the Damned,* ed. Arthur Weinberg. Excerpted in the Minton anthology, pp. 229–304. A passionate and clear, though philosophically unsophisticated statement of the hard deterministic viewpoint.

EDWARDS, PAUL, and ARTHUR PAP, *A Modern Introduction to Philosophy* (3rd ed.), section I. New York: Free Press, 1973. This general anthology of philosophical readings contains a good selection of material on the determinism-free will issue. Included is an excellent and comprehensive 16-page bibliographic essay describing the literature on the determinism-free will issue.

HOBART, R.B., "Free Will as Involving Determination and Inconceivable Without It," *Mind*, 43 (1934), 1–27. Also included in the Berofsky anthology. Hobart, a soft determinist, argues that actions can be free only when they are determined. This article is directed to the philosophically sophisticated.

HOOK, SIDNEY, ed., *Determinism and Freedom in the Age of Modern Science.* New York: Collier Books, 1961. This anthology contains the proceedings of a symposium devoted to the determinism-free will issue that took place at New York University in 1957. Many well-known philosophers and scientists were participants. Included in this anthology are the ten papers originally presented at the symposium on the general concept of determinism, the notion of determinism in physics and the notions of determinism, freedom and responsibility in ethics and law. Also included are seventeen papers by participants of the symposium in reply to these papers.

HOSPERS, JOHN, "What Means This Freedom," first published in the Hook anthology (pp. 126–42). Reprinted in the Minton anthology. A clear and provocative defense of the hard-deterministic viewpoint. In his earlier (1950) article "Free Will and Psychoanalysis" (reprinted in the Edwards-Pap and Berofsky anthologies), Hospers attacks soft determinists for neglecting unconscious influences. It would be worthwhile to compare the tougher hard deterministic stance Hospers takes in "What Means This Freedom" to the weaker stance he takes in "Free Will and Psychoanalysis."

JAMES, WILLIAM, "The Dilemma of Determinism." This 1884 Address to Harvard Divinity Students has been reprinted in many anthologies. An abridged version can be found in the Minton anthology (pp. 305–13) and a more complete version in the Edwards and Pap anthology (pp. 34–46). James argues for the acceptance of a world governed by chance. It is only in such a world, he contends, that free will and emotions of regret over what has happened make sense.

MELDEN, A.I., *Free Action.* London: Routledge and Kegan Paul, 1961. Melden argues that while human "bodily movements" are caused it is logically impossible for "actions" to be caused. In drawing a radical logical distinction between the domain of "bodily movements," which can be explained in terms of (scientific) "causes," and the domain of "actions," which can be explained only in terms of "reasons," Melden's view of the determinism-free will relationship is similar to Kant's. Melden's point of view is subjected to forceful criticism by D. Davidson in his 1963 (*Journal of Philosophy*) article, "Actions, Reasons and Causes." Excerpts from both Melden and Davidson are included in the Berofsky anthology. This controversy will appeal only to the more advanced philosophy student.

MINTON, ARTHUR, ed., *Philosophy: Paradox and Discovery.* New York: McGraw-Hill, 1976. The articles by Hospers ("What Means This Freedom"), Campbell, Hook and James, and the excerpt from Darrow, listed separately in this bibliography, are reprinted (with omissions) in this general anthology of philosophy readings. Footnote page references in this chapter are from this anthology.

OFSTAD, HAROLD, *An Inquiry into the Freedom of Decision.* London: George Allen and Unwin, Ltd., 1961. An excellent detailed analysis and survey of various positions on the determinism-free will issue for the philosophically sophisticated.

OFSTAD, HAROLD, "Recent Work on the Free Will Problem," *American Philosophical Quarterly,* 4 (1967), 179–207. An excellent and comprehensive critical analysis of different contemporary perspectives on the determinism-free will issue for the philosophically sophisticated.

SCHLICK, MORITZ, "When Is a Man Responsible?" chapter 7 of his *Problems of Ethics,* published in 1931. Reprinted in the Edwards and Pap anthology, pp. 59–66. A very clear and nontechnical defense of the soft deterministic viewpoint which I highly recommend for beginning philosophy students. Schlick is especially concerned with uncovering what he takes to be the linguistical confusions that have led philosophers to think that determinism is incompatible with freedom and moral responsibility. Schlick's contentions in this regard are challenged by Campbell in his article "Is 'Free Will' a Pseudo-Problem?" which follows the Schlick article in the Edwards and Pap anthology.

II

SOME CONTEMPORARY MORAL PROBLEMS

Of one thing we may be sure. If inquiries are to have any substantial basis, if they are not to be wholly in the air, the theorist must take his departure from the problems which men actually meet in their own conduct. He may define and refine these; he may divide and systematize; he may abstract the problems from their concrete contexts in individual lives; he may classify them when he has thus detached them; but if he gets away from them he is talking about something his own brain has invented, not about moral realities.

JOHN DEWEY AND JAMES TUFTS

Pretend what we may, the whole man within us is at work, when we form our philosophical opinions.

WILLIAM JAMES

Out of the crooked timber of humanity no straight thing was ever made.

(*attributed to*) IMMANUEL KANT

4

Sexual Morality
and the
Enforcement of Morals

Given the importance of sex in our lives, it is understandable that sexual morality—that is, the principles for distinguishing proper from improper sexual behavior—is a topic of universal concern. Since sex is connected with the bringing of children into the world, it is inevitable that sexual behavior, however private and intimate in itself, must be a concern of our social morality as well as of our own private moralities. There are many people, however, who believe that, as long as children are not involved, private consenting adult sexual behavior should be beyond the scope of legal prohibition or moral criticism. As they see it, while individuals can rightfully be condemned for such things as the dishonesty, selfishness, or exploitiveness that accompanies their sexual behavior, they cannot rightfully be condemned for their sexual behavior alone, however repulsive or unnatural it appears to the majority. Underlying the views of such individuals, one will find a strong commitment either to hedonistic utilitarian or libertarian principles. The secular utilitarian, focusing upon the consequences of different sexual practices, is considerably less apt to accept rigid moral principles in this area than those who derive their sexual morality from religious tradition. Aware that the science of anthropology testifies to large variations in patterns of sexual behavior in different cultures, such an individual is apt to be an ethical relativist when it comes to questions of sexual morality.

His conservative opponents, on the other hand, will not accept such a tolerant view. From their perspective, certain deviant sexual practices threaten the very fabric of our collective way of life. Such individuals will discard the anthropological findings of diverse sexual practices as morally irrelevant. Most who accept this point of view are religious absolutists who appeal to the revealed word of God and the patterns of personal and social behavior they believe he has ordained for us. For such individuals, God has clearly spoken and condemned certain sexual practices as immoral. Not all those who are conservative in their sexual morality, however, base their view on the belief that there is a single correct morality which derives its ultimate justification from God. As we shall see in this chapter, there are some moralists who attempt to justify a conservative attitude toward sexual morality on the basis of a utilitarian concern for the maximization of human happiness. As they see it, certain *conventions*, however arbitrary, as to proper sexual behavior are necessary to maintain the cohesiveness that is essential for social living and, in turn, for human happiness.

The first part of this chapter will be devoted to critical discussions of the morality of nonmarital sex, homosexuality, and contraception. Since the burden of moral persuasion should be on those who would have us interfere with or morally condemn others for their behavior, the primary concern here will be with the arguments that have been offered for a restrictive conservative attitude toward sexual morality. If I am correct, these arguments tend to collapse on careful analysis. Nevertheless, specific permissive liberal attitudes towards sex—as exemplified, for example, by "The *Playboy* Philosophy"—are, I think, equally incapable of "proof." The "open-marriages" and the "freedom from sexual guilt" that sexual liberals often advocate have their benefits, no doubt, but they also have their price. Given the fundamental differences in liberal and conservative thinking about sexual morality and the assumption that no single conception of proper sexual morality can be established as the solely "true" one, we shall turn our attention in the second part of this chapter to the issue of a society's right to legally enforce its predominant and pervasive moral values upon members who reject these values.

NONMARITAL SEX

With its Judaic-Christian heritage, western culture is among the more repressive of societies in its conception of proper sexual morality. Early Christian sexual morality, greatly influenced by the sexual asceticism of Saint Augustine and Saint Paul, was especially negative in its evaluation of the value of sexual behavior. Total abstention from such behavior was presented as the ideal to which humans should strive. (Because of this conception, even today, we tend to associate the notion of a "virtuous" woman with that of a chaste one.) However, given man's strong animal nature, it was granted that such an ideal was too difficult for the average man who was permitted to indulge his sexual desire only within the sacrament of marriage. As Augustine put it, "it is better to marry than to burn [in Hell]." Although today such a view would be

rejected by western religious moralists as too extreme, the intimate connection between sex and marriage will still be loudly proclaimed. Sex,
although natural and enjoyable, it is now said, should never be used
merely for physical gratification but should involve the whole person
and be an expression of deep love and affection, and should have procreation as its ultimate purpose, the more conservative would add. The
deep love and affection which expresses itself, among other ways, through
sexual behavior, conservative sexual moralists will proclaim, must furthermore be of an exclusive sort which finds its only rightful place within
marriage. As they see it, our social and affectional natures can find their
maximal fulfillment only within the institution of marriage and the family structure that it embraces. The limitation of sex to marriage, they
will say, is a necessary condition for forming and maintaining stable
family units; for such a limitation will encourage people to get married
and to stay married, and the impermissibility of sex outside marriage will
tend to strengthen the marriage.

The liberal sexual moralist, on the other hand, will challenge one
or both of the two fundamental assumptions of his conservative opponents—that sexual passion should always be connected with love or
feelings of deep affection and that one should only have sex with one
person at a time. For the moderate liberal, although human sex should
never be promiscuous and loveless, it need not be restrictive. Just as a
parent can love more than one child and find different sorts of gratification in the love of different children, so one can carry on meaningful
love affairs simultaneously with more than one person. Adherents to
such a view would argue that it is often considerably better for a person
to have sex with more than one person over some long period of time
than to engage in less deep and more fleeting successive sexual liaisons
which take place within the alleged sanctity of the marriage bed.

For the extreme liberal, it is not only the exclusivity of sex that
should be rejected, but also the assumption that it should always be connected with feelings of deep love and affection. According to this viewpoint, now that contraceptives are readily available and reliable, one
should see sex as the purely pleasurable physical experience that it can
be. Just as one can enjoy good food in a variety of settings without in-
vesting such enjoyment with the burden of moral solemnity, so one can
enjoy a casual sexual experience with someone without any feelings of
"love" or deep affection. Most adherents of this position would be quite
willing to grant that love tends to enhance sex with greater meaning.
Nevertheless, they will claim, most people at some point in their lives
find themselves sexually interested in individuals for whom they feel
little or no love. Indeed, there are many people who have no capacity
for affection or love at all, although they possess normal sexual desires.
It is much more conducive to human happiness, it will be claimed, that
such individuals be permitted to obtain whatever gratification they can
from their sexual desires, without the burden of moral guilt, as long

as they do not impose their sexuality involuntarily, hurtfully, or deceitfully upon others.

Premarital Sex

With these general sketches of the differing perspectives on sexual morality in mind, let us consider the philosopher Carl Wellman's case for the undesirability of both casual and stable premarital sex in his book *Morals and Ethics* (1975). He writes,

> The pleasantness of casual premarital sex is often reduced by certain unpleasant aspects of the experience. Unless the lovers have ready access to some fairly suitable and completely private place, the sex act is likely to be performed hurriedly and uncomfortably. Even if both partners feel no guilt, each is apt to feel anxiety about participation in a socially forbidden practice. . . . Reduced pleasure is still pleasure, of course, but it is important to note that in the case of casual premarital sex it is almost inevitably trivial pleasure. That is, the act of sexual intercourse lacks full meaning or significance for the partners because it lacks the full context of past shared activities, present joint life, and future commitment that marriage can give. . . .
>
> Some of the likely consequences of casual premarital sex . . . often make it undesirable. The sharp rise in the incidence of venereal disease in the teenage population of this country suggests that sexual promiscuity has its very real dangers. . . . Moreover, the danger of an unwanted pregnancy is always there. The existence of modern contraceptive devices makes it all too easy to ignore this possibility, but no device is completely effective. The real danger, however, lies not so much in the defectiveness of the device as in the fact that it may not be used properly or used at all. . . . In the absence of any established relationship or genuine love, neither partner may care enough to take precautions to protect the other. . . . Finally, both the insistence of sexual desire and the ideal of spontaneous love making tempt casual sexual partners to throw caution to the winds. . . . It seems to me that the values of casual premarital sex are too slight to be worth its very real dangers.
>
> It is less clear that stable premarital sexual relationships are undesirable. The existence of an established personal relationship and mutual love give the experience of stable sex a significance and meaning that the experience of casual sex lacks, and these same factors eliminate or reduce such negative factors as anxiety or the danger of venereal disease. At the same time, premarital sex within a stable relationship presents a danger of its own; it threatens to damage or impair the relationship between the sexual partners. . . .
>
> Premarital sex threatens to damage a stable personal relationship in at least three ways. First, it tends to overemphasize sexual activities . . . at the expense of other activities. . . . This danger is not limited to premarital sex. Some married couples probably share very little of their lives except the sex act itself. But this danger is less within marriage,

where the sex partners have usually had an extended period to grow as persons and to learn to share many parts of their lives, and where husband and wife necessarily participate in many joint enterprises concerning the home and family. . . .

Second, premarital sex tends to overcommit the sexual partners to each other. . . . engaging in sexual intercourse usually intensifies the emotional involvement of the sex partners and may lead them to become too deeply committed to their personal relationship too quickly. . . . It may even cause a mismatched couple to get married. . . .

Third, premarital sex, whether casual or stable, destroys one precious future possibility—the possibility of sharing in marriage something unique to that marriage. Although I do not believe that divorce is always wrong, I do firmly believe that the completeness and finality of the commitment to each other in marriage is essential to the lasting health and social value of that institution. I also think that the knowledge that sexual intercourse has been reserved for marriage gives added significance to marital sex. . . .[1]

Wellman's familiar arguments against premarital sex are quite weak. As is often the case with arguments in the area of sexual morality, my impression is that Wellman started with his position and then worked backwards to find arguments to support that position.

First, one should note that some of the potential undesirable consequences of premarital sex that Wellman fears can be rendered obsolete by new developments which can eliminate or greatly reduce these undesirable consequences—specifically, fully reliable contraceptives and the elimination of the threat of venereal disease. Although Wellman is right that all existing contraceptives are subject to failure and, consequently, that individuals who have no plan to marry and raise children stand some risk of pregnancy, it could be said in reply that today's methods of contraceptives make such a risk quite small if reasonable precautions are taken as they should be. If those who engage in premarital sex do not take reasonable precautions to avoid pregnancy, it could be said, such individuals should be faulted not for their sexual behavior but for their negligence in not taking these precautions.

If one is afraid that young lovers will (to use Wellman's expression) "throw caution to the winds," one need not jump to the conclusion that such people should abstain from premarital sex for this reason alone, but can instead insist upon the necessity of teaching young people to be more careful and responsible in their sexual relations. In addition, one could argue that mature and responsible young people who engage in premarital sex should have the right to decide whether or not to take the small risk of an undesired pregnancy. In reply, Wellman might contend that an unwanted pregnancy is not a purely personal decision since the welfare of the third party—the unborn fetus—should be con-

---

[1] From *Morals and Ethics* by Carl Wellman. Copyright © 1975 by Scott, Foresman and Company. Reprinted by permission.

sidered. As we shall see in our discussion of the abortion issue, for those who see an early fetus as "merely a mass of tissue" or, at least, as "non-human," such considerations will be rejected as irrelevant. To such individuals, an abortion, though not a preferred mode of contraception, is, at least in early pregnancy, a morally unobjectionable one. Others will strongly disagree, claiming that all abortions involve the killing of innocent "persons."

From such a perspective, the possibility of an unwanted pregnancy will provide a reason for some individuals to refrain from premarital sexual behavior. It does not, however, provide a reason why all people should avoid premarital sexual experience. Such a consideration would, for example, have no bearing upon a couple who are planning to get married and would gladly accept the birth of a child. Similarly, it would have no bearing when one or both of the potential parents would be willing to raise the child themselves or give the baby up for adoption to one of the many childless couples who would want so much to adopt it. One might think that in many cases the possibility, let us say, of a young unmarried woman or man raising a child alone is not ideal, but is that any reason for condemning it as *immoral* if the child's welfare will not be damaged by such an arrangement? It may be foolish for a person to engage in sexual behavior, willingly accepting the possibility that certain personally disruptive and undesired consequences may occur, but some other reason must be given for calling such a person immoral if he or she is willing to accept the responsibility for reasonably dealing with those consequences should they occur. After all, it is usually thought to be a person's own affair whether or not he is prepared to accept some measure of personal discomfort as the possible price of the gratification of his desires.

Wellman's claim that the pleasure of casual premarital sex is reduced by the difficulty of finding "some fairly suitable and completely private place" and by the "anxiety" that is apt to accompany such behavior is similarly very weak. Such difficulties, when they occur, after all, follow from the stigma of immorality that is often perceived to attach to premarital sex and would not exist if this behavior were considered fully acceptable. If this were the case, private places would become readily available and the anxiety of participating in a socially forbidden practice would disappear. Wellman's remarks here, though relevant to a particular person's decision to engage in premarital sex *given* a background of social disapproval of such behavior, is no argument at all for the desirability of that social attitude.

Even if one accepts Wellman's contention that casual sex is less worthwhile than sex within marriage, one may still claim that the pleasure it provides is far from "trivial." Assuming that such pleasure is less worthwhile than affectionate sex within the confines of a deeply loving personal relationship, such pleasure may be quite fulfilling relative to what is available. One can, after all, enjoy the pleasure of casual premarital sexual experience and can consider such experience as "very worthwhile" while looking for someone with whom one can have a deeper and more fulfilling sexual relationship.

Wellman's criticisms of stable premarital sexual relationships are equally weak. His claim that those who have such relationships tend to become preoccupied with sexual activities to the exclusion of other activities is a very curious one. Such an objection can be made to cut in exactly the opposite direction, for it could be said that the prohibition of premarital sex has the effect of causing those whose natural sexual desires are not offered an outlet to become overly preoccupied with thoughts of sex to the exclusion of other possible shared experiences one can have with members of the opposite sex. In claiming that those who enter stable premarital sexual relationships are apt to become "overcommitted" to each other again, Wellman seems to beg the question at issue of whether deep affection and sex should be reserved for marriage (that is, he assumes precisely the point he was supposed to establish). Liberal sexual moralists would retort that Wellman is much too sanguine about the prospects of happiness that await those who enter into marriage without any sexual experience. Rushing into marriage so as to experience the sexual pleasures that are "uniquely" in its domain, such individuals may find, once that experience has been savored, that there is little else of value to hold that marriage together.

Adultery

As a springboard for our consideration of the morality of adultery, let us turn to the popular Abigail Van Buren ("Dear Abby") who, though not a philosopher, has had a great impact upon the philosophical views of many people. Consider the following from her daily newspaper column:

> DEAR ABBY: You told a woman who was in love with a married man, "Send him home to his wife and children . . ."
>
> Abby, this is 1977. Why didn't you tell her to ask her married lover to be honest with his wife about her, and try to develop an "open marriage" that would include the girl friend too?
>
> A marriage doesn't have to be exclusive to be good. Each of us can love more than one person. Why be hypocritical? If there were fewer "either/or" ultimatums, there would be fewer divorces.
>
> After 28 years of a monogamous marriage, my wife and I decided to "open" our marriage to include others. I now encourage and help my wife to have outside relationships with other men, and she does the same for me with other women. Our open marriage has revitalized us and strengthened our marriage.
> OPEN AND HAPPY
>
> DEAR OPEN: I didn't suggest an "open marriage" because I wouldn't advise anyone to do what I myself wouldn't do. Marriage is (or should be) a sacred covenant between two persons, and to "open" it to include others is a violation of that covenant.

> It may be possible to love more than one person, but in a civilized society, it's one at a time. The "group" thing, which includes many partners, is not a "love feast"—it's a sexual smorgasbord.

While it is clearly not Ms. Van Buren's intention in her reply to give any careful defense of her position in opposition to "open marriages," it is worthwhile nevertheless to subject her remarks to scrutiny. To begin with, one should notice that when Ms. Van Buren begins her reply with the assertion that "I didn't suggest an 'open marriage' because I wouldn't advise anyone to do what I myself wouldn't do," the impression is created that she is presenting her view as a statement of personal preference, without any implication that such a position is the only rational or moral one. This impression is, however, shattered when she goes on to say that "in a *civilized* society, it's one at a time." It becomes clear at this point that Ms. Van Buren does indeed consider her position superior to the position of those who disagree. She does not, however, in any way attempt to justify her position that "marriage is (or should be) a sacred covenant between two persons." Clearly, many people in our western culture do not think that marriage should be described as a "sacred covenant" and equally clearly there are many societies which would either not describe marriage in such terms or would have an entirely different conception than Ms. Van Buren has as to the terms of this "sacred covenant." Indeed, one wonders exactly what Ms. Van Buren has in mind herself by using such a term. Since she is not against divorce, it would appear that, according to Ms. Van Buren, while this "sacred covenant" demands that one limit one's sexual relations to "one at a time," it does not prohibit sexual relations with "one after the other"— that is, not "until death do us part," but until "divorce do us part"! Although western religious tradition has considered the marriage covenant or contract to include a promise of exclusive fidelity, those who open their marriage to include others may never have agreed to such a contract or, if they had, they might have felt quite justified in openly rescinding it. Ms. Van Buren gives us no idea at all why such individuals are unjustified in refusing to commit themselves to sexual exclusivity, as she claims they should. Whatever defects open marriages may possess, they are at least free of the complex web of deceit that often accompanies an adulterous relationship. This can often prove more of a destructive force to a marriage than the adulterous relationship that led to it. Aware of this, some young couples today include the acceptance of marital infidelity into their self-composed marriage vows.

In addition, even if an adulterous relationship takes place behind a cloak of deceit or the breaking of a commitment, such actions may be capable of a utilitarian justification. It is quite possible in some situations that all parties, including the deceived one, would be better off were an adulterous relationship not brought out in the open. Realizing this, some married individuals make it clear that they would prefer not to be told, and even lied to, if their spouse were unfaithful. As unpleasant as it may be to admit, there are probably many marriages that are saved or made more bearable *to both parties* by the practice of adultery.

Comforting as it is for many of us to believe that a person can never (or "nearly" never) maximize his or her happiness by engaging in an adulterous relationship or in accepting such a relationship in one's spouse, no support for such a view can be found in the clinical or theoretical observations of psychiatrists or psychologists. Anthropological data testifies to the broad spectrum of sexual practices that seem, as far as can be discerned, to contribute equally well to the satisfaction of the basic human sexual drive. There are and have been many societies which are or have been quite tolerant of adulterous relationships either in general or in special circumstances (such as during certain ceremonials or festivals). Similarly, there are many societies which reject the view, fundamental to so many in our society, that sexual behavior should always be preceded by deep affection and commitment.[2] It may be western culture's ideal that sexual behavior ought always to be exclusive and deeply embedded within a broader framework of affection and commitment, but such an ideal cannot be shown to be the only one that maximizes human happiness in this world. One should always be wary of those who say otherwise, for their conceptions of human happiness will turn out to presuppose specific and challengeable culturally or religiously based moral conceptions of the proper ends of sexual behavior.

This is the case, for example, when adultery is condemned on the grounds that such behavior is destructive of the institution of marriage and the family, for even if this is true, such a view tacitly assumes that the traditional western conception of marriage and child rearing within a nuclear family is worthy of preservation. As obvious as this assumption may appear to some, it can be challenged. One may, for example, reject western society's conception of the monogomous marriage and the family unit, while advocating a system in which women have sexual relationships with many men (and vice versa) while the children of such unions are brought up in communal nurseries. Many of us may find such a scheme distasteful, but that, of course, may simply be a reflection of our cultural conditioning. Most advocates of adultery, however, would **not** go so far as to challenge the very pillars of western ideas of marriage and

---

[2] This is true in the Polynesian island of Mangaia. The Mangaian male is not expected by the Mangaian female to demonstrate his personal affection for her prior to sexual intimacy. On the contrary, the Mangaian girl takes an immediate demonstration of sexual virility as the first test of a male's desire for her and as a reflection of her own desirability. Personal affection may or may not result from acts of sexual intimacy, but the latter is the first step to the former, exactly the reverse of western society's ideal of the relationship of sex and affection. The man who sexually excites a Mangaian girl and then "wastes her time" with too much preliminary talking or "fooling around" is likely to be pushed away and called "uri paruparu" ("limp penis") by the irate and insulted girl.

See Donald S. Marshall "Sexual Behavior on Mangaia," in *Human Sexual Behavior,* eds., Donald S. Marshall and Robert C. Suggs (New York: Basic Books, **1971**).

family life but will instead argue that these ideas are compatible with the notion of a sexually nonexclusive marriage. For example, it will be argued that, although sexual relationships need not take place only within marriage, children should be raised in a traditional family setting and the tolerance of sex outside marriage need not undermine such a setting.

Furthermore, even if it could be shown that those who do not desire extramarital sexual relationships tend to have the most satisfying sexual lives, this would not establish that those who do desire extramarital relationships would generally be happier if they repressed their desire or terminated their marriage prior to having sexual relations with someone else. Finally, even if one could establish that the maximization of human happiness requires that one's sexual relations be confined to a single marriage partner and a traditional western family structure, this does not provide a good reason, in and of itself, to condemn those who fall short of this ideal as being immoral rather than foolish. Clearly, those who are deeply committed to such an ideal and perceive deviations from it as deviations from a moral standard do not derive their sexual morality from a secular utilitarian framework. The acceptance of this ideal stems instead from traditional Judaic-Christian morality and the biblical command that "Thou shalt not commit adultery." As we have mentioned before, however, the authority of a given bible and the proper interpretation that ought to be placed on its pronouncements is always open to challenge.

CONTRACEPTION

The Roman Catholic opposition to *unnatural* methods of contraception has been expressed in the following papal pronouncement:

> Christian doctrine establishes, and the light of human reason makes it most clear, that private individuals have no other power over the members of their bodies than that which pertains to their natural ends; and they are not free to destroy or mutilate their members, or in any other way render themselves unfit for their natural functions, except when no other provision can be made for the good of the whole body.[3]

Since the only "natural function" of the sexual organs, according to this doctrine, is procreation, it would seem to logically follow that it would be wrong to utilize any method of contraception with the sole aim of preventing pregnancy. Nevertheless, the prevailing Roman Catholic position today is that it is legitimate in some situations to engage in a

---

[3] "On Christian Marriage" ("Casti Connubil"), 1930 quoted in Ronald Atkinson, *Sexual Morality* (London: Hutchinson and Company, 1965), p. 162.

sexual act within marriage as an expression of love and affection even though it is known that a pregnancy cannot occur. According to this view, although the affectional and companionate end of sexual intercourse is a secondary end, it is legitimate when the primary end is unattainable either from natural causes—such as when one of the parties is sterile, after menopause, or during the "safe period"—or as a result of treatment that was justifiable on its own account and not performed simply to preclude the possibility of pregnancy—such as if a treatment for painful periods has rendered a woman temporarily sterile. Liberal Roman Catholic theologians are attempting to undercut such a doctrine by rejecting the view that procreation should always be taken as the "primary end" of sexual intercourse and are claiming that the affectionate and companionate function of sex, at least within the confines of marriage, is fully legitimate and need not be subject to the restrictions mentioned above. The more conservative, however, have held fast to this doctrine and its quite unclear logic. According to this doctrine, although one cannot legitimately choose to sterilize oneself or to use mechanical or chemical means of contraception with the aim of preventing a pregnancy, one can legitimately aim to avoid pregnancy through the restriction of intercourse to the "safe period." This is legitimate, it is said, because one is not employing an *artificial* means to interfere with a *natural* process.

As we shall discuss in greater detail in the context of the morality of homosexuality, the notion of what is a natural as opposed to an unnatural human act is quite unclear both in meaning and in moral relevancy. Indeed, rather than dispensing with this cloudy notion, some liberal Catholic theologians have attempted to bend it to their own moral purposes. Some, for example, have argued for the acceptability of the pill as a contraceptive measure on the grounds that this method—but not the condom or diaphragm—utilizes a "natural physiological system of fertility control" that is employed by the human body. As one person put it, "The pills provide a natural means of fertility control such as nature uses after ovulation and during pregnancy." The condom or the diaphragm, on the other hand, it is claimed, are *extraneous* devices and, as such, would be illegitimate as would be "wholly artificial chemical action." Other Catholic moralists, however, have found the extraneous character of the condom or diaphragm as a point in their favor and counting toward their "naturalness." Clearly, reference to the notion of naturalness in such claims serves only to obscure the issue. It would certainly seem to me, as it does to so many other critics of the Roman Catholic position on contraception, that once it is considered legitimate to engage in sexual intercourse with the intention of avoiding a pregnancy, no remotely plausible justification can be given for restricting legitimate contraception to the "safe periods," (which, of course, turn out not to be all that safe for some) when so much more effective and less sexually frustrating methods of contraception are available.

HOMOSEXUALITY

The Factual Background

According to anthropological data, there are and have been many societies in which homosexual behavior has been considered to fall within the range of normal sexual behavior and, indeed, in some societies such behavior has actually been encouraged. For example, in some societies young boys are introduced to sex through homosexual unions with older men at puberty and continue their homosexual conduct among themselves until they have become sufficiently mature in the eyes of their elders to have sexual relations with women. Homosexual behavior was also quite openly accepted in the ancient Greece of the famous philosopher Plato. Many a student has been surprised to find upon reading Plato's dialogue "The Symposium" that as Plato expounds upon the nature of love his attention seems to be riveted upon a young man, for Plato, it would appear, was himself a homosexual. Homosexual behavior has, however, been subject to the gravest moral and legal condemnation in Christian cultures. Presently, the majority of states in the United States have ("sodomy") laws making certain sexual practices (such as anal and oral sex, and bestiality) illegal.[4] Western society's strong condemnation of homosexuality can, without doubt, be traced to several biblical condemnations of homosexual acts. For example, the Bible tells us that homosexuality is an "abomination" (Leviticus 18:22) and that homosexuals will not "inherit the kingdom of God" (I Corinthians 6:9–10). In addition, it has always been widely assumed that the destruction of Sodom and Gomorrah mentioned in the Old Testament was a result of the general licentiousness, especially homosexuality, of these communities. Although many theologians still adhere to a strict condemnation of homosexuality, there is a growing number of theologians today who are challenging this view by attempting to attribute the unmistakable biblical condemnations of homosexuality to faulty cultural interpretation rather than to divine inspiration. For example, it has been said by some theologians that the sins of Sodom and Gomorrah were not the sins of sexual licentiousness and abuse but those of pride and inhospitality to

---

4 In March 1976, the Supreme Court in a major defeat for homosexual rights upheld a lower court's decision that the states have the authority to punish homosexual acts between consenting adults in the privacy of their own homes. On a 6 to 3 vote, the high court summarily affirmed (that is, without oral arguments and written opinions) that the constitutional right to privacy—the foundation of recent abortion and contraception rulings—does not encompass homosexual relations. In the case at issue, two Virginia homosexuals challenged a Virginia law that made anal and oral intercourse a crime punishable by up to five years in prison or a $1,000 fine. The defense claimed that such a law was both an invasion of the constitutional right to privacy and unjustly discriminatory against homosexuals, since heterosexuals were never prosecuted under such a law for the very same acts.

strangers. Similarly, Norman Pittenger of the Cambridge University School of Divinity attributes Paul's strong condemnation of homosexuality in the New Testament to the fact that the homosexuality of Paul's era "was often just licentious, not in any way a noble and moral affair as it had been among the Greeks of, say, Plato's time." The contention that homosexual behavior can be moral is also echoed by the Quakers who maintain that the standards of judgment applied to homosexuals should be no different from those that apply to heterosexuals, and that "it is the nature and quality of a relationship which matters. . . . Homosexual affection can be as selfless as heterosexual affection and therefore we cannot see that it is in some way morally worse."[5] Other theologians, in their attempt to soften the traditional Judaic-Christian moral condemnation of homosexual behavior, distinguish between voluntary and involuntary homosexuality. According to the Dutch Catechism (a liberal wing of Roman Catholicism), for example, "the very sharp strictures of Scripture . . . must be read in their context as a denunciation of a fashion that was spreading to many who were quite capable of normal sexual sentiments." The Catechism then goes on to tell us that those homosexuals who are "incapable of normal sexual sentiments" should not be subject to censure.

Psychological Theories of the Causes of Homosexuality

A survey of the psychological and psychiatric literature on the causes of homosexuality reveals wide discrepancies in the theories that presently abound in this area. It is, however, generally conceded that homosexual behavior is far more common in our society than was previously believed. Kinsey, for example, in his famous survey of American sexual behavior, found that 4 percent of white male adults were exclusively homosexual for their entire life, 10 percent had been exclusively homosexual for at least three years, and that as many as 37 percent had engaged in homosexual activity to the point of orgasm on some occasions. This would especially be the case, for example, with predominantly heterosexual people who find themselves in environments (such as prisons or armies) which preclude the possibility of heterosexual activity for long periods of time.

The simple classification of people as homosexuals or heterosexuals is itself made cloudy by contemporary psychological theory and the contemporary advocacy of bisexuality by many people. Many psychiatrists and psychologists today, for example, follow Freud in claiming that there is a basic sexual duality in human beings. The problem of sexual classification is further complicated by the biological fact that external genitals need not always correspond to genetic programming or internal sexual organs. The victims of one of the most common forms of such disorders are born with penises and an empty scrotum, but are neverthe-

---

[5] Alastair Heron, ed., *Towards a Quaker View of Sex* (London: Friends Home Service Committee, 1964).

less "girls" with respect to chromosomes (XX) and internal sexual organs and hormones. Such "girls" are usually labeled male at birth, raised as boys, and brought in for treatment when their breasts start developing at puberty. There is a male equivalent of this disorder—male in chromosomes (XY), internal gonads and hormones, but having a blind vagina and two lumps in the groin where undescended testicles are located. There are other kinds of "hermaphroditism," combining various degrees of ambiguous biological sexual components. Given such biological sexual ambiguity, the classification of behavior as homosexual or heterosexual becomes quite unclear. Are different copulatory organs alone the only necessary feature of heterosexual relations, or are different gonadal structure or genes necessary? Although such a question will strike some as pointless, it must be faced by those who condemn all homosexual acts as immoral.

However ambiguous the biological signs of gender may be, researchers have found that gender identity (that is, how one classifies oneself sexually) almost always agrees with rearing and sex assignment. In other words, whatever people are labeled and are raised to be is what they think they are and live as—no matter what the genes, internal gonads, or external genitals indicate to the contrary. Considering the primacy of learning in gender identity, the choice of sex-object, most researchers firmly believe, must also be learned. Consequently, the generally accepted view is that homosexuality, as well as many other elements in human sexuality, is not *fully* determined by physiological factors, such as heredity, genes, or hormones. For example, it seems clear that while increasing or decreasing the amount of male or female sex hormones in a person's body will affect that person's sexual excitability, it will not in itself change one's gender identity or choice of sex object, nor will it make the very shy or inhibited sexually aggressive.

Nevertheless, there are many researchers who emphasize the physiological factors that contribute to at least some types of homosexuality. For example, it has been suggested that the homosexuality of effeminate men who, from early childhood, were classified as "sissy little boys" is determined by prenatal factors. As this theory has it, there is a critical point in the development of male mammals—and in humans it is while the fetus is still in the uterus—at which the brain must be sensitized by male hormones. If not, the male will behave in an effeminate way. Those who emphasize the bearing of genetic factors on homosexuality often point to studies which seem to indicate that fraternal twins (who do not have identical genes) do not tend to be as concordant on sex-object preference as identical twins (who have identical genes). The reliability and significance of such studies have, however, been challenged.

Among researchers who accept the predominance of learning upon the development of homosexual tendencies, the predominant approach is to look for the cause of homosexuality in distorted family relationships. According to one influential theory, a large percentage of male homosexuals were, as children, treated by their fathers in a detached, hostile, and unaffectionate manner, while their mothers reacted to them in a very warm but sexually provocative manner. Arousing them to sexuality, such women would be puritanical in repressing any expression of it. It has been claimed that such boys upon maturity tend to be unconsciously afraid of any heterosexual impulse, for such impulses are associated in their minds with the incestuous sexual conflicts that were instilled in them by their dominating and seductive mothers. Many researchers, however, doubt that this theory or any other single theory of the cause of homosexuality can ever be found; the truth, they suggest, is probably that there are diverse forms of homosexuality produced by complex intertwining biological and cultural factors. Some researchers who share this point of view think that it is a fundamental mistake to assume that homosexuality and heterosexuality are two separate and distinct categories having separate and distinct causes. Sexuality, they say, should be perceived as a continuous line between the poles of exclusive heterosexuality and exclusive homosexuality. Some have gone on to assert that all of us are to some degree bisexual, although the homosexual component remains latent in most of us.

Are Homosexuals Sick?

Just as psychiatrists and psychologists disagree on the cause or causes of homosexuality, they also disagree on the normality or mental health of the homosexual. To some, homosexuality is a way of life which can in and of itself be as satisfying and conducive to mental health as can a heterosexual life. Supporters of such a view will grant that homosexuals are often quite unhappy, guilt-ridden, and socially maladjusted, but will attribute this entirely to society's reaction to them and not to the inherent inadequacy of their sexual preference. Such a view is, however, hotly contested by psychiatrists and psychologists who believe that homosexuality in and of itself is, or at least tends to be, a sign of some underlying psychopathology which limts a homosexual's capacity for a fully satisfying life.

Much of the disagreement over the mental health of homosexuals, no doubt, stems from differences in scientific beliefs about the nature and causes of homosexuality. Nevertheless, this disagreement is, to some extent, also of a conceptual nature in that individuals who share the same factual beliefs about the nature and causes of homosexuality can disagree as to whether or not these facts justify the ascription of the label of "mental health" or that of "mental illness" since they attribute different meanings to these concepts. Quite often, psychologists or psychiatrists who utilize these concepts in a particular way are unaware of the fact that their usage of these concepts may reflect *a moral commitment* to the desirability of behavioral patterns which cannot be decided merely by a consideration of the scientific facts. It is no mere coincidence, for example, that morally liberal psychiatrists and psychologists who are less willing than their more conservative counterparts to condemn lifestyles as "immoral" are also much less willing to label them as "mental illnesses."

The conceptual fog surrounding the meaning that should be attributed to the concept of mental illness (or disorder) was reflected in the widely publicized decision of the American Psychiatric Society in 1973 to remove homosexuality from its official list of mental disorders. Many psychiatrists, however, strongly dissented from this decision. For example, Dr. Charles W. Socarides, a leading authority on homosexuality, declared that "It is quite wrong for homosexuals to be treated as criminals, but it is scientific folly for psychiatry to normalize homosexual relations as if they had no psychopathology. . . . Homosexuality is a devastating disease of psychological origin." On the other hand, those who claim that homosexuality should not per se be considered a sign of mental disorder claim that psychiatrists who generalize about the psychopathology of homosexuality tend to mistakenly assume that all homosexuals are like the troubled ones who come to them for help. As such, they have no experience of those adjusted homosexuals who lead normal and, indeed, often quite distinguished lives in every other respect.

Arno Karlen in his extensive study of homosexuality[6] claims that (male) homosexuals tend to suffer from an underlying sexual insecurity over their masculinity, which gives rise to a compensating tendency toward hostility and verbal bickering, "a kind of verbal wrestling for who is on top." It is not, however, clear that the implication of this view is, as Karlen suggests, that homosexuality, in and of itself, causes these psychological characteristics. Perhaps such characteristics are nothing more than a reflection of the *normal* human reaction to being perceived as a deviant. This is the contention that would be made by many students of the sociology of deviance who see the very stigmatization directed toward a person who is labeled as homosexual as driving that person further into his deviant career. According to this view, homosexuals, because they are labeled as perverse or deviant, tend to identify with their own subculture and return the majority's hostility in a bitter, mocking, and supercilious way. One way to show this hostility, it is claimed, is to flaunt one's stigma by living up to the very stereotype that society has provided for you.

Can Homosexuals Be Cured?

Psychiatrists and psychologists also disagree on whether or not homosexuals can be cured. Again, part of the disagreement is conceptual in nature and reflects different conceptions of what is to count as a "cure." Although there are some psychiatrists and clinical psychologists who would claim that homosexuality cannot be cured, many claim that they can obtain complete change in about one-third of their homosexual patients and partial change in another third through psychotherapy

6 Arno Karlen, *Sexuality and Homosexuality* (New York: W.W. Norton & Co., Inc., 1971).

(that is, "talking" therapy). Behavioral psychologists[7] have, however, claimed up to 80–90 percent cure rate in their treatment of homosexuals through behavioral conditioning. This claim is hotly contested by psychoanalytically oriented therapists who claim that such treatments do not resolve the "underlying psychic conflicts" from which homosexuals suffer. There is also disagreement among therapists as to the ultimate aim of "successful" therapy for homosexuals. Some aim at the total eradication of a patient's homosexuality, while others aim not at changing the homosexual but at getting him "to accept himself for what he is." Other therapists take a middle stand, attempting to aid the homosexual not in repressing his attraction to members of the same sex, but in widening his field of sexual attraction to include members of the opposite sex. From this therapeutic standpoint, the problem of homosexuality is not attraction to members of one's own sex, but a flight from members of the opposite sex. Supporters of this viewpoint often believe that when a homosexual's underlying fear of members of the other sex has been removed and heterosexual relationships are established, this new form of satisfaction will make the old one obsolete and unnecessary.

The Morality of Homosexuality

It is the belief of many people in our society that homosexuals are not only "sick," but "immoral" as well. On the face of it, this is a paradoxical claim, for usually people who are described as sick are assumed to be victims of some involuntary affliction and, consequently, are not seen as fit subjects for judgments of moral blame. Certainly, if we believe that homosexuals are sick, in that they are victims of a condition that precludes a fully satisfying life, we should not subject these individuals to the added burden of being classified as immoral social outcasts without some strong justification. If, as is generally conceded, a homosexual does not voluntarily choose to be a homosexual, it would be unfair to blame him for his condition. Similarly, it would be unfair to blame a homosexual for not overcoming or working to overcome his homosexual tendencies if one believes, as some do, that homosexuals have little or no control in changing their homosexual tendencies and can choose not to

---

7 According to behavioral psychologists who accept the "learning theory" point of view, homosexual behavior is behavior that develops according to the same psychological laws of learning or association as those governing the development of normal behavior and can be "extinguished" through a reconditioning process. The learning therapist, unlike his psychotherapeutic counterpart, does not seek to remove the underlying causes of homosexuality nor to provide the homosexual with insight into his condition. Instead, he arranges a program of reconditioning in which new reinforcements are instituted in order to condition the homosexual into heterosexuality (or bisexuality). A technique often utilized to achieve this aim is "aversion therapy" in which the therapist aims at setting up an associative process between unpleasant stimuli and the thought of homosexuality.

act on these inclinations only at the heroic cost of accepting a life of great frustration and lack of fulfillment. Unfortunately, these considerations are rarely considered by those who condemn homosexuals as immoral. Let us turn to the arguments that have been offered in defense of this claim.

Homosexuality Is Offensive

No doubt, many people find the homosexual lifestyle a highly offensive one, but even if the vast majority of people in our society felt this way, this would not justify the moral condemnation of homosexuality as a way of life. This is so for two reasons. First, and most important, the mere fact that a given individual finds certain behavior offensive does not at all show that he *ought* to find that behavior offensive—that is, that he has any *justification* for his feelings. Second, there are things that we feel justified in being offended at which are clearly not moral matters. For example, most of us would find it very offensive to be in the presence of someone who never washes and emits the strongest of body odors. Such a person, short as he may find himself of friends, would not be considered an *immoral* person. Again, some reason apart from the mere offensiveness of a person's conduct must be given for its moral condemnation.

Practically all moralists, however, would agree that a society has a right to shield itself through legal sanctions from conduct which the vast majority of its citizens finds offensive, even if that conduct is not in itself immoral. For example, even though it is not immoral for a husband and wife to have sexual intercourse, most of us would find it highly offensive were we to come across a married couple in the midst of an act of sexual intercourse while we strolled with our family through a public park. We would believe that such *public conduct* ought to be legally prohibited since we, and so many others, find it offensive. Although we might very well feel that the voluntary sexual practices of people in private is "no business of the law," their public behavior, we think, is. It would seem that even the most liberal of supporters of free expression would be willing to limit public behavior that a vast majority of citizens find offensive when such behavior is thrust upon them unwillingly. Such a stand is reflected in laws relating to "public nuisancy." This is one of those areas in the law in which principles to which we give some degree of allegiance clash and consequently call for balancing. In this case, we find a person's right to freedom of expression conflicting with another individual's right to privacy and noninterference by others. At times, drawing a balance between these conflicting considerations is a difficult matter. For example, just as practically all of us would feel justified in making public heterosexual intercouse illegal in public places which can be avoided only with unreasonable inconvenience by those who would be offended by such conduct, we would feel justified in making homosexual intercourse illegal in similar circumstances. But what about public homosexual petting or kissing? Clearly, most of us would be much more tolerant and less apt to be disgusted by such public behavior when it involves heterosexuals. Even if one is willing to admit that one ought not to make such a discrimination, the fact is that most of us do—however culturally conditioned this discrimination is—and cannot easily change our feelings in this matter. Do we then have a right to protect our sensibilities when they are "flagrantly offended" in public or does the homosexual's right of freedom of expression override our right in these situations? Reasonable people will give different answers to such a question. To some, even if the vast majority of citizens finds homosexual kissing and petting offensive, that is still not sufficient justification for restricting the homosexual's right to freedom of expression. Supporters of this position may go on to suggest that we would be healthier psychologically if we were not offended by such conduct and that exposure to it might very well make us more tolerant of it. On the other hand, there are those who draw the balance sheet in favor of the offended majority and who feel quite justified in restricting such displays of sexuality to the privacy of one's home or private homosexual meeting places.

Homosexuals Are Dangerous

It is often claimed that homosexual behavior ought to be morally condemned since such behavior is in some respect dangerous to other individuals or to society as a whole. At times the defense of such a claim can appear quite ludicrous when it is subjected to scrutiny. For example, it is often argued that "homosexuality is immoral because the existence of such behavior encourages others to do the same and if everyone or large numbers of people were to become homosexuals, there would no longer be any human race." Underlying such a claim would appear to be the fear that countless people would turn to homosexuality if such behavior were free of moral condemnation[8]—so many, in fact, that the very existence of the human race would be put in jeopardy. Certainly, one should have more faith in the heterosexuality of human beings! This should especially be the case if one believes, as most opponents of homosexuality do believe, that the homosexual life is not capable of being as satisfying as that of the heterosexual life. Furthermore, in an overpopulated world, one would think that homosexuality would be quite desirable. Finally, a preference for homosexuality is not inconsistent with procreation. One can easily imagine a society of people devoted to a homosexual way of life who enter brief heterosexual unions, produce a socially required number of children, and then devote the rest of their sexual lives to homosexuality. Indeed, with the advent of artificial in-

---

[8] According to Freud, such underlying assumptions are often not brought to consciousness since they are mere rationalizations for our own fears of becoming homosexuals ourselves. The condemnation of homosexuality, on this view, helps strengthen our own heterosexuality by repressing the homosexual element that lies hidden within our unconscious.

semination and artificial wombs, such individuals would not have to engage in heterosexual activities at all.

It has also often been suggested that homosexuality is dangerous and, as such, is immoral in that such conduct tends to undermine the family unit and that this, in turn, tends to lead to a general moral breakdown. In the next part of this chapter we shall scrutinize the many unclear and questionable assumptions implicit in such a claim when we discuss a society's right to enforce its prevailing moral standards. It will suffice now to simply point out some of these questionable assumptions. First, such an argument assumes that the traditional heterosexual family unit, as found in contemporary western culture, is worthy of preservation. Second, it assumes that homosexuality poses a dangerous threat to this family unit. Those who take this view, however, are usually silent in their condemnation of nonmarital sexual relations and the easy availability of contraceptives which has contributed to the growing number of childless heterosexual marriages. Yet they would appear to provide a much greater threat to the traditional western family unit. Third, even if the tolerance of homosexuality would pose some substantial threat to the existence of the traditional western family unit, it is not at all obvious that this would, in turn, lead to other fundamental revisions in our current moral standards which should, if they were to occur, be described in the negative judgmental terms of "moral breakdown" rather than in the neutral terms of "moral change" or the positive-sounding terms of "moral evolution."

In addition to such general and abstract defenses of the dangerousness of the homosexual way of life, a much more concrete argument is often heard that homosexuals are dangerous since they tend to molest children and in general to impose their sexual preferences unwillingly on others. There is, however, simply no evidence to support the general belief that this is true of a greater percentage of homosexuals than heterosexuals. The fact that such claims are so often made with no evidence at all would seem to indicate that they are often used as rationalizations either for less easily articulated reasons or for deeper unconscious fears or conflicts.

Homosexuality Is Unnatural

Homosexuals are often subjected to moral criticism on the grounds that they practice an *unnatural* form of behavior. Unfortunately, those who make such a claim rarely attempt to clarify the meaning they wish to attribute to the notion of unnatural behavior, nor do they argue for the moral relevance of such a notion—that is, why unnatural behavior is *immoral* behavior. Indeed, it would appear that the claim that "homosexuals are immoral *because* they engage in unnatural behavior" is often utilized in a tautological manner where the notion of unnatural behavior is used synonymously with that of immoral behavior. When this is so, the critic of homosexuality may give others, as well as himself, the mistaken impression that he is giving a reason why homosexuals are immoral when he is not.

What then are we to take the notion of "unnatural" to mean in this context? Clearly, if by natural behavior all one means is behavior that is found in nature, then homosexuality as well as everything one finds in this world is natural. (In this sense the concept of unnatural is synonymous with that of supernatural.) Similarly, if we take the notion of unnatural simply to mean uncommon, the studies of Kinsey and others would seem to indicate that homosexuality is not at all unnatural to human beings. Most important of all, however, even if homosexual behavior were uncommon, this would in itself be no good reason for morally condemning such behavior. Running a four-minute mile is uncommon, but it is not immoral. It would seem that those who claim that homosexual behavior is unnatural are asserting that such behavior goes contrary to either the purpose assigned by God for the proper utilization of the sexual organs or to the proper biological and psychological role of sexuality in human beings. Let us consider these contentions in turn.

Those who claim that homosexual behavior is contrary to divine purpose assume that this world and everything in it was purposefully designed by God for some good purpose. From this perspective, God not only ordained certain descriptive laws which impose an order or pattern upon the events of this world, making scientific predictability and understanding possible, but also ordained certain "natural laws" that human beings must follow if they are to act in accord with the will of God. Those who accept this view have often assumed that homosexuality is contrary to "natural law"—that is, is contrary to the divine purpose ordained for the use of the sex organs. Since it is assumed on this view that procreation is the only legitimate purpose for the utilization of the sex organs, it would seem to logically follow that the very great number of heterosexuals who use contraceptives or engage in oral intercourse are as immoral as homosexuals. Even if one believes that God created the sexual organs and made sexual acts pleasurable in order to assure that these organs be utilized for procreation, this in no way would show that it is contrary to God's will that these organs be utilized in other ways as well. For example, if one believes that God created the human eye to enable human beings to see, this would not at all entail that a woman is "acting contrary to divine purpose" when she uses her eyes in a flirtatious manner. Just as we would assume that God does not object to this, why should he object to the nonprocreative utilization of the sex organs as a mode of expressing love or merely as a means of obtaining pleasure when this is done in a nonharmful and freely chosen manner? And if it is true that he does not object in the case of heterosexuals, simple justice would seem to demand that he not object in the case of homosexuals. Unless one is content, as I think one should not be, to accept at face value those passages in the Bible which express God's supposed moral condemnation of homosexuality but which provide no explanation for this condemnation, one must seek some justification for the special wrath that God supposedly reserves for homosexuals. Yet, I cannot see how such a justification can be given.

Not all, however, have sought their justification for the claim that homosexuality is unnatural in the alleged will of God; from a purely secular perspective, some have attributed the "unnaturalness" of homosexuality to the alleged inability of this mode of behavior to satisfy human needs or to the alleged fact that such a sexual orientation is not found in other animals. Let us consider these claims more fully. First, even if it were true that homosexuality is inherently unsatisfying, this provides no good reason for subjecting homosexuals to criticism, let alone moral criticism, for their choice of lifestyle. It might very well be, for example, that although the homosexual life would be quite unsatisfying to the majority of human beings, it is still the best or only form of sexual gratification available to homosexuals. More important, however, even if homosexuals have a "free choice" of being heterosexual and would be happier if they made this choice, why should they be subject to moral condemnation for such a choice? After all, people make all sorts of foolish choices which are not subject to moral condemnation.

Similarly, if one classifies homosexual behavior as a form of unnatural behavior on the grounds that other animals are never exclusively homosexual, such a fact, if it is a fact,[9] would appear to provide no

---

[9] The general consensus among researchers in animal behavior is that although animals may participate in what would appear to be "homosexual" activities, such behavior results either from a lack of heterosexual outlets or is nonsexual—for instance, a male may mount another male not in order to obtain sexual gratification but as a sign of friendship or as a method for asserting control. This view is not, however, universally accepted. According to Konrad Lorenz, for example,

> The capacity for homosexual behavior is part of the normal makeup of many animals. . . . In geese, falling in love and pair-bonding can be as dissociated from copulation as it can be in man. You may find a very strong homosexual bond between two male geese who behave like a pair though they cannot copulate. They never do—they always forget that the other refuses to be mounted and they try again every spring. Each goose behaves in a perfectly normal male way and, if he could speak, he would say, "I love my wife very much but she's definitely frigid."
>
> Homosexual male pairs rise very high in the rank order of a goose colony because the fighting potential of two males is superior to that of a heterosexual pair. Therefore, they are admired by unmarried females. Often when they fail to copulate because each wants to mount and neither will crouch, a loving female will crouch between them and is copulated by one or by both. This female is gradually accepted by the two males, but she gets no respect. If she succeeds in getting a nest and laying, she may awaken the parental response in both males and they may guard the nest and accept the babies. Then you have a *ménage à trois* in which two males love each other and the female loves one of them. (Richard I. Evans, *The Making of Psychology*, New York: Knopf, 1976), p. 5.

It is interesting to note that Lorenz apparently conceives of his "homosexual" geese as being unaware of the proper sexuality of their mate ("I love my wife . . . but she's . . . frigid"). As such, it is open to a critic to contend that grounds at all for the moral condemnation of the homosexual way of life. Homosexuality in humans, it might turn out, results from a unique human capacity to go beyond rigid biological sexual programming and to invest sexuality with a complexity and psychological meaning that is beyond the capacity of animals. It is indeed ironic that those who are often the loudest in proclaiming the uniqueness of human beings among the animals of this world are often the very same people who condemn homosexuals on the alleged fact that they are not sufficiently like the animals!

Homosexuals and the Law

One can believe, as many do, that although consenting adult homosexual conduct is immoral, it ought not to be subject to legal prohibition. From this perspective, when an act such as a homosexual one is private, between consenting adults and where no one is subject to physical danger, it is not in the proper domain of the law to interfere by making such action punishable. Such a position is a widespread one. The influential American Law Institute in its 1955 Model Penal Code, for example, made homosexual acts criminal only when they involved force, fraud, or a minor. Such a view is becoming more and more popular here in the United States as is evidenced by the growing number of states that have changed their laws to make consenting adult sexual behavior legal, including homosexuality. In other states, the old penalties for "sexual perversion" are being lightened. For example, North Carolina's "sodomy law" which prohibits anal intercourse and "all kindred acts of bestial character whereby degrading and perverted desires are sought to be gratified" originally called for up to 60 years imprisonment for such an offense, but when a man was sentenced in 1962 to 20 to 30 years for a private consenting, homosexual act under this law, enough of a public outcry was aroused that the law was revised, reducing the sentence to 4 months to 10 years.

Many critics of the laws which make homosexual conduct per se illegal point with disgust to the manner in which the police in various cities enforce the laws relating to homosexuality. Since it is understandably difficult to obtain evidence against consenting homosexuals, "vice squads" are often forced to use decoys to lure homosexuals into making advances and to engage in the surveillance of places in which homosexual

---

such geese are not "really homosexuals" but are instead "confused heterosexuals." This would be true only if one incorporates an intellectual awareness of the sexuality of one's mate into the definition of homosexuality. If this awareness is understood to involve an intellectual conceptual awareness that only human beings possess, it would follow that animals are actually *incapable* of true homosexuality.

behavior is likely to take place (such as in public bathrooms).[10] Such conduct has itself been loudly condemned as more "morally degrading" than the behavior it is meant to deter. Such a view is reinforced by skepticism as to the effectiveness of criminal prohibition in deterring individuals from homosexual behavior.

Nevertheless, there are many who are opposed to the decriminalization of homosexuality. According to such individuals, the law should not only protect people from the unwelcome harm or unfairness of others but should also strive to make people virtuous. For example, in the television program *60 Minutes,* James J. Kilpatrick, in reply to Shana Alexander's claim that "I would remove the penalties from all victimless crimes," argues as follows:

> Up to a point, Shana, I share your libertarian theories. I too believe an individual has a right to mess up his own life, so long as he does no harm to others. But there is such a thing as society or community or the commonwealth—a body of moral conviction developed over many centuries out of law and religion—and I believe it cannot wisely be disdained. In libertarian theory, laws against prostitution should be repealed. A woman's body is her own, and she can sell it if she wants to. But I believe society has a right to say prostitution is wrong, it's degrading; and if it can never be eliminated it should not be implicitly approved. It's the same with hard-core pornography. As a writer, I'm troubled by legal censorship. I don't like it. But I believe the community has a right to say hard-core pornography is wrong, it pollutes, and it subtly eats at the fabric of our life. You make persuasive arguments for legalized heroin, but maybe society has a right to say, out of its collective wisdom and experience: Heroin is a terrible evil; we ought not to make it easy for the weak to surrender to addiction. What I am suggesting, Shana, is that we should not flinch from setting standards of right conduct, of virtue, of public good and public evil. And we ought to shun the notion that the drunk, and drug addict, and the whore, even if they do not demonstrably harm others, do not affect others—for they do. For better or for worse, a community is influenced by each of its members. Saints and sinners, we are touching atoms. So, ask not for whom the bell tolls, Shana, it tolls for thee and me, and for all of you out there. (*Used with permission*)

Prominent among those who share Kilpatrick's sentiments are moral absolutists who believe that there is a uniquely correct set of moral standards that can be discovered through reason or religious revelation. Convinced that they possess the only true morality, and often convinced as well that it is more important to protect a person's character from

---

[10] While the courts have generally considered "entrapment" a defense to criminal prosecution, they have disagreed as to the definition and specific behavior that counts as entrapment. According to the most popular definition, "entrapment" occurs "when the criminal design originates with the officials of the government, and they implant in the mind of an innocent person the disposition to commit the alleged offense and induce its commission in order that they may prosecute."

moral harm than to protect his body from physical harm, such individuals will consider it irrational for the law to protect individuals from physical but not moral harm. It is not true, however, that all who would be sympathetic to Kilpatrick's sentiments are ethical absolutists. As is the case with Patrick Devlin, whose views we shall soon subject to scrutiny, some who believe that a society is justified in using the law to discourage consenting adults from voluntarily engaging in conduct which is considered immoral according to the prevailing moral standards of that society are ethical relativists who would be willing to grant that the morality they wish to enforce can in no way be shown to be uniquely justifiable. Accepting Durkheim's claim that morality is the cement that holds members of a society together, supporters of this viewpoint assert that without a strong, generally accepted morality or "way of life," a society tends to disintegrate. From this perspective, it is the cohesive power of a morality, and not its quality, that matters. Let us now turn our attention to this view and the traditional "liberal" one to which it stands in marked opposition.

LIBERTY AND THE ENFORCEMENT OF MORALITY

The Classical Liberal Position: John Stuart Mill's On Liberty

The classical liberal position on the legitimate scope of governmental interference with individual freedom is expressed by John Stuart Mill in his famous essay *On Liberty* (1859). In the beginning of this essay, Mill states his position, writing,

> The object of this Essay is to assert one very simple principle, as entitled to govern absolutely the dealings of society with the individual in the way of compulsion and control, whether the means used be physical force in the form of legal penalties, or the moral coercion of public opinion. That principle is that the sole end for which mankind are warranted, individually or collectively, in interfering with the liberty of action of any of their number, is self-protection. That the only purpose for which power can be rightfully exercised over any member of a civilized community, against his will, is to prevent harm to others. His own good, either physical or moral, is not sufficient warrant. He cannot rightfully be compelled to do or forbear because it will be better for him to do so, because it will make him happier, because, in the opinion of others, to do so would be wise, or even right. These are good reasons for remonstrating with him, or reasoning with, or persuading him, or entreating him, but not for compelling him, or visiting him with any evil in case he do otherwise. To justify that, the conduct from which it is desired to deter him must be calculated to produce evil to someone else. The only part of the conduct of anyone, for which he is amenable to

society, is that which concerns others. In the part which merely concerns himself, his independence is, of right, absolute. Over himself, over his own body and mind, the individual is sovereign.[11]

The rest of Mill's essay (a little over 100 pages) is devoted to a defense of this thesis. Underlying this defense was Mill's great fear of the tendency toward the suppression of individual freedom that he saw growing in the democracies of his day. It was Mill's belief that democratic social theorists, such as John Locke, in their attempt to defend majority rule over the power of an absolute monarchy, failed to place sufficient safeguards upon the possible "tyranny of the majority." It was essential, Mill believed, that the rights of minorities to unconventional styles of living and to freedom of expression should be protected, however offensive such styles of living and beliefs might be to the dissenting majority. As well as being afraid of the possibility of repressive laws, Mill was even more afraid of the indirect power of societal pressure directed against nonconforming minorities—pressures which can be strong enough to deprive people of the right to a job, to live where they choose, and to teach what they believe. Without such rights, Mill believed, a democracy would merely exchange the tyranny of absolute monarchy for the potentially even greater tyranny of the majority.

Mill's defense of individual freedom hinges upon his distinction between "self-regarding" and "other-regarding" actions. Although a society has a right to interfere with a person's conduct when it "affects others," it has no right to interfere with that part of his conduct "which merely concerns himself." Underlying Mill's uncompromising defense of his position is his utilization of the idea of "the free market-place of ideas." Borrowing the contention of the laissez-faire economists of his day that the best interests of the consumer can only be satisfied in a free economy which allows an unfettered competition of economic products, Mill argues that the on-going search for truth and happiness requires an unrestricted competition among differing ideas and lifestyles. As long as people do not interfere with the liberty of others, they should be allowed the right to be idiosyncratic and to live their lives as they choose. Since we have not obtained perfection, Mill argues, the maximization of human happiness requires that individuals be allowed the freedom to form their own "experiments in living" and not be forced into a stifling "tendency to conformity which breeds only withered capacities."

Some Difficulties with Mill's Position

Mill's classical defense of a person's right to act as he so chooses in that domain of his life which "concerns only himself" has been subjected to much criticism. First, while Mill speaks of this right being unlimited, this is not his actual position, for he concedes that

11 John Stuart Mill, *On Liberty* (Indianapolis: Bobbs-Merrill, 1956), first published 1859, p. 13.

. . . this doctrine is meant to apply only to human beings in the maturity of their faculties. We are not speaking of children, or of young persons below the age which the law may fix as that of manhood or womanhood. Those who are still in a state to require being taken care of by others must be protected against their own actions as well as against external injury. For the same reason, we may leave out of consideration those backward states of society. . . . Despotism is a legitimate mode of government in dealing with barbarians, provided the end be their improvement, and the means justified by actually effecting that end. Liberty as a principle has no application to any state of things anterior to the time when mankind have become capable of being improved by free and equal discussion.[12]

As this passage and others demonstrate, Mill intended to restrict his principle to human beings "in the maturity of their faculties." As such, the principle was not to apply to children, irrational people, barbarians,[13] and those under the influence of temporary irrational passion. This is, however, a very open-ended qualification. Although Mill wrote in an era which proclaimed the basic rationality of most human beings, we do not live in such an era today. Given the pessimistic twentieth century emphasis upon the irrationality of human beings, we are much less apt than Mill to accept his assumption that each individual is the best judge of his own interests. As the success of modern day advertising seems to confirm, it is not necessarily the best products that sell or the truth that always wins out at the end, but rather the best packaged product or that version of the truth which best appeals to the subliminal and often irrational desires of the masses. Given such a pessimistic view of human rationality, a person who accepts Mill's proviso that his principle applies only to rational and mature individuals may go on to assert that this, unfortunately, excludes most of us.

It is interesting to note in this regard that Mill believed that a commitment to the maximization of human happiness would lead in turn to a commitment to a principle allowing broad tolerance of individual freedom. The link between these principles was, for Mill, the assumption that individuals are generally the best judges of their own interests. Without this fundamental assumption, there is no longer any assurance that a commitment to the principle of utility will lead us to embrace the wide guarantees of individual freedom that Mill advocated. Instead, many would argue, a government devoted exclusively to the maximization of the welfare of its citizens would be forced by its citizens' lack of rational foresight to pass many paternalistic laws, which attempt to protect people from themselves. The choice between the principle of

12 Ibid., pp. 13–14.

13 One should note that Mill was writing during the British colonial period when Britain asserted much control over the individual freedoms of the inhabitants of the colonies. Many would today loudly protest Mill's ethnocentricity in assuming that the inhabitants of the colonies were "barbarians" who were incapable of judging their own best interests while the English were not.

utility and principles of individual freedom is one of the foremost political questions of our day. In our country today, it is those who are classified as liberals who emphasize the value of social welfare, while those who are classified as conservatives emphasize the value of individual freedom. For example, it was the liberals in Roosevelt's New Deal days who, accepting Mill's basic commitment to the maximization of human happiness, argued for the necessity of compulsory social security laws, while the conservatives, accepting Mill's commitment to individual freedom, were opposed. While the argument in Mill's *On Liberty* would have been that each individual should be free to make his own arrangements for life, old-age and disability insurance through voluntary savings or insurance plans, the liberals of the Roosevelt era would not accept Mill's belief that allowing people to make their own free decisions on this matter would ultimately work out in their best interests. They realized that those who need social security protection the most would be just those who would find it most difficult to put aside money for some indefinite "rainy day" when it could be so easily put to use immediately. As modern day conservatives are wont to proclaim, a commitment to social welfare in the twentieth century has gone hand in hand with an abridgment of individual freedom.

Certainly, there are few people today who would not be committed to some degree of paternalistic legislation which attempts to protect people from themselves. Clearly, existing laws that make suicide or euthanasia illegal or that refuse to accept consent as an excuse to assault (that is, X cannot be excused for killing Y simply on the grounds that Y asked him to) can only be justified on the paternalistic ground that society has some legitimate right to tell individuals what is for their own good.

Mill's defense of individual freedom has also been challenged on the grounds that the basic distinction between "self-regarding" and "other-regarding" actions that underlies this defense cannot be made clear. As Mill's critics have pointed out, the consequences of human actions can rarely, if ever, be isolated to one person. If, for example, a person through the use of drugs allows his body or mental capacities to deteriorate, he harms not only himself but those who care for him or rely upon him for support. Even if such a person's action does not cause direct harm to others, it may affect others by the corrupting example it provides. Mill is not insensitive to such a criticism. He writes,

> I fully admit that the mischief which a person does to himself may seriously affect, both through their sympathies and their interests, those nearly connected with him, and, in a minor degree, society at large. When, by conduct of this sort, a person is led to violate a distinct and assignable obligation to any other person or persons, the case is taken out of the self-regarding class. . . . If, for example, a man, through intemperance or extravagance, becomes unable to pay his debts, or, having undertaken the

moral responsibility of a family becomes from the same cause incapable of supporting or educating them, he is deservedly reprobated, and might be justly punished; but it is for the breach of duty to his family or creditors, not for the extravagance.[14]

According to Mill, then, in determining what is to count as an exclusively "self-regarding" action, one must first know the scope of a person's obligations to others. Mill does not seem to realize, however, that people can have very different conceptions as to how broad or narrow one's obligations to others ought to be. For example, Mill would have accepted as legitimate one's obligation not to physically hurt other people, but would have rejected as illegitimate one's obligation not to offend others. It is problematic, however, that such a position can be justified on purely utilitarian grounds, since being offended sometimes causes a person more pain than being physically hurt. While Mill, no doubt, would have said that consenting adult homosexual behavior does not "affect the interests" of disapproving heterosexuals, and consequently should not be subject to legal sanction, the fact is that many disapproving heterosexuals do indeed "take an interest" in such behavior—behavior which many of them see as a "moral abomination," contrary to the will of God. For such individuals, the presence in their community of homosexuals may cause greater pain than a physical blow. Furthermore, they will certainly consider the possibly corrupting influence of homosexuals as affecting their own vital interest in their community and especially in the bringing up of their own children. As many of them see it, the "extravagance" of homosexuality is a contagious one that poses a substantial *risk* of harm to others.

Whether or not homosexuals "violate a distinct and assignable obligation to any other person or persons" and consequently, according to Mill, whether their behavior should be seen as other-regarding will depend on the obligations we *choose* to place upon homosexuals. This in turn will depend on the importance of the social interest we see threatened by homosexuals and the degree of the risk we see them posing to this interest. As such, the distinction between self-regarding and other-regarding actions is not at all, as Mill made it appear, a morally neutral one that can be called upon to form the foundation of a simple moral principle that can guide us in deciding when to limit human freedom. On the contrary, this distinction *presupposes a moral position* on the scope of the *legitimate,* legally enforceable interests individuals can take in the actions of others. A "self-regarding action," as Mill uses this term, is simply one that he believes is not *rightfully* subject to legal coercion. Consequently, Mill's claim that self-regarding actions ought not to be subject to legal coercion is a tautology.

[14] Mill, *On Liberty*, pp. 98–99.

The Philosophy of Community:
Devlin's The Enforcement of Morals

Opposed to Mill's libertarianism is the conservative philosophy of the political philosopher Edmund Burke and the sociologist Emil Durkheim, who emphasize the human need to enfold oneself within the structure of values provided by an established community. According to this view, the very liberty and individuality which Mill celebrates tend to lead to individual unhappiness. Freed of the meaning and warmth that shared values can provide, most individuals will find themselves alone, anchorless and adrift in a sea of unstructured desires. Individual reason itself will prove sadly incapable of unifying these desires into a coherent whole and the quest for individuality will tend to lead, not as Mill thought it would, to an invigorating feeling of freedom, but rather to the cold, barren feeling of isolation. When this feeling of isolation from shared values becomes widespread in a society, the society loses its reason for existence as a collective unit and disintegrates from within.

This conservative perspective was given fresh expression in 1958, when Patrick Devlin, an English judge, gave a lecture before the British Academy in criticism of a report (the Wolfenden Report) made public the year before by a committee that was commissioned to study the justification for subjecting homosexuality and prostitution to criminal sanction. Accepting Mill's general libertarian perspective, the committee recommended that homosexuality and prostitution should not, in and of themselves, be illegal. Although not questioning the basic immorality of homosexuality and prostitution, the committee asserted that "there must remain a realm of private morality and immorality which is, in brief and crude terms, not the law's business." According to Devlin, however, there is no way of specifying or defending a clearly defined realm of private morality and immorality that should remain immune from punishment. Devlin's lecture aroused great interest and controversy and led him to write a series of supporting and amplifying essays which were published in 1965 in a book entitled *The Enforcement of Morals*. This book, in turn, generated much comment and criticism in both Great Britain and the United States. Perhaps, as Devlin himself suggested in the preface of his book, the great interest in his ideas was due in large measure to the fact that they were "an expression of orthodox views on a subject in which orthodoxy is more seldom found in print than it is in common behavior" and because his ideas were expressed at a time which found growing numbers of people uncertain as to the sexual values of an older era. There can be no doubt that Devlin expressed in these essays ideas often acted upon by others who either lack the inclination or capacity to articulate them. It is for this reason above all that Devlin's argument deserves careful attention and analysis.

Devlin's Statement of His Position

Devlin begins his inquiry by isolating the question that will be the focus of his concern: "What is the connection between crime and sin and to what extent, if at all, should the criminal law of England concern itself with the enforcement of morals and punish sin or immorality as such?" In defending his conclusion that society can properly "punish immorality as such," Devlin begins by defining a society as a collection of people who share a common morality. He writes,

> [a] society means a community of ideas; without shared ideas on politics, morals, and ethics no society can exist. . . . If men and women try to create a society in which there is no fundamental agreement about good and evil they will fail; if, having based it on common agreement, the agreement goes, the society will disintegrate. For society is not something that is kept together physically; it is held by the invisible bonds of common thought. If the bonds were far too relaxed the members would drift apart. A common morality is part of the bondage. The bondage is part of the price of society; and mankind, which needs society, must pay its price.[15]

As an example of the implication of such a claim, Devlin considers the institution of marriage, writing,

> Whether a man should be allowed to take more than one wife is something about which every society has to make up its mind one way or the other. In England we believe in the Christian idea of marriage and therefore adopt monogamy as a moral principle. Consequently, the Christian institution of marriage has become the basis of family life and so part of the structure of our society. . . . It has got there because it is Christian, but it remains there because it is built into the house in which we live and could not be removed without bringing it down. The great majority of those who live in this country accept it because it is the Christian idea of marriage and for them the only true one. But a non-Christian is bound by it, not because it is part of Christianity but because, rightly or wrongly, it has been adopted by the society in which he lives. It would be useless for him to stage a debate designed to prove that polygamy was theologically more correct and socially preferable; if he wants to live in the house, he must accept it as built in the way in which it is.[16]

The next step in Devlin's argument is his claim that every society has a right to use the law to preserve its underlying morality which is essential for its very existence. He writes,

[15] Patrick Devlin, *The Enforcement of Morals* (London: Oxford University Press, 1965), p. 10. By permission of Oxford University Press.

[16] Ibid., p. 9.

. . . an established morality is as necessary as good government to the welfare of society. Societies disintegrate from within more frequently than they are broken up by external pressures. There is disintegration when no common morality is observed and history shows that the loosening of moral bonds is often the first stage of disintegration, so that society is justified in taking the same steps to preserve its moral code as it does to preserve its government and other essential institutions.[17]

Nevertheless, Devlin is willing to admit that the rights of the individual must be balanced against society's right to "punish immorality as such." No simple principle capable of mechanical application can, however, be given for this balancing. Although "there are no theoretical limits to the power of the state to legislate against immorality," there are, Devlin asserts, three "elastic principles" supporting the rights of the individual against the state. These principles are as follows:

There must be toleration of the maximum individual freedom that is consistent with the integrity of society. . . . Nothing should be punished by law that does not lie beyond the limits of tolerance. . . . As far as possible privacy should be respected.[18]

How are the moral judgments of a society to which individual liberty must at times give way to be ascertained? Devlin writes,

It is surely not enough that they should be reached by the opinion of the majority. . . . English law has evolved and regularly uses a standard which does not depend on the counting of heads. It is that of the reasonable man. He is not to be confused with the rational man. He is not expected to reason about anything and his judgment may be largely a matter of feeling. It is the viewpoint of the man in the street.[19]

A Critique of Devlin's Argument

There is an unresolved tension in Devlin's argument between an extreme view that strong popular feeling alone suffices to justify making behavior criminal and a more moderate one which claims that behavior can be made criminal to prevent injury to society as a whole, as well as to specific individuals.

The Moderate Thesis According to the more moderate position that can be extracted from Devlin's writings, there is no single rule which should be relied upon to tell us when the state has the right to limit the freedom of its citizens. Each case must be considered separately and decided on the basis of the balancing of principles of individual

17 Ibid., p. 13.

18 Ibid., pp. 16–18.

19 Ibid., p. 15.

freedom against principles which attempt to prevent practices that are injurious either to specific individuals or to society as a whole. Although the right of the state to interfere in the actions of its citizens is limited by various principles, it is not limited in accordance with Mill's distinction between self-regarding and other-regarding actions. The law, Devlin asserts, exists not only to protect individuals from injury or annoyance, but also to protect the "community of ideas, political and moral, without which people cannot live together." As a result, Mill was wrong when he claimed that an individual cannot rightfully be compelled by a society "to do or forbear because it will be better for him to do so, because it will make him happier, because, in the opinion of others, to do so would be wise, or even right." Clearly, such a sweeping principle would be rejected by all except a small minority of very libertarian thinkers in our society today. As Devlin points out, our current laws, which make such voluntary actions as suicide, euthanasia, incest, duelling, and the killing of someone at his own request illegal, are attempts to enforce particular moral principles.[20] While many people would advocate reform of the law on some of these matters, practically no one would advocate removing all restraints on all of them.

Devlin is quite right that there is no simple principle we can appeal to in deciding upon the limits of the criminal sanction. As we have seen, Mill's pivotal distinction between other-regarding and self-regarding actions presupposes some view of the scope of a person's *legitimate* legal obligations to others. Furthermore, while Mill was adamant in restricting governmental interference with individual liberty to those actions which harm *specific* identifiable individuals, the very distinction between criminal and tort liability hinges on the distinction between public and private harm. When Devlin says that crimes are offenses "not merely against the person who is injured but against society as a whole," he is expressing the very essence of the distinction between the *punishment* we feel is appropriately applied to criminals and the *compensation* that we believe is due to those who wrongfully suffer private injury. Even if one insists that the concept of social harm must be reducible to specific harm to individuals, questions crowd in upon us as to the meaning of individual harm and the degree of it that justifies the use of the criminal sanction. For example, can the criminal law legitimately protect us from "psychic harm" or the "harm of being offended," as well as from physical harm and harm to property? How likely must the risk of that harm be? (Consider the problem of gun possession.) How direct or immediately connected to one's action must that risk of harm be? (Con-

---

20 It is an evasion to assert, as H.L.A. Hart does in his *Law, Liberty, and Morality* (Stanford, Calif.: Stanford University Press, 1963), that such laws are not, as Devlin suggests, attempts to "enforce morality as such" but are rather examples of paternalistic measures directed to protecting people from themselves. Although attempting to protect people from "harming themselves," such actions may be seen as "harmful" precisely because they are perceived as immoral.

sider the problem of criminal attempts.) When should failing to provide benefits to others count as harm to others? As well as coming to grips with such questions, we must balance the harm we hope to prevent against the degree of infringement on the *rights* of individuals the prevention of such harm will entail. For example, even if it could be shown that pornography leads to sex crimes, some would argue that it is more important to protect the right to freedom of expression than to prevent this harm.

Devlin does not, however, throw any light on how the rights of the individual are to be balanced against a society's right to preserve certain moral standards and consequently he gives us no way to determine whether or not specific laws attempting to enforce moral standards, such as those relating to euthanasia and homosexuality, are justifiable ones. In particular, the three fundamental moral principles he supplies, which aim at protecting the individual from the moral judgment of society, suffer from a degree of elasticity that would appear to rob them of any meaning whatsoever. For example, lacking any definition of what is to count as "the integrity of society," Devlin's claim that "There must be toleration of the maximum individual freedom that is consistent with the integrity of society" tells us nothing. Similarly, lacking any clarification of what "lies (or should lie) beyond the limits of tolerance," Devlin's principle that "Nothing should be punished by law that does not lie beyond the limits of tolerance," gives us no guidance. If all Devlin means to assert here is that people should punish only behavior they are *as a matter of fact* not willing to tolerate, this is trivial and clearly not a principle protective of individual freedom. If, on the other hand, Devlin's assertion is taken to mean that people should punish only that behavior which lies beyond the limits of *legitimate* tolerance, this claim reduces itself to a tautology (that is, we ought to punish only those things that ought to be punished). Devlin's third principle that "As far as possible privacy should be respected" suffers from the same indeterminancy as the others. No one, from the most tolerant to the most repressive of individual freedom, will deny that privacy should be respected *as far as possible*. They will, of course, greatly differ as to how far that is.

The Extreme Thesis Devlin's moderate position is overshadowed in his writings by a more extreme one, according to which, strong popular sentiment against certain behavior is in and of itself sufficient to make that behavior criminal. In this vein, Devlin writes,

> . . . before a society can put a practice beyond the limits of tolerance there must be a deliberate judgment that the practice is injurious to society. There is, for example, a general abhorrence of homosexuality. We should ask ourselves in the first instance whether, looking at it calmly and dispassionately, we regard it as a vice so abominable that its mere presence is an offence. If that is the genuine feeling of the society in which we live, I do not see how society can be denied the right to eradicate it. Our feeling may not be so intense as that. We may feel about it that, if

confined, it is tolerable, but that if it spread it might be gravely injurious; it is in this way that most societies look upon fornication, seeing it as a natural weakness which must be kept within bounds but which cannot be rooted out. It becomes then a question of balance, the danger to society in one scale and the extent of the restriction in the other.[21]

As we see in this passage, Devlin appears to equate behavior that is "injurious to a society" with behavior which elicits strong feelings of disgust in most members of that society. While one would have thought that a determination of whether a given form of behavior is "injurious to a society" would require some inquiry into the actual consequences of that behavior, this does not seem to be true for Devlin when he expresses his more extreme thesis. According to this position, strong general feelings of disgust are alone sufficient to make behavior criminal, without either any inquiry into the consequences of prohibition or a balancing of conflicting principles. The balancing of conflicting principles, it would seem, is supposed to take place only when popular feelings are not too strong.

Morality and Popular Sentiment   Although Devlin is right in emphasizing that moral notions grow out of strong human feelings, he fully neglects the rational component of morality. No coherent concept of what counts as a "moral principle" emerges from Devlin's writings. It will not do, for example, to equate judgments of immorality with strong feelings of revulsion, as Devlin seems to, for there are many things we feel revulsion toward that are not moral matters. By neglecting a consideration of any factors other than the depth of popular disgust, Devlin makes it impossible to evaluate moral positions on rational grounds and consequently dissolves the distinction between rational and irrational moral beliefs.

Devlin does not even seem to be too concerned that popular sentiment might prove to be inconsistent on various issues. For example, he tells us that homosexuality may properly be made illegal if it elicits strong enough feelings of disgust in the average person who accepts Christian sexual morality. What then of other sexual practices, such as adultery, which are equally contrary to Christian sexual morality? Why shouldn't they be equally subject to the strong feelings of members of our society and equally subject to their moral and legal condemnation? Devlin replies that "the fact that adultery, fornication, and lesbianism are untouched by the criminal law does not prove that [male] homosexuality ought not to be touched." Why male and female homosexuality should not elicit the same degree of revulsion Devlin does not attempt to explain, but he suggests that adultery does not elicit the degree of revulsion that homosexuality does simply because it is so much more common. For this reason, he tells us, it is "generally regarded as a human weakness not suitably punished by imprisonment." I don't find such a reason very

21 Devlin, *The Enforcement of Morals,* pp. 17–18.

convincing. Drunk driving is also a very common "human weakness," but such action is still a crime. Certainly, the best reason for not punishing adultery stems from the recognition that making such behavior illegal is unlikely to lead to happy marriages. Similarly, it is unreasonable to believe that making homosexuality illegal is likely to lead to the creation of adjusted and happy heterosexuals or celibates.

Certainly, anyone who has any respect for civil liberties would have to reject, out of hand, a society's contention that it has the right to make behavior illegal merely on the grounds that the average person in that society finds that behavior disgusting. Although Devlin tells us that such judgments of disgust ought to be given weight only when they are made "calmly and dispassionately," it is not at all easy—if not downright conceptually impossible—to imagine a person arriving at a description of a form of conduct as an "abominable vice" after "calm and dispassionate" reflection. According to Devlin, it would appear, the homosexual must subject himself to the vicissitudes of popular feeling, while those who judge him need not subject their feelings to the scrutiny of scientific understanding of the nature and consequences of homosexuality and the efficacy of the prohibition of such conduct. Clearly, popular feelings often need to be subjected to guidance and not always taken for granted. As the utilitarian Jeremy Bentham clearly put it,

> But ought the legislator to be a slave to the fancies of those whom he governs? No, between an imprudent opposition and a servile compliance, there is a middle path, honorable and safe. It is to combat these fancies with the only arms that can conquer them—example and instruction. He must enlighten the people, he must address himself to the public reason; he must give time for error to be unmasked. . . . It is to be observed, however, that too much deference for prejudices is a more common fault than the contrary excess.[22]

One wonders, furthermore, how Devlin can be so sure of the feelings of the "right-minded" or "average" Englishman; he clearly is not basing his observation on surveys. It is certainly possible that a survey might reveal that, while the average person does react with some degree of distaste or discomfort to homosexuality, the knowledge of its voluntary and private practice by others does not disgust him nearly as deeply as Devlin seems inclined to believe. One cannot be faulted for suspecting that Devlin might be projecting his own prejudices upon others rather than inquiring into people's actual beliefs. Again, as Bentham puts it,

> [Popular prejudice] serves oftener as a pretext than as a motive. It is a convenient cover for the weakness of statesmen. The ignorance of the people is the favourite argument of . . . [cowardliness] and indolence,

[22] Jeremy Bentham, *Theory of Legislation* (New York: Harcourt Brace Jovanovich, Inc., 1931), first published in 1802 in French, p. 77.

while the real motives are prejudices from which the legislators themselves have not been able to get free. The name of the people is falsely used to justify their leaders.[23]

Furthermore, one should not neglect the effect that legalization of a particular form of behavior has on leading to greater toleration of it. If, as I have suggested, no justifiable reason can be given for the strong revulsion so many of us feel toward homosexuals, exposure to homosexuals, who would no longer fear to identify themselves as such, may awaken us to the fact that our initial stereotype of them is sadly mistaken and that they are, as a whole, no less moral than the rest of us. By making human feeling the sole yardstick of legality, as Devlin does, our prejudices can be insulated and protected from a possibly disrupting clash with the facts.

A Society's Right to Preserve Itself Devlin's extreme thesis hinges on the following two claims:

1. Every society consists by definition of a group of people who live under a common morality or way of life. (a conceptual or definitional claim)
2. Every society has the right to preserve its existence and to use the criminal law to enforce the common morality which is essential for its existence. (a moral claim)

Let us consider these claims. Devlin's definition of a society as a group of people who share a common morality or way of life is not an arbitrary one, but reflects at least one common usage of this term. For example, it is this definition of a society that we seem to be employing when we say that Czarist Russia was *a different society* from Communist Russia. Nevertheless, this same fact can be expressed as well by saying that *the same* Russian society was at one time Czarist and at another time Communist. The fact is that the concept of a society does not have a single clear meaning. It would appear to me that much of the force of Devlin's argument stems from the manner in which Devlin trades upon this ambiguity in his argument. The plausibility of Devlin's moral claim that a society has "a right to preserve its existence" resides in the fact that such a claim tends to make us think of a society preserving itself from physical violence and internal anarchy. Devlin trades upon this association when he speaks of a society "disintegrating" or of its members "drifting apart."

Nevertheless, it is clear that Devlin means to include much more than the mere minimum core of law and order, which is required for the existence of any society, in his conception of those aspects of morality which are required for "the existence of a given society." Therefore, when Devlin speaks of a society having a right to preserve "its existence," his claim must be taken as asserting that a society has the broad right to

23 Ibid., p. 78.

preserve its "essential way of life" and not merely that it has the narrower right to protect itself from violence and anarchy. The failure to enforce this broader right need not, however, lead inevitably to the need to enforce the narrower right, for a society's "essential way of life" can undergo gradual or abrupt change without accompanying violence or anarchy, and, therefore, without anything that should be called "disintegration" or the "drifting apart" of its members. If "the continued existence of a society" is to be taken to mean living according to some specific shared moral code, then it will follow, by definition alone, that whenever this moral code undergoes change, a society has ceased to exist. It is intolerable, however, to assert, as Devlin seems to, that a society has the right to use the criminal sanction to prevent this change, however peaceable.

In addition, one should realize that some changes in the morality of a given society are much less threatening to the fabric of moral ideas and attitudes that comprise "its style of life" than are others. While Devlin admits that not all deviations from a society's common morality threaten its existence, he seems to have a tendency to assume that, as one critic aptly put it, a person's morality is "a seamless web" and, as such, a change in any part of this fabric is bound to affect other parts. As Devlin himself asserts, "most men take their morality as a whole." As a description of the facts, this might be true. As a prescription, however, of how people ought to take their morality, such a view should be rejected as contrary to the discriminating and refining attitude of mind that is essential for the development of good moral principles. There is no reason to believe, for example, that a person who challenges a society's sexual morality will challenge other parts of that morality as well.

Finally, Devlin is much too facile in his utilization of the notion of "the common morality" of a given society. In the Middle Ages, one could speak of "feudal morality" or "Christian morality" as "the common morality" of large groups of people, but today, especially in the United States and Western Europe, where one finds all sorts of different moralities coexisting, this makes very little sense. A clear consensus of opinion on many deeply felt moral issues will rarely be found in morally pluralistic societies like our own. In such instances, Devlin's notion of the moral feelings of "the average man" becomes a myth. If one accepts the libertarian perspective of Mill's *On Liberty,* such a fact is to be applauded. For, according to this perspective, the tolerance of divergent moral ideas and lifestyles is more conducive in the end to human happiness and development than that attitude of mind which refuses to tolerate any deviation from a single scheme of moral ideas. One will search in vain through Devlin's writings for any argument directed toward a refutation of this point of view.

DISCUSSION QUESTIONS

1. What is your reaction to the claim made by some that sexual fidelity fosters "a possessive attitude that interferes with self-realization"? Is such a claim capable of scientific verification?

2. Consider the following imaginary dialogue:

A: Although I certainly would not be so conservative as to say that adultery is always wrong, I do think that it is wrong more often than not. It seems to me that today's permissive sexual attitude has a stiff price. It tends to vulgarize sex and to detach it from deeper human feelings. "Having an affair" has become the new American pastime. People who previously might have worked harder to make their marriages work find it so easy now to "pick somebody up." Unfortunately, however, the little romp in the motel room rarely solves their problems. Indeed, it often leaves them more alienated than they were before. It wasn't sex they really wanted; it was the warmth and meaning of a caring and sharing human relationship, but such a relationship is very difficult to achieve when it is accompanied by the guilt and dishonesty of most adulterous relationships.

B: I'm sure that what you say is often true. Nevertheless, it seems to me that many affairs are much more than mere "romps in motel rooms." While some people are lucky enough to find a spouse with whom they can share all that is important to them, most people cannot. Consequently, married people often look for someone else with whom they can share dimensions of experience they cannot share with their spouses. Even when this is not the case, an affair can serve as an act of self-discovery. Frustrated married men or women who remain faithful to their spouses because of moral principle tend very often to take their frustration out on their spouses—often blaming them for problems whose source lies within themselves. People often discover this is the course of an affair. Having to face the new set of personality problems of a lover can make one more appreciative of one's spouse and the value of one's marriage. People, it seems to me, often need to experiment before they can discover what they really want. I think this is true about sexual relationships after marriage as well as before.

C: I think that both of you are overintellectualizing this matter. Adultery is often simply an escape from boredom. The very "illicitness" of an adulterous affair tends to make it exciting—a refreshing break from the monotony and staleness of a boring life or a boring marriage. People may speak of the "meaning" or "sharing of experience" that can be obtained from adulterous relationships, but it is primarily good old-fashioned repressed lust that makes adultery an exciting and often rejuvenating experience.

What do you think? What bearing do these different views have on the morality of adultery?

3. Critically consider and evaluate the following claim:

While the rigid sexual morality of my day caused much frustration and guilt, it seems to me that today's permissive sexual morality exacts a much heavier price. With today's permissive attitude, many young couples who live together claim there is no need to bother with the legal technicality of marriage, conveniently refusing to make the *commitment* that marriage entails. Hand-in-hand with our permissive sexual morality, has come a much more selfish attitude toward life. This is reflected in today's widespread preoccupation with such things as "self-realization" and "self-growth" and the proliferation of psychological movements which reflect this concern. Preoccupied with self-fulfillment, couples do not work as hard as they did in my day to make their marriages work. The sad results are increasing divorces and the unhappy children of so many of these divorces. Preoccupied with finding their own private meaning, many people fail to appreciate the meaning that comes from enveloping oneself in a fabric of shared values and responsibilities. In spite of its shortcomings, the rigid sexual morality of my day was part of such a fabric. Our current self-indulgence is reflected in so many of today's books. For example, in a book I just read, a couple traces the course of their marriage—his discovery of desires for men, her shock and anger, their therapy sessions, her discovery of desires for women, etc. Throughout the book, the couple rehashes the selfish blather we hear all the time about the joys of sex and self-realization. Ironically, while one hears more talk today about one's right to personal happiness, one was more likely to find that happiness when our **moral** principles were more rigid and less self-centered.

4. Is society justified in limiting the rights or job opportunities of individuals on the basis of their homosexuality? If so, how and why?

5. Can you think of any actions that would generally be considered highly immoral that are not prohibited by law? Should they be?

6. Which of the following reasons for compelling motorcyclists to wear helmets do you find most satisfactory?

   A: It is in the best interests of the motorcyclists. Motorcyclists should not have the right to make the clearly stupid decision not to use a helmet. I see no problem in sacrificing a person's freedom of choice whenever this is clearly in his self-interest.

   B: Laws requiring motorcyclists to wear helmets should not be seen as infringements of freedom, but as an attempt to prevent people from making capricious choices which do not reflect their own rational desires. When we tell a motorcyclist that he is required by law to wear a helmet, we are only telling him to do what he himself would choose to do if he rationally reflected on the matter.

   C: It is in the best interest of society to compel motorcyclists to wear helmets. If we did not have such a requirement, inevitably some motorcyclists would become seriously hurt and either they or their dependents would become public charges. Motorcycle helmet laws should not be seen as paternalistic laws concerned with purely self-regarding actions but should be seen instead as an attempt to prevent action that is likely to cause harm to others.

7. Which of the following laws do you favor? Why?
   a. laws forbidding gambling
   b. laws forbidding polygamy
   c. laws forbidding prostitution
   d. laws forbidding the use of marijuana

e. laws forbidding obscenity

f. laws forbidding the desecration of the national flag

g. laws forbidding the mistreatment of a corpse, including the use of a corpse for medical experimentation without prior consent

8. Consider the following general principles for restricting an individual's behavior:

   a. to prevent physical harm to others

   b. to protect the property of others and to enforce contracts

   c. to prevent psychic injury or offense to others

   d. to protect social institutions

   e. to benefit others

   f. to prevent that person from making involuntary choices

   g. to prevent harm to that person

   h. to benefit that person

   i. to prevent or punish immorality or sin

   Which of these principles would you accept? How, if at all, would you attempt to limit them? Do you think that some of the principles on this list have the same practical implications?

9. Critically consider and evaluate the following:

   A: Judged on the basis of the purely utilitarian goal of maximizing the general welfare, the Communists have succeeded spectacularly in transforming Chinese society. Nevertheless, a very stiff price in terms of individual liberty has been paid to make these achievements possible. Molded into preset collectivistic roles, the Chinese people lack the individuality and commitment to liberty that is an essential aspect of human dignity. Communism, no doubt, promises the Chinese people greater security, but only at the morally unjustified price of the forfeiture of their freedom and individuality.

   B: Your sentiments are an expression of a bourgeois capitalistic ideology. The "freedom" you so extol turns out, in practice, to be the freedom to be selfish and exploitative. True human fulfillment, and yes, "human dignity," comes not from the lonely pursuit of individual pleasures but rather from the willingness to share and sacrifice for the common good. Western philosophers may speak of "liberty" as "the first virtue of social institutions," but for the ordinary person that virtue is protection or security—a virtue that can best be achieved through a commitment to collectivistic goals that transcend our purely selfish desires.

FURTHER READINGS

ATKINSON, RONALD, *Sexual Morality*. London: Hutchinson and Company, 1965. A good analytic treatment of the topics of "free love," divorce, homosexuality, contraception, and artificial insemination, which is preceded by a general discussion of ethics and of the specific sorts of arguments encountered in the area of sexual morality (such as prudential and utilitarian arguments, arguments relating to justice, to human nature, or to natural law). The analysis is good and the general point of view liberal.

BEAUCHAMP, TOM L., ed., *Ethics and Public Policy*, section 5. Englewood Cliffs, N.J.: Prentice Hall, Inc., 1975. This anthology has a good collection of material on the question of the enforcement of morality. Included are Devlin's key essay on the enforcement of morality, a critque of Devlin's argument by his leading critic, H.L.A. Hart, a critique of both Devlin and Hart by Ernest Nagel and a more general philosophical discussion of different moral principles that can be used to justify the prohibition of behavior, by Joel Feinberg. Also included is a useful bibliography.

BERTOCCI, PETER A., *The Human Venture in Sex, Love, and Marriage*. New York: Association Press, 1949. A defense of traditional Christian sexual morality by a professor of philosophy, addressed primarily to young people contemplating premarital sex. As Bertocci sees it, unmarried young people are apt to lose much more psychologically by indulging their sexual appetites than by restraining them. Sex, he claims, provides its most enduring and enriching satisfaction only when it is a "symbolic expression of other human values," which gives it *human* significance. According to Bertocci, the human significance of sex is inseparable from feelings of love and should be restricted to marriage. He develops the idea of a "love progression," whereby love naturally leads to marriage and to procreation. The same point of view is expressed in Bertocci's 1967 book *Sex, Love, and the Person* (New York: Sheed and Ward). I would, however, recommend the earlier book as the better of the two.

DEVLIN, PATRICK, *The Enforcement of Morals*. London: Oxford University Press, 1965. A collection of Devlin's essays on the general topic of morality and the law. The key essay is "Morals and the Criminal Law," which is a slightly revised version of a lecture Devlin presented in 1959 under the title of "The Enforcement of Morals."

HART, H.L.A., *Law, Liberty, and Morality*. New York: Random House, 1963. A very clear critique of Devlin by a famed legal philosopher.

MAPPES, THOMAS A., and JANE S. ZEMBATY, eds., *Social Ethics: Morality and Social Policy*, section 6. New York: McGraw-Hill, 1977. A good collection of material on the topic of sexual morality. Included are Justice Byron White's concurring opinion in *Griswold v. Connecticut* (arguing for the unconstitutionality of a statute making it illegal for anyone to use "any drug, medicinal article, or instrument for the purpose of preventing contraception"), excerpts from the writings of the contemporary philosophers Richard Taylor and Peter Bertocci as well as from the psychologist Albert Ellis, presenting different views of the connection between "sexual passion" and "love" (Taylor, for example, objects to the common description of human copulation as "making love"). Also included is a critique of the claim that homosexuality is unnatural by Burton Leiser and an excerpt from the writings of the philosopher John Wilson, arguing that the homosexual lifestyle is "too restrictive, and, in essence, too easy."

MILL, JOHN STUART, *On Liberty*. Indianapolis: Bobbs-Merrill, 1959. Mill's classic defense of the liberty of the individual.

WASSERSTROM, RICHARD, ed., *Morality and the Law*. Encino, Calif.: Wadsworth, 1971. An excellent anthology of material on the question of "the enforcement of morals." Included are excerpts from Mill's *On Liberty*, Devlin's

"Morals and the Criminal Law," and discussions of the issues raised by the Devlin essay by the philosophers H.L.A. Hart, Ronald Dworkin, and A.R. Louch, a discussion of the justification of paternalistic laws by the philosopher Gerald Dworkin, a discussion of the American Law Institute's treatment of moral offenses in its 1962 draft of its Model Penal Code by Louis Schwartz, a law professor, and excerpts from the judicial opinions in four cases involving the enforcement of morality.

WASSERSTROM, RICHARD, ed., *Today's Moral Problems,* 2nd ed., section 4. New York: Macmillan, 1979. This anthology contains a good selection of material on sexual morality. Especially worthwhile are Wasserstrom's own article "Is Adultery Immoral?" in which Wasserstrom analyzes arguments that are made in support of the claim that adultery is immoral and uncovers their presuppositions, and Fred Berger's "Pornography, Sex, and Censorship" which analyzes and criticizes contemporary arguments in defense of the censorship of pornography. Included also are philosophically interesting judicial opinions on two cases involving sexual morality. First, there is the 1973 California Supreme Court's majority opinion in *Pettit v. State Board of Education* upholding the California State Board of Education's decision to revoke an elementary school teacher's license to teach on the grounds that her acts of sexual misconduct (oral copulation at a private "Swinger's Club") was evidence of her unfitness to teach. This is followed by the two dissents to this 5–2 judicial decision. Second, there is an excerpt from the majority opinion of U.S. Supreme Court Chief Justice Burger's 1973 opinion in *Paris Adult Theatre v. Slaton* upholding a court action to prohibit the showing of two pornographic movies at an adults only public theater, and an excerpt from Justice Brennen's dissent in this case.

WELLMAN, CARL, *Morals and Ethics,* chapter 5. Glenview, Ill.: Scott, Foresman, 1975. A very clear presentation of the arguments for and against premarital sex. As we saw in this chapter, Wellman himself sees premarital sex as generally undesirable.

WHITELEY, C.H., and W.M. WHITELEY, *Sex and Morals.* London: Bratsford, 1967. An interesting, though, in sections, dated treatment of sexual morality. The book begins with a chapter entitled "Why is There Sexual Morality?" This is followed by three chapters devoted to the patriarchal, puritan, and romantic attitudes toward sex. Chapter 5, "Unfruitful Sex," is the most interesting chapter of the book. In this chapter, the Whiteleys (husband and wife) consider forms of sexual activity that cannot lead to procreation—such as masturbation and homosexuality. A serious drawback of this otherwise good book is the Whiteleys' disconcerting tendency to make factual assertions without providing any support for them. (Some of these assertions are not generally accepted.)

5

Abortion

INTRODUCTION

In no contemporary moral issue can one find the passionate conviction and advocacy surrounding that of abortion. On one hand, many proponents of the women's liberation movement rally round this issue, seeing restrictive abortion laws as one of the many instruments of female subjugation. A woman, they exhort, should have absolute right to control her own body. On the other hand, there are those, often of a deeply religious persuasion, who see abortion as an act of wanton murder of "the most defenseless of human beings." Given such widely divergent perceptions of abortion, antagonists rarely speak directly to their opponents' arguments, rejecting their fundamental assumptions as unworthy of serious discussion. Seekers and holders of political office are besieged to "take a stand" by those passionately committed to this issue. Although interest and rhetoric abounds in this issue, there is very little attempt at principled justification and conceptual clarity. Very rarely do the antagonists come to grips with the fundamental questions that lie at the core of the abortion issue. What, for example, do we mean when we call something a *human being* or a *person?* Is a fetus a *person?* If so, when does it become one? How do we weigh the rights of the unborn against the rights of those already born? Does a fetus, perhaps, have a right not to be born? In what situations is it morally justifiable to kill the innocent? Before we grapple with these issues, let us briefly consider the biological facts and the historical and legal background of the abortion issue.

236

THE BIOLOGICAL FACTS

The union of the human ovum and sperm forms a single-celled zygote, having a full genetic blueprint for further development, half from each parent. The zygote begins a process of cellular divisions doubling the number of cells each time. As it continues to divide and grow, it slowly moves through the fallopian tube to be implanted in the uterine wall. This occurs about seven days after fertilization at about the same time that segmentation takes place—the process by which the various individuals in a multiple birth are separated. At this point the zygote is now called a conceptus. From the end of its second week, when it consists of an inner and outer layer of cells, until the eighth week, it is called an embryo. At about the third week, the various organ systems begin to form, so that by the eighth week, the embryo, which is now called a fetus,[1] begins to look human. It is also at this time that brain waves can be monitored (actually there is primitive brain activity from about the sixth week on). The next important milestone (at least psychologically) in the developing pregnancy is the mother's experience of "quickening"—the feeling of fetal movement. This occurs by about the eighteenth week. When the fetus's organ systems have developed to such an extent that it is capable of surviving outside its mother's womb and grow to maturity (with the assistance of medical technology), the fetus is said to be viable. With current medical technology, viability usually occurs around 24 weeks.

At present, pregnancy cannot be diagnosed for at least ten days after the failure of the onset of menstruation. A suspected pregnancy may, however, be terminated by a "morning after" pill which prevents the implantation of the zygote into the uterine wall. Up to the twelfth week of pregnancy, abortions are usually performed by a suction technique or by the technique of dilitation and curettage (D & C). In the suction procedure the cervix (mouth of the uterus) is dilated (stretched) until a tube can be inserted which is attached to a suction apparatus. The embryo or fetus is sucked out, being crushed or badly torn in the process. In the dilitation and curettage method, a sharp loop-shaped instrument (curette) is inserted into the dilated uterus, and the embryo or fetus is scraped out.

After the twelfth week of the pregnancy (the end of the first trimester), abortions become more complex and more dangerous to the mother.[2] The usual procedure for late abortions consists of the insertion into the mother's womb of a needle which extracts about eight ounces of amniotic fluid, replacing it with a highly concentrated salt solution which

[1] In this chapter, I will employ the standard practice of using the term "fetus" broadly to include reference to a zygote, conceptus, and embryo as well, even though these terms have distinct medical meanings.

[2] The death rate among women undergoing late abortions is 12 per 100,000, compared with fewer than 2 per 100,000 in first-trimester abortions.

usually terminates the life of the fetus. Then 8 to 72 hours later, the mother goes into labor and expels it. Occasionally, however, the fetus survives the salt solution and emerges alive. A major drawback to the use of this method is the chance that the needle may accidentally penetrate one of the mother's blood vessels, permitting the salt solution to enter her blood stream, which can cause convulsions and death. For this reason, many doctors choose to avoid this procedure, injecting a hormone-like substance called prostaglandin that causes strong uterine contractions. Only a small amount of this substance is required, so it does not necessitate the removal of any amniotic fluid. Furthermore, it is harmless, should it find its way into the mother's blood stream. This method does, however, have the consequence, unfortunate to many, of making it much more likely that the fetus will be born alive. Hysterotomy, the least often used method of late-term abortions, poses the greatest danger to the mother and is the most likely to result in a live fetus. The surgeon makes an incision similar to that for a caesarian delivery, only smaller, and extracts the fetus. Where sterilization is desired, the physician performs a hysterectomy, removing the uterus itself with the "unborn" fetus inside.

Clearly, if an abortion is to be performed, it should be done as early as possible. Nevertheless, there are some women who do not realize their condition until well along in their pregnancy. Others simply find themselves unable to come to an early decision. At times, the situation changes as the pregnancy develops (such as when the father abandons the pregnant mother or loses his job). Late abortions are also the result of the discovery that the fetus is mongoloid or suffering from some other grave defect. At present, this knowledge can only be obtained by a procedure done after the fourteenth week, called amniocentesis, in which amniotic fluid is removed and tested; approximately three weeks is required to complete the laboratory analysis.

HISTORICAL AND LEGAL BACKGROUND

There have been many societies in which abortion, and even infanticide, were considered quite morally proper. This was true, for example, in ancient Greece and Rome where deformed babies or unwanted female babies were often left to die. The early Judaic and Christian view of abortion was greatly influenced by the metaphysics of the ancient Greek philosopher Aristotle (384–322 B.C.). As Aristotle saw it, the characteristic that made a physical body human was the human soul, but he did not conceive the soul, as we do now, as a sort of immaterial "thing" or "substance" that occupies a body. Instead, Aristotle saw the soul as the *function* of the body. A body possessed a human soul, he believed, when it was capable of performing the functions that were unique to human beings. As he saw it, this was possible only when a body possessed a human shape and human organs. Accepting this view, and assuming that human fetuses did not possess a human shape or human organs until well along in the pregnancy, early Judaic-Christian thinkers believed that while immature human fetuses are alive, they are alive in ways no different from the ways in which plants and other animals are alive. In Aristotelian language, an immature human fetus possessed a vegetative or animal soul, but not a human soul. This was, for example, the view held by the Christian Medieval philosopher Thomas Aquinas (1225–1274). The Catholic Church officially adopted this position in 1322 and as a result forbade the faithful from baptizing any premature births which did not have a definite human shape.

Under the influence of erroneous scientific reports, the Church in the early seventeenth century accepted the view that a human fetus has a human body from the very moment of conception (the "preformation theory"). According to this view, the development of the fetus simply consists of a continuous increase in size of organs and bodily structures which were assumed to be fully present in microscopic form from the moment of conception. With the acceptance of both the preformation theory and the Aristotelian view of the soul, it could be assumed that the human soul was present in a human fetus from the moment of conception. The preformation theory, however, was eventually rejected, as was the Aristotelian view of the soul, which gave way as the "Cartesian dualism" of Descartes (1596–1650) gained influence. According to the Cartesian picture, soul and body are two radically different sorts of "substances," capable of existing independently. A human being, as Descartes saw it, was a combination of these two radically different and interacting substances. The soul, as he saw it, was an immortal, conscious substance that occupied or animated a body for a period of time. When this animation or ensoulment took place was an open question. Originally, it was assumed to take place on the fortieth day for males and on the eightieth day for females. Consequently, it was only after this period that abortions became a mortal sin, justifying the eternal torment of hell. An eternity of the deprived existence of limbo awaited the unbaptised fetus, tainted now forever with original sin. In 1869, Pope Pius IX decreed that all fetuses should be considered to be ensouled from conception.

There is no single moral attitude toward abortion that can be described as the "Jewish position." According to the most prevalent tradition, a fetus does not become a full person with full moral rights until it is born. Some rabbis who accept this view have advocated abortion on demand, while others have claimed that although abortion is not technically murder, it is still "akin to homicide" and "allowable only in grave cases." There is no consensus, however, among those who take this view as to what is to count as a "grave case." While some use this term narrowly, others use it quite broadly. There are some rabbis who are opposed to liberal abortion laws, not on the grounds that it is "akin to homicide," but on the grounds that such laws would have such undesirable social consequences as encouraging promiscuity, adultery, and childless marriages. In spite of the very different attitudes toward abortion in Jewish morality, there is a strong consensus that the welfare of a pregnant woman is more important than that of the fetus she is carrying. From this perspective, some rabbis have advocated the abortion of defective fetuses on the grounds of the anguish their births would cause their mothers rather than out of concern for the fetus.

In the United States, prior to the landmark Supreme Court decision in *Roe v. Wade* (1973), the various states were unlimited by constitutional restraints in the formulation of their own abortion laws. Consequently, some states had much more restrictive abortion laws than others. Arguments have been made, however, both by those in favor of and those opposed to abortion, that states should be limited in their right to formulate abortion laws by certain provisions of the Constitution. It has been claimed, for example, that a fetus should be considered a person, whose right to life is protected under the Fourteenth Amendment. On the other side, the argument has been presented that a fetus should not be considered a person under the Constitution, and that a pregnant woman has a "right to privacy" derived from the Bill of Rights which renders unconstitutional all state laws prohibiting abortions.

In *Roe v. Wade,* the United States Supreme Court came to grips with the constitutionality of abortion. According to this 7 to 2 decision, fetuses are not "full legal persons" and women do indeed have a right to privacy which gives them the right to abortion on demand during the first trimester. During the second and third trimesters when abortions become more risky, the Court declared, the states have a "legitimate interest in preserving and protecting the health of the woman," and, consequently, the right to regulate abortions, requiring, for example, that they be performed in fully equipped hospitals rather than in a doctor's office. Only in the last trimester did the Court recognize that an "important and legitimate interest in potential life" might outweigh the mother's rights and wishes. Giving no constitutional guidelines as to how these rights should be weighed, except to say that the state cannot forbid abortion in the third trimester when it is "necessary to preserve the life or health of the mother," the Supreme Court left the matter to the individual states.

The majority decision in *Roe v. Wade* is inherently unstable since its pivotal distinctions are made a function of an ever-advancing medical technology. As abortion methods become more advanced, the risk to the health of the mother might be eliminated and, consequently, the state's interest in the health of the mother and the relevance of the second trimester could drop out of consideration entirely. Similarly, the moment of viability could conceivably be brought back to conception. Yet, according to the majority decision, it is viability which presently occurs at approximately the beginning of the third trimester that marks the point where the state's interest in "potential life" can justify restricting abortion in the interests of the developing fetus. Thus, the Supreme Court decision would seem to allow the point where a fetus is given the right to life to be constantly moved back toward conception as techniques of artificial incubation become more sophisticated.

This Supreme Court decision has stirred great controversy. Various antiabortion ("right-to-life") groups are campaigning for a constitutional amendment that would ban abortions and nullify the Supreme Court decision. In addition to a woman's right to privacy, some proponents of abortion have argued that a fetus should have a legal "right not to be born" into a life which has no reasonable prospect of being a life worth living. There have been several civil suits which have been based on this alleged right, but until now they have all been rejected by the courts.

In early 1975, Dr. Kenneth C. Edelin of Boston City Hospital was convicted of manslaughter in the death of a 20- to 28-week-old aborted fetus (through the hysterotomy method). In this highly controversial case, Edelin was convicted for not making a sufficient attempt to save the life of the fetus he had the legal right to abort. This case raises the troublesome question of whether a pregnant woman has a right only to "detach herself from a dependent fetus" or has the right as well to procure its death in those situations where an ever-advancing medical science has the means to keep it alive outside her womb. The most poignant case in this regard is one of rape. One can certainly understand a woman's desire to secure the death of a fetus conceived in such circumstances. Similarly, if the fetus is gravely deformed and an abortion is desired, the desire will almost always be that the fetus die.

THE CENTRAL PHILOSOPHICAL ISSUE: IS A FETUS A PERSON?

Clearly, the most poignant of philosophical questions in the abortion issue concerns the humanity of the fetus. On one hand, we find those agreeing with the psychiatrist Thomas Szasz when he says that during the first trimester an abortion is nothing more than "the removal of a piece of tissue from the woman's body." On the other hand, one finds those who accept the Roman Catholic position that "every unborn child must be regarded as a human person with all the rights of a human person from the moment of conception." Others straddling the line between these opposing positions describe the fetus as a "potential person," possessing from conception some rights, but not the rights of a "full person." Others say that a fetus becomes a person somewhere along its gradual and continuous development within its mother's womb. Still others suggest that a newborn baby, like an unborn fetus, should not be considered a person and, consequently, should not be afforded a right to life.

Without a resolution of the fundamental question of whether the fetus should be considered a "human being" or a "person," possessing the same rights as living human beings or persons, many of the arguments used by proponents of abortion sadly miss the mark. For example, it is often argued that the state has no more right to interfere with a woman's freedom to choose whether or not to complete a pregnancy than it does

to interfere with her religious freedom. If a person is religiously or con-
scientiously opposed to abortion, she has the right not to obtain one, but
she should not have the right to impose her beliefs on those who disagree. To those who see the fetus as a person, however, the question of
abortion is not at all a question of one's freedom to choose one's own
private beliefs and practices, but one of minority rights—the right of a
defenseless innocent human being to life itself. Certainly, none of us who
deplore the immorality of racism would afford the racist the freedom to
victimize those whom he sees as inferior. To those who see the fetus as
a person, the situations are morally identical.

Similarly, if the fetus is a person, arguments which relate to the
undesirable consequences of an unwanted pregnancy seem callously out
of place. Most of those who support very liberal abortion laws would be
aghast at the proposal that the aged, deformed, retarded, and senile be
put to death when the cost of caring for them becomes burdensome.
Again, for those who see the fetus as a person, the situations are morally
identical. As one "pro-lifer" put it, "You must eliminate the problems
people have, not the people themselves." Similarly, "pro-lifers" must
reject as morally irrelevant the undeniable fact that, should abortion be
made illegal, many women would turn to illegal abortions and risk their
own deaths. This is an undesirable consequence, they will admit, but
certainly one does not justify the murder of innocent people this way!
Indeed, many "pro-lifers" would want abortion made illegal, even if
every woman who desired an abortion would obtain an illegal one, if
necessary, for they would argue that the state should not sanction the
immorality of murder. In fact, however, making abortion illegal would
certainly cut down on the number of abortions performed and on the
number of human deaths.

How does one decide whether a fetus is a human being or a person? Indeed, should the terms human being and person be used interchangeably, as many use them, or should we attach different meanings
to them, as some have suggested? In resolving these questions, it is essential that one realize that these terms do not have a single agreed upon
factual meaning; two people may totally agree on the biological characteristics of a developing organism and disagree on whether it ought to be
called a human being or a person, since they take different positions on
the *moral* relevance of these characteristics. The decision to call a fetus a
person, for example, clearly has moral implications. One will not use this
term to describe an organism unless one is willing to ascribe rights to it
—in particular, the right to life. One cannot, for example, dispose of
"persons" without at least weighty reasons. Consequently, the question
of whether a given biological organism is a person (or human being)[3] is

---

3 While many commentators on the abortion issue use the concepts of a "person" and that of a "human being" interchangeably, it is more useful and consistent with common usage to utilize the notion of a "person" as a moral concept and that of a "human being" as a purely biological one. In this usage,
to be a "person" is to be the sort of creature who is considered an appropriate

best conceived as equivalent to the moral question, "Is this biological organism sufficiently similar to a 'normal' adult human being to be afforded similar moral and legal rights?" Let us turn to various answers that have been given to this question and discuss the adequacy of their supporting arguments.

A Person at Conception

It is often argued that a fetus is a person from the very moment of conception. Given the continuity of gradual development, it is claimed, any other dividing line is clearly arbitrary. The moment of conception, however, marks a radically discontinuous step from what existed before. Of those who mark the humanity of a fetus at the very moment of conception, some base their reasons on the fetus' alleged possession of an immortal soul and others on its genetic completeness and capacity to develop into an adult human being. Let us briefly consider these positions in turn.

A Fetus Has a Soul

According to the Roman Catholic position, a fetus becomes a person when it is infused with an immortal soul. Although it is generally conceded now that this moment cannot definitely be known, one must assume that it is the moment of conception itself. Opponents of this position will point to its unverifiable nature, many claiming that the very notion of a "soul" is without meaning. The antagonists, of course, have reached a metaphysical impasse. Yet, even if we grant, for the sake of argument, that a "soul" is "infused" into the zygote at conception, what are the theological consequences of an abortion? Some Catholics have argued that if a fetus is aborted, its immortal soul, now forever incapable of receiving the salvation only baptism can provide, will be resigned to an eternity in "limbo," never to experience the joys of heaven. The quick and, to my mind, decisive objection to this view is that it seems incomprehensible that the infinitely powerful and good traditional Judaic-Christian God would allow such a thing to happen. One must realize that if baptism is required for salvation, many human souls would be deprived of salvation through no fault of their own; this would include all those children whose parents do not believe in baptism, as well as all those countless fetuses that die as a result of natural or induced abortions or whose mothers die before delivery. Certainly God should

---

bearer of rights and responsibilities, and, as such, can be considered a member of a moral community. To be a "human being," on the other hand, is to be a member of the biological species *homo sapiens*. If we accept this usage, useful distinctions become possible. We may now speak of "nonhuman persons" (such as an advanced extraterrestrial life form) and of "human nonpersons" (a human being born without a cerebrum or one in a coma).

not penalize someone for something that he or she could in no way have avoided. If the "ensouled" fetus was put in this world to face a moral test with the possibility of a heavenly reward, does it not seem reasonable that God should give that individual another chance and "recycle it into some other body?"

The Right to Life Based on Genetic Potentiality

In defense of a fetus' right to life from the moment of conception, many have pointed to the fact that it is at this moment that a complete genetic blueprint is formed that determines the future development of a specific organism. It is this point and this point alone, it is claimed, that can be marked as "the beginning" of an organism's life. Supporters of this view take the position that it is not a fetus' *current* characteristics that justify its right to life, but its genetic *potentiality* to become a person. But what is the moral significance of this potentiality? Can it not equally as well be said that an unfertilized egg or sperm has the potentiality of developing into a human being? Certainly, they cannot develop into a human being alone, but neither can the fertilized egg.[4] Granted, too, that the natural probabilities of an egg and sperm becoming part of the causal chain leading to the birth of a human being are vastly smaller than that of the fertilized egg, why should it be considered entitled to the rights of a human being until it actualizes its potentialities? An acorn, for example, has the potentiality of becoming an oak tree, but it certainly is not an oak tree. If one considers it wrong to abort a fetus simply because of its potentiality, then ought not one be opposed to all methods of contraception which prevent unfertilized eggs and sperms from developing the potentialities they would otherwise possess? If potential life has a right to be actualized, where are we to draw the line? Clearly, we do not want to say that fertile celibates are acting immorally by not attempting conception.

---

[4] Clearly, however, most of us believe that while it is reasonable to call a fertilized egg a "potential person," it is not at all reasonable to use this term to describe an unfertilized egg or sperm. Why is this so? I think there are two main reasons for this attitude. First, the union of a sperm and an egg is quite naturally seen as the beginning of a causal sequence which contains all the important causal ingredients—that is, the genes—for the development of a human being. On the other hand, an unfertilized egg or a sperm contains only part of these essential causal ingredients, and as such neither can reasonably be picked out as "the beginning" of a causal series that can lead to the formation of a human being. Second, as a matter of brute biological fact, a much greater percentage of fertilized eggs become persons in the natural course of events than do unfertilized eggs or sperms. It is interesting to note in this regard that if female reproduction were such that, instead of eliminating ova that are not fertilized in a short period of time and releasing new ones every month, a woman would retain the same unfertilized egg until it became fertilized before forming (and not simply releasing) a new one, we would be much more apt to call an unfertilized egg a "potential person" than we are now.

Implications of the View that a Fetus
Is a Person at Conception

The view that a fetus has the right to life at the very moment of conception has implications which should be considered. On this view, those who use the "morning-after" pill, which causes expulsion of any zygote that might have been conceived, are potentially intentional "killers," while those who use the various intrauterine devices which also work to expel any fertilized ova that might have resulted from contraceptive failure are responsible for the creation of a homicidal risk. In addition, a woman who negligently causes herself to miscarry should, perhaps, be held legally responsible for "negligent homicide." Consider, too, the possibility that sperms and eggs may be artificially joined in some extra-uterine environment with (let us say) about a ten percent chance to survive for the full nine-month gestation period. (The possibility of extra-uterine human conceptions surviving to be born alive became an actuality in July 1978 with the birth of Louise Brown in Great Britain.) If this were the case, should such extra-uterine fertilizations be legally prohibited as "wanton reckless homicide"? If you say no, must you not reject conception as the point at which a fetus obtains the right to life? Indeed, if extra-uterine fertilization (with ten percent chance of survival) became very common, would we not naturally begin to place less importance on the moment of fertilization and more importance on what happens afterwards?

Mental Activity and Physical Appearance

Certainly, the presence of consciousness is essential to "personhood." Indeed, as Descartes, we tend to associate ourselves with our states of consciousness (that is, our thoughts, memories, feelings, and emotions) and not with our physical bodies. If our mental life were to come to an end, so would we. Since this is so, should we not claim that a fetus has no moral significance or is not a person until it becomes conscious? Many philosophers have thought so. The existence of a primitive level of fetal brain activity probably begins about the sixth week of the pregnancy. The point at which brain activity gives rise to consciousness is, however, open to question. Nevertheless, it has been suggested by some physiologists that it is improbable that a fetus has the capacity to experience sensations, such as pain, until about the twenty-fourth to the twenty-eighth week, when its nerve endings develop their fatty myelin sheaths which seem to play some role in the transmission of nerve impulses. Assuming, then, for the sake of argument, that a fetus becomes conscious at around the beginning of the third trimester, should we, for this reason, single out this period as the point at which a fetus becomes a person?

There are difficulties with this view. One must realize that the level

245

of mental activity that exists at this point of human fetal development is quite primitive. Certainly, it is no different from the mental activity of the fetuses of other mammals, such as dogs or chimpanzees. Indeed, one may assume that this is true throughout the pregnancy. If we are then to afford a right to life to a human fetus by virtue of the existence of primitive brain activity, ought we not give an equal right to life to the fetuses of other mammals; and, conversely, if we are not to give these other fetuses such a right, how can we justify giving it to a human fetus? Clearly, what leads many to attribute the right to life to a human fetus, but not to a dog or chimpanzee fetus resides not in the level of its mental activity, but in its external physical resemblance to a human being. As the pictures of fetuses "pro-lifers" are wont to show amply demonstrate, the thought of aborting a creature that looks like a little baby, is quite disturbing to many of us, as is the thought of "cutting it to pieces" or "tearing it apart" in an abortion procedure. I must admit that this has an emotional impact on me, but is it really morally relevant? Is it not reasonable to claim that it should be mental activity, and not physical appearance, that confers personhood upon an organism? A creature from some other planet and a greatly deformed human being may have very little external resemblance to a human being, but would they not be considered persons if they had the mental capacities of persons? Conversely, is it not proper to consider a seriously brain-damaged individual who looks like a human being, but is unconscious or conscious on a very primitive level, as a "mere vegetable," and not a person?

If the mere existence of a primitive level of consciousness or the external physical resemblance to a human being does not confer "personhood" on a fetus, where are we to draw the line? What mental capacities must a fetus possess before it becomes a person? A developing fetus can have pleasant and painful experiences, but it cannot reason, have human emotions, or enter into the human socialization process. Are we then to say that a fetus is never a person, and perhaps go so far as to say that this is also true of a newborn baby, implying that neither has a right to life? This is indeed the position of Michael Tooley in his widely reprinted article "Abortion and Infanticide." According to Tooley, a creature should not be considered a person unless it "is capable of desiring to continue existing as a subject of experiences" and furthermore "possesses the concept of a self as a continuing subject of experiences and other mental states, and believes that it is itself such a continuing entity." Unfortunately, Tooley does not seem to recognize the vagueness of this notion and does not attempt to clarify it. Although I do not profess to know all that might be packed into Tooley's notion, it would seem that before a creature can be said to be a person in Tooley's sense, it must possess some concept of personal identity, have some ability to envision and desire things in the future, and must have some notion of what it is to die. If this is so, its consequence, morally shocking to most of us, would be that human beings probably do not become persons until somewhere between the ages of 2 and 5. Although Tooley makes no attempt to tell us where the line should be drawn, he is quite willing to grant that newborn babies are not persons and consequently do not have a right to life.[5]

Although Tooley is correct, I believe, in claiming that the standard for personhood should involve some minimal consciousness and mental capacity, it seems implausible to me to single out the complex sense of personal identity as the sole standard. Perhaps a good way to focus upon the characteristics essential for personhood is to imagine ourselves faced with some complex extraterrestrial life form or man-made robots of the future. What would such creatures have to be like to be called persons? Certainly, it would be essential that they were considered to be conscious beings, capable of having feelings and emotion. This is not, however, sufficient. In classifying something as a person, we would be concerned with such mental qualities as its problem-solving abilities, its capacity for reasoned self-directive activity, its capacity for introspective self-awareness and self-identity through time, and its capacity to communicate and relate to others. Although no definite answer can be given as to the relative weights that should be placed on these mental capacities in judging the personhood of a creature, as the number and degree of these capacities increase, our natural inclination to classify a creature as a person will increase. From this perspective, personhood is based not on a single characteristic but on a cluster of imprecisely defined ones which admit of distinctions as to degree, making it possible to speak of *the degree* of a creature's personhood. In addition, our *actual* tendency to classify creatures as fellow persons will also involve the degree of fellow-feeling we have for these creatures. After all the facts are in, we will have to decide whether we *choose* to afford these creatures rights which reflect our concern and respect.

Viability and Birth

Many have suggested that viability or birth should be considered the point at which a fetus becomes a person and consequently is entitled to the right to life. Those who take this perspective point to the fetus' independence or capacity to be independent of its mother, claiming that while a fetus is dependent upon its mother for its very existence, it is not really a separate and independent person. It becomes so, they claim,

---

[5] As an interesting corollary of his view, Tooley is willing to admit that adult animals may be "persons" in his sense of the term and consequently entitled to a right to life. If this is true, Tooley suggests, "one may find himself driven to conclude that our everyday treatment of animals is morally indefensible, and that we are in fact murdering innocent persons." In addition, Tooley suggests that although a fetus or newborn does not have a right to life, it may have, by virtue of its capacity to feel pain, "a right not to be tortured." Tooley does not, however, develop this idea or consider its moral implications when a method of abortion will cause a fetus pain.

either when it no longer is dependent or need be dependent upon its mother. This position is clearly inadequate. Granted that a fetus is dependent upon its mother in a unique and special way and would die if it were severed from that relationship prior to viability, this does not mean that the fetus is not a separate organism from its mother. Indeed, if one points to the dependence of a fetus on its mother, it is certainly the case that a newborn baby is dependent upon adults for its very life until well after its birth. As a fetus is born, the nature of the environment it depends upon undergoes a radical change. Instead of being dependent upon only one, its needs can now be satisfied by many, but it is still at the mercy of others just as much as it was before. Certainly, the mere fact that a child is dependent upon its parents in no way negates its right to life. If it seems morally monstrous to even suggest such a thing, is it any less morally monstrous to claim that the mere fact that a fetus is dependent upon its mother robs it of its personhood and right to life? Similarly, can one seriously suggest that the mere *capacity* for independence from its mother's womb confers personhood on an organism that otherwise would not possess this characteristic? Assuming, for example, that medical science will one day be able to keep a three-month-old fetus alive in an artificial incubator, could one seriously suggest that while it has no right to life now—and can be aborted for any reason—it would then have such a right? Similarly, can one seriously suggest that if two fetuses having the same level of consciousness differ only in the respect that one is already viable while the other is not, that the first, but not the second, has the right to life?

As a rational principle, the mere independence or capacity for independence of a fetus from its mother must be rejected as morally irrelevant to its personhood or right to life; as a psychological factor, on the other hand, one cannot doubt that the mere fact that a fetus is *hidden* within its mother's womb makes it psychologically easier for us not to see it as a person that has rights. Similarly, a woman may not perceive a fetus to be a person until she feels its movement, but certainly no one would suggest that a fetus that suffered from some type of motor paralysis, making it incapable of movement, would be less of a person than an otherwise identical fetus that could move.

THE RIGHTS OF A FETUS
VERSUS
THE RIGHTS OF ITS MOTHER

A Woman's Right to Refuse the Use
of Her Body to a Dependent Fetus

Although one may be unjustified in using viability or the moment of birth as the moment at which a fetus becomes a person, one may plausibly argue that, while dependent upon the use of its mother's body, a fetus does not have a right to the use of that body in certain circumstances and its mother has no obligation to afford it that use. This is the position of Judith Thomson in her widely reprinted article "A Defense of Abortion." Granting for the sake of argument that a fetus is a person,[6] Thomson claims that in cases where the mother's life is at stake or where the mother has been raped, or has simply engaged voluntarily in sexual intercourse but has taken reasonable precautions to avoid pregnancy, she has no obligation to accept the inconvenience of a pregnancy.[7] To make it a woman's obligation to accept these inconveniences when she has in no way voluntarily consented to her pregnant condition is, according to Thomson, to force her to be "a Good Samaritan" which the law does not force other people to become.

Granting that a fetus is a person entitled to the *full* rights of live persons, Thomson attempts to convince us that a mother's right to decide what shall happen to her own body may override the fetus's right to life through the use of an example which she claims is morally analogous. She tells you to imagine yourself waking up one morning in bed with a famous unconscious violinist whose circulatory system has been plugged into yours, so that your kidneys can be used to extract poisons from his blood stream. Having discovered that only you have the right blood type to save the ailing violinist from otherwise certain death, the Society of Music Lovers has kidnapped you and plugged you up to the violinist without your consent. You are told that the violinist will require the use of your body for nine months, after which time he will have recovered from his ailment and can be safely unplugged from you. It is quite clear to Thomson that the violinist has absolutely no right to the use of your body. Indeed, according to Thomson, even if the violinist needed the use of your body not for nine months, but only for an hour, you would have no moral *obligation* to afford him the use of your body and would not be acting *unjustly* if you refuse that use. Nevertheless, Thomson admits, if the violinist needed your body only for such a short period of time, you would be "callous" and "indecent" to refuse.

Thomson's description and moral appraisal of the violinist case is clearly Kantian in nature. The refusal to afford the use of one's body in this situation is not unjust since it is not a violation of one's (perfect) duty, but rather a refusal to provide benevolent assistance to someone to whom one has no special obligation. Reflecting the Kantian view that laws should function to assure justice and not to provide for benevolence, existing laws do not, Thomson points out, attempt to force one into

---

[6] Thomson confesses to the difficulty of determining when a fetus should be considered a person and offers no suggestion as to where that line should be drawn. She does, however, express her view that a fetus is not a person at conception and is one "well before birth."

[7] In these cases, it is Thomson's position that the mother only has the right to refuse the use of her body; she does not have the right to secure the death of the unborn fetus, if it is possible to detach it alive. This is true, she claims, even in cases of rape.

becoming "Good Samaritans" or indeed even into "minimally decent Samaritans" (when the sacrifice is small).

Counting on you to accept her moral judgment of the violinist case, Thomson believes that cases of unintentional pregnancy due to rape or even resulting from the nonnegligent failure of contraceptive methods are analogous, in every morally relevant respect, to the violinist case. Consequently, she claims, just as you would have no special obligation to keep the violinist alive by affording him the use of your body, a pregnant woman in situations of unintentional and nonnegligent pregnancy has no obligation to afford a fetus the use of her body.

Thomson's argument, I believe, is conclusive in the case of a pregnancy due to rape. But even here, one could suggest that a woman who allows a fetus resulting from rape to develop within her womb for a certain period of time has tacitly assumed an obligation toward it. Leaving aside the case of rape, however, greater difficulties arise when one turns one's attention toward unintentional pregnancies that result from voluntary indulgence in sexual intercourse. Thomson's position here seems to be that a pregnant woman has no responsibilities toward the fetus as long as she took "reasonable" precautions to avoid pregnancy. Many, however, would disagree. Unlike the violinist case and the analogous case of a pregnancy due to rape, the "victim" has some degree of responsibility for her condition. Even if one is willing to grant along with Thomson that a pregnant woman has a responsibility to a fetus only if she has failed to take "reasonable" precautions to prevent pregnancy, reasonable people can disagree as to the standard that should be used to make this determination. Since pregnancies due to rape are comparatively rare, Thomson's inadequate treatment of other types of unintended pregnancies makes her defense of abortion quite tenuous. Adequate arguments for a broadly liberal abortion policy must, I believe, center on a denial that a fetus is a full person and as such is not entitled to the full legal and moral rights afforded to living human beings, but this is precisely the question Thomson attempts to sidestep.

Direct Abortions Are Never Morally Justified: The Principle of "Double Effect"

Diametrically opposed to Judith Thomson's position that a woman's right to her body can in many circumstances outweigh a fetus' right to life is the controversial Roman Catholic position which considers all direct abortions immoral; a "direct" abortion is defined as one in which the death of a fetus is either intended as an end in itself or as a means to some other end, for example, to safeguard the health of the mother. On the other hand, an "indirect" abortion would occur if the death of a fetus is neither one's purpose nor a means to one's purpose, but is the foreknown and permitted result of some other action. The Catholic position is that although direct abortions are never justifiable, even to save the mother's life and indeed even if the fetus would die as well if the abortion were not performed, indirect abortions are morally permissible in certain circumstances. As an example of the application of this doctrine, it would be considered morally wrong for a doctor to perform a craniotomy in which the skull of a fetus in the process of being born is crushed in order to save the life of its mother—a direct abortion. If, on the other hand, a physician removes the cancerous uterus of a 3-month-pregnant woman, this would be considered an example of an indirect, and consequently permissible, abortion. Although it is known that the fetus will die as a result of the hysterectomy, this action is not directly intended; what is intended is the removal of the uterus.

The general Catholic idea that the morality of actions should be determined on the basis of the direct, and not indirect, intentions of one's actions is called the "principle of double effect," since an action can have both a directly and indirectly intended result. This general principle is in turn a corollary of the even more general Catholic doctrine that "evil is not to be [intentionally] done that good may come of it." According to the principle of double effect, it is morally permissible to perform an action, foreseeing that an evil will result as long as

1. The action is not performed in order to obtain the evil (that is, the evil is not the direct intention of the act), but in order to obtain some good result.
2. The evil is not part of the means of producing the good effect.
3. The good to be produced must be proportionate to the evil that will be produced (that is, the evil produced cannot exceed the good to be produced).

To many non-Catholics, the principle of the double effect has seemed to be complete sophistry. Some critics have claimed that this principle is devoid of clear meaning. In the context of the issue at hand, the contention is that a given act of abortion can be described in more than one way and can consequently be seen under one description as a "direct" abortion, while under another description as an "indirect" abortion. For example, although Catholic moralists have claimed that a craniotomy performed to save the life of a woman in labor is a "direct" killing where the death of a fetus is a means to the desired end of saving the mother's life, it has been suggested that the fetus' death need not be seen as a means, but as a foreseen, and in itself unwanted, consequence. What is wanted as a means, it may be said, is the removal of an obstruction, not the death of a person. Of course, the Catholic moralist would rightfully reject this description as pure sophistry. As he will see it, since the removal of an obstruction in this case *is* the crushing of a human skull, it is absurd to claim that what is directly desired as a means is the crushing of a skull, not the death of a person. While in the case of the removal of a cancerous uterus, it is at least *possible* that the three-month-old fetus could survive this procedure and be kept alive in an incubator, it is *impossible* for a fetus to survive a craniotomy. This is not, however, as clear as it may appear on the surface. While it is certainly much more within the realm of the *possibilities of medical technology* to save an early fetus that is removed along with its mother's cancerous uterus, it is at least *logically possible* and *consistent with the laws of nature* to imagine a fetus surviving the crushing of its skull and its later reconstruction through greatly advanced medical technology.

Even if we assume, however, that the principle of the double effect does have a clear meaning, many have claimed that it lacks any moral significance. As they see it, there is no morally relevant difference in the foreseen death of a fetus through a craniotomy or through the removal of a cancerous uterus, as Catholic moralists claim. Individuals who accept this point of view would consider it beyond the pale of moral justification to refrain from performing a direct abortion to save a mother's life if both mother and fetus would die if nothing were done. Yet, the typical Catholic response in this situation would be that it is better for both innocent persons to die as a result of "an act of God" than for some human being to directly intend the death of one, even if, by so doing, he can save the other.[8] (Consider the case of "the overcrowded lifeboat" in our list of moral dilemmas.) This may appear especially morally unjustified in the early weeks of a pregnancy when Catholics concede that one cannot be sure that a fetus is a person ("ensouled"). How, one may ask, can we justify allowing a woman to die, who can be saved, on the mere *chance* that by saving her we will be killing a person who will die in a short time anyway?

SOME REFLECTIONS

It is, unfortunately, much easier to bring out the inadequacies of other people's positions on the abortion issue than to offer a cogent position of one's own. The continuous development of a fetus renders untenable all attempts to objectively justify any specific time as the point where a fetus becomes a person and, as such, a bearer of moral rights.

[8] Some Catholic moralists have attempted to justify abortions performed to save the life of a mother by employing Aquinas's justification of homicide. As Aquinas saw it, while a human being never has a right to "directly intend" the death of another human being, he does have a right to kill an "aggressor" who threatens his life and cannot be stopped by any lesser means, as long as his "direct intention" goes no further than stopping the assault (that is, it does not include the desire to have the aggressor die). If one accepts this view, the question in the case of an abortion would be whether a fetus endangering its mother's life should be considered an "aggressor" properly subject to retaliation, even though it is without fault.

Any point we focus upon in the continuous development from conception to fetus to baby seems arbitrary and open to telling objections. Yet we quite rightfully feel a need "to draw a line" somewhere and the thought that all such lines are ultimately arbitrary is too difficult for most of us to accept. So we construct our arbitrary lines and try to find some justification for them, but we never really succeed. The reasons we give for our positions on the abortion issue, I suspect, are often rationalizations that we conveniently construct to hide from ourselves how *feelings of identification* more than reason motivate us in this issue. For some this feeling of identification focuses naturally on the developing fetus, while for others it focuses on the suffering or wishes of the expectant parents. For the former abortion is naturally *felt* to be immoral, while for the latter it is *felt* to be moral. Reasons are given to justify these feelings, but they prove inadequate. Those of us who, like myself, feel identification with both the developing fetus and the expectant parents, struggle to draw some reasoned intermediate position, but reason fails us no less than it fails our absolutist opponents. If one says, as I do, that it is consciousness that bestows personhood upon a fetus, one finds oneself incapable of specifying in any definite way the degree of consciousness that is required. The definite line that we seek in separating persons from nonpersons proves to be disturbingly arbitrary. Given the significance of this matter, however, we refuse to allow people to draw their own lines, free of legal restraint. Instead, we fight it out, debunking the inadequacies of our opponents' positions but conveniently overlooking the inadequacies of our own.

I certainly do not profess to have any easy answers to the abortion issue myself, but let me share with you some of my personal reflections on this issue. First, I am willing to categorically state that a fetus is not a person until it becomes conscious—that consciousness is an essential condition for personhood. I realize that I am open to the objection that if consciousness is essential for personhood, then individuals in a dreamless sleep or in a reversible coma are not persons. I am willing to accept that, but would say that they should have rights nevertheless since they are capable of regaining consciousness. This answer, I recognize, is not in itself satisfactory, for fetuses too are usually capable of gaining consciousness if they are left alone. But there seems to be a morally relevant difference in these two cases. Fetuses never were persons, whereas those asleep or in a coma were, and for that reason should have rights that the former need not be given. I am quite aware, however, that to many others this difference in the two cases is not strong enough to bear the moral weight that I impose upon it.

Since I see the presence of consciousness as a necessary condition for the personhood of a fetus, I would say that a fetus is not a person before it develops a functioning brain. Consequently, I would see no moral dilemma in affording a woman absolute rights to dispose of a developing fetus prior to this point. I would, however, begin to feel uneasy about abortions after the eighth week, feeling that the loss of a fetus at this point is more than "the mere removal of unwanted tissue from a woman's uterus," as some have described it. I must admit that I have no effective reply as to how I can justify having moral regrets over the loss of an 8- to 12-week-old human fetus, but not the fetuses of other animals whose levels of brain activity are indistinguishable. As we have seen, I do not think it is adequate simply to say that a human fetus is worthy of more respect since it looks like or is potentially a human being. Nevertheless, my feeling still persists, which indicates that these considerations do move me. However psychologically understandable my attitude may be, I find it incapable of rational justification. I think I should be less concerned about mindless fetuses that look like human beings or can be envisioned as developing into persons and be more concerned about some adult animals that are more like persons.

Certainly a human fetus during the last trimester of development should have a claim upon our moral sensibilities. Nevertheless, I would not afford it the *full rights* of a human being. I would, for example, feel no moral hesitancy in choosing the life of a normal pregnant woman over the life of a fetus, however developed. I do not hesitate to say that the mother's life is a more valuable one than that of the fetus. The fetus, unlike its mother, does not have an already developed personality, nor has it established relationships of affection and social responsibility with others. As well as giving the claims of a fetus less weight than those of the already living, I would also afford a fetus "a right not to be born," if it possesses certain clearly defined severe abnormalities; parents should be permitted to claim that right on behalf of their unborn.

Critics of abortion are likely to protest strongly that one should never attempt to weigh the relative worth of human life, for this mode of reasoning will eventually lead us down "a slippery slope" of moral reasoning which first justifies early abortions, then later ones, and eventually infanticide and the involuntary euthanasia of such individuals as the feeble-minded and senile who are seen as not fully human or as "having no prospect of a meaningful life." I have two replies to this claim—one factual, the other philosophical. As a factual matter, those countries—such as Sweden and Denmark—which have long-standing liberalized abortion laws have not, as a matter of fact, found themselves going down that slippery slope. Indeed, the practice in Sweden and Denmark is to give the best of care to all living individuals, including the physically deformed, mentally retarded, and senile. On a philosophical level, however, one cannot dismiss the claim that the logic of a position which distinguishes "the relative worth of human life" transcends the abortion issue. This is indeed true, but the relevance of this notion to such issues as infanticide and euthanasia cannot be determined before a detailed consideration of the differences as well as similarities in these issues. One must consider each issue on its own merits. Reasonable people committed to the relevance of considerations relating to "quality of life" can disagree as to the moral permissibility of various *specific* proposals relating to abortion, infanticide, and euthanasia. Certainly this concept is capable of application in ways that most of us would find morally reprehensible. This does not, however, distinguish it from many other moral concepts (such as "utility") which can be misapplied equally as well. As I have suggested in our discussion of traditional theories of normative ethics, moral values are not absolute but require always to be adjusted to each other and to the constantly changing contours of specific problems. Moral values provide us with guides, not with mechanical answers. In the hands of morally insensitive people, the best of moral guides can lead us astray.

The critics are right, however, that a consistent adherence to my mode of reasoning will have logical consequences which appear morally repugnant to some. For example, since I would consider late-term abortions morally permissible when a fetus is discovered to be severely deformed, and since I do not think that the act of birth should confer special rights to a fetus that it did not possess just prior to birth, I should, in all consistency, be willing to grant the moral permissibility of infanticide in certain circumstances. I am so willing.

DISCUSSION QUESTIONS

1. Under what conditions, if at all, would you consider (direct) third-trimester abortions morally justifiable? Would you consider infanticide morally justifiable under the same conditions? Would you be willing to grant parents the legal right to abortions and infanticides you consider wrong? How far would you be willing to go in allowing parents the legal right to make their own choices in this area? Consider the following situations:

   a. the fetus has severe brain damage which makes it certain that it will never gain consciousness.

   b. the fetus has severe brain damage which makes it unlikely that it will ever gain consciousness.

   c. the fetus has severe brain damage. Although it will grow to be conscious of its environment, it will suffer from grave physical, emotional, and intellectual retardation and will most certainly require supervision for the remainder of its life.

   d. the fetus suffers from a genetic defect. If it is born, it will develop into a normal child, but it will eventually contract a painful and crippling neurological disease that will kill it before it reaches adulthood.

   e. the fetus has a 50 percent chance of developing the neurological disease described above.

   f. the fetus has no legs and arms, but is otherwise normal.

   g. the fetus is normal, but it is unwanted by its parents who are financially and emotionally incapable of caring adequately for a new child.

h. the fetus has been discovered by amniocentesis to be developing into a normal female baby. The parents desire an abortion so that they may try again for a boy.

2. According to a recent Supreme Court decision (Planned Parenthood v. Danforth—1976), a pregnant woman need not get the father's consent before having an abortion performed. Does this seem fair to you? Are there any situations where a man's desire to have and raise his own child should be sufficient to compel a woman not to have an abortion to which she would otherwise be entitled? If not, should the law at least require the woman to inform the father that she is having an abortion?

3. In June 1977 the Supreme Court of the United States ruled that although *Roe v. Wade* gives a woman the unrestricted right to an abortion during the first trimester of her pregnancy, it is constitutional for the states to place restrictions on the use of welfare funds to pay for the abortions of women on Medicaid. Federal law, the Court declared, allows, but does not require, the states to provide elective abortions under their Medicaid plans. There has been much controversy over this ruling. Do you think this ruling was right? Why, or why not? What are your reactions to the following argument in defense of this ruling?

> During the first trimester of pregnancy, women have a right to obtain an abortion; the state may not make it a crime to perform such abortions. But there is no accompanying right to elective abortion at public expense.
>
> Analogies spring to mind. I have a right of free press. Does this mean that the government must buy me a newspaper? Every citizen has a right to free speech. Must the taxpayers hire him a hall? We have a right to the free exercise of religion. It is not contended that the Treasury must finance churches and synogogues so that the right may conveniently be exercised. There is a right to keep and bear arms. Do we have a right to free rifles?
>
> Let us move closer to the status of those on public welfare. Every indigent person has a right to travel. Such a person may want to visit Hawaii, indeed he may "need" to visit Hawaii; but for want of money it may be difficult or impossible for him to pay his own way. It is fatuous to argue that the taxpayers . . . therefore must buy the indigent a round-trip ticket to Honolulu. Yet, in principle, this is what the petitioning pregnant women have demanded in the abortion cases. (James J. Kilpatrick, reprinted by permission.)

4. Consider the following dialogue:

A: A 3-month-old human fetus is not a person; it's more like a lump of tissue or a human organ. Since it is not a conscious organism at this point, it has no moral worth.

B: But it looks so human! Just like a little baby! All the organ systems, you know, are already formed. Clearly such a being has moral worth, by virtue of what it is and what it could become. More moral worth than the fetuses of animals and indeed more moral worth than adult animals.

A: That's pure emotion. I thought we were trying to discuss this issue rationally.

B: I'm not sure we can. I wonder how rational you are about this matter yourself. Assuming that an aborted 3-month-old human fetus could be prepared as a gourmet's delicacy, would you eat it, the way you eat suckling pigs?

A: Heavens no!

B: But why? After all, you say that a 3-month-old human fetus has no moral worth. Is your reaction to the thought of eating a human fetus rational?

Does *A* have an effective reply?

5. If it were possible to safely remove from its mother's womb and to artificially incubate a fetus that is at least three weeks old, in what situations, if at all, should a woman have the right not only to free herself from a dependent fetus but also to have that fetus destroyed?

6. Assuming, as Thomson does, that a fetus is a person, possessing the same moral rights as its mother, what would your reaction be to the following defense of abortion made by a 30-year-old woman?

> I've been lucky enough to be admitted to medical school in the fall and if I continue with this pregnancy I won't be able to attend and most likely will never have another chance. The impact of having a child will be devastating upon my life prospects. Don't I have a moral right to protect myself against this sort of injury? My fetus is innocent, but so am I; I took every reasonable precaution to avoid getting pregnant. An abortion in a case like mine should be seen as an act of self-defense. If I can protect myself against physical injury, why can't I protect myself from having my life ruined?

7. What do you think of the following argument?

> It is absurd to say that abortion is contrary to the will of God since about two-thirds of conceptions result in natural abortions or stillbirths. If God were opposed to abortions, he clearly would not have allowed nature to work in this manner. Is it not more reasonable to say that God allows natural abortions—such as the natural abortion of a fertilized ovum that is incapable of successfully implanting itself on the uterine wall—as a means of weeding out possible defective organisms. On this analogy, the decision of parents to abort a genetically defective fetus is quite "natural."

8. Grassian claims that the life of a third-trimester fetus is less valuable than the life of a normal pregnant woman. Underlying his view, is

the position that a fetus, however fully developed, should be seen as less of a person than a normal adult human being. Do you agree? If so, does this mode of thinking logically lead to the view that old senile people are not full persons, and that their right to life is consequently less than it was when they were younger? Would you accept such a conclusion?

9. If consciousness is an essential condition of personhood, can any reasonable justification be given for refusing to grant the right to life to fetuses before they become conscious, but to grant this right to adults who are in a dreamless sleep or reversible coma?

10. What do you think of the following argument?

> It was right for the Joneses to abort their severely physically deformed fetus several years back. If they hadn't done this, I know they wouldn't have had any more children, and healthy, happy Johnny would never have been born. Certainly, it is better that they waited to have Johnny than to have had a defective child that would not have had the potential for a happy and healthy life that Johnny has.

FURTHER READINGS

FEINBERG, JOEL, ed., *The Problem of Abortion*. Encino, Calif.: Wadsworth, 1973. A good collection of material on the moral and legal aspects of abortion. Included are excerpts from *Roe v. Wade* and a tort action for "wrongful life" (in which a person was sued for allowing another person to be born). There are also several articles by contemporary analytic philosophers, among them the articles by Tooley and Thomson mentioned in this chapter.

MAPPES, THOMAS A., and JANE S. ZEMBATY, eds., *Social Ethics: Morality and Social Policy*, chapter 1. New York: McGraw-Hill, 1977. While practically all of the current anthologies on contemporary moral issues have a section on abortion, this collection would be best for beginning students who are seeking readable analyses of the abortion issue from diverse moral standpoints. Included are excerpts from John T. Noonan (a "conservative" viewpoint), Daniel Callahan (a "moderate" viewpoint), and Mary Anne Warren (a "liberal" viewpoint). Also included are excerpts from *Roe v. Wade*.

NOONAN, JOHN L., ed., *The Morality of Abortion: Legal and Historical Perspectives*. Cambridge, Mass.: Harvard University Press, 1970. An anthology of material by authors with a theological perspective on the historical, legal, and moral aspects of abortion.

6

Euthanasia

I see there is an instinctive horror of killing living things under any circumstances whatever. For instance, an alternative has been suggested in the shape of confining even rabid dogs in a certain place and allowing them to die a slow death. Now my idea of compassion makes this thing impossible for me. I cannot for a moment bear to see a dog, or for that matter any other living being, helplessly suffering the torture of a slow death. I do not kill a human being thus circumstanced because I have more hopeful remedies. I should kill a dog similarly situated because in its case I am without a remedy. Should my child be attacked with rabies and there was no helpful remedy to relieve his agony, I should consider it my duty to take his life.

MAHATMA GANDHI
Young India
November 18, 1926

THE CONCEPT OF EUTHANASIA

Death inevitably awaits us all. To some it comes unexpectedly and peacefully, while to others it comes in pain and dreadful anticipation. In cases of painful terminal illness or severe physical defect, is it right for a human being to take it upon himself to choose the moment and mode of death, attempting to make it as painless and dignified as possible? Such is the question at the heart of the euthanasia debate.

The concept of euthanasia is used today with varying meanings. In its original Greek meaning, "euthanasia" meant no more than an easy and painless death (*eu = well; thanatos = death*) and was later extended to refer to the work of a physician in alleviating as far as possible the suffering of dying. Today, however, "euthanasia" is often used synonymously with that of "mercy killing" and as such entails the bringing about or acceleration of death. *The American Heritage Dictionary* (1975) defines "euthanasia" as "the action of inducing the painless death of a person for reasons assumed to be merciful." As this definition demonstrates, central to our current concept of euthanasia is the idea that such

259

an action be motivated by a desire to be merciful to or to do good to the recipient. As such, when most people are asked to think of a case of euthanasia they imagine a person who is dying of a painful terminal illness, such as cancer, and is given some lethal drug or injection that is meant to "put him out of his misery."

Is it *euthanasia*, however, if doctors purposely refrain from treating a terminally ill patient in the belief that treatment would merely prolong the agony of dying? Many people would say no. As they use the term, "euthanasia" must involve some *positive* action; mere "refusals to save" or decisions to "let die," they would say, are not *acts* of euthanasia. Since the question of the relevance of the active-passive distinction is central to the euthanasia debate, it is best to use the notion of euthanasia broadly to include "intentional acts of omission" (such as the refusal to connect a person to a respirator) as well as "acts of commission" (such as giving a patient a fatal injection). Most commentators on the euthanasia issue have made this linguistic decision and consequently distinguish between "active (or direct) euthanasia" and "passive (or indirect) euthanasia." Straddling the line between active and passive euthanasia are those actions which involve the termination of life-support measures (such as unplugging a patient from a respirator). In addition, euthanasia can be distinguished as either "voluntary" or "nonvoluntary." An act of voluntary euthanasia would require the voluntary consent of the recipient, whereas nonvoluntary euthanasia would encompass both those cases where consent cannot be obtained (such as when the patient is comatose) or where euthanasia is applied contrary to the wishes of the recipient (such as euthanasia of the irrational, retarded, and senile).[1] It is only the latter type of nonvoluntary euthanasia which should properly be said to be involuntary, although both are often so described.

While the motive of "acting for the sake of the patient" is central to our contemporary concept of euthanasia, it is quite questionable that this motive is behind the often-made decision not to utilize "artificial" life-support measures for those in hopeless comas. Yet deaths resulting from such decisions are often cited as examples of euthanasia. If we are to accept this common usage, euthanasia should be defined as "an act of inducing or permitting death to occur, when death, if not a benefit, is at least not an evil, to the recipient." (Notice, too, that we have deleted reference to a *painless* death in the preceding definition since individuals who are "allowed to die"—that is, passive euthanasia—often die in pain.)

MEDICAL AND LEGAL REALITIES

The rapid progress in the development of ever more sophisticated means of life support poses an especially acute moral dilemma for to-

---

[1] One should note that in cases where consent is denied, it will be very difficult (some would say impossible) to show that the act is a *kindly* one and consequently can be properly described as an act of euthanasia.

day's doctors. A generation ago, a patient died when his heart stopped and "extraordinary" treatment consisted of an injection of adrenalin. Today, however, with the advent of such means as respirators, heart-lung machines, and organ transplants, patients who would otherwise most certainly have died, can be kept alive much longer, and maybe before long indefinitely. Given the possibility of prolonging life, doctors must often make painful choices. To some, a doctor's hippocratic commitment to the treatment and cure of disease necessitates that he always do all in his power to prolong life. Others, emphasizing instead the hippocratic commitment to the relief of suffering, see the prolongation of life in some cases as nothing more than the futile and cruel prolongation of suffering. Others, of a practical bent, focus upon the vast potential cost of the absolute commitment to the prolongation of human life. Is it worth the immense cost, they wonder, to connect 1,000 people to a respirator for long periods of time when the chances are perhaps that only one might—just might—survive? Could not this immense amount of money if spent on medical research be of much greater long-range value to the ideal of elimination of human suffering and the prolongation of human life?

The utilization of passive euthanasia in hospitals is widespread. Physicians routinely decide whether treatments should be applied or life supports utilized or withdrawn. It is common procedure in hospitals, for example, for doctors to indicate (in code) on the charts of terminally ill patients that they should not be resuscitated should their hearts stop beating. In some cases, decisions to withhold treatment are made in a very circuitous manner. Instead of unplugging a hopelessly ill person from a respirator, for example, a physician may order that antibiotics not be used if the patient develops some expected infection, like pneumonia. Wary of the possible legal consequences of their actions or seeking to soothe their own consciences, some doctors employ devious plots to accomplish their benevolent purposes. Instead of switching off the respirator, they may order instead that the oxygen tank not be replaced when empty. Other doctors, hardened by their constant exposure to death and dying, can be quite callous in the choices they make, allowing patients to die whenever the effort to save them becomes personally burdensome.[2]

An especially difficult decision that doctors must face is that of withholding treatment from a patient who is unable to express his or her wishes. Such decisions are particularly controversial in the case of infants born with severe mental or physical defects. The decision to withhold treatment from a newborn infant is made most easily in cases of extreme mental defect—the most extreme of which is anencephaly, the complete absence of a cerebral cortex. As Dr. John Freeman of Johns Hopkins put it, "With the best of care they live for only a few months, so many

---

2 "Do you mind if this patient dies?" the doctor asked of one emergency case. "The respirator's on the fifth floor and the nurse says it's a pain in the ass. . . ." (quoted in *Newsweek,* November 3, 1975, p. 67)

of us believe it is acceptable to withhold feeding and treatment of infections." There have, however, been cases of infants born with severe mental defects whose parents were forced to avail themselves of the lifesaving techniques of medical science. Among these cases was that of David Patrick Houle, who was born without a left eye and ear canal, various neurological disorders, and a stomach disconnected from the esophagus. Admitting that if David should live he probably would be blind, deaf, palsied, and might never have gained consciousness "as we know consciousness," the hospital in which he was born sued his parents after they refused to allow corrective surgery. Siding with the hospital, the Maryland court ordered the operation, saying that parents "have no right to withhold such treatment and that to do so constitutes neglect in the legal sense. The basic right enjoyed by every human being is the right to life itself." The surgery, which consisted of the implantation of a food tube in David's stomach, was performed. A second operation, to connect the baby's esophagus to his stomach, was to have been performed, but David died—15 days after he was born.

Courts have also ordered corrective surgery in cases of mongoloid infants (Down's syndrome). Many of these infants are born with gastrointestinal or cardiac defects that would be fatal unless surgically repaired. Although doctors have often accepted parents' decisions not to operate in such cases, there is growing opposition to this practice and court cases have resulted. Of course, for each court case, there are countless noncontested decisions that parents and doctors make every day. Many infants whose potentiality for normal mental development is unimpaired are refused medical treatment for physical abnormalities which are capable of surgical correction. Dr. Jordan Weitzman of the University of Southern California School of Medicine recalls the case of a child born with no genitals, intestines, or bladder who was left to die even though his condition was treatable. According to Weitzman, "Nobody said a word." This was so, he reflects, "because we live in an era of the Body Beautiful, so the sight of a kid with almost nothing below the waist gave everybody pause."

There is much controversy among doctors on the appropriate treatment for infants born with spina bifida—an opening in the spine. In serious cases, (about 2 per 1,000 live births), the infant is born with a protruding unclosed sac in the lower back which contains nerve tissue and cerebrospinal fluid. As a consequence of the spinal cord deformity, the infant has no bladder and bowel control and is usually paralyzed from the waist down. Such infants are also often born with hydrocephalus ("water on the brain") which, if not treated, will lead to severe mental retardation. For some doctors, the appropriate medical response to such unfortunate infants is aggressive medical intervention, including many operations. Yet even with such vigorous intervention, more than 50 percent of such children die before they are 16. Those who survive usually have low IQ's and face the pitiful prospect of continued operations, full or partial paralysis, severe problems of incontinence, and recurring urinary infections. Furthermore, such children tend to create great strain on their families. In many cases, their parents forgo having further children so that they can devote themselves more fully to their defective child. Focusing on the personal cost of aggressive medical intervention, some doctors strongly advocate doing nothing. As they see it, it is better for both the spina bifida child and its parents for "nature to take its course" in such cases. With no medical intervention, they point out, approximately 90 percent of such children will die before their first birthday. On the other hand, advocates of aggressive medical intervention point to the fact that the 10 percent that do survive without intervention will have a much lower quality of life as a result of not being treated. Furthermore, while most treated infants face the bleak prospect of retarded intellectual development and gross physical defects, not all do. If we are to do nothing to help children born with severe spina bifida, other doctors have pondered, would it not be kinder to directly kill them? If nature is to be allowed to take its course, they ask, is it not best that nature be helped to take her course more quickly? Other doctors focus on the vast economic cost of treatment for such children and ponder over its social utility. How, so many doctors wonder, are we to weigh the unclear and conflicting demands of morality in such cases?

As we turn from nonvoluntary to voluntary euthanasia, we also find great controversy. For example, the courts have taken conflicting positions on the right of patients to refuse lifesaving treatments. While the courts have generally respected "competent" adults' wishes that treatment be withheld in their own cases, they have not always done so. In addition, the courts have often intervened to ensure that minors be given lifesaving treatments in spite of their own and their parents' objections, even when based on religious grounds. For example, the courts have intervened against Jehovah's Witnesses who have refused blood transfusions for their children. The courts are, however, united in their opposition to active euthanasia (mercy killing) which is legally classified as an unjustifiable homicide. Nevertheless, there have only been two cases of doctors coming to trial in the United States for active euthanasia. In 1949, Dr. Hermann Sander of New Hampshire was accused of injecting air into the veins of a cancer patient and, in 1973, Dr. Vincent A. Montemaro of New York was charged with giving a cancer patient a lethal dose of potassium chloride. Sympathetic juries acquitted both.[3]

---

[3] There have been about a dozen cases of lay individuals being brought to trial for the active (both voluntary and nonvoluntary) euthanasia of relatives. In the majority of these cases, the defendant was either acquitted or found "temporarily insane" by jurors who clearly were guided more by their sympathies than by the law. While jurors in the U.S. often are forced by their sympathies for the defendant to ignore the law in euthanasia cases, many European countries, unlike the U.S., permit a reduction of the level of homicide in mercy killings, allowing, in most cases, for a suspended sentence. The Uraguayan penal code is more direct, allowing the motive of mercy to be a complete excuse to homicide in certain cases. According to this code, "The judges are authorized to forgo punishment of a person whose previous life has been honorable where he commits a homicide motivated by compassion, induced by repeated requests of the victim."

Although there are probably many physicians who have clearly participated in active euthanasia, there are many more who use circuitous methods of avoiding this charge. Many, for example, administer increasing doses of narcotics to terminally ill patients with the full knowledge and intention that the drug will not only relieve pain, but will also kill. Sometimes, doctors simply leave pills for patients with the warning, "I have something for your pain. If you take too much, it will be harmful," allowing the patient to make his own decision. Dr. Joel Posner of Pennsylvania describes the case of a man on a respirator who was so sick that the respirator tube would slip out of his throat several times a day, causing him to turn blue from near suffocation. Seeing the man's suffering, Posner decided that further care on the respirator was pointless and that it would be better for him if he died. Although Posner would have had no legal problem if he simply turned off the respirator, he perceived this course of action as a cruel one since it might take the patient a half a day of choking before he died. Since morphine to put him to sleep and suppress his respiration would be active euthanasia, Posner decided to turn off the respirator, while administering pure oxygen to the patient. The effect was the same, yet, as Posner puts it, "somehow more legal."[4]

THE RELIGIOUS CASE AGAINST EUTHANASIA

Suicide

While, as we shall see, liberal euthanasia policies have been rejected on the basis of their alleged dangerous consequences (disutility), the most forceful, and historically most influential, objections to euthanasia come from the traditional Judaic, Christian, and Islamic condemnation of suicide as a grave sin. Some religions and societies, however, have perceived certain suicides as honorable and brave actions. The Greeks and Romans took this view as do many Eastern religions. In such religions, actions such as "suttee" in which a wife throws herself on the funeral pyre of her dead husband and "hara-kiri" invest suicide with honor and embellish it with ritualistic dignity.

Stoic and Epicurean philosophers of the ancient world considered the choice of the time and mode of one's own death as the ultimate expression of human freedom, dignity, and rationality. For example, the Roman stoic Seneca (4 B.C. ?–65 A.D.) wrote,

> As I choose the ship in which I will sail and the house I will inhabit, so
> I will choose the death by which I leave life. In no matter more than
> in death should we act according to our own desire. . . .
> If I can choose between a death of torture and one that is simple and

---

[4] *Newsweek*, November 3, 1975, p. 67.

easy, why should I not select the latter? Why should I endure the agonies of disease when I can emancipate myself from all my torture? I will not depart by death from disease as long as it may be healed and leaves my mind unimpaired, but if I know that I will suffer forever, I will depart, not through fear of pain itself, but because it prevents all for which I live.

Western religion's condemnation of suicide can be traced to the conception that we are God's "property" and that the physical world we briefly inhabit is a testing ground provided by God for the development of our moral virtue. As such, we have no right to take it upon ourselves to leave this world and consequently to leave unfinished the tasks God intends for us. In the words of the philosopher John Locke,

> . . . men being all the workmanship of one omnipotent and infinitely wise Maker; all the servants of one sovereign Master, sent into the world by His order and about His Business; they are His property, whose workmanship they are made to last during His, not another's pleasure.
> . . . Every one . . . is bound to preserve himself, and not to quit his station wilfully. . . .[5]

Kant echoes the same sentiments, writing,

> We have been placed in this world under certain conditions and for specific purposes. But a suicide opposes the purpose of his creator; he arrives in the other world as one who has deserted his post. . . . Human beings are sentinels on earth and may not leave their posts. . . .[6]

Relating such sentiments directly to the euthanasia issue, a contemporary Catholic writes,

> . . . euthanasia is murder and as such can never be permitted . . . it must be resolutely refused to the sick person . . . however intense his suffering, however small the hope of recovery. God alone is lord over life and death. It is not God's will and is neither permitted to us mortals, nor indeed possible for us, to strip death of all its terror and pain; death is meant to be the last and greatest test we have to undergo here on earth.[7]

I must admit that I find these sentiments unconvincing and cruel in their implications. If one consistently believed that all life's sufferings were a necessary part of an omnipotent and benevolent God's plan,

---

[5] John Locke, *Second Treatise of Government* (Indianapolis: Bobbs-Merrill, 1952), pp. 5–6.

[6] Immanuel Kant, *Lectures on Ethics* (New York: Harper & Row, Pubs., 1963), p. 154.

[7] Everhard Welty, *A Handbook of Christian Social Ethics*, II (London: Nelson, 1963), pp. 130–31.

would it not follow that all human attempts to alleviate suffering are an unjustified interference with that plan?[8] If we say, with the mainstream of Western religious thought, that it is God's will that we alleviate suffering, how can one be convinced that God totally prohibits human beings from "quitting their stations" when life offers them nothing but suffering? How can anyone who has witnessed the slow, painful, and hopeless physical and mental wasting away of a human being plausibly claim that in such cases the victim is undergoing his "last and greatest test." What, may I ask, is the point of such a test and what is it to "pass" such a test? I find no plausible answer to this question.

If God condemns all suicides, he should have good reasons for his condemnation. But one can search in vain through the writings of Locke and Kant for plausible reasons for this condemnation. The first sustained Christian condemnation of suicide can be traced back to Saint Augustine (354–430) who claimed that such action was a violation of the divine Commandment that "thou shalt not kill." Historically, Augustine's stand against suicide can be seen as a reaction to the suicidal tendencies of many Christians of his day. Given Christian theology, such tendencies were quite understandable. Since, for the Christian, this world was merely preparatory for the afterlife, providing a moral testing ground to sort out those who would ultimately go to heaven or to hell, the supreme personal aim for each Christian was to assure that he "pass" this test. Since the way to accomplish this end was by avoiding sin, and since the world and one's natural desires made it all too easy to sin, many Christians committed suicide for fear of succumbing to temptation. Some accomplished this by purposely provoking infidels to martyr them, while others did it more directly by casting themselves from cliffs. If suicide were not itself ruled out as a sin, Augustine recognized, such action would be quite reasonable. Indeed, the most logical course of action for those singularly bent on assuring their own place in heaven would be to commit suicide right after a sin-cleansing baptism. Augustine's assumption that there was an absolute divine prohibition of suicide served to deny the validity of this line of reasoning.

---

[8] This sort of reasoning has been used by those who have opposed the use of anesthetics and other medical treatment as an unjustified interference with God's perfect plan. Since God has made us suffer, they argue, such suffering must be essential for some greater good and consequently any alleviation of that suffering, while immediately beneficial, is bound, in the long run, to be detrimental. Believers in the traditional Judaic-Christian conception of an all-powerful, all-knowing, and perfectly good God must give some plausible reason why such a God would approve of our alleviation of suffering, while he himself allows this suffering to exist. This sort of question poses a serious challenge to the existence of the traditional Judaic-Christian God. It has been claimed by some critics that this challenge is unanswerable and brings out the logical incompatibility of the existence of the traditional Judaic-Christian God, given the suffering that exists in this world. The question of the ultimate rationality of belief in the traditional Judaic-Christian God, given the suffering that exists in this world, is known by theologians and philosophers as the "problem of evil."

The most influential Christian condemnation of suicide is found in the following passage from the Medieval philosopher Saint Thomas Aquinas's (1225?–1274) *Summa Theologica:*

> It is altogether unlawful to kill oneself, for three reasons. First, because everything naturally loves itself, the result being that everything naturally keeps itself in being. . . . Wherefore suicide is contrary to the inclination of nature. . . . Hence suicide is always a mortal sin, as being contrary to the natural law. Secondly, because every part . . . belongs to the whole. Now every man is part of the community, and so, as such, he belongs to the community. Hence by killing himself he injures the community. . . . Thirdly, because life is God's gift to man, and is subject to His power, Who kills and makes to live. Hence whoever takes his own life sins against God, . . . as he who usurps himself judgment of a matter not entrusted to him. For it belongs to God alone to pronounce sentence of death and life.[9]

We have already touched upon the inadequacy of Aquinas's third reason. If, as Aquinas claims, only God can rightfully decide when a human life should come to an end, could not one argue as well that one is "usurping God's province" when one decides to prolong one's life as well as to shorten it? Such a view, as Hume pointed out in his essay *Of Suicide,* would imply that "If I turn aside a stone which is falling on my head, I disturb the course of nature and I invade the peculiar province of the Almighty by lengthening out my life beyond the period, which . . . he has assigned to it." In addition, one can construct an argument for the morality of suicide which is logically analogous to Aquinas's, as the Roman scholar Pliny (23–79) did. As Pliny put it, the existence of poisonous herbs with which one may so easily kill oneself, is a benevolent gift from God. Clearly, Aquinas would reject such a view, claiming that we are usurping the province of God when we act to shorten our life but not when we act to preserve it. As Aquinas would see it, God gives us life, an instinct for survival, and a moral injunction that it is wrong to take one's life. When, despite our efforts, he takes us, it is his doing, not ours; but when we fail to avert danger, etc., it is our abuse. This is, however, simply a statement of a position, and not an argument for it.

Aquinas's first and second reasons fare no better. First, all suicide victims would appear to be refutations of Aquinas's claim that "everything naturally keeps itself in being." Indeed, even if everyone did *as a matter of fact* have a stronger natural inclination to live than to die this would not entail that they *morally ought* to act on that inclination. Certainly, Aquinas would not say that we ought always do what we are most strongly inclined to do. (Consider in this context the Catholic requirement that priests be celibate.) Aquinas's reply would no doubt be that the notion of what is natural should not be equated with "everything

---

[9] Thomas Aquinas, *Summa Theologica,* vol. II, part II, question 64, article 5.

that occurs in nature" but rather with "that which is in accord with *natural law*"—that is, the commands of God concerning *proper* human behavior. But lacking an independent characterization and justification for the demands of "natural law," Aquinas's claim that suicide is unnatural reduces to an *unjustified assertion* that suicide is morally wrong since it is contrary to the will of God, for there is no reason he gives for God's will on this matter.[10]

Second, although a person may have a moral obligation to tolerate great personal suffering if this is a necessary condition for the fulfillment of a specific social obligation, it would appear to be absurd to say that all suicides must "injure the community" as Aquinas (echoing Aristotle) declares. While many suicides are, no doubt, quite selfish actions which cause great psychological suffering to those who loved the suicide victim, it can by no stretch of the imagination be reasonably claimed that most suicides hurt society as a whole in any appreciable concrete way. Though our self-esteem may like it otherwise, few of us are indispensable. On a deeper, less concrete level, however, suicides can be seen as an insult to a community. As one commentator put it,

> Suicide shows a contempt for society. . . . This most individualistic of all actions disturbs society profoundly. Seeing a man who appears not to care for the things which it prizes, society is compelled to question all it has thought desirable. The things which make its own life worth living, the suicide boldly jettisons. Society is troubled, and its natural and nervous reaction is to condemn the suicide. Thus it bolsters up again its own values.[11]

I suppose this is the best defense that can be made for Aquinas's claim that suicide "injures the community." Yet I doubt very much that occasional suicides in *healthy* societies would be that "profoundly disturbing" to the values of members of that society. Indeed, in such societies one could very well see suicide as a process of purification by which society rids itself of misfits and sources of misery. There are times, all too sadly, when the suicide of some especially troubling person comes as a (secret) relief to those who suffered his existence. On the other hand, if there are large numbers of suicides, people ought to be disturbed and seek to discover and eradicate the underlying sociological or psychological causes of these suicides.

Aquinas's classic discussion of suicide in the *Summa Theologica* also suffers from his failure to settle on a clear definition of this concept. In this discussion, Aquinas seems to be employing a broad definition of suicide as "intentionally doing or omitting to do something that results in one's death, either with the desire that one die or the knowledge that one's death is a very likely consequence of this action or omission which

---

10 Recall Bentham's criticism of "intuitionism" in ethics and our own discussion of the claim that homosexuality is unnatural.

11 H. Romilly Freeden, *Suicide,* quoted in Glanville Williams, *The Sanctity of Life and the Criminal Law* (New York: Knopf, 1957), p. 267.

is chosen as a means to some other end." If this definition is accepted, however, all acts of heroic self-sacrifice would become instances of suicide. For example, a soldier who sacrifices his life for his comrades, a spy who swallows a lethal pill in order not to divulge vital information under torture, and a person who steers his automobile over a cliff and toward his almost certain death in order to avoid killing a group of children in its path, would all have to count as suicides under this definition. Aquinas seems willing to accept the characterization of such acts as suicidal and hence unjustified, for he does explicitly claim that the heroic self-sacrifice of Samson was a suicide and was not a sin only because he was "acting under a command of God." While Aquinas seems unbending in his characterization of acts of heroic self-sacrifice as suicides which can be justified only if they are directly commanded by God, he does not take the same line in his subsequent discussion of the morality of killing the innocent. In this discussion, Aquinas employs the principle of double effect that we discussed in connection with the abortion issue. According to this principle, accepted today by Roman Catholic moralists, suicide can be more narrowly defined as an act whose direct intention is the taking of one's life; as such Samson's act would be described as a nonsuicidal one since his direct intention (purpose) was not to take his life, but was to thwart the actions of his enemies. As we have seen, however, the distinction between direct and indirect intention is unclear.

While one should approach the question of the morality of suicide with an open mind that allows for the possibility that some acts of suicide may turn out to be rational, justifiable, and praiseworthy, Catholic moralists approach this question burdened by the unchallengeable dogma that suicide is wrong. They may try, as Aquinas did, to argue for such a view, but, ultimately, they accept it on faith. Yet, like the rest of us, there are acts of heroic self-sacrifice that they want to praise (such as Samson's act). So they either turn to unverifiable assumptions as to God's commands in particular situations, as Aquinas did, or attempt to find some definition of suicide that makes the actions they want to praise nonsuicidal, and hence not subject to automatic censure. The principle of the double effect is supposed to do that job, but it doesn't do it well. For example, Catholic moralists, like the rest of us, tend to recoil at the thought of censuring the brave action of Captain Oates, a member of Robert Scott's last fatal expedition to the South Pole, who walked into the Antarctic snow to die because his frostbitten legs made him a life-threatening handicap to the rest of Scott's party. As Scott himself wrote of Oates in his journal,

> He slept through the night . . . hoping not to wake; but he woke in the morning. . . . It was blowing a blizzard. He said, "I am just going outside and may be some time." He went out in the blizzard. . . . We knew that poor Oates was walking to his death, but although we tried to dissuade him, we knew it was the act of a brave man . . .[12]

---

[12] *Scott's Last Expedition,* 2nd ed. (New York: Dodd, Mead, 1964), p. 155.

Did Oates commit suicide? Some Catholic moralists have said no. "He did not kill himself," they say, "the blizzard did." Since he did not directly intend his death, his act is not a suicide. But what does this mean? Clearly, Oates knew that his act would lead to his death and this is precisely what he chose as a means of freeing his comrades from the burden he created. He knew his action would cause his death as much as a self-inflicted series of bullets to his head. Yet the same Catholic moralists would feel compelled by the principle of double effect to describe Oates's action as a suicide if he shot himself and hence would feel compelled to morally condemn it. But the blizzard is somehow supposed to be different. Why? Because it takes longer to die that way? If so, does this mean that a person who puts her head in a stove and turns the gas on slowly can protest as she dies, "I didn't do it, the gas did." After all, she may be motivated, as Oates was, with the desire to rid others of a burden. Catholic moralists have tried to point to some relevant moral difference that can explain why Oates did not *directly intend* his death, while people who shoot themselves or put their heads in gas-filled stoves do, yet they never succeed in giving some coherent explanation that they are willing to consistently employ in all cases. Is such an explanation, however, at all possible, or does the distinction between direct and indirect intentions serve more to obscure than to clarify the difficult moral choices we sometimes have to make? I certainly think it does.

Euthanasia: Killing versus Letting Die

As we turn from western religion's general condemnation of suicide to its more specific condemnation of euthanasia, one finds little reliance upon the distinction between direct and indirect killing and much on that between (actively) killing and allowing to die. At its simplest, the claim has been made that although you are never justified in committing active euthanasia, passive euthanasia, where you simply refrain from offering someone essential life support is justified. In this case, it is said, it is not you who are (responsible for) killing, but the disease or condition from which the victim suffers. This simple characterization is clearly inadequate. In some cases, deaths which result from intentional omissions are as much *acts* for which we are morally responsible as shooting or poisoning. Certainly, the decision to refuse feeding a newborn baby should be described strongly as *an act of killing* the infant and not one of merely *permitting it to die.* No justification can be given for claiming that it is morally better to refuse to feed an infant than to kill it directly with some lethal injection. On the contrary, it is morally better to give the injection since this is much quicker and much less painful to the infant.

The distinction between *killing by some positive action* and *refusing to save by some omission* also proves inadequate as a morally relevant distinction in those cases of euthanasia involving a decision to terminate an already initiated life-support measure. A doctor, for example, who unplugs a respirator from a pain-racked terminally ill patient has certainly *done* something. Yet when death follows such an action, many of us refuse to describe the doctor's action as one of *killing* his patient. No, we tend to say, the doctor did not *kill* his patient, his underlying condition did that; the doctor simply decided no longer to try *to save him* and *let him die.* Clearly, the fact that the doctor did rather than omitted to do something plays no part in the widespread hesitancy to describe his action in the active terms of killing rather than the passive terms of letting die or not saving. (Notice that the description of an act as one of killing rather than letting die tends to carry along in our minds the implication of greater moral responsibility.)

Most of us quite rightfully recognize that there can be no moral or legal justification for giving a doctor the right to refuse to connect a patient to a respirator and yet to refuse him the right to disconnect a patient already so connected. Certainly, it would be absurd to suggest that if respirators, by some chance, required periodic recharging, a doctor would have the right in certain circumstances not to recharge the respirator—an omission—but would not have the right in the same circumstances to unplug a continuously operating respirator—an action. Seeing no morally relevant difference in such actions and omissions, we describe them equally as instances of refusals to save individuals or of letting them die, and not as instances of killing them. Clearly, as commonly used in the context of the euthanasia issue, the notion of *allowing to die* or *refusing to save* may involve something other than a failure to act. Just as we tend to describe the act of unplugging a respirator as one of refusing to save rather than of killing, so we tend in certain circumstances to call the act of moving a patient out of an intensive care unit a refusal to save rather than an act of killing even though we may well know that such an action is bound to result in a patient's death. In spite of the element of *action* in these cases, we tend to classify them as *refusals to treat* patients rather than as *acts of killing* them. Although doctors have a moral obligation, we tend to believe, to provide *ordinary* assistance to their patients (such as feeding a newborn baby), they do not have a moral obligation to render *extraordinary* (or *heroic*) assistance in all cases. Since we tend to consider doctors responsible for providing *ordinary* assistance, when it is not provided we describe the failure to act as one of *killing.* On the other hand, when the failure to act is one of not providing *extraordinary* assistance, we tend to call it an act of *not saving* or *letting die,* and attribute whatever deaths result from such failures to act to the patient's underlying condition rather than to the action or omission of the physician.

It is this often invoked distinction between ordinary and extraordinary or heroic means of life support that the late Pope Pius XII relied upon in his influential discussion of the euthanasia issue in a speech before a group of doctors and medical students.[13] The Pope claimed

---

[13] "Papal Allocation to a Congress of Anaesthetists," 24 November 1957, *Acta Apostolicae Sedis,* 1027–33.

that while we have no moral right to omit the utilization of ordinary means of life support (and to do so would be equivalent to killing), we do have such a right when it comes to extraordinary life-support measures (and to refuse to use such measures is not killing, but simply permitting to die). In explaining the meaning of an extraordinary lifesaving measure, the Pope claimed that such a measure is one that "cannot be obtained or used without excessive expense, pain, or other inconvenience for the patient or for others, or which, if used, would not offer a reasonable hope of benefit to the patient." This statement was left, however, without clarification. The key notions here are "excessive inconvenience" and "reasonable hope of benefit to the patient." To begin with, we should notice that if the Pope's statement is taken literally, one has no obligation to avail oneself of means which *either* are excessively inconvenient *or* do not provide a reasonable hope of benefit to the patient.

Let us now consider each of these two key notions separately. First, the notion of "reasonable benefit to the patient" is open to both liberal and conservative analyses. To those who support a liberal euthanasia policy, any life-support measure that leaves a patient without a meaningful or dignified life would qualify as being without benefit. On the other hand, to the very conservative, any measure which improves any condition or disease from which the patient suffers in however limited a degree could count as a benefit. Without any clarification as to what is to count as "a reasonable benefit to a patient," the Pope's use of this notion does not offer any guidance. The same can be said of the other key notion, "excessive inconvenience." Although the Pope is certainly correct in stressing the cost and potential pain a lifesaving method may entail as factors that we implicitly use in our determination of its "extraordinary" nature, it would seem that the condition of the patient and certainty and scope of the effect of the treatment are also relevant to whether a lifesaving measure ought to be used. Certainly, most of us would feel a strong moral obligation to use expensive and inconvenience-causing methods that are likely to enable a person to live a normal or close-to-normal life and would for that reason alone hesitate to call it an extraordinary life-support measure.

It is very important to realize that while such factors as the cost, scarcity, probable pain, certainty, and scope of result and possible side effects of a treatment are all relevant in judging the extraordinariness of that treatment, reasonable people can weigh these factors differently. It would seem to me that the description of a treatment as extraordinary does not justify our judgment that doctors have no moral obligation to utilize it, but rather is often used as a mere vehicle for expressing that judgment. As often utilized, "an extraordinary treatment" simply means "a treatment that we have no moral obligation to provide." When so used, the claim that "we have no moral obligation to provide extraordinary treatments" is a mere tautology. We do not tend to first decide whether an action or omission involves ordinary or extraordinary measures, without the utilization of any moral considerations, and then use this nonmoral determination as the standard for justifying the imputation of moral obligation. On the contrary, our decision as to the standards to be utilized in determining what is to count as an extraordinary as opposed to ordinary life-support measure is often itself based upon some moral judgment. For example, the decision as to whether or not intravenous feeding of terminally ill patients should count as extraordinary treatment clearly involves taking some moral stand as to what one ought to do in such circumstances.

In addition to the implicit moral judgments that often go into the determination of whether a given mode of treatment in a given situation is extraordinary, it is important to realize that for many a mode of behavior is considered extraordinary only when it is perceived as something which interferes *artificially* with the familiar pattern of events. As such, the perception of a medical technique as being extraordinary tends to vary inversely with one's exposure to that technique and its availability. Years ago, antibiotics were widely perceived as extraordinary since they were a new introduction into the arsenal of medical treatments. Today respirators and dialysis (kidney) machines may be considered as such by laypersons, but are less apt to be considered so by physicians who are more used to them. In the future, especially if their cost goes down relative to newer methods, they will tend to be seen as ordinary and the newer methods as extraordinary. There is no reason, however, to believe that the ever-shifting popular conception of which specific treatments are extraordinary and which are ordinary is at all a coherent one from a moral point of view. For example, although people may tend to classify mechanical devices, such as respirators and dialysis machines, as extraordinary much more readily than they so classify drugs, there is no good reason to believe that such a distinction can provide a rational basis for distinguishing those treatments that ought to be utilized from those that need not be.

As we have seen, the commonly invoked distinctions between killing and letting die and between ordinary and extraordinary life-support measures are quite unclear. Although one can attempt to clarify them in a manner that makes them morally relevant, these distinctions seem to me to cloud the moral waters rather than to clear them. As our discussion of existing medical practice indicates, doctors attempting to adhere to these notions often act in circuitous ways for which, I think, no moral justification can be given. It may presently be, as the sensitive Dr. Posner put it, "somehow more legal," but it seems the height of moral insensitivity to me to claim that Posner would have been morally justified in unplugging the respirator from the terminally ill patient, but not in giving him the morphine. The only morally relevant distinction I can see is that the latter method of euthanasia is a kinder one and, as such, the morally preferable one. Similarly, it strikes me as cruel and morally pointless not to directly give a person with a terminal condition a wanted injection that will peacefully kill him but to wait instead until he inevitably contracts some infection and then not treat it. Again, the only relevant moral difference is that the passive method of euthanasia is the crueler one.

I can only ask those of you who condemn all forms of active euthanasia to empathize with a slowly dying and physically deteriorating terminal patient who cries out that he wants to die in peace and with some semblance of dignity and then honestly consider whether you can hold firmly to your absolute condemnation of active euthanasia. I also ask those of you who would feel justified in refusing to initiate an extraordinary treatment (such as connecting a person to a respirator), but not in terminating such treatment, to realize that the net effect of such a distinction, if given legal effect, would be to make physicians much more hesitant in initiating treatments in cases for which there is little hope. Certainly, it would be better to initiate treatment and be allowed the legal option of withdrawing that treatment than not to begin it at all. It may be easier on many people's consciences to perceive their action as one of *allowing a person to die* rather than as one of *killing him,* for one's action can then be perceived as less immediately connected to the person's death and less apt to be thrust upon unwilling eyes. Nevertheless, one should not escape the responsibility that one's action is in both cases a cause of death and, as such, one should accept responsibility for the consequences.

In Great Britain today, there are 30 facilities called "hospices" for the terminally ill which are committed to passive euthanasia but which shun active euthanasia. There are also a growing number of hospices in the United States, especially in California. A spokesman for the idea of hospices, Dr. Richard Lamerton of Great Britain, was in Los Angeles in April of 1976. Lamerton is reported by the *Los Angeles Times* (April 21) to have told an audience of health professionals at the U.C.L.A. School of Public Health that regular hospitals do not treat terminally ill patients appropriately. Giving an example of the "appropriate" treatment for a terminally ill patient, Lamerton related the case of a young man with cancer of the neck who suddenly hemorrhaged because the cancer had eroded the tissues in his neck and had exposed a major blood vessel. Most doctors and nurses probably would have attempted to stop the bleeding, but, according to Lamerton, such care would have been inappropriate. Stopping the bleeding would not alter the patient's terminal condition and the hemorrhaging would inevitably have recurred within a few days, causing the patient and his wife to face the ordeal a second time. The "correct" treatment, Lamerton claimed, was to cover the patient with a blanket so that nobody would see the bleeding and to sit with him until he died. As I read this in the *Times,* my immediate reaction was to wonder how long the bleeding would take, hoping that the ruptured blood vessel was indeed a major one and that death would be rapid. As I thought about this case, I had a morbid picture in my mind of a man slowly bleeding to death and of some nurse routinely changing the blankets. If I were that nurse and such a man cried out that he did not want to see himself slowly die, but wanted instead to be peacefully put out of his misery, there would be no doubt in my mind that the morally correct thing to do in this case would be to respect the man's wishes.

The active-passive distinction is no better a moral guide in cases of nonvoluntary euthanasia. For example, commentators almost universally condemn the notorious case at Johns Hopkins of an infant born with Down's syndrome and duodenal atresia (a closure in the upper part of the small intestine). While the atresia could have been corrected easily surgically, the child's parents refused and the infant was allowed to slowly starve to death over a period of 15 days. Clearly, such an action was an evil to the poor child and as such was not, as we have defined it, an act of euthanasia. But leaving aside this linguistic point, and assuming that parents should be given the legal right to refuse treatments for certain congenital defects of their mongoloid offspring, is it not clear that when such a refusal will cause a slow, painful, and inevitable death, morality demands that we make death quick and painless through active euthanasia?

If I am correct in my contention that the distinction between killing and letting die does not serve as an adequate moral guide in the euthanasia issue, why then are there distinctions so commonly invoked? No doubt, there is a psychological factor involved here. People simply do not *feel* as responsible for their omissions as they do for their actions. This feeling is capable of a general justification. Any practical morality must limit one's sphere of responsibility and hold people to higher standards of responsibility within their special spheres. While one can encourage and praise people for helping those to whom they are not bound by special responsibilities, it is too much to morally require individuals to render aid to others in all situations where the principle of utility would require it. An important way we attempt to limit people's responsibilities to others is by drawing a distinction between one's responsibilities for acts and for omissions—a moral distinction that is also reflected in the law. For example, while Jones has a legal obligation not to strike Smith, unless he has some special responsibility toward Smith he generally has no legal obligation in our society to render him aid. Indeed, this would be true even *if* Jones knew that rendering that aid would require no effort or sacrifice on his part and that without it Smith would die. Although practically all of us would consider Jones' omission morally reprehensible, we do not make it punishable. This is not unreasonable, however, for if the law accepted a general obligation to render aid to strangers in need, such an obligation might prove too vague and diffuse to be practical. As one group of legal commentators put it,

> It is true that the man who, having abundance of wealth, suffers a
> fellow creature to die of hunger at his feet, is a bad man—a worse man,
> probably, than many of those for whom we have provided very severe
> punishment. But we are unable to see where, if we make such a man

legally punishable, we can draw the line. If the rich man who refuses to save a beggar's life at the cost of a little copper is a murderer, is the poor man just one degree above beggary also to be a murderer if he omits to invite the beggar to partake of his hard earned rice? Again: if the rich man is a murderer for refusing to save the beggar's life at the cost of a little copper, is he also to be a murderer if he refuses to save the beggar's life at the cost of a thousand rupees? . . .

It is indeed most highly desirable that men should not merely abstain from doing harm to their neighbours, but should render active services to their neighbours. In general, however, the penal law must content itself with keeping men from doing positive harm and must leave to public opinion, and to the teachers of morality and religion, the office of furnishing men with motives for doing positive good. It is evident that to attempt to punish men by law for not rendering to others all the services which it is in their duty to render to others would be preposterous.[14]

Given such considerations, the law attempts to limit a person's obligation to "be his brother's keeper." In general, the law says that we have obligations to render aid only to those to whom we stand in special relationships of responsibility—such as our children, parents, spouses, charges, and those whom we have harmed. For example, our "callous passerby," Roger Smith, in our list of moral dilemmas, would generally have no legal obligation in our society to rescue the teenage boy. (Whether he should have is, of course, another matter.) On the other hand, in a case that went before the Indiana Supreme Court in 1942 (*Jones v. State*), a defendant was held responsible for the murder of a twelve-year-old girl whom he had raped. The girl, distracted by pain and grief, fell or jumped into a creek where she drowned. The defendant abstained from rescuing her although he could have done so at no risk to himself. The Supreme Court of Illinois, affirming a conviction of second degree murder, declared, "Can it be doubted that one who by his overpowering criminal act has put another in danger of drowning has a duty to preserve her life?" If a person dies as a result of the neglect of that duty, the Court implied, such neglect can be said to be "the cause" of the resultant death.

So, we see, the law does not, as a matter of fact, consider the distinction between acts and omissions relevant in those cases where the person who omits to act has a special responsibility to the person who requires his aid. Clearly, this is the relationship of a doctor to his patient. I would suggest that, at least to some extent, the commonly invoked distinction between acts and omissions in the euthanasia issue stems from an uncritical importation of a general moral and legal doctrine to an area where it should have no application. The decision not

---

[14] Macauley and other Indian Law Commissioners, a penal code prepared by the Indian Law Commissioners (1837) quoted in Monrad G. Paulsen and Sanford H. Kadish, *Criminal Law and Its Processes* (Boston: Little, Brown, 1962), pp. 227–28 (omitted from the third edition).

to stop the young man's bleeding made in Lamerton's hospice should have been perceived as a decision to *kill* that young man as much as the decision of the rapist not to rescue his victim or of a mother not to feed her baby. Indeed, while the rapist may be said not to have intended the death of his victim, this cannot be said of those who refrained from stopping the man's bleeding in Lamerton's hospice. Clearly, they *wanted* the poor man to die in this instance. If, by some chance, the bleeding had stopped by itself this time, they would have been disappointed for, as they would have perceived it, this would have been simply a cruel postponement of the inevitable fatal hemorrhage.

THE CASE FOR ACTIVE EUTHANASIA

Underlying the pleas that have often been made for active euthanasia is the belief that it is not mere human consciousness that has value but "the quality" of that consciousness. As the advocates of active euthanasia see it, in many terminal illnesses the physical and mental anguish that often accompanies a slow death can strip life of any remnant of promise or beauty, making consciousness a personal injury and death a benefit. As many opponents of active euthanasia see it, however, there is always the possibility that beauty and meaning will be found in human consciousness, however filled with suffering. The supporters of active euthanasia will dismiss such romantic sentiments as, at times, quite unjustified, claiming that meaning and beauty is rarely found as a pernicious disease eats away at one's body and mind. Nevertheless, such a claim is not apt to convince their opponents who accept a much more optimistic attitude toward the value of human consciousness, in and of itself. We have reached at this point the moral bedrock of deep subjective feeling and commitment that rational argument builds upon but cannot easily alter. It is for this reason that arguments as to the "personal benefit" to be derived from acts of euthanasia tend to founder as divergent moral standpoints come into conflict.

The strongest case to be made for active euthanasia must be sought not in the notion of utility, but in the Kantian notion of rational self-determination. Those who believe that they can find meaning in the suffering of a terminal illness or who believe that consciousness itself is a "thing of precious beauty" should not be prevented from seeking that meaning or beauty, but neither should terminally ill individuals be forced to seek a meaning or beauty that they believe cannot be found. The immorality of refusing to accept a rational patient's voluntary plea to be afforded active euthanasia comes from the fact that we have no right to make him endure the physical and mental anguish of a terminal illness against his will, and from the cruelty of refusing to render him assistance in painlessly taking his life when he is incapable of doing it himself.

A NONRELIGIOUS CASE AGAINST EUTHANASIA

Professor Yale Kamisar of the University of Minnesota School of Law would object strongly to the preceding plea for voluntary active euthanasia. In a clearly written and cogently argued article,[15] Kamisar grants that "as an ultimate philosophical proposition, the case for voluntary euthanasia is strong."[16] As far as the patient is concerned, voluntary euthanasia, Kamisar admits, would be a morally justified course of action if the "person is *in fact* 1) presently incurable, 2) beyond the aid of any respite which may come along in his life expectancy, suffering 3) intolerable and 4) unmitigated pain and of a 5) fixed and 6) rational desire to die."[17] Although Kamisar does not deny that such cases exist,[18] nevertheless, "abstract propositions and carefully formed hypotheticals are one thing; specific proposals designed to cover everyday situations are something else again!"

The problem, as Kamisar sees it, is two-fold. First, although one can imagine cases of terminally ill patients for whom voluntary euthanasia would be the preferred mode of response, any law which attempts to specify the conditions under which euthanasia can be practiced is bound to be vague and subject to mistakes and abuse, resulting in the morally unjustified utilization of euthanasia in some instances. In order to protect potential victims of vague euthanasia laws, Kamisar is willing to sacrifice those who "*in fact* have no desire and no reason to linger on." Secondly, Kamisar fears that laws allowing for voluntary euthanasia will most likely lead to laws allowing the involuntary euthanasia of the feeble-minded, insane, and senile. Acceptance of the principal behind voluntary euthanasia that there is such a thing as a life not worth living tends to brutalize us, Kamisar claims, making it easier for us to "dispatch" all whom we find troublesome—as the Nazis did in their comprehensive euthanasia program. Let us consider these objections in greater detail.

First, Kamisar is quite skeptical of the standards that would be

---

[15] "Some Non-Religious Views Against Proposed 'Mercy-Killing' Legislation," 42, *Minnesota Law Review*, 969–1042 (1958).

[16] Kamisar does not make a distinction between active and passive euthanasia in his article. It would appear that his objections are meant to apply to both.

[17] Kamisar, "Against Proposed Mercy Killing," p. 975.

[18] He does not, on the other hand, explicitly affirm that they do. Taken literally, it is doubtful that cases fitting Kamisar's standard will be found. Certainly with the availability of pain-killing drugs, it is doubtful that anyone will suffer "unmitigated" pain. Similarly, in most cases, one cannot rule out the possibility that "a respite may come along" during the patient's lifetime, although one can often justifiably say that the chances of this happening are close to nil. Yet, it is most likely that Kamisar does not adhere too strictly to his standard and does admit, more loosely, that there are individuals who "have no desire and no (rational) reason to linger on."

utilized to determine when a patient's decision to choose euthanasia is a truly voluntary and rational one. In this context, Kamisar quotes with approval someone else's claim that those who advocate voluntary euthanasia expect the decision to be made "only if the victim is both sane and crazed by pain." Kamisar asks,

> By hypothesis, voluntary euthanasia is not be be resorted to until narcotics have long since been administered and the patient has developed a tolerance to them. When, then, does the patient make the choice? While heavily drugged? Or is the narcotic relief to be withdrawn for the time of the decision? But if heavy dosage no longer deadens pain, indeed, no longer makes it bearable, how overwhelming is it when whatever relief narcotics offer is taken away, too? . . .
>
> Even if the patient's choice could be said to be "clear and incontrovertible," do not other difficulties remain? Is this the kind of choice, assuming that it can be made in a fixed and rational manner, that we want to offer a gravely ill person? Will we not sweep up, in the process, some who are not really tired of life, but think others are tired of them; some who do not really want to die, but who feel they should not live on because to do so when there looms the legal alternative of euthanasia is to do a selfish or cowardly act? Will not some feel an obligation to have themselves "eliminated" in order that funds allocated for their terminal care might be better used by their families or, financial worries aside, in order to relieve their families of the emotional strain involved?[19]

In addition, Kamisar is skeptical of a patient's and his doctor's decision that his case is "hopeless." Under any euthanasia law, Kamisar believes, there are bound to be victims of euthanasia whose conditions would have improved had they lived. But even if laws could be precisely formulated to protect individuals from becoming unjustified recipients of euthanasia, Kamisar fears that voluntary euthanasia is likely to be but the "first wedge" to measures to which he is firmly opposed. Realizing that the wedge argument that something which is, in iteslf, not bad will lead to something worse and then to something worse yet is often an unwarranted one, Kamisar believes that the argument should not be taken too lightly in this instance since the "parade of horrors" that constituted the Nazi euthanasia program began with a program of the euthanasia of incurables.

> Even before the Nazis took charge in Germany, a propaganda barrage was directed against the traditional nineteenth-century attitudes toward the chronically ill, and for the adoption of a utilitarian . . . point of view. . . . Lay opinion was not neglected in this campaign. Adults were propagandized by motion pictures, one of which . . . deals entirely with euthanasia. This film depicts the life history of a woman suffering from multiple sclerosis; in it her husband, a doctor, finally kills her to the accompaniment of soft piano music rendered by a sympathetic colleague

[19] Kamisar, "Against Proposed Mercy Killing," pp. 986–87, 990.

in an adjoining room. Acceptance of this ideology was implanted even in the children. A widely used high school mathematics test . . . included problems stated in distorted terms of the cost of caring for and rehabilitating the chronically sick and crippled. One of the problems asked, for instance, how many new housing units could be built and how many marriage-allowance loans could be given to newly wedded couples for the amount of money it cost the state to care for "the crippled, the criminal, and the insane . . ." The beginnings at first were merely a subtle shift in emphasis in the basic attitude of the physicians. It *started with the acceptance of the attitude, basic in the euthanasia movement, that there is such a thing as life not worthy to be lived.* This attitude in its early stages concerned itself merely with the severely and chronically sick. Gradually the sphere of those to be included in this category was enlarged to encompass the socially unproductive, the ideologically unwanted, the racially unwanted, and finally all non-Germans. But it is important to realize that the infinitely small wedged-in lever from which this entire trend of mind received its impetus was the attitude toward the nonrehabilitatable sick.[20]

A Critical Reply

Kamisar's criticisms against voluntary euthanasia are helpful in making us focus upon the pitfalls of an overly zealous rush into the legalization of euthanasia, but they do not justify the total prohibition of laws allowing euthanasia that Kamisar advocates. First, Kamisar's skepticism over the possibility of formulating laws which require the voluntary and rational consent of a potential recipient of euthanasia is overdrawn. Given his hesitancy of counting as truly voluntary the pleas for euthanasia of a pain-racked patient, Kamisar should have carefully considered the possibility that the pain-racked patient before becoming ill may have signed a statement requesting euthanasia if he contracts an incurable disease or develops a totally disabling condition.[21] Yet Kamisar certainly does not give this case adequate consideration. In reply to the claim that "where a pre-pain desire for euthanasia is re-

---

20 Ibid., pp. 1031–32. Kamisar quotes this from Alexander, "Medical Science Under Dictatorship," *New England Journal of Medicine*, 241 (1949).

21 A way of doing this is by signing and having witnessed a "living will" provided (free of charge) by the Euthanasia Educational Council (250 W. 57th Street, New York, N.Y. 10019). Since active euthanasia is currently illegal, this document only relates to the utilization of "heroic" measures.

The idea behind a "living will" is gaining legal recognition. For example, the California legislature passed in 1977 a "Natural Death Act" which permits a competent adult to sign a directive authorizing physicians to withhold or discontinue "mechanical" or "artificial" life-support equipment if he or she is in a "terminal" condition and "death is imminent." (Notice that this bill does not deal with comatose patients whose deaths are not imminent.)

affirmed under pain there is the best possible proof of full consent,"
Kamisar has only the following to say:

> Perhaps. But what if it is alternately renounced and reaffirmed under
> pain? What if it neither is affirmed nor renounced? What if it is only
> renounced? Will a physician be free to go ahead on the ground that the
> prior desire was "rational" but the present desire "irrational"?[22]

After raising his questions, Kamisar lets the matter drop, nowhere
amplifying the "perhaps" admission he made prior to raising his questions. These questions[23] serve to sidestep us from the issue at hand
which is the bearing on the voluntariness of a terminal patient's decision for euthanasia *when* such a decision serves to reaffirm a similar prior
decision. Whatever we are to make of Kamisar's enigmatic answer of
"perhaps" to the question of whether such a decision should count as
a truly voluntary one, certainly such a decision should at the very least
strongly *count toward* the voluntariness and rationality of a person's
death-bed decision.

Furthermore, Kamisar is quite unjustified in his caricature of the
patient who opts for euthanasia as "sane, but crazed with pain." With
modern drugs, pain is rarely constantly "intolerable and unmitigated."
Even while in pain, terminal patients can often show a lucidity and
keenness of judgment that is often lacking in those embroiled in the
mundane and selfish cares of life. More fundamentally, Kamisar is wrong
in suggesting that euthanasia could only be the appropriate mode of
response for those suffering "intolerable and unmitigated" pain and
consequently in concluding that modern pain-killing drugs have to a
large extent obviated the need for euthanasia.[24] Although modern drugs
often can eliminate pain for long periods, they do so at high cost—the
cost of living long periods in a twilight state of wakefulness and drugged
stupor, while suffering various side effects of the drugs such as severe
nausea and vomiting. In addition to these side effects, there are other
miseries associated with terminal illnesses. For example, many terminal
cancer patients have to endure foul smelling malignant fungus-like
growths on their bodies and have to endure as well such miseries as

---

22 Kamisar, "Against Proposed Mercy Killing," p. 990.

23 These questions are subject to straightforward answers. If the prior decision
is renounced or alternately renounced and reaffirmed, euthanasia should not
be permitted. If the prior decision is neither affirmed nor renounced, one would
assume that the patient must (because of unconsciousness or some mental disability) be incapable of doing either. If this is the case, the prior decision should
be respected.

24 Kamisar does not mention that patients develop tolerances to narcotic pain-
killing drugs, necessitating larger and larger dosages for the same result. Sometimes the dosages required will considerably speed up the death of the patient or
induce it immediately. Some doctors are unwilling to administer such massive
dosages.

incontinence, obstruction of the bowels, and severe difficulty in swallowing. The process of slow death by illness, is, unfortunately, often a very ugly business. If severe physical pain is capable of justifying euthanasia, I do not see why these agonies cannot justify it too, especially when it is coupled with the suffering that comes from the realization of one's hopeless plight. I also do not see why it is inappropriate, as Kamisar suggests, for patients whose lives must continue at such personally costly prices to consider it to be an unjustifiable financial or emotional burden to impose upon their families. In addition, Kamisar fully neglects the much more common situation of terminal (but not "pain-racked") patients choosing to die rather than to continue with the extensive and debilitating treatments they have suffered through (such as cancer-leukemia patients). While some people might consider such refusals to continue with treatment justifiable since they involve passive and not active euthanasia, Kamisar's objection to euthanasia seems to cut across any such distinction.

The best protection against the unjustified self-sacrifice to euthanasia of those who are not hopelessly ill is the provision that concomitant to a patient's consent should be the judgment of several doctors that he is indeed suffering from such a disease or condition. Indeed, both the English and American Euthanasia Societies provide elaborate safeguards in their euthanasia proposals to insure, as much as possible, that the patient's consent is both informed and voluntary and that his condition is truly hopeless, given current medical knowledge. The American Euthanasia Society, for example, provides that a person over 21,

> "suffering from severe physical pain caused by a disease for which no remedy affording lasting relief or recovery is at the time known to medical science" petition for euthanasia in the presence of two witnesses and file same, along with the certificate of an attending physician, in a court of appropriate jurisdiction; said court to then appoint a committee of three, of whom at least two must be physicians, "who shall forthwith examine the patient and such other persons as they deem advisable or as the court may direct and within five days after their appointment, shall report to the court whether or not the patient understands the nature and purpose of the petition and comes within the (act's) provisions": whereupon, if the report is in the affirmative, the court shall—"unless there is some reason to believe that the report is erroneous or untrue"—grant the petition; in which event euthanasia is to be administered in the presence of the committee, or any two members thereof.[25]

25 Notice that the American Euthanasia Society, by requiring that a patient be "suffering from severe physical pain," does not make provision for those terminal patients whose pain can be deadened by pain-killing drugs, but only at a personally unacceptable cost or for those comatose patients who have suffered irreversible and major brain damage but have previously made their wishes for euthanasia in such a situation known. Cases such as these are also not included in the proposal of the British Euthanasia Society, which requires that a patient should be "suffering from a disease involving severe pain and of an incurable and fatal character."

Surprisingly, Kamisar, although quoting the provisions of both the American and English Euthanasia Societies, does not actually take a stand as to whether they provide sufficient safeguards against the mistake and abuse he fears. His main criticism is directed instead toward Glanville Williams' proposal for euthanasia as described in his book *The Sanctity of Life and the Criminal Law.* According to Williams, the safeguards of the Euthanasia Societies are too drawn-out and cumbersome in operation, and should be replaced by a much simpler proposal. According to Williams,

> The reformers might be well advised . . . to abandon all their cumbrous safeguards . . . giving the medical practitioner a wide discretion and trusting to his good sense. . . . The essence of the bill would then be simple. It would provide that no medical practitioner should be guilty of an offense in respect of an act done intentionally to accelerate the death of a patient who is seriously ill, unless it is proved that the act was not done in good faith with the consent of the patient and for the purpose of saving him from severe pain in an illness believed to be of an incurable and fatal character. Under this formula it would be . . . for the prosecution to prove that the physician acted from some motive other than the humanitarian one allowed him by law.[26]

Now, I would certainly agree with Kamisar that Williams' proposal is fraught with the danger of mistake and misuse. As Kamisar suggests, one's personal physician may not be "a sufficient buffer between the patient and the restless spouse or overwrought or overreaching relative, as well as a depository of enough general scientific know-how and enough information about current research developments and trends, to assure a minimum of error in diagnosis and anticipation of new measures of relief." One would expect that after dismissing Williams' proposal as being too apt to be misused, Kamisar would turn his attention to the particular provisions of the English and American Euthanasia Societies, but he does not. My own belief is that these proposals provide ample safeguards. It would seem to me that the legal machinery provided by the American Euthanasia Society is amply quick and potentially easy in operation. Indeed, the period of time (about one week) that would be required from the moment a patient gives his consent to the actual implementation of euthanasia is desirable in providing a period for reconsideration. The added pain and anticipation of death that potential euthanasia patients will face during that week is well worth the price.

A bill such as that proposed by the American Euthanasia Society is also the best protection against the possibility that a cure might exist or be found for a patient's apparently hopeless condition. One would expect that the doctors on the euthanasia committee would have full access to information as to any new medical research which might have

26 Glanville Williams, *Sanctity of Life,* pp. 339–40.

some bearing on a euthanasia applicant's case and this knowledge would be communicated to the patient and his doctors. Of course, as opponents of euthanasia are wont to stress, there is always the chance that a recipient of euthanasia could have been saved from some painful and terminal condition by a medical breakthrough that was not known at the time he was subjected to euthanasia. We should not, however, exaggerate this possibility. In the final stages of a terminal illness, it will practically always be too late for a treatment to be effective, especially a new one in the experimental stage. At any rate, it seems unjustified to me to refuse the pleas of the vaster number of people whom we would be condemning to needless pain, for the sake of the few whose lives would be unnecessarily taken, if euthanasia were made legal. At any rate, such a gamble is best left with the patient. For some, one chance in a thousand or even a million of a lifesaving breakthrough may be worth the wait, while for others, one chance in a hundred or even ten may not be worth the certain agony that the wait entails.

Let us turn now to Kamisar's contention that all proposals for voluntary euthanasia should be rejected, since, if enacted, they are likely to lead us down a "slippery slope" toward the involuntary euthanasia of the senile, retarded, and insane and, finally, the useless and unwanted. One must always be skeptical of "slippery slope" ("wedge") arguments such as this, many of which are fallacious. For example, during Roosevelt's New Deal days, Social Security was often criticized on the grounds that it would lead to greater and greater socialism, until the United States became a completely socialistic state. This does not seem to be happening, however. The "slip" from one socialistic measure to another is far from inevitable. The United States has proved to be much less inclined to embrace the socialistic measures that other western democracies such as Great Britain and the Scandinavian countries have, and there is every reason to believe that in the foreseeable future the economic choice for the United States will not be that of pure capitalism versus pure socialism, but rather one of proper balance in a mixed economy.

No doubt, as Kamisar claims, euthanasia laws would always be subject to misuse and overextension. This, however, is the case with all laws. For example, existing laws allowing for the civil commitment of the dangerously mentally ill and laws allowing for voluntary human experimentation are capable of grave misuse and overextension, and have, as a matter of fact, been misused and overextended. Yet few would suggest that such laws should be eliminated.

Although a slippery slope argument is often the last refuge of the doctrinaire conservative, such arguments cannot be dismissed out of hand and each must be considered on its own merits. Kamisar's impassioned invocation of a slippery slope argument in the context of the euthanasia issue clearly derives its force from the association of euthanasia with the Nazi experience. There are no good reasons, however, to think that contemporary proposals for voluntary euthanasia are at all likely to lead to any of the many Nazi horrors. The often brutal killings the

Nazis engaged in were justified on the basis of a cold-blooded social utility, often perceived on purely economic terms. Untroubled by any concern for individual rights, the Nazis had no principled objection to involuntarily taking the lives of the socially troublesome and useless. On the other hand, current-day advocates of voluntary euthanasia who perceive such action as a benevolent response to a suffering individual which, by requiring his voluntary consent, acts to maximize human freedom, would have to abandon their moral principles of individual justice and benevolence in order to embrace the Nazi practices of involuntary merciless killings. Granted that the Nazis often hid their merciless principles of social utility behind the cloak of benevolence, and that kindness, especially when divorced from consent, can often turn to cruelty, the horrors of the Nazi experience, rather than providing a path for us to follow, should act as a beacon bidding us to be more vigilant in establishing safeguards to prevent us from slipping away from principles of justice and kindness. The best safeguard for this is the informed consent of the euthanasia recipient.

The greatest danger of slipping into the Nazi practice of sacrificing human lives for nebulous and short-sighted visions of "the common good" comes from nonvoluntary euthanasia. As we have seen, the nonvoluntary euthanasia of defective newborn infants is not a threat that lurks in the future; it is, rather, an actuality. The law at present deals with this problem primarily by overlooking it. When it is forced by litigation to look, its decisions are not guided by adequate moral principles. For example, was it not wrong for the law to compel surgery on David Houle against his parents' wishes? On the other hand, was it not wrong for the law not to intervene in the Johns Hopkins case either to compel surgery or, at the very least, to compel that the child be killed directly and mercifully rather than indirectly and cruelly? While it is perhaps too much, given the widespread divergent moral sentiments in this area, to expect any general consensus of when nonvoluntary euthanasia is morally appropriate, consensus is much more likely on the extreme cases, and that is where we must begin.

Slippery slope arguments to the contrary, strong advocates of active voluntary euthanasia may very well change sides when it comes to a consideration of *particular* proposals for nonvoluntary euthanasia—for there are ethically relevant differences in the two cases. Given the need to observe the implications of our proposals in action and the widespread opposition that the thought of active euthanasia engenders in the minds of many, it is unwise to attempt to answer all questions at once. The answers to some questions are best left to the future, while we move cautiously forward a step at a time, ready to learn from experience and to adjust our ideas accordingly. Although the future will always be filled with pitfalls for the uncautious and self-deceived, our concern and fear of the possible future effects of our actions should never drive us into a paralysis of action that often seems to be the strict logic of many slippery slope arguments.

Let us also not lose sight of the fact that doctors, who are not especially trained in moral matters, are, as a matter of fact, presently making daily under-the-counter decisions concerning who should live and who should die. These decisions and the moral principles that are used to justify them should not be hidden from public scrutiny as they presently are, but discussed and debated in the open. The result of this process of public debate should be the creation of a law relating to euthanasia that doctors can respect and appeal to as a guide for their actions. The present widespread divergence between medical practice and professed moral and legal principle is a sham. Certainly, the current practice of surreptitious and conscience-salving actions of doctors should be replaced by an honest reliance on uniform legal principles, arrived at after careful public discussion and debate. Decisions relating to euthanasia may be easier when they are swept under the rug or delegated to doctors who often make their decisions behind closed doors, but this is a very poor way of arriving at good decisions.

If active euthanasia should never be made legal, we must ask ourselves why. Are we afraid, as Kamisar is, of the vagueness of possible euthanasia laws and the difficulties of their practical administration? If so, are such difficulties worse than the difficulties that now face us? If we are afraid, as Kamisar is, of introducing a principle into the law that "some lives are not worth living," we must face the fact that such judgments, as a matter of fact, implicitly come into play in decisions as to the extraordinariness of a given treatment. If we have a principled objection to active euthanasia that goes beyond these practical difficulties, we must scrutinize the rational basis of this objection. If our objection is a religious one, based on the belief in a divine prohibition against suicide, we must inquire as to its meaning and justification. (Is a person committing *suicide* when she refuses lifesaving treatment?) Even if we can find, as I think we cannot, some rational religious basis for an absolute moral prohibition against active euthanasia, we must ask ourselves if we have a right to impose our religious beliefs in this matter upon those who disagree. Does the value of human autonomy override whatever harm active euthanasia is likely to bring in its wake? Such are the questions that must be tackled if we are to come to a reasoned resolution of the euthanasia issue.

DISCUSSION QUESTIONS

1. Do you believe that a physically healthy individual's decision to commit suicide can ever be a fully voluntary and rational one? Consider, in particular, the possibility that someone very dear to you decides to commit suicide. Under what circumstances, if any, would you be willing to accept such a decision as voluntary and rational?

2. If you believe that the suicides of physically healthy individuals are sometimes justifiable actions, is it justifiable, nevertheless, that young

people be trained to believe that they have a moral obligation not to commit suicide and consequently to make people naturally disposed to feel guilty when they contemplate suicide? Would the consequences of removing the natural aversion to suicide be desirable or is there some middle ground?

3. Consider:

A: Infanticide is best capable of justification in the case of the very severely mentally retarded, for such individuals are not, and never can become, persons.

B: I don't agree. As long as such human beings are physically healthy, it is generally implausible to claim that death will be more of a benefit to them than their limited life. While you and I might prefer to be dead rather than to become severely mentally retarded, since we know the value of the mental capacity we would be losing, we have no right to claim that a severely mentally retarded person who knows nothing else would prefer death to life. On the other hand, I think infanticide is much more capable of justification in the case of mentally normal infants born with severe physical abnormalities. In such cases, death can be a benefit to an infant who faces the bleak prospect of continual physical suffering, made all the worse by her recognition of her sad fate.

What do you think?

4. Consider the following moving description of the agony hospital staffs endure when they are forced to watch the slow death of newborn infants whose parents refuse to consent to lifesaving surgery:

> . . . When surgery is denied [the doctor] must try to keep the infant from suffering while natural forces sap the baby's life away. As a surgeon whose natural inclination is to use the scalpel to fight off death, standing by and watching a salvageable baby die is the most emotionally exhausting experience I know. It is easy at a conference, in a theoretical discussion, to decide that such infants should be allowed to die. It is altogether different to stand by in the nursery and watch as dehydration and infection wither a tiny being over hours and days. This is a terrible ordeal for me and the hospital staff. . . . (Shaw, A., "Doctor, Do We Have a Choice?" *The New York Times Magazine,* January 30, 1972, p. 54).

Do you think hospital staffs would feel less agony if such infants were quickly and painlessly put to death by some lethal injection? Is this the right thing to do in such situations? Why or why not?

5. In cases where the state will incur the cost of lifesaving treatment for a newborn infant as well as the cost of lifelong institutionalization should it survive, do you think the state should ever have the right to refuse to pay for such treatment even if the parents would want it performed?

6. Joseph Fletcher, a Protestant spokesman for voluntary euthanasia writes,

> A commission of American Protestants recently concluded that the mass extermination of civilians by atom bomb blasts can be 'just,' although many members of the commission would hesitate to agree that fatal suffering could be ended righteously for one of the victims burned and charred externally and internally, not even as a response to the victim's pleas.

Fletcher thinks that such a view is morally absurd. How do you think the commission members would have defended their view? Do you find this defense plausible? Why, or why not?

7. Consider:

A: It would have been so much better if the doctors had given Father a lethal injection to end his misery. We all knew that there was no hope. The cancer had spread too far. Instead, Father was left to die a slow, painful, and undignified death.

B: If the doctors had given Father a lethal injection, it would not have been the cancer which killed him, as it did, but the injection they administered. It's one thing for doctors not to interfere with a disease process that is killing a person and consequently to let that person die, but it is something quite different for a doctor to initiate a death-producing causal process. You can't expect doctors to play the role of executioners.

A: If doctors are to be perceived as "executioners" when they give terminally ill patients lethal injections, they should be seen as executioners when they refuse to act to prolong a terminally ill patient's life out of a desire to spare him the additional agony that the prolongation of his life would entail. At any rate, if Father's doctors did not want to take the responsibility of directly killing him, they should have left some lethal pills for Dad to swallow himself, with our aid.

B: While I am willing to admit that there are cases where active euthanasia is preferable to passive euthanasia, it would be too dangerous to accept a general practice of active euthanasia. Such a practice runs too great a risk of undermining respect for human life.

A: I admit that the acceptance of a general legal rule, permitting active euthanasia in particular circumstances, is fraught with difficulty and the potential for misuse, but it seems to me that there is at least as much difficulty and potential for misuse in attempting to hold fast to the absolute prohibition of active euthanasia. In our overriding desire to prevent unjustifiable active euthanasia, we tend to assume much too readily that the distinction between active and passive euthanasia carries more moral weight than it does. Consider, for eample, the Mongoloid infant who was denied a simple operation and was allowed to starve to death.

B: Clearly, one needs to restrict the range of legally permissible passive euthanasia, but this is much easier than attempting to restrict the range of legally permissible active euthanasia. No doubt, you are quite right that there are cases where active euthanasia is justifiable and even more cases where it is excusable, but these are still relatively exceptional cases. It is quite important that we see these cases as exceptional ones that *defy our normal moral universe.* As jurists have often observed, "hard cases make bad law." In these hard cases, juries often rightfully refuse to punish those who engage in mercy killings, in spite of what the law says. That's the way it should be.

A: While juries often find those who commit mercy killings "temporarily insane," this is usually dishonest since most so acquitted were mentally competent and morally responsible at the time of their act. A verdict of this sort is simply a convenient way of refusing to apply an overly broad general rule. Rather than countenance this dishonesty, it would be better to modify the general rule.

Critically discuss.

8. Do you think voluntary euthanasia should be restricted to those who are dying from some terminal illness or should it be allowed in other situations as well? If so, when? If euthanasia is to be restricted to the "dying," how would you define this concept?

9. Which of the following legal alternatives do you favor? Why?

    a. Doctors should be legally permitted in certain circumstances to actively kill their patients.

    b. Doctors should not be legally permitted to actively kill their patients, but should be allowed to provide patients who are terminally ill and mentally competent with the means to take their own lives.

    c. Doctors should be legally prohibited from assisting suicide but should not have a legal duty to take precautions to prevent terminally ill and mentally competent patients from committing suicide (such as by making it difficult or impossible for the patient to disconnect his oxygen bottle).

    d. Doctors should have a legal duty to take precautions to prevent patients, even if terminally ill and mentally competent, from committing suicide.

10. Do you favor the American Euthanasia Society's proposal for active euthanasia? Would you modify it in any way?

11. Consider:

A: In 1971, Delores Heston, 22 and unmarried, was severely injured in an automobile accident in New Jersey. While incoherent herself, her mother informed the hospital that Delores was a Jehovah's Witness and would be opposed to a blood transfusion but not to the surgery the doctors said was necessary. In spite of the lack of consent, the hospital successfully petitioned to get legal permission for the transfusion. The surgery and transfusion were performed and Delores recovered. On appeal (*John F. Kennedy Memorial Hospital v. Heston*), the New Jersey Supreme Court affirmed the lower court decision on the grounds that "there is no constitutional right to choose to die." As the court saw it, a Jehovah's Witness who refuses a lifesaving blood transfusion is attempting suicide. Since attempted suicide is a crime in New Jersey, the court reasoned that Jehovah's Witnesses do not have a right to refuse blood transfusions. The court saw no relevant legal or moral distinction in "passively submitting to death and actively seeking it." This was a mistake. Miss Heston did not want a blood transfusion, but *she did not want to die*. Consequently, her act should not be seen as suicidal.

B: I don't think it's as easy as that. In a sense, one could say that practically all those who attempt suicide would prefer to live *if only the prospects of their lives were better*. Mrs. *X*, for example, may decide to take her life after her husband has died and her children have abandoned her, only because life under such conditions appears unbearable to her. Nevertheless, she would not want to die if she felt there was somebody who really cared. Just as Miss Heston did not want to live at the price of a blood transfusion, so Mrs. *X* does not want to live at the price of being alone. You and I may think that Mrs. *X*'s act is "irrational," but this is a purely subjective statement of personal preference; Mrs. *X* has as much right to her opinion as we do to ours. If Jehovah's Witnesses should be allowed to choose death rather than life at an unbearable price, so should those who base their choice on nonreligious grounds.

C: There is a morally relevant difference in the two cases. In Mrs. *X*'s case, death is actively chosen, whereas in the case of Miss Heston, it was simply accepted as a byproduct of the intention to avoid doing evil—remember the principle of the double effect.

D: I think we also make a distinction in the two cases because we believe there is a good chance that we can—and should try to—get through to Mrs. *X* and persuade her to see things differently. Consequently, we tend to see her as blinded by depression and see her suicidal choice as not a truly voluntary one. On the other hand, we are willing to take Miss Heston's choice as a voluntary expression of her "true self" and do not feel justified in trying to dislodge her religious convictions.

E: I'm not at all sure what Miss Heston really wanted. I remember reading that deep down, many Jehovah's Witnesses really want to be forced to submit to lifesaving blood transfusions. This way they can both live and be free of the responsibility of making what they take to be a sinful choice. Consequently, they are relieved when doctors take the burden of responsibility off their shoulders. This is certainly a possibility we should not lightly dismiss.

Critically discuss.

12. Should lifesaving blood transfusions be imposed on Jehovah's Witnesses with dependent children on the grounds that they have an obligation to care for their children? Why, or why not?

FURTHER READINGS

ABELSON, RAZIEL, and MARIE-LOUISE FRIQUEGNON, eds., *Ethics for Modern Life*, chapter 2. New York: St. Martin's Press, 1975. This anthology contains an abridged version of Kamisar's article in the *Minnesota Law Review* and an abridged version of Glanville Williams' reply to it in the same journal.

AQUINAS, ST. THOMAS, *The Summa Theologica of St. Thomas Aquinas*, part II, question 64: "Of Murder," pp. 195–212. London: Burns, Oates and Washbourne Ltd., 1929. The classic Roman Catholic position on the morality of homicide and suicide.

BEHNKE, JOHN A., and SISSELA BOK, eds., *The Dilemmas of Euthanasia*. Garden City, N.Y.: Anchor Books, 1975. An anthology of clear and nontechnical articles on the historical, sociological, medical, and legal aspects of euthanasia directed to a wide lay audience. Especially informative are the articles by lawyers David Meyers and Norman Cantor on the legal issues surrounding voluntary and nonvoluntary euthanasia. These articles, as well as the others in this anthology provide a valuable factual background for conceptual analysis and moral appraisal of the euthanasia issue.

HUME, DAVID, "Of Suicide," in *Essays, Moral, Political, and Literary*, pp. 585–96. London: Oxford University Press, 1963. Hume's classic argument for the morality of suicide. Hume is especially concerned with refuting the view that suicide is a crime against God, but he also argues that it is not necessarily a violation of our duties to society or to ourselves.

KAMISAR, YALE, "Some Non-Religious Views Against Proposed 'Mercy-Killing' Legislation," *Minnesota Law Review*, 42 (1958), pp. 969–1042. An influential and clearly written argument against euthanasia on nonreligious grounds.

KANT, IMMANUEL, "Suicide," in *Lectures on Ethics*. New York: Harper & Row Pubs., 1963. Kant's classic argument that suicide is always wrong. As Kant defines it, one commits suicide only when one acts with "the intention to destroy oneself." Using this definition, Kant does not count as suicidal a decision to fight against one's enemies even though one knows that this will result in one's death, as long as one does not fight with the desire (purpose) that one die.

KOHL, MARVIN, ed., *Beneficent Euthanasia*, Buffalo, N.Y.: Prometheus Books, 1975. An excellent anthology of articles pro and con on the issue of euthansia by philosophers and experts in the fields of theology, law, and medicine.

KUBLER-ROSS, ELIZABETH, *On Death and Dying*. New York: Macmillan, 1974. Kubler-Ross is a psychiatrist who has devoted herself to psychotherapy with dying patients. This book is a report of her observations on the psychological processes the terminally ill go through in learning about and accepting their terminal condition. Reading a psychiatrist like Kubler-Ross's description of the despair that terminally ill patients often experience will tend to undercut Kamisar's naive caricature of the terminally ill patient who requests euthanasia as being "pain-crazed."

LADD, JOHN, ed., *Ethical Issues Relating to Life and Death*. New York: Oxford

University Press, 1979. An anthology of essays by contemporary analytic philosophers on the conceptual and moral issues connected with euthanasia. Most of the essays are highly abstract and directed to the philosophically sophisticated.

MAPPES, THOMAS A., and JANE S. ZEMBATY, *Social Ethics: Morality and Social Policy*, chapter 2. This anthology contains an abridged version of Kamisar's article in the *Minnesota Law Review* and an abridged version of Williams's reply to it in the same journal. Also included is an excerpt from Justice Muir's judicial decision refusing to grant the Quinlans' request that their daughter Karen be freed of a mechanical respirator helping her to breathe. Included, too, is an article by James Rachels, arguing for the position that there is no morally relevant distinction between killing and letting die and a criticism of this article by Tom Beauchamp.

RAMSEY, PAUL, *Ethics at the Edges of Life*, part II, New Haven, Conn.: Yale University Press, 1978. An analysis of the euthanasia issue (including specific legal cases) by a very influential contemporary religious moralist who is especially interested in problems in medical ethics. Like much of Ramsey's work, this book is incisive and thought-provoking, but, at times, convoluted and vague. Secular moralists will also find Ramsey's underlying religious moral perspective too dogmatic. In addition, the general reader may be disconcerted to find that much of Ramsey's discussion is directed to criticisms of the writings of others. In spite of these drawbacks, I highly recommend this book for serious students of the euthanasia issue. Unlike the polemic quality of much of the writing on euthansia, one is bound to learn from Ramsey's book.

WILLIAMS, GLANVILLE, *The Sanctity of Life and the Criminal Law*, chapters 7 and 8. New York: Knopf, 1957. A clearly written discussion of the historical and legal background and moral arguments relating to suicide and euthanasia by a legal scholar who advocates their decriminalization (including the "unselfish abetment of suicide").

WILLIAMS, GLANVILLE, " 'Mercy-Killing' Legislation—A Rejoinder," *Minnesota Law Review*, 43 (1958), pp. 1–12. Williams's reply to Kamisar.

7

Racial and Sexual Discrimination and the Problem of "Reverse Discrimination"

The civil rights movement of the early 1960s has served to bring the question of discrimination to the fore of the American consciousness. Blacks, women, and other groups who perceive themselves as oppressed, cry out for the equality that the American dream promises all but does not seem to deliver. Their pleas often strike a sympathetic chord upon the consciences of a wide spectrum of white affluent males who share their equalitarian ideals and admit that the future should see a much greater participation of women and minority groups in those occupations in our society that have up until now been almost exclusively the domain of white males. Rather than complacently accepting the fruit of generations of discrimination, they are willing to make amends. But how is this to be done? What does our society owe to groups who have been treated unjustly in the past and carry the legacy of that injustice today? Should they be compensated for the injustices of the past? If so, what form should that compensation take, how great should it be, and how long should it last? Is it right to compensate people at the price of temporary injustice or inequality to others? Is it right for a white man to be penalized today for the injustices perpetrated against women and the nonwhite in the past, even though he himself may not have participated in or profited from those injustices himself? Can preferential treatment of individuals who are victimized by the lingering effects of prior discrimination be squared with the constitutional provision for "equal treatment"? Can we sacrifice some degree of present equal treatment for a greater equality in the future? Is that "fair"? If it isn't, can the social utility that may result from efforts to eliminate discrimination outweigh the injustice of those efforts? Such is a sampling of the questions that face us today as we ponder the advisability of "affirmative action programs," as their proponents tend to call them, or "reverse discrimination," as their opponents tend to label them. These questions are, of course, the most fundamental of moral ones, but as is often the case in debates over complex moral issues, positions on this matter tend to be defended by appeal to moral principles which, though reflecting legitimate strands of our collective moral common sense, seem to point us in conflicting directions. Uncritically accepting our own moral principles and neglecting those of our opponents, we fail to come to grips with their meanings, implications, and presuppositions. It is this essential task which will occupy us in this chapter.

THE EQUALITARIAN IDEAL: EQUALITY OF OPPORTUNITY

In its most basic and ordinarily used form, the concept of justice is associated most closely with that of equality. The central idea here is that justice demands that we *treat like cases alike.* Since any given case will resemble other cases in some respects and differ from them in others, until it is established what resemblances and differences are *relevant,* the command to treat like cases alike remains merely the empty form of a principle, devoid of specific content. As the current debate over the relevance of race or sex in deciding who is to be admitted into certain professional schools or occupations indicates, people can strongly disagree as to which characteristics are relevant and which are irrelevant.

Deeply a part of the American ethic, however, is the belief that justice requires equality of opportunity. At the core of this ethic is the view that competition for the most desirable positions in our society should be a fair and open one in which all participants are afforded equal access to educational opportunities and other social benefits. When this is so, we believe, it is only fair that individuals should go as far as they can and be rewarded differentially in accordance with their *individual merit.*

There are, however, serious difficulties with this basic equalitarian ethic. First, as is often pointed out, the ideal of equal opportunity in this country is certainly not a reflection of the social realities of our society. Although we proudly proclaim the equalitarian ideal of equal access to educational and social benefits, it is clear that the rich reap much more of these benefits than the poor. As such, a great deal of competition in our society is unfair. Since the advantages of inherited wealth or the disadvantages of inherited poverty create gross inequalities in opportunities to compete, it is unfair to expect persons from deprived, poverty stricken backgrounds to compete equally with those from affluent, highly advantaged backgrounds. This commonplace criticism, as we shall see, is at the very heart of the arguments utilized by those who support affirmative action programs. Less obvious, however, is the problem of *natural,* as opposed to socially induced, inequalities, for just as poverty can work against an individual, so too can innate biological handicaps. While we say that "people are born equal" and often interpret this to mean that most people are born with the same or insignificantly different abilities, this, many would say, is simply not the case.

The question of the relative infleunce of "nature" (heredity) and "nurture" (environment) in developing one's personality and abilities has been a perennial philosophical one. Nevertheless, it would be generally conceded that the contribution of inborn abilities or predispositions cannot be fully discounted and that these inborn characteristics which depend on "the luck of the genetic draw" create advantages for some and disadvantages for others. Given the undeserved inequalities of environment and inborn abilities, is it not unfair to base financial rewards on achievement? The proper indicator of one's individual merit, it has been said, should be effort, not achievement. From this point of view, a truly just society which cannot eliminate the inequalities of genetic or environmental factors would have to reward people not on what they accomplish, but on how hard they work to accomplish what they do.[1] For example, Edward Bellamy, in his novel *Looking Backward* (1889) imagines a society where all workers receive the same salary for doing their best, regardless of what they actually accomplish. Just as citizens today of Communist China or of an Israeli kibbutz, the citizens of Bellamy's imagined community are motivated to do their best not by the promise of higher financial rewards but by their devotion to the common good, by feelings of patriotism and pride and by the desire for recognition. Karl Marx, too, envisioned a society where reward would not be based on achievement. For Marx, however, the principle of proper distribution in such a society was not to give each person the same share of the benefits of that society, for some people needed those benefits more than others. The proper principle of distribution, he believed, was that each person should receive in proportion to his need. As Marx put it, "from each according to his ability, to each according to his need."

As Bellamy and Marx realized, the often quoted equalitarian view that people *deserve* to be rewarded in accordance with achievement is built on the presuppositions of equal environmental opportunity and equal natural ability. If either of these two presuppositions is denied, it becomes reasonable to deny that justice or fairness demands that one be rewarded in accordance with one's achievement. From this point of view, it is plausible to think that justice demands that people should in some way be compensated for their undeserved disadvantages which prevent them from fairly competing with others. As we shall see, such a claim is

---

1 But even this, some will claim, is not "just" since the effort people exert is itself dependent upon hereditary and environmental conditions which "one does not choose." (Recall our discussion of the hard deterministic view in the chapter on free will.)

often made by those who defend affirmative action programs where the focus is on environmental disadvantage. One should not forget, however, that individuals also suffer from inherited disadvantages as well. If a person can rightfully demand compensation for being poor, can he not also rightfully demand compensation for being born a moron? Is this not equally a demand for justice? Similarly, if we have a moral obligation to eliminate as best we can environmental inequalities that contribute to differing abilities, do we equally have a moral obligation, once genetic engineering becomes technically possible, to eliminate genetic differences which contribute to differing abilities?

Another grave difficulty with the view that justice demands that individuals be rewarded in terms of their merit lies in the fact that one's conception of meritorious qualities is culture-bound and dependent upon shifting social needs and desires. What would be considered meritorious qualities in one society may not be so considered in another society. For example, Abdul-Jabbar's undeniable merit as a basketball player would have gone unrecognized at the Court of Versailles. Consequently, "having merit," at least to some extent, implies being lucky enough to be in the right place at the right time. As the products, services, and forms of entertainment of a society change, so too do those qualities which are deemed meritorious and, for that reason, subject to special reward. One's conception of "merit," especially in a free enterprise system, is especially vulnerable to the vicissitudes of supply and demand. As many new Ph.D.s entering the teaching profession and aerospace engineering in the early 1970s poignantly discovered, qualities that were up until then considered quite meritorious and, as such, qualifications for prestigious jobs in our economy, no longer seemed to be in demand and consequently no longer were a badge of merit or a key to special rewards. Since such individuals may have worked very hard to obtain their Ph.D.s and could not reasonably have been expected to anticipate the new "glut of Ph.D.s" that hit the American economy in the early 1970s, they certainly did not see their plight as a just one.

RACIAL AND SEXUAL DISCRIMINATION

Since justice demands that individuals be treated equally unless some *relevant* difference exists which can justify their unequal treatment, if individuals are treated differently on the basis of irrelevant differences, an injustice has been committed. While it is often claimed today that it is unfair to deny jobs to individuals simply because of their race or sex, this statement is too strong. For example, we would not think it unfair to restrict parts in some play or movie to people of a particular race or sex. Similarly, sex is clearly decisive in determining who should be hired as a wet nurse. Apart from such special cases, it would generally be conceded that race or sex is not a relevant ground, in and of itself, for excluding individuals from most positions in our society. Nevertheless, some would claim that while individuals cannot rightfully be excluded from the desirable positions of our society simply on the basis of their race or sex, *as a matter of biological fact* the race or sex of an individual often has an important bearing on his or her ability to perform well in these positions. For example, according to the philosopher Aristotle, it is man's "nature" to rule, while it is woman's "nature" to be ruled.

Sexual Equality: The Argument from Nature

Aristotle's sexist view is still shared by many people. For example, it is not uncommon to hear people say today, "No woman should ever be President of the United States; women are too emotional for such responsibilities." Such a claim reflects the still common belief that the sex of an individual is very highly correlated with psychological characteristics and, as such, may be used as an indicator of an individual's capacity to perform certain tasks. As a result of this belief women are often treated unequally in our society.

This belief is, however, currently the subject of heated controversy. On one side of this controversy are those who, like Aristotle, believe that there are various psychological differences between the sexes which are biologically caused and make women "by their very nature" unequal to men in certain significant respects. On the other side, there are those who, like John Stuart Mill in the nineteenth century,[2] deny either that such sexual psychological differences exist, or if they do exist, that they are inborn. According to the latter claim, whatever psychological differences exist between the sexes is caused by environmental factors. From this point of view, if it is true that women tend to be considerably less aggressive than men, this is a result of the fact that society encourages or pressures women to accept passive roles while men are encouraged or pressured to accept more aggressive roles. Therefore, these differences are artificially induced and are not based on any natural sexual inequalities.

Such a claim is, however, challenged by those who argue for the existence of fundamental biological differences in the sexes which result in differing psychological attributes. For example, according to psychoanalytical views, a person's experience of his or her own body has an important affect on personality development. Some psychiatrists have drawn analogies between genitals and sex roles. Since a vagina, they say, is passive and a penis is aggressive, this naturally leads women to see themselves as passive, while men see themselves as aggressive. The argument has also been made that certain hormonal differences in the sexes make men inherently more aggressive than women. For example, Steven

[2] Mill was an early strong defender of women's rights. While a member of the English Parliament, he submitted the first bill on the enfranchisement of women to the House of Commons. His essay "The Subjection of Women" is a classic feminist defense.

Goldberg defends this thesis in his book *The Inevitability of Patriarchy*. As Goldberg sees it, man's inherent greater aggressiveness guarantees male domination of the high status roles in society. Furthermore, according to Goldberg, if society did not attempt to socialize women away from competing with men for such roles, then although some women would be aggressive enough to succeed in the competitive struggle, the vast majority of them would be failures—socialized to desire high-status positions but incapable of achieving them. As Goldberg puts it,

> . . . one need merely consider the result of society's *not* socializing women away from competitions with men, from its *not* directing girls toward roles women are more capable of playing than are men or roles with status low enough that men will not strive for them. No doubt some women would be aggressive enough to succeed in competitions with men and there would be considerably more women in high-status positions than there are now. But most women would lose in such competitive struggles with men . . . and so most women would be forced to live adult lives as failures. . . . Now I have no doubt that there is a biological factor that gives women the desire to emphasize maternal and nurturance roles, but the point here is that we can accept the feminist assumption that there is no female propensity of this sort and still see that a society must socialize women away from roles that men will attain through their aggression. For if women did not develop an alternative set of criteria for success their sense of their own competence would suffer intolerably.[3]

Even if we assume that Goldberg is right that there are innate hormonal differences between the sexes which account for significant psychological differences, he does not establish his point that our society *should enforce the acceptance of sex roles* where women are socialized to be passive and not aggressive. Even if one assumes with Goldberg that women will *tend* to lose out in the competitive struggle with men for high-status positions, it requires more argument to show that women would *on the whole* be happier if they were socialized away from the desire to compete with men for these positions than they would be if they were encouraged instead *to make their own choices* as to the roles they would like to follow, free of any social encouragement or pressure. If there are significant psychological differences in the inherent aggressiveness of the sexes, as Goldberg claims there are, it is natural to expect that women would tend to freely choose the less aggressive roles in our society, without any external force having to be applied. Indeed, Goldberg concedes this point, but he does not seem to perceive the possibility that nature itself will see to it that those women who are most likely to lose out in the competitive struggle for high-status positions would not choose to enter that struggle without any social encouragement or pres-

[3] Steven Goldberg, *The Inevitability of Patriarchy* (New York: Morrow, 1973), p. 107.

sure. As Mill so aptly put it in "The Subjection of Women," "The anxiety of mankind to interfere in behalf of nature, for fear lest nature should not succeed in effecting its purpose, is an altogether unnecessary solicitude."

One should not lose sight of the fact that if there are natural psychological differences in the sexes which make women on the whole less aggressive than men, this will not be *universally* the case. Although women *may on the average* be less aggressive than men, there will be some women who turn out to be quite capable of successfully competing with very aggressive men for those roles in our society which require such attributes. It is far from clear that society has a right to systematically deny these roles to those women who would be quite capable of winning a free competitive struggle for them for the benefit of those women who would not be so capable. First, one could argue that even if Goldberg is right that women as a whole would be worse off if they were not socialized away from competition for these positions, it is unfair, and for that reason wrong, to penalize those women who would succeed in the competitive struggle for the benefit of the greater number who would not (that is, one could assume a deontological standpoint where the value of justice outweighs the disutility of a social practice). From this perspective, justice demands that each individual be judged on the basis of individual merit and not on the basis of the average psychological makeup of that individual's sexual group.

Furthermore, Goldberg's utilitarian claim that the lack of socially enforced sex roles is apt to result in a lesser quantity of happiness for women as a whole than would be obtained were these sex roles socially promoted is more complex than he makes it appear. According to Goldberg's utilitarian argument, in order to maximize the happiness of women a society would have to encourage women to accept the view that it is their nature to be less aggressive than men and, consequently, that it would be unwise for them to compete with men for the high-status positions in our society. Goldberg's conclusions would follow, however, only if one assumes that the happiness that would be gained by socializing women away from unsuccessfully competing with men for high-status positions would be greater than the happiness that would be lost to those women who are socialized away from entering a competitive struggle they could have won and otherwise would have entered. There is, however, as far as I know, no evidence that would support (or refute) such a claim. Goldberg's argument seems to me to rest more on an act of faith than on any scientific fact, and as such tends to lend support to the contention that arguments from nature for male dominance in our society function as myths for making this dominance acceptable to male and female alike. At the very least, our commitment to the value of individual autonomy should be strong enough to require that any person who advocates restricting free choice on utilitarian grounds should have the burden of providing strong evidence that the consequences of such a restriction would indeed contribute to "the greatest good for the greatest number." This is a burden that has not been met, as far as I can see, when it comes to encouraging social acceptance of sex roles.

Racial Equality:
The Nature versus Nurture Question

Just as those who defend male dominance of the positions of influence in our society rest their claim on alleged innate biological differences between the sexes, those who defend racial subjugation point to alleged innate differences to account for the alleged superiority or inferiority of certain races. For example, the typical justification for Negro slavery in this country rested on the belief that Negroes suffered from a genetically inherited racial inferiority which accounted for their childlike and irresponsible natures. Given this widely accepted stereotype of the "essential nature of the Negro," slavery could be perceived as a benevolent institution which provided the Negro with the fully protective environment that was essential for his survival in a "civilized society." This view of genetic Negro inferiority was the predominant one among educated as well as uneducated whites in this society until the early twentieth century. Its influence began to wane, however, as the environmentalism of the developing behavioral sciences gained influence in educated circles in the late 1920s and 1930s and became the predominant view in these circles in the 1940s and 1950s. The tendency, during this period, was to deny the validity of the typical "Sambo" personality of the black man as docile and loyal but irresponsible and lazy, humble but chronically given to lying and stealing. Instead an emphasis was placed on the black man's courage and rebelliousness against strong odds. By the 1950s and 1960s, it was generally taken as beyond question that the innate inferiority of the Negro had been fully discredited by modern science and that blacks differed at birth from whites only in color pigmentation. As Kenneth Stampp put it in his influential study of slavery, *The Peculiar Institution* (1956), "Negroes are, after all, only white men with black skins, nothing more, nothing less."

Not, all, however, shared Stampp's view that the "Sambo" personality was a pure myth created to justify Negro subjugation. Given the environmental intellectual temper of the times, scholars who believed that the "Sambo" personality was not a pure myth but reflected some truth about the "typical" Negro personality during and after slavery in this country turned to environmental explanations of its source. It was claimed, for example, that this personality type was a direct result of the "savage" environmental conditions of African tribal life. Yet anthropological observations of the energy, resourcefulness, and dignity of African tribal life tended to undercut such a perspective. In addition, although such noble Negro qualities did indeed tend to be crushed for those Negroes who became slaves in the United States, this did not seem to be the case in Latin America and the West Indies. Why was this? According to Stanley Elkins in his influential book *Slavery* (1959), it was the

American slavery system itself which created the "Sambo" type. Borrowing the sociological concepts of "role theory," Elkins claimed that the American Negro during slavery, unlike his Latin American counterpart, tended to display the typical "Sambo" characteristics because in the United States, unlike in Latin America, this was the only role the Negro would be rewarded for playing. Since he was rewarded for playing up to the role of a person who was incapable of being trusted with the full privileges of freedom and adulthood, the American Negro tended to display these characteristics which could then in turn be used as evidence for his inherent inferiority and as a justification for his continued subjugation.

Throughout the 1960s, the view that there was a genetic base for differences in the abilities of members of various races was almost universally rejected in academic circles. In 1969, however, Arthur Jensen published an article[4] which asserted that blacks as a group have lower I.Q.s than whites. In this and later articles, Jensen elaborated his view that the mean black I.Q. is about 15 points (one standard deviation) below that of whites. Heredity, Jensen claimed, accounts for some 80 percent of I.Q. variance, while environment (including prenatal environment) accounts for only 20 percent. Since such a claim struck at the very heart of the faith of the equalitarian liberalism of the 1960s, Jensen's article was widely and vehemently denounced in academic circles. Yet Jensen too had his supporters,[5] and a new round in the nature versus nurture debate began in the 1970s.

There are good reasons for one to be skeptical of the claims that are now being made again about the inherent intellectual inferiority of blacks. Similar claims were made not long ago about other minority groups, only to be finally refuted. For example, in the early days of I.Q. tests, immigrant Poles, Russians, and Jews were found to score on the average about 25 or 30 points lower on these tests than the Nordics from Northwestern Europe. Such a fact fueled the belief that there was a genetic reason for such differences. But as these various supposedly in-

---

[4] "How Much Can We Boost IQ and Scholastic Achievement?" *Harvard Educational Review*, 39, 1–123.

[5] In particular, see William Shockley, "Dysgenics, Geneticity, Raceology: A Challenge to the Intellectual Responsibility of Educators," *Phi Delta Kappan*, January 1972, 297–307 and R. Hernstein, *I. Q. in the Meritocracy* (Boston: Little, Brown, 1973). Shockley, Hernstein and Jensen's concerns are, however, quite different. Jensen's main concern has been with ways of changing the educational system. Shockley has been concerned with what he calls "dysgenics"—that is, the genetic downbreeding of the population. As he sees it, the less able elements in society tend to breed faster than the more able elements, producing more and more offspring who cannot take their productive place in a technological society. Hernstein's concern has been with the implications of the equalitarian ideal of providing equal environmental opportunities to all. As Hernstein sees it, if all environmental inequalities were removed and individuals freely competed for the best jobs on the basis of *individual merit,* then occupational level and social class level would ultimately be determined solely by the genes, resulting in a *meritocracy* of inherited social class based on genetics.

tellectually inferior minority groups became assimilated into American culture, the I.Q. differences disappeared. As environmentalists have charged, standard I.Q. tests may be culturally biased ones that are slanted to favor the sort of conceptual abstract thinking that is a product of the environmentally enriched and not disadvantaged home.

Nevertheless, it is important that we realize that there are quite a few very competent people who would strongly take issue with the standard liberal dogma that a society that provided equal environmental opportunities to all would be a society in which all the various racial and ethnic groups would be represented in the different sectors of our economy in proportion to their percentage of the total population. This is a quite questionable assumption not only on genetic grounds but also on the basis of cultural differences in values and styles of living. Such cultural differences can be greatly diluted in the United States "melting pot" but they do not tend to disappear fully. Since many people who have the opportunity to assimilate themselves into the more diffuse mainstream of American culture often voluntarily choose to remain faithful to their older cultural traditions, it is doubtful that mere equality of opportunity would eliminate these cultural differences and whatever other differences they bring in their wake.

However, even if different racial or ethnic groups would "naturally" gravitate to different professions or sectors of the economy, it would be unjust to deny particular individuals equal environmental opportunities and the chance to compete for particular positions on such grounds. However much heredity or cultural differences account for differing abilities, there will be some members of all racial and ethnic groups who would succeed in the competitive struggle if they were given a chance. Jensen, for example, is explicit in his commitment to equal opportunity for individuals regardless of their racial heritage. In an interview with the psychologist Richard I. Evans, Jensen declares,

> I'm a strong advocate and always have been of equal opportunity, of civil rights. I've been opposed to racial or social class segregation. I believe in treating people in terms of their own individual characteristics, rather than in terms of their group membership. . . . every person is a unique combination of genes. Your genetic background can produce so many different combinations even within one family . . . that you have to think of yourself in terms of what you, yourself, are and not in terms of your origins. I think it's racist thinking to think of yourself in terms of your group or your ancestry: What about a Japanese fellow, say, who's six feet three inches. Should he worry about the fact that the Japanese population as a whole is shorter than, say, the Scandinavian population as a whole? He's six feet three inches, which is tall enough to be a basketball star. Now if he were five feet four inches, he'd never make it as a basketball star, not because he's Japanese, but because he's five feet four inches. It's the same thing in the intellectual realm.[6]

[6] Richard I. Evans, *The Making of Psychology* (New York: Knopf, 1976), p. 65. Even if one accepts Jensen's sincerity in being committed to equal opportunity, his research can still be criticized—see question 14 on p. 335.

THE QUESTION OF "PREFERENTIAL TREATMENT" FOR VICTIMS OF SOCIAL INJUSTICE

Introduction

As a result of the Civil Rights Act of 1964, federal and state governments have embarked upon various affirmative action programs which aim at eliminating discrimination and improving the condition of disadvantaged minorities[7] in our country. At first, these programs aimed at eliminating deliberate barriers which denied to some minority groups the opportunities that were afforded others. In addition, there was an attempt to root out the more subtle types of discrimination that are often not recognized as such. For example, it has often been suggested that standards which might be good predictors of performance for members of one group might turn out to be poor predictors of performance for other groups. Similarly, attention has often been directed to the unfair utilization of beliefs that race and sex are correlated with other features that would seem to justify discriminatory practices. For example, it has been said that it is unfair to discriminate against a woman on the grounds that, unlike a man, she would be likely to eventually have child care or other domestic responsibilities which would limit the time she could devote to her job.

In addition to the various governmental programs which aimed at eliminating explicit and more subtle discriminatory practices, there was the general realization that certain minority groups should be compensated for the educational, social, and economic disadvantages that made it impossible for them to equally compete with others who were provided greater opportunities. Fairness dictated that minorities that were denied equal opportunities in the past be provided these opportunities now. Such was the underlying sentiment behind the federal affirmative action program launched by Lyndon Johnson in 1965. As President Johnson put it,

> You do not take a person who, for years, has been hobbled by chains and liberate him, bring him up to the starting line of a race, and then say, "You are free to compete with all the others," and still justly believe that you have been completely fair.

Educational programs were instituted, such as the federal "Headstart" program, which attempted to provide prekindergarten learning ex-

---

[7] As we shall later discuss, the meaning of "disadvantaged minority" and the groups it refers to is itself a subject of debate. As this term is usually used, it is taken to refer to blacks, Spanish Americans, American Indians, and, at times, women. Often no distinction is made as to the relative degree of disadvantage of individuals within these groups; instead, merely belonging to one of these groups is taken to qualify an individual for a special affirmative action program.

periences to economically disadvantaged children, and the New York State "Seek" program, which provided free college preparatory courses and allowances for economically disadvantaged high school graduates who were judged capable of doing college work but would not ordinarily gain admittance to colleges in New York on the basis of their grades and test scores.

Since such remedial programs did not seem to result in any appreciable and immediate minority participation in the various professions and skilled trades, some governmental programs encouraged the hiring of members of minority groups or their admission into educational programs on the basis of criteria other than those normally used. This generated widespread criticism. It was unfair, the critics protested, to attempt to remedy the injustices of the past by utilizing unfair discriminatory practices in the present. Individual merit, such individuals protested, should be the only standard utilized in deciding who should receive jobs and positions in professional schools. Just as it would be wrong to prevent a person from obtaining a job or being admitted to a professional school simply because he or she was a member of some minority group, it would be wrong, they argued, to favor certain minorities at the expense of more qualified candidates. It was especially wrong, such critics affirmed, to guarantee groups a set number of places in some trade or professional school. Affirmative action "goals," they asserted, had the tendency in practice to become unfair "quotas." The idea of "racial quotas," seemed especially immoral to many members of other minority groups, such as Jews, who were themselves in the past often denied jobs or admission to professional schools on the basis of quotas. If some individuals are to be rewarded on the basis of quotas, they argued, others must necessarily be unjustly penalized as a result of these same quotas.

On the other hand, those who defended "preferential treatment" or specific quotas for minority groups saw such programs as morally justified for various different reasons. For some, such programs were seen as a just way of compensating individuals or groups for past injustices or for present disadvantages stemming from past injustices. Others saw the requirements of justice in a different light. While being willing to admit that such programs would indeed result in injustices being perpetrated against individuals for some period of time, they saw such programs as an essential means for eliminating the injustices of the past and for that reason as morally justifiable. Still others saw such programs as justifiable on purely utilitarian grounds. As they saw it, such programs were required as a means of bringing about certain future goods, such as providing for diversity of ideas in the various professions or as a means of providing "role models" for disadvantaged minorities to help break the grip of self-fulfilling expectations that they cannot succeed in certain areas.

The conflict over what "justice" or "utility" requires in the setting of standards for allocating scarce jobs or openings in professional schools has become a politically explosive one which fuels the passions of both those who demand their "fair share" of the American dream and those who see themselves as unjustly threatened simply on the basis of their race or sex. Such treatment, they argue, is contrary to the equal protection guaranteed every American by the Fourteenth Amendment of the Constitution. It is precisely this claim that was put before the Supreme Court in the cases of Alan Bakke and Brian Weber, cases that have generated much controversy and have divided groups that pride themselves on their commitment to justice for minority groups. It would be instructive, however, if we turn our attention first to the case of Marco DeFunis who, in 1971, filed a lawsuit against the University of Washington Law School, claiming that he had been unfairly and unconstitutionally denied admission on the basis of the fact that he was a white male. Appealed through the court system, this case (*DeFunis v. Odegaard*) became the first "reverse discrimination" case to come before the United States Supreme Court.

The DeFunis Case

In his lawsuit against the University of Washington Law School, DeFunis contended that he had been denied admission to the law school while minority applicants, defined on racial standards, who were less qualified by virtue of lower college grades and lower Law School Admission Test scores were admitted. This, he claimed, was contrary to the Fourteenth Amendment which provides that "[No state may] deny to any person within its jurisdiction the equal protection of the laws." The Washington trial court that heard DeFunis's case ruled in his favor and granted an injunction enabling him to enroll in the University of Washington Law School. On appeal, however, the Washington State Supreme Court reversed the lower court decision, ruling in favor of the University of Washington Law School's admission policy.

In defending this judgment, the court contended first that it was quite reasonable for a law school to depart from a "mechanical" consideration of test scores and grades when considering minority applications, for this

> . . . does not always produce good indicators of the full potential of such culturally separated or deprived individuals, and that to rely solely on such formal credentials could well result in unfairly denying to qualified minority persons the chance to pursue the educational opportunities available at the University.

Although the test scores and grades of minority applicants admitted to the Law School were generally lower than those of many rejected applicants, their records, nevertheless, showed that they were qualified to compete in the law school program, the court declared. In addition, the court continued, the University did not violate DeFunis's right to equal protection under the Fourteenth Amendment by granting preferential treatment to certain racial categories of applicants. In defense of this claim, the Court pointed out that according to Supreme Court decisions, racial classifications are not always unconstitutional. Indeed, according to *Brown v. Board of Education*,[8] there are times when race must be utilized by public educational institutions as essential to bringing about racial balance in the schools. While a racial classification is a "suspect classification" subject to "strict scrutiny," such a classification is legitimate constitutionally when its utilization is essential to some "compelling state interest."[9] The utilization of racial classifications in the admission policy of the University of Washington Law School was indeed essential for a "compelling state interest," the court declared, asserting,

> It can hardly be gainsaid that the minorities have been, and are, grossly underrepresented in the law schools. . . . we find the state interest in eliminating racial imbalance within public legal education to be compelling. . . .
>
> The legal profession plays a critical role in the policy making sector of our society. . . . That lawyers, in making and influencing those decisions, should be cognizant of the views, needs, and demands of all segments of society is a principle beyond dispute. The educational interest of the state in producing a racially balanced student body at the law school is compelling.
>
> Finally, the shortage of minority attorneys—and, consequently, minority prosecutors, judges, and public officials—constitutes an undeniably compelling state interest. If minorities are to live within the rule of law, they must enjoy equal representation within our legal system.

[8] In this momentous 1954 decision, the Supreme Court addressed itself to the question of whether "segregation of children in public schools solely on the basis of race, even though the physical facilities and other 'tangible' factors may be equal, deprive the children of equal educational opportunities." Claiming that segregated schools are "inherently unequal" and consequently contrary to the equal protection clause of the Fourteenth Amendment, the Supreme Court answered, "yes."

[9] As interpreted by the courts, the equal protection clause of the Fourteenth Amendment limits the types of classifications states can utilize in determining how to distribute their various benefits and burdens. In most cases, as long as there is some "rational relationship" between the classification utilized and a permissible legislative purpose, the courts, in deference to the legislative judgment of the states, have allowed classifications to stand, even when there might be good evidence that some other type of classification would better serve their purpose. However, when a classification infringes on a basic constitutionally guaranteed right, the courts look harder at whether a legitimate purpose exists and whether the classification serves that purpose. In such cases, the classifications are said to be "suspect" and subject to the "strict scrutiny" test. According to this test, a state has the burden of showing that its classification "is the least restrictive means toward furtherance of a compelling state interest." As far as the issue at hand is concerned, some claim that the racial and ethnic classifications utilized in special admissions programs should be subjected to the "rational relationship" test, while some claim that they should be subjected to the stiffer "strict scrutiny" test. Yet others claim that some intermediate standard of appraisal should be utilized.

In reply to the claim that a minority admissions policy is not necessary for the achievement of these objections, the court replied,

> It has been suggested that the minority admissions policy is not necessary, since the same objective could be accomplished by improving the elementary and secondary education of minority students to a point where they could secure equal representation in law schools through direct competition with nonminority applicants on the basis of the same academic criteria. This would be highly desirable, but 18 years have passed since the decision in *Brown v. Board of Education* . . . and minority groups are still grossly underrepresented in law schools. If the law school is forbidden from taking affirmative action, this underrepresentation may be perpetuated indefinitely. No less restrictive means would serve the governmental interest here.

DeFunis appealed the Washington Supreme Court's decision to the United States Supreme Court which heard the case in 1974 and in a 5 to 4 decision declared the case moot since DeFunis was, at that time, in his last quarter at the law school and as such did not stand to gain from a favorable verdict.

The Bakke Case

In 1973 and again in 1974, Alan Bakke, a white, thirty-six-year-old civil engineer, applied for admission to the medical school at the University of California at Davis, but was rejected. Since Davis, during these two years had accepted minority students whose college averages and test scores were considerably lower than his, Bakke went to court, claiming that the University of California had denied him admission, while granting admission to less qualified students, solely on the grounds that he was white. This, he charged, was a violation of the equal protection clause of the Fourteenth Amendment. In particular, Bakke claimed, it was unconstitutional for the U.C. Davis Medical School to put aside a quota of 16 out of its 100 places in its first-year student body for minority group applicants.[10]

[10] Applicants to medical schools are required to take the Medical College Admissions Test which consists of four tests (verbal, quantitative, general information, and science). Alan Bakke's scores on the tests and his average were quite high relative not only to "minority" admittees, but also to regular admittees. For example, in 1973,

	Overall GPA	Verbal	Quanti- tative	Science	General Information
Alan Bakke	3.51	96	94	96	72
Averages of Regular Admittees	3.49	81	76	83	69
Averages of Special Admittees	2.88	46	24	35	33

The University of California filed a cross-complaint, asking the court to determine that their special-admissions program was valid. Minority group status, the University contended, was only one factor out of several in the selection process. In particular, minority students were considered for admission under the special minority program only when they suffered from financial disadvantage. Granting that some minority admittees may have been less qualified than nonminority rejectees such as Bakke, the University asserted that this program nevertheless served a "compelling state interest." This was so, the University argued, in that the minority program served to promote diversity in the student body, to expand the opportunities for medical education to minorities who came from economically and educationally disadvantaged backgrounds, to provide for greater representation of minorities in the medical profession, and to increase the number of doctors serving the minority community. Since such purposes, the University contended, served a "compelling state interest," the special admissions policy instituted to achieve them did not violate the equal protection clause of the Fourteenth Amendment. Furthermore, the University contended that racial classifications should be seen as "suspect classifications" requiring "strict scrutiny" only when they result in "invidious discrimination." Using the courts' own standard of "invidious discrimination" as the utilization of a method of classification which "excludes, disadvantages, isolates, or stigmatizes a minority or is designed to segregate the races," the University contended that white applicants denied admission were not so stigmatized.

In September 1976, the California Supreme Court ruled (6 to 1) that the University of California's special admissions programs for minorities at the Davis Medical School was unconstitutional. The court ordered the program abolished and that Bakke be admitted to the Davis Medical School. The California Supreme Court, by reputation one of the most liberal in the country, declared that the equal protection clause of the Fourteenth Amendment is incompatible with granting preferential treat-

---

While test scores and grade point averages were by far the most important factors considered for nonminority applicants, the Davis Medical School's Admissions Committee also took into consideration an applicant's extracurricular and community activities, his work experience, his personal comments on his application, and the two letters of recommendation that each applicant is required to have submitted on his behalf. After considering these factors, the Admissions Committee determined whether the applicant showed sufficient promise to warrant a personal interview. (Bakke was interviewed both years that he applied. It has been claimed that his age was a strong factor in his rejection.) In addition to the regular admissions procedure, the university operated the "special admissions program" which, although described simply as one whose aim is to "increase opportunities in medical education for disadvantaged citizens," had been used only to aid "minority" group students. Students identified as "minorities" (black, Chicano, American Indian) were placed in a separate admissions pool to compete only against each other for the 16 places reserved for them.

ment to individuals on the basis of their race.[11] Agreeing that the use of racial criteria in the University of California special admissions programs would be constitutional if a "compelling state interest can be demonstrated and there are no viable nonracial alternative methods available," the court ruled that the University of California had not, as a matter of fact, exhausted alternative methods of achieving its legitimate goal of greater minority enrollment. Among such alternative methods, the Court suggested, would be more aggressive recruitment of "fully qualified" minority applicants, remedial educational programs, lessening the emphasis on grades for all students, or increasing the number of medical school places. If such methods should, however, prove inadequate, it would be permissible for the University to grant preferential treatment to students on the basis of educational and economic disadvantage, but not race, the Court declared.

It was "abundantly clear," the Court declared, that whites suffered a grievous disadvantage "when they were excluded from the University's Medical School on racial grounds." The fact that they were not also "invidiously discriminated against in the sense that a stigma was cast upon them because of their race" was irrelevant. In reply to those who claimed that racial classifications may be used for "benign" or "favorable" purposes, the Court replied that the special admissions program was not benign to Bakke and other nonminority applicants who were denied admission as a result of it. There should only be one standard utilized for all 100 places at the Davis Medical School, the Court contended. Because he was white, Bakke was unable to compete for the 16 places reserved for minority applicants. This was wrong, the Court declared. Bakke was entitled to have his application evaluated without regard to his race or the race of any other applicant.

Given the California Supreme Court's ruling on Bakke's behalf, the University of California appealed to the United States Supreme Court. Let us turn to a brief summary of the arguments presented by the University of California and by Bakke to the Supreme Court and to the Supreme Court's resolution of this case.

The University of California's Position

Utilizing the same standard that it presented to the California Supreme Court, the university claimed in its brief to the U.S. Supreme Court that the Fourteenth Amendment does not prohibit "race-conscious

11 In the sole dissenting opinion, Justice Matthew O. Tobriner upheld the university's position, claiming that the court ought to distinguish between "invidious" and "benign" racial classifications. "Our society cannot be completely color blind in the short term if we are to have a color-blind society in the long run," he wrote. The "benign" racial classifications utilized by the special admissions program were used not to exclude any particular racial group "but to assure that qualified applicants of all racial groups were actually represented in the institution." Consequently, they were not a violation of the Fourteenth Amendment, Tobriner agrued.

state action that is neither hostile or invidious, and which is closely tailored to achieving a major public objective." Even though the Davis Medical School does provide quotas on the number of white students it admits, it does not discriminate against them in a manner precluded by the Fourteenth Amendment, for such quotas do not "stigmatize them as inferior." The special admissions program, furthermore, is not unfair, as some have contended, allowing unqualified students to enroll at the expense of qualified ones, but simply exercises discretion among groups of qualified students who differ by degree. No persons are admitted under the special minority admissions program unless they are deemed qualified to succeed in the professional programs.

If increasing minority enrollment is a legitimate public objective, as even the California Supreme Court conceded, there simply is no way to achieve this goal other than through the use of racial classifications, the University of California argued. In particular, the California Supreme Court's suggestion that it should open its special admissions program to all disadvantaged students regardless of race, "founders on the rock of reality," the University contended. The problem is that far more low-income whites apply for medical and law schools than low-income members of minority groups. For example, the University cited a study by the Association of American Colleges showing that in 1976, of medical school applicants from families earning less than $10,000 annually, 71 percent were white and 29 percent were members of minority groups. Indeed, if the University of California were to open its special enrollment program to all disadvantaged students, the figures would be even more strongly slanted against minority groups, as the University would find itself swamped with the applications of an "enormous number of whites who do not now apply because they know their grades are too low." In addition, disadvantaged whites not only far outnumber disadvantaged minorities, but also tend to outperform them in grades and admission test scores. Attributing the lower academic performance of blacks to the inferior and segregated schools they are often forced to attend, the University argued that being black should not be equated for moral purposes with being poor, for it is blacks and not the poor who "have been compelled by unconstitutional laws to attend segregated and inferior schools."

Bakke's Position

The arguments presented to the Supreme Court supporting Bakke fell into two groups. First, there were those who claimed that the Fourteenth Amendment requires state-run professional schools to choose among their applicants solely on the basis of their "individual qualifications," without any consideration being given to their race or ethnic background. Bakke was denied his Fourteenth Amendment right to be considered on his merits as an individual since the Davis Medical School admitted minority students who were clearly "less qualified" than he, as evidenced by Bakke's far superior academic credentials.

Not all who supported Bakke, however, claimed that only the "most qualified," as judged by academic credentials, should be admitted to medical and law schools. For example, Reynold H. Colvin, a Bakke attorney, in oral argument before the Supreme Court, conceded under questioning that, in his opinion, the Davis Medical School's special admissions program would be constitutional if it aimed at aiding all disadvantaged students and not only those who are members of minority groups. According to this line of reasoning, considerations of *compensatory justice,* can override the principle of rewarding people according to *individual merit* based on academic credentials, but the equal protection clause of the Fourteenth Amendment prohibits the direct utilization of racial standards in any admissions policy. What general category of "disadvantage" then should warrant compensation? For most who took this point of view, including Colvin, the relevant category was that of economic disadvantage, while for others, this category should be conceived more broadly, to include the disadvantages that result from racial segregation and racial prejudice as well, as long as such factors are not considered exclusively.

The Supreme Court's Decision on the Bakke Case

On June 28, 1978, the Supreme Court of the United States presented its ruling in the Bakke case. First, it ruled 5 to 4 that the admissions program at Davis was unlawful and ordered Bakke admitted. Second, it ruled 5 to 4 again (but with a different majority) that race may properly be considered a factor in admissions programs. Justice Lewis Powell had a pivotal role in this decision, joining Justices Stevens, Rehnquist, Stewart, and Burger in striking down the Davis program and in ordering Bakke admitted, but leaving their fold to join Justices Brennan, Blackmun, Marshall, and White in permitting universities to consider race as an element in their admissions policies.

As Stevens, Rehnquist, Stewart, and Burger saw it, there was no need to consider the constitutionality of Davis' admissions program under the equal protection clause of the Fourteenth Amendment since this program was unlawful under Title VI of the Civil Rights Act of 1964. Although the words of the Fourteenth Amendment may be open to different interpretations, the directive of Title VI, they declared, "is crystal clear" in forbidding federally funded universities from "excluding individuals on the ground of race, color, or national origin." Since the University of California could not meet the burden of proving that Bakke was not excluded on the basis of his race, he should be admitted, the Stevens-Rehnquist-Stewart-Burger bloc declared.

On the other side, Justices Brennan, Blackmun, Marshall, and White claimed that the Davis admissions program was legal under both Title VI of the Civil Rights Act and the equal protection clause of the Constitution since it was an essential means for remedying "societal discrimination" against blacks and other minorities. As these justices saw it, university admissions policies which place some weight on an applicant's racial or ethnic background are unlawful only when they serve to "stigmatize" or "stamp as inferior" a particular group of people. This, they declared, is not the case with the admissions policy employed at Davis, which legitimately attempts to overcome "the handicap of past discrimination" and to remedy the "substantial and chronic underrepresentation of minority groups in medical school."

Justice Powell began his opinion with a discussion of Title VI of the Civil Rights Act. Believing that the types of racial classifications prohibited under Title VI are exactly those prohibited under the equal protection clause of the Fourteenth Amendment, Powell then turned his attention to the equal protection clause. He began by rejecting the view that this clause should be taken as directed only to certain minority groups who are deserving of more protection than others, declaring that "the guarantee of equal protection cannot mean one thing when applied to one individual and something else when applied to a person of another color." On this basis, Powell strongly rejected the University of California's argument, accepted by the Brennan, Blackmun, Marshall, and White bloc, that the Court should adopt the view "that discrimination cannot be suspect [of a violation of the equal protection clause of the Fourteenth Amendment] if its purpose can be characterized as benign [that is, if it does not 'stigmatize' and serves some legitimate purpose]." The equal protection clause is not framed in terms of "stigma," he stated:

> [This notion] reflects a subjective judgment that is standardless. All state-imposed classifications that rearrange burdens and benefits on the basis of race are likely to be viewed with deep resentment by the individual burdened. The denial to innocent persons of equal rights and opportunities may outrage those so deprived and therefore may be perceived as invidious. . . . One should not lightly dismiss the inherent unfairness of, and the perception of mistreatment that accompanies, a system of allocating benefits and privileges on the basis of skin color and ethnic origin.

Powell then went on to point out that the "white majority" is itself a collection of minorities, many of whom were themselves subjected "to a history of prior discrimination at the hands of the state and private individuals." There is no principled basis, he declared, for deciding which groups should merit "heightened judicial solicitude" and which should not under a special minority admissions program. Davis, for example, was unable to explain why it had singled out only those minority groups that it did, Powell noted.

Nevertheless, Powell was not willing to rule out consideration of race and ethnic status entirely. Instead, he took the view that although the Constitution protects all individuals from discrimination on the grounds of race and ethnic background, it is still possible for universities to utilize such classifications as a factor in their admissions programs. Such classifications, he claimed, are "suspect ones," which require "strict scrutiny."[12] Powell then went on to consider the various goals proposed by the University of California as justifications for its special minority admissions program, rejecting as unconstitutional all but the goal of obtaining a diverse student body. Universities have a "countervailing constitutional interest" to select those students who will contribute the most to the "robust exchange of ideas," he declared.

Powell did not, however, accept the view that the goal of a diverse student body can be constitutionally achieved by the utilization of racial and ethnic quotas which, he believed, place too much emphasis upon race and ethnic background to the exclusion of other relevant factors. Racial and ethnic origin is but a "single element" in the "far broader array of qualifications and characteristics" that contribute to academic diversity, he asserted. As examples of these other qualities, Powell mentioned unique work experience, leadership potential, maturity, demonstrated compassion, and a history of overcoming disadvantage. Although race may properly be considered by universities in judging who should be admitted, a university must "adhere to a policy of individual comparisons" as opposed to a method that results in a systematic inclusion of certain groups. In such an individualized, case-by-case process, "the file of a particular black applicant may be examined for his potential contribution to diversity without the factor of race being decisive when compared, for example, with that of an applicant identified as an Italian-American if the latter is thought to exhibit qualities more likely to promote beneficial educational pluralism," Powell wrote. Since the Davis admissions program "prefers the designated minority groups at the expense of other individuals who are totally foreclosed from competing for the 16 special admissions seats," it is unconstitutional, Powell declared. Powell then went on to commend the Harvard College admissions program which attempts to recruit a diverse student body without setting any racial or ethnic quotas. At Harvard, Powell approvingly pointed out, "the race of an applicant can tip the balance in his favor, just as geographic origin or life spent on a farm may tip the balance in other candidates' cases." Such a program, unlike the one employed at Davis, Powell noted, does not insulate "the individual from comparison with all other candidates for the available seats."

Powell's opinion in the Bakke case is a logically fragile one. While Powell sees a major difference between the admissions program employed at Harvard College, which utilizes race and ethnic background as *a factor* to be weighed in a university's admissions policy, and the admissions

---

[12] The Brennan-White-Marshall-Blackmun bloc rejected both the strict scrutiny and rational relationship standards, utilizing instead the intermediate standard that racial and ethnic classifications "must serve important governmental objectives and must be substantially related to achievement of these objectives."

program employed at Davis which utilizes racial and ethnic *quotas*, this difference is, as Justice Blackmun described it, "a thin and indistinct one." Indeed, Justice Brennan suggested that it is entirely illusory, writing:

> There is no sensible and certainly no constitutional distinction between, for example, adding a set number of points to the admissions rating of disadvantaged minority applicants as an expression of the preference with the expectation that this will result in the admission of an approximately determined number of qualified minority applicants and setting a fixed number of places for such applicants. . . . there is no basis for preferring a particular preference program simply because, in achieving the same goals that the Davis Medical School is pursuing, it proceeds in a manner that is not immediately apparent to the public.

Brennan has logic on his side. There is no justification for saying, as Powell does, that admissions programs that utilize racial quotas violate *individual rights,* while this is not true of admissions programs that consider race as a factor. Clearly, in the latter programs, as long as race counts, nonminority students, who would otherwise have been admitted, will lose places to minority students. As such, race will be an admissions handicap to nonminority students. Until one knows how much race is to count in such programs, one will be unable to determine whether nonminority students will be better off under such programs where their race is a handicap for all positions than they would be under programs where it will be no handicap for a smaller number of positions. If admissions programs which consider race as a factor do not necessarily violate the individual rights of applicants, as Powell claims, then neither should racial quotas.

In its self-description of its admissions program, Harvard College declared,

> a truly heterogeneous environment . . . cannot be provided without some attention to numbers. . . . 10 or 20 black students could not begin to bring to their classmates and to each other the variety of points of view, backgrounds, and experience of blacks in the United States. Their small numbers might also create a sense of isolation among the black students themselves. . . . Consequently, when making its decisions, the Committee on Admissions is aware that there is some relationship between numbers and achieving the benefits to be derived from a diverse student body, and between numbers and providing a reasonable environment for those students admitted.

So numbers do matter at Harvard College after all! Does Harvard then do covertly what Davis does overtly? Although Justice Powell concedes the possibility that flexible university admissions programs can be utilized to disguise racial and ethnic quotas, he is willing, he tells us, to presume that universities will operate on "good faith." But what this means when the standard they are supposed to use is itself terribly vague he does not at all suggest. It is clear, however, that Powell is concerned with *what appears to be just* to the general public as well as with what actually is just. After telling us that the Davis admissions policy "will be viewed as inherently unfair by the public generally, as well as by applicants for admissions to the state university," Powell goes on to quote from the late Supreme Court Justice Frankfurter that "Justice must satisfy the appearance of justice." Is the great virtue of the Harvard program, then, not that it *is* more just than the Davis program, but that it merely *appears* that way to the general public?

The Weber Case

On June 27, 1979, a year after its Bakke decision, the Supreme Court spoke again on the issue of reverse discrimination in the case of *United Steel Workers of America v. Brian F. Weber*. In this less heralded, although potentially more significant case, a majority of the Supreme Court ruled that private employers are acting within the law when they utilize racial quotas to "eliminate conspicuous racial imbalance in traditionally segregated job categories," even though they are not guilty themselves of racial discrimination.

The Weber case had its roots in a 1974 agreement between Kaiser Aluminum & Chemical Corporation and the United Steelworkers of America to initiate on-the-job skilled-craft training programs at 15 Kaiser plants, open to unskilled Kaiser workers. Prior to these programs, Kaiser hired as skilled workers only those who had prior craft experience. Because they had long been excluded from craft unions, few blacks had such experience and consequently were greatly underrepresented among Kaiser's skilled workers. For example, in the plant in Gramercy, Louisiana, where Weber was employed as an unskilled worker, only 2 percent of the skilled craftsmen were black, even though blacks comprised 39 percent of the local work force. The Kaiser training programs were initiated to overcome this racial imbalance. Black craft hiring goals were set for each Kaiser plant equal to the percentage of blacks in the respective local labor forces. In order to achieve this goal, each training program was to reserve 50 percent of its openings for blacks (until the goal was met), with black and white applicants to be selected on the basis of their relative seniority within their racial groups. When Kaiser announced that it was offering a total of 9 positions in three of these on-the-job training programs at the Gramercy plant, Weber applied for all three programs, but was not selected. When he learned that 2 of the 5 successful black candidates had less seniority than he, Weber brought suit in the U.S. District Court of Louisiana, alleging that use of the 50 percent minority admission quota to fill vacancies in Kaiser's craft training programs violated Title VII of the Civil Rights Act. The section of Title VII that speaks directly to this issue provides that

> It shall be an unlawful employment practice for any employer, labor
> organization, or joint labor-management committee controlling
> apprenticeship or other training or retraining, including on-the-job
> training programs to discriminate against any individual because of his
> race, color, religion, sex, or national origin in admission to, or employment
> in, any program established to provide apprenticeship or other training.

Both the U.S. District Court and Appeals Court agreed with Weber, prohibiting further use of Kaiser's racially based training program. As these courts saw it, while employers who have themselves utilized racially discriminatory employment or promotional policies may be compelled by a court to compensate the victims of these discriminatory policies, Title VII forbids employers who are not guilty of racial discrimination from using race as a factor in deciding whom to employ or promote. A majority of the Supreme Court disagreed.

Since the Weber case did not involve state action, the Supreme Court did not turn, as it had in the Bakke case, to a consideration of the Fourteenth Amendment's equal protection clause. Instead, it turned to the narrower legal question of whether Title VII prohibits the use of Kaiser's racially based training program. In a 5 to 2 decision, the Supreme Court ruled that it did not. (Justices Powell and Stevens excused themselves from this decision.) Justices Brennan, Marshall, Blackmun, and White who took the position in the Bakke case that the utilization of racial quotas in universities is constitutional were joined by Justice Stewart. While Justice Stewart, along with Justices Burger, and Rehnquist, had claimed in Bakke that the Civil Rights Act prohibits the use of *state imposed* racial quotas, Stewart's position in the Weber case indicated that he did not see the Civil Rights Act as prohibiting private employers from voluntarily utilizing racial quotas to redress racial imbalance. Burger and Rehnquist strongly disagreed.

The Supreme Court's Weber decision came as a relief to many large companies who were unsure of the legality of their affirmative action programs. On one hand, they found themselves pressured by the federal government—through the fear of loss of federal contracts—to increase the number of their minority employees. On the other hand, the district and appeals court in Weber ruled that they could not grant special preferences to underrepresented groups unless they had discriminated against these groups in the past. If they did not admit to this discrimination and proceeded, nevertheless, to grant special racial preferences, they invited legal suits for reverse discrimination from passed-over whites. Yet, if they admitted prior discrimination, they invited suits from the alleged victims of their previous discrimination. Clearly this situation was intolerable.

Justice Brennan wrote the majority opinion in the Weber case. While admitting that a "literal interpretation" of Title VII would prohibit the Kaiser training program, Brennan claimed that such an interpretation would be inconsistent with the spirit behind the Civil Rights

Act—the advancement of blacks in the American economy. In defense of his contention that Congress did not intend that Title VII prohibit employers with racially imbalanced work forces from granting preferential treatment to racial minorities, Brennan pointed to the fact that Title VII does have a section which explicitly provides that nothing contained in Title VII "shall be interpreted to require any employer . . . to grant preferential treatment to any [racial] group." If Congress intended not to *permit* as well as not to *require* employers to grant preferential treatment to underrepresented racial minorities, it could easily have said so. Since it did not, Brennan argued, "[t]he natural inference is that Congress chose not to forbid all voluntary race-conscious affirmative action."

Rehnquist began his sarcastic 37-page dissent (about three times the length of Brennan's majority opinion) by comparing Brennan's reading of Title VII to George Orwell's novel *1984,* where government officials distort the meanings of words to make them conform to shifting government policies. While Kaiser's racially discriminatory admission quota is flatly prohibited by the plain language of Title VII, and as such should make it unnecessary to inquire into the usually murky question of legislative intent, in this case, however, Rehnquist claimed, "the legislative history of Title VII is as clear as [its language] . . . and it irrefutably demonstrates that Congress meant precisely what it said . . . —that *no* racial discrimination in employment is permissible under Title VII. . . ." The bulk of Rehnquist's opinion is devoted to a very detailed review of the legislative history of Title VII, including an abundance of direct quotations from Congressmen who participated in the debate over passage of the Civil Rights Act. As Rehnquist convincingly demonstrates, while the clause prohibiting the imposition of racial preferences was motivated by the fear of many Congressmen that federal officials might interpret any racial imbalance in a work force as a sign of racial discrimination and impose racial preferences to remedy that alleged discrimination, many supporters of the 1964 Civil Rights Act argued that federal agencies could not *require* racial preferences *since* Title VII clearly *prohibited* them.

While it is difficult to speak of "the intent of Congress" since the intent of the members of Congress who pass a given bill may be quite different, the devastating force of Rehnquist's direct quotations makes it clear that even if there were some members of Congress who assumed that Title VII did not prohibit the voluntary utilization of racial quotas to help underrepresented racial minorities in private industry, many clearly thought that it did. Equally clearly, in 1964, there would have been no chance for the Civil Rights Act to pass if it were generally assumed that this act would later be used, as it was, by the federal government as a prod to *encourage* private employers to embark upon *voluntary* affirmative action programs giving special preferences to racial minorities. This is quite understandable, for in 1964 the goal of supporters of the Civil Rights Act was to put a stop to the explicit racial discrimination that prevented blacks from having *equal access* to jobs. It was only later that the belief became widespread that the cause of racial assimilation required more.

While Rehnquist is right in his reading of the general congressional intent in 1964, he does not mention, however, that as America's perception of the relevance of race has changed, so has that of Congress. Even though Congress has had ample opportunity to resolve the issue of whether the Civil Rights Act should be taken to mean what it seems to be saying, it has chosen not to do so. Indeed, rather than making it clear that this act prohibits the granting of racial preferences as a means of remedying racial discrimination, Congress passed a public works program in 1977 which requires racial preference. In this program, Congress mandated that at least 10 percent of grants for local public works projects should be spent for "minority business enterprises" defined as businesses 50 percent of which are owned by "Negroes, Spanish-speaking [Americans], Orientals, Indians, Eskimos, and Aleuts." (The constitutionality of this program will be before the Supreme Court in its 1979–1980 term.) Clearly, it would appear that the congressional intent in 1964 was not the intent in 1977. As a matter of legal principle, Rehnquist and Burger are quite right that if the 1964 Civil Rights Act should not be taken now to prohibit the granting of racial preferences, it should be Congress, and not the Supreme Court, that says so. If the Supreme Court had upheld the Appeals Court's decision in the Weber case, however, it would have been intolerable to employers engaged in affirmative action programs if Congress did not come to grips with this issue quickly. Whether they would have been able and willing to resolve this politically explosive question is another matter.

An Analysis of the Moral Arguments

The Demands of Compensatory Justice

While the notion of compensatory justice is often appealed to as a justification of affirmative action programs, this notion has been used, in this context, in two different, and often not clearly distinguished, ways. For some, this notion is a purely backward-looking one that demands that individuals be "paid back" for the unfair burdens they have suffered in the past. In this view, compensation is the payment of a *debt* rightfully *owed* to those who were wronged by those who were either responsible for that wrong or who profited from it. On the other hand, some see the demands of compensatory justice from a forward-looking perspective. As they see it, affirmative action programs are attempts to alleviate unfair or undeserved disabilities, whatever their source, that prevent people from competing on equal terms. In this view, it is not the unfair burdens individuals *have suffered* which in themselves justify compensation, but rather *the effect* these unfair burdens have had in preventing people from competing on equal terms.

From this perspective, compensatory justice is an attempt to neutralize the *present* competitive disadvantages caused by unfair burdens so as to *create* a more equalitarian society.

Those who rely on the notion of compensatory justice also disagree over whether groups as well as individuals should be granted compensation (however understood). For example, if blacks as a group have been victimized in the past by injustice, does compensatory justice demand that blacks as a group be compensated for this injustice, or does it require instead that only those blacks who were victimized by this injustice be compensated? One will find supporters of both positions. For example, many of those who see compensation as a backward-looking debt assume that this debt is one owed by continuing groups (such as whites) to other continuing groups (such as blacks). If one accepts the idea of group responsibility and group entitlement to compensation for the injustices of the past, one must come to grips with the thorny question of how far back in the past one should go in one's attempt to compensate for injustices. Furthermore, since we cannot eliminate all the injustices of the past, which ones should we attempt to "erase"? Is it not impossible to "erase" some injustices of the past, without creating new injustices?

While some see the compensation of individuals for the injustices suffered by their group as just, others do not. Beneficiaries of compensatory justice, they believe, should themselves be victims of the injustices for which they are being compensated. For example, although one cannot deny that blacks as a group have been and continue to be victims of unjust discrimination, there is no invariable connection between being black and suffering from unjust discrimination. Should a middle class black who himself has not suffered the injustices suffered by blacks as a group be given preferential treatment in the name of compensatory justice over a white person who has suffered great economic injustice (such as a person who fought his way out of the grinding poverty of Appalachia)? Many have thought not.

Any system of affording preferential treatment only to members of particular minority groups is bound to be unfair to those victims of severe injustice or undeserved disadvantage who happen not to fall into any of these groups. For example, in September 1977, a California lower court enjoined the University of California at Davis to admit Rita Clancey to its medical school. Ms. Clancey, like Bakke before her, had brought suit against the University of California, charging that she was denied a place in the 1977 first year class at the Davis Medical School as a result of their special admissions program and that this program violated the equal protection clause of the Fourteenth Amendment.

Ms. Clancey, number one on the U.C. Davis Medical School's waiting list, on any reasonable standard, was a victim of far greater undeserved disadvantage than many of the students who were admitted as "disadvantaged minorities." Indeed, at one point, officials at the Medical School considered her for their special program, but in the end rejected her since she was white and as such did not qualify as a "disadvantaged *minority.*" (Being female does not qualify one for minority status at the Davis Medical School.) Ms. Clancey, an A– psychobiology graduate from U.C.L.A., was born in Russia to parents who had survived imprisonment in concentration camps. She came to the United States at fourteen able to speak only Hungarian and Russian. After the Clanceys emigrated, Rita's father, a bookkeeper, was incapacitated by brain surgery. The family then went on welfare and Rita worked her way through school. If members of certain "minority groups" can justly demand compensation for previous "unfair" disadvantage, why shouldn't Ms. Clancey have this right too? In reply, some have defended restricting special admissions programs to specific "minority" groups on the basis of the high correlation between being a member of these groups and having suffered from injustice. It would be too difficult administratively, they have claimed, to attempt to make such discriminations on an individual basis. If one takes this line, however, then it is not justice alone which is being used to justify such programs, but utility as well.

In addition, although restricting special admissions programs to members of particular minority groups might appear to be quite simple administratively, this may turn out not to be the case as administrators of such programs argue over which groups should qualify as disadvantaged minorities and how membership in these groups should be defined. For example, given the vast amount of interracial offspring, what is to count as being "black" is quite unclear. Similarly, if special preference is to be afforded "Spanish Americans," it is unclear how membership in this group should be defined. Persons with Spanish surnames, for example, may not be Spanish at all or even though they have some Spanish ancestry, they may be more French or Italian than Spanish and may not be able to speak Spanish or have any Spanish cultural heritage.

Furthermore, if individuals can justly demand compensation on the grounds of environmental disadvantage, can they equally justly demand compensation on the grounds of hereditary disadvantage? For example, if Mr. Jones can demand compensation on the grounds that through no fault of his own he was unjustly the victim of poverty and racial discrimination, then should Mr. Smith also be able to demand compensation on the grounds that he was born with an inferior intellectual capacity? Although hereditary handicaps can be as unfair to their possessor as environmental ones, we tend to feel an obligation to compensate individuals for the latter, but not the former. Clearly, the source of our distinction here stems from the fact that environmental injustices are created by and can be consciously affected by human actions, while the same, at this time, is not usually true of hereditary disadvantages. It is not, however, obvious that such a fact can justify the basic "fairness" of affording compensation to those who suffer from environmental injustices but not from hereditary disadvantages.

Just as people can disagree as *to whom* compensation is justly due, they can argue as well over the question of *from whom* this compensation should be exacted. For example, many supporters of Weber and

Bakke have argued that it is quite unfair to place the burdens of remedying the injustices of the past upon the shoulders of young white males who are attempting to enter careers, while those white males who have already established themselves in their careers are not expected to make any similar sacrifice. Indeed, some who are asked to bear the cost of compensation may not themselves have contributed at all to the injustices for which they are being made to compensate. In reply to this last point, those who support preferential treatment for specific minority groups on the grounds of compensatory justice have claimed that even though Weber and Bakke may not have been responsible for the injustices that some minority groups have suffered, they nevertheless have profited from them. If these injustices had not existed, they would have found themselves facing much keener competition from members of these minority groups. According to this view, individuals who have suffered from injustices can exact from white males such as Weber and Bakke a compensation commensurate with their unfairly lost ability to compete on equal terms. Some who accept such a point of view have contended that compensatory justice demands that minority groups who have been denied a fair opportunity to compete with others should be given the number of places in professional schools that they would have fairly won *had they been given an equal opportunity to compete.* There is, however, simply no standard that can be utilized to determine what this hypothetical number should be. In addition, there clearly must be some threshold level of minimum competence which limits the utilization of such a principle of justice. It clearly will not do, for example, to admit a minority candidate to medical school who in point of fact lacks the requisite academic qualifications, on the grounds that he would have had them if he had been given a "fair chance."

It is for this reason that a forward-looking notion of "compensatory justice" which aims at providing equality of opportunity and not to pay debts for the actions of the past is, in my opinion, a much more inviting view. As many who accept a forward-looking view of compensatory justice see it, the way to achieve compensation is not through the setting aside of a fixed number of positions in professional schools and trades but rather through special training, remedial education, and scholarships to victims of injustice or undeserved disadvantages at general taxpayer expense. After such compensation is afforded, they claim, the demands of compensatory justice have been met and one can then allow a fair and open competition to decide upon the relative representation of different groups in different jobs and different trades.

But a critic is sure to reply, "such remedial programs cannot erase a lifetime, or indeed generations, of unfair discrimination or economic injustice, and, as a result, it will still be unfair, even with such programs, to subject those who have in the past been victimized by grave injustice to the same standards that we apply to those who have not been victimized by grave injustice." But even if one accepts this view, it still does not necessarily follow that the proper way to compensate victims of injustice is by making it easier for them to gain admission to professional schools or to obtain scarce jobs, especially when such a policy of compensation may place unfair burdens upon those who are displaced by such a policy. Instead, one might argue, for example, that Congress should pass legislation granting tax exemptions or governmental allowances to the victims of injustice. At least such a policy would have the virtue of spreading the burden of compensation fairly upon the general taxpayer and not unjustly upon certain individuals.

The Demands of Distributive Justice

If compensatory procedures which go beyond providing special training and education programs are required to redress certain minorities for the injustices of the past, how are we to determine when such compensatory procedures should come to a halt? It would appear that many who call for compensation for certain minority groups tacitly assume that such procedures should continue until the goal of "reasonable representation of minorities" in professions and trades is achieved. From this point of view, affirmative action programs which grant special privileges to certain minorities should aim at providing for a more just distribution of the goods of our society among different groups. Since some groups do not share in the goods of our society in a manner proportionate to their percentage of the general population, it is often assumed that this must be the result of the fact that they have not received their "fair share." For many who accept this point of view, the goal of achieving *social justice in the future,* which requires that the goods of our society be justly distributed, can morally justify the tolerance of a certain level of *individual injustice in the present.* From such a perspective, while it is individually unjust both that some white males such as Weber and Bakke are made to accept a special burden of redressing the injustices of the past and that some minority members are given advantages that they may not individually deserve, such results are required for the advancement of particular groups as social justice demands.

Although programs which aim at providing particular groups with percentages of the goods of society in proportion to their numbers may seem fair to some, to others the logical consequence of such programs would be the creation of quotas which unfairly restrict the shares of other groups. If, for example, "fairness" dictates that 11 percent of the doctors in our country be black since blacks form 11 percent of our population, then it would seem to be equally "unfair" as well that the percentage of Jewish doctors in our country is far greater than would be justified on the basis of their percentage of the general population. Is it right then to restrict the number of new Jewish doctors? Such a proposal would be greeted with widespread moral abhorrence. While we may be willing to use quotas to help specific minorities gain greater opportunities, we do not want to use quotas to restrict the opportunities of specific minorities. Is this not because we realize that certain minority groups might indeed "deserve" more of certain positions in our economy than their percentage of the population would indicate? Do we not implicitly accept the possibility that there may exist genetic or deeply ingrained cultural differences in lifestyles and general value commitments among different minority groups that would exist even if all groups were given the same access to environmental opportunities?

The view that the goal of affirmative action programs is to obtain for minority groups their "proportionate share" of the goods of our society also founders when we attempt in some principled way to determine which groups can rightfully demand their "fair share." In particular, if every racial or ethnic group can make such a demand, why shouldn't other groups that cut across racial or ethnic lines (such as orphans or ghetto residents) be allowed to make similar demands. But since people fall into overlapping classes, a given individual will necessarily opt for that classificatory system which gives him the greatest share. For example, although Jones may be a white male, he may also be the first generation son of immigrants. If a black man can point to the indisputable fact that blacks are vastly underrepresented in proportion to their percentage of the population in prestigious professional schools, why can Jones not point to the equally indisputable fact that the same is true of first generation children of immigrants? Indeed, it might very well turn out that such individuals are even more underrepresented than blacks.

In addition, in determining what is to count as a "reasonable representation of minorities" in professions and trades, it is important to realize that there is great variance in the average age of members of different racial and ethnic groups. For this reason, it is a mistake to assume, as many do, that a minority group's percentage of the general population can reasonably be used as a basis for determining what its percentage in the work force ought to be. Furthermore, the percentages will differ from one geographical area to another. Understandably, each minority will use that geographical area that is most favorable to itself. For example, at a 1972 Berkeley minority student caucus attempting to arrive at a fair distribution of minorities at the University of California at Berkeley's law school, blacks looked to national population figures, Chicanos to California ones, and Asian-Americans to the San Francisco Bay area. Together, they demanded, in the name of justice, about half the places in Berkeley's entering law class.

Who Is a Qualified Applicant:
The Utilitarian Underpinnings
of the Notion of Individual Merit

According to the most often heard argument against providing "special privileges" in the allocation of scarce jobs or admission to professional schools for members of racial or ethnic minorities, the very notion of affording any *group special preferences* is incompatible with the basic American philosophy that people should be rewarded solely on the basis of *individual merit*. A scarce job or opening in a professional school should go to the "most qualified" applicant regardless of his or her racial or ethnic background or any other group affiliation, it is often said. But how is "merit" to be determined? According to most critics of special university admissions programs for racial and ethnic minorities, grades and test scores are the only standards that can properly be used to determine who as *individuals* "deserve" or "merit" admission to medical and law schools. But, since some people find it much easier to accomplish some things than others, achievement is not a good indicator of *moral merit*.

It is clear that we are interested in grades and test scores not as indicators of what individuals deserve for what they have done, but rather as predictors of how they are likely to perform in school and in their professions. A decision to admit only those with the highest grades and test scores reflects the belief that this *group* of individuals is most likely to make the best doctors and lawyers. The question as such is not one of individual versus group rights, but rather what type of groups should be admitted. Should it be solely the group of those with the highest grades and test scores or should some other classification system be employed? Since tests and grades are used essentially as predictors of performance, it has been argued that performance should be measured on a broader yardstick. Supporters of this view have argued that grades and test scores, though clearly relevant, should not be decisive in deciding who are "the most qualified" to become good doctors and lawyers.

It has often been suggested that the Law and Medical School Admissions Tests are unfair indicators of the abilities of minority students. Such tests, it is said, put a premium on accumulated knowledge that has little bearing on law and medical school testing. Indeed, even if it is granted that most individuals who are admitted to law and medical schools on special minority programs tend to cluster at the bottom of their medical and law school classes, one should realize that being a good doctor or lawyer involves more than doing well on tests; it also involves the ability to serve one's clients in ways that require human qualities as well as the abstract knowledge of law and medicine which is tested in medical and law schools. In a society in which racial and ethnic identities play an important role in everyday life, it has been suggested, a lawyer's or doctor's racial or ethnic background may have an important bearing on his ability to serve his client. Many of the tasks, for example, that lawyers perform for their clients require an understanding of the social context in which their clients' problems arise. Given the distinctive subcultures within our society, it is said, it is essential that lawyers be trained who understand the problems of their clients and "speak their language." Such qualifications for a good lawyer are most likely to be found, it is claimed, among lawyers who share their clients' racial or ethnic identity. Similarly, a good doctor for a minority community would have to be able to communicate with his patients and both understand and empathize with their special physical and psychological problems.

Utilitarian Arguments for Preferential Treatment of Minorities

Many supporters of preferential treatment programs for minorities, while willing to concede that such programs create some individual injustice, would claim that they are nevertheless justified as the essential or best means for bringing about certain future goods. Such utilitarian arguments can take many different forms, depending on the intrinsic goods one is willing to accept. For example, those who accept as an intrinsic good the creation of a society where economic goods and political power are more evenly distributed, tend to see these programs as essential to the eradication of racial and sexual discrimination, which they see as standing in the way of the creation of a just society. For such individuals, the future good of the creation of a just society may be seen as being of sufficient importance to justify "short-term measures" which cause injustices to particular individuals who find themselves displaced by "less qualified" members of minority groups. This is indeed the position of some. However, as we have seen, not all supporters of preferential treatment programs for minorities would take the view that those admitted under such programs are "less qualified" than those who are admitted under different standards.

Many who take this view (especially in reference to university admissions) would claim that we need not turn to an appeal to the goal of creating a more just society in the *future* as a justification for such programs, but need turn only to an appeal to the desirable *current* benefits of such programs. For example, it is claimed that:

1. Integration of the classrooms can provide for a diversity of ideas and values and as such for a broader and more valuable educational experience. This would be especially the case in law schools where minority members may bring valuable perspectives on the functions of law in society. The representation of minority members in the student bodies of professional schools and then in the professions will act to create a much more widespread awareness among professionals of the needs of the minority community.

2. The integration of minorities into the larger economic and political framework which will result from their integration into the professions and skilled trades will act to widen or alter the perceptions of other members of society, making them more aware and responsive to the special needs of minority communities and less apt to think in terms of unflattering stereotypes.

3. Minority lawyers or doctors are more likely than others to serve their own minority communities which are often badly in need of their services and to take an interest in their special legal and medical problems. Furthermore, minority lawyers and doctors are likely to have the greatest rapport with members of their minority communities and thus can best serve them.

4. The existence of minority professionals can provide "role

models" to young people in minority communities, demonstrating to them that they too can overcome the handicaps of past discrimination.

Utilitarian Arguments Against Preferential Treatment of Minorities

The critics of preferential treatment programs for minorities also use utilitarian arguments to justify their position. For example it has been claimed that:

1. Rather than tending to eradicate racism, such programs will make us classify ourselves and others in racial or ethnic terms. Such programs tend to cause racial friction as different minority groups vie to catch the public eye and to play the game of power politics in order to gain special consideration for themselves. Since there is no agreed-upon standard for determining which minority groups should be granted special preferences, the result will be claims and counterclaims by various groups which are incapable of principled resolution. In pleasing some groups by granting them special consideration, we will displease those who are denied this special consideration and now perceive themselves as victimized by unjust discrimination. Therefore, the policy of granting special consideration to certain minority groups is apt to be a very unstable one which generates widespread dissatisfaction.

2. Admitting minority applicants to professional schools whose academic credentials are considerably lower than those of nonminority admittees is apt to result in a general erosion of academic standards. For example, minorities, enrolled under special affirmative action programs, who would otherwise have been rejected, tend to cluster at the bottom of their medical or law school classes. In addition, they tend to fail the bar exam in much greater proportions than graduates who were admitted under normal admissions policies that are based on grades and test scores. In the face of this, some supporters of affirmative action have claimed that the bar exams in the various states are "unfair" since they favor those who can "think, act, and react from a white, middle-class mold." Such claims are often made as rationalizations for failure. Bar exams are usually quite fair and favor those who can "think, act, and react as good lawyers." If thinking like a good lawyer is defined as a type of "middle class" thinking, then the charge that bar exams have a "middle-class bias" is true, but it is trivially true and clearly not to be morally condemned. If, however, we are to accept this claim in a nontrivial way, how is the "middle class bias" of bar exams to be removed? Are we to have two bar exams just as we now have two admissions policies, or are we to lower the passing grades? Although the first proposal may be more in line with the logic of special minority admissions programs, the second seems to be the direction in which we are moving. For example, the Pennsylvania State Board of Bar Examiners lowered the passing grade, allowing around 90 percent instead of the previous 70

ercent who took the exam to pass. In California, the "Third World Coalition for Justice in the Legal System" is calling for a similar lowering of the bar exam passing grade. If they get their way, it is claimed, the result will be a general erosion in the quality of legal services.

3. The utilization of special minority preferences for admission to professional schools and skilled trades will tend to perpetuate the discrimination and stigmatization that it is meant to eliminate. The unmistakable impression will be created that certain minority groups are inferior and cannot make it on their own.

4. Many of the utilitarian arguments for special minority admissions policies are unsound. The goal of the truly equalitarian society that we should be striving toward is not one with black doctors and lawyers for blacks, Chicano lawyers and doctors for Chicanos, etc., but a society where *good* lawyers are available to all. It is untrue that minorities are so culturally insulated that outsiders cannot "speak their language." In addition, the way to attract doctors and lawyers to minority communities and the problems that especially concern them is not through the very indirect and unpredictable method of setting aside a certain number of places for minority candidates in medical and law schools, but rather through the more direct way of making government financial subsidies available to all qualified doctors and lawyers who are willing to work where there is a special social need for them. This objective can also be achieved if governmental scholarships are made available to all needy, but academically qualified, students who, regardless of race and ethnic origins, are willing to make a pledge to work a certain number of years under a general governmental public service program that assigns lawyers and doctors to those areas where their services are especially needed.

Some General Reflections on the Justification of Preferential Treatment of Minorities

Given the moral and factual complexities surrounding it, the issue of "reverse discrimination" is an exceedingly difficult one to satisfactorily resolve. It is precisely those who are most convinced of the rightness of their positions who so readily utilize such notions as *racist, individual merit* and *qualified applicant* with no sense of their problematic meanings. For example, opponents of special minority admissions programs in medical and law schools often take it as obvious that those who benefit from these programs are less qualified than those they displace, giving no thought to the possibility that grades and test scores may not always be the best indicator of an applicant's potential to be a good doctor or lawyer. On the other hand, supporters of such programs tend to dismiss their opponents much too glibly as racists, while they do not reflect that it is they and not their opponents who support the use of racial categories. The concepts that we so easily bandy about in arguments about "reverse discrimination" are rarely clarified in the heat of moral arguments that touch upon the raw nerves of self-interest or deep ideological commitment. While I am not certain of my own answers to the questions we have been discussing, let me share my general reflections with you, with the hope that they will help to clarify your own.

While the strongest pleas for preferential treatment for minorities are made on behalf of the demands of "compensatory justice," when we attempt to apply this abstract concept to the issue of preferential treatment, we find ourselves facing a morass of unanswerable questions when it comes to deciding which individuals should be granted compensation, what form that compensation should take, how much it should be and at whose expense it should be exacted. The notion of "compensation" can be most easily applied in those cases where both the victims and responsible parties to an injustice are easily identifiable and the degree of injury is measurable. All of these elements are, however, quite unclear in the issue at hand.

First, it is not clear what principles should be used in determining those who merit compensation. Clearly, those who are born in poverty suffer from an undeserved disadvantage, but so do those who are born retarded or ugly or of uncaring parents. Where is the line to be drawn? I cannot draw it. Second, it is not clear who should pay that compensation. For example, if Jones, a black, can exact compensation for the injustices of slavery that continue to be his legacy today, should the children of immigrants have to pay a portion of that compensation? Finally, it is not clear how we are to determine the amount of compensation due. While the law conceives "compensation" as an attempt to restore a person to the position he held prior to suffering an injustice or misfortune, in the case at hand we are attempting to compensate people for what they, because of social injustice, never were or had in the first place. Consequently, there is no norm we can appeal to in determining how much compensation is required.

It is also not obvious that this compensation should take the form of jobs and university positions. It is important to realize that such a method of exacting compensation aids only those minority members with marketable skills, leaving unaffected those who are perhaps most deserving of compensation. Furthermore, it exacts that compensation usually from young and lower-middle-class whites entering the job market, while it leaves both the more established and more affluent whites unaffected.

In addition, many who defend special admissions programs for minority groups on the basis of compensatory justice assume that such programs are necessary either for the elimination of racial discrimination or to prevent the lingering debilitating effects of racism from being passed on to generations yet unborn. I am not so sure, however, that this is true. No doubt, as Justice Marshall claimed in his opinion on the Bakke case, the ideal of racial equality should be "a state interest of the highest order." The question at issue, however, is that of means. Given the conflicting sociological views of the underlying factors interfering with the realization of the ideal of racial (and ethnic) assimilation and the likely effects of various remedies, one cannot be too sure of how this ideal can be best achieved. That there are deep racial injustices in our society, however, we should not deny. As Justice Marshall passionately relates in his opinion in the Bakke case:

> A Negro child today has a life expectancy which is shorter by more than five years than that of a white child. The Negro child's mother is over three times more likely to die of complications in childbirth. . . . The median income of the Negro family is only 60 percent that of the median of a white family, and the percentage of Negroes who live in families below the poverty line is nearly four times greater than that of whites. . . . For Negro adults, the unemployment rate is twice that of whites, and the unemployment rate for Negro teenagers is nearly three times that of white teenagers. . . . Although Negroes represent 11.5 percent of the population, they are only 1.2 percent of the lawyers and judges, 2 percent of the physicians, 2.3 percent of the dentists, 1.1 percent of the engineers, and 2.6 percent of the college and university professors.
>
> The relationship between those figures and the history of unequal treatment afforded to the Negro cannot be denied. At every point from birth to death the impact of the past is reflected in the still disfavored position of the Negro. . . .
>
> The dream of America as the great melting pot has not been realized for the Negro; because of his skin color he never even made it into the pot.

While it may not be true that a "just" society would see blacks represented in the various sectors of our economy in direct proportion to their percentage of the general population, there can be no doubt that much of the statistical discrepancy Marshall mentions must be attributed to racial injustice. One's perception of the social realities of being black in America should not, however, be uncritically projected upon other groups that are often classified as "disadvantaged minority groups" in affirmative action programs.

The strongest case for affirmative action programs rests not on the backward-looking assertion that specific minority groups are "owed" a certain compensation or percentage of desirable places in our economy, but rather on the forward-looking assertion that such programs are required to achieve an integrated society in which people are not denied opportunities simply on the basis of their racial or ethnic background. The notion of "diversity" that Justice Powell made the focal point of his decision in the Bakke case cannot suffice to replace the most morally compelling reason for affirmative action programs which the Brennan-Marshall-Blackmun-White bloc rightfully saw as the attempt "to remedy the effects of past societal discrimination." It is questionable, after all, that Powell's notion of "diversity" has as much place in scientifically oriented medical schools as it does in law schools and liberal arts colleges whose curricula are more value-laden. Similarly, the notion of "diversity" cannot reasonably be used to justify the preferential hiring and promotion of members of minority groups in private industry. If we want racial diversity, for example, in the construction trade, it is not because this diversity leads to better constructed houses, but rather because we hope it will lead to a better constructed society.

It is important that we see affirmative action programs as attempts to remedy social and not individual injustice. Since it is impossible for us to alleviate all individual injustices, we must of necessity restrict ourselves to the alleviation of those injustices we see as important social problems and whose alleviation we hope will contribute to the creation of a more just society, less troubled in the future by that type of injustice. It is not "desert" that justifies the preferential treatment of minorities, but the utility that preference promises for the achievement of a more integrated society in the future.

In addition, we should not lose sight of the fact that the notion of who is "most qualified" or who "merits" admission to professional schools cannot be separated from utilitarian judgments as to who can best fulfill the goals of our society. As such, "the brightest" as measured by grades and test scores are not necessarily "the best." Even though the first step in any adequate academic admissions program should be to screen out those candidates who do not meet certain minimum standards of academic achievement as measured by grades and test scores, the fact that there are so many more applicants for law and medical schools than there are places for them has raised these minimum standards in some schools to unreasonably high levels which tend to screen out a high percentage of disadvantaged students who might make the very best of lawyers or doctors.[13] Clearly, there are innumerable reasons why an applicant with a lower grade-point average and test scores than some other applicant may still be considered the "more promising" law or medical student. In particular, the disadvantages with which a student had to contend, be they the disadvantages of poverty, or racial discrimination, or of a physical disease, can themselves be predictors of his chances of succeeding, since a person's academic achievement is measured not only by how high he stands but also by how far he had to climb to get to where he is.

Although Justice Powell's opinion in the Bakke case is not "the definitive decision" many hoped would be reached in this case, perhaps the very vagueness of this decision is its principle strength. No doubt, this decision does not provide us with any guidance in resolving the issue of how much race and ethnic background should count in a university's admissions program. But do we really want a definite answer to this question, and if we do, can it be answered any way other than in terms

---

[13] On the other hand, it is quite important that we do not overly downplay the importance of grades and test scores, as many supporters of affirmative action programs do. Unfortunately, the academic discrepancies between regular and special admittees often turn out to be substantial and not easily discounted.

of the numbers of specific racial and ethnic minorities we desire to be admitted? Indeed, as long as considerations other than grades and test scores are to be considered relevant to university admissions, it would appear that race and ethnic background will have to be considered relevant, indirectly if not directly, regardless of what the courts say. The black student who is admitted to a university seeking diversity in its student body may not be said to be admitted because he is black, but rather because he has, let us say, "special interests" or "special perspectives," but it will be his blackness that makes us attribute these interests and perspectives to him. Such individuals as farmers, the physically handicapped, and homosexuals, after all, also have "special interests" and "special perspectives," but one doubts that as much weight will be placed on such types of diversity as will be placed on *racial* diversity. Clearly, there is no rational basis in a society such as ours, where race and ethnic background are important social forces, to exclude considerations of a university applicant's racial and ethnic background while considering such things as his geographical background in attempting to achieve diversity in a student body.

In the debate over preferential minority treatment, the choice before us is not one between "a right" and "a wrong," as so many disputants make it appear, but one of the proper balance between conflicting moral values. The quest for social justice, unfortunately, often requires unfair moral burdens and unpleasant social turmoil. This may be the case with the goal of ending racial discrimination. The ideal of racial assimilation, especially of blacks, deserves the taking of some risks and the imposition of some temporary unfair burdens. In deciding how far minority preferential treatment should go, we must balance our vision of justice tomorrow with our conception of the needs and rights of individuals today. As is the case with all conflicts of basic values, there is no uniquely reasonable and right way of weighing these values against each other.

DISCUSSION QUESTIONS

1. Consider the following imaginary dialogue:

   A: What people deserve depends on what they would have achieved if they were given a fair chance.

   B: Even if we could agree on what is to count as "a fair chance" and had some basis for determining what individuals *would have achieved* under different circumstances, I still would not accept your moral principle. While Jones may have been capable of achieving more than Smith, if he were given the same environmental opportunities, the fact of the matter is that Smith has worked much harder and accomplished much more than Jones and consequently *deserves* more for *what he has done.* Indeed, because of his extra opportunities and his response to them,

Smith has developed a more meritorious character than Jones. We don't live in hypothetical worlds but in this one.

A: Smith may have a better character than Jones but that's only because he had more undeserved environmental opportunities. Consequently, he doesn't *deserve* to be rewarded for his character.

B: In your sense, no one will ever "deserve" anything.

Critically discuss.

2. Consider and evaluate the following claim:

> The ideal of complete equality of opportunity conflicts with the ideal of individual autonomy. For example, it is the ideal of individual autonomy which justifies allowing parents to choose how many children they should have. In making this choice, parents realize that the more children they have, the less they will have to give each child. If complete equality of opportunity is our prime goal, would it not follow that family size should be strictly controlled? Furthermore, while one may, through strict social controls, equalize the financial opportunities parents can provide for their children, there is no way one can hope to equalize the vast differences in opportunities for psychological and intellectual growth that parents provide their children within the setting of the traditional family unit. The ideal of complete equality of opportunity, then, would seem to be achievable only in a social system where children are raised in communal nurseries. Yet how many of us would welcome such a scheme?

3. How would you reply to the following plea of Jones, a lower-middle-class white?

> I grant that I have indirectly benefited from the injustices of racial discrimination at the expense of blacks, but then again, whites born of rich parents have benefited from the injustices of differential wealth and the inheritance of wealth at my expense. Consequently, if I owe blacks a debt, rich whites owe me one.

4. In what respects do the disadvantages women have suffered as a result of sexual discrimination differ from the disadvantages blacks have suffered as a result of a racial discrimination? Are blacks more deserving of special preferences than women?

5. Grassian claims that Rita Clancey "was a victim of far greater undeserved disadvantage than many of the minority students who were admitted [under the Davis special admissions program] as 'disadvantaged minorities'." Is this true? In what morally relevant respects, if any, do the disadvantages Rita Clancey suffered from differ from those suffered by the various minority groups that are usually included in preferential admissions programs?

6. Consider the following claim:

> . . . the slaves had an indisputable moral right to the products of their labor; these products were stolen from them by the slave masters, who ultimately passed them on to their descendants; the slaves presumably have conferred their rights of ownership to the products of their labor to their descendants; thus, the descendants of slave masters are in possession of wealth to which the descendants of slaves have rights; hence, the descendants of slave masters must return this wealth to the descendants of slaves with a concession that they were not rightfully in possession of it.
>
> It is not being claimed that the descendants of slaves must seek reparation from those among the white population who happen to be descendants of slave owners. This perhaps would be the case if slavery had produced for the slave owners merely hoards of gold, silver, or diamonds, which could be passed on in a very concrete way from father to son. As a matter of fact, slavery produced not merely specific hoards, but wealth which has been passed down mainly to descendants of the white community, to the relative exclusion of the descendants of slaves. Thus, it is the white community as a whole that prevents the descendants of slaves from exercising their rights of ownership, and the white community as a whole that must bear the cost of reparation.[14]

Do you agree? Why or why not? Is every American black a victim of discrimination? Is every American white a beneficiary of it?

7. Consider the following claim made by Professor Thomas Sowell, a black professor of economics at UCLA:

> the actual harm done by quotas is far greater than having a few incompetent people here and there—and the harm that will actually be done will be harm primarily to the *black* population. What all the arguments and campaigns for quotas are really saying, loud and clear, is that *black people just don't have it,* and that they will have to be given something in order to have something. The devastating impact of this message on black people—particularly black young people—will outweigh any few extra jobs that may result from this strategy. Those black people who are already competent, and who could be instrumental in producing more competence among the rising generation, will be completely undermined, as black becomes synonymous—in the minds of black and white alike—with incompetence, and black achievement becomes synonymous with charity or payoffs.[15]

Do you agree? Why, or why not?

[14] Bernard Boxill, "The Morality of Reparation," *Social Theory and Practice*, 2, No. 1 (Spring 1972), 113–22. (Also reprinted in R. Wasserstrom, *Today's Moral Problems.*)

[15] Thomas Sowell, *Black Education, Myths and Tragedies* (New York: McKay, 1972), p. 292.

8. Consider the following argument:

> The sad truth is that without an affirmative action program for
> minorities at the UCLA Law School, we would have absolutely no black
> or Chicano students. This is, however, morally intolerable for a publicly
> supported law school located in an area which contains such a high
> percentage of blacks and Chicanos. It is very important that minorities
> participate in the legal process which now often neglects, demeans, and
> discriminates against them. At every turn of the legal process, criminal
> justice is to a large extent discretionary. Police exercise discretion in
> deciding whom to arrest or search, prosecutors in pressing or dropping
> charges, juries in finding facts, judges in sentencing, wardens in awarding
> time off for good behavior, and parole boards in granting parole. In every
> discretionary step, however, racial bias may, and often does, play some
> role. For this reason, there is some justification for the widespread
> minority perception of the law as an instrument of white oppression. The
> only way to remedy this is by a race-conscious attempt to increase minority
> representation in the legal community. Lawyers, we must realize, wield
> enormous political power in the United States. For example, most
> legislators are lawyers. The almost total exclusion of minorities in the
> legal profession must come to an end, and soon.

What do you think?

9. Consider the following imaginary dialogue:

> **A:** I'm just as concerned as you with eradicating the lingering effects of
> racial discrimination. In the past, when universities and industries em-
> ployed racial quotas to exclude certain groups, we were both against them.
> We agreed that it was wrong to base employment and admissions policies
> on an applicant's race. But you seem to forget all this now, when you
> favor today's policy of preferential treatment toward members of particu-
> lar races. It seems to me that you're being inconsistent. If racism was
> wrong before, it is wrong now.

> **B:** It was "racism" before, but it is not "racism" now. We were both opposed
> to racial policies before because they were part of a social system which
> aimed at unjustly excluding individuals from the mainstream of our so-
> ciety simply on the basis of their race. The situation is quite different,
> however, in the case of those white individuals who are excluded on the
> basis of preferential treatment programs that favor racial minorities. It
> is absurd to say that they are being "oppressed" by such policies as were
> the minorities that these policies attempt to help. It is unfortunate that
> qualified white people are being bypassed as a result of these programs,
> but they are being bypassed in order to create a more just society and
> not to perpetuate injustice. That's why it's absurd to call such programs
> "racist."

What do you think?

10. Is it right to compare the admissions policy of an undergraduate
liberal arts college with that of a medical school as Justice Powell

does in his opinion in the Bakke case? Why, or why not? Does the
same apply to law schools? Why, or why not?

11. Is Powell's notion of "diversity" any less subjective and standardless
than the notion of "stigma" which he rejects? What do you think
Powell would say to a university that decides to restrict the number
of Jewish medical students on the grounds that the goal of diversity
demands such restriction? What would you say?

12. Consider and evaluate the following argument for utilizing quotas in
some industry:

> Unlike the universities, there are no natural standards for evaluating
> the qualifications of young people seeking apprentice positions. Formerly,
> those with "pull" were those who got in. Since those in the industry were
> almost exclusively white, their friends were almost exclusively white too.
> Indeed, even those whites in positions of influence who prided themselves
> on their lack of racial prejudice naturally tended to choose other whites
> as the most "promising" employees, simply because they, without realizing
> it, were socially conditioned to see as most promising those who looked
> and acted like themselves. The enforcement of minority quotas is the
> only way to break the subtle and self-perpetuating grip of racism in
> our society.

13. What do you think of the following claim?

> It is ludicrous to assert that Bakke was no more qualified to be admitted
> to the Davis Medical School than the minority student who was admitted
> in his place. The discrepancy between Bakke's test scores and those of
> the special minority admittees is so glaring as to dim into insignificance
> any other possible factor. Especially glaring is Bakke's 96 percent score on
> the science test as compared to the average 35 percent score for the minority
> admittees. It is quite unreasonable to think that such a discrepancy does
> not really matter. "Patient rapport" and "empathy" may be among the
> qualities one would expect of a good doctor, but they are not nearly as
> important as scientific knowledge. Bad bedside manners may make us feel
> uneasy and even aggravate our conditions, but they rarely kill us, while
> ignorance does.

14. Consider the following criticism of Arthur Jensen's research into inherited racial intellectual differences:

> Jensen may indeed be committed to equal opportunities for all racial
> groups, as he says. He does not seem to realize, however, that there is
> a great difference between being a very intelligent black fellow and being
> a 6'3" Japanese fellow who has the capability of becoming an excellent
> basketball player. The Japanese fellow's tallness is an obvious physical
> characteristic, observable by all. This is not true, however, of the black
> fellow's native intelligence. The belief that blacks are generally less
> intelligent than whites is apt to make blacks feel inferior and be looked

upon as inferior by whites, preventing them from achieving their
potential and helping to create precisely the racial intellectual differences
that will be attributed mistakenly to genetic causes. It is very important
that we do not allow such general racial perceptions to distort equal
environmental opportunities. It is for this reason that I strongly believe
that it is wrong for people like Jensen to engage in research attempting
to uncover genetically caused racial differences. Public funds should never
be used to finance such research. I can forsee no possible benefit of such
research that would outweigh its likely undesirable consequences.

What do you think?

FURTHER READINGS

COHEN, MARSHALL, THOMAS NAGEL, and THOMAS SCANLONG, eds., *Equality and
Preferential Treatment.* Princeton, N.J.: Princeton University Press, 1977.
An anthology of articles by contemporary philosophers on the morality
of affording preferential treatment to particular minority groups.

ENGLISH, JANE, ed., *Sex Equality.* Englewood Cliffs, N.J.: Prentice-Hall, Inc., 1977.
An anthology of material on the issue of sexual equality. Classical philosophical positions are represented (such as, Plato, Aristotle, Locke, Mill,
and Engels), as well as contemporary philosophical arguments and expressions of popular viewpoints. Such specific issues as natural sex differences, sex roles, the role of the family, equal opportunity, and reverse
discrimination are discussed. An excerpt from Goldberg's *The Inevitability of Patriarchy,* discussed in the preceding chapter, is included.

GOLDBERG, STEVEN, *The Inevitability of Patriarchy.* New York: Morrow, 1973.

GROSS, BARRY, ed., *Reverse Discrimination.* Buffalo, N.Y.: Prometheus Books,
1977. Another anthology of articles by contemporary philosophers on the
morality of affording preferential treatment to particular minority groups.

MAPPES, THOMAS A., and JANE S. ZEMBATY, eds., *Social Ethics: Morality and
Social Policy.* New York: McGraw-Hill, 1977. This excellent anthology
on contemporary moral issues contains a section on "Discrimination and
Reverse Discrimination" as well as a section on "Sexual Equality" which
includes an excerpt from Goldberg's *The Inevitability of Patriarchy.* The
editors begin each section with relevant judicial opinions which provide
an effective backdrop for consideration of the moral issues.

MILL, JOHN STUART, and HARRIET TAYLOR MILL, *Essays on Sex Equality,* edited
with an introduction by Alice S. Rossi. Chicago: University of Chicago
Press, 1970. This little book contains J.S. Mill's classic essay "The Subjection of Women," (1859) his wife Harriet Taylor Mill's "Enfranchisement of Women" (1851), and "Early Essays on Marriage and Divorce"
by both (1832). The introduction by the editor presents the interesting
story of the relationship of the two Mills.

The Monist, 57, no. 1 (January 1973). This issue is devoted to articles by contemporary philosophers on issues relevant to "Women's Liberation."

The Philosophical Forum, V, nos. 1 and 2 (Fall and Winter, 1973–74). These
issues contain articles by contemporary philosophers on the oppression
and liberation of women.

THALBERG, IRVING, "Visceral Racism," in *The Monist,* 56, no. 4 (October 1972). Also reprinted in the Mappes and Zembaty anthology. A provocative philosophical discussion of the concept of "visceral racism" which Thalberg (a white) defines as a set of unacknowledged attitudes that leads whites who pride themselves on being "unprejudiced" to misrepresent or distort "social inequalities which are glaringly evident to black observers." Thalberg attempts to uncover the "protective cocoon of ignorance and distortion" with which "visceral racists" structure events. For example, Thalberg claims that the "visceral racist" tends to overlook the violence perpetuated against blacks while he much too readily perceives as "violent" (instead of "self-defensive") any aggressive black counter-response.

WASSERSTROM, RICHARD, ed., *Today's Moral Problems* (2nd. ed.). New York: Macmillan, 1979. This is another excellent anthology which contains a good section on preferential treatment. The section begins with Powell, Brennan, Marshall, and Blackmun's opinions (some edited) in the Bakke case. This is followed by articles by four philosophers representing diverse opinions on the moral and constitutional justification of preferential treatment for disadvantaged minorities.

WASSERSTROM, RICHARD, "Preferential Treatment," in *Philosophy and Social Issues: Five Studies* by Richard Wasserstrom. Notre Dame, Ind.: University of Notre Dame Press, projected 1980. An excellent and clearly written defense of preferential treatment. In defending his view, Wasserstrom carefully distinguishes the empirical, logical, and moral questions that can be asked about such programs and criticizes arguments that have been raised against them.

WEITZ, SHIRLEY, *Sex Roles.* New York: Oxford University Press, 1977. A well-balanced and factually informative survey of the causes, nature, and future of sex roles by a social psychologist who sees biological as well as social factors contributing in a complex way to maintenance of traditional sex roles. Accepting a nondogmatic interdisciplinary approach, Weitz critically considers various different theories of sex roles and also discusses the connection between sex roles and the family and the contribution of symbolism to the maintenance of sex roles. In the final chapter she presents a cross-cultural look at several societies (U.S.S.R., China, Israel, and Sweden) that have instituted sex role changes in this century, and presents, as well, a brief historical survey of the history of feminist thought in the U.S.

Punishment
and
Rehabilitation

Punishment is punishment, only where it is deserved. We pay the penalty because we owe it, and for no other reason; and if punishment is inflicted for any other reason whatever than because it is merited by wrong, it is a gross immorality. . . .

F. H. BRADLEY, *Ethical Studies*

What is past is but one act; the future is infinite. The offense already committed concerns only a single individual; similar offenses may affect all. In many cases it is impossible to redress the evil that is done; but it is always possible to take away the will to repeat it; for however great may be the advantage of the offense, the evil of the punishment may be always made out to outweigh it.

JEREMY BENTHAM, *The Theory of Legislation*

"He is a delightful man," continued the interpreter, "but he has suffered terribly from" (here there came a long word which I could not quite catch, only it was much longer than kleptomania) "and has but lately recovered from embezzling a large sum of money under singularly distressing circumstances; but he has quite got over it, and the straighteners say that he has made a really wonderful recovery; you are sure to like him."

SAMUEL BUTLER, *Erewhon*

INTRODUCTION

As the popularity of recent books on punishment, such as the well-known psychiatrist Karl Menninger's *The Crime of Punishment*, demonstrates, people are very much concerned about our response to crime. There is more involved in this concern than intellectual curiosity; moral questions relating to such issues as abortion or euthanasia, though personally agonizing for some, are not nearly as universally pressing as crime. Who has not had the experience of hearing or reading about some ghastly crime and shuddering inwardly with the realization of our own vulnerability? We are frightened and quite skeptical about the general effectiveness of our system of criminal justice. Our fear and distrust is amply justified by a look at the bleak statistics. In the bigger cities, the law-abiding feel compelled to arm themselves and barricade their homes, fearful of the invisible menace outside. Fearful of our own safety, we feel that something is seriously wrong when we become aware that so few criminals are apprehended and fewer still punished. We react with disgust when we learn of clearly guilty criminals being released because of some "legal technicality." We are annoyed at the slow movement of a criminal justice system which often seems more concerned with the rights of criminals than with the control of crime. The price of such justice, many of us strongly feel, is increased crime, and we suspect that the price is too high—that not enough attention is being given to the rights of the victims or potential victims of crime.

As well as criticisms directed to the effectiveness of our criminal justice system in controlling crime, there is widespread dissatisfaction at the unfair results of the practical workings of the law to those criminals who are eventually punished. For example, there is widespread dissatisfaction with the great and unguided discretion afforded judges in the setting of sentences and to its resultant injustices. Similarly, there is widespread dissatisfaction with the practice of "plea bargaining," where a defendant pleads guilty to a lesser offense for fear of being found guilty of a greater one; such a practice, it is clear, has very little to do with justice and much to do with the practical pressures facing overworked courts.

The current dissatisfaction with our punishment system, however, goes much deeper than a skepticism over its effectiveness and the nature of the justice which it, as a matter of practice, dispenses; the very conceptual and moral justification of our entire punishment system is being questioned. We wonder whether punishment really deters crime or serves any justifiable purpose. Psychiatrists and psychologists, such as Karl Menninger and B.F. Skinner, and criminologists and lawyers, such as former United States Attorney Ramsey Clark, speak out against the immorality and ineffectiveness of traditional conceptions of "retributive punishment" which they see as a barbaric and useless relic that merely satisfies our urge for revenge. Most who take such a point of view attack the very philosophical foundation of our criminal justice system on hard deterministic grounds. Our criminal justice system, they contend, based as it is on the illusions of moral responsibility and free will is incapable of moral justification. The progress of the deterministic sciences, they claim, has made such concepts obsolete. The behavior of a human being is simply the determined response of an object to the forces which act upon it. The relationship of these stimuli and responses can be studied and controlled scientifically. Instead of attempting the philosophically impossible task of measuring the "fault" connected with some act in the past, we should turn our attention to the future rehabilitation of the criminal and to the prevention of crime. These sentiments are often expressed by saying that a system of *treatment* ought to replace our present *punishment* system.

Let us turn our attention to the philosophical questions that are now being raised about the justification of punishment. We shall first briefly consider the meaning of the concept of punishment and its traditional retributive and utilitarian justifications, and then turn to a critical consideration of those elements of our criminal justice system that the critics of punishment would like to see changed. Finally, we shall critically consider the proposals of the critics.

THE CONCEPT OF LEGAL PUNISHMENT

As we have repeatedly seen in our discussions of both abstract and practical ethical issues, the first essential task of a philosopher in attempting to come to grips with a particular ethical issue is that of clearly defining the various central concepts in which that problem is formulated. This is especially the case when we consider the question of the justifiability of punishment. For example, although many denounce legal punishment as immoral or ineffective, it is not at all clear what it is they are denouncing or what they might be offering as a substitute when they speak, as they often do, of replacing our punishment system with one devoted to the treatment of offenders. Until we know what this distinction amounts to, we cannot attempt to consider the merits of such a proposal. Is the critic of punishment, for example, really advocating that we should not punish criminals at all, or is he, perhaps, advocating a particular form of punishment which dispenses with *certain* features presently associated with the concept of punishment. If, for example, it is the retributive element of punishment that he wishes to see eliminated, cannot one still punish people for purely utilitarian reasons? After all, utilitarian philosophers, such as Bentham, as well as retributivists, such as Kant, have offered philosophical defenses of punishment. Yet when many denounce punishment, it seems clear that what they are really denouncing is *retributive* punishment.

It is essential then that we come to grips with the meaning of the concept of legal punishment, before we attempt to discuss its moral justification. As is often the case, however, with deeply value-laden concepts which are embedded in complex and ever-changing social processes, the concept of legal punishment is a very vague one. A cluster of considerations incline us to apply this concept—considerations which are assigned varying weights by people with different moral perspectives. It is for this reason that conceptions of the "nature of punishment" provided by such systematic moral philosophers as Bentham and Kant are *philosoph-*

ically theory-laden conceptions which presuppose the acceptance of a specific underlying theory of moral obligation. For example, Kant's view of punishment follows logically from, and cannot be understood apart from, his conception of the legitimacy of political obligation, while Bentham's view follows directly from his commitment to the principle of utility. For Kant, punishment was defined as a *debt deservedly* exacted from a lawbreaker for his violation of a social duty rightfully required of him, while for Bentham, punishment was one of four different remedies for crime which is distinguished from the others by its *aim*—"to prevent like offenses whether on the part of the offender or of others." If one accepts such theory-laden definitions of punishment, however, the question of the *meaning* of punishment cannot be kept distinct from that of its justification, for what is perceived to be the very moral justification of a punishment system is built into the definitions of punishment offered by Bentham and Kant. Such definitions do not merely *describe* what is ordinarily meant by calling something a legal punishment, but are attempts to *prescribe* how this concept ought to be used from the perspective of a particular theory of moral obligation. Such definitions are, of course, open to challenge by those who reject that theory of moral obligation.

In their attempt to clearly separate the question of the definition of punishment from that of its justification, several well-known contemporary philosophers, including the famed English legal philosopher H.L.A. Hart, have attempted to offer a neutral definition of punishment which reflects our ordinary usage of this term and does not presuppose some theory of normative ethics. According to Hart, the standard case of punishment exhibits the following defining features:

1. It must involve pain or other consequences normally considered unpleasant.
2. It must be for an offense against legal rules.
3. It must be of an actual or supposed offender for his offense.
4. It must be intentionally administered by human beings other than the offender.
5. It must be imposed and administered by an authority constituted by a legal system against which the offense is committed.[1]

Let us consider this definition. The first feature Hart mentions is the one most closely associated with the concept of "punishment," for punishment, we all realize, is by its very nature something that is *meant* to be unpleasant. Today, of course, the unpleasantness of punishment usually takes the form of imprisonment, but this has not always been the case. In the past, offenders were generally imprisoned only while awaiting trial. They were then sentenced usually to be fined, flogged,

---

[1] H.L.A. Hart, "Prolegomenon to the Principles of Punishment," in *Punishment and Responsibility* (London: Oxford University Press, 1968), pp. 4–5.

pilloried, mutilated, exiled, or put to death.[2] Hart's second feature seems to be equally essential to our concept of *"legal* punishment," for we think of people being punished *for* specific *conduct* that violates certain legal rules, and that, one might think, is what Hart means when he speaks of an *"offense* against legal rules." This will not do, however, since people may be punished for what they *are* ("crimes of status") as well as for what they *do*. Such punishments have often been accepted in Anglo-American law. For example, it has often been a "crime" subject to punishment to *be* a vagrant or a drunk or a narcotic addict.[3] Consequently, if we are to define the concept of legal punishment in a way that is consistent with traditional legal usage, the notion of an *offense* must be broadly understood to include crimes of status as well as the more typical crimes involving specific conduct. Although Hart's third feature is central to contemporary Anglo-American law, it does not seem that this feature should be taken as an essential feature of punishment since many primitive cultures have allowed for "vicarious punishments" (that is, one person is intentionally "punished" for someone else's crime). Hart, of course, is quite aware of this and would say that this is in some sense a "substandard" case of punishment. Similarly, Hart would say that such things as collective, parental, divine, and self-punishment are "substandard" instances of punishment. He does not, however, provide any rationale for distinguishing standard from substandard cases of punishment. Clearly, Hart's definition should not be taken as a definition of "punishment," per se, but of existing Anglo-American *"legal* punishment."

But even on this assumption, Hart's definition seems seriously incomplete, for, as stated, it would seem to encompass things that most of us would not want to count as punishment. Consider, for example, a mentally ill person who is involuntarily civilly committed to a mental hospital where he is to be subjected to the unpleasantnesses of both involuntary confinement and of shock therapy. While Hart might contend that such a person would not fit his definition since he has not committed a legal offense or that the unpleasantnesses inflicted upon him are not for that offense, this is not at all clear. As we have seen, an offense can be said to be anything—be it conduct or status—that violates

---

[2] The identification of imprisonment with punishment can be traced to the efforts of liberal reformers in the nineteenth century who saw imprisonment as a much more humane way of treating criminals. As they saw it, criminals should be sent to quiet places to do penance for their criminal offenses. The religious origins of these places, appropriately called "penitentiaries," can still be seen in the churchlike spires and windows of some of today's older penitentiaries.

[3] The constitutional legitimacy of crimes of status has been challenged in the courts. For example, in a very important case *(Robinson v. Calif.* 370 U.S. 660 [1962]), the United States Supreme Court declared unconstitutional a California law which made it a crime to be addicted to narcotics on the grounds that this would be "cruel and unusual punishment" prohibited by the Eighth Amendment. Following this lead, other lower courts have held that other statutes making it an offense to be a drunk are similarly unconstitutional.

some legal rule or norm, and one may assume that the mentally ill person is being civilly committed for his failure to satisfy the legal rule or norm that he not be a danger to himself and others. Nevertheless, most of us would not call this punishment if our response to such a person stems primarily from a desire to help him rather than from a desire either *to prevent similar offenses in the future* (the justifying aim of punishment according to the utilitarian) or to maintain justice by giving a person *what he deserves for wrongfully violating a legal duty* (the justifying aim of punishment according to the retributivist). If this is so, the very *meaning* of "punishment" involves reference to its justifying purposes—whether they be utilitarian or retributive. Although questions concerning the relative importance of these two purposes or whether one should be eliminated entirely are normative ones, open to moral debate, the presence of one or both of these aims, it may be said, are part of the very *meaning of* "punishment." This is, for example, the position taken by the late Herbert Packer, a Professor of Law at Stanford University, in his book *The Limits of the Criminal Sanction.* According to Packer, in addition to Hart's five defining characteristics of punishment, a sixth should be added which reads as follows: "It must be imposed for the dominant purpose of preventing offenses against legal rules or of exacting retribution from offenders, or both." Many will find this definition not fully satisfying either. For example, let us turn back to our involuntarily civilly committed mental patient again, but this time assume that the dominant purpose of our response to him is not to help him (perhaps he simply cannot be helped), but rather to help ourselves by isolating a potentially dangerous person. Is such a person being punished? Packer would say yes, but many of us would feel uncomfortable with such a description, feeling, perhaps without being able to clearly articulate it, that judgments of moral guilt and blameworthiness and feelings of moral disapproval, resentment, and righteous indignation are essential aspects of punishment. Certainly, those who cry out for the elimination of punishment are tacitly assuming that the concept of punishment requires reference to such traditionally retributive notions, for they are clearly not advocating the elimination of the involuntary confinement of the dangerous.

Many sociologists and psychiatrists share the view that punishment is essentially a vehicle for the expression of community judgments of moral disapproval and feelings of righteous indignation. For example, according to the famous sociologist Emile Durkheim in his classic study *The Division of Labor in Society* (1893), every society is bound together by a collection of moral beliefs and feelings which he called "the common conscience." As Durkheim saw it, it is "the common conscience" that provides a society with "the social solidarity" that binds it together as a group. Punishment, in his view, was a passionate reaction to offenses against the common conscience. Its prime function, he claimed, was to provide a socially accepted ritualistic channel for the expression of community feelings of hostility and outrage toward those who have violated the common conscience, feelings which, if not expressed, would "result in the breakdown of social solidarity." As Durkheim writes,

> . . . we must not say that an action shocks the common conscience because it is criminal, but rather that it is criminal because it shocks the common conscience. . . .
>
> . . . whenever a directive power is established, its primary and principle function is to create respect for the beliefs, traditions, and collective practices; that is, to defend the common conscience against all enemies within and without. . . . And in truth, punishment has remained, at least in part, a work of vengeance. It is said that we do not make the culpable suffer in order to make him suffer; it is none the less true that we find it just that he suffer. Perhaps we are wrong, but that is not the question. We seek . . . to define punishment as it is or has been, not as it ought to be. . . .
>
> Punishment, thus, remains for us what it was for our fathers. It is still an act of vengeance since it is an expiation. What we avenge, what the criminal expiates, is the outrage to morality. . . . It is sufficient, moreover, to see how punishment functions in courts, in order to understand that its spirit is completely passionate, for it is to these passions that both prosecutor and defense-attorney address themselves. The latter seeks to excite sympathy for the defendant, the former to awaken the social sentiments which have been violated by the criminal act. . . .[4]

According to many psychiatrists following Freud, punishment is a moralistic response brought about by the internal conflicts of the law-abiding. Since the desires that the criminal has dared to act upon are present in the ordinary citizen, he is a source of hidden envy, for he has done what we would have done had our instinctual desires had their way. As Freud put it,

> The human code of punishment . . . rightly presumes the same forbidden impulses in the criminal and in the members of society who avenge his offense. Psychoanalysis here confirms what the pious were wont to say, that we are all miserable sinners.[5]

Faced with similar latent criminal desires ourselves, Freud and his followers tell us, we react with moral indignation and resentment toward those who dare to act on these desires; furthermore we feel it necessary to prove to ourselves that "crime does not pay." As Flugel writes,

> . . . the criminal by his flouting of law and moral rule constitutes a temptation. . . . it is as though we said to ourselves, "if he does it, why should not we?" This stirring of criminal impulses within ourselves calls for an answering effort on the part of the super-ego [our conscience], which can best achieve its object by showing that "crime doesn't pay." This in turn can be done most conveniently and completely by a

[4] Emile Durkheim, *The Division of Labor in Society*, 2nd ed. (Glencoe, Ill.: Free Press, 1960), originally published 1893, pp. 88–90.

[5] Sigmund Freud, *Totem and Taboo* (London: Routledge & Paul, 1950), p. 12.

demonstration on the person of the criminal. By punishing him we are not only showing him that he can't "get away with it" but holding him up as a terrifying example to our own tempted and rebellious selves. . . .[6]

In addition, psychiatrists have claimed that punishment provides an outlet for aggressions which can be hidden behind a facade of morality. It has been claimed that limitations upon this expression of aggression may cause the aggression to be expressed in criminality itself. According to this view, a punishment system represses dangerous expressions of aggression and channels them into the punishment of the criminal. Indeed, in punishing the criminal there may be an opportunity of vicariously committing the very crime that is to be punished. As Freud claimed, ". . . punishment will not infrequently give those who carry it out an opportunity of committing the same outrage under colour of an act of expiation."

The insights of Freud and Durkheim have been incorporated into contemporary sociological views of punishment which see the punitive reaction to crime as growing out of the moral indignation of the public. Punishment, according to such views, is a ritual expression of the sentiments which uphold the institutionalized values the criminal has violated. This ritual expression serves to consolidate those sentiments and to strengthen them in that part of the population which has latent criminal tendencies.

The preceding psychoanalytic and sociological views of punishment stress two important, often neglected, facts. First, one of the aims of punishment, as the philosopher Nietzsche (1844–1900) saw, "is to improve him who punishes." Second, criminal punishment presupposes the existence of a community of individuals who psychologically and socially identify with each other within a background of mutual cooperation. Within such a community, a violation of certain community interests by members from within is seen as a moral issue since the offender of these interests, the criminal, is seen as having a moral obligation to respect these interests. For this reason, a community's reaction to a criminal carries with it a judgment of moral censure and is unlike the mere hostility directed to a source of danger from without (such as natural forces, animals, and, often, prisoners of war) who are not seen as having any moral obligation to the community whose interests they threaten. The criminal is not seen merely as an enemy, but as a traitor to the community to which he is tied by the bonds of moral obligation.

PHILOSOPHICAL THEORIES OF PUNISHMENT

Since the concept of legal punishment defies a precise descriptive analysis and since an unbiased study of our present system of legal punishment indicates that it has many values and serves many different pur-

---

[6] John C. Flugel, *Man, Morals, and Society* (New York: International Universities Press, 1945), p. 174.

poses—purposes and values which can on occasion generate internal conflict, if not internal inconsistency, philosophers have provided theories of punishment. These theories are attempts to provide some comprehensive framework of moral principles from which the practice of punishment can be precisely defined and justified. These comprehensive frameworks can then, in turn, be used as a basis for the critical appraisal of our present punishment system.

The Retributive Theory

As Freud and Durkheim clearly saw, central to the concept of legal punishment is the idea that a criminal has exacted something unfairly from the law-abiding and therefore owes them something in return. In punishing a criminal, we say that "he is paying his debt to society" or "getting what's coming to him," that is, we see punishment as something that a criminal *deserves*. The notion that punishment is essentially a debt deservedly exacted from a criminal for his wrongdoing is the central idea of various *retributive* theories of punishment. (The concept of retribution has its etymological roots in the Latin *retribuere = to repay*.) Although, as scientists attempting to understand the underlying psychological and sociological meaning of the practice of legal punishment, it was not Freud and Durkheim's task to justify this practice, those who accept the retributive theory of punishment have attempted precisely this. For the retributivist, punishment is not simply something that ordinary people tend to see as "deserved"; it is something that *ought* to be so seen.

While all "retributivists" share the belief that a society's right to punish derives from a principle of justice and not utility, there is no single "retributive" theory of punishment. "Retributivism" is often described in the philosophical literature as the view that punishment is justified purely on the grounds that *wrongdoing merits punishment,* that it is *morally fitting that a person who does wrong should suffer in proportion to the degree of his moral blameworthiness* (or to use a California court's stronger language, "moral turpitude"). Such a view, however, is not held by Kant, who is generally considered the best example of a retributivist. As we have seen in our discussion of Kant's general ethical theory, for Kant, political societies exist not to maximize utility, nor indeed to proportion reward and punishment to moral desert, but to maximize liberty. As such, the way Kant saw it, criminals should be punished not for their *wickedness,* but for their *injustice—* that is, for upsetting a balance of benefits and burdens which is essential for the maximization of freedom in a community. However "bad" a person may be, a state has no right, Kant firmly believed, to punish him unless he *intentionally acted* to upset that balance. If the state were to attempt to punish for "moral blameworthiness" (which depends ultimately on one's motives) as well as injustice, liberty would not be maximized—indeed it would be greatly restricted as the state attempted to discover the underlying motives of individuals as well as their intentions and actions. Furthermore, Kant was very skeptical of the possibility of discovering the underlying motives behind individual actions. For this reason, Kant, in spite of the highly moralistic tone in much of his writings, was surprisingly hesitant about ultimate judgments of moral worth—judgments which, he believed, can be made reliably only by God.

Retributivists such as Kant are deontologists who see morality as the fulfillment of obligations and duties. Living in a society requires mutual cooperation which in turn demands regulation of conduct involving self-restraint, for one's personal interest at a particular moment often conflicts with one's obligation to do what is in the ultimate interest of all. A legal system, in the retributive view, is a reciprocal affair in which individuals gain the benefits of noninterference by others at the cost of self-restraint. The criminal, in this view, is a parasite who has accepted the benefits of a legal system while refusing to pay the price of self-restraint. Such a person owes the law-abiding a debt and is a proper object of resentment, for he has gained an unfair advantage over them. Matters are not even until this advantage is erased. Punishment, for the retributivist, is the means of exacting that debt and is a demand of justice—the restoration of a condition of equality between the lawbreaker and society.

Furthermore, for such retributivists, the severity of punishment should be proportional to the social importance of the duty violated and the ease with which that duty might have been fulfilled. Though for some retributivists, such as Kant, just punishment is unconditionally binding and not to be mitigated by any utilitarian consideration, a retributivist can consider the disobedience of a law as creating a right, but not an inescapable duty, to punish and may even consider it desirable to punish only when it is useful. Nevertheless, it will always be a criminal's desert which provides the upper bound of morally permissible punishment. It is only because punishment is recognized as deserved, the retributivist will claim, that the notions of forgiveness and mercy are deeply a part of the language of punishment, for to be merciful or to forgive is to let an offender off of part or all of his deserved punishment. The law, the retributivist will argue, should always treat individuals as sources of rightful claims and never merely as instruments for the promotion of utility. The only people who can justly be punished are the guilty, that is, those who have shirked an obligation of reciprocity justly demanded of them. Punishment of those who are not guilty is wrong, not because it results in more unhappiness than happiness, but because it does not treat such individuals justly.

The most influential of all retributivists is the philosopher Kant. Since criminal punishment is an infringement of human liberty in a quite brutal form, it can, for Kant, only be rightfully inflicted on a criminal who has himself unjustifiably interfered with the liberties of others. In punishing the criminal, we attempt, as best we can, to do to him what he has done to others. In Kantian terms, we attempt to demonstrate to him the implications of the universalization of the maxim under which he has acted. As such, for Kant, the justification of punishment is directed to the criminal himself who is to be shown that he has "brought his punishment upon himself." We do this, according to Kant, by applying the criminal's maxim of action to the criminal himself. If he murders, he must be executed; if he steals, he must be stolen from, etc.

Kant's retributive sentiments are best expressed in the following often-quoted passage:

> Judicial punishment can never be used merely as a means to promote some other good for the criminal himself or for civil society, but instead it must in all cases be imposed on him only on the ground that he has committed a crime; for a human being can never be manipulated merely as a means to the purposes of someone else. . . . He must first be found to be deserving of punishment before any consideration is given to the utility of this punishment for himself or for his fellow citizens. The law concerning punishment is a categorical imperative, and woe to him who rummages around in the winding paths of a theory of happiness looking for some advantage to be gained by releasing the criminal from punishment or by reducing the amount of it. . . . If legal justice perishes, then it is no longer worthwhile for men to remain alive on this earth. If this is so, what should one think of the proposal to permit a criminal who has been condemned to death to remain alive, if, after consenting to allow dangerous experiments to be made on him, he happily survives such experiments and if doctors thereby obtain new information that benefits the community? Any court of justice would repudiate such a proposal with scorn . . . for . . . justice ceases to be justice if it can be bought for a price.
>
> What kind and what degree of punishment does public legal justice adopt as its principle and standard? None other than the principle of equality (illustrated by the pointer on the scales of justice), that is, the principle of not treating one side more favorably than the other. Accordingly, any undeserved evil that you inflict on someone else . . . is one that you do to yourself. If you vilify him, you vilify yourself; if you kill him, you kill yourself. Only the law of retribution (*jus talionis*) can determine exactly the kind and degree of punishment. . . . All other standards . . . cannot be compatible with the principle of pure and strict legal justice.[7]

There are three basic points that Kant makes in this passage, all of which are integral parts of his retributive theory. First, the only acceptable reason for punishing a person is that he is guilty of a crime and, therefore, is deserving of punishment. Although Kant is adamant that utility cannot justify either the infliction of punishment or its degree, once a criminal's punishment and its degree are justified on the

---

[7] I. Kant, *The Metaphysical Elements of Justice,* John Ladd, translator (Indianapolis: Bobbs-Merrill, 1965), pp. 100–101.

basis of his desert, this punishment may then be utilized in order to serve utilitarian goals. However, it is never these utilitarian goals themselves, Kant insists, that confer upon us *the right to punish;* only criminal desert can do that. Second, the only acceptable reason for punishing a person in a given manner and degree is that the punishment inflicted is equal to the crime which the criminal has committed. Third, it is not only wrong to punish people who do not deserve punishment or to punish them more than they deserve; it is also wrong to "let a person off" his justly deserved punishment or some measure of it, even if such punishment can be given no utilitarian justification. A person's guilt *demands* punishment and if we refuse to exact that demand, we "may be regarded as accomplices in this public violation of legal justice," Kant declares.

The Utilitarian Theory

Whereas the retributivist will see the practice of punishment as justifiable independent of its consequences, utilitarians, such as Bentham, have considered it a painful necessity, justified only by its ability to prevent crime. From this point of view, the retributive insistence upon seeing punishment as in some way deserved, apart from any consideration as to its consequences, is usually dismissed as nothing more than an intellectual rationalization for a primitive and morally unjustified desire for revenge. The end of legal punishment, as the end of all justifiable legal institutions, utilitarians such as Bentham have declared, must be "to augment the total happiness of the community." From this perspective, the justification of legal punishment is not directed, as it is by the retributivist, to the criminal himself, but is directed instead to the personally uninvolved citizen whose aim is to live in a society where the general happiness is maximized. Crime, according to this perspective, is a form of *mischief* which interferes with the general happiness, and *punishment* is a specific *remedy* for the suppression of this mischief. As Bentham saw it, punishment is one of the four following remedies for crime: 1) *preventive,* 2) *suppressive,* 3) *satisfactory,* 4) *penal remedies* or *punishment.* A *preventive remedy,* according to Bentham, would be one which attempts to prevent crimes from ever happening by eliminating some of their essential causes (such as the confiscation of weapons and tools that can be used for the commission of crimes, and reeducating people away from possible criminal lives). A *suppressive remedy,* on the other hand, would be one utilized after a criminal act has been initiated but not completed (such as grabbing a would-be killer's gun from him). Once the crime has been completed, a *satisfactory remedy* would be one which "consists of reparations or indemnities, secured to those who have suffered from offenses" (that is, a victim of a crime is compensated for his loss or suffering). Finally, *punishment* may be inflicted upon a criminal who has committed an offense. For Bentham, *punishment* differs from *satisfactory remedies* for crime in that its purpose is not one of compensating the victim, but rather "to prevent like offenses, whether on the part of the offender or of others." As Bentham put it,

> . . . punishment which, considered in itself, appears base and repugnant to all generous sentiments, is elevated to the first rank of benefits when it is regarded not as an act of wrath or vengeance against a guilty or unfortunate individual who has given way to mischievous inclinations, but as an indispensable sacrifice to the common safety.[8]

The aim of the crime prevention, Bentham claims, can be achieved through the incapacitative, deterrent, and rehabilitative power of punishment. First, punishment provides an incapacitative function by temporarily (such as by imprisonment) or permanently (such as by death) making it physically impossible for the criminal to commit again the same or similar criminal actions. Second, punishment acts as a deterrent by giving the criminal himself a motive (fear of being punished again) to refrain from similar criminal activities in the future (specific deterrence). And most important of all, for Bentham, the punishment of the criminal can act as a source of intimidation to the rational self-seeking potential offender who requires the fear of punishment as a restraint on his own behavior (general deterrence). Finally, punishment can serve its rehabilitative function when its imposition can so change the desires or values of a criminal that he no longer desires to commit similar criminal actions. Unlike the deterred offender, a rehabilitated offender has undergone some type of personality change which makes the external restraint of fear of criminal punishment unnecessary.

Since, for Bentham, punishment is in itself, apart from a consideration of its beneficial consequences, an evil, it would be wrong to inflict it in any situation where its infliction would likely cause more harm (*mischief*) than good or where that good could be achieved at a *cheaper rate* (that is, at less of a utilitarian cost). Once the infliction of punishment is justified on utilitarian grounds, its manner and degree must also be so justified. For example, Bentham argues that it is necessary to set penalties in such a way that a person will have more motivation to commit a crime which produces less harm rather than one that produces more.

While Bentham saw general deterrence as "the chief end of punishment," contemporary utilitarians are often quite skeptical of the value of punishment as a deterrent. As they see it, this view rests on the mistaken assumption (clearly made by Bentham) that most people rationally decide whether to be criminals—balancing its possible dangers against its possible rewards. Such a view of human beings, they claim, has been

---

[8] J. Bentham, *The Rationale of Punishment,* quoted in Edmund L. Pincoffs, *The Rationale of Legal Punishment* (Atlantic Highlands, N.J.: Humanities Press, 1966), p. 22.

refuted by the psychological and social sciences. Skeptical of the value of deterrence, such utilitarians often emphasize the rehabilitative aim of punishment. Since many who emphasize rehabilitation over deterrence tend to see the justification of criminal rehabilitation at least as much in terms of the betterment of the offender as in terms of the goal of crime suppression, and, furthermore, tend to assume, as Bentham did not, that retributive notions are essential to the concept of punishment, defenders of this viewpoint often advocate the elimination of punishment and its replacement by a fully forward-looking treatment-oriented mode of dealing with criminals. (For the sake of clarity, let us refer to those utilitarians who accept such a viewpoint as *rehabilitationists.*)

Not all contemporary utilitarians, however, dismiss the effectiveness of punishment as a deterrent. As some see it, a belief in deterrence is quite compatible with contemporary psychological views which downplay the role of rational calculation and emphasize the emotional and unconscious factors that influence human behavior. As we have briefly discussed, current sociological and psychoanalytic theories of the nature of punishment emphasize the power of punishment as an unconscious deterrent. It is by means of a ritualistic law which is deeply connected with moral feelings, Durkheim, Freud, and their followers have claimed, that the moral impropriety of criminal behavior is emphasized and internalized by the general community. Specific punishments may have little immediate effect upon specific and general deterrence, but the practice of punishment may have a long-run general deterrent effect upon the suppression of criminalistic tendencies, it has been suggested.

Some Reflections on Utilitarianism and Retributivism

As we have seen in our discussion of normative ethics, utility and justice are both essential moral values. Utilitarians and retributivists emphasize one of the two values at the expense of the other; by so doing, they achieve a uniformity of theory which is inadequate to the complexities of the moral life. It is a mistake to insist upon one theory at the expense of the other. If, on one hand, we insist upon a purely retributive theory of punishment, unlimited by any utilitarian considerations, we will never be able to clearly distinguish our unrelenting demand for "retribution" from the primitive urge for "revenge." Similarly, if we insist upon perceiving the principle of "equality" of crime and punishment as a principle which can be applied without any appeal to utilitarian considerations, we will be incapable of distinguishing this principle from the primitive principle of "an eye for an eye, and a tooth for a tooth" and will be at a loss, at times, to know how to apply such a principle at all. For example, what do we do to the rapist, the embezzler, the mass murderer, or a person who is responsible for a reckless or negligent homicide?

If, on the other hand, we insist upon a purely utilitarian theory of punishment, unlimited by principles of individual justice, there can be no principled objection to subjecting individuals to unjust punishment whenever this can serve the aims of crime prevention. In particular, as retributivists have pointed out, there can be no principled utilitarian objection to punishing an innocent person in certain circumstances. For example, let us assume that there is a widespread outbreak of a particular crime and that none of the guilty parties can be found. Nevertheless, there is a pressing need for someone to be punished to serve the aim of general deterrence. Why, then, should we not sacrifice an innocent person, if the "mischief" of his punishment is less than the "mischief" of the crime that his punishment can serve to deter? Even if, as utilitarians have suggested, *a systematic practice* of punishing the innocent would, in the long-run, cause sufficient insecurity and general disrespect for the law as to outweigh the short-term good of such unjust punishments, it is simply false to assert that the punishment of innocent individuals could never be justified on purely utilitarian grounds *in certain special circumstances*—such as in those situations where there is every reason to believe that the knowledge of the punished person's innocence can be kept quiet and thereby not tend to subvert general respect for law or generate mass insecurity. (Recall our criticism of rule-utilitarianism.)

If laws aimed only at utility, legislators would be justified in passing many laws requiring strict liability (liability without fault), laws which are presently resisted out of a sense of their injustice. Similarly, the utilitarian legislator might very well have good reason to punish negligent manslaughter caused by drunken drivers much more severely than most premeditated murders, for the former is generally more deterrable and dangerous to more people than the latter. Yet the murderer is punished more severely since he, unlike the drunk driver, intended to kill. It is our sense of justice and not a utilitarian calculation that instinctively assumes that guilt should depend upon intent as well as the effect produced. In addition, if utilitarian considerations were the sole judicial concerns, it would be perfectly proper in some situations to allow the sentence for a given crime to be constantly adjusted in accord with the shifting demands of general deterrence—for instance, whenever there is a general outbreak of a particular crime, its punishment would be made more severe. Again, it is our sense of justice that recoils at the thought of "using the criminal *merely as a means* for promoting the good of others" and of allowing his punishment to be varied according to the vicissitudes of social need, without any relation to his degree of desert or fault.

Nevertheless, must we not agree with the utilitarian that it is wrong to punish criminals simply because they deserve it, even when the general welfare would be better served by not doing so. While such individuals may "owe us a debt," is it right for us to exact it regardless of the consequences? It is, after all, one thing to say that only the guilty *may* be punished and something quite different to say that the guilty *must* be punished, as Kant does. In addition, the utilitarian seems quite justified in rejecting the Kantian view that the penalty "appropriate" for a given crime should be determined apart from a consideration of consequences. On the contrary, our notion of the appropriateness of penalties must ultimately reflect our conception of the relative seriousness of crimes which can either be understood in terms of the purely psychological notion of the degree of revulsion they tend to generate in the minds of the law-abiding or in terms of the relative harm they tend to produce. Certainly, the degree of revulsion people feel toward specific crimes should be subject to appraisal according to some rational principle; this principle should be the utilitarian one of grading crimes according to the degree of harm they are likely to cause.

Although utility and justice may be competing values, they are not mutually exclusive. Punishment is always best when it is both useful and just. Nevertheless, there are times, in both the legislative and judicial realms, where these values conflict and we must choose between them, depending upon our own ultimate moral preferences. For example, a judge must often weigh the competing values of justice and utility against each other, trying not to blind himself to one value or the other. Yet, in the end, he must often choose, guided to some extent by precedent and to some extent by his own moral preferences. As such, some judges tend to see themselves more as stern balancers of the scales of justice, whose responsibility it is to give people what they *deserve* and not primarily what is *best,* while other judges see themselves more as "social engineers," who, working within the constraints of the laws they are sworn to uphold, attempt to accomplish as much good as possible in particular cases. Even though such different perceptions of one's role as a judge often generate differences in particular sentencing policies, this is not always the case, for quite often both justice and utility can be seen as pointing toward the same resolution of a particular problem. For example, both retributivists and utilitarians have justified punishing individuals more for crimes involving deliberation than for those done "in the heat of passion." For the retributivist, this will be seen as justified in terms of the greater moral culpability of a person who acts with deliberation, while for the utilitarian, this will be seen as justified in terms of the greater deterrability or dangerousness of those who deliberate over those who do not.

It is the fashion nowadays to dismiss retributivism as "nothing but a rationalization for revenge." This is sadly mistaken. As we shall see in our discussion of the rehabilitative ideal that is now in the forefront of discussions of punishment, the retributive model may be the only protection a criminal can have against a utilitarianism gone mad, for this model, unlike the utilitarian one, treats individuals as *free agents* who have *rights* protecting them from being completely at the mercy of someone else's conception of *the common good* or of what it is to be an *adequate* human being. A complete devotion to the utilitarian model, unlimited by principles which distribute rights to individuals and which aim at minimizing the state's interference in the liberty of its citizens cannot help but invite the worst horrors or Orwell's *1984* or Huxley's *Brave New World.*

On the other hand, on grounds of political philosophy, I prefer emphasizing utilitarian principles rather than retributive ones, for I fear that an emphasis upon the concepts of justice and desert can generate a smug self-righteousness which considers the practice of punishment as being immune from scientific support or criticism and does not look for more efficient and humane ways of reducing crime. As the philosopher John Dewey once claimed,

> No amount of guilt on the part of the evildoer absolves us from responsibility for the consequences upon him and others of our way of treating him, or for our continuing responsibility for the conditions under which persons develop perverse habits.[9]

I am also led away from the retributive view on more substantial philosophical grounds. The retributive model of a rational offender who receives his deserved punishment for upsetting a justly balanced scale of benefits and burdens, though reflecting a model of human beings and society as they ideally ought to be, cannot be made to fit human beings and society as they actually are.

Punishment as retribution makes sense in a community of equal individuals bound together by freely and commonly accepted legal rules. It is for this reason that the retributive view has often been associated with a commitment to a "social contract" theory of the grounds of legal obligation which looks upon society as if it were based upon a pact between rational individuals who have assented to subject themselves to a system of mutually beneficial rules. (Such "social contract" theories do not assume that people *in fact* have consented to these rules, but that it would have been *rational* for them to do so, if they were given the choice. Consequently, these theories function as models of *rational decision,* such as those found in contemporary decision and game theory.) These rules are to be imposed and enforced so impartially and fairly that no person subject to them can justifiably claim that he is being victimized. As such, the retributivist is open to the Marxist challenge that existing societies, with their crime-breeding economic and social injustices, do not live up to this requirement. Certainly, in this country, those minority groups that are most given to crime do not have the same social benefits as the more affluent majority. As Anatole France put it, "The law in its majestic equality forbids the rich as well as the poor to sleep under bridges, to beg on the street, and to steal bread." A retributivist may agree with this criticism, claiming that the retributive model is an ideal to which existing society ought to strive.

The retributivist is, however, open to the more serious challenge that no society can, on psychological grounds, ever live up to his ideal.

[9] John Dewey, *Human Nature and Conduct* (New York: Holt, Rinehart & Winston, 1922), pp. 18–19.

Surely, if a given legal system is to be fair, all who are punished should be capable of conforming to the law and should be punished to a degree proportionate to their degree of power to so conform. Although such power varies greatly among individuals, the retributivist, as well as all existing legal codes, tend to assume a society of persons with roughly equal powers to conform to the requirements of law. It is on the basis of this assumption that the retributivist and existing legal systems tend to attribute the characteristics of a mythical "average man" to criminal offenders, in spite of the fact that this is often not the case. Quite often, a skeptic will claim, criminals tend to have far less power to conform to the law than the law-abiding. Consequently, the retributivist is unjustified in his basic assumption that the criminal is *morally worse* than the rest of us, since we have exercised self-restraint, whereas he has not, for often exercising that self-restraint was simply easier for us. As we learn more about the causes of human behavior, our skeptic will say, we will begin to realize that most offenders have much less power to do otherwise than the retributivist is willing to admit. The moral distinctions the retributivist insists upon are merely a function of our empirical ignorance and will disappear once that ignorance has been dispelled.

One's position on the free-will issue has a great influence on one's position on the justification of punishment. A person who believes that man is not free to act otherwise than he does will reject the retributive view and maintain that one can with no more justification speak about just retribution against a criminal than one can speak about just retribution against a dangerous dog. Though a person with such sentiments will not himself look upon punishment as a deserved infliction of suffering upon the morally guilty, he may be forced, on purely utilitarian grounds, to advocate a system of punishment like our own in which retributive notions have an important place. Realizing that retributive feelings are a fundamental part of most people's natures, such a utilitarian may see the retributive language as serving a social purpose. While the general community will see retributive punishment as morally called for, he will see it as an orderly outlet for the desire for retribution which either cannot be suppressed or can only be suppressed at the cost of dangerously lessening in the general populace the largely unconscious behavior controls provided by feelings of guilt, remorse, and indignation.

THE ASSAULT UPON THE NOTION
OF CRIMINAL LIABILITY

Introduction: The Concept of a Crime

Our criminal justice system is today caught up in a wave of ideological criticism directed toward its fundamental philosophical foundation. "Treat criminals, do not punish them," the critics often exhort. We must, they say, fully uproot the notion of retributive punishment with its emphasis upon the *moral guilt* or *fault* incurred by a *free agent* who *deserves* to be punished in a particular manner and degree for his criminal act; instead, our response to crime should be flexible and oriented toward the differing needs of the criminal. The criminal, they say, should not be seen as a *responsible* and *blameworthy* individual who is "paying his debt to society," but rather as a *sick* individual who needs to undergo some "therapeutic regime for personal betterment."

Among those who hold such a position, there is much dissatisfaction with the manner in which our existing criminal law attempts to distinguish legally responsible from legally nonresponsible offenders and attempts to distinguish varying degrees of legal responsibility. Before we inquire into the nature of this dissatisfaction, let us briefly see how the law presently defines "crimes" and "criminal liability."

Traditionally, a "crime" has been defined as a voluntary act or omission (in Latin, an *actus reus*) accompanied by some "mental element" which renders the offender blameworthy (in Latin, *mens rea* = *guilty mind*). In applying this definition, the law tends to count all acts as voluntary as long as they are chosen, regardless of how forced that choice may be. From this perspective, the law would count as involuntary behavior (for which there can be no criminal liability) conduct occurring while one is asleep, unconscious, or in a state of "automatism," but would count as voluntary an act performed under extreme coercion. It is the *mens rea* requirement of criminal liability which attempts to distinguish blameworthy voluntary acts from nonblameworthy ones. For some crimes, the *mens rea* requirement is that the voluntary act was done purposely (that is, the actor knew what would happen and wanted it to happen), or knowingly (that is, the actor knew what would happen), or recklessly (that is, the actor knew that there was a good chance that the result would occur and unreasonably disregarded that risk), or negligently (that is, the actor was not aware of the possibility of the result, but "a reasonable person in his situation" would have been aware). For other crimes, a more specific *mens rea* may be required (such as premeditation for first degree murder). In this century, however, there has been a growing tendency in the criminal law to dispense with the *mens rea* requirement and to allow "liability without fault" or, as it is called, "strict liability." For example, it is common now to punish individuals for manufacturing, distributing, or selling adulterated foods, even if they did not know nor could not have reasonably been expected to know that those foods were adulterated.

Even if all the defining elements of a crime are present, a person's act is not a crime if it is capable of justification or excuse. In calling an act justifiable, the law asserts that under the circumstances it was the right thing to do, while in excusing an act the law asserts that even though it was wrong, it would be improper to punish it. For example, if a policeman kills an armed robber in self-defense, this would be a justifiable homicide, while if the policeman nonnegligently kills an innocent bystander while attempting to shoot at a fleeing killer, this would be considered an excusable homicide. While there is disagreement as to its definition and extent, the criminal law accepts a principle of "necessity" which affords a general justification for conduct that would otherwise constitute an offense. In its broadest formulation (such as that formulated in the American Law Institute's Model Penal Code) such a principle of general justification can be utilized *whenever* a person's action is necessary to avoid a "greater evil." More commonly, however, such a justification is limited to the avoidance of specific grave evils, such as death or bodily injury. Nevertheless, if a person is faced with a choice of unpleasant alternatives and makes a choice which the law considers to be wrong, he may still be legally excused if his choice was made under the influence of such duress (coercion) that "a person of reasonable firmness" in his situation would have been unable to resist.

The Insanity Defense

Recognizing that there are persons who, on any common sense notion of justice, are not morally blameworthy for their actions, not because of specific external pressures, but rather because of their grossly abnormal personalities, the law also accepts the excuse of insanity (the insanity defense). Although the plea of duress is directed to "average" citizens who are assumed to be capable of accepting the obligation to obey the law as a rational one and are assumed to have roughly similar capacities to reason, to judge consequences, and to exercise self-restraint, the insanity defense is directed to individuals who are so different from the rest of us that we do not consider them as members of our moral community. If they do something that adversely affects our interests, we try to stop them, very much as we would stop animals or small children whom we do not morally blame for their actions.

Although utilitarians have attempted to justify the existence of the insanity defense on the grounds that some individuals are nondeterrable and consequently there would be no utilitarian justification in punishing them, such a view is fraught with difficulties. First, one could plausibly argue that even if some individuals are "nondeterrable" (whatever this is taken to mean), the acceptance of such an excuse might encourage persons who have some power to refrain from their actions to either simulate such an excuse or to deceive themselves into thinking that they are powerless to refrain from their actions and consequently not subject to punishment (that is, punishing the nondeterrable might have a beneficial effect upon general deterrence). More fundamentally, however, if we accept the principle that only deterrable criminals should be punished, this would seem to lead us to the paradoxical conclusion that "ordinary incorrigible criminals" should not be punished, even though most of us would want to say that such individuals *deserve* their punishment, whereas the insane do not. In addition, the common assumption that those whom we tend to consider as insane cannot respond to threats of punishment seems to be refuted by the fact that those committed to mental hospitals for their insanity are quite often capable of responding to the suspension of privileges, ridicule, corporal punishment, and unpleasant jobs no less than "ordinary criminals."[10]

It would certainly appear that utilitarian considerations are really not what lead us to accept an insanity defense; it is rather our sense of the injustice of punishing the innocent that retributivists so strongly insist upon. Recognizing this fact, contemporary rehabilitationists have often strongly denounced the justification of the insanity defense. The confusion surrounding the principles presently utilized to distinguish insane from sane offenders, they claim, amply demonstrates the impossibility of distinguishing the sick from the bad or the nonresponsible from the responsible. The insanity defense, they say, must be abolished and, along with it, the traditional retributive insistence upon the moral guilt of criminal offenders.

The insanity rule utilized in Great Britain and about thirty states in the United States is the famous M'Naghten rule which was formulated in Great Britain during the reign of Queen Victoria in the mid-nineteenth century. According to this rule,

> . . . to establish a defense on the ground of insanity, it must be clearly proved that, at the time of the committing of the act the party accused was labouring under such a defect of reason, from disease of the mind, as not to know the nature and quality of the act he was doing; or if he did know it, that he did not know he was doing what was wrong.

In spite of the fact that the M'Naghten rule has become a focal point in the contemporary controversy surrounding the insanity defense, there has been little judicial interpretation of its meaning. For example, even though psychiatrists and psychologists often disagree as to what, if anything, the concept of "mental illness (disease)" means, the courts have not taken a definite stand as to what is to count under M'Naghten as "a defect of reason from disease of the mind." The generally accepted view among legal commentators has been that this notion should be taken as synonymous with the psychiatric notion of a "psychosis." Unfortunately, however, this notion does not have a single accepted psychiatric meaning. As any psychiatrist will attest, the standards for distinguishing psychoses from neuroses or for distinguishing cognitive from affective and motivational defects are far from clear. Although it is common for people to assume that the distinguishing difference between a psychosis and a neurosis is that only the former results in a defect of reason, such an assumption is not in accord with psychiatric usage. For example, the elaborate rationalizations of many neurotics are often described by psychiatrists as defects of reason.

The interpretation to be given the phrase, "he did not know he

---

[10] See, for example, Erving Goffman, *Asylums: Essays on the Social Situation of Mental Patients and Other Inmates* (New York: Doubleday, 1961).

was doing what was wrong" has been the subject of much controversy in the debate over the M'Naghten rule. The critics, mainly psychiatrists, have tended to assume that according to this rule the mere emotionally detached ability to recognize that one's action would be condemned by others as wrong qualifies one as sane, even though one may have an extremely inadequate understanding of the moral and physical implications of one's act and no emotional appreciation of it (such as feelings of guilt, shame, or inner moral conflict). The critics often distinguish this narrow concept of knowledge from a broader psychiatric one which involves having some insight into the nature and implications of one's act and some degree of emotional appreciation of it. In spite of the widespread assumption that the law imposes a narrow interpretation of "know," this is mistaken. In most jurisdictions, the jury is simply given the words of the rule, without explanation, and left to give it their own "common-sense" interpretation. Those jurisdictions that do address themselves to the question have tended to favor rather broad interpretations of "know." Some courts have taken the "nature and quality" clause as supporting a broad interpretation. This clause is, however, rarely treated by the courts as if it adds anything to the "know . . . wrong" clause; indeed, some courts omit this phrase entirely. While many courts are willing to assume that "knowing one's act is wrong" requires some insight and/or emotional appreciation of one's action, they have not attempted to specify how much of this broader knowledge is required for criminal responsibility nor have they offered any rationale as to why only those who lack this broader knowledge as a result of "a defect of reason, from disease of mind," should be exculpated, while "ordinary" criminals should not.

Since M'Naghten is directed only to those offenders who in some sense lack knowledge of the moral or physical nature or consequences of their actions and, since it is widely assumed that a person who has such knowledge might still be "incapable of controlling himself," in many states in the United States M'Naghten is supplemented by some type of "irresistible impulse" rule. This often-used term is misleading in mistakenly suggesting that such rules require that actions be a product of sudden impulses. There is no single "irresistible impulse" test; indeed, most tests do not utilize this term at all, directing themselves to whether an offender "was capable of controlling himself" or whether he had "freedom of choice." As we have seen, however, in our discussion of the free-will issue, such phrases have no agreed-upon meaning. As in the case with M'Naghten, their interpretation is usually left to the "common sense" of the jury. The only precise interpretation of these phrases has been supplied by the military courts which require conduct which would not be prevented even by a "policeman at the elbow" of the defendant. Yet the only acts which probably satisfy this strong requirement are acts which the law would recognize as "involuntary" and hence acts which would make an insanity plea unnecessary. For example, though one may assume that the capacity to control tests are directed toward excusing those whom psychiatrists would call "compulsive neurotics" (such as kleptomaniacs), it is generally recognized that an exceedingly compulsive kleptomaniac will not steal in the presence of a policeman.

As our little excursion into legal analysis has amply demonstrated, the meaning of the M'Naghten and irresistible impulse rules are far from clear. Indeed, since many, if not most, "ordinary" criminals either lack insight or emotional appreciation of their actions and their consequences or are very limited in their capacity to do otherwise, many or most criminals would seem to qualify as insane, if they could be said to suffer from some mental illness. But most ordinary criminals, many will surely protest, are not mentally ill. This depends, however, on which psychiatrist or psychologist one asks. The classification of someone as "mentally ill," whether made by psychiatrists, psychologists, or lay people, often does not reflect a diagnosis of the cause of his behavior, thoughts, and feelings, but rather reflects *a decision* to look upon him in a certain way—a decision that the person is not to be blamed but helped. Since psychiatrists and psychologists have been trained to help people, it is not surprising that many of them are tempted to see all deviant behavior as a sign of mental illness. The following are extreme statements of this attitude:

> Theft, like rheumatic fever, is a disease of childhood and adolescence, and, as in rheumatic fever, attacks in later life are frequently in the nature of recurrences.[11]

> Using medical terms, delinquency can be described as a very widespread illness, affecting mainly young people and causing gross symptoms.[12]

> The time will come when stealing or murder will be thought of as a symptom indicating the presence of a disease, a personality disease. . . .[13]

The thrust of these statements is clearly that all offenders are mentally ill and that, consequently, an insanity defense which attempts to distinguish the "blameworthy" from the "sick" is attempting to distinguish the indistinguishable. Although the concept of "mental illness" was once largely restricted to those severe psychological disorders that required hospitalization (that is, to what psychiatrists would today call "organic or functional psychoses"), today the concept of mental illness has been so extended that it now is often taken to include individuals who experience problems in social adjustment or vague feelings of dissatisfaction, lack of fulfillment, or lack of a sense of self-identity. If a

[11] John Boulby, "Forty-four Juvenile Thiefs: Their Characters and Home Life," *International Journal of Psychoanalysis*, 25 (1944), p. 19.

[12] Michael Balint, "On Punishing Offenders," in George Wilbur and Warner Muensterberger, eds., *Psychoanalysis and Culture* (New York: International Universities Press, 1951), p. 254.

[13] Karl Menninger, "Medicolegal Proposals of the American Psychiatric Association," *J. Criminal Law and Criminology*, 19 (1928), p. 367.

psychiatrist is today asked to define "mental illness," he might very well reply that a "mental illness" is anything that is listed in *The Diagnostic and Statistical Manual of Mental Disorders* of the American Psychiatric Association. Yet if one looks at this manual, one discovers that all types of behavioral disorders and deviance are listed here (such as alcoholism, inadequate personality, emotionally unstable personality, transient situational personality disturbance, and dyssocial reaction—that is, cultural deviance). These disorders are defined as being medical in nature, meaning that their treatment can become the exclusive concern of psychiatrists. (Consequently, it is quite understandable that psychologists, the main competitors for the psychotherapeutic franchise, have been most vocal in advocating the redefinition of behavioral disorders and deviance as being nonmedical.)

The courts, in their attempt to restrict the insanity defense to those who suffer from a "mental illness," have often learned that this notion is subject to conflicting psychiatric interpretations. In an important insanity trial in the District of Columbia (*Blocker v. United States*, 1959), for example, psychiatrists first testified that psychopaths did not suffer from a mental disease; then, after a weekend of reflection, decided that they did. Though the basis for this decision was not given, one can be assured that it was not a result of a new medical discovery. This sorry state of affairs prompted the appeal judge, Warren Burger (who later became Chief Justice of the U.S. Supreme Court) to remark, "This is reminiscent of Lewis Carroll's classic utterance, 'When I use a word,' Humpty Dumpty said, in rather a scornful tone, 'it means just what I choose it to mean—neither more nor less,' " and he could have added with Alice, "The question is . . . whether you can make words mean so many different things."

Although for an ordinary person, "psychopaths" are the very model of wicked individuals who intentionally and of their own free will commit criminal acts which they know to be wrong and could easily refrain from if they wanted to, psychiatrists often see such individuals as sick people who "cannot help themselves." As Barbara Wootton, a contemporary English magistrate and leading critic of our punishment system puts it, "The psychopath now prays in aid of his defense the very qualities which in the case of the wicked would but serve to blacken his record."[14] Certainly when one sees the psychopath described by those who have studied him as ". . . an antisocial, aggressive, highly impulsive person who feels little or no guilt and who is unable to form lasting bonds of affection with other human beings,"[15] one can well see the justification for Wootton's remark. Yet there are psychiatrists who would

[14] Barbara Wootton, "Diminished Responsibility: A Layman's View," *Law Quarterly Review*, 76 (1960), pp. 224–39.

[15] William McCord and Joan McCord, *The Psychopath* (New York: D. Van Nostrand, 1964), p. 3.

claim that the psychopath is not only mentally ill but seriously so.[16] Indeed, the psychopath, given his impulsiveness and lack of internal moral restraints, would seem to be the very model of a nondeterrable individual who lacks any emotional appreciation of the significance of his acts. Consequently, under a broad interpretation of the M'Naghten rule or under an irresistible-impulse rule, he would seem to qualify as insane. Yet to the general community, such a judgment will appear quite unjustified—for the psychopath appears so "normal" and so "bad."

For the hard determinist, this inconsistency is quite understandable, for once we delve into the causes of the behavior of even the most seemingly wicked of criminals, we will ultimately come to some cause for which he cannot reasonably be held responsible. This is true, the hard determinist would say, not only for those whom the ordinary person would perceive as mentally ill, but also for those apparently mentally healthy individuals who are victims of any one of the many unfortunate unlucky breaks of life, such as that of being born poor or into a subculture that rejects the values of the predominant majority. Such individuals also often grow up incapable of accepting or appreciating the moral standards that form the foundation of our law and incapable of feeling the sort of guilt, shame, and inner moral conflict that the "ordinary" criminal is supposed to feel when he commits a crime. Since such individuals did not choose to be brought up as they were, why should they be considered any more responsible or morally blameworthy for their actions than those whose actions result from what would commonly be called a mental illness, our hard determinist will rhetorically ask. His question is one that cannot easily be answered.

Indeed, psychiatrists who do not challenge the insanity defense on general hard-deterministic grounds have posed fundamental questions concerning the justification of assuming, as insanity rules tacitly do, that there is something special about mental illness that tends to rob persons of their free will. Today, there are many psychiatrists and psychologists who would consider this assumption quite mistaken.[17] From their point of view, one should reject the typical medical model of mental illness as some type of psychic cancer which "involuntarily invades and afflicts" a person and is responsible for the abnormal patterns of thought, feel-

---

[16] See, for example, H. Cleckley's *The Mask of Sanity*. According to Cleckley, the psychopath suffers from an *inability* to care about others or to empathize with their plight, which is so severe that he is incapable of understanding the "ultimate significance and intention of words and phrases," and is consequently unable to "integrate and appreciate his experience"; this, Cleckley claims, is a "psychosis." Indeed, many psychiatrists have claimed that the distinctive uncaring, impulsive, and remorseless attitude of the psychopath "is not really his fault," but is the result of the deprivation of parental love suffered in early childhood.

[17] See, for example, Thomas Szasz, *The Myth of Mental Illness* (New York: Dell Pub. Co., Inc., 1961) and R.D. Laing, *The Divided Self* (New York: Penguin, 1960).

ings, and behavior that form the symptoms of the disease from which the person suffers. Instead, they claim, one should see most mentally ill patients as free agents who *choose* their neuroses or psychoses as a way of life, which, like others, is usually partially successful in obtaining for the individual what he wants from the world and, as such, may be considered a strategy for living in a world not of one's own making. For such psychiatrists, it is not the model of nonresponsibility and victimization, which is reflected in the insanity defense, that threatens to swallow up the "ordinary" criminal, but it is rather the traditional legal reliance upon responsibility and free choice that threatens to swallow up the insanity defense. For example, the psychiatrist Bernard Diamond (who testified on behalf of Sirhan Sirhan, the assassin of Robert Kennedy) has suggested that in some cases people *choose to become psychotic* in order to commit crimes which they want to do but otherwise would lack the courage to do. Are we then to hold people responsible, at least in some cases, for choosing to become mentally ill? As psychiatrists ponder such questions, the distinction between those who should and those who should not be considered morally responsible for their actions fades into obscurity.

Objective versus Subjective Liability: The Doctrine of Diminished Responsibility

Until quite recently, if a mentally ill offender wanted to utilize his psychological abnormality as a factor in his defense, he would generally be able to do so only through a plea of insanity. This has been the result of the widespread adoption of the "objective theory" of criminal liability, which assumes that the differences in the psychological capacities of noninsane adults should be disregarded in the determination of the existence and degree of criminal liability. For example, most jurisdictions require, for a successful plea of self-defense, both that the defendant honestly believed at the time of his act that his life was in immediate danger and that this belief was "reasonable" in the circumstances, where the standard of "reasonableness" is "objective" (that is, the relevant question is whether "the reasonable man"—who is not assumed to have the defendant's psychological incapacities—would have thought that his life was in danger). However, in some jurisdictions, the objective theory of liability is giving way to a "subjective theory" of liability, which inquires into a defendant's actual psychological capacities. For example, a few jurisdictions now permit a jury to take some of the defendant's psychological characteristics into account in deciding what "the reasonable man" would have done "in the defendant's situation." The movement away from the objective theory of criminal liability has, however, been most noticeable in the growing number of jurisdictions which allow evidence of mental illness to reduce the degree of certain crimes—most notably in homicide cases, through what has come to be known as a plea of "diminished responsibility (capacity)." Indeed, in England and California, where this doctrine is most developed, it has, to a large extent, replaced the insanity defense. Before we consider the meaning of this doctrine, let us briefly consider how the various degrees of homicide are presently distinguished.

The Degrees of Homicide

Every unjustifiable and inexcusable killing of a human being by another human being is either manslaughter or murder. Traditionally, it is the absence of "malice aforethought" which distinguishes manslaughter from murder. Although until the early seventeenth century, "malice" was construed in its popular sense as "ill will" and implied a certain wickedness of motive, the meaning of this term has been greatly broadened through the years by the introduction of the notion of "implied malice." In the United States, the law generally is that all intentional criminal homicides satisfy the "malice" requirement for murder unless the defendant killed under "legally sufficient (adequate)" provocation and "in the heat of passion." In determining whether a given provocation is "legally sufficient" for a verdict of manslaughter, the law generally uses an objective standard, inquiring into whether the provocation "might render reasonable (or ordinary) men liable to kill in the same circumstances," evidence of the defendant's particular psychological characteristics being considered inadmissible. Considering the widespread differences in peoples' moral conceptions of when an "ordinary" person's loss of self-control should justify the mitigation of blame and punishment, it is not surprising that there is general disagreement on what specifically should count as legally sufficient provocation. As one critic wrote,

> The reasonable man's answers to the question of how he would react to a given set of circumstances have varied as he stepped from one jurisdiction to another. In some states, if he has suffered an assault, it will be sufficient provocation to reduce his killing to manslaughter; in others he must have been the victim of an assault and battery before his blood reaches the heat necessary to dispel any malice from his system; and in still other situations, even if an assault and battery has been committed upon his person, he may still as a matter of law be judged guilty of murder. We find this diversity of decision in almost every other situation in which the question of the adequacy of provocation is raised. The reasonable man tells us that he does not become sufficiently provoked when his California or Georgia or Iowa wife tells him she has been unfaithful but the provocation becomes unbearable when the scene is shifted to Kentucky, Mississippi, or South Carolina.[18]

Generally, in intentional homicides, if there is no legally sufficient provocation, malice aforethought is implied and a "murder" has been

[18] "Manslaughter and the Adequacy of Provocation: The Reasonableness of the Reasonable Man," 106, *Univ. of Penn. L. Rev.* 1036–37 (1958).

committed. The majority of U.S. jurisdictions recognize two degrees of murder. The standard for distinguishing first and second degree murder was first formulated in 1974 by a Pennsylvania court which declared that "all murder, which shall be perpetrated by means of poison, or by lying in wait, or by any other kind of . . . deliberate or premeditated killing, or which shall be committed in the perpetration, or attempt to perpetrate any arson, rape, robbery, or burglary shall be deemed murder in the first degree." Subject to minor variations, this is the law in all those states which distinguish degrees of murder. Since some jurisdictions have taken the view that "there need be no appreciable space of time between the intention to kill and the act of killing" for premeditation and deliberation to be said to exist, the conceptual distinction between "impulsive" and "premeditated and deliberate" homicides is not at all clear.

The justification of the traditional distinction between degrees of homicide has been defended on both utilitarian and retributive grounds. As the utilitarian has traditionally seen it, the justification for punishing individuals less for homicides committed in situations of provocation is that in these situations one's act, to a large extent, can be attributed to an external provocation which overwhelms one's normal self-control and is not, for that reason, a good reflection of one's normal character and consequently of one's dangerousness. Similarly, utilitarians have claimed that acts resulting from deliberation and premeditation would seem to be better reflections of one's normal character than acts committed impulsively, and, again, a better reflection of one's degree of dangerousness. For the retributivist, the acceptance of degrees of homicide is a reflection of our common-sense belief that the more a person's act can be attributed to his character, as opposed to some external provocation of temporary impulse, the more morally guilty that individual is. The utilitarian or retributive justification for distinguishing degrees of murder on the basis of the distinction between deliberate and impulsive killings has, however, widely been called into question. As the critics have pointed out, there is no invariable correlation between one's degree of deliberation and premeditation and one's degree of dangerousness or moral guilt. As the American Law Institute put it in formulating its highly influential Model Penal Code,

> . . . we think it plain that the case for a mitigated sentence does not depend on the distinction between impulse and deliberation; the very fact of long internal struggle may be evidence that the actor's homicidal impulse was deeply aberrational, far more the product of extraordinary circumstances than a true reflection of the actor's normal character, as, for example, in the case of mercy killings, suicide pacts, many infanticides, and cases where a provocation gains in explosive power as the actor broods about the injury. . . . And apart from such disturbance of the actor, we think it no less clear that some purely impulsive murders may present no extenuating circumstance. As Stephen put it long ago . . . :
> "As much cruelty, as much indifference to the life of others, a disposition at least as dangerous to society, probably even more dangerous, is shown

by sudden as by premeditated murders. The following cases appear to me to set this in a clear light. *A,* passing along the road, sees a boy sitting on a bridge over a deep river and, out of mere wanton barbarity, pushes him into it and so drowns him. A man makes advances to a girl who repels him. He deliberately but instantly cuts her throat. . . . In neither of these cases is there premeditation . . . but each represents even more diabolical cruelty and ferocity than that which is involved in murders premeditated in the natural sense of the word."[19]

The California Doctrine of Diminished Responsibility

California differs from most other states in requiring that a person who pleads "not guilty by reason of insanity" must first be tried for the crime charged and found guilty of that crime before the question of insanity can be raised in a second trial. In the first trial for the crime charged, the defendant is assumed to be sane. If he is found guilty, there is a second trial on the issue of whether or not he was insane at the time of his act. At first, the California courts refused to consider any evidence directed to establishing that the defendant, because of mental abnormality, did not have the capacity to have the mental state required to commit the crime charged (that is, the *mens rea* required for that crime). The position of the courts was that such evidence belonged only in a trial directed exclusively toward establishing the sanity or insanity of the defendant. Such an evidential restriction was, however, challenged on constitutional grounds. It was claimed that this restriction could lead to serious individual injustices and as such was a violation of the Fourteenth Amendment's guarantee of "due process." For example, it was claimed, it would be unjust to prevent a mentally abnormal offender who is charged with first degree murder from offering evidence of his mental abnormality in order to defeat the charge of premeditation. If such a person happened to plead insanity and was found sane, he would be guilty of first degree murder despite the fact that evidence of his mental abnormality might very well have established that his act was not "premeditated" and consequently that it was not first degree murder. This reasoning was accepted by the California courts in *People v. Wells* (1949) which declared unconstitutional the restriction of evidence of mental abnormality to the insanity trial.

With the Wells decision, the California courts were forced to come to grips with the question of the bearing of mental abnormality upon the existence of the specific mental states (*mens rea*) required to commit specific crimes, and the California doctrine of "diminished responsibility" slowly emerged. In a very important case in the development of this doctrine, *People v. Wolff* (1964), the California courts faced the question of the bearing of mental abnormality upon a defendant's capacity to premeditate. The California courts had in previous cases developed the principle that "the true test of the premeditation and deliberation re-

---

[19] Sanford H. Kadish and Monrad G. Paulsen, *Criminal Law and Its Processes,* 3rd ed. (Boston: Little, Brown, 1975), p. 221.

quired to sustain a first degree murder charge is not the duration of time as much as it is the extent (quality) of the reflection." (Such a principle is quite reasonable when one considers that some people deliberate much more incisively and quickly than others.) This principle was further developed in the Wolff case. Wolff, a schizophrenic 15-year-old boy whom psychiatrists described as suffering from a "complete dissociation between intellect and emotion," was convicted of the brutal first degree murder of his mother. He appealed, and the appeals court ruled in his favor, reducing his crime to second degree murder. In its decision, the court declared that the ultimate rationale for distinguishing various degrees of homicide stems from our recognition that there are important differences in the "quantum of personal turpitude" or "personal depravity" of different offenders. Consequently, the court declared, the premeditation and deliberation required to justify a first degree murder conviction does not refer merely to the extent of time "during which the thought must be pondered before it can ripen into an intent which is truly deliberate and premeditated" but also must "include consideration of a defendant's ability to *maturely and meaningfully* reflect upon the gravity of his contemplated act." Of Wolff, the court said

> . . . the defendant had ample *time* for any normal person to maturely and appreciatively reflect upon his contemplated act and to arrive at a cold, deliberated, and premeditated conclusion. He did this in a sense —and apparently to the full extent of which he was capable. But indisputably . . . this defendant was not . . . a fully normal . . . mentally well person. He knew the difference between right and wrong. . . . But the extent of his understanding, reflection upon it, and its consequences, with realization of the enormity of the evil, appears to have been materially—as relevant to appraising the quantum of his moral turpitude and depravity—vague and detached.[20]

In another important case, *People v. Conley* (1966), the California courts considered the bearing of mental abnormality upon the "malice aforethought" which distinguishes murder from manslaughter. In overturning the first degree murder conviction of Conley, the court declared that "if because of mental defect, disease, or intoxication. . . , the defendant is unable to comprehend his duty to govern his actions in accord with the duty imposed by law, he does not act with 'malice aforethought.' "[21] This principle, one should notice, sounds very similar to the M'Naghten rule for insanity. Considering that the California courts have encouraged a broad interpretation of M'Naghten, it is unclear why the Conley court thought, as it clearly did, that this rule would encom-

[20] Ibid., pp. 235–36.

[21] According to the British Homicide Act of 1957, the law of Great Britain also provides for a reduction of murder to manslaughter when a defendant kills while "suffering from such abnormality of mind . . . as substantially impaired his mental responsibility."

pass mentally abnormal killers who would not qualify for M'Naghten. In addition, the Conley court did not consider the bearing of its decision upon the Wolff decision. If, as the Wolff court claimed, lack of emotional appreciation due to mental illness precludes mature and meaningful premeditation and hence can reduce first degree murder to second degree murder, the Conley court did not explain why this lack of emotional appreciation cannot reduce second degree murder to manslaughter according to their principle. Considering the fact that the California provision for separate trial of the guilt and insanity issues was passed in order to simplify matters for the jury and to diminish appeals to jury sympathy in the guilt phase of the trial, the lack of clarity surrounding the principles to be employed in determining the bearing of mental abnormality upon the degree of homicide is a quite ironic development.

The Proposal for the Elimination of the Insanity Defense and the Mens Rea Requirement for Criminal Liability

Until recent years, the direction of reform in the determination of the criminal responsibility of mentally abnormal offenders has centered on broadening the insanity defense and allowing evidence of mental abnormality to reduce the degree of homicide. Today, however, there are a growing number of critics who believe that this trend of reform is philosophically and dangerously misdirected. The difficulties we have seen in developing an insanity defense and in attempting to correlate the degree of punishment with an offender's moral guilt, these critics contend, cannot be patched up, since they are ultimately tied to the illusion of human free will. The remedy is not in better tests of insanity or degrees of diminished responsibility, but rather in completely discarding the traditional retributive insistence that "only the morally guilty should be punished" and that "individuals should be punished in accordance with their degree of moral guilt." It is these principles that are the motivating force behind the insanity defense and the movement toward subjective liability, which the critics see as incapable of a utilitarian justification. In particular, the critics see the movement toward subjective liability (such as, the developing doctrine of diminished responsibilty) as quite inconsistent with the utilitarian aim of punishing individuals in accordance with their degree of dangerousness. Unlike a successful plea of insanity, which often calls for indefinite commitment until "cured" or "no longer dangerous," a subjective approach to the determination of criminal liability is bound to have the undesirable utilitarian consequence of reducing the length of imprisonment of persons who have difficulty in restraining themselves and are, consequently, particularly dangerous. As the critics see it, it is quite often precisely those whom psychiatrists are apt to describe as suffering from some mental abnormality which "substantially impairs their responsibilty" who are the most dangerous offenders. The aim of the law, such critics argue, should not be the impossible one of attempting to proportion one's punishment to one's moral guilt, but rather that of social protection and individual rehabilitation.

As the critics see it, all crimes should require strict liability. Since actions attributable to negligence, accident, or innocent ignorance can be as dangerous as the most premeditated and malicious of actions, the law's traditional concern with the moral blameworthiness of offenders serves no useful purpose. The whole notion of *mens rea*, they claim, should be uprooted from the law. All dangerous actions should be subject to criminal control, regardless of the perceived moral culpability of the offender. All inquiries into a defendant's mental state at the time of his crime should be reserved for *a post conviction* dispositional analysis of how an offender can best be treated so as to prevent a recurrence of the forbidden act. Let us consider this view.

THE REHABILITATIVE IDEAL: THE ELIMINATION OF PUNISHMENT

United by their rejection of both the traditional retributive insistence upon viewing criminals as morally blameworthy individuals who must pay for their wrongdoing and the traditional utilitarian insistence that general deterrence is the main justification for punishment, the critics emphasize the rehabilitative goal of punishment. The common slogan, "treat the criminal, not the crime," best captures the essence of the rehabilitationist philosophy which has gained much support in recent years among psychiatrists, psychologists, sociologists, probation officers, and lawyers alike. Although there are important differences in the views of different supporters of this general point of view, there are certain interrelated principles that seem to form the core of the rehabilitationist philosophy. First, rehabilitationists tend to be hard determinists who assume that since all human actions, be they criminal or noncriminal, are fully determined, free will and moral responsibility are illusions. As the psychologist B.F. Skinner puts it in his widely read book *Beyond Freedom and Dignity,*

> The concept of responsibility is particularly weak when behavior is traced to genetic determiners. We may admire beauty, grace, and sensitivity, but we do not blame a person because he is ugly, spastic, or color blind. Less conspicuous forms of genetic endowment nevertheless cause trouble. Individuals presumably differ, as species differ, in the extent to which they respond aggressively or are reinforced when they effect aggressive damage, or in the extent to which they engage in sexual behavior or are affected by sexual reinforcement. Are they, therefore, equally responsible for controlling their aggressive or sexual behavior, and is it fair to punish them to the same extent? If we do not punish a

person for a clubfoot, should we punish him for being quick to anger or highly susceptible to sexual reinforcement? . . . The concept of responsibility offers little help. The issue is controllability. We cannot change genetic defects by punishment. . . . What must be changed is not the responsibility of autonomous man but the conditions, environmental or genetic, of which a person's behavior is a function.

Although people object when a scientific analysis traces their behavior to external conditions and thus deprives them of credit and the chance to be admired, they seldom object when the same analysis absolves them of blame. . . . The mistake . . . is to put the responsibility anywhere, to suppose that somewhere a causal sequence is initiated.[22]

Second, since criminals are not ultimately morally responsible for their actions, they should be looked at as unfortunate victims of their environment or heredity who require help in becoming productive members of society. Since the behavior of human beings is subject to scientific understanding and control, this help should be provided by experts in the behavioral sciences. Third, our response to offenders should be directed not primarily to the nature of his crime and the aim of general deterrence, but to the suppression of his criminalistic tendencies, and, if this is not possible, to his physical restraint. Fourth, since one should reject the retributive view that criminals must pay a particular price for their crime, proportionate to the moral gravity of their crime and their guilt in committing it, and since our response to criminals should be oriented instead to their needs for rehabilitative treatment, the nature and length of a criminal's sentence should be left primarily in the hands of correctional experts. Since there are vast differences in the treatability of individuals who commit the same crime, it is absurd for legislatures to be given the responsibility for deciding what mode and duration of treatment should be allowed for a given crime, and it is equally absurd to give a judge the responsibility for determining the specific mode and duration of treatment that should be afforded a given criminal. If treatment is to be individualized, as it should be, this discretion belongs in the hands of correctional experts. Ideally, sentences should be indeterminate in length, criminals being released only when cured or no longer dangerous.

Is commitment to the rehabilitative ideal the hope of a scientific and humane future less victimized by the constant threat of crime, as its supporters claim, or is it the latest threat to human dignity and freedom, as its detractors warn? Unfortunately, as with other moral issues that have caught the mood of our time, although passionate rhetoric abounds on this issue, careful analysis and well-thought-out proposals are rare. Much of the literature, especially the most popular, suffers from philosophical, legal, and psychological confusions and most of all, from a tendency toward oversimplification and vagueness. It is very easy to

22 B.F. Skinner, *Beyond Freedom and Dignity* (New York: Bantam, 1971), pp. 70–72.

point out the glaring inadequacies of our current system of criminal justice, but something much more difficult to suggest a practical way of overcoming them. Ironically, those who cry out loudest against the unscientific, irrational, and ineffective nature of our current dealings with criminals have the least to offer in concrete proposals. Their suggestions for change are described in a very sketchy manner which generates many unanswered questions.

If offenders are to be subjected to treatment, for example, what will its ultimate aim be? Will it be educative or will it be directed to methods of behavioral conditioning which bypass the intellectual processes? If behavioral conditioning is to be used, will it be isolated to extinguishing particular socially undesirable learned behavior or will it aim at fundamental personality reorganization? Will the aim not only be to develop socially desirable behavior controls but also to create greater effectiveness and personal comfort for the offender? Can this be accomplished in a context of forced deprivation of liberty? Will certain limits be placed on the type of treatment that may be inflicted upon an offender? Will a criminal have a right to refuse a treatment that promises to change his personality and to request punishment instead? How are the demands of general deterrence to be weighed against the demands of individual rehabilitation? If sentences are not to reflect guilt and are to be indeterminate, what standards are to be used to determine when an offender is cured or no longer dangerous and should consequently be released? What are we to do when the offense is minor and the treatment very long or nonexistent? Sadly, most critics of punishment ignore these questions. Let us turn to some of them. By so doing, I think we will discover that what is needed at this moment is not an extension of the rehabilitative ideal, but the development of legal principles for subjecting this ideal to the restraints of a just law.

The Criminal as Sick and Nonresponsible

Supporters of the rehabilitative ideal often suggest that we should cease conceiving of crime as the result of the free and responsible acts of wicked people, but rather as a sign of "defective functioning" or "mental illness" for which the criminal is not responsible. For example, former Attorney General Ramsey Clark declares,

> The goal of modern correction must be not revenge, not penance, not punishment, but rehabilitation. The theory of rehabilitation is based on the belief that healthy, rational people will not injure others. Rehabilitated, an individual will not have the capacity—will not be able to bring himself—to injure another nor to take or destroy property. . . . Rehabilitation is also the one clear way that the criminal justice system can significantly reduce crime. We know who the most frequent offenders are; there is no surprise when they strike again. Even if nothing but selfish interest impelled us, rehabilitation would be worth the effort. When it

works, it reduces crime, reduces the cost of handling prisoners, reduces the cost of the criminal justice system, and even relieves pressure to provide the basic and massive reforms that are necessary to affect the underlying causes of crime.[23]

Clark's claim that "The theory of rehabilitation is based on the belief that healthy, rational people will not injure others" is, on its face, ludicrous. Leaving aside Clark's tacit equation of criminals as those "who injure others" (which may leave out "victimless crimes" such as prostitution), can one seriously suggest that no rational or healthy person would ever commit a crime or injure someone else? When one considers the great range of activities that can be criminally prohibited, from brutal, premeditated mass murder to income-tax evasion, are there any of us who have not committed, or cannot easily imagine ourselves committing, a crime? Does it follow then, that we are all irrational and mentally ill? If Clark's claim is taken literally, self-defense and all acts of war would become signs of underlying irrationality or mental illness. Since one can be reasonably sure that Clark would not want to accept such a conclusion, we must assume that his remarks are not to be taken literally. But then, how should they be taken? Does Clark think that no one, non-criminal as well as criminal, is morally responsible for his actions, as Skinner does? One cannot help but suspect that Clark himself has not adequately thought out the meaning, presuppositions, and implications of his own proposals.

Similar remarks may be made about the hard deterministic sentiments expressed by Skinner in the passage quoted on p. 369. As hard determinists often do, Skinner confuses the notion that individuals are not ultimately responsible for the desires they find within themselves with the quite different notion that individuals are incapable of modifying these desires or controlling them. Clearly, there is a difference between having a clubfoot and being "quick to anger" or "highly susceptible to sexual reinforcement." When Skinner raises his rhetorical question: "If we do not punish a person for a clubfoot, should we punish him for being quick to anger or being highly susceptible to sexual reinforcement?" the proper reply should be, "We don't punish a person *for being susceptible* to outbursts of anger or to sexual reinforcement, but for *succumbing* to that susceptibility when he has the power to refrain." Although "we cannot change genetic defects by punishment," as Skinner claims, this does not mean that we cannot change human behavior that is *not fully determined* by genetic defects through punishment.

As we have seen, many philosophers would reject the hard deterministic perspective assumed by Skinner as a confused one, but even if we grant that in some "deep" sense, no one is "really morally responsible," no one "really to blame" for his actions, one should not neglect the fact that the very act of holding some people morally responsible may act

[23] Ramsey Clark, "When Punishment Is a Crime," *Playboy Magazine,* 17, no. 11 (November 1970), p. 102. Originally appeared in *Playboy Magazine;* copyright © 1970 by Ramsey Clark.

as a causal determinant in their behavior. Inanimate objects do not respond to being held morally responsible, but most human beings do. Perhaps, if the criminal law were to give official support to the idea that no one is morally responsible and blameworthy for his actions, this would have a highly detrimental effect upon the behavior of individuals who have a certain disposition to criminality but, by accepting responsibility for their actions, are capable of controlling themselves. Must we not be concerned with such people? What if, as many psychiatrists suggest, a majority of us are like this? Surprisingly, the critics of "moral responsibility" rarely face this question. As we shall see, although behavioral psychologists, such as Skinner, would treat criminals by employing behavioral conditioning techniques which bypass their sense of responsibility and capacity for reasoned self-determination, this is certainly not the case with the various methods of psychotherapy (talk-therapies) that other critics of punishment and moral responsibility advocate. Psychiatrists recognize that the help that they have to offer a person is dependent upon his acceptance of responsibility for what has happened to him and what will happen to him in the future. The psychiatric patient is told that he can control his future by his own educated choices and should not see himself as a helpless object whose behavior is fully controlled by forces beyond his control.

Given the psychological role of the concepts of moral responsibility, guilt, resentment, and indignation in controlling human behavior and in giving vent to natural human attitudes, any attempt to eliminate them may prove impossible as well as undesirable. Ironically, Karl Menninger, who passionately tells us that the criminal is not wicked but sick and as such is no more deserving of moral condemnation than a victim of cancer, also says,

> In serious offenses there is another element itself ordinarily powerful enough . . . to control those capable of being influenced by deterrents of any sort. That is the profound feeling of social disapproval, involving moral disgrace, manifested toward crimes considered grave.[24]

Rehabilitation as the Sole Response to Crime

Supporters of a rehabilitative nonpunitive response to criminal behavior, such as Clark and Menninger, seem to totally neglect the general deterrent aim of the criminal law. Some critics have claimed that punishment simply does not deter.[25] But there is no empirical evidence for this claim, clearly contrary to common sense. It would appear that the critics of deterrence tend to mistakenly direct their attention only to those criminals who have already committed criminal acts and have conse-

---

[24] Karl Menninger, *The Human Mind*, 3rd ed. (New York: Knopf, 1946), p. 44.

[25] In support of this claim, the critics often point to the many pickpockets who practiced their craft in the crowds that gathered in early nineteenth century England to watch the hanging of captured pickpockets.

quently not been deterred, rather than to the much greater number of people who refrain from criminal activities possibly because they have been deterred. It is one thing, after all, to claim that a great portion of crime is committed in situations where deterrence is not effective; it is an entirely different matter when one reflects on what the crime rate would be if we approached the situation from a purely nonpunitive point of view which looks solely at the rehabilitative needs of the criminal, while neglecting the demands of general deterrence.

What are we to do, for example, in a totally rehabilitatively oriented system, to those offenders who at the time of sentencing are no more dangerous or in need of rehabilitation than the average citizen? We might, for example, find ourselves dealing with a premeditated murderer who has succumbed to a unique set of circumstances and has become so affected by the gravity of his crime that he now feels total aversion to acts of violence. If rehabilitation were our sole concern, such an individual would be released. Such an action, however, may have dire repercussions on general deterrence. One shudders to think of the effect release would have on potential murderers who might be tempted to rid themselves once and for all of some particular person and who believe that they would never find themselves tempted to do such a thing again.

Similarly, the supporters of rehabilitation have neglected the question of the connection that should exist between the crime committed and the possible length of involuntary confinement and treatment. Many critics have claimed that criminals should be subject to indeterminate sentences and released only when *no longer dangerous* or when *cured*. They do not, however, attempt to clarify these concepts nor do they point out that correctional experts notoriously disagree on how they should be applied. The critics of punishment seem to be characteristically blind to the implications of their proposals. What shall be do, for example, to a petty offender whose criminal action (such as exhibitionism or disturbing the peace by singing in the middle of the night) is caused by personality disturbance which is either incurable or subject to cure only through long and drastic methods of personality change?

The critics are also silent about the connection that should exist between one's state of mind in committing one's criminal act and the sort of "personality deficiencies" that should be subject to treatment. Will a person who is convicted of negligently causing an accident be subjected to psychological and psychiatric diagnosticians only for the purpose of ascertaining his "accident proneness" or will the inquiry be broader in scope? What are the authorities to do, for example, if they find that a person who negligently committed a minor crime has homicidal tendencies? Do we subject him to treatment for these tendencies? If so, why restrict inquiry only to those who through some fortuity find themselves in the "clutches" of the law? It is certainly an exceedingly small step from such a procedure to the general provision that all citizens should undergo periodic examinations to determine whether they are potentially dangerous and need to subject themselves to some type of "compulsory regime for social protection and personal betterment." Indeed, as long as the treatment which is imposed upon an offender is conceived not only as a means of social protection but as something which attempts to "make an offender better," there will be a natural tendency toward a not too rigorous standard for potential dangerousness and great pressure toward not requiring any overt act at all.

If, on the other hand, some inherent connection is to be made between the state of mind of an offender at the time of his crime and the scope of the inquiry into an offender's potential dangerousness and treatability, will we not have to begin speaking again of his *guilt* in committing the act in question? It would certainly appear that if we are not to totally neglect the demands of justice, we must inquire into precisely the issues that critics of punishment tell us we should avoid. The critics, in their dedication to the ideal of rehabilitation, do not seem at all concerned with the dictates of justice. Indeed, Karl Menninger says,

> The very word *justice* irritates scientists. No surgeon expects to be asked if an operation for cancer is just or not. No doctor will be reproached on the grounds that the dose of penicillin he has prescribed is less or more than *justice* would stipulate. Behavioral scientists regard it as equally absurd to invoke the question of justice in deciding what to do with a woman who cannot resist her propensity to shoplift, or with a man who cannot resist an impulse to assault somebody. This sort of behavior has to be controlled . . . it has to be *stopped*. This (to the scientist) is a matter of public safety . . . not of justice. The question . . . is not what would be *just* . . . but what would be effective in deterring them![26]

This is a truly astounding claim. Can one seriously say that *involuntarily* inflicted treatments can never be judged just or unjust? If the shoplifter were *stopped* by the coercive use of mind-altering drugs that drastically numbed and interfered with her intellectual and emotional processes, would not one say that she has been treated unjustly? Would not Menninger say so, if she were his wife or daughter? Is it not the case that treatment can be quite *effective* in the limited sense of successfully eliminating or deterring criminalistic tendencies, but quite *ineffective* from a broader perspective? Effectiveness, after all, can only be measured relative to some purpose—a purpose whose moral worth cannot be discovered simply by "scientific investigation." Although notions of justice are not scientific in nature, they need not be inconsistent with the findings of science. If a scientist finds himself "irritated" by such notions, then he ought not to be addressing himself to the question of the *morality* of punishment, as Menninger does.

[26] Karl Menninger, *The Crime of Punishment* (New York: Viking, 1969), pp. 17–18.

Methods of Rehabilitative Treatment

The most serious question left unanswered by the proponents of the rehabilitative ideal concerns the methods of rehabilitation that should be employed and the rights, if any, a criminal should have to refuse certain treatments. Let us consider the possible forms the rehabilitation of criminals might take.

Psychotherapy and Vocational Training

The least morally troublesome type of rehabilitative treatment would consist of some form of psychotherapy (talk-therapy) and vocational training. In such a scheme, the criminal would essentially be subjected to an educative process, learning about both himself and some marketable skill. While this type of treatment of criminals is, perhaps, the one most widely suggested or hinted at by the critics of punishment, it is the most ineffective of the various rehabilitative techniques. Furthermore, the high cost and limited supply of psychiatrists and clinical psychologists would at present rule out the possibility of providing individualized psychotherapy to all criminals. Given the practical realities, group psychotherapy, where groups of inmates are given an opportunity to talk out their problems in the presence of a therapist who may exert much or little control on the reflections of the group, is all that can be provided. Such sessions for criminals are already established procedure in many progressive states. Unfortunately, the results are not very impressive. Indeed, it has been claimed that even individualized psychotherapeutic sessions are generally quite ineffective as a method of rehabilitating criminals.

First, the effectiveness of such treatment is dependent upon the voluntary cooperation of its participants. Second, the generally understood purpose of the various methods of psychotherapy—such as classical psychoanalysis—is self-knowledge. There is no guarantee, and certainly many psychotherapists would not insist upon the abstention from criminality as a necessary condition of "successful treatment." For the psychoanalyst, for example, what is important is that the offender, free of unconscious fears, anxieties, and repressions, should make *his own* rational and informed decisions as to whether to continue his criminal activities. Given the limitations of an offender's environment, criminal activity may in some situations be quite rational from the offender's point of view. Furthermore, even if the problem of crime could be controlled by a combined program of psychotherapeutic education and vocational training, as individuals like Menninger would have us believe, it is certainly the height of injustice and disutility to provide psychotherapeutic and vocational services to criminals that are not provided to the law-abiding. Consequently, those who advocate such services for criminals ought to concern themselves with making these services freely available to all those who may want to avail themselves of them. Understandably, those who loudly demand these services for criminals, do not direct their attention to the vast cost of these services if they are to be made available to all who need them, nor to the political reality of the general unwillingness of voters to incur such costs. If psychotherapy were a clearly effective method for eliminating much of crime, the cost would be well worth it; unfortunately, there is no reason to believe that this is so.

Behavioral Conditioning (Aversion Therapy)

It would surely seem that if rehabilitative treatment is to become the prime justification for what is now called punishment, with the realistic hope that it can be effective in controlling crime, the criminal will be *made to undergo* methods of treatment which aim at changing his desires, emotions, and attitudes in ways which do not require his consent.

Presently, the most widely used method of nonpersuasive therapy is aversion therapy. Such treatment is based on a conditioning process where an association is set up between unpleasant or painful experiences and the behavior which it is designed to eliminate. Aversion therapy is used today in many state prisons and mental hospitals. In California, there was a widespread outcry in 1970 against a particularly harsh form of aversion therapy utilized on inmates of Atascadero State (Mental) Hospital and Vacaville, California's psychiatrically oriented prison. During a five-year period, 154 inmates were subjected to the drug Anectine that paralyzes the body and stops breathing for up to two or three minutes, causing, as one practitioner euphemistically called it, "an extremely negative experience." The victim of the drug remains conscious throughout his ordeal and, according to aversion therapists, is quite susceptible to suggestions and conditioning. While the inmate was under the influence of the drug, he would be repeatedly admonished by the therapist about the act for which he was being punished and was told that similar acts would result in similar treatments.

Surgical, Biochemical, and Electrical Methods of Control

The most fascinating and morally troublesome methods of rehabilitation involve the use of various surgical, chemical, and electrical methods of control. During the 1950's, for example, psychosurgical procedures such as the now generally discredited frontal lobotomy, were widely used methods for eliminating or controlling undesirable behavior. Today, those uncontrollable patients who would have previously been candidates for a frontal lobotomy and electroshock treatment can be kept sedated by the use of various powerful tranquilizing drugs. The art of psychosurgery, where laser beams may soon replace the surgeon's scalpel, has become increasingly advanced since the 1950s. The sophisticated practices of brain mapping and electrode implantation described in Michael Crichton's *The Terminal Man* are not science fiction. Hundreds of men and women have had up to a dozen or more needle-thin electrodes implanted into their brains. These electrodes can trigger various behaviors. One famous practitioner of this technique, Dr. Jose Delgado of the University of Madrid, has publicly demonstrated this technique by stopping charging bulls in midflight.

Two psychologists, Ralph Schwitzgebel of Harvard and his brother Robert at Claremont, in California, have worked extensively with electronic monitoring devices which are capable of the constant surveillance of individuals. In addition to monitoring a person's location, the device is capable of monitoring voice, blood pressure, heartbeat, and other physiological activities. Electrode implantation and electronic surveillance fit together quite well and could lead to the ultimate in aversion therapy. Researchers have envisioned a sophisticated system where dangerous criminals who are allowed to walk the streets are monitored by transmitters which report their location and physiological reactions to some central computer which decides upon the appropriate response, including the activation of implanted electrodes (or drugs) which can calm emotions such as hostility or send pleasurable or unpleasurable "messages" to the criminal. Supporters of these techniques claim that their use would be cheaper and safer for society than the present prison system. Some have suggested that these techniques should be provided only as a voluntary alternative to prison. If a criminal is unwilling to accept the restraints of electronic surveillance and control, he can simply stay in jail and serve out his sentence or be executed. On the other hand, some have suggested that these techniques would be immoral since they would rob the criminal of his human dignity, turning him into a nonmoral agent—a mere "clockwork orange"—who cannot be praised or blamed for his conduct.

Rehabilitation and the Rights of the Criminal

Given the morally awesome power that the rehabilitative techniques of the future may provide, one should react with alarm when Menninger writes,

> Do I believe there is effective treatment for offenders, and that they *can* be changed? *Most certainly and definitely I do.* Not all cases, to be sure; there are some physical afflictions which we cannot cure at the moment. Some provision has to be made for incurables—pending new knowledge —and these will include some offenders. But I believe the majority of them would prove to be curable. The willfulness and the viciousness of offenders are part of the thing for which they have to be treated. These must not thwart the therapeutic attitude. It is simply not true that most of them are "fully aware" of what they are doing, nor is it true that they want no help from anyone, although some of them say so.[27]

[27] Menninger, *Crime of Punishment*, pp. 261–62.

The implications of such a remark are shocking. One wonders, for example, how political dissenters would fare in such a system. Are all who disagree with those who have political power to be looked at as "sick" and then compulsorily "cured" of behavior which they believe to be right? (Consider the present day Soviet practice of committing political dissidents to *mental hospitals* to be *cured* of their *unhealthy* political views.) Surely, we can never rule out as morally irrelevant a person's desire not to be forcibly turned into what he does not want to be. Most of the critics of punishment, I am sure, will deny that their proposals have such chilling implications; nevertheless, without any concrete proposals as to the rights a criminal will have against the rehabilitative techniques which are now being developed, one can justifiably fear that a wholesale acceptance of the rehabilitative point of view of such individuals as Menninger cannot help but allow the revengeful, brutal, callous, or merely frightened among us to sacrifice human liberty to the demands of social protection. As Supreme Court Justice Louis Brandeis once perceptively warned,

> Experience should teach us to be most on our guard to protect liberty when government's purposes are beneficent. Men born to freedom are naturally alert to repel invasions of their liberty by evil minded rulers. The greatest dangers to liberty lurk in insidious encroachment by men of zeal, well meaning but without understanding. (*Olmstead v. U.S.* 1928)

It is surely unjust that we are quite willing to grant that detention which is conceived as "penal" must be limited, yet, at the same time, are quite willing to assume that detention which is conceived as "therapeutic" need have no limits at all. We must be on guard against the great possibility for self-deception that exists in the tendency to utilize the language of therapy to justify the taking of preventive measures which would be rejected as unjust if seen as punitive. Such self-deception is seen today in the various sexual psychopath laws which indiscriminately classify the violent rapist and the harmless exhibitionist as "sexual psychopaths," who are then, in the name of nonexistent treatment facilities, indefinitely deprived of their liberty in a mental hospital which is indistinguishable from most prisons. As Sol Rubin puts it,

> The constitution gives the defendant in a criminal case certain enumerated rights . . . embraced under the heading of due process of law, without observance of which he cannot be convicted and his liberty cannot be encroached. The law evades . . . these requirements by calling the procedure . . . noncriminal, hence not requiring criminal due process. How is this accomplished? Only by the magic word formula. We go after the criminal, and process him without the final declaration that he is a criminal. . . . Meanwhile we skip some of the procedural protections he would have if he were dealt with as a criminal, and then we proceed to punish him more severely than we could under the criminal law—a longer

term of incarceration, lessened eligibility for probation or parole, no better treatment.[28]

As Rubin so aptly puts it, while quoting the words of the King from Rogers and Hammerstein's *The King and I,* "If allies are strong with power to protect me, might they not protect me out of all I own?" One can well understand a criminal's plea to be afforded a just retributive punishment instead of being "helped" in ways that he does not want.

Some Reflections

The current debate as to the merits of a "rehabilitative" as opposed to "punitive" reaction to criminals has resulted in an extreme and oversimplified polarization of attitudes. What the future calls for is not a passionate commitment to slogans, but the practical wisdom to proceed cautiously and with moral sensitivity. Instead of blindly urging us forward toward an evanescent panacea, supporters of the rehabilitative ideal should seek to develop the new concepts and standards that such a commitment entails. They must face the questions we have posed. Is it right, for example, that petty criminals should be involuntarily subjected to a longer and more unpleasant mode of rehabilitative treatment than the offender who has committed a much more serious crime? Does not justice demand that we maintain some upper bound on the length of involuntary treatment that may be imposed on an offender? Should criminals always be given the right to refuse treatments and the use of monitoring devices and to accept a fixed jail sentence or, perhaps, even death instead? If some or all criminals are to be allowed to refuse certain treatments, what is to count as "informed" and "noncoercive" consent? Are prisons and mental hospitals "inherently coercive," as many have suggested? Does a person, perhaps, have a right to refuse treatment on the basis of a fundamental constitutional right to keep his own personality inviolate to involuntary change—does the criminal, to put it bluntly, have a right to be bad, if he so chooses? How are we to weigh the demands of general deterrence against the needs of individual rehabilitation? The questions abound; yet careful answers are nonexistent. Without answers to these questions, substituting the euphemistic notion of treatment for that of punishment may lead a society to feel justified in interfering with any behavior which it finds offensive but would have found too unjust to punish. Let us hope that our desire for crime control never becomes so strong that we are willing to completely ignore the ideals of a free society in our attempt to achieve it.

[28] Sol Rubin, *Psychiatry and the Criminal Law* (Dobbs Ferry, N.Y.: Oceana Publications, 1965), pp. 154–55.

DISCUSSION QUESTIONS

1. It is an almost universal legal practice to punish people more for a completed crime than for an attempt to commit that crime. This is true even if the criminal has done everything in his power to commit that crime and fails as a result of some unforeseen circumstance (for example his gun jams). Can a utilitarian justification be given for this practice? A retributive one?

2. How would a utilitarian distinguish the punishment of criminals from the forfeiture of liberty associated with the quarantine of infectious carriers of disease? How would a retributivist see it? Which view do you find more adequate? Why?

3. Critically discuss the issue involved in the following dialogue:

   A: While retributivists are right that moral guilt is a necessary condition of punishment, utilitarians are right that it is not a sufficient condition. Punishment should be inflicted only when it has a utilitarian justification.

   B: I don't agree. The guilt of a criminal is often itself a sufficient condition for punishment. Eichmann, for example, deserved to be punished, even though his punishment had no utilitarian justification. It would have been unjust for him not to have been punished.

4. What justification would a utilitarian give for the legal practice of punishing negligent behavior less than intentional behavior? How would the retributivist see it? What do you think?

5. Should the direction of penal reform be more toward strict liability (that is, liability for harm done with no concern for individual blameworthiness) or toward greater subjective liability (that is, liability based on the actual blameworthiness of individuals which reflects their individual psychological capacity to conform to the law they have violated). Defend your position.

6. Assuming that we had reliable tests for determining which individuals were prone to certain types of criminality, how would a utilitarian analyze the problem of the desirability of involuntarily subjecting people to such tests? How would a retributivist analyze the problem? What do you think?

7. Is it realistic to hope that we may someday find a method or methods for "curing" most criminals? Can criminals be cured on a large scale without general societal reform? Would certain societal reforms alleviate the need for criminal reform?

8. Should "prisons" be seen more as "mental hospitals" or "mental hospitals" more as "prisons"? Why?

9. What principle would you employ to distinguish those intentional criminal homicides that should be punished the most? Would you prefer to divide intentional criminal homicides into first and second degree murder and voluntary manslaughter as most American jurisdictions do, or would you prefer to follow the English procedure of not distinguishing different degrees of murder? Why, or why not?

10. Critically evaluate the following proposal:

> Imprisonment is a very costly and quite ineffective response to crime. Instead of "warehousing" criminals in "schools of crime," criminals should be forced to work to compensate their victims for the harm they have caused. While the idea that the state, and not the victim, should have the power to prosecute criminals was motivated by a desire to make punishment impersonal—to take revenge out of the hands of the victim, we ought to move back to the old conception of punishment as compensation. As things stand now, the victims of crime are forgotten, as criminals are punished in the impersonal name of the state. Most crimes, however, are primarily affronts to individuals and not to the state. The law should return to a recognition of this fundamental truth. The victim of a crime should be named as a co-plaintiff alongside the state. If a conviction results, the court's judgment should provide for an enforceable order of compensation for the victim and a reimbursement to the state for the cost of bringing the case to trial. In most cases, a jail sentence will be unnecessary.

FURTHER READINGS

BENTHAM, JEREMY, *An Introduction to the Principles of Morals and Legislation,* chapters XIII-XVII, (eds., J.H. Burns and H.L.A. Hart). London: University of London, 1970. *The Theory of Legislation,* pp. 239–472, ed. C.K. Ogden. Bentham's classical discussion of punishment is found in both books which contain much overlap. These detailed discussions are directed to the philosophically sophisticated and not the general reader. Nevertheless, the detailed table of contents in both books make them ideal as reference sources for serious students of the classical utilitarian theory of punishment.

BUTLER, SAMUEL, *Erewhon and Erewhon Revisited.* New York: The Modern Library, 1927 (third edition, orig. pub. in 1901). Butler satirizes the traditional view of the criminal as morally responsible by imagining a society where criminals are considered to be victims of "disease" and subject to "treatment" by "straighteners," while those with physical illnesses are considered to be morally blameworthy individuals rightly subject to punishment.

FEINBERG, JOEL, "The Expressive Function of Punishment," in *Doing and Deserving,* pp. 95–118. Princeton, N.J.: Princeton University Press, 1970. Originally published in *The Monist,* 52 (July 1965), 397–423. Feinberg contends that "punishment" is by definition "a conventional device for the expression of attitudes of resentment and indignation, and of judgments of disapproval." It is only by realizing the expressive aspect of punishment, Feinberg argues, that some of the functions of punishment and some of the conceptual problems it raises can be made intelligible. After describing some of the expressive functions of punishment, Feinberg relates these functions to the constitutional problem of defining criminal punishment and the problem of strict criminal liability. He also argues against that form of the retributive theory of punishment which insists that the ultimate justification of punishment is "to give each criminal offender exactly that amount of pain the evil of his offense calls for, on the alleged principle of justice that the wicked should suffer pain in exact proportion to their turpitude." As Feinberg sees it, such a view turns out, on analysis, to be incoherent, its incoherence resulting from its failure to distinguish between the hard treatment aspect of punishment and its expressive function. The article is very clearly written and is highly recommended for beginning students. It had a great influence in setting the direction of my own philosophical thoughts about criminal punishment.

GOLDSTEIN, ABRAHAM S., *The Insanity Defense*. New Haven, Conn.: Yale University Press, 1967. An excellent, clearly, and nontechnically written historical and analytic study of the insanity defense by a professor of law.

HART, H.L.A., *Punishment and Responsibility*. London: Oxford University Press, 1968. A collection of the legal philosopher H.L.A. Hart's essays on punishment, criminal responsibility, and the rehabilitative assault on punishment. Especially recommended are Hart's essays "Prolegomenon to the Principles of Punishment" and "Legal Responsibility and Excuses." In these articles, Hart considers the meaning, justification, and proper scope of criminal punishment. As he sees it, utilitarians are right that punishment must be justified in terms of its beneficial consequences. However, Hart sees the traditional retributive (Kantian) concern with the maximization of freedom as a "limiting condition" on the proper scope of criminal punishment. Also recommended is Hart's essay "Changing Conceptions of Responsibility" which discusses and criticizes Wootton's proposal for strict-liability.

KADISH, SANFORD H., "The Decline of Innocence," 26, *Cambridge Law Journal* 273–90 (1968). A critique by a professor of law of proposals to eliminate "punishment"—in particular, Wootton's proposal.

KADISH, SANFORD H., and MONRAD G. PAULSEN, *Criminal Law and Its Processes, Cases and Materials* (3rd). Boston: Little, Brown, 1975. An excellent collection of cases and material on the substantive and administrative principles of the criminal law. The excerpts at the beginning of the book on the different underlying philosophic approaches to punishment and the rehabilitationist assault upon punishment are quite good.

KANT, IMMANUEL, *The Metaphysical Elements of Justice*, pp. 99–107 and 131–33. Indianapolis: Bobbs-Merrill, 1965. This work contains Kant's most thorough treatment of punishment. Nevertheless, Kant has things to say about punishment in his other writings, not all of which seem to be consistent with his "official" theory in *The Metaphysical Elements of Justice*. For example, in his *Lectures on Ethics* (Harper & Row, Pub., pp. 55–56), Kant, sounding very much like a utilitarian writes that "All punishments imposed by governments are pragmatic. They are designed to correct or make an example. Ruling authorities do not punish because a crime has been committed, but in order that crimes should not be committed."

LEWIS, C.S., "The Humanitarian Theory of Punishment," 6, *Res Judicatae*, 224–30 (1953). A passionate critique against the rehabilitationist philosophy from a retributivistic point of view.

MENNINGER, KARL, *The Crime of Punishment*. New York: Viking, 1968. A well-known psychiatrist's indictment of our punishment system and a defense of the rehabilitationist philosophy directed to a wide lay audience.

MORRIS, HERBERT, ed., *Freedom and Responsibility*. Stanford, Calif.: Stanford University Press, 1961. An excellent anthology of interdisciplinary material representing the fields of philosophy, law, psychiatry, and sociology on the general issue of moral and legal responsibility.

MURPHY, JEFFRIE G., ed., *Punishment and Rehabilitation*. Encino, Calif.: Wadsworth, 1973. An excellent anthology of material on the issues of this chapter by philosophers (both classical and contemporary), lawyers, psychiatrists, and psychologists.

PACKER, HERBERT, *The Limits of the Criminal Sanction*. Stanford, Calif.: Stanford University Press, 1968. An excellent and nontechnical exposition by a professor of law of the rationale, processes, and limits of criminal punishment which is geared to the general reader.

PINCOFFS, EDMUND L., *The Rationale of Legal Punishment*. Atlantic Highlands, N.J.: Humanities Press, 1966. An excellent analytic study of the justification of legal punishment. Pincoffs discusses the classic debate between retributivists and utilitarians over the justification of legal punishment and attempts to arrive at some integrated theory. There is a chapter on the punishment-versus-treatment issue.

SKINNER, B.F., *Beyond Freedom and Dignity*. New York: Bantam, 1971. A very influential contemporary behavioral psychologist's widely read (hard-deterministic) criticism of the traditional picture of human beings as "free and morally responsible." Continuing with the theme of his bestselling utopian novel *Walden Two*, Skinner advocates a societal commitment to behavioral engineering.

SZASZ, THOMAS S., *Ideology and Insanity: Essays on the Psychiatric Dehumanization of Man*. New York: Anchor Books, 1970. A collection of the widely read and influential psychiatrist Thomas Szasz's essays critical of the classification of people as "mentally ill." Included is Szasz's most famous essay "The Myth of Mental Illness," in which Szasz claims that "mental illnesses do not exist." What are now commonly called "mental illnesses," Szasz claims should be seen instead as "problems in living." This essay (included in the Murphy anthology) has generated much controversy in psychiatric circles.

SZASZ, THOMAS S., *Law, Liberty, and Psychiatry*. New York: Macmillan, 1963. A forceful critique against the possible tyranny implicit in the rehabilitative ideal. Szasz is especially concerned with uncovering what he sees as the tendency of psychiatry to promote moral and political values which are mistakenly presented as value-free "health values." The psychiatric "treatment" of criminals and those who are civilly committed should be seen, Szasz argues, not as "medicine" but as "social engineering" which can be, and has been, used to suppress individual freedom and dissent.

WASSERSTROM, RICHARD, ed., *Today's Moral Problems* (2nd ed.) chapter 6. New York: Macmillan, 1979. This anthology has an excellent collection of material expressing diverse viewpoints on the punishment issue. First, there is John Rawl's "Two Concepts of Rules." In this very influential article, Rawls, arguing like a rule-utilitarian, contends that it is important to distinguish the justification for the institution of punishment from the justification within that institution for punishing individuals. As Rawls sees it in this article, utilitarian arguments are appropriate in justifying the practice of punishment, while retributive arguments fit the application of particular rules to particular cases. Second, there is an excerpt from Barbara Wootton's *Crime and the Criminal Law,* advocating a rehabilitationist philosophy. Third, there is Herbert Morris' article "Persons and Punishment," which defends a retributive position on punishment. Morris, a professor of law and philosophy, delineates the features of our present punishment system—with its retributive underpinnings—and compares this system to a therapy system—which sees crime as a symptom of disease. Morris then argues, very much in the Kantian tradition, that retributive punishment, unlike treatment, respects the *dignity* of human beings. Fourth, there is an article, "Marxism and Retribution," by the philosopher Jeffrie Murphy. Murphy, although believing that "retributivism can be formulated in such a way that it is the only morally defensible theory of punishment," also accepts the Marxist view that, given the social injustices of most existing societies, such a theory is largely inapplicable. The radical conclusion Murphy draws is that "modern societies largely lack the moral right to punish."

WOOTTON, BARBARA, *Crime and the Criminal Law.* London: Stevens and Sons, 1963. In this very readable and short book, Wootton, an English lay magistrate, argues for a rejection of the traditional retributive elements of punishment and advocates a system of total strict liability. In her proposed system, individuals will be held criminally liable for all of their dangerous actions, however faultless. Once a person has been convicted of some dangerous act, he will be turned over to a team of behavioral scientists who will determine the kind of treatment he should receive in the interests of crime prevention. (Excerpts of this book can be found in the Murphy and Wasserstrom anthologies.)

9

The
Death
Penalty

Among all the issues of penal policy, there is none that has generated the storm of controversy and passion that surrounds capital punishment. In the strongest of words, its adherents have praised the death penalty as an essential instrument of justice and the prevention of crime, while in equally strong terms, its opponents have condemned it as inhumane, unfair, and useless, if not actually harmful. Millions of words have been written, arguments stated and restated; yet, the issue of capital punishment still finds itself clouded in moral ambivalence and empirical uncertainty which is reflected in my own thinking about this issue.

THE LEGAL BACKGROUND

The number of executions in the United States has steadily declined through the years. In the 1930s, the annual average of executions was 166; in the 1940s, 127; in the 1950s, 71. The number of executions continued to decline during the 1960s and came to a halt in 1967, as the states awaited a Supreme Court decision on the constitutionality of capital punishment, which finally came in 1972. At that time, 39 states had a death penalty, 5 of which restricted it to exceptional cases, such as murder of police officers or prison guards or for second offenders. The methods of execution employed by the states were electrocution, lethal gas, and hanging. In Utah, a person condemned to execution had the option of choosing death by a firing squad as an alternative to hanging. This was the dramatic method of execution chosen by Gary Gilmore, who was executed in January 1977, the first person executed since 1967.

The constitutional objection to capital punishment stems from the Eighth Amendment to the Constitution, which prohibits the federal government from inflicting "cruel and unusual punishment."[1] Since there is substantial legal authority to the effect that the Eighth Amendment is incorporated within the due process clause of the Fourteenth Amendment, which applies to the various states, the prohibition against "cruel and unusual punishment" can then be applied to the states as well as to the federal government. The argument was placed before the Supreme Court that the death penalty is "cruel and unusual punishment." In June 1972, the Supreme Court in *Furman v. Georgia* made its long-awaited decision concerning the death penalty. In a 5 to 4 ruling, with each justice writing his own opinion, the death penalty was declared unconstitutional in the state of Georgia. Given the differing arguments of the majority, however, the implications of this important decision were not clear. Only Marshall and Brennan argued that capital punishment was unconstitutional in all circumstances. Marshall, appealing to his reading of the popular will, claimed that the death penalty is "cruel and unusual" since "it is morally unacceptable to the people of the United States at this time in their history." For Marshall, the test of moral acceptability did not rest on prevailing opinion, "but on whether people who were fully informed as to the purposes of the penalty and its liabilities would find the penalty shocking, unjust, and unacceptable."

As Brennan saw it, the "cruel and unusual" clause "prohibits the infliction of uncivilized and inhuman punishments." Such punishments, he claimed, are those that do not treat persons "with respect" or "comport with human dignity." The death penalty is such a punishment for several interrelated and converging reasons, he declared. First, it is "excessive." A punishment is excessive, he wrote, when it is "unnecessary . . . when it is nothing more than the pointless infliction of suffering." This is the case, he claimed, with the death penalty since there is no reason to believe that this severe penalty serves any justifiable penal purpose more effectively than does the less severe punishment of long imprisonment. Second, it is arbitrarily applied. Third, as evidenced by its infrequent use, its "rejection by contemporary society is virtually total." Fourth, it is too "severe" a punishment. Apart from its excessiveness, Brennan wrote, "the deliberate extinguishment of human life by the State is uniquely degrading to human dignity." This is so, he claimed, given the irrevocable nature of the death penalty and the physical and mental anguish it causes. The severity of the death penalty would in itself be sufficient grounds for judging it "cruel and unusual punishment" were it not for its long-standing usage, Brennan claimed. Believing that it is the convergence of the features of severity, excessiveness, arbitrari-

---

[1] Although the Eighth Amendment speaks of "cruel *and* unusual punishment," judicial interpretations of this phrase indicate that it is actually taken as a disjunction, prohibiting "cruel *or* unusual punishment." This, indeed, is the phrase used in the California Constitution.

ness, and popular rejection that make the death penalty unacceptably degrading to human dignity, Brennan turned to the complex principle that "It is a denial of human dignity for the State arbitrarily to subject a person to an unusually severe punishment that society has indicated it does not regard as acceptable, and that cannot be shown to serve any penal purpose more effectively than a significantly less drastic punishment." On the basis of this principle, Brennan concluded that "death is today a 'cruel and unusual' punishment."

The other three members of the majority, Douglas, White, and Stewart, were more guarded in their opposition. It was not the punishment of death itself they objected to, but its erratic and discriminatory method of application. The death penalty, Douglas emphasized, operates in a cruel and unusual fashion because it gives judges and juries the discretion to decree life or death, which they use in an arbitrary manner, unjustly applying it in many cases to members of minority or unpopular groups, while others, equally deserving, escape. Stewart and White, interpreting the notion of cruelty as the "unnecessary infliction of suffering," argued that the death penalty was a cruel punishment since, given its seldom use, it could not serve as a credible threat or deterrent. It was "unusual," they claimed, by virtue of its capricious application. To be sentenced to death, Stewart declared, is essentially, "like being struck by lightning." The dissenters in this decision were Burger, Blackman, Powell, and Rehnquist. Their objections rested on two basic grounds. First, it is the task of the legislatures, who are more in touch with the will of the people, and not the courts, to decide "which penalties best serve the ends of penology." Second, the majority's objection of erratic infliction of the death penalty could be overcome if legislatures would provide clear and unequivocal standards for juries and judges to follow in applying the death penalty.

As most interpreters of the Furman decision saw it, states could now maintain the death penalty only by making it mandatory for certain specifiable categories of offenders in certain states. Several states changed their laws to accomplish this end. In California, for example, in a referendum posed to the voters, a measure to reinstate the death penalty passed by a 2 to 1 margin. As a result, the state legislature designed and passed a death penalty statute that made the death penalty mandatory in certain circumstances, which included, among others, murder for hire, killing of a police officer, murder to prevent a witness from testifying, killing during a commission of a robbery or a kidnapping or a rape, and a prior conviction of murder.

The prevalent belief that the Supreme Court would require mandatory death penalties was, however, proven wrong when the Supreme Court reconsidered the capital punishment issue in various cases argued before the bench in July 1976. In some cases, the death penalty was upheld, while in others it was rejected. Nevertheless, the swing was clearly toward upholding the death penalty, as was evidenced by the 7 to 2 majority votes in upholding the death penalty provisions of Georgia, Florida, and Texas. The central guiding principle behind the reasoning of the majority justices in these decisions was that the states could not make the death penalty mandatory and consequently go too far in curtailing discretion, nor could they go too far in the opposite direction by allowing so much discretion so as to make the decision a capricious one. Exactly how much discretion a jury should be given, the Court did not say. The justices generally thought that Georgia's law concerning the death penalty was the best of the cases they had before them. The discretion of the jurors was, in this state, Stewart claimed, effectively "channelled" by requiring them to consider "mitigating" as well as "aggravating" circumstances and requiring the existence of at least one aggravating circumstance before conviction. (Georgia follows the American Law Institute's proposal in its 1959 Model Penal Code in this regard.) In addition, it was required that the state Supreme Court scrutinize every capital case and be prepared to overturn a death sentence when this sentence was not applied in previous similar cases. In the Texas case, Stevens declared that any sentencing system that allowed a jury to consider only aggravating circumstances and not mitigating ones would be too mandatory and hence unconstitutional. Given the imprecisely defined line the Supreme Court has drawn, it is unclear how this new law will affect various states. In light of this recent Supreme Court decision, however, the California high court declared unconstitutional the California death penalty statute passed after Furman which did not allow for mitigating circumstances. As a result, the California legislature refashioned and overwhelmingly passed a new death penalty statute.

Let us turn our attention to the arguments that have been offered for and against the death penalty. We shall proceed by first sketching the arguments on both sides of the death penalty issue and then shall subject these arguments to analysis and criticism.

THE ARGUMENTS FOR THE DEATH PENALTY

Justice Demands the Death Penalty for Certain Criminals in Certain Crimes

Although this type of argument is not fashionable today, there can be no doubt that people cling to the death penalty because of the feeling that death is the only appropriate response to certain criminals in certain heinous crimes. Many of a religious persuasion quote certain passages of the Bible as divine authority for the unique appropriateness of the death penalty. Certainly, when one considers a criminal, such as Adolf Eichmann, who is sentenced to death for his heinous crimes, it is clear that this sentence is not motivated by utilitarian considerations, such as general deterrence or societal protection, but by the feeling that such a man *deserves* to die, that to allow him to spend his life in prison is to give him less than he deserves, to somehow cheat the dictates of justice. Seldom clearly articulated, this feeling runs deep.

The Death Penalty Is Needed as a Deterrent

The strongest case that can be made for the death penalty is that it is required as a deterrent for certain crimes. For example, Burton Leiser writes,

> . . . it is evident that certain major crimes cannot possibly be deterred by any other penalty. The revolutionary who contemplates blowing up a school bus as a means of terrorizing the population is not likely to be deterred by the threat of life imprisonment, for he believes that even if he is caught he will be released and be given a hero's welcome by his fellow revolutionaries when the revolution succeeds. Similarly, the potential traitor in wartime will not be deterred from betraying his country by fear of life imprisonment, for he believes that when his country is "liberated" by the enemy, his imprisonment will be brought to an end. The same must be true of criminals who are already serving life sentences in prison. The threat of yet another lengthy sentence is meaningless and can therefore have no effect at all upon the lifer who contemplates doing in his cellmate or the guard on duty in his cell block. If anything at all will deter such men from the crimes they are contemplating, nothing less than the death penalty will do.[2]

According to the testimony of police officers and F.B.I. agents, many captured criminals have admitted that after committing offenses punishable by life imprisonment, it was only the fear of capital punishment that induced them to refrain from murder, even though such action would have increased their chances of escape. It is this same fear, criminals have also admitted, that caused them to refrain from carrying deadly weapons in the serious crimes they have committed. If the death penalty were abolished, it is urged, it would be to the self-interest of a criminal who has already committed a crime subject to life imprisonment, such as kidnapping or rape, to kill any witnesses to his crime. The death penalty is also essential, it has been claimed, for repeat murderers for whom imprisonment has proved insufficient deterrent and who might otherwise kill guards and fellow inmates in prison with impunity. This claim leads us to the next argument.

Some Criminals Are Too Dangerous to Be Allowed to Live

Some supporters of the death penalty do not argue that some criminals "deserve" to die or can be used to deter others, but rather argue on the basis of the social utility of eliminating dangerous individuals who cannot reasonably be expected to be rehabilitated. Such individuals should often be perceived, it is said, as dangerous animals who

---

[2] Burton M. Leiser, *Liberty, Justice and Morals,* 2nd ed. (New York: Macmillan, 1979), pp. 242–43.

must be exterminated for the safety of the law-abiding. As Jacques Barzun puts it,

> It is all very well to say that many of these killers are themselves "children," . . . Doubtless a nine-year-old mind is housed in that 150 pounds of unguided muscle. Grant, for argument's sake, that the misdeed is "the fault of society," trot out the broken home and the slum environment. The question then is, What shall we do, not in the Utopian city of tomorrow, but here and now. The "scientific" means of cure are more than uncertain. The apparatus of detention only increases the killer's antisocial animus. Reformatories and mental hospitals are full and have an understandable bias toward discharging their inmates. Some of these are indeed "cured"—so long as they stay under a rule. The stress of the social free-for-all throws them back on their violent modes of self-expression. . . .
>
> As in all great questions, the moralist must choose, and choosing has a price. I happen to think that if a person of adult body has not been endowed with adequate controls against irrationally taking the life of another, that person must be judicially, painlessly, regretfully killed before that mindless body's horrible automation repeats. . . .
>
> . . . what are we to say of the type of motive disclosed in a journal published by the inmates of one of our Federal penitentiaries? The author is a bank robber who confesses that money is not his object:
>
>> My mania for power, socially, sexually, and otherwise, can feel no degree of satisfaction until I feel sure I have struck the ultimate of submission and terror in the minds and bodies of my victims. . . . It's very difficult to explain all the queer fascinating sensations pounding and surging through me while I'm holding a gun on a victim, watching his body tremble and sweat. . . . This is the moment when all the rationalized hypocrisies of civilization are suddenly swept away and two men stand there facing each other morally and ethically naked, and right and wrong are the absolute commands of the man behind the gun.
>
> This confused echo of modern literature and modern science defines the choice before us. Anything deserving the name of cure for such a man presupposes not only a laborious individual psychoanalysis, with the means to conduct and sustain it, socially and economically, but also a re-education of the mind, so as to throw into correct perspective the garbled ideas of Freud and Nietzsche, Gide and Dostoevski. . . . Ideas are tenacious and give continuity to emotion. Failing a second birth of heart and mind, we must ask: How soon will this sufferer sacrifice a bank clerk in the interests of making civilization less hypocritical? And we must certainly question the wisdom of affording him more than one chance.[3]

The recidivism rate is simply too high, it has been said, to afford us the luxury of allowing certain dangerous criminals to live. If we attempt to remedy this problem by sentencing some people to life im-

---

[3] Jacques Barzun, "In Favor of Capital Punishment," in *The Death Penalty in America,* ed. Hugo Bedau (New York: Doubleday, 1967), pp. 159–60. Reprinted from *The American Scholar,* Volume 31, Number 2, Spring 1962. Copyright © 1962 by the United Chapters of Phi Beta Kappa. By permission of the publishers.

prisonment, without the possibility of parole, then such a punishment would be more inhumane than death itself. Furthermore, we should realize that life imprisonment does not eliminate the risk that these dangerous criminals provide to other criminals and to guards.

A death penalty is also required, it has been said, for certain political criminals who, if allowed to live, might become a focal point for dangerous revolutionary agitation. As Sidney Hook puts it,

> There is an enormous amount of historical evidence which shows that certain political tyrants, after they lose power, become the focus of restoration movements that are a chronic source of bloodshed and civil strife. . . . I did not approve of the way Mussolini was killed. Even he deserved due process. But I have no doubt whatsoever that had he been sentenced merely to life imprisonment the Fascist movement in Italy today would be a much more formidable movement, and that, sooner or later, many lives would have been lost in consequence of the actions of Fascist legitimists.[4]

It Is Too Costly to Keep Prisoners in Jail for Long Periods of Time

Some supporters of the death penalty see it not only as a way of permanently eliminating very dangerous people from our society, but as a measure of cold-blooded economics. It simply costs too much money, they say, to keep criminals in jail for very long periods of time, especially if the criminal is a violent or mentally unstable one who requires special psychiatric or custodial facilities. Prisons are too overcrowded already and we ought to alleviate this overcrowding by using the death penalty on nonreformable criminals who would otherwise be sentenced to life imprisonment. Certainly, the countless thousands of dollars that will be required to imprison a person like Charles Manson over a long period of time could be better spent on more socially desirable causes, such as the attempt to eradicate the sociological and psychological roots out of which such individuals as Manson grow.

THE ARGUMENTS AGAINST THE DEATH PENALTY

The Death Penalty Is Inhumane

Just as most of us would reject torturous punishments as inhumane even if it could be shown that such punishments are a better deterrent than imprisonment or relatively painless death, so too should we reject

---

[4] Sidney Hook, "The Death Sentence," in *The Death Penalty in America,* ed. Bedau, p. 151.

the intentional and cold-blooded killing of a criminal as inhumane. When we kill a criminal who has killed someone else, we, along with him, have contributed to a cheapening of the value of human life. Instead of reinforcing society's concern for the sanctity of human life, we have struck a blow against this most central of moral principles.

If the infliction of death itself is not inhumane, the drawn-out procedure of appeal, reappeal, and postponement that accompanies a sentence of death certainly is. The average time between the imposition of the death penalty and execution is almost four years—four years of uncertainty of the most agonizing nature. This is a type of torture that no civilized society should allow, it is claimed.

The Death Penalty Is Unjustly Applied

A study of case histories of individuals sentenced to death shows the vast injustice of the process by which we decide who shall live and who shall die. Professional killers, the rich and powerful, are, when infrequently caught, able to get lesser sentences through astute criminal representation. Those who are perceived as "wild beasts" generally escape death through a judgment of insanity. This, however, is not always the case. Some whose horrid crimes make the public cry out for vengeance are executed as ruthless criminals instead of being perceived as the sick and helpless victims they really are. If a defendant facing the death penalty has the money, however, he can employ psychiatrists who can paint a sympathetic picture of him. But, if he is poor, he is at the mercy of the psychiatrists the state chooses to supply. In addition, he is always at the mercy of the prejudices of the jury that will decide his fate. If he is poor or black or a member of some unliked minority group, the odds are greatly increased that the jury will not find the same sympathy for him that they are apt to find for other criminals. There is no greater injustice than taking the life of one man and sparing the life of another, no more deserving, simply because he happens to be richer, more powerful, or white. Yet, this happens regularly.

The Death of Innocents

Inevitably, if there is to be a death penalty, some individuals will be executed for crimes they did not commit. There are many case histories of evidence clearing an innocent individual being found too late to save him from execution. There is no way, given the irreversible nature of death, for us to attempt to compensate an executed man for our error. The death penalty must be abolished to prevent an innocent person from ever being executed again, it is claimed.

The Death Penalty Does Not Deter
More than Long-Term Imprisonment

As practically all official government studies on capital punishment, both in this country and others, have found, the death penalty is not a greater deterrent than long-term imprisonment. Statistical studies have confirmed this time and time again. Common sense also indicates that we should not expect it to be a more effective deterrent. As most penologists have emphasized, the deterrent power of a given penalty depends more upon the likelihood of its application than it does upon its harshness. If a person thinks that there is an excellent chance that he will escape punishment, no punishment, however harsh, is apt to deter him. Yet that is precisely the situation today, as most criminals escape apprehension entirely. A rational offender will also often realize that even if he is apprehended there is a good chance that he will escape a death sentence since the percentage of individuals who are actually executed will be small compared to the numbers of individuals who commit similar crimes. Consequently, if the criminal is a rational offender who carefully deliberates over his course of action, the mere existence of a death penalty is not apt to play any appreciable role in his deliberations.

As well as failing to frighten the rational, the death penalty will clearly fail to deter the unpremeditated homicides which are often committed by either mentally unstable people or individuals in the grip of temporary passion. Yet most homicides are of this nature. It also clearly will not deter those criminals who do not care if they die or who actually want to die. Yet there are many criminals like this. Indeed, the very existence of the death penalty might incite mentally unstable people who want to die to commit capital crimes with the hope that the state will take their lives for them. For example, some individuals accused of capital crimes have admitted that before committing their crime, they attempted, or lacked the courage to attempt, suicide. Other mentally unstable individuals commit capital crimes as a way of achieving some degree of recognition—even if it must be of notoriety—from a world that has up until now ignored them.

When one subtracts all those individuals for whom the death penalty cannot reasonably be expected to function as a deterrent, one is left only with those who are sane and cautious enough to weigh the risk of punishment against the anticipated gain from crime and then decide that the risk is worth taking if the penalty is long imprisonment, but not if the penalty is death. It is unreasonable to assume that any appreciable numbers of such people exist, if any, it is claimed.

The Existence of the Death Penalty Has a Profoundly
Disturbing Effect upon the Administration of Justice

The sensational aspects of many capital crimes attract a press eager to publicize details of capital crimes which make a fair trial difficult, if not impossible, to obtain. Capital trials are exceedingly wasteful of time and money. The process of empanelling a jury for a capital case is a prolonged and difficult affair. Given the practice of appealing and re-appealing death sentences, a sentence of death results in a drawn out process of litigation which has caused the average length of time spent under sentence of death to steadily increase through the years while the actual numbers of individuals executed decreases. There are only two ways to avoid this unacceptable consequence. We may either abolish the death penalty or reduce the due process afforded a criminal subject to execution. The latter alternative is unacceptable, for we should not tamper with the rights of a person subject to a death sentence. The abolishment of the death penalty is then our only recourse, it is claimed.

ANALYSIS OF THE ARGUMENTS

Justice Demands

Underlying the view that justice at times demands the death penalty is the principle central to retributive theories of punishment that morality demands that a punishment should fit a given crime. The simplest formulation of this principle is found in the ancient code of Hammurabi which prescribes "an eye for an eye and a tooth for a tooth." As critics of the retributive point of view have pointed out, however, there is no way to justify the assertion that a given punishment is the only one which "fits" or is "equal to" a given crime. We may feel that death is the appropriate penalty for certain murders but that can, of course, be explained by our attachment to tradition and not by any principle of reason. Clearly, the simple "eye for an eye" principle reduces itself to absurdity when one considers such crimes as rape, since we obviously do not want to rape the rapist. In addition, what conceivable penalty is fitting to a mass murderer such as Adolf Eichmann? Certainly, he cannot be killed millions of times over. And even if we could in some way measure the degree of suffering a criminal has caused to his victims, most of us will react with moral revulsion at the thought that justice demands that we sadistically kill a sadistic murderer so that he be made to suffer to the degree that he made others suffer. While many of us feel this way in moments of passion, most of us would shudder to live in a society where these sentiments are reflected in law.

The retributive principle of the equality of punishment to crime is not, to be sure, an entirely empty notion, but reflects a fundamental principle of justice that one's punishment should reflect one's degree of guilt and not be allowed to vary depending on the vicissitudes of utilitarian considerations, such as deterrence (for instance, we should not punish X at time A more than Y at time B simply because there was a greater need to deter offenders at time A than at time B). The idea behind this principle is that our ranking of punishments from the harshest at one extreme to the most lenient at the other should be made to directly correspond to our perceived ranking of the moral gravity of a crime (for instance, if crime *A* is "morally worse" than crime *B,* then *A* ought to be more harshly punished). This principle does not tell us, however, as some retributivists would have us believe, how harsh or lenient our scale of punishments should be. In the past, "simple death" was considered an inappropriately lenient punishment "unequal" to the gravity of certain offenses. Elaborate and brutal tortures often awaited a condemned man who would cry out for the release of death. "Justice" demands that the "worst" criminals get the "worst" punishments, but our notion of "humaneness" helps determine what that punishment is.

Given our present moral sensibilities, the torturous executions of the past are ruled out as "inhumane," regardless of their possible "utility" or "appropriateness." Why then do so many of us believe that "justice" requires death rather than long-term imprisonment? I suspect that this belief derives from a feeling that a special punishment is required for certain heinous crimes. Some criminals, we believe (for example, Eichmann) require a qualitatively different sort of punishment than the routine imprisonment we inflict upon countless criminals whose crimes are immeasurably less in moral magnitude. Even life imprisonment, without the possibility of parole, will not suffice to satisfy our feeling that these moral monsters be punished in some special way. Again, one can understand such feelings, but they are feelings that can never be fully satisfied. Even if we were to set aside a special "qualitatively different" punishment for the gravest of crimes, among these crimes some will still appear "immeasurably worse" than others and will consequently call forth the feeling that some special penalty be applied in their cases. This reasoning can then be applied ad infinitum, as we seek harsher and harsher penalties to reflect the unbounded human capacity for evil.

The Death Penalty Is Inhumane
and Results in the Death of Innocents

Those who cry out about the inhumanity of capital punishment and speak of "the sanctity of human life" are often silent when it comes to opposing wars which result in far greater loss of human lives and, in this case, of innocent ones. Since most opponents of capital punishment are not morally opposed to all use of lethal force, such as in situations of self-defense, their invocation of the principle of "the sanctity of human life" in the context of the death penalty issue rings hollow. The acts of criminals sentenced to death for murder are the clearest example of inhumanity. If capital punishment is a superior deterrent to imprisonment for these acts of criminal inhumanity, and if the number of people that are deterred from these acts exceeds the number of people executed, then capital punishment should be perceived as a measure of social self-defense which aims not at the destruction of human life, but at its preservation. Our concern for the loss of convicted criminals' lives should not blind us to the lives of the potential innocent victims of crime we could save if capital punishment is indeed a superior deterrent to long-term imprisonment.

Similarly, although we should do everything within our power to avoid convicting and executing an innocent person, we must weigh the minute number of such innocent lives that would be lost against the lives of those innocents who would otherwise be killed if we were to abolish the death penalty and it turned out to have deterrent value. There are many more substantial risks of the death of innocent people that we are willing as a society to take. For example, we license people to drive automobiles, knowing that a number of them will kill innocent victims. We try to screen out the bad risks, but we do not stop driving cars.

Although the death penalty is so often loudly condemned as "inhumane" and "irreversible," it is not at all clear that long-term prison sentences are more humane and reversible. One can certainly sympathize with a criminal who, out of pride for his *dignity,* prefers death to the subhuman condition of long-term imprisonment that might be awaiting him in a given prison. Although the critics of capital punishment often offer imprisonment without the possibility of parole as a "humane" alternative to death, they will rarely be willing to allow the criminal the right to choose which of these two penalties he would prefer. Imprisonment without the possibility of parole may be easier on the critics' consciences, but not necessarily more compatible with the "human dignity" of the criminal. In addition, what could possibly suffice as "compensation" for a person whose innocence has been established after his having served ten or twenty years of his sentence? Yet, this, too, sometimes happens. Such is the price we must pay for the fallibility of the judicial fact-finding process.

The Death Penalty Is Unjustly Applied

There is no doubt that prejudice more than justice has often been the prime motivating factor behind a death sentence. This is, however, not a sound criticism against the death penalty itself, but rather against the basic principles of the administration of justice and, in particular, the jury system. Sentences of long imprisonment are no less apt to be motivated by the prejudice of jury members than the sentence of death. If we are especially concerned with such miscarriages of justice when the death penalty is involved, we should require, as the current Georgia statute requires, that every sentence of death be subject to higher-level judicial scrutiny and should be overturned if there is any indication that this sentence is not consistent with those in other legally similar cases. Furthermore, while one should look with regret at the large percentages of minority group members who are sentenced to death, one should not forget that their victims are often minority group members as well. It is for this reason that Illinois State Senator Ewing, who is himself black, refused to vote for a moratorium on the death penalty in Illinois, declaring, "I realize that most of those who face the death penalty are poor and black. . . . I also realize that most of their victims are poor and black . . . and dead."

It Is Too Costly to Keep Prisoners in Jail for Long Periods of Time

It is not at all clear that society would reap any, let alone any appreciable, financial savings by having a death penalty. First, there are many lifers who settle down to productive jobs that more than pay for their upkeep. Second, there is great financial cost associated with capital punishment, including the cost of prolonged trials, and special facilities in prisons, including the various instruments of execution. It is questionable that these costs are less than the cost of prolonged imprisonment.

If financial cost is to be one of our prime concerns, we should give serious consideration to the various methods of psychophysical control and rehabilitation that were discussed in the previous chapter. If a person's behavior could be subjected to change or control to such an extent as to render him no longer a threat to society, some will argue that such a person should be freed from the constraints of a prison and allowed to live and work outside, perhaps paying a percentage of his earnings to the families of his victims or to society as a whole. As was mentioned in the previous chapter, if individuals are to be given the right to refuse having their personality changed against their will, a person could be given the option of choosing this sort of treatment in lieu of long imprisonment or a death sentence, if capital punishment is to be retained. The problem, however, of deciding when a choice of this sort is truly "voluntary" and "informed" will prove to be a very vexing one. Although some civil libertarians would doubtlessly oppose a movement in this direction on the basis of their concern for criminal rights, others of a different orientation will argue that methods of behavioral and psychophysical control, if they are not to be too unpleasant to their recipients, will cheat society both of its retributive desire to give a criminal his "just deserts" and of its utilitarian objective of furthering general deterrence. Consequently, such methods, to be feasible and generally accepted, would have to be perceived as undesirable enough to be a credible deterrent and a "just retribution," but not so undesirable that no rational person would voluntarily choose it as an alternative to long-term imprisonment or death. Developing legal principles which reflect this requirement would be formidable indeed.

Some Criminals Are Too Dangerous to Be Allowed to Live

Again, one response to very dangerous criminals is the use of the various techniques of behavioral control and rehabilitation. Drugs have already been utilized on an involuntary basis in prisons as a method of control. The justification of such procedures are the subject of current judicial litigation and legislative debate. Leaving aside the vexing question of behavioral modification, the fears that lead many to envision murderers as exceedingly dangerous individuals whose recidivism rate is higher than that of other offenders is without justification. This is borne out by the statistics as well as the first-hand observations of correctional officials.[5]

It is important to realize that the closer one comes to the image of a murderer as a "crazed" and "uncontrollable wild beast," the closer one comes to the image of "insanity." Yet, our current punishment system with its deep conceptual connection to retributive notions of moral guilt and desert leads us to the acceptance of an insanity defense which attempts to weed such individuals out of the criminal process entirely. While our current criminal law considers it morally inappropriate to treat such individuals as "dangerous animals" to be "exterminated," this is the sentiment behind Barzun's proposal quoted on p. 391. In essence, he proposes that capital punishment should be perceived not as a retributive measure, but rather as the preventive or "prophylactic execution" of potential murderers. Such an idea was defended by George Bernard Shaw in his 1922 essay "The Crime of Imprisonment." As Shaw put it, "persons who give more trouble than they are worth will run the risk of being . . . returned to the dust from which they sprung."

Some will protest that to treat a human being in the way in which Barzun and Shaw suggest is immoral; I would not, however, take this line myself. Regretfully, I must admit that some creatures who possess the bodies of human beings should indeed be perceived more as "animals" than as persons who can reasonably be expected to be part of a moral community. If there is no possibilty of turning these creatures into moral agents, I feel a strong pull toward Barzun and Shaw's view. However, since we do not at present know how to make reliable predictions as to a person's potential dangerousness, and will not be able to do so in the foreseeable future, such a view is fraught with the potential for misuse. At best, one could reasonably claim that the state should have the option to use capital punishment (or behavioral modification) on those who, after being sentenced to prison for murder, murder again either upon release or while serving their sentence. The determination of the appropriateness of utilizing that option should center not on the degree of such a person's guilt, but rather upon the risk society takes in allowing him to live.[6]

5 See, for example, Sara R. Ehrmann, "The Human Side of Capital Punishment," in *The Death Penalty in America,* ed. Bedau, pp. 492–519.

6 Consider, for example, the case of Joseph Morse of San Diego, who received the death penalty for killing his mother and sister but was given life imprisonment following a retrial. While awaiting transportation back to prison, he killed a fellow inmate over a few packs of cigarettes. He received a death penalty for that, which was reduced again to life imprisonment when California's death penalty statute was declared unconstitutional. What, one may reasonably ask, other than death or drastic behavioral modification, is to prevent such a man from killing again?

The Question of Deterrence

Some who argue against the death penalty on the grounds that it does not deter rest their claim on the more general assertion that all punishments fail to deter. This is, however, certainly false. The question is not whether the death penalty deters, for it most certainly does, but whether it deters more than long-term imprisonment for those crimes we deem most serious. (Obviously, a death penalty would be a very effective deterrent for parking violations!) Also not at issue is the question of whether there are more effective deterrents than the death penalty (such as death preceded by torture). Given our current moral sensibilities, such punishments would be ruled out as too inhumane to be contemplated, regardless of their deterrent efficacy.

What are we to make of the conflicting claims as to the deterrent power of the death penalty? Both sides rely on conflicting pronouncements of common sense and conflicting readings of the various statistical studies. Although there have been many statistical studies which have attempted to throw some light upon the question of the deterrent effect of the death penalty, it is difficult to know what to make of them. These statistical studies have been of various sorts. Some have simply compared the homicide rates in states having and not having the death penalty. Such studies are of doubtful value since it is quite possible that the differences in homicide rates in different states are not dependent upon the presence or absence of a death penalty, but rather upon underlying socioeconomic conditions. For example, perhaps due to its special socioeconomic conditions, state A has a lower homicide rate than state B. Clearly, any statistical analysis would be mistaken that focuses on the fact that A has a lower homicide rate than B and attributes this to the fact that A has a death penalty, while B does not.

More meaningful statistical studies have restricted their comparisons to the following:

1. adjacent states, having roughly the same socioeconomic conditions, one (or more) of which has the death penalty for murder, and one (or more) of which does not.
2. homicide rates in a given state before and after abolition.
3. homocide rates in a given state before, during, and after a capital trial and/or execution.

These studies are, however, also beset with problems of interpretation. First, most are studies of general homicide rates and make the questionable assumption that this rate directly corresponds to the rate of capitally punishable homicides. Secondly, there can be no doubt that the causes of crime and of homicide in particular are quite complex. One cannot "simply look at the figures" to arrive at reliable interpretations. If, for example, the homicide rate in state X drops after it abolishes the death penalty, an abolitionist might interpret this as offering evidence for the assertion that the existence of a death penalty actually incites people to homicide rather than deterring them. This, however, could be false; it is quite possible that the drop in the homicide rate in state X is causally independent of the abolition of the death penalty (for instance, perhaps when state X abolished their death penalty, other penal reforms were also instituted which account for the drop in the homicide rate). Similarly, if X's homicide rate increases after abolition, retentionists are apt to interpret this as evidence of capital punishment's deterrent efficacy. Again, this need not be the case; perhaps X's homicide rate would have increased anyway due to other factors, regardless of the existence or nonexistence of the death penalty. Indeed, it is possible that even though the homicide rate has increased in state X, the abolition of the death penalty has served to reduce it, for if the death penalty had been maintained, the homicide rate would be even higher.

The general consensus of those who have analyzed these statistical studies has been that they are inconclusive and give no evidence to support the view that capital punishment is a superior deterrent to imprisonment for the crime of murder. Some have gone further, asserting that the statistics *establish* or *support* the view that capital punishment is no better a deterrent than imprisonment for the crimes for which it is used as a penalty. Some have even gone so far as to assert that the statistics indicate that capital punishment actually incites more to violence than it deters. Largely on the basis of these statistical studies, the vast majority of governmental studies of the desirability of the death penalty have concluded that there is no good reason to assume that the death penalty is a superior deterrent to long-term imprisonment. This conclusion is, however, denied by Professor Isaac Ehrlich of the University of Chicago who in a recent study concluded that between 1933 and 1967, "an additional execution per year . . . may have resulted (on the average) in seven or eight fewer murders." Ehrlich's claim has, in turn, been contested by critics, and the debate continues. Given such conflicting pronouncements and the ambiguity of the data itself, I think we must discount these statistical studies entirely. It might very well be that the existence or nonexistence of the death penalty has such a negligible effect upon the general homicide rate as to prove statistically insignificant.

Leaving aside the ambiguity of the statistics, what can we say of the various "common sense" arguments for and against the deterrent efficacy of the death penalty? First, the abolitionists are, no doubt, correct in arguing that it is unreasonable to expect that many individuals who would not be deterred by the threat of long imprisonment will be deterred by the remote threat of death when they most likely think they will get away with their crime anyway. Second, Leiser's claim that revolutionaries provide a prime example of individuals who can be deterred by the threat of death but not of long imprisonment does not seem reasonable. Indeed, revolutionaries like Gandhi are, perhaps, the best example of individuals who are so committed to their cause as to be nondeterrable by any punishment that can be inflicted upon them. The same is often true of the idealistic traitor. The less idealistic traitor who turns on his country for more materialistic considerations, one would suppose, does so generally in the belief that he will escape any punishment. Third, Leiser's claim that the death penalty is the only deterrent for criminals who are already serving a life sentence is simply false. There are many rewards and punishments that can be utilized on those sentenced to life imprisonment that can act as deterrents, including the possibility of early parole, solitary confinement, and the forfeiture of some of the conveniences that make prison life more bearable, such as the privilege of having visitors.

However, we should not so easily discount, as many abolitionists do, the direct testimony of captured criminals to law enforcement officials that the threat of death deterred them from either killing a potential witness to a crime already punishable by life imprisonment or from carrying or using a lethal weapon even though to do so would have increased their chances of escape. Although one can well imagine a criminal, such as a kidnapper, who does not kill his victim out of a regard for human life, which is independent of the existence or nonexistence of a death penalty, one can equally as well imagine a cold-blooded kidnapper who refrains from killing his victim only because of his fear of the death penalty. No doubt, as abolitionists claim, such a cold-blooded criminal would most likely never have embarked upon his criminal activities if he believed that there was a substantial risk of being caught. Nevertheless, if the kidnapping does not go as planned, such an individual may later become very much concerned with the possibility of his capture, a possibility which now appears much greater than it once did.

No doubt, as abolitionists point out, criminals who tell law enforcement officials that they were deterred from murder by the existence of a death penalty are often telling these officials what they want to hear and these officials often, like everyone else, hear what they want to hear. This has been supported by the wardens of such prisons as San Quentin and Sing Sing who report that criminals have often admitted to them that they lied when they made those remarks. Consequently, some skepticism must be employed in weighing the value of the pronouncements of law enforcement officials as to the important deterrent effect of capital punishment, but we would be rash to fully discount their pronouncements.

The moral choice we must face is whether we should risk abolishing the death penalty and risk losing the lives of those innocents who would otherwise be spared should it prove to be a better deterrent to murder than long imprisonment. This is a choice each of us must ponder for ourselves. Certainly, however, our sympathy for those who are condemned to capital punishment and whose plight is visibly presented to us should not blind us to the invisible victims of murderers whom we could save if capital punishment is a better deterrent to murder than long imprisonment. On the other hand, if we are to opt for capital punishment in the hope that it proves a superior deterrent, weighing against our wager will not only be the lives of those guilty of the most serious crimes, but some innocent individuals as well—those who are unjustly executed and those who die at the hands of those who are incited to crime by the existence of a death penalty. Do we have a reasonable basis for assuming that their numbers will be less than the numbers of innocent lives saved which can be attributed to the superior deterrent efficacy of capital punishment? This question has no clear answer.

If we decide to maintain the death penalty, gambling on the belief that the death penalty is a superior deterrent to murder than long imprisonment, we should realize that it is a gamble and not a certainty with which we are dealing; and we should not exaggerate the possible deterrent value of capital punishment as many law enforcement officials do. It is easy to mask one's frustrations at controlling crime by a passionate commitment to capital punishment, but the existence of such a penalty cannot be expected to have a significant effect upon the difficulties facing law enforcement officials and certainly it should not blind us, as citizens, to the causes of crime, whose eradication will have a profoundly greater effect upon crime control.

DISCUSSION QUESTIONS

1. Do you believe the death penalty is justified? Why, or why not?

2. What do you think of the following argument:

   Individuals have a moral right to kill in self-defense. If individuals have a moral right to kill in self-defense so does a nation. *The death penalty is a measure of national self-defense.* Therefore, it is right to use the death penalty.

3. Do you think the death penalty has a "brutalizing effect" on society as many have suggested? If so, how important is this factor relative to the possible beneficial consequences of the death penalty?

4. Which of the following arguments do you find more convincing?

   A: The most basic of human rights is the right to life. It is purely speculative whether the death penalty has a deterrent value and as such can save lives. The utilization of capital punishment, on the other hand, is a clear infringement on that most basic of human rights. One is never justified in violating a person's right to life on the basis of a purely speculative good. Therefore, the death penalty is unjustified.

   B: It is unclear whether more lives are saved or lost with capital punishment, but since the life of a potential victim of crime should be valued more than the life of a convicted murderer, the death penalty is justified.

5. Assuming that an "insane" killer poses a substantial threat of killing again and can only be contained through physical chains or biochemical or electrical intervention with his mental processes which

will reduce him to a "zombie-like" existence, should either of these means be utilized or would it be better that such an individual be painlessly put to death, or are none of these alternatives morally justifiable?

6. Do you think the execution of a terrorist murderer can be justified on the grounds that her imprisonment is likely to cause other terrorists to threaten the death of innocent hostages as a price for her release? Would this be justifiable if the terrorist had committed a lesser crime?

7. Should the death penalty be allowed as a voluntary alternative to life imprisonment without the possibility of parole? As a voluntary alternative to some lesser penalty?

8. Argue for or against Justice Brennan's claim that "the deliberate extinguishment of human life by the State is uniquely degrading to human dignity."

9. Do you think the Israelis were right in executing Adolf Eichmann for his responsibility in the extermination of the Jews? How would you have treated him? Why?

10. a. According to legal practice, if a criminal who is sentenced to death becomes physically ill, he is treated for his physical illness and then killed at the appointed time of his execution. Do you find this practice justifiable? Why?

   b. Similarly, do you find any justification for the legal practice of postponing the execution of those criminals who "go out of their mind" in jail until they are of "sound mind"?

11. Some Supreme Court justices (such as Rehnquist) have claimed that the constitutional prohibition of "cruel and unusual punishment" should be taken to prohibit only those punishments that the framers of the Constitution would have considered to be "cruel" (such as the thumbscrew and the rack, but not whipping). Most Supreme Court justices, however, have taken the position that this prohibition should be interpreted in terms of evolving moral standards. Supporters of this point of view are divided as to how the courts should determine these standards. Some justices (such as Burger) think the courts should rely on legislative enactments and the sentencing behavior of juries as the standard of what punishments *are as a matter of fact found acceptable* "under contemporary standards of decency." On the other hand, some justices have taken the view that the standard of "cruelty" should be a *normative* one. For example, Justice Marshall takes the view that the courts should turn not to what people will as a matter of fact say about a given punishment, but rather to what they would say if they *were fully informed*. Which of the above views do you find most acceptable? Why?

12. In 1977 and 1978, legislation was passed in the states of Oklahoma, Texas, and Illinois to substitute painless lethal injections for the standard and more dramatic forms of capital punishment. If the death penalty is to be maintained, do you think that this is advisable? Why, or why not?

FURTHER READINGS

BEDAU, HUGH ADAM, ed., *The Death Penalty in America* (rev. ed.). Garden City, N.Y.: Doubleday, 1967. An excellent and comprehensive interdisciplinary anthology of material on the pros and cons of the death penalty, representing religious, philosophical, sociological, law enforcement, legal, and psychological perspectives. The anthology begins with a presentation of the historical background of the death penalty and ends with a presentation of case histories of people sentenced to death which Bedau, himself an abolitionist, selected to demonstrate "the inhuman side of capital punishment in America." Included in this anthology are Sidney Hook's "The Death Sentence" (pp. 146–54) and Jacques Barzun's "In Favor of Capital Punishment" (pp. 154–65), which were referred to in this chapter. Bedau criticizes Hook and Barzun in his own article "Death as a Punishment" (pp. 214–31).

BEDAU, HUGO ADAM, and CHARLES M. PIERCE, eds., *Capital Punishment in the United States.* New York: AMS Press, Inc., 1975. A collection of material on psychological and sociological research on the death penalty that has appeared since the Supreme Court's *Furman v. Georgia* ruling in 1972.

BEDAU-VAN DEN HAAG, Debate (see Van den Hagg below).

BLACK, CHARLES L., JR., *Capital Punishment: The Inevitability of Caprice and Mistake.* New York: W.W. Norton & Company, Inc., 1974. Black, a law professor, argues for abolition on the grounds that it is impossible to eliminate arbitrariness and mistake in the infliction of the death penalty.

McCAFFERTY, JAMES A., ed., *Capital Punishment.* New York: Lieber-Atherton, 1972. An anthology of material on the pros and cons of the death penalty by philosophers and people directly involved in the administration of the criminal law.

MAPPES, THOMAS A., and JANE S. ZEMBATY, eds., *Social Ethics: Morality and Social Policy,* chapter 3. New York: McGraw-Hill, 1977. This anthology has a well-rounded selection of material on the death penalty consisting of selections from Marshall's and Burger's judicial opinions in *Furman v. Georgia,* Hook's, Barzun's, and Bedau's articles on the death penalty (also included in the Bedau anthology) and an article by David Conway, written as a dialogue between an abolitionist and retentionist. The retentionist presents various arguments for the death penalty on deterrent grounds which are challenged by the abolitionist (who seems to be Conway himself).

RACHELS, JAMES, ed., *Moral Problems* (3rd ed.), part IV. New York: Harper & Row, Pub., 1979. This anthology also has a good collection of articles on the death penalty. Included are excerpts from Justice Stewart's majority opinion and Justice Douglas's dissent in *Gregg v. Georgia* (the 1976 case where the death penalty statute of Georgia was declared constitutional by the U.S. Supreme Court), Barzun's article in favor of the death penalty and an article by Victor H. Evjen which very clearly presents and defends various arguments against the death penalty. Both articles are directed to a wide lay audience.

RADIN, MARGARET JANE, "The Jurisprudence of Death: Evolving Standards for the Cruel and Unusual Punishments Clause, 126, *Univ. of Penn. L. Rev.* 989–1064 (May 1978). A study of the principles utilized by various Supreme Court justices for determining whether capital punishment is "cruel and unusual punishment." Radin defends the abolitionist point of view.

VAN DEN HAAG, ERNEST, "On Deterrence and the Death Penalty," *Ethics*, 78, no. 4 (July 1968), 280–87. A defense of the death penalty on deterrent grounds. Van den Haag's article is criticized by Hugo Bedau in his "The Death Penalty as a Deterrent: Argument and Evidence," *Ethics*, 80, no. 3. (April 1970), 205–16. Van den Haag provides a brief and heated rebuttal to Bedau in his "Deterrence and the Death Penalty: A Rejoinder," *Ethics*, 81, no. 1 (October 1970), 74–75 and Bedau even more briefly replies in his "A Concluding Note" in the same issue, p. 76.

WASSERSTROM, RICHARD, ed., *Today's Moral Problems* (2nd ed.), part six. New York: Macmillan, 1979. Another good collection of articles on the death penalty can be found in this anthology. Included are portions of Justices Douglas, Brennan, Powell, and Burger's opinions in *Furman v. Georgia*. In addition, there are articles by Steven Goldberg and George Schedler which argue for conflicting viewpoints on the bearing of considerations of deterrence on the moral justification of the death penalty. Originally printed in philosophical journals, these articles are directed to an audience with some philosophical background.

10

The Morality
of
War

INTRODUCTION: THE TRAGIC AND IRRECONCILABLE CLASH OF MORAL PRINCIPLES INVOLVED IN WARS

The question of the morality of war is a deeply troubling one. For some, the very notion of "a moral war" is a contradiction in terms, for war, as they see it, is by definition a brutal struggle for survival which reduces human beings to a primitive amoral level of existence whose only guiding principle is that of self-preservation. For others, questions relating to the morality of war, however practically difficult they may be to resolve, are at least *in principle* resolvable, given sufficient factual information and moral understanding. For still others, like myself, who see the moral life as being built upon more than one basic moral principle and accept the possibility of irreconcilable conflict between these moral principles, questions relating to the morality of war bring home, in an acutely disturbing way, the potentiality for tragic and unresolvable moral conflict.

For the utilitarian, the brutality of war, and in particular the killing of innocent human beings that it involves, can be morally justified whenever such a measure is an essential means for securing a greater good. For the Kantian, however, who sees the demands of justice in absolutist and immediate terms, war must be condemned as the very model of immorality. What better example is there of treating individuals "as mere means"—which Kantian ethics forbids us ever to do—than to intentionally drop bombs that one knows will kill innocent civilians, including babies, in order to achieve some "greater good." When one thinks of the death and horror inflicted on so many innocent people in wartime, a morally sensitive person must feel some pull toward the Kantian view that some things are wrong, regardless of the consequences. If one could not feel morally justified in shooting an innocent child at point-blank range, even if this were essential as a means to achieve some "greater good," how can one feel morally justified in dropping bombs that will kill thousands of innocent children, as the Allies did in their obliteration bombing of German cities and in the American nuclear bombing of Hiroshima and Nagasaki in World War II? Doubtlessly, it is *psychologically easier* to drop bombs than to fire a gun point-blank at the head of a helpless child whose little frightened face one cannot help but see. The bomber pilot may not see the countless little frightened children, but he has killed them nevertheless. Although one's moral horror over the results of one's actions may vary inversely with one's distance from that horror, one's moral responsibility certainly does not. If one focuses squarely on the immense human horror of modern war, on the colossal forfeiture of human rights that it involves, one may understandably feel strongly inclined toward the view that modern wars are always morally wrong. Better that we should die or be victimized by the injustices of others than that we should intentionally will the stupendous injustices of modern wars. Such a moral view may not be best suited to assure our survival or happiness in this world, but it is essential, one may feel, if we are to maintain our humanity as moral beings.

Nevertheless, the utilitarian pull is also very strong, for few of us believe, as Kant did, that justice must be done even "if the heavens are about to fall." No doubt, many wars that have been waged and the means utilized in waging them have not been justified on utilitarian grounds, but some certainly seem to have been. For example, when one thinks of the possibility of the triumph of Nazism and the vast inhumanity that such a triumph would have assured, can one so easily say that the Allied obliteration bombings of German cities and the vast numbers of innocent civilians killed by these bombings were unjustified *if* such measures were essential for defeating the Nazis? As Einstein and those atomic scientists who urged that our country undertake the construction of an atomic bomb believed, in spite of one's moral revulsion at the thought of using such a bomb, its use would be morally justified *if there were no other way* of winning the war against Hitler. In order to preserve the value of justice and of human life for this and future generations, justice and human lives would have to be sacrificed.

It is precisely because most of us are responsive to both the utilitarian and Kantian ways of moral thinking and are at times subject to their irreconcilable demands, that the question of the morality of war is an especially difficult one. The ultimate moral tragedy of war is that it produces choices that our utilitarian moral intuitions tell us we must make and our Kantian intuitions tell us we never can. As the contemporary philosopher Thomas Nagel puts it in his sensitive essay "War and Massacre," when we squarely face the question of the morality of war, we also come squarely face to face with the possibility "that these two forms of moral intuition are not capable of being brought together into a single, coherent moral system, and that the world can present us with situations in which there is no honorable or moral course for a man to take, no course free of guilt and responsibility." As Nagel clearly sees, whatever decision we make in such situations must be made with a sense of tragic loss, guilt, and agony over the cost of one's decision. A totally committed utilitarian or Kantian who sees morality as being built on a single basic moral principle need not feel any moral guilt or regret as long as he observes that basic moral principle, but for those of us who accept a plurality of independent and possibly conflicting basic moral principles, there is always the possibility of having to face a moral dilemma, all of whose options involve choosing something which violates a basic moral principle and for which we will feel deep guilt and regret for the remainder of our days. Such is the tragic condition of life in this world—a tragic condition that cannot be escaped by any morally sensitive person who attempts to assess war in moral terms.

THE DISTINCTION BETWEEN THE MORAL JUSTIFICATION FOR WAGING WAR AND THE MORALITY OF THE MEANS OF WAGING WAR

Since the waging of war involves grave injustices, unlike anything we are willing to condone in any other context, many would question the very possibility of assessing war in moral terms. For example, consider the following remarks made by Bayard Rustin:

> I have said to these young men that they make too much of American brutality. The Viet Cong is equally brutal. Whether one is among the battling Pakistanis and Indians, or in Watts, or in warfare anywhere, the law of violence is such that each side becomes equally vicious. To try to distinguish which is more vicious is to fail to recognize the logic of war.[1]

According to Rustin, it would appear, it is not simply that human beings *as a matter of fact* refuse to subject the means used in waging war to principles of moral assessment, but that the very "logic of war" makes this assessment *impossible*. Although one may distinguish, perhaps, between moral (or just) and immoral (or unjust) reasons for waging wars, it simply *makes no logical sense* to speak of morality or justice in the waging of war, Rustin seems to believe. The distinction between the justice of war (*jus ad bellum*) and justice in wars (*jus in bello*) was a central one for medieval moralists who reflected on the morality of

---

[1] Quoted in Michael Walzer, "Moral Judgment in Time of War," in *War and Morality*, ed. Richard A. Wasserstrom (New York: Wadsworth, 1970), p. 54.

war. It was, they believed, very important for us to morally appraise both the reasons nations have for waging war and the means they adopt in waging it. For Rustin, however, a distinction between moral and immoral ways of waging war cannot be meaningfully drawn. As the familiar saying goes, "All's fair in love and war"—that is, any kind of deceit in love and any kind of violence in war. Although Rustin's claim is no doubt psychologically comforting to those who share responsibility for waging war, it flies in the face of the fact that we often do make the distinction between moral and immoral ways of waging war.

For example, many of us condemned as immoral the Pakistani way of waging war in Bangladesh in 1971. Whether or not Pakistan had any justification for attempting to repress Bangladesh's movement for autonomy, their *manner of repressing* that movement for autonomy was loudly morally condemned. It was wrong, so many of us said, to turn an army loose to massacre innocent civilians as Pakistan did. It was beyond moral justification for an army to rampage freely, burning, raping, and killing as it saw fit. It was wrong for it to compile "death lists" of political, cultural, and intellectual leaders of Bangladesh and then to systematically slaughter them. Although the entrance of India on the side of Bangladesh was doubtlessly, at least in part, motivated by India's own strategic interests, many who cared little or nothing about these interests rallied on the Indian side, seeing their action as called for by a humanitarian concern to stop the Pakistanis from waging a type of war that was beyond the pale of moral justification.

Just as it is possible for a just war to be fought unjustly, it is possible for an unjust war to be fought justly. For example, although Rommell was fighting for the unjust cause of Nazi Germany, he, unlike so many other German generals, adhered to some basic principles of morality in waging his war. For example, he burned the Commando order issued by Hitler which laid down that all enemy soldiers encountered behind the German lines were to be killed at once.[2] One may morally condemn the justice of Rommell's cause, but morally commend him for fighting justly.

Although one can often separate the question of the morality of a nation's reasons for waging war from the question of the morality of its means of waging war, these questions are clearly intertwined. From a utilitarian perspective, a war waged for quite morally justified purposes may become immoral when the means of waging that war involves more harm than the good that can be achieved by it. For example, such a situation often arises when a foreign influence finds itself fighting guerrillas that have some degree of local support. As Michael Walzer puts it,

> Foreigners fighting local guerrillas are likely to find themselves driven
> to justify, or rather to attempt to justify, virtually every conceivable action

2 See Ronald Lewin, *Rommell as Military Commander* (Princeton, N.J.: D. Van Nostrand, 1968), p. 242.

against a hostile population—until they reach that climactic brutality summed up in the orders issued by General Okamura, Japanese commander in the struggle against Communist guerrillas in North China during World War II: "Kill all! Burn all! Destroy all!"

At this point, the question of morality in war and of the morality of a particular war come together. Any war that requires the methods of General Okamura, or anything approaching them, is itself immoral, however exalted the purposes in the name of which it is being fought.[3]

Conversely, from a utilitarian perspective, the more morally justified one's reasons for waging war, the more individual injustice one should be willing to tolerate to win that war. For example, considering the clear and pressing moral justification for defeating Nazi Germany and the far from clear and pressing need to defeat the Viet Cong in Vietnam, the United States might have been justified in the obliteration bombing of German cities, but not in the bombing of Vietnamese villages and cities.

THE UTILITARIAN VIEW OF THE MORALITY OF WAR: THE NOTIONS OF PROPORTIONALITY AND MILITARY NECESSITY

For a utilitarian, in deciding upon the morality of waging a particular war in a particular way, one must weigh the harm that is likely to be caused as a result of waging this war against the good that is likely to be achieved by waging it. In principle, then, it becomes possible that the harm likely to be produced through the waging of a war can exceed whatever good consequences a country hopes to achieve by waging and winning that war. If this is the case, such a war can be given no utilitarian justification.

In practice, however, nations tend to assume that the utility of their aims is so immense that any means can be justifiably utilized from a utilitarian standpoint to achieve them. This is especially the case when nations see their enemies as incarnations of evil "who must be crushed at any cost" and see themselves, as they often do, as waging a war for some supreme ideal—such as "making the world safe for democracy" or "waging a war to end all wars"—that far overshadows in utility the immediate suffering and death that individuals will be forced to endure in a war to achieve this ideal. Although history clearly attests to the fact that these supreme ideals seem elusively unachievable through the horrors of war, we cling to this illusion, nevertheless, for with it we can escape the essential utilitarian need to weigh the utility of our means in waging war against the utility of our objectives.[4] Instead we simply assume that

---

[3] Walzer, "Moral Judgment in Time of War," p. 59.

our objective is of such overriding importance that it can justify whatever means are essential to achieve it. From such a perspective, the utilitarian question reduces itself to that of choosing those means essential for achieving one's objective at the "cheapest" utilitarian price (that is, one must choose the means for achieving one's ends that have the least disutility). Nations are rarely, however, willing to grant that the undesirable consequences of waging a war are likely to be greater than any good consequences that waging that war are likely to achieve. Unwilling to accept this possibility, nations assume they can do *anything* they must to win, as long as what they do is actually related to winning. This view is captured in the notion of "military necessity," which is a key notion in the various international laws of war which attempt to specify the scope of a nation's legitimate means for waging war. In essence, the laws of war which allow nations to do everything "militarily necessary" to win their war rule out only purposeless or wanton violence. This is not, however, a small achievement, for there can be no doubt that much of the violence of war does not serve any useful purpose. Military history, unfortunately, is a sad tale of wanton brutality beyond the bounds of any plausible utilitarian justification.

Our moral intuitions (and the various laws of war which reflect them), however, go beyond the utilitarian notion of "proportionality" and "military necessity." However entitled countries may be to win their wars, we do not believe that they are entitled to do anything whatever that contributes to this objective. Certain things, many of us deeply believe, are wrong regardless of the beneficial consequences they are likely to achieve. For example, it has been said that the prospect of plunder and rape is "a spur to the courage of the troops." The plausibility of such a claim would be strongest in the case of mercenaries who are hired to aid a country in fighting a war. For example, a group of mercenaries fighting with the Free French forces in Italy in 1943 was responsible for raping a large number of Italian women. (An incident of such

---

4 The psychological processes by which human beings convince themselves, often without any adequate justification, of the importance of their ends is considered by Ralph K. White, a social psychologist, in his insightful book *Nobody Wanted War: Misperception in Vietnam and Other Wars* (New York: Doubleday, 1968). In his book, White describes the typical, recurrent misperceptions that often make war possible, even when on both sides there is an urgent desire to avoid it. Paramount among these misperceptions, according to White, are the recurring tendencies to see one's enemy as some type of devil ("The Diabolical Enemy-Image") and to see oneself as motivated by the highest of unselfish and noble motives ("The Moral Self-Image"). In addition, White asserts, the desire to avoid humiliation and to be seen as strong is often a very strong motivating force in a nation's decision to wage war. ("The Virile Self-Image"). In many wars, governments are acutely conscious of the danger of backing down or seeming to back down, while they are much less aware of the pain and death of the countless human beings who will have to pay the price of their virile self-image ("Selective Inattention" and "Absence of Empathy").

rape was dramatized in the movie *Two Women* starring Sophia Loren.) Now, although one can argue on utilitarian grounds with great plausibility that the license to rape is "a rather inefficient spur to masculine courage," the point is that even if such a spur were an essential means to motivate an army to fight on, most of us would loudly condemn such means, regardless of its beneficial consequences. As Kant before us, we would say that it is wrong to offer an innocent woman as a sacrifice to some soldier's lust, for to do so is not to treat her as a person but as a mere object—a mere prize of war. This is a morally unjustifiable violation of her rights and dignity as a human being. The only alternative to the slippery and overly permissive utilitarian notion of proportionality, it has often been said, is the position that there are certain prohibitions against types of violence that can never have any rightful exceptions, regardless of the consequences. Paramount among these prohibitions is the prohibition against using (and especially killing) the innocent. Let us critically consider this view.

THE KANTIAN CASE FOR THE IMMORALITY OF WAR: THE KILLING OF THE INNOCENT

The strongest case for an absolute moral condemnation of war in the modern era of sophisticated military technology comes from the vast numbers of innocent human lives that are inevitably lost in modern wars. Although the question of who is truly "innocent" in times of war is open to debate (for instance, are civilian supporters of a government waging war innocent?), most of us make a basic distinction between those people—such as soldiers, government officials, and workers in munitions factories—who are directly involved in the waging of war and those who are not and as such have done nothing that can justify the violation of their right to be left alone. However we are to make the distinction between the innocent and the noninnocent in times of war, everyone would agree that there are some people in any country who clearly are innocent and as such must meet any reasonable standard of innocence that is proposed. The best example of such innocents, all would agree, are defenseless children. In the days when the means for waging war were more primitive—such as bows and arrows or swords—one could wage a war with the realistic hope and expectation that innocent lives could be spared. Modern military technology, however, makes it impossible to limit the sphere of destruction of one's weapons. Inevitably, when we drop our bombs and shoot our guns from great distances, we know that innocent people, including little children, will die as a result of what we do. For those fully committed to the Kantian way of thinking, such actions appear to be incapable of moral justification, regardless of how essential they are as a means to achieve however noble an end.

Just as we would react with moral outrage at the prospect of sacrificing the lives of a few innocent children to medical experiments which promise to eventually save the lives of a much greater number of children, we should react with moral outrage at the thought of sacrificing children for whatever beneficial consequences we hope to achieve through the waging of war. Indeed, even if we were *absolutely convinced that the only way* to save thousands of potential victims of a childhood disease would be by the sascrifice of only a very few innocent children, our sense of justice would lead most of us to loudly condemn such an action as immoral. It is simply wrong, so many of us would believe, to attempt to justify the violation of an innocent human being's right to life in terms of the utility of such a violation in a particular situation. If we are to accept such a moral perspective in this case, consistency would seem to demand that we morally condemn as well all wars that we know will result in the death of innocent human beings. From such a point of view, our commitment to the values of justice or of human freedom demands that we never sacrifice for "the common good" innocent individuals who have in no way given their consent to be so sacrificed. To assume otherwise is inconsistent with respecting the dignity of such individuals as persons but is rather to treat them "as mere means," the very essence of immorality for those committed to the Kantian moral framework.

For those who take such a point of view, one can only remain morally pure by refusing to "dirty one's hands" with the injustice of modern wars which inevitably cause the death of the innocent. The grave difficulty with this view, however, is that our utilitarian instincts pull us to accept our responsibility for the consequences not only of our actions, but also of our *failure to act* to defend our values from violation by others. For example, can a pacifist committed to "the sanctity of human life" remain "morally pure" when by his refusal to fight a war he allows others such as Hitler to flagrantly violate this value. If one were sure that the only way to prevent Hitler from engaging in a worldwide program of genocide would be by waging a war to stop him, a war which would doubtlessly cost innocent human lives but far fewer lives than would be lost if this war were not waged, what should a person who values innocent lives do? Surely, those of us who would consider it morally justifiable to wage war against Hitler must accept responsibility for those innocents who will die as a result of our decision, but must not those who refuse to wage that war accept responsibility for those innocent lives that one might have saved? I would think so. To assume that one remains morally pure by refusing to use evil means is to assume that one cannot be morally responsible for *letting people die* as long as one does not *kill them* oneself, and this squarely conflicts with our utilitarian moral intuitions. As I have suggested, if the moral purity that many who absolutely condemn war seek is a way of acting for which one should feel no moral regret or guilt, then moral purity is, I am afraid, sometimes impossible to achieve in this imperfect world.

THE CLASSICAL CATHOLIC POSITION
ON THE MORALITY OF WAR:
THE DOCTRINE OF THE DOUBLE EFFECT

Although there have been many Christian pacifists who have considered all wars immoral on the grounds that "evil may not be done as a means of achieving good," the classical Christian position toward war is reflected in the writings of Thomas Aquinas and other Catholic moralists of the Middle Ages who, by means of the principle of the double effect, attempted to reconcile the absolute prohibition against killing the innocent with a utilitarian concern for the consequences of one's acts and omissions. According to this classical doctrine, it is morally permissible to perform an action likely to have evil consequences (such as the killing of the innocent) provided that one does not directly aim at these evil consequences (either as an end or as a means) but instead aims at morally acceptable consequences (such as the killing of enemy soldiers or the destruction of military installations). Furthermore, one must believe that the likely good effects of one's actions are sufficiently good to compensate for allowing the evil effect (that is, the utilitarian notion of proportionality). On the basis of such a principle, contemporary Catholic moralists have justified aerial bombardment. Even though it is inevitable that such action will result in the death of innocents, it is nevertheless justified, they have said, as long as one does not directly aim at such deaths and can justify such actions on utilitarian grounds. Such a position does not, however, do justice to our Kantian moral intuitions and therefore the reconciliation that it attempts to provide is a specious one.

It is not at all clear that the distinction between the direct intentions of one's actions and their foreseen, but unintended, consequences should always be considered to have moral relevance, let alone that it should have decisive moral relevance. Does it really matter, after all, whether innocent deaths are a direct or an indirect effect of our actions, as long as we know equally as well in both cases that they are bound to occur? It will hardly matter to our victims. If we know in advance that we are likely to kill many innocent people and go ahead anyway, can we be morally blameless if we do not "intend" to kill these people and believe our action is justified on purely utilitarian grounds? Is it better to drop bombs that one knows will unintentionally kill *thousands* of innocent persons than to intentionally kill *a few* innocent persons who are in some way unwittingly contributing to the enemy's cause or are being forced to so contribute against their will? I would think not. Yet according to the doctrine of the double effect, the latter action is absolutely immoral, whereas the former one is capable of moral justification. No doubt, it will often prove more psychologically difficult for us to intentionally kill innocent persons than to direct our intention exclusively toward some good consequence of our action, while accepting the deaths of innocents that one knows will inevitably result from one's action, for it is much easier not to think about these deaths this way; but this does not show that the latter action is a more morally justifiable one. As the sorry spectacle of religious apologists for the U.S. war in Vietnam amply demonstrated, the doctrine of the double effect can simply justify too much. For example, it was common American military practice to subject areas which harbored enemy soldiers to devastating aerial bombardment. Such bombardment could be seen as having a "double effect"— enemy soldiers were killed, but so were many innocent civilians who happened to be in those areas. It was not the intention of those who ordered such actions to kill those civilians, of course, for they were acting out of a concern for their own soldiers. Yet such actions should not be complacently accepted as being morally justified, even if they could be justified on the broader moral standard of utilitarian proportionality as the doctrine of the double effect requires. Such a moral standard does not do justice to our deep moral feeling that a soldier must accept certain risks to himself and indeed to the very cause for which he fights in order to preserve the rights of those innocent people who are caught up in a war, *regardless of the apparent disutility* of such a concern in particular circumstances.

There are many situations in the context of a war when we expect soldiers to take risks to themselves in order to save innocent civilian lives without calculating the utilitarian costs of such an action. For example, consider the following from Frank Richards' memoirs of his experiences as a soldier in World War I:

> When bombing dug-outs or cellars, it was always wise to throw the bombs into them first and have a look around them after. But we had to be very careful in this village as there were civilians in some of the cellars. We shouted down to them to make sure. Another man and I shouted down one cellar twice and receiving no reply were just about to pull the pins out of our bombs when we heard a woman's voice and a young lady came up the cellar steps. . . . She and the members of her family . . . had not left [the cellar] for some days. They guessed an attack was being made and when we first shouted down had been too frightened to answer. If the young lady had not cried out when she did, we would have innocently murdered them all.[5]

If Richards and his fellow soldiers felt themselves morally restrained only by the dictates of "military necessity," it would have been much more prudent for them to throw their bombs without any warning, for if there had been German soldiers in the cellar, they might very well have rushed out, firing as they came. Yet Richards would most clearly have considered such a course of action wrong, regardless of its immediate disutility. Even if he were convinced that a policy of bombing without warning in situations such as this would in the long run be jus-

---

[5] Quoted in Michael Walzer, *Just and Unjust Wars* (New York: Basic Books, 1977), p. 152.

tified on purely utilitarian grounds, he, like so many of us, would still most likely consider such an action an *unjustified murder*. As Michael Walzer puts it in considering this case, "He was acting as a moral man ought to act; his is not an example of fighting heroically, above and beyond the call of duty, but simply of fighting well."[6] Yet according to the doctrine of the double effect, Richards would have been quite justified in bombing without warning if he thought such an action were justified on purely utilitarian grounds. If such actions were required as *essential* means for winning a just war, most of us would agree, but we would not agree simply if the utilitarian gains of such actions outweighed their utilitarian costs. Yet it is precisely this type of utilitarian calculation that supporters of the doctrine of the double effect would have us use in those situations where we do not *directly intend the death of innocents*. Such a moral doctrine, I fear, makes the moral choices that soldiers inevitably face too easy, for it does not give as much weight as it deserves to the immense injustice that innocent people unintentionally suffer in war.

SOME CONCLUDING REFLECTIONS

Even if there is no single unified moral theory that we should rely upon to resolve questions relating to the morality of war, this does not mean that all answers to such questions are equally valid—that each side is "right from its own point of view." When one attempts to appraise war in moral terms, one commits oneself to a mode of discourse, governed by indefinite and at times conflicting rules that often allow us to offer plausible moral justifications for conflicting moral positions; but it does, nevertheless, serve to limit the sphere of things that can be said in defense of a given position and, at times, forces those attempting to justify their actions to say things that are simply false. For example, although people can reasonably argue over who was the aggressor in many wars, there are some wars where all reasonable and informed people would agree as to which side merits this label. Hitler's invasion of Poland, for example, was clearly an aggressive act by any reasonable definition of this term. It was precisely because this was the case that Hitler invented an elaborate charade to disguise his naked aggression.[7] The truth in this situation simply could not be clothed in moral garb.

The assumption that it is impossible to subject one's decision to wage a particular sort of war to moral appraisal makes it much too easy for us to desensitize ourselves to the horrendous price we often choose

---

[6] Ibid., p. 154.

[7] According to this charade, Germans were dressed up as Polish soldiers who then staged a mock attack on a number of German border outposts. Hitler's little charade was staged simply as a pretext for his invasion of Poland, which had been planned well in advance of this episode.

to pay for our military victories. If one allows oneself to empathize with the countless victims of war, one cannot help but realize how difficult it is to morally justify most of the wars that crowd upon us through the pages of history. For some, this price can never be rightfully paid. But even if one believes, as I do, that it can be, history amply testifies to the fact that it is paid much more than it should be. Nations have often been willing to pay these unjustifiably high prices for their victories precisely because they have refused to subject their military decisions to the constraints of moral criticism.

Refusing to subject their ends and the means that are essential to achieve them to moral criticism, government officials can allow themselves to do things in the name of "political realism" that they would never do in the name of morality. Such an amoral point of view is, for example, implicitly advocated in Henry Kissinger's *A World Restored.*[8] Rejecting "a faith in universal values," Kissinger advocates a "coldblooded and unsentimental submission of our values to the facts." National leaders, he tells us, must attempt to "harmonize the just with the possible." Although he does not explicitly tell us what this cryptic phrase means, in context it would appear to mean that national leaders should choose whatever means are essential to their ends, untroubled by the restraint of "universal values." It is this manner of thinking that made it much too easy for government officials in the United States to accept the immeasurable human cost of the death and destruction that our military technology brought to Vietnam as an acceptable price for the lofty ends we professed. In their minds, a concern for the victims of their military decisions took second place to more abstract speculations about the future of democracy and communist containment. This in turn led to a much too facile tendency to rely upon coldblooded and abstract calculations of "future goods" to justify very concrete charred human bodies. A moral person should, however, shudder as he thinks of the *certain* massive sacrifice of innocent persons that political leaders and civilians alike have often been willing to accept with no apparent sense of guilt and anguish on the basis of nebulous utilitarian calculations that such actions would *probably* lead to some greater good in the future. We are much too apt, it would appear, to trade certain evils for speculative future goods which often prove to be more difficult to obtain than we expected. Although no precise formula is possible here, a certain evil should always weigh much more heavily in our minds than a greater but speculative future good. Yet the game of international power politics that political leaders so readily play seems to lead them to act on the very opposite principle, weighing their conception of the future good much more heavily than the certain evil they often employ as means to achieve these goods.

The assumption that a nation's ends are of such momentous value

---

[8] Henry A. Kissinger, *A World Restored* (Boston: Houghton Mifflin Company, 1957).

as to outweigh whatever evil is essential to achieve them is undoubtedly psychologically comforting to those who so often unthinkingly make this assumption. With it, one can maintain one's moral self-image as one chooses whatever means are essential to achieving one's ends, regardless of their price. Unwilling to contemplate the possibility that this price may be too high, we tend to close our minds to moral arguments, as too many of our government officials did for too long during the Vietnam war. Seeing their responsibility to their country's "vital self-interests" as overriding all their other obligations, such government officials could perceive themselves as conscientious civil servants who "must do what their duty demands," however hard it might initially be. (In this, they were no different from the Nazi Eichmann who also saw himself as a conscientious civil servant who "merely did his duty."[9]) Of course, as we become increasingly used to such a mode of thought, we tend to make ourselves callous to the evil we cause, as we more and more coldbloodedly attempt to accomplish our ends in the most "efficient" manner, untroubled by the nagging moral questions of our responsibility to humanity, to God, or to certain universal values that transcend our national borders.

Although questions of morality are no doubt unwelcome intruders to our peace of mind and self-esteem when we contemplate the "megadeath" of modern war, it is through them that we are forced to examine the ultimate justification for our actions and in the process are often forced to bring to consciousness the many implicit assumptions that underlie our perception of our situation and motivate us to resort to war as an arbiter of our international conflicts. Similarly, by subjecting our decision to wage war to moral scrutiny and debate, we are much more apt to empathize with the motives of our antagonists and often forced to come to the psychologically disturbing recognition that we are motivated by no more loftier interests and ideals than they. If a peaceful resolution of our conflict is not now possible, our recognition of the ambiguities of our situation should make it much more difficult for us to justify our decision to wage war, but that is the way it should be, for the moral justification for waging war should never be an easy matter. If we decide to opt, as most of us will, for an essentially utilitarian solution to our moral dilemmas concerning war—weighing more heavily our vital national interests than the rights of those who stand as obstacles to it— we must not be free of guilt for what we do. A moral theory that allowed us to make the decision to wage war, without any guilt for violating the rights of the innocent, might be easier to live with and be more coherent; but it would not do justice to our moral sensibilities which often lead us to want to say both "yes" and "no" to the moral choices that face us when it seems that we have no choice but either to allow others to interfere with our legitimate interests or to fight for them and in the process kill and maim those with whom we have no right to interfere.

9 See Hannah Arendt's insightful book *Eichmann in Jerusalem: A Report on the Banality of Evil* (New York: Viking, 1964), revised and enlarged edition.

DISCUSSION QUESTIONS

1. What standard should be used for distinguishing the "innocent" from the "non-innocent" in time of war? Are all civilians "innocent"? What of workers in munitions factories, writers of propaganda, and farmers, all of whom contribute in some way to the war cause (for instance, farmers supply the food that soldiers must eat)?

2. "Obliteration bombing" has been defined as follows:

> It is the strategic bombing, by means of incendiaries and explosives, of industrial centers of population, in which the target to be wiped out is not a definite factory, bridge, or similar object, but a large section of a whole city, comprising one-third or two-thirds of its whole built-up area, and including by design the residential districts of workingmen and their families.[10]

Such bombing was carried out on a massive scale by the Allies during World War II against such German cities as Hamburg, Berlin, and Dresden. Its intent was not only to destroy military targets but also, by its sheer massiveness, to terrorize civilians and undermine their morale. The moral justification for such obliteration bombing was utilitarian in character. Some claimed that it was essential for victory itself, while others claimed that even though the war could be won without it, it would hasten the war's end and minimize the final count of war dead. Still others, however, disagreed, arguing that such bombing was not likely to have any appreciable effect on the war. Indeed, some claimed that obliteration bombing would stiffen the resistance of the Germans just as the German bombing of England had stiffened the resistance of the English and would make the German people so hateful toward the Allies that it "might engender . . . a volume of hatred which not even the peace will be able to assuage." Some also argued that the economic and social problems likely to result from the terror bombing of large German cities would prove to more than outweigh, in the long run, whatever possible good such bombing would achieve in the short run.

Let us assume, however, that it was indeed reasonable to believe that such bombing would be likely to shorten the war and minimize the ultimate number of war dead, even though the war could be won without it. If this were so, do you think that the decision to utilize such bombing against densely populated German cities was a morally justifiable one? Would it make any difference in your mind (as it would to those who accept the doctrine of the double effect) whether the death of innocent civilians was essential if such bombing were to achieve its intention of undermining German morale? What would

10 John C. Ford, S.J., "The Morality of Obliteration Bombing," in *War and Morality*, ed. Wasserstrom, p. 24.

be your reaction to a supporter of the doctrine of the double effect who said the following:

> The intent of such bombing was not to kill civilians in their homes but merely to destroy their homes. Even though we knew that innocent civilians would doubtlessly be in their homes when their homes were destroyed and would consequently be killed themselves, it was not our intent to kill these civilians. Since we merely foresaw their deaths and did not intend them, our act was a morally justifiable one, but it would not have been morally justified if we intended to kill civilians.

3. In offering his justification for using the atomic bomb against Japan, President Truman declared the following in an address to the American people on August 12, 1945:

> We have used [the bomb] against those who attacked us without warning at Pearl Harbor, against those who have starved and beaten and executed American prisoners of war, against those who have abandoned all pretense of obeying international laws of warfare. We have used it in order to shorten the agony of war.

On the surface, Truman, in claiming that the atomic bomb was "used in order to shorten the agony of war," seems to be offering a straightforward utilitarian justification of this action. If this is the case, why does he refer to Japan's alleged "war crimes" in justifying his action. Does he mean to assert that since the Japanese, but not we, were to blame both for beginning the war and for disobeying the laws of war, we were not morally obligated to subject our manner of waging this war to as rigid a moral appraisal as would otherwise have been required? Does he believe that, given the Japanese aggression in beginning the war and in waging that war in an illegal manner, Japanese civilians can rightfully be deprived of certain basic rights with less moral justification than would otherwise be required? Do you see any plausibility in such a claim? If, by some chance, we were losing the war and it was the Japanese who had the bomb, what do you think Truman would have said had they used it on American cities, killing tens of thousands "in order to shorten the agony of war"? Would Truman not have considered such an act as another one of Japan's "war crimes"? If so, can Truman's sentiments be rendered into any reasonable moral principle?

4. Let us now consider the dominant utilitarian strand of Truman's argument. As the story has it, the choice facing Truman was whether to utilize the atomic bomb or to prepare for an invasion of the Japanese islands which would meet fierce Japanese resistance and would

be far costlier in both American and Japanese lives.[11] Churchill, for example, described the atomic bomb as "a miracle of deliverance" which promised to "avert a vast, indefinite butchery . . . at the cost of a few explosions." There is, however, possibly a serious flaw in this utilitarian argument, for the Americans were apparently unwilling to accept anything less than an unconditional surrender of Japan. If less than this were asked of the Japanese, they might very well have surrendered without either an invasion or the use of the atomic bomb. Assuming this to be the case, was it morally justifiable for the Americans to refuse to accept anything less than an unconditional Japanese surrender? What undesirable consequences of a conditional Japanese surrender would outweigh, on a purely utilitarian moral ledger, the vast human costs of utilizing the atomic bomb against Japan?

5. Consider the following hypothetical case:

> Either an invasion of Japan or the use of the atomic bomb will be necessary to obtain even a conditional Japanese surrender. Either way, the defeat of Japan is assured. If the atomic bomb is dropped, about one million Japanese civilians will perish. No Americans, however, would die. If an invasion is chosen, about 50,000 American soldiers will die, as well as 80,000 Japanese soldiers, and 20,000 Japanese civilians.

Since victory is assured in either case, a utilitarian American military strategist would seem to have to be committed to choosing to invade

---

[11] This story is not universally accepted as true. According to the revisionist historian Charles Mee, Jr., in his *Meeting at Potsdam*, (New York: M. Evans & Company, 1975), neither an invasion of the Japanese islands nor the use of the atomic bomb was necessary to obtain the unconditional surrender the Americans demanded. Why then was the atomic bomb used? According to Mee, the major reason for its use was political: "to make Russia more manageable in Europe," as then Secretary of State Byrnes put it. With an atomic bomb that "worked potently on the imagination," Truman felt that he could intimidate the Russians into dealing with him in a more conciliatory manner in the resolution of post-war questions concerning the future of Europe and the Far East. As Mee puts it,

> The psychological effect on Stalin was twofold: the Americans had not only used a doomsday machine; they had used it when, as Stalin knew, it was not militarily necessary. It was this last chilling fact that doubtlessly made the greatest impression on the Russians. (p. 239)

According to Mee, many military figures did not want to use the atomic bomb against Japan. For example, General Eisenhower said that Japan was already so utterly defeated that the bomb was "no longer mandatory as a measure to save American lives," and to drop it was "completely unnecessary." Admiral King and Generals Arnold and LeMay also agreed. Admiral Leahy, Mee tells us, "was at a loss to explain the determination to use the bomb and thought it was 'because of the vast sums that had been spent on the project.' " With its use, Leahy asserted, Americans "had adopted an ethical standard common to the barbarians of the Dark Ages."

Japan, on the grounds that Japanese lives should count no less than American lives. Doubtlessly, however, American officials would consider themselves as having a greater responsibility to save American lives than to save Japanese ones. If this is so, how are American lives to be weighed against Japanese lives? Is it right, for example, to sacrifice one hundred Japanese soldiers to save one American soldier, when the outcome of the war will not be affected by such a choice? Where would you draw the line? Would it make any difference to you if the choice were one of sacrificing Japanese *civilians* or sacrificing American *soldiers?*

6. In the 1950s, the philosophers Bertrand Russell and Sidney Hook debated the question of unilateral disarmament in the nuclear age. The question at issue in this debate was whether it would be morally preferable to die in a nuclear war or to surrender and live under Soviet domination—that is, "Is it better to be red or dead?" According to Hook, death was preferable to life under Soviet communism, while for Russell, life under almost any kind of political system was preferable to death. Since, as Russell saw it, nuclear war promised the end of the human race or a significant part of it, he opted for universal disarmament, while Hook strongly disagreed. If the only alternatives were living under Soviet communist domination or fighting a war which would destroy one quarter to one half of our population, most of us, I suspect, would agree with Russell, but, of course, the choice between being "red or dead" is not at all a forced one, since we hope, through a policy of nuclear deterrence, to avoid either of these two alternatives. The threat of nuclear slaughter, it is hoped, will prove to provide "a balance of terror" which prevents either side from ever having to use its nuclear weapons. Some have argued, however, that the utilization of such a threat is itself immoral. As the philosopher John Bennett rhetorically asks, "How can a nation live with its conscience and know that it is preparing to kill twenty million children in another nation if the worst should come to the worst?" Do you agree that the threat of nuclear war is incapable of moral justification? What if the chances are roughly only one in one hundred that nuclear weapons will eventually be used on a massive scale? What about one in ten or one in three? Do you think the chance of nuclear war is too great to risk today? Would a truly moral person in our country have to opt for unilateral nuclear disarmament if worldwide nuclear disarmament is not possible? Why, or why not?

7. Let us now suppose that our policy of nuclear deterrence has failed and that Soviet missiles have been launched against us. Several million Americans will probably be killed or gravely injured as a result of this nuclear attack. We can either do nothing or massively retaliate. If we choose to do nothing, we will have forfeited our military equality to the Soviets who will now be unquestionably the number one world power. On the other hand, if we strike back, we are assured of

"neutralizing" whatever advantage the Soviets have gained, but only at the cost of unleashing a massive nuclear war which will kill millions more Americans as well as millions of Soviet citizens. The devastation of such a nuclear war will be so vast that it would be impossible to think of either side emerging "victorious" from this war. Does morality not clearly demand that we refuse to retaliate and absorb our losses as best we can, or is it in some way morally fitting that our enemy be made to pay for his aggression? If, in abstract reflection, you shudder at the thought of a person who demands an "eye for an eye" in responding to a nuclear attack, do you think that you might change your tune if you were the President of the United States and were actually faced with such a choice? What do you think most people would do in such a situation? Would most act as you think morality demands that they act?

8. Do you think that any reasonable principle can be given for distinguishing between moral and immoral weapons of war? For example, can some reasonable grounds be given for claiming, as some have claimed, that biological weapons are not moral, whereas chemical ones are? Is the use of napalm and antipersonnel shrapnel, as was used in Vietnam, immoral? Why, or why not? What of bombs such as the controversial neutron bomb that have the special capability of killing people without destroying property? (Such a bomb, it has been suggested, could be especially useful in repelling an invading Soviet army in Western Europe.)

9. It has often been said that a nation has a right to wage war *only* in self-defense to repel acts of aggression by other countries. What do you think the notions of "self-defense" and "aggression" should be taken to mean when applied to the actions of nations? Can one, for example, speak meaningfully of economic, political, or ideological aggression or self-defense? If so, how would you define these notions? Assume that nation *A*, fearful that nation *B* might obtain the advantage of striking the first blow, preemptively strikes that first blow itself. Is nation *A* acting in self-defense or aggressively in such circumstances? If you think this depends on more specific circumstances, on what exactly do you think it depends? Assuming that Hitler posed no threat to any other country and had the full and open support of a majority of German citizens in his extermination of the Jews and other "undesirable" groups of people, would a country be acting aggressively if it dropped its own armed paratroopers on German soil to rescue large numbers of intended victims of the Nazi extermination program who were waiting to die in Nazi concentration camps, and then destroyed those camps? Why or why not?

FURTHER READINGS

BEAUCHAMP, TOM L., ed., *Ethics and Public Policy*, chapter 4. Englewood Cliffs, N.J.: Prentice-Hall, Inc., 1975. This general anthology on contemporary moral issues contains an excellent selection of philosophical articles on the morality of war. The opening selection is Donald Wells's article "How Much Can 'The Just War' Justify?" In this provocative article, Wells argues that a modern formulation of Aquinas' conditions for a "just war" cannot be made applicable to modern war. This is followed by a brief rejoinder by Richard Purtill who attempts to patch up Aquinas' conditions so as to escape Wells' criticisms. Next comes Richard Wasserstrom's article, "The Laws of War," which criticizes international laws of war as seriously incomplete. As Wasserstrom sees it, a reliance on these laws tends to desensitize us to the immorality of conduct that is legitimate according to the laws of war. The final selection consists of Thomas Nagel's "War and Massacre." In this article, Nagel criticizes utilitarian views of the morality of war. While Nagel is quite sympathetic to an absolutist view that certain acts of war are wrong, regardless of the consequences, he is not willing to totally embrace the absolutist position and accepts the inevitability of "moral blind alleys" which provide us with unavoidable choices between "morally abominable courses of action."

COHEN, MARSHALL, THOMAS NAGEL, and THOMAS SCANLON, eds., *War and Moral Responsibility*. Princeton, N.J.: Princeton University Press, 1974. An anthology of articles by philosophers, lawyers, and political scientists that originally appeared in the philosophical journal *Philosophy and Public Affairs*. The first part of this anthology contains articles on the general problem of the sorts of moral restraints that should be placed on wars. The second part consists of articles discussing the special circumstances of World War II, the justifiability of the Nuremberg Trials, and selective conscientious objection.

GINSBERG, ROBERT, ed., *The Critique of War*. Chicago: Henry Regnery, 1969. An anthology of articles, primarily by philosophers, on the causes, justification, and alternatives to war.

The Monist, 57, no. 4 (October 1973). This issue of this philosophical journal is devoted to discussions by philosophers on the topic of the philosophy of war.

WALZER, MICHAEL, *Just and Unjust Wars*. New York: Basic Books, 1977. An excellent study of the morality of war by a professor of government at Harvard University.

WASSERSTROM, RICHARD A., *War and Morality*. Encino, Calif.: Wadsworth, 1970. An excellent anthology of material on the morality of war, representing diverse viewpoints.

Index